Communication for Development and Social Change

Edited by
Jan Servaes

SAGE Los Angeles • London • New Delhi • Singapore
www.sagepublications.com

Original title: Approaches to Development, directed by Jan Servaes

First published by the United Nations Educational, Scientific and Cultural Organization (UNESCO), 7, place de Fontenoy, 75352 PARIS 07 SP, France.
© UNESCO, 2003

The present edition has been published by SAGE Publications by arrangement with UNESCO and Jan Servaes.

 SAGE Publications India Pvt Ltd
B1/I-1 Mohan Cooperative Industrial Area
Mathura Road
New Delhi 110 044, India
www.sagepub.in

SAGE Publications Inc
2455 Teller Road
Thousand Oaks
California 91320, USA

SAGE Publications Ltd
1 Oliver's Yard, 55 City Road
London EC1Y 1SP, United Kingdom

SAGE Publications Asia-Pacific Pte Ltd
33 Pekin Street
#02-01 Far East Square
Singapore 048763

Second Printing 2008

Published by Vivek Mehra for SAGE Publications India Pvt Ltd, typeset in 10/13 pt Nebaraska by Star Compugraphics Private Limited, Delhi and printed at Chaman Enterprises, New Delhi.

Library of Congress Cataloging-in-Publication Data

Communication for development and social change/Jan Servaes.
    p. cm.
Originally published by the United Nations Educational, Scientific and Cultural Organization (UNESCO) ... under the original title: Approaches to development: studies on communication for development/directed by Jan Servaes.
    Includes bibliographical references and index.
1. Communication in economic development. 2. Communication in community development. 3. Social change. 4. Communication—Developing countries. 5. Communication—Social aspects—Developing countries. I. Servaes, Jan, 1952–

| HD76.C6523 | 338.9001'4—dc22 | 2007 | 2007036649 |

ISBN: 978-0-7619-3609-1 (PB)   978-81-7829-772-9 (India-PB)

SAGE Production Team: Sugata Ghosh, Vaijayantee Bhattacharya and Girish Kumar Sharma

Disclaimer
The designations employed and the presentation of material throughout this publication do not imply the expression of any opinion whatsoever on the part of UNESCO concerning the legal status of any country, territory, city or area or of its authorities, or the delimitation of its frontiers or boundaries.

    The authors are responsible for the choice and the presentation of the facts contained in this book and for the opinions expressed therein, which are not necessarily those of UNESCO and do not commit the Organization.

Dedication

To Patchanee, Fiona, Lisa and the millions of strong women and girls who often remain invisible as the real change agents in today's world.

Contents

List of Tables

List of Figures

List of Boxes

List of Abbreviations

ABC	Abstinence, Be faithful, Condom use
ABCFM	American Board of Commissioner for Foreign Mission
ACCE	African Council for Communication Education/Conseil Africain d'Enseignement de Communication
ACCT	Agence de Cooperation Culturelle et Technique/Agency for Cultural and Technical Co-operation
ACD	Applied Communication Division
AKAP	Awareness, Knowledge, Attitudes and Practices
ALAIC	Asociación Latinoamericana de Investigadores de la Comunicación
AMARC	Association Mondiale des Radiodiffuseurs Communautaires/World Association of Community Radio Broadcasters
AMAS	Antwerp Minor Asylum Seekers
AMIC	Asian Mass Communication and Information Centre
ASEAN	Association of Southeast Asian Nations
ASTINFO	Regional Network for the Exchange of Information and Experiences in Science and Technology in Asia and the Pacific
CAP	Community Access Programme
CAM	Christian Aids Ministry
CARSTIN	Caribbean or Regional Network for the Exchange of Information and Experience in Science and Technology
CATS	Community Audio-Tower Systems
CBO	Community-Based Organization
CDSC	Communication for Development and Social Change
CESO	Centre for the Study of Education in Developing Countries
CESPA	Centre de Services de Production Audiovisuelle
CESPAC	Centro de Servicios de Pedagogía Audiovisual para la Capacitación
CFSC	Communication for Social Change
CIDA	Canadian International Development Agency
CIESPAL	Center for Advanced Studies and Research for Latin America
CM	Community Media

CMC	Community Multimedia Centre
CNN	Condom use, sterile Needles, safer sex Negotiation
CPF	Cultural Projects Fund
CRAD	Centre for Development Research and Action
C4D	Communication for Development
DOI	Diffusion of Innovations
DSC	Development Support Communication
DSCS	Development Support Communications Service
ECREA	European Communication Research and Education Association
EDSA	Epifanio de los Santos Avenue
EE	Entertainment Education
EPI	Expanded Programme on Immunisation
ERDF	European Regional Development Fund
EST	Experience in Science and Technology
EU	European Union
FAO	Food and Agriculture Organization
FES	Friedrich Ebert Stiftung
FFS	Farmer Field School
FGM	Female Genital Mutilation
GKN	Global Knowledge Network
GNP	Gross National Product
HBM	Health Belief Model
HIV/AIDS	Human Immunodeficiency Virus/Acquired Immune Deficiency Syndrome
IAMCR	International Association for Media and Communication Research
IAP	Information Access Points
ICPD	International Conference on Population and Development
ICTs	Information and Communication Technologies
ICT4D	Information and Communication Technology for Development
IDRC	International Development Research Centre
IEC	Information, Education and Communication
IIC	International Institute of Communication
IIEP	International Institute for Educational Planning
ILO	International Labour Organization
IMF	International Monetary Fund
IMPACS	Institute for Media, Policy and Civil Society
INFOLAC	Information Society Programme in Latin America and the Caribbean
IPAL	Instituto Para America Latina
IPDC	International Programme for the Development of Communication
IPM	Integrated Pest Management
IPS	Inter Press Service

IT	Information Technology
ITU	International Telecommunications Union
JRS	Jesuit Refugee Service
KAP	Knowledge, Attitudes and Practices
LDC	Least Developed Countries
MCT	Multipurpose Community Telecentre
MDG	Millennium Development Goal
MPCC	Multi-Purpose Communication Centre
MPCT	Multi-Purpose Community Telecentre
MPTC	Multi-Purpose Telecentre
MSSRF	M.S. Swaminathan Research Foundation
NAPAC	Northern AIDS Prevention and Care Program
NGO	Non-Governmental Organization
NWICO	New World Information and Communication Order
OECD	Organization for Economic Co-operation and Development
OFTDP	On Farm Trial and Demonstration Programme
PCARRD	Philippine Council for Agriculture, Forestry and Natural Resources Research and Development
PlanOps	Plan of Operations
PO	Post Office
PRA	Participatory Rural Appraisal
PRCA	Participatory Rural Communication Appraisal
PRI	Institutional Revolutionary Party
PRODERITH	Programa de Desarrollo Rural Integrado del Trópico Húmedo-Program for Integrated Rural Development in the Tropical Wetlands
PSA	Public Service Announcement
PSC	Protestant Social Center
RACO	Regional Applied Communication Offices
RBM	Results-Based Management
R&D	Research & Development
RH	Reproductive Health
RINAF	Regional Informatics Network for Africa
RINAS	Regional Informatics Network for the Arab States
RINSCA	Regional Informatics Network for South and Central Asia
RINSEAP	Regional Informatics Network for South-East Asia and the Pacific
RMCT	Rural Multipurpose Community Telecentres
RNTC	Radio Nederland Training Centre
RSF	Reporters Sans Frontières Reporters Without Borders
RTI	Right To Information
SADC	South African Development Community

SAKS	Sosyete Animasyou Kominikasion Sisyal
SCT	Social Cognitive Theory
SIDA	Swedish International Development Co-operation Agency
SIF	Social Impulse Fund
SMR	Sender-Message-Receiver
STIs	Sexually Transmitted Infections
TOT	Transfer of Technology
TRA	Theory of Reasoned Action
TRAI	Telecommunications Regulatory Authority of India
UNDP	United Nations Development Programme
UNESCO	United Nations Educational, Scientific and Cultural Organization
UNFA	Uganda National Farmers' Association
UNFPA	United Nations Population Fund
UNGASS	United Nations General Assembly Special Session
UNHCR	United Nations High Commissioner for Refugees
UNICEF	United Nations Children's Fund
UNIDO	United Nations Industrial Development Organization
UNOCHA	United Nations Office for the Coordination of Humanitarian Affairs
USAID	United States Agency for International Development
VERCON	Virtual Extension, Research and Communication Network
VIPP	Visualisation in Participatory Programmes
VPA	Visual Problem Appraisal
WACC	World Association for Christian Communication
WANAD	West and Central Africa News Agencies Development/Developpement des Agences de Presse en Afrique de l'Ouest et Centrale
WEF	World Economic Forum
WFS	World Food Summit
WFS	Women's Feature Service
WFUNA	World Federation of United Nations Associations
WHO	World Health Organization
WIF	Worldview International Foundation
WSIS	World Summit on the Information Society
WTO	World Trade Organization

Introduction

JAN SERVAES

Development Communication is the study of social change brought about by the application of communication research, theory, and technologies to bring about development.... Development is a widely participatory process of social change in a society, intended to bring about both social and material advancement, including greater equality, freedom, and other valued qualities for the majority of people through their gaining greater control over their environment.

—Everett Rogers, 1976

Communication for development is a social process, designed to seek a common understanding among all the participants of a development initiative, creating a basis for concerted action.

—UN FAO, 1984

The planned use of communication techniques, activities and media gives people powerful tools both to experience change and actually to guide it. An intensified exchange of ideas among all sectors of society can lead to the greater involvement of people in a common cause. This is a fundamental requirement for appropriate and sustainable development.

—Colin Fraser and Jonathan Villet, 1994

There has been no sustainable, effective social development in which the principles of leadership from within the peoples most affected; a strong and independent voice in public debate, private dialogue and decision making fora by people most affected; and the people most immediately involved defining and agreeing the development agenda, have not been core, central components of the action.

—Warren Feek, Communication Initiative, 2006

Communication for Social Change [CFSC] is a process of public and private dialogue through which people themselves define who they are, what they need and how to get what they need in order to improve their own lives. It utilizes dialogue that leads to collective problem identification, decision making and community-based implementation of solutions to development issues.

—CFSC, 2006

Development communication involves creating mechanisms to broaden public access to information on reforms; strengthening clients' ability to listen to their constituencies and negotiate with stakeholders; empowering grassroots organizations to achieve a more participatory process; and undertaking communication activities that are grounded in research.

—World Bank, 2006
(http://sitresources.worldbank.org 2006)

What is communication for development and social change? Scholars and practitioners may differ in the wording they use to define the subject, but their intent is constant. Put simply, development programmes cannot produce change without an ongoing, culturally and socially relevant communication dialogue among development providers and clientele, and within the recipient group itself.

Therefore, all those involved in the analysis and application of communication for development and social change—or what can broadly be termed 'development communication'—would probably agree that in essence development communication is the sharing of knowledge aimed at reaching a consensus for action that takes into account the interests, needs and capacities of all concerned. It is thus a social process. Communication media are important tools in achieving this process but their use is not an aim in itself—interpersonal communication too must play a fundamental role.

This basic consensus on communication for development and social change has been interpreted and applied in different ways throughout the past century. Both at theory and research levels, as well as at the levels of policy and planning-making and implementation, divergent perspectives are on offer.

The relationship between the practical application of communication processes and technologies in achieving positive and measurable development outcomes is an emerging subject of research, discussion and conjecture. While media professionals, opinion-shapers and development assistance policy-makers have often sought to utilize communication systems for social mobilization and change, a lack of understanding of the complexity of behavioural, societal and cultural factors on end-user consumption patterns has more often led to ineffective, or even counterproductive, outcomes.

Experienced practitioners and communication scholars point to the need for a close study of society and culture in formulating media and outreach strategies, thus ensuring that target audiences are reached in an appropriate manner to effect knowledge transfer. This is particularly so in developing countries, where access to information supporting health, agriculture, HIV/AIDS, literacy and other initiatives can be vital.

In establishing communication for development programmes, professionals have, in the past, often laboured under a misunderstanding commonly held by policy-makers and counterparts relating to the nature of the discipline. Lay persons, understandably, confuse the subject with public relations, public information, corporate communications and other media-related activities. However, while communication for development may incorporate skill-sets from those areas of information dissemination, the subject reaches far deeper and broader into the entire communication process.

At the research and theory levels this could easily be illustrated as follows:

In her Ph.D. thesis Jo Ellen Fair (summarized in the journal, *Gazette*, 1989) examined 224 studies of communication and development published between 1958 and 1986, and found that models predicting either powerful effects or limited effects informed the research.

Development communication in the 1958–1986 period was generally greeted with enthusiasm and optimism:

> Communication has been a key element in the West's project of developing the Third World. In the one-and-a-half decades after Lerner's influential 1958 study of communication and development in the Middle East, communication researchers assumed that the introduction of media and certain types of educational, political, and economic information into a social system could transform individuals and societies from traditional to modern. Conceived as having fairly direct and powerful effects on Third World audiences, the media were seen as magic multipliers, able to accelerate and magnify the benefits of development. (Fair, 1989:145)

Three directions for future research were suggested: to examine the relevance of message content, to conduct more comparative research and to conduct more policy research.

As a follow-up to this research, Jo Ellen Fair and Hemant Shah (1997) studied 140 journal articles, book chapters and books published in English between 1987 and 1996. Their findings are quite illuminating:

> In the 1987–1996 period, Lerner's modernization model completely disappears. Instead, the most frequently used theoretical framework is participatory development, an optimist postmodern orientation, which is almost the polar opposite of Lerner who viewed mass communication as playing a top-down role in social change. Also vanishing from research in this latter period is the two-step flow model, which was drawn upon by modernization scholars .... Both periods do make use of theories or approaches such as knowledge gap, indirect influence, and uses and gratifications. However, research appearing in the years from 1987–1996 can be characterized as much more theoretically diverse than that published between 1958–1986. (Fair and Shah, 1997:10)

In the 1987–96 study, the most frequent suggestion was 'the need to conduct more policy research, including institutional analysis of development agency coordination. This was followed by the need to research and develop indigenous models of communication and development through participatory research' (Fair and Shah, 1997:19).

Therefore, today almost nobody would dare to make the optimistic claims of the early years any longer. However, the implicit assumptions on which the so-called dominant modernization paradigm is built do still linger on and continue to influence the policy and planning-making discourse of major actors in the field of communication for development, both at theoretical and applied levels.

From Modernization, over Dependency, to Multiplicity

After the Second World War, the founding of the United Nations stimulated relations among sovereign states, especially the North Atlantic Nations and the developing nations, including the new states emerging out of a colonial past. During the Cold War period, the superpowers—the United States and the former Soviet Union—tried to expand their own interests to the developing countries. In fact, the USA was defining development and social change as the replica of its own political-economic system and opening the way for the transnational corporations. At the same time, the developing countries saw the 'welfare state' of the North Atlantic Nations as the ultimate goal of development. These nations were attracted by the new technology transfer and the model of a centralized state with careful economic planning and centrally-directed development bureaucracies for agriculture, education and health as the most effective strategies to catch up with those industrialized countries.

This mainly economic-oriented view, characterized by endogenism and evolutionism, ultimately resulted in the *modernization and growth* theory. It sees development as a unilinear, evolutionary process and defines the state of underdevelopment in terms of observable quantitative differences between so-called poor and rich countries on the one hand, and traditional and modern societies on the other hand (for more details on these paradigms, see Servaes 1999).

As a result of the general intellectual 'revolution' that took place in the mid 1960s, this Euro- or ethno-centric perspective on development was challenged by Latin American social scientists, and a theory dealing with *dependency and underdevelopment* was born. This dependency approach formed part of a general structuralist re-orientation in the social sciences. The 'dependistas' were primarily concerned with the effects of dependency in peripheral countries, but implicit in their analysis was the idea that development and underdevelopment must be understood in the context of the world system.

This dependency paradigm played an important role in the movement for a New World Information and Communication Order from the late 1960s to the early 1980s. At that time, the new states in Africa, Asia and the success of socialist and popular movements in Cuba, China, Chile and other countries provided the goals for political, economic and cultural self-determination within the international community of nations. These new nations shared the ideas of being independent from the superpowers and moved to form the Non-Aligned Nations. The Non-Aligned Movement defined development as political struggle.

Since the demarcation of the First, Second and Third Worlds has broken down and the cross-over centre-periphery can be found in every region, there is a need for a new concept of development which emphasizes *cultural identity and multidimensionality*. The present-day 'global' world, in general as well as in its distinct regional and national entities, is confronted with multifaceted crises. Apart from the obvious economic and financial crisis, one could also refer to social, ideological, moral, political, ethnic, ecological and security crises. In other words, the previously-held dependency perspective has become more difficult to support because of the growing interdependency of regions, nations and communities in our so-called 'global' world.

From the criticism of the two paradigms above, particularly that of the dependency approach, a new viewpoint on development and social change has come to the forefront. The common starting point here is the examination of the changes from 'bottom-up', from the self-development of the local community. The basic assumption is that there are no countries or communities that function completely autonomously and that are completely self-sufficient, nor are there any nations whose development is exclusively determined by external factors. Every society is dependent in one way or another, both in form and in degree. Thus, a framework was sought within which both the Centre and the Periphery could be studied separately and in their mutual relationship.

More attention is also being paid to the content of development, which implies a more normative approach. Another development questions whether 'developed' countries are in fact developed and whether this genre of progress is sustainable or desirable. It favours a multiplicity of approaches based on the context and on the basic felt needs, and the empowerment of the most oppressed sectors of various societies at divergent levels. The main thesis is that change must be structural and occur at multiple levels in order to achieve these ends.

Therefore, we start this book with three more general contributions which, each from a multidimensional perspective, set the stage for a more detailed analysis of the issue of communication for social change.

Pradip Thomas reminds us that there are about 1.3 billion people worldwide living in absolute poverty, that is to say, people who cannot meet their basic needs. About a third of the population in the so-called developing countries falls in this category, and even in the United States of America and the European Union, 15 per cent of the population is living below nationally-determined poverty levels.

At first sight, the problem of poverty might appear insolvable, but the World Bank has estimated that it would require only 1 per cent of developing countries' consumption to abolish extreme poverty, which it defines as an income of less than US$ 275 per person per year. According to the Food and Agriculture Organization (FAO) of the UN it would need US$ 13 per person per year to solve the problem of poverty. Furthermore, it would require a transfer of just 3 per cent of the total consumption in developing countries to eliminate poverty in general, defined as an income of less than US$ 370 per person per year. Poverty and its related social disintegration were key themes at the World Summit on Social Development held in Copenhagen in 1995, and of the

World Food Summit held in Rome (at FAO) in 1997. At this World Food Summit the world leaders agreed to set the objective of reducing the number of hungry to around 400 million by the year 2015.

Cuban President Fidel Castro was one of the few dissident voices. He scorned 'the modesty of this objective as shameful'. He referred to the US$ 700 billion a year spent on arms, even after the end of the Cold War. He finished his statement as follows: 'The bells that presently toll for those starving to death every day will tomorrow toll for the whole of humanity, which did not want to, know how to, or have the wisdom to save itself from itself.'

Pradip Thomas argues that the worldwide poverty situation could be solved by participatory communication. The use of participatory communication education mechanisms could bring about social change and development through sustained improvements in agriculture, health, education, politics and economics over a sufficiently long enough time to make a considerable proportion of the population less poor, both in material as well as immaterial ways.

Also the recurrent themes of human rights, culture and development have to be addressed in a book like this. Jan Servaes and Chris Verschooten start by revising the often discussed 'dichotomies' of tradition versus modernity, universalism versus relativism, and individualism versus collectivism. They arrive at similar conclusions as those advocated by the World Commission on Culture and Development, chaired by the former UN Secretary General Javier Perez de Cuellar (1995).

Local and Global Perspectives

Processes at local and global levels have further complicated the above developments. The vision of an era of global communications seems especially pertinent when changes in other spheres of human societies are taken into consideration. The 1990s, with the fall of the Berlin Wall and the explosive growth of the World Wide Web as preludes, have been marked by the collapse of the physical, virtual and institutional barriers, which had kept people apart over the previous several decades. The ever closer trade relationships among nation-states, the growing number of transnational corporations, ICTs, the Internet and discussions on e-commerce and e-governance, the emergence of global health and environmental issues, and a common style of consumption of material and cultural products have all helped to bring about what is described as the 'globalization' of our world. In general, globalization is considered as the widening, deepening and speeding up of worldwide interconnectedness in all aspects of contemporary social life.

But, beyond a general awareness and agreement of this global interconnectedness, there is substantial disagreement as to how globalization is best conceptualized, how one should think about its causal dynamics, how one should characterize its structural, socio-economic consequences, and what implications it has on poverty alleviation, culture and human rights, state power and governance.

The three different theses on globalization—(hyper)globalist perspective, a sceptical or traditionalist perspective, and a transformationalist perspective—outlined in the chapter by Servaes and Lie can all be found in several other chapters of this book.

Diffusion versus Participatory Communication

The above, more general, typology of the so-called development paradigms can also be found at the communication and cultural levels. The communication media are, in the context of development, generally used to support development initiatives by the dissemination of messages that encourage the public to support development-oriented projects. Although development strategies in developing countries diverge widely, the usual pattern for broadcasting and the press has been predominantly the same: informing the population about projects, illustrating the advantages of these projects, and recommending that they be supported. A typical example of such a strategy is situated in the area of family planning, where communication means like posters, pamphlets, radio, and television attempt to persuade the public to accept birth control methods. Similar strategies are used in campaigns regarding health and nutrition, agricultural projects, education, and so on.

This model sees the communication process mainly as a message going from a sender to a receiver. This hierarchical view on communication can be summarized in Laswell's classic formula—'Who says What through Which channel to Whom with What effect?'—and dates back to (mainly American) research on campaigns and diffusions in the late 1940s and 1950s.

The American scholar Everett Rogers is said to be the person who introduced this diffusion theory in the context of development. Modernization is here conceived as a process of diffusion whereby individuals move from a traditional way of life to a different, more technically developed and more rapidly changing way of life. Building primarily on sociological research in agrarian societies, Rogers stressed the adoption and diffusion processes of cultural innovation. This approach is therefore concerned with the process of diffusion and adoption of innovations in a more systematic and planned way. Mass media is important in spreading awareness of new possibilities and practices, but at the stage where decisions are being made about whether to adopt or not to adopt, personal communication is far more likely to be influential. Therefore, the general conclusion of this line of thought is that mass communication is less likely than personal influence to have a direct effect on social behaviour.

Newer perspectives on development communication claim that this is still a limited view of development communication. They argue that this diffusion model is a vertical or one-way perspective on communication, and that active involvement in the process of the communication itself will accelerate development. Research has shown that, while groups of the public can obtain information from impersonal sources like radio and television, this information has relatively little effect on behavioural changes. And development envisions precisely such change. Similar research has led to the conclusion that more is learned from interpersonal contacts and from mass communication techniques that are based on them. On the lowest level, before people can discuss and resolve problems, they must be informed of the facts, information that the media provide nationally as well as regionally and locally. At the same time, the public, if the media are sufficiently accessible, can make its information needs known.

Communication theories such as the 'diffusion of innovations', the 'two-step-flow', or the 'extension' approaches are quite congruent with the modernization theory. The elitist, *vertical or top-down orientation* of the diffusion model is obvious.

The participatory model, on the other hand, incorporates the concepts in the framework of multiplicity. It stresses the importance of cultural identity of local communities and of *democratization and participation at all levels*—international, national, local and individual. It points to a strategy, not merely inclusive of, but largely emanating from, the traditional 'receivers'. Paulo Freire (1983:76) refers to this as the right of all people to individually and collectively speak their word: 'This is not the privilege of some few men, but the right of every man. Consequently, no one can say a true word alone—nor can he say it for another, in a prescriptive act which robs others of their words'.

In order to share information, knowledge, trust, commitment and a right attitude in development projects, participation is very important in any decision-making process for development. Therefore, the International Commission for the Study of Communication Problems argues that 'this calls for a new attitude for overcoming stereotyped thinking and to promote more understanding of diversity and plurality, with full respect for the dignity and equality of peoples living in different conditions and acting in different ways' (MacBride, 1980:254). This model stresses reciprocal collaboration throughout all levels of participation.

Also, these newer approaches argue, the point of departure must be the community. It is at the community level that the problems of living conditions are discussed, and interactions with other communities are elicited. The most developed form of participation is self-management. This principle implies the right to participation in the planning and production of media content. However, not everyone wants to or must be involved in its practical implementation. More important is that participation is made possible in the decision-making regarding the subjects treated in the messages and regarding the selection procedures. One of the fundamental hindrances to the decision to adopt the participation strategy is that it threatens existing hierarchies. Nevertheless, participation does not imply that there is no longer a role for development specialists, planners, and institutional leaders. It only means that the viewpoint of the local groups of the public is considered before the resources for development projects are allocated and distributed, and that suggestions for changes in the policy are taken into consideration.

From Sender to Receiver

Also the perspective on communication has changed. It is more concerned with process and context, that is, on the exchange of 'meanings,' and on the importance of this process, namely, the social relational patterns and social institutions that are the result of and are determined by the process. 'Another' communication 'favors multiplicity, smallness of scale, locality, deinstitutionalization, interchange of sender-receiver roles (and) horizontality of communication links at all levels of society' (McQuail, 1983:97). As a result, the focus moves from a 'communicator' to a more 'receiver-centric' orientation, with the resultant emphasis on meaning sought and ascribed rather than information transmitted.

With this shift in focus, one is no longer attempting to create a need for the information one is disseminating, but one is rather disseminating information for which there is a need. The emphasis is on information exchange rather than on the persuasion in the diffusion model.

To illustrate this shift, Alfonso Gumucio-Dragon presents us with an interesting selection of participatory projects.

The second part of the book further discusses and details the above typologies and findings. Sujatha Sosale adopts a discourse approach to identify two strategies of power on communication and development. One is the power to survey, and the other is the power to remain invisible. She concludes that 'a critical tension continues to exist between guided social change signified by policy, and alternate possibilities that might fall outside the realm of policy or are at best located at its fringes'.

Roy Colle traces the seven 'threads' or origins which have contributed to the complexity of the development communication field. He starts with an appreciation of the pioneering work on development support communication by Erskine Childers and his colleagues in the late 1960s, and continues with the approaches of extension and diffusion, participatory communication, population and health communication, social mobilization, institution-building, and information and communication technologies. Colle concludes that these threads convey a sense of evolving into a development communication fabric. He identifies eight characteristics which together help to define what development communication for the future is about: a focus on beneficiaries, the consideration of various stakeholders, participation, emphasis on outcomes, data gathering and analysis, systematic models, strategy, and a multi-channel versatility.

In similar ways and by way of summary of the most important arguments and findings of the first set of contributions, Jan Servaes and Patchanee Malikhao then present the main perspectives on development communication both at the general development levels, as well as at the more specific communication level.

Robert Huesca zooms in on the concept of participatory communication. He argues that, despite its widespread use, the concept is subject to loose interpretation. Therefore, by tracing the history of participatory communication approaches to development from a Latin American perspective, he aims to present a variety of directions for future research and practice.

Communication for Development and Social Change

At a more applied level, several perspectives on communication for development and social change could be identified, as presented in the third and fourth part of the book.

A first perspective could be of communication as a process, often seen in metaphor as the fabric of society. It is not confined to the media or to messages, but to their interaction in a network of social relationships. By extension, the reception, evaluation and use of media messages, from whatever source, are as important as their means of production and transmission.

A second perspective is of communications media as a mixed system of mass communication and interpersonal channels, with mutual impact and reinforcement. In other words, the mass media should not be seen in isolation from other conduits.

One could, for instance, examine the role and benefits of radio versus the Internet for development and democracy. Both the Internet and the radio are characterized by their interactivity. However, if, as many believe, better access to information, education and knowledge would be the best stimulant for development, the Internet's primary development potential is as a point of access to the global knowledge infrastructure. The danger, now widely recognized, is that access to knowledge increasingly requires a telecom infrastructure that is inaccessible to the poor. Therefore, the digital divide is not about technology, it is about the widening gaps between the developed and developing worlds and the info-rich and the info-poor.

While the benefits offered by the Internet are many, its dependence on a telecom infrastructure means that they are only available to a few. Radio is much more pervasive, accessible and affordable. Blending the two could be an ideal way of ensuring that the benefits accruing from the Internet have wider reach.

Another perspective of communications in the development process is from an inter-sectoral and inter-agency concern. This view is not confined to information or broadcasting organizations and ministries, but extends to all sectors, and its success in influencing and sustaining development depends to a large extent on the adequacy of mechanisms for integration and co-ordination.

Therefore, different agencies have evolved distinct approaches and strategies for putting the principles into operation with differentiated policy bases, planning models and terminologies. As a result, it is often difficult for specialists within particular agencies to understand precisely what others are trying to express or to achieve, as presented in the chapter on governmental and non-governmental agencies by Jan Servaes.

FAO's Communication for Development Group has arguably been one of the foremost practitioners of applied communication for improving agriculture and related sectors in the developing world (for example, forestry, environment and nutrition), since its establishment in 1969. During these three decades the role of communication has undertaken a dramatic shift from a one-way, top-down transfer of messages by agricultural technicians to farmers, to a social process designed to bring together both groups in a two-way sharing of information among communication equals—in short, participatory communication. In recognizing that rural people are at the heart of development, by seeking their views and involving them from the start, participatory communication has become what many consider to be the key link between farmers, extension, and research for planning and implementing consensus-based development initiatives. Too often, however, it has been a missing link and many projects have failed as a result.

Along with communication, it is also now widely accepted that a parallel investment in human resources through education and training of adults is essential for project success. Awareness raising, knowledge acquisition, attitude change, confidence building, participation in decision-making and action, all require processes of education and communication. And all are essential for effective development—they are not just desirable options.

In this spirit, the chapter by Gary Coldevin and others traces the growth of participatory communication and adult learning in FAO's field programmes, along with examples drawn from other agencies, and provides snapshots of notable successes. With a view on the current push towards networking the developing world, a concluding section draws on the lessons emerging from the application of traditional and older electronic media format, as guidelines for constructive use of the Internet in rural settings.

Neill McKee, Erma Manoncourt, Chin Saik Yook and Rachel Carnegie summarize the UNICEF experience, They start from very basic questions such as 'Why are people's behaviours so difficult to change?', and 'Why do development communication interventions often fall short of their behaviour altering goals?'. Basing themselves on an integrated approach towards involving people in evolving behaviour, and an analysis of several cases, they conclude that many processes and factors must converge in order to facilitate behaviour change. They also emphasize the importance of building effective and responsive communication elements into development programmes right from the start of all projects: 'While communication on its own will not bring about change and development, neither will change happen without development communication. We need to integrate all our efforts'.

HIV/AIDS Communication

Many practitioners believe that they can achieve the greatest understanding by combining more than one theory or developing their own conceptual framework. Where previous perspectives did not succeed in reconciling economic growth with social justice, an attempt should be made to approach problems of freedom and justice from the relationship of tension between the individual and the society, and limits of growth and sustainability are seen as inherent to the interaction between society and its physical and cultural ecology.

The so-called *Copenhagen Consensus Project* is worth mentioning in this context. Though still dominated by economic perspectives and researchers (some of them Nobel prize winners), the panel of experts evaluated a large number of development recommendations, drawn from assessments by UN agencies, and identified 10 core challenges for the future:

- Civil conflicts
- Climate change
- Communicable diseases
- Education

- Financial stability
- Governance
- Hunger and malnutrition
- Migration
- Trade reform
- Water and sanitation

The major challenge identified by this panel was the fight against HIV/AIDS. (For more details, see a number of reports in *The Economist*, April–June 2004, or visit www.copenhagenconsensus. com).

As HIV/AIDS is increasingly becoming identified as one of the major challenges for communication for development and social change advocates and practitioners, the fourth part of the book presents three chapters which together summarize the core issues from both theoretical and applied perspectives. Rico Lie reviews three shifts in thinking about appropriate HIV/AIDS communication: (1) a shift away from mainstream HIV/AIDS mass media campaigning towards culturally appropriate responses to HIV/AIDS and the use of local community media; (2) a shift away from seeing HIV/AIDS primarily as a health problem towards seeing it as a development problem, and (3) a shift from a primary focus on behavioural change to a primary focus on social change. These shifts overlap and are connected. As a consequence of these shifts in the underlying philosophical principles and paradigmatic thinking about communication, a shift in research and intervention strategies is also suggested. This shift concerns an evolutionary moving on from the use of dominant (theoretical) models to loose conceptual frameworks and common principles.

Patchanee Malikhao illustrates these shifts in the case of Thailand. After a brief historical overview of the situation of HIV/AIDS prevention campaigns in Thailand, she describes the communication strategies that Buddhist and Christian leaders employ to operate HIV/AIDS prevention campaigns in two separate villages in the northern part of Thailand (Chiang Rai province) where the numbers of people who died of AIDS are the highest in the country. Also, Thomas Tufte addresses the changes in communication perspectives and strategies. He analyses the case of Soul City in order to discuss how an *entertainment-education based communication strategy* can contribute to a participatory development process. Soul City is the name of the media and health NGO behind the large, ongoing, goal-oriented, media-driven information and training initiative that works for social change in the South African society. First, he introduces the history and development of Soul City. Second, he provides a brief historical overview of the developments within entertainment-education in relation to the general discussions of communication for development. Finally Tufte explores how Soul City contributes to the further development of entertainment-education strategies in both theory and practice. As so often seen before, practice comes prior to theory, and he thus argues that what Soul City is de facto doing is anticipating the theoretical advancement he wishes to argue for entertainment-education (EE).

Furthermore, according to Ronny Adhikarya (in *The Journal of Development Communication*, 1997:22), there appears to be at least two main problems which limit development communicators' effectiveness in contributing successfully to achieving development objectives or goals:

The first problem is related to the main tasks normally assigned to communication specialists. Most of them are expected to produce mainly publicity, public relations, and/or multi-media materials without much involvement at the information needs assessment, communication strategy and planning, message positioning, treatment, and design, and/or multi-media mix selection processes. The second, and more critical, problem is their lack of a holistic, integrated, multi-disciplinary and inter-sectoral approach in analysing communication problems as well as in designing and planning communication strategies in support of the broader development objectives or goals.

As academic and professional training programmes in development communication emerge (they are already established in the Asia region, and are growing elsewhere), these frequently emphasize one set of approaches and vocabularies, without looking comparatively at alternatives. This inhibits cross-fertilization, comparative analysis, and mutual learning, but the most significant obstacle that it creates is to collaborative, inter-agency working, at a time when integrated approaches to development are emphasized, and coordination is important for reasons of economy, efficiency, and maximization of impact.

Special Cases

Two additional cases which need attention are the role and place of the often-overlooked community media, and the role of the mass media in ethno-political conflicts.

In the first case Carpentier, Lie and Servaes argue that the multiplicity of media-labelled 'community media' necessitates different approaches towards a definition of community media.

They start from the 'working definition' of community radio adopted by AMARC, the World Association of Community Radio Broadcasters. This organization encompasses a wide range of radio practices in the different continents. In Latin America, the AMARC-members are termed popular radio, educational radio, miners' radio or peasants' radio. In Africa, they refer to local rural radio. In Europe, it is often called associative radio, free radio, neighbourhood radio or community radio. In Asia, they speak of radio for development, and of community radio; in Oceania of aboriginal radio, public radio, and of community radio. In AMARC's attempts to avoid a prescriptive definition, a community radio station is labelled 'a "non-profit" station, currently broadcasting, which offers a service to the community in which it is located, or to which it broadcasts, while promoting the participation of this community in the radio' (AMARC, 1994:4).

Finally, Georgios Terzis and Myria Vassiliadou argue that, as a result of their ability to reach and participate in the opinion-building process for large numbers of people, the media carry immense power in shaping the course of an ethno-political conflict. Although many past and present examples of the media's negative contribution to the escalation of violent conflicts exist, fair and accurate journalism and media programming that build confidence and counteract misperceptions have a significant positive role to play in both conflict prevention and transformation. They attempt to investigate the potentials of the media in situations of ethno-political conflict, and concentrate on three different forms of projects: training, provision of media hardware, and production of peace-oriented media programming.

Communication and Development for Whom and for What?

Colin Fraser and Sonia Restrepo-Estrada (1998) sum it all up: the successes and failures of most development projects are often determined by two crucial factors, that is, communication and people's involvement. 'Even though communication for development came into being in the 1960s, and has clearly shown its usefulness and impact in change and development actions, its role is still not understood and appreciated to the point that it is routinely included in development planning' (Fraser and Restrepo-Estrada, 1998:39). Many well-intended projects are thought out in places far remote from the actual context in which they are supposed to be implemented. Consequently, they fail to understand the complex power relationships and the cultural and communication processes existing at these local levels.

Therefore, most authors in this collection argue that authentic participation directly addresses power and its distribution in society. Participation involves the more equitable sharing of both political and economic power, which often decreases the advantage of certain groups. Structural change involves the redistribution of power. In mass communication areas, many communication experts agree that structural change should occur first in order to establish participatory communication policies.

Hopefully this collection offers interesting insights and examples to prove that the field of communication for development and social change is still alive and kicking.

Acknowledgements

An earlier version of this book, entitled *Approaches to Development: Studies on Communication for Development* was published in March 2003 by UNESCO's Communication and Information Sector under the guidance of the late Lluis Artigas de Quadras. This edition, which was also distributed on a CD-ROM, was highly successful and soon out of print. We are grateful to UNESCO's Assistant Director-General for Communication and Information, Dr Abdul Waheed Khan, for allowing us to transfer the copyright to SAGE Publications India Pvt Ltd. All of the chapters in this new version have been updated, most of them have gone through major rewriting and editing. Some new texts have been added to this volume. We thank the SAGE team, Sugata Ghosh, Vaijayantee Bhattacharya and Girish Kumar Sharma, for their support and perseverance in getting this new version out.

References

Adhikarya, R. 1997. 'Improving Farmers Education and Training: Challenges for Development Communicators', *The Journal of Development Communication*, 20–41.

AMARC-Europe. 1994. 'One Europe-Many Voices'. Democracy and Access to Communication Conference Report, AMARC-Europe Pan-European conference of Community Radio Broadcasters, Ljubljana, Slovenia, 15–18 September 1994, Sheffield: AMARC.

de Cuellar, J.P. (ed.). 1995. *Our Creative Diversity: Report of the World Commission on Culture and Development*. Paris: UNESCO.

Fair, Joe Ellen. 1989. '29 Years of Theory and Research on Media and Development: The Dominant Paradigm Impact', *Gazette*, 44:129–150.

Fair, Joe Ellen and Hemant Shah. 1997. 'Continuities and Discontinuities in Communication and Development Research since 1958', *Journal of International Communication*, 4(2):3–23.

Feek, W. 2006. Communication Initiative Website: www.comminit.com.

Fraser, C. and J. Villet. 1994. *Communication—A key to human development*. Rome: FAO.

Fraser, C. and S. Restrepo-Estrada. 1998. *Communicating for Development: Human Change for Survival*. London and New York: I.B. Tauris Publishers.

Freire, P. 1983. *Pedagogy of the Oppressed*. New York: Continuum.

MacBride, S. (ed.). 1980. *Many Voices, One World: Communication and Society. Today and Tomorrow*. Paris: UNESCO.

McQuail, D. 1983. *Mass Communication Theory*. London: Sage Publications.

Mody, B. (ed.). 1997. 'Communication and Development: Beyond Panaceas', *The Journal of International Communication*, 4(2):138.

Quebral, N., R. Colle, R. Adhikarya et al. 1997. 'Development Communication: What the "Masters" Say' (special issue), *The Journal of Development Communication*, 8(2):179.

Rogers, E. 1976 (ed.). 1976. *Communication and Development: Critical Perspectives*. Beverly Hills, California: Sage Publications.

Servaes, J. 1999. *Communication for Development. One World, Multiple Cultures*. Cresskill: Hampton Press.

UN FAO. 1984. *Expert Consultation on Communication for Development*. Rome: FAO.

World Bank. 2006. 'Development Communication.' Available online at http://www.worldbank.org/WBSITE EXTERNAL TOPICS/EXTDEVCOMMENG/0,,menu PK:34000201~pagePK:34000189~piPK:34000199~theSitePK:423815,00.html.

Part I

Introduction

Communication and the Persistence of Poverty: The Need for a Return to Basics

1

PRADIP THOMAS

Regular readers of the press in India will have noticed an alarming increase in suicides within communities of traditional weavers and agriculturalists in India, throughout the country. In fact, a recent report by India's leading 'poverty journalist' P. Sainath (2006:2) indicates that the problem is nationwide and that it has begun to affect even the most prosperous states in the country, including Maharashtra, whose capital Mumbai is the financial nerve-centre of India. Writing on farmer suicides in Vidharba district, Maharashtra, he observed that '... the number of farmer suicides in the region since June 2005 has crossed the 760 mark'. This journalist, in an earlier article (2001:45), recorded deaths in Andhra Pradesh, the rice bowl of India: 'Recent government figures show that in Anantapur, just one district of Andhra, 1,826 people, mainly farmers with very small holdings of two acres or less, committed suicide between 1997 and 2000'.

The suicides do not normally make headline news, although it does when the issue is occasionally raised in the Parliament. There seems to be a pattern to these suicides, irrespective of the community. A combination of factors—rising costs of inputs, low returns, landlessness, increase in the prices of essential commodities, food grains in particular, the lack of subsidies, an increase in debt payments, the lack of back-up social services, and the dismantling of the welfare economy—seem to be the key factors that have contributed to the suicides. It is alarming that in a country that is feted universally for moving up the ladder of development, 320 million people remain in real poverty.

In direct contrast to this image of pre-colonial penury, is the image of the new Andhra Pradesh on the move that was manufactured by the national and global media. It is an image of a technological paradise, of software engineers, of dotcom companies, of the stern, laptop carrying ex-Chief Minister, Chandra Babu Naidu, of e-commerce, software parks, Cyberabad (the new name for the capital city Hyderabad) and electronic democracy. Along with the two other South Indian states of Karnataka and Tamil Nadu, Andhra Pradesh is in the vanguard of the information revolution in India.

While it is imperative that countries like India maximize their investments in, and hopefully returns from, the Information Technology (IT) revolution, such investments need to be seen in a macro perspective, from the point of view of returns to the majority rather than to any minority group. The analysis of the results of the parliamentary elections held in 2004, particularly from Andhra Pradesh, does suggest that one reason for the resounding defeat of the incumbent party was their inability to speak in the language of the majority voters who care more about regular supplies of drinking water, employment opportunities and low prices for food grains, than about investments in IT or the fibre optic cabling of the state.

The persistence of poverty can often lead to upheaval. The 1 May 2001 demonstrations in Manila, by the mostly poor supporters of the disgraced former President Estrada, was a clear reminder of the real gaps that exist between the rich and the poor in the Philippines. Four out of every 10 Filipino are classified as poor. In 1997, 20 per cent of the population accounted for 52 per cent of national income while 20 per cent had access to only 5 per cent of that income. Sheila Coronel (2001:13–14), while attempting to explain the reasons for the uprising by the poor in support of an ex-President who was notoriously corrupt, believes that his pro-poor stance and perceived ill-treatment at the hands of his middle class incarcerators were the catalysts that led to the Epifanio de los Santos Avenue (EDSA) 3 rally, that was in terms of numbers, greater than numbers at the EDSA 2 people power rally that led to Estrada's fall from power. 'Metro Manila's vast shanty towns, home to some four million people, provide the starkest evidence of the magnitude of poverty and the kind of vision, resources, and political will needed if the poor are to have immediate relief'. EDSA is the main highway in Manila, where the first EDSA rally was held and that resulted in the overthrow of the Marcos regime in 1986.

The obvious paradox of death, distress and the dotcom is arguably also the paradox of communication in the twenty-first century. There have been tremendous advancements in the field of Information Technologies, and the many advantages and applications of digital forms of information have resulted in qualitative changes in the lives of many people around the world. The stories of IT applications in development are now legion and appear regularly in the media from a diverse range of countries and locations—from tiny villages in Brazil to cities in Senegal to hamlets in Sri Lanka. There are other macro stories of IT-derived applications including the potential medical benefits from the 'human genome' project to the actual benefits of electronic democracy experienced in some Scandinavian countries and the many significant, public service aspects of the World Wide Web. It would seem that the cumulative growth of these technologies will result in many possibilities for using IT in the context of the democratization and development of societies. From the romanticized, near-mythical, Zapatistas on the Net, to the avalanche of electronic mail messages that deluged and disabled the White House site—a global response to President Bush's recalcitrance to the Kyoto Agreement, worldwide networks of ordinary people now have the means to leverage policy-makers and make the difference. This, at least, is the hype of netizens involved in global and national governance.

The Persistence of Poverty

However, all things are not equal. Organizing around the Net, although a growing activity, does not necessarily lead to social change. One can argue that while there is, on the one hand, a surfeit of communication, there is also on the other, a large, growing reservoir of people for whom the information glut and the content of that information are irrelevant, simply because it does not address their concerns and needs. As the annual United Nations Development Programme (UNDP) Human Development Reports have periodically reminded us, poverty is a characteristic feature of the world in which we live. While poverty levels may have remained constant during the last five years, the percentage of people living in seriously vulnerable situations seems to be increasing rather than decreasing. In other words, the gaps between the very poor and the poor, let alone the gaps between the very poor and the relatively poor, have become painfully visible in many parts of the world. Poverty is not limited by geography. In fact, the wealthiest country in the world, the USA, is also home to pockets of poverty, such as that experienced by poor Blacks and Hispanics living in the Bronx, New York. It took hurricane Katrina to expose the reality of poverty in the USA, beyond the veneer of jazz and good times in New Orleans. Every mega-metropolis: Mexico City, Sao Paulo, Kolkata and Mumbai, and almost every major city from Nairobi to Manila to Johannesburg, is home to huge agglomerations of shanty towns. Dharavi, in Mumbai, is the largest of its kind in the world. More than half of the population of Mumbai live in similar environments.

Poverty is conceptualized from a variety of perspectives and as a result the preferred solutions are also varied. These approaches to poverty include the following:

Poverty as a Mindset

This approach, influenced by a largely psychologistic interpretation of poverty, often resulted in a 'blaming the victim' policy. While such approaches are thankfully in decline, in the context of global development scenarios characterized by rapid change on the one hand, and little change on the other, there remains a tendency to blame people rather than to query the models and priorities, or tools and technologies of change (Thomas, 2006).

Poverty as a Lack of Resources

This remains the most widespread understanding of poverty. It affirms that people are poor relative to others because they do not have the means to develop themselves, or to sustain their development over time because they do not have recourse to significant and sufficient resources. The means are normally identified in economic or material terms, for example, in terms of a person who lives on less than an average amount per year, in terms of a person's access to health resources, communication resources, physical resources, educational resources, and so on. UNESCO traditionally defined communication deprivation in terms of ownership of radio sets and access to newspapers per hundred of any given population. While the absolutization of this definition of poverty has been criticized, it nevertheless remains the dominant model and, irrespective of its critics and limitations, offers the most visible, vivid, readily communicable understandings of poverty. The image of a starving child somewhere in sub-Saharan Africa, a favela in Brazil or a peasant herdsmen in Mongolia does denote poverty, even if it is of a limited, fleeting surface kind. After all, affordable access to and consumption of regular supplies of food signifies a child that is not starving. In other words, such snapshots of poverty and the co-relational models used to determine poverty, in spite of real limitations, does capture aspects of poverty. What these models fail to account for are the structural reasons for poverty.

The solution to poverty then in this model is inputs—food supplies, shelter, health-care centres, the creation of employment opportunities, information, and so on. This is the favoured model of poverty alleviation adopted by international agencies, governments and NGOs. The role of information technologies in poverty alleviation, despite the paucity of evidence from the field, is treated as a given, and often regarded as an all-sufficient, substitute that will solve all the problems of rural poverty. In a paper presented at the *International Association for Media and Communication Research* (IAMCR) Conference in Cairo (2006), I had commented on the requisite need for a larger, enabling environment that is needed to make the necessary qualitative difference to telecentre and e-governance projects in India.

It is clear that a range of variables, dependent and independent, impact on the success of information and communication technology-based projects. These range from the quality of intra-project human relationships, local capacities, resourcing and sustainability, the availability of technical know-how, the availability of infrastructure including the supply of electricity, access and affordable use of these technologies, the computerisation of back-end services and access to a range of online material, an equitable social context of access and use, a supportive political environment, adequate levels of inter-sectoral computerisation, existing policies that facilitate the translation of information into real benefits and the exercise of social power. (Thomas, 2006:6)

Poverty as a Lack of Access

There is a growing body of literature on the potential benefits accruing from, and related to, the enabling of access to a variety of inputs in the context of alleviating poverty. Access is often linked to empowerment. The rationale for this approach is as follows. Poverty is not only an indication of a lack of resources but is also, rather fundamentally, about the lack of awareness on the part of a people of their own role in the fight against poverty. For instance, the lack of access to legal advice or information on a country's land reform legislation or minimum wages prevents vast numbers of rural farmers around the world from demanding what is rightfully theirs.

Access to information is, of course, the basis for the right to information movement in India. A key issue is the need for transparency, so that ordinary people can read for themselves the details of public expenditures, and if there are anomalies, demand explanations from the concerned authorities. Admittedly, right to information legislations the world over are still in their infancy. While governments and, in some cases, the civil society are required to be transparent, corporations are not. Notwithstanding such lacunae, access to information is an important right for it can become the basis for the enjoyment of related rights and securities: in education, shelter, access to food grain and employment opportunities. Access to 'survival' resources—for example, food and shelter are of course critical to human survival. For communities who have lived subsistence lives as hunter-gatherers, access to a forest's resources are necessary for survival. The lack of access to such traditional, life enhancing resources is one of the rallying calls for popular mobilizations in the context of the movements against the building of large dams in Thailand, China, India, Malaysia and many other parts of our world.

In other words, the notion of access suggests that when people become aware of their rights, they are empowered to confront and deal with the many reasons that continue to keep them in poverty. In contrast, in the poverty as lack of resources model, the poor are often seen as beneficiaries of government largesse or charity and are not given opportunities to use these resources in a meaningful manner and over a long term. However there is a significant caveat in the access model. The promise and delivery of 'access' across a range of sectors is of course vital to the maintenance of societies in the developed world. Access to essential services, to education, to employment opportunities and so forth, are among the major planks of government policy in the developed world. While in the developed world, the guaranteeing of enhanced access is at the very core of the democratic contract between the state and its citizenry, in the developing world, given the reality of poverty and other divides in society, access to essential services continues to remain a luxury for large sectors of the population. Furthermore, while access to information services in theory ought to open doors to other services, this is not always a certainty, given that in the developing world, there are visible disjunctures and lags in infrastructural growth and the provision of development services between and within different sections of the development apparatus. Development policy, resource availability and implementation are often the result of external and internal pressures, from governments, aid and multilateral agencies, political expediency and the availability of public finances at any given time. To place it in starker terms, when a government makes welfare cuts to its rural health and education budgets because of pressures from the World Bank, the International Monetary Fund (IMF) and other proponents of economic liberalization, access becomes a prime casualty. When, in response to such pressure, governments in the developing world affirm their commitment to technological solutions, the absurdity of development becomes that much more pronounced.

Poverty as a Lack of Human Rights

While the access model is important on its own right, it can be argued that its delivery is conditioned by the state of poverty and development legislations in any given country by the political will demonstrated by the state and the ability of civil society to enforce this will. In other words the quality and nature of access remains an issue. While the efforts of the Bangladesh-based Grameen Telecommunications to subsidize the ownership of cellular phones by poor, rural women, who, in turn have used it for accessing market information and for extending public services, remains a sterling example of access and the democratization of new technologies—it still remains to be seen whether access to information services has been complemented by other improvements in public services—in the success of land reforms, watershed conservation and management and so on, that is critical to development and social change.

Unlike other models, the poverty and human rights model is conversant with the politics of 'entitlement', the legal, political and administrative arrangements that allows ordinary citizens to fulfil their immediate and long-term needs. These arrangements vary—from welfare models on one end of the spectrum, mixed-models to completely privatized models. Entitlement is all about political will, the setting of priorities, preferential options. Dreze and Sen (1989:9), in the context of their work on famine, define entitlement as follows:

> What we can eat depends on what food we are able to acquire. The mere presence of food in the economy, or in the market, does not *entitle* a person to consume it. In each social structure, given the prevailing legal, political, and economic arrangements, a person can establish command over alternative commodity bundles.... These bundles could be extensive, or very limited, and what a person can consume will be directly dependent on what these bundles are.

The nature of entitlement does impact on the realities of poverty and wealth in any given context. It becomes acute in the context of the developing world, where entitlements have been steadily whittled away for the majority of people as a consequence of structural adjustment policies, the privatization of bio-diversity, the costs of mega-development projects, landlessness, the high costs of agricultural inputs and the low costs of outputs and low purchasing power.

The notion of poverty as a lack of human rights is based on earlier models of development—development as structural, human transformation that was popular, at least in the 1970s. The unpopularity of this model was linked to its rather radical understanding of the means of tackling global poverty. Its proponents were not happy with the piecemeal, incremental understandings of poverty alleviation but believed in transformative changes to a country's economic system in the light of the critical needs faced by the majority of people. If the access model makes change within the system possible, the human rights model is a radical model with maximum guarantees for the fulfilment of basic needs. The fact that there are relatively few takers for this model, except perhaps in the case of Cuba, and small-scale initiatives around the world, is not surprising, given the many people who stand to loose from any changes to the existing order: with its priorities, values, certainties, and economic interests. In spite of the limitations of the Cuban model of development, their attempt to create a level playing field against tremendous odds, has elicited support from a most unlikely source—the former President of the World Bank, James Wolfenson (Lobe, 2001) who had affirmed that 'Cuba has done a great job on education and health. They have done a good job, and it does not embarrass me to admit it'.

Most civil society organizations work within the 'access' model, in spite of the fact that their rhetoric comes close to the 'human rights' model. This is a familiar constraint, not in the least because most NGOs and other civil society organizations work within the parameters of the democratic consensus on social change. It is interesting to note that NGOs are rarely effective in the context of extreme poverty situations where people, because of their circumstances, opt for a more radical solution to their problems. Examples include the Maoist movements in Nepal and India.

Communications in Development

Communication interventions in poverty are under-girded by one or another understanding of poverty and the means to overcome it. The *communication resource* model has of course been the dominant model exemplified by the early UNESCO approaches, the *diffusion* model and the latter-day approaches to development communication based on 'marketing' and 'communication inputs'. The latest in this line of thinking is the IT intervention in *development* model which continues the tradition of conceptualizing information as an adequate and complete resource in development. It is not too difficult to understand the reasons for the worldwide dissemination of this model of development. Given the salience and impact of information technologies and information processing in every aspect of human life and at the heart of an extensive range of productive processes, IT has been granted an extraordinary role in global development.

The *psychologistic, behaviouristic model* best associated with the theories of Daniel Lerner and others, although not as widespread as it was in earlier years, is still very much a reality in many parts of the world. This model assumes that the refusal to adopt innovations or modify behaviour is a consequence of a traditional mindset, of a people's inability to empathize with or adopt modern sensibilities. It is assumed that such ways of thinking are an obstacle to modernization. There is a huge corpus of literature on the subject especially in the context of agricultural extension, family planning and communication-based strategies in the context of health/nutritional change.

The models of *participatory communication* are closely related to both the access and the human rights approaches to development. Stemming from the theories of the Brazilian pedagogist Paulo Freire and the many experiments with alternative communications that appeared in the late 1960s and 1970s—this model explicitly affirms that people's participation in communication is vital to the success of any given project. It is based on a conscious effort to involve people in their own development. The success of this model is self-evident. There have been numerous attempts at documenting participatory communication projects in Latin America, Africa and Asia. The use of popular theatre in development, community radio and, recently, IT-based projects witness this success.

However, the very success of 'participatory' approaches needs to be seen against the gradual institutionalization of the NGO movement in large parts of the world and the many attempts by governments to co-opt and dilute the notion of participatory change—from its original meaning rooted in the idea of grassroots, people-led, inclusive, autonomous change to that of people-led change defined by NGOs and governments. What is significant about the latter approach is the absence of a political agenda explicitly linked to the transformation of structures and practices responsible for poverty. In other words, this model privileges access within imposed models of development. For instance, rural radio stations in Cameroon do provide opportunities for local people in programming and in creating content. However, these stations are not owned by specific communities nor do they encourage the mobilization of people in support of large-scale change. Similarly, the many IT-based projects in parts of Africa, Asia and the Pacific, supported by inter-governmental agencies are strong on access but weak on situating these interventions within a long-term, integrated approach to the development of communities. One of the central para-doxes of IT interventions in development is that 'access' has not dramatically affected the feudal constancy of the rural political economy in contexts around the world.

However, in direct contrast to this restrained notion of participation adopted by the majority of NGOs in development, there are numerous community-based communication projects that are owned and run by local communities. In these projects, participation is the means to a larger end and that larger end is often linked to the achievement of justice, human rights, equitable development. Good examples of this approach are the radio projects supported by the Toronto-based World Association for Christian Communication in Haiti—Radio Inite, Radio Sel, Radio Flambeau and Radio Lakay. While the first three stations are networked through the Port-au-Prince-based Centre for Development Research and Action (CRAD), Radio Lakay is part of a community radio network run by the *Sosyete Animasyou Kominikasion Sisyal* (SAKS). In both cases, these stations are run by local communities who have placed radio at the heart of development. Not only is radio used for development in a traditional sense, it has become central to the preservation and dissemination of traditional culture and religion and is also used as an early warning system to inform people of weather extremes. It is the basis for numerous attempts at investigative journalism aimed at exposing police/military brutality, government corruption; has helped reinforce local security, and is used as an information kiosk for 'lost and found' messaging and for community education. Most importantly, the local radio platform in each of the instances is run by local volunteers and managed by people who are representatives of the local community.

While the foregoing introduction to communication-based interventions in poverty alleviation suggests diversity and universality, it is clear that many of these interventions have not led to the desired outcomes. While delivery systems have undergone change, with IT being the preferred delivery system today, the larger contextual issues related to politics, economics, power and social change continue to be ignored. A neutral attitude to poverty alleviation, favoured by many governments and NGOs, merely results in incremental development. Such projects rarely, if ever, affect the constancy and continuity of existing power relationships. This neutrality is part of a larger political consensus that suggests that a combination of democracy in politics and a free market in economics provides the ideal framework for development.

The Politics of Common Sense

Let us briefly deal with some of the myths that have been generated by this politics of neutrality.

The Market as the Great Leveller

There is a near-universal belief in the primacy of the market as the great leveller in development. According to this notion, the more the people involve themselves in market-based transactions, the better their chances of becoming part of the global consuming public. In other words, there is an assumption that consumption will inevitably lead to prosperity, to a levelling, and to a closing of existing economic gaps between the rich and the poor.

While there is no denying the importance of, and the links between, the market and development, the paradox of the market is that it is both inclusive and exclusive. It is inclusive in the sense that it caters to every community that can afford to buy or sell something or the other. It is exclusive in the sense that it discriminates against people who live below the poverty threshold— the millions of people who cannot buy or sell in the market. While the market has become a part of even the remotest of rural communities, it can be argued that the change in consumption habits and lifestyles is more a consequence of the profit-seeking habits of corporations rather than the change-seeking mentality of the rural poor. Take for instance Hindustan Lever, which, in terms of earnings and profits is among the largest companies in India. Their vast consumer portfolio includes detergent soaps. While the company has expended time and energy branding their detergent soap bars for rural consumers, they have also at the same time persuaded the same buying public to consider the virtues of the detergent powder—which is, at least in terms of branding and status, one step higher from the detergent soap. Hindustan Lever's concerns however begin and end with the buying public. They are not concerned with the non-buying public for the obvious reason that it would not make economic sense. This business attitude is affirmed by all sellers in rural markets. However, in the context of the growing populations of the poor, such exclusions merely contribute to the accentuation of the divides between the rich and the poor. What makes this situation even more desperate is the present moves by governments to back away from their public policy commitments. Take for instance, the liberalization of telecommunications in India that has led to the privatization of services. It has also resulted in the government handing over some of its public service commitments—for instance, the provision of universal services to the private sector. While in the country's new telecommunications law, the private sector is, in return for a licence, required to also connect poorer communities in their operating areas, there is absolutely no way of guaranteeing the implementation of such services. While the Government of India has established an overseer—the Telecommunications Regulatory Authority of India (TRAI)—to monitor the role of the private sector in providing rural services, TRAI is not independent enough to enforce this measure.

In other words, the market as a leveller is currently Gospel truth. While there is no denying that in an era of cable and satellite television, more and more people are being exposed to modern habits and lifestyles and are even changing their consumption behaviour, this again affects only those who have disposable incomes in hand. It would be difficult to find such change in some of the areas that the journalist Sainath (see Sainath, 1996) has visited—parts of Orissa, Bihar, and even Maharashtra and Andhra Pradesh.

The Neutrality of the Development Enterprise

There are, at any given moment, a slew of development initiatives supported by multi-lateral aid agencies and governments. The contemporary effort by some governments in Africa to raise a digital solidarity fund is one such example. There are many others in the areas of watershed development, bio-diversity conservation, animal husbandry, micro-credit, gender-based development, and so forth, that combine both macro and micro initiatives directed at the development of people. However, and this is the crux of the problem—many of these projects are based on the relativization of poverty. Poverty is often seen as a macro phenomenon affecting people across the board. Those who then become the targets for development are those who are perceived to be poor, relatively speaking, but who also have access to land and resources and who are seen to be capable of rising above their circumstances. In other words, there is a typical gravitation towards families who will contribute towards the government's or agency's anti-poverty success statistics. This kind of an approach inevitably leads to the marginalization of people living in remote areas or of those who have no access to land and resources. In the context of South Asia and sub-Saharan Africa, those who rank among the absolute poor can be counted in the millions. In other words poverty schemes rarely affect those who are the most vulnerable. That is an axiom that has remained constant in spite of millions of aid dollars.

The sectorality of the development enterprise, which is a consequence of funding from specialist aid agencies and current thinking on development, is often an obstacle to planned, integrated development. While the issue of gender, its relationship to domestic violence, violence against women in society, and the inequitable gender-based distribution of resources in a family environment—need to be seen as problems on their own right, they also need to be seen as symptoms of a larger violence in society. The lack of education, resources, access to land and employment, discriminatory religious and social customs, the reality of class and caste divides, the situation of institutionalized violence, the break down of local welfare schemes in the areas of health and education as a result of privatization and debt repayments, the degradation of land and soil resources, natural calamities related to change in the climate and environment, the persistence of feudal environments and opportunistic, corrupt politics at local and national levels—all these factors contribute to that larger violence that creates victims among women, children and men.

The sectoralization of development is an instance of neutrality. It is based on the belief that it is better to focus on a specific area rather than on the whole. It is based on the perspective that incremental change will lead to changes in other sectors—to a sort of domino effect. However, such predictions rarely work in a macro sense. Poverty cannot be tinkered with. Its root causes are related to inequitable power flows, ownership of resources and access to services. This may seem like an unfashionable statement—but if one ignores this reality, what one is left with are schemes built on the edifice of neutrality.

The Information Technology Fix

While the debate about the usefulness of technology or otherwise, especially IT in development, is an ongoing one, it would seem that this debate does have a central blind spot. The focus on the usefulness or otherwise of technology is, I believe, the wrong end of the stick. Satellite technology can be used to track hurricanes and map land areas belonging to indigenous populations but it can also be used for military purposes. What is important and often neglected are engagements with the policy implications supportive of the use of IT in development, for instance the logic of cost-effectiveness and efficiency. Take for instance the use of IT in education—through distance learning and in the context of local learning initiatives. The logic that is frequently used to favour distance learning over conventional education is ease of delivery, universality and cost-effectiveness. Although this logic is impeccable in the context of remote areas and difficult terrains, in less difficult geographical contexts, policy decisions in favour of IT in education usually impact on the recruitment, training and prioritizing of teachers in rural education. In most cases, while not openly acknowledged, IT becomes a substitute for teachers and part of a self-fulfilling circle—where the lack of teachers is weighed against the cost-effectiveness and availability of IT, leading to the edging out of the teaching fraternity. While in contexts characterized by wide employment opportunities, re-skilling and employment are a real possibility, such scenarios do not hold true for rural contexts in the South, where employment opportunities relate to a fixed number of professions.

In other words, cost-effectiveness related to the induction of IT and virtual learning environments can lead to the death of 'expendable' professions, like that of teachers, resulting in poorer learning environments bereft of face to face learning opportunities. Such policy initiatives are in turn a consequence of the many pressures to centre IT at the heart of development efforts. There are hidden strings attached to such efforts as IT-based applications are a significant part of the mantra of globalization. Current IT inductions in development fit perfectly with current policies that are anti-subsidy, anti-welfare and pro-World Trade Organization. Such applications often fulfil the free market conditionalities imposed by the World Bank and the IMF on indebted governments.

In the words of Adair Turner writing in *Prospect* (April 2001:25), this accent on IT is misplaced because it really does not deal with fundamentals.

Africa may lag 15 years or so behind US levels of PC and internet penetration, but it lags more like a century behind in basic literacy and health care. Anti-malaria programmes or, good schools, and the attainment of clean government are far higher priorities for the world's poor countries than avoiding a digital divide. Africa could be an economic disaster zone even with mobile phone and internet access as widely spread as in Europe today.

Tackling Poverty

So, what can be done to bring poverty back into the agenda of communication specialists, in particular those involved in using communications in development? The following suggestions are by no means exhaustive but merely point to the basis for another use of communication for development:

Training for Rural Journalists

What is perhaps significant from the point of view of journalism is that—in direct proportion to the commercialization, specialization and lifestyle focus of modern journalism, there has been a decrease in the coverage of less exotic stories, for instance, the coverage of poverty, unless it is of a sufficient magnitude, and is predicted to lead to significant political repercussions. It is often the case that issues related to poverty are covered/reported by journalists who reside in the urban centres. The poverty beat is not a favoured one and as a result there are only a handful of journalists around the world who actively report on poverty-related issues. While their con-tributions have been important, it would also make sense to train local people in journalism. Local writers are best suited to report on local realities that they understand better than outsiders. Additionally, such training will allow their voices to be heard in contexts far away from their reality, in locations and environments where decisions are taken. Rural journalism was a theme of the late 1970s. It needs to be revived but focussed on the training of the most vulnerable people.

Focus on Integrated, Participatory Communication Projects

There needs to be an accent on communication projects that are at the centre of community development and that address the critical justice and equity issues facing the community. The meaning of access, in this context, is related to the affirmation of this larger objective.

Investments in Community-based Communication Projects

Communication can no longer be seen as a luxury. It is central to development efforts. Governments need to invest in community media projects just as they support local development initiatives such as the Panchayat system in India. Support for community radio needs to become a routine part of the government's support to rural development. While in the Indian case, there have been recent initiatives aimed at locating information kiosks in rural centres—it is nevertheless necessary that such initiatives be open to and accessed by all people, rather than by the privileged few. Support for local cultural diversity and right to language needs to be seen as integral parts of investments in communication for community.

Involvement of Local People in Local Planning for Communications

This may look obvious but the fact remains that communication initiatives for the poor rarely are planned with input and participation from the poor. For example, the proposed information kiosks in India are state-based initiatives that have been planned and executed by technocrats and bureaucrats. While such initiatives will be of some benefit—for example to farmers who need regular information of prices of farm produce—it is bound to be less useful to the landless who may have other types of information needs.

The Poor and Their Rights to Information/Communication

With a few exceptions, most countries around the world are yet to enact significant, inclusive, right to information legislations. While the right to information (RTI) Act (2005) in India and the various state-level RTI legislations have certainly opened opportunities for the poor in India to access information necessary for the enjoyment of a range of human rights, the combination of a top-heavy bureaucracy and institutionalized corruption remain obstacles in the way of equitable, rural development. The implementation of the RTI in India offers one of the best hopes for the rural poor to fulfil their right to development. The right to information movement is, in my way of thinking, a grassroots expression of communication rights. The operationalization of this right is a significant cause for hope.

References

Coronel, S. 2001. 'Hot House of Rebellion', *The Investigative Reporting Magazine*, VII(2):12–16.
Dreze, J. and A. Sen. 1989. *Hunger and Public Action*. Clarendon: Oxford.
International Association for Media and Communication Research (IAMCR). Cairo. Available online at http://www.aucegypt. edu/conferences/iamcr/main.html.

Lobe, J. 2001. 'Learn from Cuba, Says World Bank', *Third World Network Features*, June 9:1–3.
Available online at: http://www.hinduonnet.com/fline/stories/20060908004500400.htm.

Sainath, P. 1996. *Everybody Loves a Good Drought: Stories from India's Poorest Districts*. New Delhi: Penguin Books.

———. 2001. 'None So Blind as Those Who Will Not See', *The UNESCO Courier*, June:44–46.

———. 2006. 'Withering lives', *Frontline*, 23(17):1–4. Available online at: http://www.hinduonnet.com/fline/stories/20060908004500400.htm.

Thomas, P.N. 2006. 'Bhoomi, Gyan Ganga, e-Governance and the Right to Information: ICTS and Development in India'. Paper presented at the Participatory Communication Section, IAMCR, 23–28 July, Cairo.

Turner, A. 2001. 'Not the e-Economy', *Prospect*, April: 22–26.

WACC. 2000. *Kreyon Pepe La Pa Gen Gonm: The People's Pen Has No Eraser: Communication Stories from Haiti's Grass Roots*. London: WACC Publications.

Hybrid Interactions: Human Rights and Development in a Cultural Perspective

2

JAN SERVAES AND CHRIS VERSCHOOTEN

Human rights increasingly form part of a wider network of perspectives which are shared and exchanged between the North and South, centers and peripheries, in multiple, creative and sometimes conflict-ridden ways. Human rights have become 'universalized' as values subject to interpretation, negotiation, and accommodation. They have become 'culture'.

—Ann-Belinda S. Preis, 1996

The question of empowerment is central to both culture and development. It decides who has the means of imposing on a society the view of what constitutes culture and development.

—Aung San Suu Kyi, 1995

A conference, held in November 1998 in Istanbul by a group of scholars, lawyers, development specialists and human rights activists, focussed on 'how compatible a universal normative approach to development is with respect to the right of peoples and communities to self-determination as well as with respect to organisations' autonomy (Donders, 1999:1). We are obviously faced here with a complex matter. Therefore, this chapter attempts to provide an introductory overview of recent thoughts on human rights, development and culture. We realize, however, that this complexity cannot be dealt with exhaustively within the scope of a single chapter (for a comprehensive overview of the most important declarations and covenants, see Hamelink, 2004; Linden, 1997; Mutua, 2002).

Human rights, development and culture are continuously evolving concepts. For instance, the civil and political rights are often referred to as the first generation of human rights. A second generation of rights emerged at the turn of the twentieth century, emphasizing the economic, social and cultural rights of people. Among others, the right to work, education and cultural participation belong to this set of rights. Since the 1950s, the demand for collective, solidarity or third generation rights has been voiced by the South as the result of anti-colonial revolutions. These new rights emphasize national self-determination and non-discrimination.

Development and culture too are dynamic concepts. A complete historical survey, however, would carry us too far. In this chapter, we will limit ourselves to a revision of three conventional 'dichotomies': (a) tradition versus modernity, (b) universalism versus relativism, and (c) individualism versus collectivism.

Two basic assumptions are made. First, human rights, development and culture are interdependent phenomena, which should not be separated in practice. Second, individuals are not only objects of human rights or development, but active agents, participating in, and constituting these phenomena through their interactions with other individuals and institutions.

Tradition and Modernity

For a long time, cultures were seen as homogeneous and bounded entities. This view, perhaps epitomized in the description of cultures as a list of traits, led to an instrumental and mechanical approach vis-à-vis human rights and development. If cultural traits were incompatible with human rights or modern ideas about development, then culture was seen as an obstacle. If the traits were compatible, then culture could be used as a surplus to development.

This chapter proposes a more integrated approach that views culture as a constructive and creative force which encompasses both development and human rights. The underlying idea is that cultures are not homogeneous and bounded entities, but rather dynamic, heterogeneous and open-ended. Some level of cultural coherence must always exist, but this has often been overstated. Deviance, inconsistency, contradiction and disagreement are parts of any culture. They move cultures forward from within, while intercultural contact moves cultures from without.

Apart from economic and political mechanisms, two basic human principles seem at work. On the one hand, people have an inward tendency to associate or identify with a specific culture or subculture (probably as a result of socialization processes). On the other hand, people tend to look to other cultures in order to establish alliances as well as to reinforce differences. In today's globalized context, intercultural contact has become particularly important (Servaes, 1989, 1999).

Modernization has introduced human rights and the conventional Western concept of development (as a linear, mainly economic, process) nearly everywhere. Colonialism and globalization are major forces that have made a large number of cultures 'creole' or 'hybrid'. In hybrid contexts, simple models such as *traditional versus modern* or *Western versus non-Western* are no longer valid. Western views on development and human rights often remain caught in these dichotomies. But many cultures now overlap and blend into each other as never before due to new modes of communication, trade and transport.

In the contemporary world, cultures are not isolated. They interact and influence each other. The intercultural dynamics is set in motion by contemporary processes of globalization, which lead, not without tension, to the emergence, consolidation or reformulation of specific cultural and ethical values common to the various cultural areas. Any culture in relation and comparison with other cultures may find its own idiosyncrasies and peculiarities, its strong and weak points.

The assumption has been made that as societies develop, they will loose their separate identities and cultural differences and tend to converge towards one common type of society. This is considered to be a result of industrialization and urbanization, which are identified as the main causes of this historical movement from diversity towards conformity, towards one global village. This global village is characterized by a secular culture and decline of religion, considerable geographic and social mobility, the predominance of the nuclear family, a high division of labour, with growing levels of formal education, economies based on industry, nowadays driven by the so-called 'knowledge' or e-economy, and so forth.

However, many studies contradict these assumptions. In the case of Thailand, for instance, Suntaree Komin (1988, 1991) found that certain so-called 'traditional' values and 'superstitious' behaviours like 'fortune-telling' and 'lucky numbers' are practiced more among Bangkokians than among farmers. No difference was observed in terms of educational level. 'This casts some doubt on the theory that postulates a negative correlation between education and supernatural belief and behaviour. However, it is a dominant value behaviour characteristic of the Thai' (Komin, 1988:171).

Therefore, the global village concept reflects an abstract and idealized image of a fully modern society. Several authors have come to the conclusion that modernization does not necessarily change cultural values. Modernization and indigenous culture can walk parallel, not simply convergent, paths (for example, Barbero, 1993; Barker, 2000; Hannerz, 1996; Harindranath, 2006; Howard, 1993; Miller, 1995; Servaes and Lie, 1997; Tomlinson, 1997; Werbner and Modood, 1997).

The way Islamic law and human rights discourses have met in recent years is a good example of how hybridization really works. In Afghanistan, women defend their right to education and health care by drawing on Western discourses about human rights. At the same time, however, many of them insist on being faithful to Muslim traditions at home (Ignatieff, 1998). Elsewhere, many young Islamic women insist on wearing veils because it makes them less vulnerable to reproaches of westernization and allows them to go out for work or study (Postel-Coster, 1994). They are not necessarily on their way to a complete assimilation of Western ideas.

The norms, worldviews, institutions and behavioural patterns that they face—and others in other cultures—are not simply given, but construed. Geertz (1973) and others have shown that cultures are symbolic constructions created within social contexts. Foucault (1980), for example, pointed out that power is at play here. Different cultural discourses are in competition with each other at various levels.

The debate in India about the practice of *sati* is a good example. *Sati*, originally the Sanskrit word for 'virtuous woman', was the practice whereby women burnt themselves on their husband's funeral pyre. *Sati* was abolished by the British Raj in 1829 after numerous cases had been recorded, particularly in the state of Bengal. Lati Mani (1987), who analysed the debate preceding this decision, shows that *sati*, as a cultural practice, was interpreted in three different ways by three different groups. She distinguishes between (1) the British colonial discourse, (2) a conservative indigenous discourse and (3) a progressive indigenous discourse. Mani demonstrates how each position represented a particular construction of *sati*. Each construction was based on different parts of Brahman scriptures and ignored particular Hindu customs, thus creating an illusionary sense of coherence. The point here is that women were used as a 'site on which tradition is debated and reformulated' (Mani, 1987:153), while they themselves were completely absent from the debate. In the 1980s, a number of cases of *sati* in the north of India brought the old debate back. Feminists pointed out that *sati* was now encouraged by some for economic reasons: to acquire the widow's dowry and to gain profit by turning it into a tourist attraction (Narayan, 1997). The example shows how a single cultural practice can be used for different purposes and can have different meanings for different people across time.

There are numerous other examples. Many discourses constructed by the tourism industry, governments, elites and Western activists alike—for moral, idealistic, commercial or other reasons—reduce people to uni-dimensional cardboard figures. If these people belong to minorities, whose voice is suppressed, they have a hard time resisting these constructions. The rights of individuals have often been violated that way. For instance:

> It is at least ironic to see largely Westernized elites warning against the values and practices they have adopted. At their best, such arguments tend to be dangerously paternalistic. For example, 'villagization', which was supposed to reflect traditional African conceptions, was accomplished in Tanzania only by force, against the vocal and occasionally even violent opposition of much of the population. (Donnelly, 1989:119)

The antidote to such harmful views begins with a critical look at one's own cultural constructions and at conventional views of 'us' and 'them':

> What is needed is a willingness to interrogate, politically and historically, the apparent 'given' of a world in the first place divided into 'ourselves' and 'others'. A first step on this road is to move beyond naturalized conceptions of spatialized 'cultures' and to explore instead a production of difference within common, shared, and connected spaces. (Gupta and Ferguson, 1997:45)

First of all, we have to come to grips with our past. Edward Said's (1995) captivating overview of the way in which Asian societies and philosophies throughout the ages were perceived by the West starts from the thesis:

> That the essential aspects of modern Orientalist theory and praxis (from which present-day Orientalism derives) can be understood, not as a sudden access of objective knowledge about the Orient, but as a set of structures inherited from the past, secularized, redisposed, and re-formed by such disciplines as philology, which in turn were naturalized, modernized, and laicized substitutes for (or versions of) Christian supernaturalism. In the form of new texts and ideas, the East was accommodated to these structures. (Said, 1995:122)

Therefore, academics and the people they study 'construct stylized images of the occident and orient in the context of complex social, political, and economic conflicts and relationships ... these stylized images are not inert products. Rather, they have social, political, and economic uses of their own, for they shape people's perceptions, justify policies, and so influence people's actions' (Carrier, 1995:11).

Those participating in a culture are often not aware of the discourses surrounding them, of how they have been constructed, and of how these discourses operate within a power structure. This relates to the difference between participants and observers. Observers can take a critical distance from their own cultural practices. This need not imply that they have to become outsiders. They can remain participants in their own culture, but will be more aware of what is happening around them, and more capable of determining their own path to development. Harmful cultural practices, such as female circumcision, can probably only be countered successfully by turning *participants* into *observers*. Note that:

> the increase of this kind of social reflexivity and the growth of criticism which allows members of a society and culture to challenge these practices in the name of some normative standards is one of the sociological constants of the transition from tradition to modernity. Modern societies allow their members to be at once observers of and participants in their normative orders. (Benhabib, 1995)

Universality and Relativism

Human rights emerged in the West when the modern state and capitalist economy started to develop. They represent a particular vision on human needs and human potential, based on early 'natural rights' and later on the 'rights of man' which reflected the rationalism, humanism and individualism of the European Enlightenment. The so-called first generation of rights, reflected in the Covenant on Civil and Political Rights, can be directly related to a Western bourgeoisie liberating itself from feudal and aristocratic powers. In the nineteenth century, Western socialist thinkers inspired a second generation, reflected in the Covenant on Economic, Social and Cultural Rights (see, for example, Donnelly, 1989; Galtung, 1994). Given these roots, human rights have always been under attack from cultural relativists. Relativists see the Universal Declaration and the Covenants as Western, ethnocentric lists of rights and freedoms, with limited value for the Majority World.

The debate between relativists and universalists, largely a philosophical and ethical issue, continues till today. East-Asian countries, which did not contribute significantly to the Universal Declaration, take what is probably the most critical view on human rights. The introduction of Asian values has been one of the most important issues fuelling the universalist-relativist debate during the 1990s. Asian values are put forward as a cultural alternative to human rights. They emphasize tolerance, harmony, consensus, collective rights and the right to development.

However, Asian values seem to serve other considerations. It should not come as a surprise that these are mainly economic and political, since the Asian values critique largely comes from government officials. This critique should not lead, however, to a complete rejection of the concept of Asian values, or worse, imply that Asian people have no values. As Tommy Koh (1999), the executive director of the Asia–Europe Foundation, explains:

> Some of East Asia's political leaders have given Asian values a bad name by seeking to justify their abuses of power and the inequities of their societies in the name of Asian values. For example, corruption, collusion and nepotism should be condemned by all Asians. They have nothing to do with Asian values. To put it more accurately, they have everything to do with bad Asian values but nothing with good Asian values. This leads me to my point that it is essential to distinguish between good Asian values and bad Asian values. Not all Asian values are good values just as not all Western values are good values. There are good Asian values and bad Asian values, just as there are good Western values and bad Western values. (ibid.:10)

Various attempts are made to reconcile universalism and cultural relativism. If the radical positions of either side are conceptualized as two extremes of a single continuum, then intermediate positions can be found somewhere in between.

Cultural relativism is based on the empirical fact of cultural and historical variability. In its most radical form, cultural relativism opposes all absolutes, considers cultures to be unique and therefore to be the only valid source of values, rights and duties. This position is no longer held by many. According to Janusz Symonides (2000), former director of the Human Rights Division at UNESCO, the results of the Vienna Conference confirm that this kind of cultural relativism is in retreat on many fronts. In more moderate forms, cultural relativism remains a valuable correction of the seemingly natural tendency towards ethnocentrism, evaluating one's culture as superior to others, or taking one's own values for universal values. Moderate relativism seems compatible with moderate universalism, but not with radical universalism.

Radical universalists deny the historical and cultural specificity of human rights. They claim that human rights are grounded in human nature and that we are all alike. Thus, human rights are moral rights of the highest order, applicable to all at all times. Universalist theories state that human rights are:

> ... held by all human beings, irrespective of any rights or duties one may or may not have as citizens, members of families, workers, or parts of any public or private organization or association.... If all human beings have them simply because they are human, human rights are held equally by all. And because being human cannot be renounced, lost or forfeited, human rights are inalienable. (Donnelly, 1993:19)

In its most extreme form, universalism can easily lead to imperialism. In more moderate forms, however, it emphasizes a global ethics of people 'being bound and motivated by shared commitments' (Perez de Cuéllar, 1995:34) who draw on a variety of cultural resources. This position comes close to moderate relativism.

Radical relativism, which excludes this possibility, is hard to accept today, if not from a moral or philosophical perspective, then certainly for pragmatic and functional reasons. There is a nearly worldwide consensus on many of the values that the Universal Declaration wants to protect. Almost all states have adopted the declaration—at least rhetorically—thus giving its rights in practice a substantial and nearly universal basis. Many countries have used them in anti-colonial struggles. The Western origin of human rights does not mean that they are irrelevant elsewhere or cannot have universal value. It does not imply that westernization is needed to realize human rights, or that the West is at some advanced stage, or has some universal moral authority.

Although the particular notion of human rights may be said to be Western in origin, basic human needs and various concepts of human dignity around the world can serve as a valuable basis for defending and promoting human rights (for a discussion on needs and rights, see Galtung, 1994). But we do need to acknowledge that 'rights' as instruments for development are an alien concept to many cultures. The Universal Declaration of Human Rights is often unknown and perceived as highly abstract. That is why several authors have argued for the localization of human rights. Baxi, for instance, in a strong critique of the universality claim of human rights, pleads for making peoples and communities the primary authors of human rights (Baxi, 2002:101). According to Bell, translating human rights into local cultural contexts has five important advantages. First, it leads to long-term commitments. Second, it helps to find the social groups that are most capable of bringing about social and political changes. Third, human rights are easier to justify. For instance,

> if it can be demonstrated that according to traditional Confucian conceptions of political rule governments have an obligation to alleviate suffering and avoid cruelty, this may help to persuade self-identified 'Confucian' rulers to avoid committing torture. (Bell, 1996:655)

Fourth, it helps activists to find the right attitude. Finally, it increases sensitivity to local mechanisms appropriate for the protection of human rights.

The concern to make human rights more applicable across different cultures has led to such notions as 'critical universalism', 'inclusive universalism' and 'weak cultural relativism'. Theories based on these concepts accept universals at a general level, but simultaneously recognize the need for cultural accommodation. Cultural diversity is seen as a positive factor contributing to the universality of human rights. For some scholars this implies a transformation of the system itself, for others cultural accommodation should mainly be seen in terms of a flexibility of the current standards.

Donnelly, who coined the term 'weak cultural relativism', distinguishes between three levels of cultural variation: variation in (1) the substance of the list of human rights, (2) the interpretation of individual rights, and (3) the form in which rights are implemented. For Donnelly, the three concepts represent hierarchical levels. His proposal allows for variations primarily at the lowest level of the form. For instance, whether the right to equal protection of the laws requires free legal assistance is a formal matter about which no universal claims can be made (particularly in developing countries it is often a matter of available resources). Cultural variations in form, however, are limited by the levels of interpretation and substance. At the level of interpretation, Donnelly accepts that 'culture provides one plausible and defensible mechanism for selecting interpretations' but adds that 'there are strong limits on the acceptable range of variation':

> The meaning of the 'right to political participation,' for example, is controversial, but the range of controversy is limited by the substance of the concept: an election in which a people were allowed to choose an absolute dictator for life ('one man, one vote, once,' as a West African quip put it) is simply an indefensible interpretation. (Donnelly, 1989:117)

Substantive differences lead to changes to the list itself. According to Donnelly, these should only rarely be made. Essentially, there are no reasons not to allow changes to the list of human rights. Since human rights address needs, and these needs may vary across time and culture, new human rights may be desirable and may improve the human rights system. There is little to be gained, however, by introducing new rights that remain insignificant at the operational level. In practice, a proliferation of rights may ultimately reduce the value and legitimacy of the human rights discourse.

A truly cross-cultural approach should not only be concerned with the *content* of rights, but also focus on the *construction*. Galtung notes that human rights are also Western in their construction. Among others, he points to 'the ultimate, universal normative emission in one sender (United Nations General Assembly), and the delicate balance between enacting rights and cashing in on duties in one receiver only (the state)' (Galtung, 1994:19). Galtung suggests 'not to let the state off the hook of accountability, but to extend accountability to other world actors' such as international organizations and corporations, and 'to spin a dense normative web of norms by and large pointing in the same (basic human needs) direction, dispersing both authority and credit' (ibid.:20).

This has become a very important issue since states are rapidly loosing power due to globalization. Multinational corporations increasingly control the economic and everyday life of an individual, but are hardly accountable. They can easily turn their back on human rights. NGOs can pressurize these groups to implement human rights standards. This is not an easy thing to do as economists and other professionals in these organizations tend to separate human rights and economic considerations.

That approach is very deeply rooted not only in the institutional mythology of most, if not all, of the international agencies, but is also strongly reinforced by the philosophical underpinnings of many economic theories and by the methodological approaches used by the great majority of economists. (Alston, 1988:18)

This critique has also been voiced by Amartya Sen. The problem can be countered by bringing together economists, lawyers and cultural specialists in multidisciplinary teams.

Individualism and Collectivism

A discussion on culture inevitably leads to the traditional debate on individualism and collectivism. The premise is well known: while the Western cultural position is said to be based on 'the sacredness of the individual body, and spirit of the individual' (Galtung, 1994:15), non-Western societies are supposed to emphasize the loyalties and responsibilities towards the community. Many scholars agree with Kagitçibasi who suggests that there is 'an individualistic ethos in the Western world' while 'the majority of humankind share at least some aspects of collectivism' (1997:4, 5).

Since the 1990s, collectivism has been put forward as one of the Asian values. The general assumption is that Asian societies tend to favour the interests of the community, while the West emphasizes the individual. This relativist position was reflected in the Bangkok Declaration of April 1993, adopted at the Asian regional preparatory meeting for the World Conference on Human Rights in Vienna. The Vienna Declaration, however, adopted by consensus by the World Conference, confirmed the universality of human rights and rejected the notion of cultural relativism.

The individualism-collectivism dichotomy can be linked to another set of presumed 'opposites': first-versus-second-generation rights. The separation of these two types of rights—in a nutshell, food versus freedom—has been the cause of many heated debates, first between the East and the West, now between the South and the North. Liberal-capitalist ideologies traditionally emphasized civil and political rights, while Marxist thinking tended to focus on second-generation rights. The current insistence on free elections by Western donor countries and the introduction of Asian values has revived the debate. Western countries are criticized for giving priority to civil and political rights over social, economic and cultural rights. Asian countries in particular have argued that the West now uses civil and political rights to cut aid and undermine development. But Asian governments are said to contest universal human rights 'as a bargaining tool vis à vis the West' and 'to pursue globalization without internally democratising their societies' (Ravindran, 1998:54).

African nations have emphasized collectivism too. The African Charter on Human and Peoples' Rights includes collective rights, and points towards the duties of individuals towards the community

(Ama Ankumah, 1992). But the demand from many non-Western countries for universal solidarity rights has not fared well so far. The demand for these rights emerged through anti-colonialist revolutions and is concerned with self-determination and non-discrimination. Solidarity rights pertain primarily to certain collective concerns, such as peace, culture, development and ecological balance. So far, with the exception of the right of peoples to self-determination, the International Bill of Human Rights includes only individual rights.

There are two important reasons why, apart from the right to self-determination, no collective rights have been adopted at the international level. First, states fear that giving rights to groups may foster secessionist movements (this is also the reason why they limit self-determination). In this age of globalization, where states are loosing power to higher levels already, groups with collective rights within their borders might weaken their strengths even more. Second, group rights are a potential threat to current human rights. Collective freedoms may easily be claimed against, or over, individuals. It is a very serious problem:

> Appeals to the rights of the people collectively are most often used by oppressive, paternalistic regimes to ignore or repress the desires, or to deny the rights of, real, concrete people. The rhetoric of the rights of peoples or the masses too often seems to have little purpose other than to justify the denial of most specific (human and other) rights of most people. The dangers of political abuse are especially strong when the collective body held to possess these third generation human rights is the state. (Donnelly, 1989:145–146)

The Forum for Human Rights and Development, an NGO network based in Bangkok, defends a more grass-root position. They argue that supporting community rights against individual rights is in practice used against Asian communities by denying them their rights.

Nevertheless, we need to take the demands for collective rights seriously. Concerns, such as peace, culture, development and a healthy environment are important enough. Many countries in the world have minority groups that are seriously threatened. Due to globalization, an increasing number of immigrant groups are demanding the right to freely express their cultural particularities within nations dominated by another culture (Lukes, 1993). One might argue that most of their demands are already covered by existing individual human rights, which is true to some extent. But not always. For instance, the individual right to education does not give a group the right to institutionalize its own educational system. In addition, collective rights might help to correct structural injustices. As Tomasevski points out:

> Access to remedy for human rights violations is still—and likely to remain so—exclusively individualistic: remedies can be sought by the individuals whose individual rights have been (allegedly) violated. This is obviously insufficient to challenge structural and policy problems in development. (Tomasevski, 1993:191)

Ultimately, the question is whether rights of a group can be human rights (since groups are not human, but a collection of human beings), and whether they can be compatible with existing human rights. Jones (1999) proposes a distinction between 'collective groups' and 'corporate groups'. A collective group has no moral standing of its own. The attribution of a right to the group is motivated only by the separate but identical interest of the individuals which form the group. A corporate group is a single, integral entity with a moral standing of its own. Jones argues that corporate group rights cannot be accepted as human rights because the moral unit is a group and not a human being. Nations or 'peoples', therefore, cannot have human rights. Groups based on a collective conception, however, might enjoy human rights because these rights can be traced back to individuals. These rights of the collective group cannot write:

> ... individuals out of the moral calculation. If we adopt the collective theory, the claims of the few may have to yield to those of the many, but at least the claims of the few will be heard and counted. (...) Thus, morally, there is no group that has an existence independently of, and that can hold rights against, its own members. There are only individuals who hold rights jointly, and, by common consent, right holders cannot hold rights against themselves. Rights held by individuals jointly, like those held individually, must be rights directed 'outward' at other individuals or groups of individuals rather than 'inward' to the right holders themselves. (ibid.:93–94)

Jones' proposal is largely to see groups and individuals not in opposition to each other, but rather as complementary. Lukes (1993) agrees:

> To defend human rights is to protect individuals from utilitarian sacrifices, communitarian impositions, and from injury, degradation, and arbitrariness, but doing so cannot be viewed independently of economic, legal, political, and cultural conditions and may well involve the protection and even fostering of collective goods.... For to defend human rights is not merely to protect individuals. It is also to protect the activities and relations that make their lives more valuable, activities and relations that cannot be conceived reductively as merely individual goods. (ibid.:30)

It is a fact that we are all individuals within *groups*, and that many groups need protection because they are seriously threatened. Whether solidarity rights are really needed, remains to be seen. At the conference in Istanbul on human rights (Donders, 1999) most participants questioned the inclusion of collective rights into the human rights canon. Galtung (1994) looks at the future from a historical perspective:

> In the Western countries human rights have generally first been articulated by civil society, and the state has received the norms only when they can be seen as being sent from above, and usually without any enthusiasm. The civil-political rights were promoted by powerful individuals and civil groups from the emerging bourgeoisie who then became majorities in the national assemblies, transforming monarchies into presidential systems or constitutional monarchies. The economic-social-cultural rights were promoted by working-class parties before the ruling classes could accept them from a national assembly. In the same vein, the most

articulate and meaningful civil society organizations today are probably in the fields of development, environment, and peace, promoting norms about goals and processes that sooner or later will be accepted by the state system. (Galtung, 1994:150)

Conclusion

Some of the issues discussed above, it is hoped, can help to establish a cautious but more effective approach in the field of human rights and development. Five major issues are thought to be essential to any human rights and development policy. It is suggested that:

1. Cultures are increasingly hybrid. This forces us to deal with conventional dichotomies, such as traditional versus modern, in a more creative and hopefully more productive way.
2. Culture is a multi-dimensional discourse with a power structure. To understand oppressive discourses, people need to become observers of their own culture. Observation leads to more knowledgeable participation.
3. Human rights should be translated into local cultural contexts. This is not in opposition with universality, provided one accepts a moderate universalism.
4. There is little to support a division of rights. Limited resources and cultural particularities require choices to be made, but these should ideally be made at the level of the form or interpretation of a right, not by cutting rights from the list.
5. There are a number of reasons *not* to support collective human rights. At least at the level of a corporate group, collective rights are a potential threat to existing human rights.

References

Alston, P. 1988. 'Making Space for New Human Rights: The Case of the Right to Development', *Harvard Human Rights Yearbook*, 1:3–40.

Ama Ankumah, E. 1992. 'Universality of Human Rights and the African Charter on Human and Peoples' Rights', in *Universaliteit en Mensenrechten. Fundamenteel en Controversieel*, pp. 23–38. Leiden: NJCM.

Barbero, J.M. 1993. *Communication, Culture and Hegemony. From the Media to Mediations*. London: Sage Publications.

Barker, C. 2000. *Cultural Studies. Theory and Practice*. London: Sage Publications.

Baxi, U. 2002. *The Future of Human Rights*. New Delhi: Oxford University Press.

Bell, D.A. 1996. 'The East Asian Challenge to Human Rights: Reflections on an East West Dialogue', *Human Rights Quarterly*, 18(3):641–667.

Benhabib, S. 1995. 'Cultural Complexity, Moral Interdependence, and the Global Dialogical Community', in M. Nussbaum and J. Glover (eds). *Women, Culture and Development. A Study of Human Capabilities*, pp. 235–255. Oxford: Clarendon Press.

Carrier, J.G. 1995. *Occidentalism. Images of the West*. Oxford: Clarendon Press.

Donders, Y. 1999. Human Rights, Culture and Development. Report of the conference organized by Women for Women's Human Rights and Novib, Istanbul, 25–27 November 1998. The Hague: Novib.

Donnelly, J. 1989. *Universal Human Rights in Theory and Practice*. Ithaca: Cornell University Press.

———. 1993. *International Human Rights*. Boulder: Westview Press.

Foucault, M. 1980. *Power/Knowledge: Selected Interviews and Other Writings 1972–1977*, in C. Gordon (ed.). Translated by C. Gordon, L. Marshall, J. Mepham and K. Soper. New York: Pantheon.

Galtung, J. 1994. *Human Rights in Another Key*. Cambridge: Polity Press.

Geertz, C. 1973. *The Interpretation of Cultures*. London: Fontana Press.

Gupta, A. and J. Ferguson. 1997. 'Beyond "Culture": Space, Identity, and the Politics of Difference', in A. Gupta and J. Ferguson (eds). *Culture, Power, Place: Explorations in Critical Anthropology*, pp. 33–51. Durham: Duke University Press.

Hamelink, C.J. 2004. *Human Rights for Communicators*. Cresskill: Hampton Press.

Hannerz, U. 1996. *Transnational Connections*. London: Routledge.

Harindranath, R. 2006. *Perspectives on Global Cultures*. Berkshire: Open University Press.

Howard, M. 1993. *Contemporary Cultural Anthropology*. New York: Harper Collins.

Igantieff, M. 1998. 'Out of Danger. Human Rights at 50: Overview', *Index on Censorship*, 27(3):21–29.

Jones, P. 1999. 'Human Rights, Group Rights, and Peoples' Rights', *Human Rights Quarterly*, 21(1):80–107.

Kagitçibasi, C. 1997. 'Individualism and Collectivism', in J.W. Berry, M.H. Segall and C. Kagitçibasi (eds). *Handbook of Cross-Cultural Psychology, 3, Social Behavior and Applications*, pp. 1–49. Boston: Allyn & Bacon.

Koh, T. 1999. 'Differences in Asian and European Values', *Asian Mass Communication Bulletin*, 29(5):10–11.

Komin, S. 1988. 'Thai Value System and Its Implication for Development in Thailand', in D. Sinha, D. and H. Kao (eds). *Social Values and Development. Asian Perspectives*. New Delhi: Sage Publications.

———. 1991. *Psychology of the Thai People. Values and Behavioral Patterns*. Bangkok: National Institute of Development Administration.

Linden, A. 1997. 'Communication and Human Rights in Developing Countries', *Culturelink*, August, 22:149–166.

Lukes, S. 1993. 'Five Fables about Human Rights', in. S. Shute and S. Hurley (eds). *On Human Rights: Oxford Amnesty Lectures*, pp. 19–40. New York: Basic Books.

Mani, L. 1987. 'Contentious Traditions: The Debate on Sati in Colonial India', *Cultural Critique*, 7:119–157.

Miller, D. (ed.). 1995. *Worlds Apart. Modernity through the Prism of the Local*. London: Routledge.

Mutua, M. 2002. *Human Rights. A Political and Cultural Critique*. Philadelphia: University of Philadelphia Press.

Narasimhan, S. 2002. *Sati. Widow Burning in India*. New York: Doubleday.

Narayan, U. 1997. *Dislocating Cultures. Identities, Traditions and Third World Feminism*. New York: Routledge.

Perez De Cuéllar, J. (ed.). 1995. *Our Creative Diversity. Report of the World Commission on Culture and Development*. Paris: UNESCO.

Postel-Coster, E. 1994. 'Women and Culture: An Ambivalent Relationship', *Culture Plus*, 14:7–10.

Preis S., A.B. 1996. 'Human Rights as Cultural Practice: An Anthropological Critique', *Human Rights Quarterly*, 18(2): 286–315.

Ravindran, D.J. 1998. *Human Rights Praxis: A Resource Book for Study, Action and Reflection*. Bangkok: The Asian Forum for Human Rights and Development.

Said, E. 1995. *Orientalism*. Harmondsworth: Penguin Books.

Samuels, H. 1999. 'Hong Kong on Women, Asian values and the Law', *Human Rights Quarterly*, 21(3):707–734.

Servaes, J. 1989. 'Cultural Identity and Modes of Communication' in J. Anderson (ed.). *Communication Yearbook*, 12, pp. 383–416. Beverly Hills: Sage Publications.

———. 1999. *Communication for Development. One World, Multiple Cultures*. Creskill: Hampton Press.

Servaes, J. and R. Lie (eds) 1997. *Media and Politics in Transition. Cultural Identity in the Age of Globalization*. Leuven: Acco.

Suu Kyi, A.S. 1995. *Freedom from Fear* (Revised Edition). London: Penguin Books.

Symonides, J. 2000. 'Towards a Human Rights Agenda for the 21st Century', in J. Servaes (ed.). *Walking on the Other Side of the Information Highway. Communication, Culture and Development in the 21st Century*, pp. 74–85. Penang: Southbound.

Tomasevski, K. 1993. *Development Aid and Human Rights Revisited*. London: Pinter.

Tomlinson, J. 1997. *Internationalisation, Globalisation and Cultural Imperialism*. London: Pinter.

Werbner, P. and T. Modood (eds). 1997. *Debating Cultural Hybridity. Multi-cultural Identities and the Politics of Anti-racism*. London: Zed Books.

Media Globalization through Localization 3

JAN SERVAES AND RICO LIE

Neither history nor ideology has come to an end. The advocates of capitalism and free trade see globalization as a positive, progressive force generating employment and ultimately raising living standards throughout the world. The critics see it as a means of expropriating the resources of poor countries by drawing them into debt, encouraging the use of sweated labour, and accelerating environmental degradation. The protagonists will turn increasingly to history for support. The obligation now falls on historians to ensure that the history cited is based on evidence rather than on honorary facts, and to consider they can apply arguments about the present to improve our understanding of the past.

A.G. Hopkins (2002:9)

In recent years we have come to witness interesting, albeit somewhat puzzling, developments in the world of media communications: the transnationalization of national, and even local, television in several parts of the world; local appeal as a success formula for television but not for cinema; the digitalization and convergence of both old and new information and communication technologies (ICT); and media globalization and localization as concurring phenomena (see for a recent account Wang, Servaes and Goonasekera, 2000).

These developments have painted a communications landscape that is quite different from what we were familiar with. They pointed to new directions for changes and exposed significant inadequacies in the framework of analysis that was employed in the past. It is only with a good look at the industry, the audience, the product and the policies that we may be able to demystify some of the clouds surrounding media globalization and assess its impacts.

What is New?

As an idea, globalization is not a product of the 1990s, or even the twentieth century, as some researchers have pointed out (Gardels, 1997; Hall, 1995; Hopkins, 2002). Held, McGrew,

Goldblatt and Perraton (1999:414) conclude that 'globalization is neither a wholly novel, nor primarily modern, social phenomenon. Its form has changed over time and across the key domains of human interaction, from the political to the ecological. Moreover … globalization as a historical process cannot be characterized by an evolutionary logic or an emergent telos'.

Over the years the word has increasingly been used to refer to a process through which the entire human population is bonded into a 'single system' (Wallerstein, 1990, 1997), a 'single society' (Albrow, 1990), or 'the structuration of world as a whole,' as defined by Robertson (1990). This 'single system', then forms the framework for individual activities and nation-state operations. It is conceived both as a journey and a destination—with arrival at the globalized state a finality (Featherstone, 1990; Ferguson, 1992; Giddens, 1990) which constitutes a unit of analysis in its own right.

This vision of an era of global communications seems especially pertinent when changes in other spheres of human societies are taken into consideration. The 1990s, with the fall of the Berlin Wall and the explosive growth of the World Wide Web as preludes, have been marked by the collapse of the physical, virtual and institutional barriers which had kept people apart over the previous several decades. The ever closer trade relationships among nation-states, the growing number of transnational corporations, ICTs, the Internet and discussions on e-commerce and e-governance, the emergence of global health and environmental issues and a common style of consumption of material and cultural products have all helped to bring about what is described as the 'globalization' of our world. In other words, this perspective considered globalization as the widening, deepening and speeding up of worldwide interconnectedness in all aspects of contemporary social life.

Globalists, Traditionalists or Transformationalists?

But, beyond a general awareness and agreement of this global interconnectedness, there is substantial disagreement as to how globalization is best conceptualized, how one should think about its causal dynamics, how one should characterize its structural, socio-economic consequences, and which implications it has on state power and governance. This debate, which has been summarized in a number of books edited by Held and others (1999, 2000), has developed three different theses on globalization: a (hyper)globalist perspective, a sceptical or traditionalist perspective, and, a transformationalist perspective.

These perspectives could be summarized as follows (Cochrane and Pain, 2000:22–23):

Globalists see globalization as an inevitable development which cannot be resisted or significantly influenced by human intervention, particularly through traditional political institutions, such as nation-states.

Traditionalists argue that the significance of globalization as a new phase has been exaggerated. They believe that most economic and social activity is regional, rather than global, and still see a significant role for nation-states.

Transformationalists believe that globalization represents a significant shift, but question the inevitability of its impacts. They argue that there is still significant scope for national, local and other agencies.

The globalists could be divided into optimists and pessimists. The optimists, with neo-liberal arguments, welcome the triumph of individual autonomy, and the market principle over state power. They emphasize the benefits of new technologies, global communications and increased cultural contacts. Neo-Marxists tend to be more pessimistic in their globalist discourse. They emphasize the dominance of major economic and political interests and point mainly to the uneven consequences of globalization. However, both groups share the belief that globalization is primarily an economic phenomenon.

Traditionalists believe that globalization is a myth and emphasize continuities between the past and present. There is nothing really new. Whatever the driving forces for globalization, they contend that the North-South 'gaps' increase. All we are witnessing is simply a continuation and progression of evolutionary change.

The transformationalists can be found somewhere in-between. They recognize the complexity of the phenomena and try to move beyond the sometimes-arid debate between the globalists and the traditionalists.

Our interpretation of this classification is that the globalist and the traditionalist perspectives are both very extreme in their views. The globalists advocate that the world changes towards a more homogenous global culture and towards all kinds of new global structures. The traditionalists take the other extreme stance and advocate that nothing really revolutionary is happening. Still in our opinion, the transformationalist perspective is not so much a compromise between the two as it is a less extreme and more modest interpretation of what is happening. Transformationalists argue that the world does go through changes—in a sense, as she has always gone through changes—but they do believe that some of these changes form a conglomerate of changes that does account for something to be interpreted as new.

Elsewhere, Lie (1998) made an inventory of such a conglomerate of changes in a cultural atmosphere and identified the following components: (1) the interrelated processes of the emergence of interdisciplinarity, (2) the increasing role of the power of culture, (3) the birth of a new form of modernization, (4) the changing role of the nation-state, and (5) the emerging attempts to address the link between the global and the local. The total conglomerate of changes accounts for something new, but especially the last issue of linking the global with the local was identified as a central point of change. But how can this conglomerate of global changes be linked to development and political-economic and social change at local levels and from within local levels?

Homogenization, Polarization, or Hybridization?

This more general typology can also be found at the communications and culture level. The globalist perspective assumes a unified, homogeneous global culture. From a neo-Marxist and functionalist point of view (Wallerstein, 1990; Chew and Denemark, 1996; Hirst and Thompson, 1996), globalization, a product of capitalists' drive to expand markets and maximize profits, only serves to perpetuate the hegemony of the few Western powers. The world of communications has become a perfect stage for the workings of capitalism. Once a single system, there will be no longer a need for every nation to maintain its own communications industry (Mittelman, 1996).

Others, especially those with a sociology and cultural studies background (Featherstone, 1995; Hall, 1992; Harindranath, 2006; Mato et al., 1996; Robertson, 1992; Said, 1993; Waters, 1995), have emphasized the plurality of cultural development as a result of the anti-colonialism movement. Instead of losing one's 'sense of place' because of increasing global influences, the importance of locality was underlined in the constructing and deconstructing, embedding and disembedding of social forces.

As pointed out by Featherstone (1995:6), globalization suggests simultaneously two views of culture. The first, taking a monoculturalist point of view, treats globalization as the 'extension outward of a particular culture to its limits, the globe,' through a process of conquest, homogenization and unification brought about by the consumption of the same cultural and material products. The second one, adopting a multiculturalist stand, perceives globalization as the 'compression of cultures'.

The monoculturalists' interpretation of globalization is often noted for its resemblance to the modernization and media imperialism theories (Servaes, 1999). Both focussed on the economic and technological forces in change, and suggested a one-way uni-linear impact of Western—or American to be specific—media on their audiences. Economic incentives and technological developments have also been believed to be the major driving forces for globalization (Featherstone, 1995:7; Robertson, 1990:22). For the communications industry, the purported globalization process was fuelled by yet another factor: policy deregulation. Although many would argue that nation-states are still capable of keeping things under control, this control is undeniably much less than it used to be (Servaes and Wang, 1997; Wang, 1997).

Globalization, Localization or Something Else?

While the meaning of globalization remains ambiguous, 'media globalisation' or 'global media' have quickly become clichés in communications studies. Two questions can be raised about the use of such terms, however. First, what is meant by a globalized communications industry, and secondly, can we assume that a genuine globalization of the industry has already taken place? More precisely, what is the direction of changes that we can observe now—globalization, localization, or something else?

All too frequently when the term 'global' is used in conjunction with the communications media or industry, it refers primarily to the extent of coverage, with the popularity of satellite television and computer networks serving as evidence of the globalization of communications.

Indeed, never before in human history has a single television channel been available in over 150 nations, nor has there been any communications medium which managed to attract hundreds of million of users. However, as Ferguson has pointed out, the linkages brought about by the so-called globalization process are largely confined to Organization for Economic Co-operation and Development (OECD) and G7 member countries, which constitute one-third of the world population. And even when a medium, for example, CNN, can put over 150 countries on its map, the rate of penetration and actual consumption can present rather a different picture. As Street (1997:77) has said, the fact that a product is available everywhere is no guarantee that it achieves the same level of popularity, let alone acquires the same significance, meaning or response (Featherstone, 1990:10). It is no secret that CNN's audiences normally account for only a small fragment of a nation's population.

However, the meaning of a globalized industry would be seriously distorted if other dimensions were left out of the discussion. These dimensions, including the dynamics of the market, modes of production, the contents and messages transmitted, are closely related to the perception of the role and function of communications in the globalization process, the direction of change in the industry, and ultimately, the cultural images presented by the theories of globalization.

There is no denying that competitive pricing is a major reason for the availability of American and Japanese programmes in most parts of the world. However if prices were the single most important factor at work, those companies which produce the cheapest and most attractive products, with the most extensive global distribution networks and best promotional skills would have become the sole suppliers for the global market, leaving very little to the smaller, less competitive national and local players. To critical theorists, communications media can be viewed as industries which commercialize and standardize the production of culture (Kellner, 1989). This definition highlights an important property of the media: a business that produces, distributes and sells marketable products. But the recognition of this property is not to overlook the media's other equally important characteristic: its being cultural.

Cultural products, more than any other, reflect the cultural values of their producers and the social reality in which they were produced. Viewing a television programme or listening to the radio, therefore, cannot be seen as a simple act of consumption; these acts involve a rather complex process of decoding cultural meanings. Although competing prices may contribute to the wide availability of certain cultural products, the purchase of cultural products differs from the purchase of typical consumer goods in that, considerations—such as product quality—may bear little significance in the decision to watch, or not to watch, a television programme.

The cultural products' market, therefore, does not operate on economic forces alone. Following a similar logic, communications technologies, the other purported major force for globalization, also have their blind spots in explaining all changes—a conclusion which we can derive, without too much difficulty, from the discussion of the significance of 'place' and 'local cultures' in the literature on globalization.

Some neo-Marxists view globalization as a process where the feeling of belonging is no longer connected to different places; they argue that the sense of belonging is to one single global society. Therefore it is fair to say that the local culture and the local 'place' is still more important to most people than the global. 'Even if cultural globalization, as Giddens pointed out, is an important part of globalization and even if local culture is constantly challenged, there are few signs of one homogenous global culture' (Lie, 1998:144).

Therefore, most scholars today see globalization as interlinked with localization. But although scholars agree *that* globalization and localization are linked, sometimes referred to as glocalization, there still remains a lot of uncertainty and discussion around the question on *how* these two concepts are linked (Bauman, 1998).

Viundal (2000:6) describes this linkage by using the analogy of a tree:

As the tree grows stretches out and widens its horizon, its roots at the other end also need to grow stronger. In my case, going to Australia, stretching out my branches, as a way of globalising, my awareness of my cultural background and roots as a Norwegian have at the same time grown stronger, as a sign of localising. Consciously or unconsciously my culture might have been challenged or changed due to my exposure to other cultures, but in this process my Norwegianness also tends to be confirmed.

This coincides with what Giddens (1995a) pointed out about human nature. He suggested that humans want, or maybe need, a place to belong to, but that they at the same time want to reach out to what is found outside this 'place'.

Cultural Identity

What globalization really is and what it means to human beings with regard to (cultural, national, ethnic ...) identity is a matter of discussion. Thomas Eriksen (1993:150) starts from the assumption that identity is locally constructed, and that 'people still live in places'. This indicates that the connected world is a stage where people with different cultures and identities meet.

Therefore, cultural identity has become a crucial concept in the debate on globalization. If we adopt Lull's (1995:66) definition of culture—'a particular way of life shaped by values, traditions, beliefs, material objects and territory'—and Anderson's (1983) idea of imagined communities, we have to accept that culture and identity are an evolving process, positioning the individual as an active participant in the consumption of information. The subconscious references and choices that we make on a daily basis, that attach meaning to the information we receive, is related to our concept of self and other. This view emphasizes the exchange of meaning taking place in the local consumption of global messages. As Katz (1980) notes, context and the individual reading of the message become the focus with a shift from 'what the media do to the people to what the people do to the media'. Globalization is thus restricted to describing the expansion and coverage of the means of communication, not its consumption.

For Example: Pokemon

In the case of Pokemon, aspects of Japanese culture could be transmitted to other countries where the game has been introduced. However, cultural transmission is seldom prominent in such exchanges. Pokemon has undergone a cleansing of its cultural aspects to make the game more appealing (marketable) to its overseas recipients, an attempt to hide its 'Japan-ness'. 'We tried not to have violence or sexual discrimination or religious scenes in the U.S.,' says Kubo of Kubo Publishing (on the Pokemon website). 'Some graphic sequences involving punching were taken out. The names of the characters and monsters were westernised.' The production of popular culture and cultural mixing makes the original source of consumer goods irrelevant (Iwabuchi, 2000).

This demonstrates the trend of globalization through localization. The global market is an aggregation of local markets and maximization of market share is obtained by penetrating as many local markets as possible. This is done by the merger of, or co-operation among, trans-national corporations of different countries of origin (ibid.). Local subsidiaries often specialize in giving trans-national products a 'local' feel.

Thus, though the potential for cultural enrichment through globalization is great, in reality most products are stripped of their cultural values in order to make the product more marketable. This 'cultural striptease' makes products, in potential, more appealing to more cultures. But, this does not necessarily mean that the product is simplified. The product is differently encoded by the producer (or better sub-producer) and is encoded in such a way that it becomes more multi-culturally interpretable (Ito, 1990). It offers the possibility for multi-cultural interpretations. Such a process leads of course to the loss of national or cultural identity of the original product, and in this way simplifies processes of intercultural communication. But, taking the other end of the communication process into consideration, it does not mean that the phenomena is part of a homogenous worldwide pop culture. The active process of cultural localization includes a process of interpretation that accounts for local cultural embedding of multi-cultural products.

Advertising is everywhere, cultivating particular attitudes to problems or creating problems where none existed previously (Young, 1990:2). When advertising is aimed at children, the emotional and irrational drives of young children can be exploited. Minors are not capable of defending themselves against such an onslaught. In this case, the advertiser is seen as the seducer and the child is cast in the role of the innocent (ibid.:18).

In the case of Pokemon advertising, trans-national communication could be considered exploitative. Pokemon has steadily maintained its popularity through its television series and movies. This is especially true of the after-show section of its TV series called 'Who's that Pokemon?' which is used to advertise new monsters for children to add in their collection. Even in the case of the official Pokemon website, it is used to advertise new products and as a place for children to purchase or auction Pokemon products.

Pokemon was the latest in a series of fad toy preferences for children. These fads are the result of trans-national communication through advertising, the linking of cultures through globalization, the penetration of local markets through localization, and the targeting of children by advertising. These fad toy preferences probably have little long-term effects on culture or society. Though many problems have arisen around the Pokemon craze, these are generally viewed as symptoms of general cultural troubles, not the cause.

Future Research Directions

The theories of globalization have been challenged, criticized and modified, but few would deny that they do offer a fertile ground for research. In Servaes and Lie (2000), we adopted a convergent and integrated approach in studying the complex and intricate relations between globalization, consumption and identity. Such an approach would allow problems to converge at key crossings or nodal points. Researchers then are rid of the burden of studying linear processes in totality, for example, production and consumption of global products, and instead are allowed to focus on the nodal points where processes intersect.

Several such nodal points were identified, including production, regulation, representation, consumption, action and local points of entry into the communications flow. The nodal points approach highlights the richness of globalization as an area of research. However, it is also important to note that all these dimensions do rest on certain axial principles. They do point out important features of the world cultural industries that converge on several points.

In this purported era of global communications, culture remains an important factor, either facilitating the trans-nationalization of national or local cultural industries, or impeding further growth of global media. Global media may be largest in terms of coverage—however, their size shrinks significantly if measured in terms of viewing rate. In many regions of the world the most important development in the communications industry has not been the further dominance of global media, but the emerging of cultural-linguistic media (mainly television) markets. As the influence of trans-national television tends to rest on a quite superficial level of cultures, no global culture or global identity—not in the fullest sense of the words—has been fostered.

As Hall indicated, it is human nature to want a place to which one feels he or she belongs; however, it is perhaps also human nature to want to reach out to the strange unknown world outside of this 'place'. Audiences may prefer home programmes, but these are not all they watch. While some national programmes are successful because of their distinct cultural characteristics, others may achieve similar success by promoting foreign values. It is the capitalist nature of the industry that made American products available everywhere. But this capitalist character failed to make them accepted everywhere.

It is difficult still to determine if communications has helped to offer a 'place,' as suggested by Featherstone, where cultures meet and clash, or has in fact enhanced the cultural context in which individuals find the 'place' that they feel attached to. Perhaps a closer analysis will show that here again, communication serves as a double-edged sword and which of the two roles becomes more prominent will be extremely variable, from situation to situation.

The danger here is treating culture and language as another set of powerful, determining factors in communication studies, thus undermining the importance of others. In fact, no single factor, nor a group of factors, can fully explain what has, is, or will, take place. Globalization may be inadequate to describe the current process of change, but neither would localization nor regionalization suffice. As co-production further blurs distinctions between the global and the local, it is important to note that the two are dialectically opposed conceptually, but not necessarily in reality.

During a dynamic process of change, it is the interaction of factors that brings about endless possibilities.

References

Albrow, M. 1990. 'Globalization, Knowledge and Society', in M. Albrow and A.D. King (eds). *Globalization, Knowledge and Society*. London: Sage Publications.

Anderson, B. 1983. *Imagined Communities: Reflections on the Origin and Spread of Nationalism*. London: Verso.

Bauman, Z. 1998. *Globalization. The Human Consequences*. New York: Columbia University Press.

Chew, S.C. and R.A. Denemark (eds). 1996. *The Underdevelopment of Development: Essays in Honor of Andre Gunder Frank*. Newbury Park: Sage Publications.

Cochrane, A. and K. Pain. 2000. 'A Globalizing Society?', in David Held (ed.). *A Globalizing World? Culture, Economic, Politics*, pp. 5–45. London: Routledge in association with the Open University.

Eriksen, T.H. 1993. *Ethnicity and Nationalism. Anthropological Perspectives*. London: Pluto Press.

Featherstone, M. 1990. 'Global Culture: An Introduction', in M. Featherstone (ed.). *Global Culture: Nationalism, Globalism and Modernity*, pp. 1–4. London: Sage Publications.

———. 1995. *Undoing Culture*. London: Sage Publications.

Ferguson, M. 1992. 'The Mythology about Globalization', *European Journal of Communication*, 7:69–93.

Gardels, N. (ed.). 1997. *The Changing Global Order*. Oxford: Blackwell.

Giddens, A. 1990. *The Consequences of Modernity*. Stanford, CA: Stanford University Press.

———.1995a. *Modernity and Self-Identity. Self and Society in the Late Modern Age*. Cambridge: Polity Press.

———. 1995b. 'New Cultures for Old', in D.I. Massey and P. Jess (eds). *A Place in the World?*, pp. 176–211. England: Milton Keynes.

Hall, S. 1992. 'The Question of Cultural Identity', in S. Hall, D. Held, and T. McGrew (eds). *Modernity and Its Future*. Cambridge: Polity Press.

Harindranath, R. 2006. *Perspectives on Global Cultures*. Berkshire: Open University Press.

Held, D. (ed.). 2000. *A Globalizing World? Culture, Economic, Politics*. London: Routledge in association with The Open University.

Held, D., A. McGrew, D. Goldblatt and J. Perraton. 1999. *Global Transformations. Politics, Economics and Culture*. Cambridge: Polity Press.

Hirst, P. and Thompson, G. 1996. *Globalization in Question: The International Economy and the Possibilities of Governance*. London: Polity Press.

Hopkins, A.G. (ed.). 2002. *Globalization in World History*. London: Pimlico.

Ito, Y. 1990. 'Mass Communication Theories from a Japanese Perspective', *Media, Culture and Society*, 12:423–464.

Iwabuchi, K. 2000. 'To Globalise, Regionalise or Localise Us, That is the Question: Japan's Response to Media Globalization', in G. Wang, J. Servaes and A. Goonasekera (eds), *The New Communications Landscape Demystifying Media Globalization*. London and New York: Routledge.

Luil, J. 1995. *Media, Communication, Culture. A Global Approach.* Cambridge: Polity Press.

Katz, E. 1980. 'On Conceptualizing Media Effects', *Studies in Communication*, 1:119–141.

Kellner, D. 1989. *Critical Theory, Marxism and Modernity.* Cambridge: Polity Press.

Lie, R. 1998. 'What's New about Cultural Globalization?... Linking the Global from within the Local', in J. Servaes and R. Lie (eds), *Media and Politics in Transition. Cultural Identity in the Age of Globalization*, pp. 141–155. Leuven: ACCO.

Mato, D., M. Montero and E. Amodio (eds). 1996. *América Latina en tiempos de globalización. Procesos culturales y transformaciones sociopolíticas.* Caracas: CRESALC.

Mittelman, J.H. (ed.). 1996. *Globalization: Critical Reflections.* London: Routledge.

Robertson, R. 1990. 'Mapping the Global Condition: Globalization as the Central Concept', in M. Featherstone (ed.). *Global Culture: Nationalism, Globalism and Modernity*, pp. 15–30. London: Sage Publications.

———. 1992. *Globalization: Social Theory and Global Culture.* London: Sage Publications.

Said, E. 1993. *Culture and Imperialism.* New York: Vintage.

Servaes, J. 1999. *Communication for Development. One World, Multiple Cultures.* Cresskill: Hampton Press.

Servaes, J. and R. Lie. 2000. 'Globalisation: Consumption and Identity. Towards Researching Nodal Points', in G. Wang, J. Servaes and A. Goonasekera (eds). *The New Communications Landscape. Demystifying Media Globalisation*, pp. 307–332. London: Routledge.

Servaes, J. and G. Wang. 1997. 'Privatization and Commercialization of the Western-European and South-East Asian Broadcasting Media', *Asian Journal of Communication*, 7(2).

Street, J. 1997. 'Across the Universe: The Limits of Global Popular Culture', in A. Scott (ed.). *The Limits of Globalization*, pp. 75–89. London: Routledge.

Viundal, J.E. 2000. *Traces of National Identity in Cyberspace.* Sydney: Macquarie University (Paper Transnational Communication Course).

Wallerstein, I. 1990. 'Culture as the Ideological Battleground of the Modern World-system', in M. Featherstone (ed.). *Global Culture: Nationalism, Globalism and Modernity.* London: Sage Publications.

———. 1991. 'Culture is the World-system: A Reply to Boyne', in M. Featherstone (ed.). *Global Culture: Nationalism, Globalism and Modernity*, pp. 63–66. London: Sage Publications.

———. 1997. 'The National and the Universal: Can There Be Such a Thing as World Culture?', in A.D. King (ed.). *Culture, Globalization and the World-system*, pp. 91–105. Minneapolis: University of Minnesota.

Wang, G. 1997. 'Beyond media globalization', *Telematics and Informatics*,14(4):357–364.

———. 1998. 'Protecting the Local Cultural Industry: A Regulatory Myth in the Global Age', in A. Goonasekera and P.S.N. Lee (eds). *TV Without Borders: Asia Speaks Out*, pp. 259–273. Singapore: AMIC.

Wang G., Servaes J. and A. Goonasekera (eds). 2000.*The New Communications Landscape. Demystifying Media Globalization.* London: Routledge.

Young, Brian. 1990. *Television Advertising and Children.* Oxford: Clarendon Press.

Vertical Minds versus Horizontal Cultures: An Overview of Participatory Process and Experiences

4

ALFONSO GUMUCIO-DAGRON

Introduction

It happened at a very small village west of Koudougou, in Burkina Faso. The name of the village is not very relevant. Not even the name of the country. It could have been any other country in Africa. I was visiting a small radio station, one of the six 'local radios' that President Thomas Sankara had set up when he was Minister of Information during the early 1980s. Outside the mud-brick small room that housed the station I found lying on the bare floor, under the rain, long rows of post office (PO) boxes, in several hundreds. My local contact saw a big question mark on my expression and immediately provided an explanation: 'Oh, these are for the new post office building, which will be built here. It's a donation from Germany'. Rust was already taking care of the donation. I inquired: 'How long ago did you get them?' He replied: 'Last year. But you know, the government has not yet started to build the post office, I'm not sure they will ever do it.'

Certainly, I thought, if I was the government I would never do it either. What kind of brain can conceive a post office building, with hundreds of luxurious post office boxes 'Made in Germany', in a small village with no more than 300 families, mostly illiterate peasants? I couldn't imagine any of them keeping a key for the PO box, and visiting the post office once a week to retrieve non-existent letters. I couldn't see many of them writing any letters either. The whole concept seemed to me imported and imposed by people who don't know much about how communication flows in rural areas of developing countries.

On the other hand, I could imagine the role that the local community radio could play, besides its typical role of airing music. If by any chance a letter came to the community, it will go straight to the radio station, and a short message would alert the family to whom the letter has been addressed. Actually, many community radio stations in the world started to build their constituency by providing precisely these kind of services to the community.

I've seen too many of these grotesque perversions of development in countries like Africa, Asia and Latin America. Mostly the result of imposed projects, by irresponsible donors that care more about an annual report on development cooperation that looks good and glossy, rather than caring about people. Very few governments in the Third World will say no to funds from cooperation agencies. Some of them, better prepared for negotiations with international or bilateral development agencies, will put the country priorities forward, but these are only a few. Many other governments will just take anything offered to them, because of corruption or because they themselves are not aware of national priorities in development.

What does this have to do with communication? Actually, everything.

Vertical Minds, Horizontal Cultures

During the past 20 years, the whole discourse of development has begun to experiment deep changes, from a very vertically imposed and rigid model of 'assistance' from international and bilateral development agencies to more flexible alternatives, that take into account what people really need, or at least, what governments say that their people need (which often is not the same).

The real needs of the so-called 'beneficiaries' have seldom been taken into account. International and bilateral cooperation agencies offer readymade packages and summon our countries: 'Take it or leave it'. We have learnt to identify many of the bilateral cooperation agencies by their agenda, which does seldom correspond with our priorities. For example, one of USAID priorities has been to control AIDS and STDs in developing countries. Many millions have been spent in many programmes of reproductive health and family planning (birth control) even in countries where the number one health priority is diarrhoea or malaria. Take it or leave it.

As communication is building its own personality as a discipline for development, its influence is being noticed by cooperation agencies, at least in the discourse, though the practice is yet to change. Even World Bank documents show in recent years much concern about development models that were embarrassing failures mainly because they failed to identify what people really wanted, let alone what they really needed (which often is not the same thing).

The whole concept of development and international cooperation is in crisis and is being reviewed, while more democratic governments displace the authoritarian regimes and civil society empowers itself to put an end or at least to denounce corruption.

The vertical minds that guided international cooperation were shaped during colonial times. They just 'knew' what was best for countries in Africa, Asia or Latin America, until they found some countries that had their own ideas about development.

Vertical minds have no room in a world of horizontal cultures. This was actually well understood as new pressures came on developing countries with the force of a tidal wave: globalization. In spite of being pervasive in the economic and trade arena, it has encountered great resistance in culture and civil society. Numerous cultures in the world are not ready to let it go. People hold on to their mother tongue, they hold on to their dress, to their music, to their religious practices. Still, the tidal wave can be powerful enough to wipe many off the globe in the long term, if there is no reaction to it now. Here again, communication in development and participation has much to look ahead. It is a resource with a potential that has only been slightly uncovered.

The problem of communication, as it has been conceived through so many decades, is that it was not meant to communicate, just to inform, conform and deform. Inform as a one-way flow of content towards the passive receiver (the old paradigm is very much alive); conform as a way of adjusting the behaviour of people to the needs of expanding markets and/or for political purposes; and deform as distorting history, memory, truth and culture, for the purpose of domination either by local privileged classes or by multinational conglomerates (the former 'banana republics' of central America did learn a lot from those years).

Still today, English language doesn't clearly differentiate information (one way) from communication (multiple ways), let alone communications (the technology) from communication (the human factor). This is very annoying considering most of the literature on communication is written in English. Mass information media is often referred to as 'mass communication'. The horizontal and dialogic components in content flows, which are essential to the act of 'communicating', are simply not taken into consideration. The whole concept of participation, which etymologically is in the core of the word communication, has been for many years bluntly ignored.

Communication was until very recently the fifth wheel in the car of development, not even the spare tire, seldom part of the development process; and this maybe because development was not even perceived as a process itself. The lack of communication and its basic principle, dialogue, has prevented many projects from succeeding. That is, if we understand 'success' as people democratically guiding the process of progress for their own community, for the benefit of the majority.

So why is the relationship between development and communication beginning to change? Why is the car of development now starting to use the spare wheel to redress its direction? It is not because the discourse is changing within the international cooperation, and even less because some scholars started writing about it. Actually, both have come to represent, digest and popularize what has been already happening at the community level for many years. Better late than never.

Participation in development has finally shattered institutional barriers, and participatory communication is helping to make of it a clear expression from communities. International or bilateral cooperation agencies can no longer ignore what the subjects of development have to say. Moreover, they need them if they want to claim any sustainability in their programmes. Without peoples' participation, no project can be successful and last long enough to support social change. This may sound as an obvious truth, but it was amazingly ignored for decades, and still is in many development projects where donor's agendas are imposed over people's needs.

Imperfect, difficult to label (which makes scholars feel uneasy), culturally diverse and mostly escaping from institutional control, participatory communication is feeding a new approach to communication and to development as well. Participatory communication is fragile; it is often contradictory—which conspires against the ready-to-replicate model exercises, but in the end is as live as the communities that use it as a means to promote dialogue and networking on issues that are important for the community life: development, yes, but also culture, power and democracy.

Process of Participation

We hold tight to words and concepts; that is what most of us do for living. Maybe it's time to be more flexible, to imagine that definitions can also be a burden when trying to define something that we don't fully understand. Let's take, for an example, 'participatory project', which already encapsulates a contradiction. 'Project' is already something that has to be designed in advance, with a clear understanding of all its phases and results. It's actually a very academic and intellectual exercise, maybe which is why we like to use the word: research project, development project, and even sentimental project. Participation, on the other hand, is a wide-open window towards a collective goal that we can only imagine over the horizon. By its very nature, participation is a *process* and when we refer to a participation project we are actually thinking on a participatory process.

It is true that often a participation process starts with a project that aims to encourage participation. Actually, this is more likely to happen when dealing with development communication. The very fact of implicating communication with a participatory purpose can make a development project different. If a communication initiative is seeking for participation with the aim of involving the community of beneficiaries to the point of them becoming the owners of a project, then a communication process has to unwind over the time to make it possible. The 'ownership' of the development project—and first, of the communication component, is what helps to establish the difference from the typical interventions in development communication projects, which reproduce the sender and receiver paradigm, only with a more progressive content.

Unfortunately, research on participatory communication has often very little 'sync' with what is actually happening on the ground. Research comes late or never. It is partial and tends to generalize based on very few examples. There are several reasons for that:

- Most of the research is done in Europe and the United States/Canada, while the subjects of research, the participatory communication experiences, are located in developing countries.
- Researchers can only spend short periods of time visiting developing countries, so they tend to pick only very few experiences for their case studies.
- Many researchers work on information readily available on the Web or in other published case studies and information, which limits enormously the scope of their research, and also highlights excessively only a handful of experiences, in detriment of many other.
- Most researchers speak only English, which limits their research to sources in English and/ or to countries where English is spoken. And even in those countries the researcher may face many difficulties in communicating with the local population, which is only fluent in the local language.

- Researches from the North (Europe and North America) have a whole system of values that prevents many of them from understanding local culture and local values of the South, thus reflecting a limited comprehension in the resulting research documents.
- Many local participatory communication experiences remain invisible because they are not promoted, funded or anyhow related to the mainstream international cooperation agencies.
- Very few research projects involve local researchers who can provide valuable insights on the social, political, economic and cultural context.

While preparing a report on participatory communication[1] I ran across many experiences that were unknown and neglected by researchers. However, my own main discovery was realizing that I could only see and show others the tip of the iceberg. I am convinced that every developing country is rich in community-based participatory experiences where communication is an important factor, but very little of this is acknowledged by researchers in North America and Europe, who too often prefer to recycle in their writings the same few case studies that a few have prepared. I personally believe that the only way to report and to understand these experiences is by being there and trying to capture at least some of the context and culture.

The analysis on participatory communication, more than any other analysis, has to deal with the context as much as with the media or communication tool being utilized. Project documents and success stories do not provide that insight. Those very academic attempts to systematize or theorize based on what others have written can only contribute to transform the original experience into an intellectual and speculative exercise that has little to do with reality. Often, enthusiasm for the novelty eclipses the description of the complexities that are found at the level where the communication process is actually taking place.

Waves of Change

If I had never been at *Radio Kwizera*, I would have had difficulties to understand the importance of this participatory communication experience in the context of a refugee situation. The small station located at Ngara, near the Tanzanian border to Rwanda and Burundi, is the most important media for half million refugees that can't go back to their countries, and can't go out of the refugee camps to join the Tanzanian or any other African society. Nobody wants them. The radio station, which was set up by the Jesuit Refugee Service (JRS), gives at least a sense of identity to the refugees, besides supporting very concrete activities related to environment, health, education, human rights, water and sanitation, among others. Considering the number of refugees, this is by any standard a 'big' communication project in terms of the captive audience. But even if it were smaller, as small as *La Voz de la Comunidad* in Guatemala or the *Community Audio Towers* in the Philippines, it would still be the most important communication tool for the community, and from their perspective, that is what is needed.

Only a few thousand people are reached by a *Community Audio Tower* (CAT), just as many as can be reached by the sound that travels from the cone speakers mounted on a high mat, to the homes that are scattered over a 4 or 5 kilometre radio. Many in the success-oriented world of international cooperation would tend to minimize the importance of this type of local media, considering it 'too small' to invest any funds on it. But if they would listen to what the community has to say, maybe their perspective would be different. For example, when I visited the CAT at Tacunan, in Davao del Norte, people at the *barangay* meeting told me they were certain that without their cone speakers they could have never progressed as they did in a few years. They got potable water, electricity and a new road. And I would add to it: pride and a voice to express their culture and identity.

La Voz de la Comunidad basically airs music and short messages for its constituency, the poor neighbourhood of San José Buenavista, hanging on the slopes of a ravine under the Incienso Bridge, not far from the very centre of Guatemala City. As other 80 community radio stations, *La Voz de la Comunidad* has been under government pressure to 'legalize' its status, which really means paying the equivalent of several thousands of US dollars to buy a FM licence. Instead, the station decided to place the transmission antennae in the lowest spot of the ravine, so to avoid the signal to reach further than the communities for whom the transmission is intended.

During the struggle against the Apartheid, radio was instrumental in defending local culture and building the sense of democracy in South Africa. *Bush Radio, Radio Zibonele* and the multimedia programme *Soul City* had to fight their way towards legal recognition. Both *Bush Radio* and *Radio Zibonele* were shut down as 'illegal' and only surfaced again in 1995. Women of Mouse Mpumalanga Province organized, often against the will of men, to create *Moutse Community Radio Station*, a rural enterprise also contributing to the peace and reconciliation process. Many other radio stations have joined since, making South Africa one of the most fertile grounds for participatory communication experiences.

Radio is generally the most successful communication tool in developing countries and usually the first to be experimented by communities that are in search of their own 'voice'. Before 1998, for example, there was no radio station at all in Kiritimati, one of the islands of the Republic of Kiribati, deep in the Pacific Ocean. A water and sanitation project supported by the Australian cooperation allowed the community to build a small radio station in just a couple of months. The *Tambuli Radio Network* in the Philippines represents a cluster of 20 small stations scattered throughout remote islands of the archipelago, all of them serving the social and cultural interests of small communities.

Images of Identity

Similar 'isolated' experiences are using video or theatre or the Internet as the communication tool. We are yet to see participatory television experiences in developing countries, but it may happen when the current video experiences develop their broadcast capacity. Take for example *TV Maxambomba* in Brazil and *TV Serrana* in Cuba. These are two communication experiences that, in spite of including 'television' in their name, are not broadcasters. Which doesn't mean at all that they don't reach people. Yes they do, and certainly with much more quality than many broadcast channels. Quality, because people participate in the video exhibitions with a sense of community, a very different type of access than having a TV control in their hands that allows them to zap and forget. What the two experiences have in common, along with *TV Viva*, also in Brazil, is that their communication action is not limited to documenting reality or producing educational videos, but mainly reaching people and interacting with communities, offering poor neighbourhoods (*TV Viva*, *TV Maxambomba*) or rural areas (*TV Serrana*) a programming that deals with their problems, their culture and their daily lives, which are never portrayed or taken into account by commercial broadcasters, not even by the public service networks, forced to broadcast for a 'general' public, thus ignoring the particularities of the various cultural and social settings of communities.

Video is also cleverly used as an instrument of community research, revealing internal problems and seeking solutions through community participation. The example of *Maneno Mengi* in Tanzania is better known, because it has supported several peasants or fisher folks communities to improve their living conditions by strengthening their organizations and their capacity to deal with authorities. Similarly, poor women in India (*Video SEWA*) and Egypt (*Video and Community Dreams*) have structured to use video as an organization tool. Video has also been an important communication tool for peasant communities in Chiapas, in the South of Mexico, the scenario of confrontation between the government and the Zapatista Army, and for some Indian tribes of Brazil (*Kayapo Video*) to re-invent their culture and face the challenges of modernization and the risks of loosing their territory to multinational and government developers.

More related with an institutional framework, several video 'projects' with a participatory component have been successful in engaging a long-term process of education and communication. *Action Health* (Nigeria), uses video for AIDS prevention and reproductive health, training groups of youth to interact with their peers through video. Video supports other activities, like drama and inter-personal communication, allowing young Nigerians to openly discuss issues related to their sexuality. In Bolivia, the *Lilac Tent* project has also been dealing with reproductive health and sexuality through video and a series of other interpersonal communication activities, which include games, quizzes, and entertainment. A huge lilac circus tent travels from one community to the next offering a wide range of communication activities involving the villagers as well as the local authorities, teachers, health staff and even police and army officials.

For at least four decades, the United Nations Food and Agriculture Organization (FAO), has supported long-term video projects aimed to support community mobilization around development projects. Three are notable experiences: the *Centro de Servicios de Pedagogía Audiovisual para la Capacitación* (CESPAC) in Perú, which originated in 1975; the *Programa de Desarrollo Integrado del Trópico Húmedo* (PRODERITH) in Mexico, which started in 1978, and the *Centre de Services de Production Audiovisuelle* (CESPA), in Mali, which was set up in 1989 and had less impact than the other two. The three projects are a similar mix of video training and video production of 'pedagogic packages' meant to facilitate exchanges of knowledge between grassroots communities and project managers and technicians. Hundreds of videos dealing with agricultural problems and solutions were produced by these projects, whereas the participatory aspects were not fully developed.

The video shows organized to mobilize communities are interesting examples of community-based dialogue facilitated by a new technology. In this case video has little to do with broadcast television and is in fact closer to community theatre, which is another important communication tool in Third World countries. Often, drama representation is already part of the local culture and part of the internal communication processes.

Drama in the Roots of Culture

There is hardly a community, rural or urban, that doesn't already have a form of participation and communication through music, dance or drama. Even the poorest do. They will have to be much less than poor to have lost the last mark of identity and culture. Unfortunately there are, of course, some of those that have been cut away from their roots, forced to migrate to urban areas for work or because of war, deprived of their language and customs, and their culture gone flat under the pervasive effect of globalization. This is what happened in the 1970s to small indigenous tribes from the Eastern tropical lowlands of Bolivia, which were left without land and migrated to the capital city, Santa Cruz, to become in only few years prey of alcoholism and prostitution.

In Colombia, *Teatro Kerigma* has found a way to strengthen cultural identity, or maybe even re-invent it, in poor barrios of Bogotá, made mostly of migrants that arrived from rural areas since the early 1960s. Since 1978 the Kerigma association has been using street theatre to mobilize the local population around cultural and human values. *Teatro La Fragua* in Honduras, and *Teatro Trono* in the outskirts of La Paz, Bolivia do something similar, just to mention three examples of community theatre groups in Latin America that have organized their work around the needs of marginalized population made mostly of migrants to the capital cities. The three projects include not only theatrical activities, but also a wide range of social and cultural manifestations.

The long tradition of performing arts in Asia and the Pacific has enormously facilitated the establishment of drama groups that go deep into historical memory and tradition in search of cultural values that relate with today's social problems. *Nalamdana*, a drama group operating in poor neighbourhoods of Chennai, has developed intense activity that goes far beyond researching, scripting and performing community drama to create awareness on health and social issues. The group is also involved in conducting workshops and developing educational materials and television dramas on STDs and HIV, especially for illiterate men and women.

In the high plains of Nepal, the *Aarohan Street Theatre* has developed a network of community-based drama groups that use local traditions and modern contents to promote dialogue and discussion about voting rights and democracy, environmental and sanitation issues, as well as other health-related problems.

With only 'one small bag' to carry props and costumes, *Wan Smolbag* is a theatre group in Vanuatu, Solomon Islands, that has also been dealing with issues of governance, representing, among other plays, a few related with voting rights and child rights. The environment is no less important for *Wan Smolbag* and several drama groups that have been trained during the past decade to create awareness on marine life under threat. Their influence now extends over numerous islands through more than 50 different plays that have been created to tackle the topics mentioned above, as well as AIDS/STDs and other health-related issues. In recent years *Wan Smolbag* has diversified its activity, including books, radio programmes and videos.

Theatre groups tend to multiply at the community level, as they represent a genuine form of local participatory communication. The concept of community theatre or popular theatre, as it is called in Latin America, has so little to do with conventional theatre as video with broadcast television. In a country like Nigeria, where even radio and television does not effectively reach the majority of the population, local drama groups have been instrumental in supporting health programmes of immunization and prevention. In the early 1990s, UNICEF supported the training of local drama groups and the development of plays based on 'Facts for Life', dealing with safe motherhood, malaria, sanitation, AIDS, nutrition, and other health-related issues. Each play was locally adapted not only in terms of language or dialect, but also taking into account the culture, rites and practices. Around 46 local drama groups were active, touring from one rural community to the next.

Gadgets or Tools for Development?

It is clear that the participatory communication process can adapt any tool or technology to support the process of community participation. Although several decades ago there was a tendency to refuse new technologies based on the assumption that they would have a pervasive influence on local cultures, reality shows that any technology can be appropriate to a social change and development process if used to articulate local needs and local contents. One of the most powerful examples is the use that Bolivian miners made of community radio for 50 years, since 1948. But there are many other examples to support the idea that technology can be adapted and 'appropriated' by local communities. Video in the hands of market women in India or the Kayapo Indians in Brazil are also encouraging examples.

A powerful new trend has been developing in recent years under the worldwide impact of the new information and communication technologies (ICTs). Agitating the banners of 'e-mail for all' or 'Internet for all', many governments, multinational corporations and international development agencies have teamed to provide 'access' to computers and the Internet to every community in the world. The chant of sirens of technology saving the world from poverty has been heard in Africa, Asia and Latin America. Millions are being invested in strengthening national networks and setting tele-centres or 'information shops' in the most remote rural areas, where there is no electricity or telephone available. ICTs have become the latest fashion in the development jargon.

Unfortunately, the large majority of ICTs projects are not being set up for the benefit of intended communities. An important part of the trend is just 'business as usual', meaning, companies selling by thousands pieces of hardware and software, and other intermediaries benefiting from the transfer of technology: consulting firms from Europe and the US, Third World government bureaucrats and a few universities. The ICTs 'instant remedy' to underdevelopment and social exclusion sounds too much like the trendy 'diffusion of innovations' of the 1970s. Again, transfer of technology is seen as the panacea, the ultimate solution, regardless of social, economic and political causes, and also regardless of the cultural implications of introducing new technologies that carry within, as a Trojan horse, the culture of globalization.

In the frenzy of competition to provide computers and connectivity, most of ICTs projects are overlooking obvious facts. It is almost boring to repeat what we all now know, but it is still worth doing it because many are just reluctant to be confronted by the evidence: the huge mass of information known as the World Wide Web that can be accessed through the Internet protocols, 90 per cent is in English and 99 per cent is irrelevant to 99 per cent of the population of the world; 80 per cent of the world's population never made a phone call; only 6 per cent of the world population uses the Internet; 90 per cent of all Internet users are in industrialized countries; Internet users in Africa and the Middle East together account for only 1 per cent of global Internet users; 52 per cent of Internet world users are non-English speakers; while 40 per cent of households in the US have access to Internet, only 0.005 per cent of the population of Bangladesh uses it. Do we need to continue with more examples?

In the name of 'digital divide' great business is being made and the so-called divide is widening. As long as the 'digital divide' is reduced to a technological gap, we will witness the widening of the social divide, the economic divide, the political divide, and so forth, thanks to new technologies.

Fortunately, parallel to the expanding wave of mercantilism that uses ICTs as the point of the lance, new critical voices are joining both in developing and industrialized countries, seriously warning about the consequences of pushing new technologies over Third World countries irrespective of priorities, needs and the local capacity to make good use of them. Today, we can clearly draw the line between those projects that are part of the technological frenzy and the ones that understand ICTs as one more instrument to be put in use for the benefit of development and social change. It is increasingly clear that Internet connectivity projects that do not include, as a mainstream force, the creation of local contents, are doomed to failure. Ironically enough, the future of the Internet for development is not the World Wide Web, but the infinite Local Community Networks that should be created in tune with language, culture and society. Only the development of local databases and appropriate local contents can meet the needs of those thousands of poor rural and urban communities that have been graced by ICTs and do not exactly know what to do with it. As many reports indicate, users are more interested in making phone calls or photocopies than in any other feature offered by a given Internet shop.

Other than the voices that are drawing the line in the debate around the 'digital divide', recent experiences are showing the way for an appropriate use of ICTs in development and social change. It is true that there is only one of these projects for every 100 that are set up with no regards for community needs and culture; however, the experience of well-planned community-based initiatives may positively influence the communities where computers were dumped by ICT pushers or ICT naïve promoters who thought something magical could happen in 'poverty reduction' when people would access the Internet. Unfortunately, by the time communities realize that there is a different way of dealing with the Internet, it is likely that thousands of computers that have been parachuted over rural and urban communities will be obsolete.

Internet-based development communication experiences are rather new and mostly unknown, in spite of a large number of reports that have been issued. Two or three years of development are usually not enough to evaluate the social impact of a communication tool. However, the eagerness of some researchers to immediately assess the operation of ICTs at the community level is bringing enormous benefits. I see this research trend as 'research with a purpose'—meaning—a purpose that defies the academic exercise and contributes to redress the evolution of ICTs experiences as they develop by the immediate devolution of a critical mass of information obtained at the community level. The research that grows and modifies itself in parallel with the experience that is being acquired by Internet-based development projects, can only benefit the course of action. India and South Africa are two countries that are outstanding in terms of the use of ICTs for social development, and the two have benefitted from early research 'with a purpose' of looking at each experience with the eyes of the community.

One of the most outstanding programmes is, no doubt, the one known as *Village Knowledge Centres*, in Chennai, India, implemented by the M.S. Swaminathan Research Foundation (MSSRF). Formerly called 'information shops', the *Village Knowledge Centres*—operated by individuals on a semi-voluntary basis, were established to take advantage of new technologies to provide information to the rural population on agricultural issues such as: health (availability of vaccines and medicines in the nearest health centre, preventive measures); relief information (issue of loans, availability of officials); inputs for agriculture (prices and availability, costs, risks and returns, local market price for the rural produce); transport information; micro-meteorological information (relating to the local area); surface and ground water-related data, pest surveillance and on agronomic practices for all seasons and crops (based on queries from the rural families); maintenance and update of data on entitlements of the rural families (vis-à-vis public sector welfare and infrastructural funds). The training and materials are in Tamil, the local language. The *Village Knowledge Centres* enable farming families not only to produce more without associated ecological harm, but helps everyone in the village to create a hunger-free area. The villagers themselves identify who the hungry amidst them are; 12 to 15 per cent of the families fall under this category.

Similar projects have been promoted in other parts of Asia, as well as in Africa and Latin America, with mixed results. At least, they aim to be established as community development tools and instead of simply seeing the community as potential user, they also see it as provider of information and cultural parameters. The telecentres in Gasaleka and Mamelodi in South Africa, the *Nakaseke Telecentre* in Uganda, the *InfoDes* project in Peru, the experience of El Limón in Dominican Republic, are only a handful of growing community-based experiences that are signalling the way for new technologies of information and communication.

Taking Further the Good Intentions

The changing discourse of international development agencies should evolve parallel to changing development practices in relation to communication. If communication is not understood as the oil that will allow the new discourse to effectively move the machinery of development and social change, little will actually change in the development practices.

How does the new development discourse of international cooperation agencies affect the programmes and projects supported? Are things really changing or is it always 'business as usual'? There are some requisites and conditions to make changes happen. Are donors, development agencies and governments ready to make changes that go beyond the discourse and the good intentions?

One of the indicators of real changes, for example, would be the allocation of budget lines to communication activities in every programme or project. What we generally see in development projects is that communication is absent from the budget. What we may find is insufficient, to say the least. We may find a small budget for 'promotion' of the overall project, which is more related with public relations than with development communication. Often, budget lines of 'information' are used to organize press conferences or to support journalists or media houses. None of these really has any influence in changing the way things are done inside each project. A neat line needs to be drawn between information activities that aim to build the external 'image' of a programme or project, and the communication activities that should be inseparable of programme activities at the community level. We are of course referring to programmes of health, agriculture, human rights, poverty reduction, water and sanitation, or any other that includes activities directly involving beneficiaries. A communication budget should ideally represent a minimum established percentage of the overall budget, and should allow communication activities to take place from the inception of the project, and all along the implementation phases.

A logical consequence of budgeting communication in a development programme would lead cooperation agencies to reflect on their human resources, particularly those in charge of administering the fund allocated to communication activities. In recent years, some development organizations, such as the World Health Organization (WHO), have increased their allocations to communication activities, but without changing the profile of the staff in charge. Doctors and other health personnel are improvised as development communicators and given the responsibility to follow-up on communication activities. As a result, very often these communication activities do not correspond to a coherent communication strategy. They are just a sum of improvised activities aimed to spend the fund allocated. Such a mechanical implementation of communication resources may not contribute to any deep changes, until cooperation agencies fully understand that communication is a specialized field of development. Some organizations, acknowledging their lack of expertise, have turned towards external consultants, with mixed results. Too often, advertising agencies are hired to conduct information activities that are more in line with social marketing and image making, than with community participation. It is obvious: advertising agencies do not have the experience and the skills to do otherwise.

Only very few international development organizations have an understanding of the profile of communicators that are needed to deal with development issues. At different levels, these organizations have placed people that are in a better position to contribute to participatory development. UNICEF, for example, besides having an important cluster of information and communication specialists in its headquarters in New York (although very much diminished under the administration of Carol Bellamy), also has communication officers in the field, in every single country where the organization is present. The communication staff at the field level is known under various names (at one point, UNICEF identified around 50 variant titles): information officers, communication officers, social mobilization officers, social marketing officers, community mobilization officers, and so on. These are a clear indication of the lack of definition that exists. But names and titles are only the tip of the iceberg. Job descriptions tend to be even more confusing, and the whole recruitment process depends usually on people that are not sufficiently knowledgeable about communication. The result: among the hundreds of information and communication officers that UNICEF has in the field, the large majority has no development communication background and experience. Many of them are journalists, media-oriented, which partly explains UNICEF strength in working with media houses, and its weakness in working with communities.

Other development organizations have no tradition of having communication staff at the field level, but they are supportive of development communication from their headquarters and regional bureaus. Just to mention two other United Nations agencies, FAO and UNESCO have made important contributions in terms of training and setting up projects where participatory communication is the mainstream driving force. We have already mentioned the video centres that FAO has supported during long periods in Peru, Mexico and Mali. The organization has also promoted important 'think tanks' and publications. UNESCO is exceptional in terms of having communication at the same level as culture, science and education. In spite of its limited budget and overgrown bureaucracy, UNESCO has made the difference supporting development communication activities worldwide, including many community radio initiatives besides others.

A look at the main players in international development, both the funding institutions and the development agencies, bilateral and multilateral, show little improvement in terms of providing enough room in their programmes for the growth of development communication initiatives. Many have attempted to leapfrog from nothing to 'ICTs for development', with very mixed results. Once more, improvising ICT managers that may know a lot about technology, but little about knowledge and culture does not contribute to changes in the usual practices at the community level. Communication, which should be central to the introduction of new information and communication technologies, is actually grossly overlooked. The sudden abundance of ICT projects is obscuring the problem of communication for social change. Just by sowing computers and connectivity doesn't mean these projects will harvest anything else but old and outdated machines in three or four years.

Participation is Dialogue

The bottom line is that development organizations should look closer to what has been already happening during the past decades at the field level, in terms of communication and participation. At one point we thought their discourse was changing because of their acknowledgement that the place where development really happens is the community. However, the new discourse seems to be already getting stiff due to the lack of exposure to reality.

If there is only one thing that we can all learn from participatory communication experiences and their mixed results, it is that dialogue is the key for development. If civil society is to take a larger role in conceiving and working for development, then dialogue is unavoidable. If development organizations are ready to change their practices and their relation with governments and the civil society, then dialogue is essential at the community level. Participatory communication movements are an invitation to dialogue, which ought not to be refused.

Note

1. 'Making Waves: Participatory Communication for Social Change', The Rockefeller Foundation, New York, 2001.

Part II

The Theoretical Underpinnings of Development Communication

The Panoptic View: A Discourse Approach to Communication and Development

5

SUJATHA SOSALE

Agreat deal of scholarly inquiry has addressed the ways in which development would enable worldwide democratic communications. Conversely, many modern communications media were, in themselves, considered to be indicators of development. Communication and development have been viewed as closely intertwined phenomena, where one is believed to guarantee the other. In this chapter, I explore the constructed nature of communication and development from a discourse perspective that encompasses democratic communications as both cause and effect of development. Here, 'communication and development' is treated as a discourse that dominated the global space for many decades.

Specifically in this study, I examine the strategy of framing employed by agents and institutions that were historically in a position to establish the dominant meanings of communication and development. Here, I refer to two sets of actors—first, there are the critical policy advocating groups, media owners, and others from the developed world promoting what are seen now as more traditional approaches to development. Secondly, the decision-makers and administrators in developing regions also contributed to the construction of dominant meanings of communication and development. From their vantage points of power, these regions were 'enframed' as needing development aid of many kinds (Escobar, 1995). Framing involves creation of a defined space and placement of objects within for full visibility and scrutiny by the viewer positioned outside the frame. Fundamental to this inside/outside relationship is the naturalizing of the inside/outside positions.

This notion of the frame, or the politics of the gaze, translates to the viewing position of those in power and the object position of the (relatively) powerless who are viewed. In the context of the recent history of communication and development, the agents and institutions involved in defining dominant meanings of the idea of development used discursive devices (or strategies) to make the object of study—the developing regions—transparent. The argument is that full knowledge of such regions is required to be able to aid them along certain paths towards certain definitions of material and cultural progress. Exercising this power that shapes the relations between developed and developing nations is not necessarily intentional (this is the naturalizing power of ideology), nor is the use of discursive strategies always carefully and consciously planned; however, a particular ideological bent is evident in the language, meanings, institutions and social practices that constituted the discourse of communication and development.

From the standpoint of the present era of high globalization, international development constitutes a period of time in recent world history. International hierarchies that emerged from this period endure. The study of communication and development is important in that globalization, for many regions of the world, has exacerbated the economic differences that have resulted from earlier development practices during a period when concerns about world development occupied centre stage in national and supranational deliberations. A study of the historical legacy of communication and development from a discourse perspective provides insights into the knowledge and power nexus that facilitated the establishment of a powerful signifier such as development, a signifier that continues to mark differences in the global arena.

Two caveats are needed here. First, it is acknowledged that any discursive construction is not an assemblage of events and instances that come together to assert certain meanings of phenomena like development. Rather, contesting the dominant meanings and practices is equally constitutive of the discourse. The dominant signifier of communication and development has been amply challenged and continues to be challenged by scholars and activists worldwide (refer, for example, Hamelink's contributions, particularly in the 1980s; the publications of Nordenstreng in the 1970s when debates about democracy and development were at their peak; the corpus of works by Schiller; the Third World Journalists' Seminar Report, 1975. Contemporary cases in point include the emerging robust literature on participatory communication, gender issues in development and social change, and more recently, human rights and new social movements in relation to development communication). Negotiations of meanings about implications for media practices have also taken place (as documents on the New World Information and Communication Order [NWICO] debate suggest). In numerous ways, many development agencies are hastening to modify their earlier development practices that did not provide the intended relief. Given this larger configuration of the discourse, to impose some scope on the chapter, the focus is retained mainly on reading strategies of visibility used to construct dominant meanings in the international arena. Secondly, the discourse of communication and development does possess a genealogy of at least half a century, starting in the 1950s. This chapter does not offer a survey of the entire period; rather, it focusses on the 1970s and early 1980s when the debates about democracy and development were pursued most seriously by several nations and a key supranational institution—the UNESCO—in a quest for a new world communication order. The debates demonstrate the configuration of the discourse of communication and development from dominant, resistant and negotiating viewpoints and this decade has been examined in a larger research project from which this chapter is an excerpt.

I begin with an explanation of a discourse approach to communication and development, followed by two sections that examine the panoptic view, or the politics of the gaze at work. I conclude with a note on resistant and negotiating moves in the critical responses to communication and development and the status of communication and development in relation to globalization.

A Discourse Approach to Communication and Development

The modern idea of 'development' is not an innocent term, condition, or state of society (Banuri, 1990; Escobar, 1995; Mohanty, 1991; Shohat and Stam, 1994). It entails a relatively narrow geo-history of construction and contestation. That 'developmentized democracy' (Escobar, 1995) is a product of the European and the Euro-colonial historical experience is widely acknowledged now. A discourse approach to studying communication and development would allow us to see the constructed nature of what has come to be considered as 'natural,' universally applied historical and social evolution and its consequences for democracy in the international sphere.

When talking about a discourse of communication and development, I refer to the larger and more visible reality that has been constructed in an overarching discourse, to the meanings and practices that define communication and development and the links between the two concepts in the context of this study. As Doty, in her work on representation in international relations, explains it, '[A discourse] is a structured, relational totality.... A discourse delineates the terms of intelligibility whereby a particular reality can be known and acted upon' (1996:6). Discursive formations are effectively understood by examining the strategies that enable this formation in the first place.

The chapter rests on the premise that the ideological hold of communication and development is expressed in discourse. A dominant discourse labours continuously to suppress the 'other' (or multiple others) (Hall, 1985). In the process, a centre emerges from which power is exercised through various means (Beechey and Donald, 1985). I refer to these means as discursive strategies, intelligible in the process of articulating an ideology. A dominant discourse emerges from the power to define meanings, create institutions to reproduce and sustain these meanings (and practices) and create a 'corpus of ... statements' which would be 'already formulated' for the Third World (Ferguson, 1994). This corpus of already formulated statements would chart a certain path for social change for all regions of the world to pursue.

Scholars have drawn on Foucault's analysis of the metaphor and the politics of the gaze to understand what Escobar has termed as 'the production of the social'. Foucault employs the concept of the panopticon to explain uneven social power relations. A type of architecture used for institutions of discipline and correction, the panopticon is conceived of as a technology of power, and as Spurr (1993:16) explains it, 'has bearing on any occasion where the superior and invulnerable position of the observer coincides with the role of affirming the political order that makes that position possible' (also Foucault, 1980). Originally the eighteenth century legal scholar Jeremy Bentham's creation, the panopticon was designed for penal institutions where inmates housed in cells along the inner perimeter of the construction were 'visible' to the supervisor located in the central watch tower, but were denied the right to return the supervisor's gaze due to the architectural design. The individual occupying the position of power thus remained 'invisible' to the inmates. Thus the 'exercise of power and, simultaneously, "the registration of knowledge"' of the prison inmates' actions occurred through the gaze (Foucault 1972:148)—literal in the case of Bentham's panopticon; metaphorical in its adaptation to critically analyse other domains such as colonialism or development. With the aid of this metaphor, we see that in the domain of communication and development, developing nations are rendered transparent on many fronts—economic, social, cultural and so on—through the deployment of media, technologies, and the production of certain types of knowledge through certain strains of communication research. Simultaneously, those who assess or devise modes and methods of assessment reserve for themselves the privilege of invisibility from the occupants of the lower spaces in the international/global arrangement by naturalizing the discourse of communication and development and hence rendering their presence and actions as a given.

The panoptic view enables scrutiny of regions and nations within a 'field of visibility' (Escobar, 1995:196). Communication media, at times, are used as tools for surveillance, and at other times, media technologies constitute an index of 'development.' Thus, communication media become both the object of the gaze as well as the instruments facilitating the gaze. At the same time, the panoptic view is designed to ensure that the viewer is placed beyond the gaze of the observed, thus reducing or denying opportunities to return the gaze. A history of self-placement outside the enframed space has rendered the viewer's position as 'natural'. The panoptic view demonstrates the vertical arrangement of nations, economies, and cultures in the world system. An examination of communication and development through this lens would yield some insights into how a certain broad 'mainstream' idea of development through communication came to be inscribed in the social imaginary (Tomlinson, 1993) of various publics.

To demonstrate the shaping of the discourse through the panoptic view, I provide a critical and interpretive reading of a few texts as detailed examples. This chapter is an excerpt from a larger study; texts for the larger study were selected from the following sources: (a) an extensive bibliography on the contributions to the NWICO debate from multiple perspectives published by the United Nations(1984), (b) the reports compiled by the MacBride Commission report and related studies, and (c) the NAMEDIA conference reports (1983). Specific texts were selected on the basis of their relationship to the themes of communication and development, such as social development, culture and development, communication technology for development, and so on.

Two strategies of power are apparent in the panoptic view. One is the power to survey, and the other is the power to remain invisible. The two have been artificially separated for analysis purposes and are termed as surveillance and invisibility. The themes most apparent in the strategy of surveillance pertained to the production of knowledge of a certain kind about Third World communication, knowledge yielded by satellite technology and specific types of communication research. The strategy of invisibility manifested itself in the economically powerful nations' efforts to 'guide' development through communication, in their self-appointed role as parent, and as having reached a stage of maturity in modern communication. Additionally, it must be acknowledged that the First World's historical role in the colonial economies of the developing world has also contributed to naturalizing its presence outside the frame imposed by the panoptic view.

Surveillance

The use of satellite technologies to survey geographical areas and national resources and compile databanks from these surveys is one manifestation of the panoptic view at work. Rhetoric on satellite communication and its uses for development worked to make Third World economies appear transparent. Discussions on satellite technology and communications focussed on making geographical terrain in the Third World as completely visible as the technology would allow it, for determining natural resources.

Prominent among the discussions of satellite technology are the reports on the UN seminars held in Addis Ababa and Buenos Aires. In the seminar in Addis Ababa, scientists and development specialists from both developed and developing regions detailed the ways in which satellites would aid in detecting natural resources because 'space platforms … [can] provide us with a unique capability to see and interact with large parts of the earth simultaneously' (United Nations, 1981, Addis Ababa, A/AC.105/290:4). Remote sensing for targeted surveillance areas of the economy such as agriculture, rural demography, economic geology, forestry, livestock, and water resources would prove beneficial.

Forms of visual communication such as air photos, radar imagery, and satellite pictures produced by various technologies were compared for costs, versatility, accuracy, and extent of information they could yield about resources of a given nation/region/continent. Superior technology for image enhancement and expertise in reading the subtler shades of images procured by such technology were pivotal to surveillance through remote sensing. To enable the use of satellite imagery in cartographic surveys and thematic maps, strategic pieces of visual communication on a nation's natural resources that have profound influences on its economy are first secured and then converted to data; the data then constitute a type of 'manufactured' resource. Since this type of resource production requires large investments (possible, for the most part, for economically advanced countries), the poorer countries found themselves in the position of purchasing knowledge about their own resources from foreign sources. The confluence of power and visibility (Escobar, 1987) is evident in the conversion of such images to strategic knowledge made available for sale.

Two remote-sensing centres were established for agricultural (in Rome) and non-agricultural satellite data (in New York). These centres were intended to serve as archives for collecting, storing, and dispensing (selling) data. Thus, full visibility of many strategic resources would be available to the centres located in areas of the globe designated as developed. The centres would catalogue, store and interpret remote-sensing data, circulate information, provide advice and assistance to projects, and organize special training courses for users and decision-makers in developing regions. The costs incurred by many Third World countries in purchasing this data have been a thorny issue with client nations and in the NWICO debates.

The vocabulary used in relation to modern satellite communication apparatuses in general was also extended to traditional media by the state in developing regions. Traditional media are transformed from cultural practices (which may serve functional or aesthetic/creative purposes, or both, something determined by the practitioners as well as the local communities using the media) into vehicles of development. In one instance, traditional folk songs with newly inserted development themes intended for rural populations were scrutinized, evaluated, and checked by the central government wing that was devoted to maintaining the cultural heritage of such media and simultaneously, in this case, utilizing them for development purposes (Malik, 1983).

Similarly, in the case of Egypt, a study commissioned by the UNESCO generated a report describing the entry points available with traditional media for promoting development (Hussein, 1980). Parallels were drawn between traditional and modern media to enable understanding of the use of traditional media also for development purposes. Source credibility (for example, religious leaders presiding over numerous folk and rural media programmes) and opportunities for inserting subliminal messages in certain traditional folk forms capable of inducing mind-altering states in group situations were identified. Traditional media thus constituted a field of visibility where their functional value for development purposes could be examined.

The question may arise as to what other means one would use to address the information needs of rural populations. The discursive strategy of surveillance operates largely under the assumption that rural populations and communities do not possess the capacity to survey and commandeer their own cultural expressions for needs they might consider a priority. The urgency apparent in documents that address the powerful role of traditional media in mainstream development tends to marginalize the possibility of other modes of and reasons for existence of these indigenous media.

A plethora of research projects and initiatives for development were generated to aid or hasten development in the Third World. Evaluations of project successes and failures, and recommendations to create stronger projects in the future have also been offered (for example, Hornik, 1988; Stevenson, 1988). Knowledge about communications in the developing world-infrastructure, capabilities, potential, target populations—have been discovered, measured, analysed, and evaluated through systematic research. This vein of research contributed substantially to constructions of 'development' and a frame within which to compare various regions using external standardized criteria that could not necessarily produce an accurate description of a particular socio-cultural communication system. Such criteria served as accurate devices for evaluating social systems. The contributory value of the knowledge and insights about diverse social systems gained from these criteria and method are not in question. However, elevating these criteria to sole international benchmarks for measuring the degree of development of a given nation legitimated the production of certain types of knowledge about that society. In the process, the discursive effects of such tools on constructing an image of world imbalances were not considered; the mainstream notions of development that emerged out of such practices have been questioned (see for example Jacobson, 1996). Communication capacities in developing regions thus constituted a field of visibility. Research activities and execution of these projects designed to generate knowledge about developing regions find an analogy in Spurr's explanation of 'non-corporeal' power in the panoptic principle.

An example would be the communication indicators of socio-economic development developed in the late 1970s (UNESCO, 1979). About 103 indicators of development were identified, including communications, education, urbanization, income distribution, industrialization, technology, growth potential, and demography.

Measurements of communication included newspaper circulation per capita, newsprint consumption per capita, telephones per 100,000 population, radio receivers and television sets per 1,000 population, and so on. While such data indeed contribute to understanding the communications picture of various nations and regions, the assumption of comparability of regions within these established categories reflect a particular (European) history of industrialization that served to define mainstream models of communication and development. Comparability of development indices was constructed in two ways. First, the construction pertained to the criteria set by the developed countries against which the degree of development would be measured. Second, such criteria not only set a universal standard for comparison, but they also served to make countries within developing regions comparable with one another. Thus, communications research projects carried out by development agencies enabled constructions of frames within which communications resources of developing regions were rendered visible to subsequently allow mapping, planning, monitoring, and mobilizing prescribed types of social change.

Other recommendations to integrate communications into the development project included the treatment of communications as a resource, thereby integrating communications with economics (Jussawalla and Lamberton, 1982).[1] A call for 'a better conceptualization and measurement of the communications sector as a macro input for development' indicates that communication was primarily an economic resource rather than a practice. As with all resources, full knowledge of communications capacities, technologies, and output was required. This knowledge constitutes a field of visibility, particularly in the context of the development project in the global system.

Invisibility: Outside the Frame

Leaders and other members of the development machinery demonstrated a 'parent' mentality from their positions as administrators, experts and in other power-conferring roles (Doty, 1996). In this family analogy, the parents are naturalized into positions of power and they exert authority over the children. The parents possessed the privilege of inspecting and examining various dimensions of communications in developing regions, for development and development policy purposes.

Extending Spurr's analysis of the politics of the gaze in colonial discourse to the discourse of communication and development, we see that looking without being looked back creates an 'economy of uneven exchange' with the object of the gaze (Spurr, 1993:13). Critics of the mainstream idea of development have pointed out that the treatment of the developing countries as children in this forced economy of uneven exchange has perpetuated the idea that an ideal developed society signifies adulthood; in this stage, people and institutions are facile users of modern media and new technologies. Whatever the combination of elements respective countries could select to 'arrive', a need was seen to naturalize and orchestrate the efforts for helping nations enter adulthood. The collective social agreement prevalent in most cultures that parents know best and that they possess the authority to check, scrutinize and admonish is extended to the domain of communication and development.

A conference report on satellite communications emphasized the need for space education by pointing out that this was the 'ongoing practice in all the countries that are developing any measure of capability in the area of space science and technology' (United Nations, 1981; Addis Ababa, A/AC.105/289:5) and that Africa should follow. The problem of capital outlay for such operations was not the main concern; instead, African countries were warned that it was not a question of not being able to afford the technology, but not being able to afford going without it. Skills for survival in the technological (world) order were needed to be taught. In such instances, other knowledge that might have had their own beneficial outcomes for non-Western societies were denied existence; pre-modern knowledge also was rendered obsolete by this discourse.

Another factor illustrating the discursive strategy of invisibility is the mystique surrounding the idea of a 'developed' society for the large rural and poor populations in developing regions. Hints at unlimited progress characteristic of the tone and aspirations of modernity suggested infinite advancement towards a relatively unknown end, and the idea that progress breeds further progress also formed a subtext. For example, Pelton (1983) described a futuristic picture of the global telnet, the telecity. Attractive though this idea may seem, for national policy-makers in the developing countries a global telecity on a large scale benefiting their vast populations and ensuring appropriate literacy and access to participate in the telecity lifestyle painted a destination that is yet to be reached with full success even in the technologically advanced nations.

As a strategy, invisibility serves to '[embed] the universals of the discourse' of communication and development (Escobar, 1995:160). Capturing a vantage point to see and maintain a shielded presence while scrutinizing, at the same time escaping scrutiny in return enables the viewer to map the terrain of communications in the Third World, a space and place that constitute the object of that scrutiny.

Conclusion

It has been argued that to figure in the discourse itself is a form of visibility. Deconstructing frames of visibility enables us to see the construction of a discourse. Here the chapter has not addressed the negotiation/resistance side of the equation in the formation of the discourse of communication and development. However, through the tropes of both surveillance and invisibility we can see that communication and development, in the form of research and intervention projects, policy debates, seminars, and studies renders communications in all its dimensions a field of visibility in the dominant discourse. Both tropes work together to create a global space where the dependent status of Third World countries was reiterated and the role of the economically powerful nations as providers, adults and/or guides acquired a natural authority.

Communication and development has constituted a composite running theme in the history of international communications until the recent past, when the contours of this theme changed to one of globalization and the culture industries. Noticeable was a new extension of concerns that went beyond many aspects of the materiality evident in the discourse of communication and development to the symbolic aspects of what Appadurai (1993) has termed a global cultural economy. Critical reactions to the exacerbated chasm between developed and developing regions because of globalization include assertions of identity in symbolic arenas. The work on new social movements and the increasing dominance of the local, the popular, the everyday (Escobar, 1992; Huesca, 1995; Melucci, 1990) are cases in point. However, questions pertaining to communication and development have not disappeared; instead, they have dispersed into various domains, but continue their interplay. For example, questions about intellectual property rights over software constitute part of the agenda for the World Trade Organization meetings and policies (Braman, 1990). Such questions tacitly assume the existence of certain types of development—primarily technological and economic—among all participants of the debate (with the premise 'all else being equal' driving the information market), or speak primarily to those nations in full possession and significant control of such developments.

A critical tension continues, between guided social change through policy and alternate possibilities that might fall outside the realm of policy or are at best located at its fringes. Increasingly, an emergent alternate literature and documentation at both the theoretical and activist levels bring to our attention the workings of such alternate communications situations, with a focus on the local and the popular.[2] Alternate visions continue to grapple with problems related to democracy and development raised in the last few decades in international communication.

Economics and technology, once part of the overall practice of conducting social life, have acquired a centrality around which meanings and practices of development revolve (Sachs, 1992). Critiques of development are often addressed to this centrality of technology or economics or a combination of both as the dominant definitions of 'development'. Social change is planned, interpreted, and intervened upon from the perspectives of technology and/or economics. The dominant discourse in the domain of communication also reflects this centrality. Alternate 'development' discourses suggested by scholars and activists such as Sachs (1992) and Marglin and Marglin (1990, 1996) do not preclude the possibility of social change. A complete return to the pre-modern is neither realistic, nor in most instances, possible, nor even desirable. Rather, the source from which an articulation of the need for change emerges becomes central. Transformed definitions of development and change within local contexts and histories, and ecologically sympathetic and compatible processes and types of social change are being pursued by development agencies and grassroots communities alike as more fruitful paths to desired social change.

Notes

1. For the parallels between economics and development, and indeed, one substituting for the other, see Sachs, 1992.
2. Huesca's (1995) research on Bolivian tin miners and participatory radio, and a film (Drishti, 1997) documenting the successful outcome of a state-wide rural women's movement in the state of Andhra Pradesh in India are examples.

References

Appadurai, A. 1993. 'Disjuncture and Difference in the Global Cultural Economy', *Public Culture*, 2(2):1–24.
Banuri, T. 1990. 'Modernization and Its Discontents: A Cultural Perspective on Theories of Development', in F.A. Marglin and S. Marglin (eds). *Dominating Knowledge: Development, Culture, and Resistance*, pp. 73–101. Oxford: Clarendon Press.
Beechey, V. and J. Donald. 1985. *Subjectivity and Social Relations: A Reader*. Milton Keynes: Open University Press.
Braman, S. 1990. 'Trade and Information Policy', *Media, Culture and Society*, 12:361–385.
Doty, R.L. 1996. *Imperial Encounters: The Politics of Representation in North–South Relations*. Minneapolis: University of Minnesota Press.
Drishti Media Group. 1997. http://home.dti.net/foil/resources/drishti.htm.
Escobar, A. 1987. 'Power and Visibility: The Invention and Management of Development in the Third World.' Doctoral Dissertation. Berkeley: University of California.
———. 1992. 'Imagining a Post-Development Era? Critical Thought, Development, and Social Movements', *Social Text*, 31/32:20–36.
———.1995. *Encountering Development: The Making and Unmaking of the Third World*. Princeton, NJ: Princeton University Press.
Ferguson, J. 1994. *The Anti-politics Machine: 'Development,' Depoliticization, and Bureaucratic Power in Lesotho*. Minneapolis: University of Minnesota Press.
Foucault, M. 1972. *The Archaeology of Knowledge and the Discourse on Language* (Translated by A. Sheridan). New York: Pantheon.
———. 1980. *Power/Knowledge: Selected Interviews and Other Writings 1972–1977* (C. Gordon (ed.). Translated by C. Gordon, L. Marshall, J. Mepham and K. Soper). New York: Pantheon.
Hall, S. 1985. 'The Rediscovery of "Ideology": Return of the Repressed in Media Studies', in V. Beechey and J. Donald (eds). *Subjectivity and Social Relations: A Reader*, pp. 23–55. Milton Keynes: Open University Press.
Hornik, R. 1988. *Development Communication: Information, Agriculture, and Nutrition in the Third World*. New York: Longman.
Huesca, R. 1995. 'A Procedural View of Participatory Communication: Lessons from Bolivian Tin Miners' Radio', *Media, Culture & Society*, 17:101–119.
Hussein, S.M. 1980. *Main Forms of Traditional Communication: Egypt, International Commission for the Study of Communication Problems*. Paris: UNESCO.
Jacobson, T. 1996.'Development Communication Theory in the "Wake" of Positivism', in J. Servaes, T.L. Jacobson and S.A. White (eds). *Participatory Communication for Social Change*. New Delhi, Thousand Oaks, London: Sage Publications.
Jussawalla, M. and D.M. Lamberton. 1982. *Communication Economics and Development*. New York: Pergamon Press, with The East-West Center, Hawaii.

Malik, M. 1983. 'Traditional Forms of Communication and the Mass Media in India', *Communication and Society*, 13. Paris: UNESCO.

Marglin, F.A. and S. Marglin. 1990. *Dominating Knowledge: Development, Culture, and Resistance.* Oxford: Clarendon Press.

———. 1996. *Decolonizing Knowledge: From Development to Dialogue.* Oxford: Clarendon Press.

Melucci, A. 1990. 'Liberation or Meaning? Social Movements, Culture, and Democracy', in J.N. Pieterse (ed.). *Emancipations Modern and Postmodern.* London, Newbury Park, New Delhi: Sage Publications.

Mohanty, C.T. 1991. 'Under Western Eyes. Feminist Scholarship and Colonial Discourses', in C.T. Mohanty, A. Russo and L. Torres (eds). *Third World Women and the Politics of Feminism*, pp. 51–80. Bloomington and Indianapolis: Indiana University Press.

NAMEDIA. (1983). Final report and documents of the Media Conference of the Non-aligned, New Delhi, 9–12 December. New Delhi: NAMEDIA.

Pelton, J. 1983. 'The Communication Satellite Revolution: Revolutionary Change Agent', *Columbia Journal of World Business*, 19(1):77–84.

Sachs, W. 1992. Development, in W. Sachs (ed.). *The Development Dictionary: A Guide to Knowledge as Power.* London: Zed Books.

Shohat, E. and R. Stam. 1994. *Unthinking Eurocentrism: Multiculturalism and the Media.* London: Routledge.

Spurr, D. 1993. *The Rhetoric of Empire: Colonial Discourse in Journalism, Travel Writing and Imperial Administration.* Durham, NC: Duke University Press.

Stevenson, R. 1988. *Communication, Development, and the Third World.* New York: Longman.

Tomlinson, J. 1991. *Cultural Imperialism: An Introduction.* Baltimore: The Johns Hopkins University Press.

———. 1993. *Cultural Imperialism: An Introduction.* Baltimore: The Johns Hopkins University Press.

UNESCO. 1979. *Communication Indicators I: Communication Indicators and Indicators of Socio-economic Development.* Summary of the study by Rita Cruise O'brien, Ellen Cooper, Brian Perkes, and Henry Lucas. CC-79/WS/134. 85 p. Paris: UNESCO.

United Nations. 1981. Report of the United Nations, Economic Commission for Africa Regional Seminar on Remote Sensing Applications and Satellite Communications for Education and Development (Addis Ababa), A/AC.105/290, New York: United Nations.

———. 1984. *The New World Information and Communication Order: A Selective Bibliography.* Bibliographical Series No. 35. New York: Dag Hammarskjöld Library.

Threads of Development Communication 6

ROYAL D. COLLE

In this chapter, we concentrate heavily on the patterns of actions that reflect how development communication has evolved over the last half century. As we explore communication in the real life context of agricultural, health and community development, we skirt the many excellent discussions by theorists and academicians who present a more abstract picture of this evolution. (For example see Casmir, 1991; Mody, 2003; Gumucio-Dagron and Tufte, 2006; and various chapters in this volume.) We will trace seven threads that have contributed to that fabric we call 'development communication'.

Communication and Development

Communication is a vital partner in initiatives that involve *voluntary behaviour* change. The two words 'voluntary' and 'behaviour' are very important in understanding what unfolds in the pages of this chapter. Where behaviour is forced, communication may be necessary for reminding people of the rules or in training them to carry out the behaviour. However, most of the effort we put into development communication involves helping people develop themselves and their communities, and this inevitably involves voluntary actions. The word *behaviour* covers a wide variety of phenomena, ranging from believing something will improve a family's welfare to using a condom or adopting (or avoiding) biotechnology-developed seed varieties. Where people have options to change their ways of life, communication becomes important in informing, persuading, listening, data gathering, educating, training, and managing change.

Thus, we emphasize the idea that development communication is 'strategic communication'— a concept applied recently to efforts to combat the HIV/AIDS problem. According to health communication experts McKee, Bertrand and Becker-Benton (2004), strategic communication is a promising response to the HIV/AIDS epidemic that has been vastly under-utilized to date.

The systematic nature of strategic communication contrasts sharply with the ad hoc practice of designing an occasional poster or radio spot for a given cause. It combines a series of elements—extensive use of data, careful planning, stakeholder participation, creativity, high-quality programming, and linkages to other programme elements and levels, among others—that stimulate positive and measurable behaviour change among the intended audience.

Government officials, academics, practitioners and others working in the development field may have different perceptions of what the defining characteristics of development communication are. Early in its history, some spoke of it as 'development support communication' suggesting that the communication function was a sub-component of various development sectors. Today some argue that development communication should itself be a sector.

The suggestion has also been made that development communication is interpersonal communication and that mass communication is something else. Others would argue that a 'development communication' approach dominated by face-to-face communication has inherent limitations if one measure of success is widespread change of behaviour in short periods of time, a goal that might be highly appropriate in some circumstances. Framing the discussion as mediated communication versus face-to-face communication is probably not the best approach. After weighing empirical data and considering the conventional wisdom about the effectiveness of communication channels, Robert Hornik concludes:

> Both data and complementary arguments suggest that the allocation of resources among channels should reflect not only relative effects but also reach, cost, managerial feasibility, and sustainability. In many contexts those considerations will lead away from an emphasis on interpersonal channels and toward increasing reliance on mass media channels.
>
> So long as the truism—media for awareness, field agents for practice change—is accepted, and so long as communication planners fail to admit the difficulty of organizing and sustaining such agent networks, communication programs are unlikely to succeed as motivators of behavior change. (Hornik, 1989:329)

A group of communication professionals, including representatives from the UN Specialized Agencies and academics who met periodically during the past decade as a Roundtable on Development Communication, concluded that its domain is best described by the phrase 'communication and development'. This suggests that both mediated and non-mediated forms of communication are relevant to the development issue. This compromise is especially useful with the growing importance for development of the new information and communication technologies—led by computers, the Internet and the World Wide Web—which cannot easily be classified exclusively as mass or interpersonal communication.

When one looks at development communication as *communication-and-development* there are significant examples of successes. Some of these have been documented on the Communication Initiative web page (www.comminit.com). Examples include:

1. Capital Doctor—Uganda

A call-in radio show that reaches a general audience of 5 million, physically covering ap-proxi-mately 75 per cent of the population, and 65 per cent of these are believed to be outside of Kampala. As of March 1998, 2,200 questions had been answered on-air. Seventy per cent of respondents at an STD clinic had listened to Capital Doctor. Ninety per cent of reported condom users were listeners to the programme, 71 per cent of those who reported to 'always' use condoms were listeners. Those who listened to Capital Doctor were more likely than non-listeners to use condoms.
http://www.comminit.com/id01-7of99/sld-485.html

2. Sanjeevani—Nepal

Attitudinal changes occurred due to this TV drama on child health issues and gender equality in education. 57.6 per cent of respondents said that they learnt that female education is of primary importance for the development of the community. 22.5 per cent learnt that health education is necessary, 12.5 per cent learnt that there should be no gender discrimination and that daughters and sons should have equal rights. 5.8 per cent learnt that knowledge should be shared with others in the community.
http://www.comminit.com/idmay15/sld-2307.html

3. Mass Media Family Planning—Turkey

A national multimedia project. Ten per cent of married women visited a clinic as a result of the programme, 20 per cent said they intended to. Modern contraceptive use increased from 38.6 to 42.8 per cent. Intra Uterine Device (IUD) use increased from 16 per cent to 22 per cent, condom use decreased by 2 per cent, oral contraceptive decreased by 3 per cent, withdrawal method decreased by 3 per cent.
http://www.comminit.com/idmay15/sld-2296.html

4. Measles Communication Programme—Philippines

A national multimedia project. Proportion of fully vaccinated children of ages 12–23 months increased from 54 per cent to 65 per cent. Average number of vaccinations that a child under two years received increased from 4.32 to 5.10. Sixty-four per cent of mothers who knew of the campaign had their children immunized, 42 per cent of mothers who did not have the knowledge of the campaign had their children vaccinated.
http://www.comminit.com/idmay15/sld-2293.html

5. Accessing Mass Media on Reproductive Behaviour—Africa

Namibia: Sixty-one per cent of married women regularly exposed to radio, TV and print media are currently using contraception; compared with 25 per cent exposed to two of those media, 20 per cent exposed to one of the media and 12 per cent exposed to no media.

Kenya: Fifty-three per cent of rural married women regularly exposed to radio, TV and print media are currently using contraception; compared with 42 per cent exposed to two of those media, 33 per cent exposed to one of the media and 22 per cent exposed to no media.

Zambia: Fifteen per cent of married women with no education regularly exposed to radio and TV are currently using contraception compared with 9 per cent exposed to one of those media and 7 per cent exposed to no media.

Burkina Faso: All women regularly exposed to radio, television and print media desire a mean number of children of 3.7; compared with 4.2 for women having regular exposure to two of those media, 5.7 for one of the media, and 6.3 for no exposure to any media.

Ghana: Rural women regularly exposed to radio, television and print media desire a mean number of children of 3.9; compared with 4.2 for women having regular exposure to two of those media, 4.6 for one of the media, and 5.3 for no exposure to any media.

6. Social Marketing of Vitamin A in West Sumatra

Indonesia—Daily consumption of dark green leafy vegetables increased: 19 per cent to 32 per cent among pregnant mothers; 14 per cent to 33 per cent among nursing mothers; 10 per cent to 21 per cent among 5–12-months olds; 17 per cent to 27 per cent among 13–60-months olds.
http://www.comminit.com/usaidimpact/sld-1931.html

7. Music Project—Nigeria

Included the production and commercial launch of two family planning songs, six TV public service announcements (PSAs) and six radio PSAs. Respondents who were highly exposed to the campaign were three times more likely to communicate with their spouses about family planning, five times more likely to have positive family planning attitudes, and almost twice as likely to use family planning when compared to those who were unexposed. Rural respondents with high exposure were seven times more likely to have positive family planning attitudes when compared to those who were unexposed.
http://www.comminit.com/idmay15/sld-2358.html

Millennium Development Goals and World Summit on the Information Society

Our exploration begins abruptly at the twenty first century although later in the chapter we will go back to explore the various threads of development communication as they emerged a half century earlier. Two of the most influential forces driving development communication in the early years of this century have been the Millennium Development Goals (MDGs) and the World Summit on the Information Society (WSIS).

The MDGs became an important political and moral force when they were adopted by more than 190 nations whose representatives convened in New York at a Millennium Summit in September 2000. The subsequent Millennium Declaration listed specific development targets to be met by the year 2015. They included cutting world poverty in half, universal primary education, reducing child mortality by two-thirds, reducing by two-thirds the proportion of the population without clean drinking water, combating the incidence of malaria and HIV/AIDS, and other development goals. Parallel to and intersecting with this great attention to the MDGs was the two-part World Summit on the Information Society. Held in two phases—Geneva, Switzerland in 2003 and Tunis in 2005—WSIS laid out challenges and applications related to the use of information and communication technologies for accelerating progress towards the MDGs.

While there are people who question the investment in information technologies rather than clinics and medicines, dramatic examples of the value of information and communication resources make a strong case for what is called ICT4D, or Information and Communication Technology for Development. For example, in West Africa, computers and satellite radio help to control river blindness. Local inhabitants send information from sensors along 50,000 kilometres of rivers to entomologists who use the data to make decisions on when to spray against the blackfly. The anecdote in the accompanying box illustrates the experience of a poor farmer in China.

Box 6.1 ICT Helping Chinese Farmers

In the village of Wu'an in Hubei Province ... farmer Li Suotian received continually updated market information [through the Internet]. He found out that Israeli breeds of tomatoes sold well in Hubei. He then grew more than 1 mu (0.07 hectares) of tomatoes and obtained an annual income of 3,500 yuan (US$ 421) from them. That income was eight times his normal income from grain growing. www.i4donline.net, May 4, 2004.

During the lifespan of the MDGs, governments, civil society and the private sector will be building broadband infrastructures, public digital databases and other resources to provide people with the kinds of information and communication services that may help us meet a variety of important economic and social goals. Already, the English language shows movement in this direction with new words like 'eGovernment', 'eHealth', 'eEducation', 'eCommerce' and 'eDevelopment'. A major challenge for many nations, however, will be to help poor people gain access to appropriate and relevant ICT resources. We take this up in one of the threads that follow.

Seven Threads

Obviously communication has become an important aspect of development initiatives in health, nutrition, agriculture, family planning, education and community economics. We now turn to an exploration of seven threads that have gone into the make-up of this communication-and-development fabric (for which we will, incidentally, use the term 'development communication').

1. The UNDP Thread and Erskine Childers

Among the earliest pioneers in the field we now call development communication was a United Nations unit called the Development Support Communications Service (DSCS) which operated under the aegis of the United Nations Development Programme (UNDP). DSCS was based in Bangkok (although its successor organization, the Development Training and Communication Planning Programme shifted to Manila). It was in DSCS where the ideas began to come together to form a distinctively new approach to communication as part of development interventions and Erskine Childers was the key person in the UNDP operation.

Childers died in August 1996 leaving behind him almost 30 years of service to the United Nations; 22 as a UN staff member and seven more with the World Federation of UN Associations (WFUNA). He dedicated effort, energy, enthusiasm and his life to the ideals of the UN. Many knew him best for the pioneering work he did in advocating communication as an integral component of development projects. An example of this is the paper he and his wife Mallica Vajrathan directed at UN organizations in 1968 which is reproduced below.

While Childers wrote no books directly related to development communication like those of Lerner, Schramm and others prominent in the field, he wrote the papers and made presentations that foreshadowed some of the concepts, principles and methods that have emerged in the past several decades. FAO's Silvia Balit summed it up well: 'He was not only the founding father of development support communication, but also a true master and an example for us all'.

Perhaps the strength of his leadership in development communication is demonstrated best in Childers' own words. In *Sharing Knowledge*, FAO's video programme on communication for sustainable development, Childers said:

If you want development to be rooted in the human beings who have to become the agents of it as well as the beneficiaries, who will alone decide on the kind of development they can sustain after the foreign aid has gone away, then you have got to communicate with them, you have got to enable them to communicate with each other and back to the planners in the capital city. You have got to communicate the techniques that they need in order that they will decide on their own development. If you do not do that you will continue to have weak or failing development programmes. It's as simple as that.

Childers spent his early career as a writer, doing scripts for radio and television, especially on topics related to international affairs and the United Nations. Former UNICEF communication specialist Jack Ling says that Childers was a conceptualizer and a prolific writer who should be 'fully recognized' for his pioneering role in development communication.

Between 1967 and 1975, Childers was based in Bangkok where, with wife Mallica Vajrathan and others, he developed the ideas and processes that became development support communication. From his post as Director of the UNDP/UNICEF Regional Development Support Communication Service (Asia-Pacific), he urged the UN Specialized Agencies and national governments to put more resources into communication, for, as he wrote in 1968, 'No innovation, however brilliantly designed and set down in a project Plan of Operations, becomes development until it has been communicated.'

One side of Childers' character was reflected by Brian Urquhart, who worked with Childers towards the welfare and reform of the United Nations. Urquhart wrote in *The Independent* soon after Childers' death: 'His biting humour and his strong opinions were splendidly stimulating to those he worked with.'

Many who had the opportunity to interact with Childers' during the past decade on the Development Communication Roundtable would echo those observations, remembering the challenges he issued and the wisdom he provided in these discussions. One Roundtable member and long-time UNFPA communication expert, O.J. Sikes, says:

Erskine was a true champion of the people. He didn't invent the concept of participation, but he and Mallica breathed life into it. He drew global attention to the importance of women's rights. Today, these concepts, unpopular when he first espoused them in the 1960s, have become widely perceived as keys to development.

Urquhart well sums up this side of Childers' character:

He was, by nature and by inheritance, a champion of the oppressed and the less fortunate. He stood up for the developing countries and their peoples. He fought for their place on the international scene and for the programmes and activities that would help them attain it.

Childers and Vajrathan wrote the following text in June 1968 while they were at DSCS in Bangkok. Entitled *Development Support Communications for Project Support*, it was one of a collection of papers Childers was to write in the next few years advocating communication as a vital component of development planning. A major value of this piece is that it reflects lessons he and his wife learned from the field. Strikingly, with only an update of the technology mentioned, the paper is as important and relevant today as it was almost three decades ago. For example, the authors anticipated D.C. Korten and N.T. Uphoff's 'bureaucratic reorientation for participatory rural development' of the 1980s (Korten and Uphoff, 1981), the importance of planning and strategy, and the imperative often found in social marketing to start with a firm foundation of social science research and analysis. Significantly, many of the measures he proposed have found their ways into the practices of some UN agencies. Although the unpublished paper was principally addressed to the UN Family in 1968, it deserves and can serve a much wider audience today.

Childers and Vajrathan begin their paper by noting a variety of circumstances in development that call for systematic communication support, such as the following:

'the need for far greater involvement of the local people in the project'
'confusion among farmers arising from conflicting and inaccurate information'
'resistance from the public due to traditional attitudes and suspicion of authority it has proven difficult to convince key officials in other departments of the success of the pilot projects and the need to budget for its expansion'
'a widespread popular view that these [communication] occupations are of inferior status compared to white-collar jobs.'

We shift now to the text of the paper (which was unpublished).

For the past ten years and more, references like those set down [above] have been appearing with increasing frequency in project reports from developing countries assisted by the UN-Family; or the difficulties epitomised in such phrases have been the coinage of countless discussions among UN development personnel. Each type of obstacle to project implementation encompassed by such familiar phrases is an obstacle of communication. It would be hopelessly optimistic to state that greater attention to the use of communication techniques in development projects would eliminate these recurring reports altogether. But it can be no exaggeration on the accumulated evidence to state that perhaps no other instrument in the development process has been so grossly neglected.

There are, of course, UN-assisted projects in which there is no need for special, supporting information and communications work. But when these and a few other limited categories of projects are set apart, it must be said that virtually all others contain a very large element of communication. They are, after all, planned efforts to introduce and diffuse innovations among communities or cadres—and to do so intensively and economically in order to telescope timespans of growth and change that would otherwise encompass entire generations, with limited funds.

No innovation, however, brilliantly designed and set down in a project Plan of Operations [PlanOps], becomes development until it has been communicated. No input or construction of material resources for development can be successful unless and until the innovations—the new techniques and surrounding changed attitudes which people will need to use those resources—have been communicated to them.

Once thus stated, the point appears to be crushingly obvious. Yet it has not been obvious in project formulation. Every project of the kind under discussion here carries a number of built-in assumptions or requirements for its success. When one or more agencies of the UN-Family assists in the design and construction of a material input—for example, a hydroelectric dam, or complex of irrigation canals—the objective is not to build a dam or canals. It is to provide new material resources which people, as rapidly as possible after physical completion, can begin to use and benefit from. The project PlanOps may be strictly for the design and construction; the terms of reference may not in any way call for UN Family effort to ensure the diffusion of the necessary accompanying innovations to use the input. Yet even in such cases, and even assuming that it could be argued that we should not seek to ensure that others—i.e. national authorities—will plan and phase in the diffusion of these innovations, even so, we are involved in communications.

From the moment a stranger appears in someone's field bearing government authority, a theodolite, and some stakes, and drives the stakes into that ground, a long chain-reaction of communication has been launched. It begins with the first villager who sees the stake, wonders about it, speculates with a neighbour, begins asking questions that ripple out to a rapidly increasing community of profoundly concerned people. Is 'Government' going to take their land? Will they get any compensation? Is it something to do with water? Will an ancestral burial ground be flooded? Is the new water for the landlord or for us? When will 'it' happen? The Agricultural Extension Officer has been telling us to start a cooperative. Is it worth it now? 'They' want us to build a new school house: will we be here, on our land, in five years' time; and if not, why put energy into a new school?

The engineers who drew up the design and specifications, the time schedule and materials-logistics for this UN-assisted project were not asked—and should not have been asked—to contemplate such immediate consequences from the first act of construction. But was anyone else asked to contemplate, to draw up an accompanying information plan—a plan for purposive support communications both to explain 'the stake' and all that would follow to the surrounding community, in time, and to begin the diffusion of needed innovations among them in time?

In another entire category of projects, communication is their very raison d'etre: planned efforts to diffuse innovations among the largest possible number of ordinary people, or by training new cadres both in historically very short periods of time. The whole web of health, agricultural, vocational and other training, adult and out-of-school education, and in school education development projects falls within this definition. All of these projects consist, first and foremost, of bodies of new information or techniques, in the hands of a relatively small number of UN and counterpart personnel, that are to be communicated to people who need them. The funda-mental premise of all this assistance is that innovations can be introduced and that people will adopt them through special and accelerated effort—rather than leaving the process to 'several generations of wider and better schooling,' and so forth.

Yet the corollary of this premise in all such development work is, surely, that special and accelerative means of diffusing the innovations will be needed—every possible means that can be devised. Many, indeed most, of the innovations have been designed from experience in more developed societies. In those societies, no self-respecting planner of a training programme for a cadre of people automatically more capable of absorbing a given innovation would dream of ignoring, say, the question of advance-planning of suitable films/slides/ charts and other aids to the communication process. Yet, the plain fact is that to date, we in the UN Family have been engaged again and again in the exercise of launching training projects for diffusion of breathtakingly 'big' innovations to people far less ready to absorb them, with only the most rudimentary aids to the communication process. To put this neglect in a nutshell: the developing countries are now strewn with cine and slide projectors supplied by UN and bilateral aid agencies—but with miserably few films or slides remotely relevant to the intended audiences. As in so many respects, the 'nuts and bolts' have been furnished, but not the innovations that can make them usable.

One crucial time factor in the communication process of development has already been mentioned—that we are trying to telescope the time-span of innovation and change from a matter of generations to a matter of years. Within this, there is a second vital time-factor— the actual phasing of a project. Whether the project-audience is a whole community or selected trainee-cadres, the innovations to be diffused are supposed to be phased over a period of perhaps five years, at most, either absolutely or per diffusion-cycle. The nature of a great many such projects leave no margin for delay in any of the logistics. Experts are phased in by project years; newly-trained cadres from one year are supposed to begin their innovation-diffusion the next; a new irrigation canal is filled with water at a date when the surrounding farmers are supposed to be ready to begin using it, first for one new kind of cultivation, then for a second crop, and so on.

By the nature of what all such development projects are trying to achieve, therefore, there can be no more margin for delay in the communications-logistics than in any other, nowadays automatically, programmed element of the PlanOps. Yet this very day, all over the developing regions, there are irrigation canals filled with water and not yet being used; experts and instructors for Phase-Year X of projects who can only begin to discover what communications aids they ought to have when their phase is nearly ended; and newly-trained cadres of project-implementation personnel going out to their diffusion–points with no more to help them than the (quite unsuitable) texts and charts they acquired in their courses. The authors of this paper witness these problems every day of the year, in every sector of development now under UN (as other) external assistance.

In short, a great many UN-assisted projects contain, as a very precondition of efficient and effective use of the investment mode, information or communications 'components' that ought to be advance-planned as carefully as all the other, now automatic logistics. The PlanOps of such projects should specify such a component, itemizing the resources that will be required; when they will be needed relative to project phases; who will provide the resources, as between UN and Government; what kinds of information materials (they may range from flip-cards and flannel graphs to films in the relevant language); and of course, the already familiar item, what communication equipment is to be supplied.

The range of Development Support Communications in which project planners and then field executors ought to be concerned is very wide—far, far wider than is covered by considering what are called 'the mass media' in the Western region. Media of Development Support Communications must be seen to include, potentially, every channel along which bodies of needed new information and ideas can be transmitted to the particular project audience. The hierarchies of government personnel in the functional or development ministries themselves are vital media. So may be a simple traditional village fair; a traditional midwife; a folk performance that may contain a potential for adaptation to a development innovation, far more powerful than a loudspeaker address by a technician from the city.

The technique of communication that may be vital in a given project need not be costly or require complicated modern equipment. We have seen communication obstacles—visibly vitiating an entire development aid investment—that are as simple as public health education personnel not knowing how to speak to an audience. They have been well trained in the content of the health innovations they are supposed to diffuse to the people: they know the technology perfectly but they simply do not know how to address audiences of thirty or forty village women.

It is equally important for project planners and for the new teams of specialists in Development Support Communications which the UN Family desperately needs to realize that the 'project-audience' for a given act of communications support varies enormously. It is by no means only 'the people' en masse, whether on a national or district scale. Nor is it only the actual trainees in training projects. Echelons of government personnel who are, or who ought to be, involved in project implementation, may also need purposive, planned support communication for a variety of reasons. The moment we get away from thinking in purely Western terms, of 'mass media' (publishing, radio, film, television, and so forth), and consider the total network of communication that needs to be activated for a development project, the point becomes obvious. The network will certainly include the mass media: the infrastructures of such mass communications need to be developed as rapidly as possible and used for Development Support even while being expanded with UN assistance or encouragement. But in this kind of communication, for example, it may be far more important for a given project to reach, motivate, and orient a precisely defined echelon of civil servants as a first phase of communications; then to devise communications programmes and materials addressed to 'the people'.

It will be apparent from the above that for professionals in Development Support Communications, 'media' or channels are also audience. While this is in reality true for information-communication anywhere, the traditional concepts and practices of Western mass communications tend to create a distinction that may have helped produce the terrible neglect of this element in development work.

It is also an axiom of this work that every act of development support communication, and the materials selected and produced for it, have to be tailored very carefully to the intended audience. Development is the deliberate introduction of a (relatively) massive disturbance in the lives, attitudes, work patterns, and socio economic relationships of given groups of people—a disturbance deliberately telescoped, too, into unusually short periods of time. Precisely what and how much, and how quickly, and on what mental and material-incentive premises workers can ask a defined group of human beings to do is the very essence of the entire process. Consider a dairy farming film presenting electric milking machines to farmers who do not have them and have not the remotest prospect of having them. Yet the communication act of screening such a film for those farmers could involve the act of 'asking' them to contemplate electric milking as an innovation. In a real case, the farmers were in fact profoundly angry about this film: they felt they were being insulted and humiliated. Development came to an angry halt at that moment.

Certain fundamental premises of development support communications follow from this. 'Know your audience', a concept familiar in Western commercial advertising and public relations, but less so in the Press or Broadcasting or Films, is a first precept of this development work. The need to know the 'stretch potential', or the innovation-absorption capacity of given groups of people within any one phase of a project, is absolutely vital. In a great many cases, above all for support communications directly addressed to whole communities, prior socio economic research and field testing of assumptions is very important indeed.

Another crucial premise is that development support communications programmes and aids (i.e., a film, or poster, or radio broadcast) should propose only those innovations that are feasible for the audience in terms of their present actual resources (and those that a project may be injecting). Having said this, it needs hardly to be mentioned that information—communication materials made on the other side of the world, in industrialised countries for those countries depicting totally alien people doing totally alien things within alien cultures and at wholly fantastic economic and technological levels, are not only of little relevance   they may, as in the dairy film case, be counter-innovatory. And it follows inexorably from this that UN Family development projects need to have communication support materials made afresh, indigenously or within comparable situations in other (and culturally acceptable) developing countries. This is not an absolute rule: there are certain kinds of materials, on certain subjects, that can be usefully imported from advanced-technology countries; and films and other materials from such countries may be extremely useful at later phases of a project. But it may be stated as an excellent general rule of thumb that the early acts of innovation communications in UN-assisted development projects ought to be with materials depicting the innovation in the country concerned, carried out by fellow countrymen.

Types of Development Support Communications

A broad assembly of the experience of development in the field indicates many categories of repeatedly needed support communication efforts. The following outline list is not presented in order of priority nor of action, nor are all these types of communication necessarily needed for every project. The priorities, the chronology of communication efforts within a project's time span, and the combinations of programmes will vary with each project.

1. Broad public motivation. Every UN project is attempted, with national counterpart, in a general 'reservoir' of public attitudes towards development in general, or the particular sector involved. The UN Family should automatically seek to assist in and encourage development support communication programmes that will motivate the public more effectively. In sectoral terms, a project may be launched at a time when, by sheer coincidence, public attention to that sector of development may be low—the national information media may never, nor not for several years, have presented the need for development in the sector concerned. It is often true that the first support communications requirement for project implementation is simply (not necessarily easily) to 'get people thinking about' the sector concerned.

2. Motivation-orientation of project implementers. To date, it has almost invariably been assumed in project planning and implementation that if a given national ministry has requested the project and signed a PlanOps, all civil servants concerned will implement it automatically. Once so stated, the assumption is obviously nonsense: yet the neglect of support communications for national project-implementing personnel amounts to such an assumption.

We should assess every project to determine what help—by idea and/or material aid—the national authorities may need to ensure that the relevant echelons of civil servants, from capital city outwards, are properly informed and motivated about the project. In very many cases, all that presently happens is that one more flood of crudely stenciled paper is distributed through the echelons, plus such word-of-mouth briefing as the specialists within the department may be able to provide.

In our experience, for projects of any size in investment, in geographical scope, and in project-community, one of the earliest needs may be a complete information-communications programme designed for these levels—quite possibly an orientation motivation film for government personnel; a pamphlet; a basic PlanOps chart; perhaps a radio or TV programme. UN Family field personnel presently have to spend grossly wasteful amounts of time simply trying to ensure that even a small number of over burdened, under-paid civil servants know even the elementary facts about a project—who is running it; what the chain of command and trouble shooting is; where supplies come from; what the roles of possibly two or three UN agencies are; what needs to be accomplished in Year One, and then and only then in Year Two, and so on. All of this is development support communications for project implementation. At present, we leave the whole crucial process, in the overwhelming majority of projects, to the word-of-mouth and formal correspondence efforts of a tiny handful of UN project field officers who do have a few other things to do as well.

3. Specific elite and government-level information. There are other often absolutely vital kinds of support locations at these levels—without proper attention to which, as the authors have witnessed in countless instances, an entire project runs into trouble. Among many, we would cite here:

Inter-departmental awareness of a given project and of its needs now and in the phased future is immensely important. More and more UN-assisted projects are bi- or multi-sectoral, requiring for their very functioning the coordination of several ministries at national and field levels. This simply does not happen because it is stipulated in a PlanOps. It happens only as a result of consistent, advance-planned, purposive communication—inevitably requiring special materials in one or more media. It is almost in the nature of sectorally organised government authorities everywhere not to coordinate. The idea that lack of coordination occurs only in developing countries is among many myths. But in efficient and cost effective project implementation, it is in such countries that we and they can least afford uncoordinated effort. UN field personnel talk themselves hoarse on this subject day after day because, to date, we have furnished them with nothing except their voices and formal correspondence office capacity to try to communicate this need of inter-departmental coordination.

Motivation for expansion and follow-up is another problem that is sheer communication in development Project Implementation at elite and government-service levels. It follows from the above needs and actions, but it ought to be planned in advance. At certain fairly precise dates in the forward 'history' of a project, decision-makers and financial controllers in Government have to authorize further steps without which the original project-investment may become largely a nonsense. More counterpart personnel must be authorised, budget-allocated, and recruited and trained; Government has to take over [technical assistance] costs; physical and human resource investments of other kinds have to be implemented by Government. All of this may have been foreseen and set down in the PlanOps. That does not mean that it will happen when it should happen. Once again, the first requirement is communication to the relevant decision-makers (and decision-influencers, even outside Government, through press and other media) of the approaching needed actions, and of the progress of the project that justifies those actions.

Anyone in the UN Family who has worked in development in the field will be all too familiar with this problem and how, invariably too late because it was never advance-planned, the need is perceived for some decent press reporting on the project a set of good slides, at the least, that can be used by the fully committed government officers to persuade and convince their key associates to authorize the necessary budget in time. It is [characteristic] of this problem, like so many others in development support communications, that the people who need to be reached cannot be physically brought to a place where the purpose and progress of the project can be seen by them with their own eyes. The project has to be brought to them—again, an exercise in planned communications using modern techniques and materials.

4. Project cadre–training communication needs. The project-field where perhaps the greatest awareness of the role of planned, purposive support communications has been evident is, of course, in training. But here again, as (by now) literally thousands of UN-recruited training instructors and their counterparts could relate, we can perceive neglect in quality and quantity that is far, far more serious for training in developing countries than in industrialized ones. We have referred earlier, in the introduction, to this special phenomenon of the diffusion of innovations in developing countries inherently needing more systematic exploitation of modern techniques of communication than in the countries from which the innovations derive. Our instructors are in need of every conceivable kind of ads—films, slides, better charts and other printed ads—designed for their trainees.

Many UN-recruited instructors have experience in making audio-visual aids: but all too often we learn of such personnel imploring headquarters, from their field posts, for possibly quite minute extra sums of money to finance production of better teaching aids—and of months passing during which the very training course itself expires before authorisation is given, if it is given at all.

We believe that it can be stated categorically that no training project should be formulated without, there and then, its locally-attuned training-aids component having been assessed, budgeted, and production planned. This will in many cases (as with virtually every other element of this new [approach] of Development Support Communications) require prior survey and appraisal in the project country concerned by experts in communication techniques. Only by such local assessment can any realistic appraisal be made of the extent to which the national media can produce the aids needed in time and the extent to which the UN agency concerned will have to supplement national-resources. Such prior survey will cost money (less if the experts already stationed at regional level to serve all such project-appraisal and implementation needs). But any clinical assessment of the effectiveness of existing training projects will quickly show that the aid-investment in them has in very many cases been vitiated by neglect of this element. We believe it is entirely legitimate to assert that in training, as in all other kinds of projects under discussion in this paper, the time has come for decision to invest in communication in order to save UN assistance funds.

Communication support for training projects embraces many needs beyond the actual aids in the class of demonstration site. Among these we would mention trainee recruitment: without planned communication, no training project can possibly select the best candidates from the optimum number and level of applicants drawn from the geographical base actually envisaged for the project. We and our national partners repeatedly face the element of urbanisation in this field the problem of training people who will stay (or at least are more likely to stay) in rural areas or at least provincial towns. Formulation of training projects should include a planned programme, worked out with Government in advance, for the widest possible dissemination of the opportunities offered.

Occupation-status improvement is another widespread need in such projects, and is again a problem of communication. More especially in ex-colonial countries, generally throughout developing regions, the status image of needed occupations by no means conforms to known manpower requirements. The topsy-turvy ratio of doctors to nurses in countries where nursing is frowned upon for girls is a well-known example. We know of a vocational training scheme that is finding it extremely difficult to recruit trainees for carpentry because wood-working has become a lesser-status occupation. A planned and country-tailored communications programme may not, by itself, resolve these very complex problems.

What is quite certain is that nothing else will even begin to apply the effort to resolve them, for in most such cases it is not economic incentive that is missing; if the job opportunity were known and the social stigma were removed or lessened, potential recruits would learn that the pay or reward was superior to their otherwise likely income. In whatever project, a problem of the social status of a given occupation is, in part if not in whole, a problem of communications.

(Even with UN-assisted projects that do not include an overt PlanOps stipulated component of training, effective implementation may call for systematic and advance-planned effort in this field of occupation status. In a given country at a given period, a UN agency may only be involved, let us say, in expanding one element of health services. But if that element actually depends upon the availability of more nurses, assistance to or at least stimulus of Government in a communications effort to enhance the status of nurses may be vital for project implementation).

5. Applied research dissemination.   Another and widespread example of the factor immediately above-referred may be seen in the case of the numerous UN-assisted institutes for applied research in a given development sector. The PlanOps may have been only for the establishment and development of the institute itself, with the implicit assumption that Government (and educational establishments) would separately see to the dissemination of the practical technology produced in the institute. In some cases, such institutes do carry a project element of industrial-use dissemination but not, for example, extension-dissemination.

The field observations of the authors of this paper compel two suggestions about such projects. At the very least, the UN Family should plan to ensure that the work of the institute and the innovations it develops be made generally known to the public and elite through a commu-nications document (film, brochure, as may be judged best) that can also be used in schools and colleges.

At the most, we are bound to put forward the question whether, in the appraisal of all requests for such institute projects, the Family ought not to adopt the standard discipline and criterion-question to Government: 'Precisely how will the technology to be developed be disseminated for urgent practical use for development?' If once this question is asked as an automatic exercise, we believe that in many cases the judgement and the shaping of the project itself may alter. Accumulating practical experience indicates that it is from many such institutes themselves that the best chain of innovation-diffusion (possibly the very organization and cadre-training of extension personnel, for example) will flow, if so planned and agreed. At the least, we believe that experience shows that it is in the early life of such institute projects, before the UN element is phased out, that concrete programming of innovation diffusion located somewhere in very close nexus with the institute should begin. It is extremely likely that if the whole UN investment is to be maximally effective, the UN agency concerned should be prepared to assist in this innovation-diffusion as well.

In all such cases it will be obvious by now that the same kind of advance-researched, advance-planned Support Communications Programme should be built into the project PlanOps as an outright component the experts' permanent counterpart personnel, the materials to be produced, and the appropriate share of financing needed. Institutes are ivory towers without planned communications.

6. Close project-support communications.   Finally, in this necessarily broad summary of types of support needs, there is what we call 'close-support' work for projects of all kinds. In virtually all UN-assisted projects under discussion here, there are fairly specific 'project communities' and implementing cadres. A project may be nation wide in scope, but it usually has defined sectors, and often operates either phased by expansion-phase or in one specific district or region entirely (i.e., a dam, a river-valley development, etc.). Assuming that the communications work at Government-services level is in hand, and that there are broad national awareness and receptivity, the project still needs very considerable close-in communications support.

At this as at other levels, we and our partners in national development service have scarcely begun to use the potential of planned, project-attuned communications techniques. At very little extra cost per project-year, we could be helping to equip each such project with a properly researched and phased schedule of information-communication aids, first, to prepare the project-community for the very 'arrival' of the project (for example, that matter of the 'surveyors' stakes); second, to explain to the people what the project seeks to achieve for them, in their terms of reference at that time, and to answer both the easily anticipated questions they will have and (by proper prior socio-economic research) the deeper worries which the project-disturbance will unleash; third, to motivate the people to participate for reasons that are tangible to them, and to demonstrate to them what resources of their own they can bring to bear on the effort; fourth, in careful phasing with the actual forward history of the project, to introduce to the community the specific innovations—in production, work methods, environment-exploitation and management, hygiene, whatever the sector—their adoption of which can alone make the project successful.

It needs to be heavily emphasized that, at present, the overall picture of project implementation at this level is extremely deficient in the above methods and in communication aids that are fashioned from them.

National Capability for Development Support Communications

It is, of course, fundamental in UN Family project policy that we do not, and could not, ourselves and alone undertake development support communications in member-countries. But against the overall neglect of these instruments to date, and the size of the problem even strictly in terms of UN-assisted projects, the present capabilities of national media should not be overestimated. Very much more could usefully be done to provide support communications from existing national resources, given an effective communications discipline in project appraisal and formulation. But we should be under no illusions whatever as to the magnitude of extra, external assistance that ought to be brought to bear as well.

A detailed, country-by-country study of the present role and capability of national media in what we mean by Development Support Communications is quite beyond the scope of this paper. From the aggregate experience of the authors in the several regions, however, we believe that we can make a number of legitimate general observations.

1. Project level support.[1]   In the majority of countries receiving UN development assistance, the national authorities are constantly seeking to create a broad climate of opinion in support of development to motivate the people to participate in and contribute to economic and social progress. We have cited this kind of broad, national motivation as very important even for project implementation. But the 'even' is crucial. Broad, national support communication does not by itself provide support communication at project implementation level; it may even lose its impact if not complemented by project-level support.

A man can be generally motivated for just so long, and just so far—and then he needs help that is tangible to him in his particular area, for his particular occupation and need, and feasible within his particular resources. A 'Grow More Food Campaign', conducted across the length and breadth of a nation becomes real only when farmers in specific crop and climate and soil areas then receive the inputs and innovations they need.

We must emphasise as crucial to the entire subject of this paper that this is one of the hidden 'flaws' in much of the work done by national authorities today in the field of development support communications. Again and again, in discussion with our national counterparts in development—whether in planning commissions or functional ministries, or even information media themselves—we find a lack of understanding of the distinction we have drawn above. The development process is intimate, local and particularistic at the point of action, which is the point of project implementation. This is now widely recognized in respect of all the other logistics of projects. It is by no means yet recognized in respect of support communications, as we shall illustrate further.

2. *Reaching villages.*   Among national officials who actually administer development programmes, including those receiving UN assistance, there is not only the universal tendency to neglect the power of communications techniques. There is a widespread assumption that, since their own ministries possess infrastructures of civil servants reaching down to district and even village level, 'we are in very close touch with the people already.'

This view is in no way unique to the civil services of developing countries, but the reality behind the view is far more severe in them. The senior civil servant in the capital city has a picture of a nation-wide network of 'outlets to the people' in serried echelons below him. Those 'outlets' are in fact underpaid and often overworked junior officers, usually reluctant to be working in rural or lower-status areas; operating in poor working conditions and with indifferent transport; and showered with unending and often barely legible stenciled directives about one programme and administrative problem after another.

We have studied the lines of communication of merely basic, factual information about new development projects down through these networks in many different sectors. The usual picture is that the information about the new project forms only one small element in that week's routine administrative problems, to be transmitted further down the hierarchy towards 'the people'. By the time transmission has experienced heat or cold, rain or dust, vehicle breakdowns or rotten overnight accommodation; and by the time the lower field echelons have coped with all the other merely routine administrative data, the new project has lost a good deal of its capital-city glory. When the news then has to be filtered through local community leadership—for example, through the village elders or council chairman, also beset by his level of 'red tape'—the new project may be lucky to enjoy two minutes of attention en passant. Not least of the problems is that from the first moment of word-of-mouth communication, inaccuracies and omissions of vital facts that may affect community response are all too common.

3. Development communication specialists.   The assumption described above that there are built in communications for development in a country's civil service—combines in many places with a lack of awareness that modern communications techniques can be instruments of development. The view is still prevalent among many decision-makers and budget controllers that media like radio, films, and television are 'consumer amenities that must wait for adequate economic growth'—not instruments that can virtually contribute to growth. With relatively few exceptions, what we may call the technical information arms of national governments are the cinderellas [beneficiaries] of budgeting—both as to expansion and as to annual operating funds.

Apart from the deficiencies in basic infrastructure and equipment that this view perpetuates, it also produces poor morale and often indifferent calibre among government information personnel. In any country where there is any kind of private or commercial communications industry—radio, TV, feature films, privately owned newspapers—the result is that the best talent seeks the highest pay outside of Government. By definition, this talent is almost entirely lost to communications for development.

The process is, of course, a vicious circle. Poorly paid and second-level information personnel, working with meagre budgets, are not very likely to stimulate new interest and respect for their development roles among decision makers and purse controllers in Government.

4. Skills for development communication.   These factors mesh, in turn, with another very powerful influence currently working against the kind of development support communications we have described as so urgently needed. Existing national information personnel are still overwhelmingly urban, middle-class (or above), and Western-oriented in their concepts of communication. We discern a whole series of practical consequences that flow from this:

a. The dominant assumption is that the job is one of disseminating 'news' and/or 'publicity'; and usually in Press terms, since most information people have either come from the Press world to Government or have received journalism training that has remained print oriented. Production of information material is widely based on the concepts of the duplicated release 'for the Press', as often as not with photographs of a Minister or other high dignitary. The same approach still dominates in radio and in newsreel styles of film for cinemas and/or television.

Again, there is a vicious circle. This is what most national information personnel do and are seen to do; this is what most national authorities think they are paid to do; this is what they are consequently expected to go on doing if they want next year's budget. This is all the information workers have the incentive, or often the equipment, or the time, to do. It is not at all uncommon, for example, to find a film unit with only two cameramen expected to produce up to 20 newsreel-style 'documentaries on development' per year, along with a weekly newsreel proper.

b. Urban (or urbanised) themselves, working in cities, under the constant administrative influence and pressure of like people, and working in a technology that is infused with the inevitably urban outlook of Western society where it originated, these national infor- mation practitioners inevitably tend to produce for urban audiences. Running through all their work is the inchoate feeling that 'the people who count' must see their production, and the people who count are also in the cities. It is, for example, extremely significant that, with very rare exceptions, the film equipment of national information media is almost entirely at 35 mm dimension. The films produced have as their first objective screening in cinemas—overwhelmingly urban, in countries where the overwhelming majority of the population (the people needing to be involved in development) are rural.

c. Further consequences flow from all this. The 'news release' orientation makes the content of materials very broad and generalised. The dominant notion of 'national propaganda' of needing to speak to an entire nation in a given document—has the same effect. But since the people producing the material have little real or deep contact with the overwhelming, rural majority of the nation, the generalisation becomes, in fact, urban. If a film is produced with a cinema audience in mind, it has to be very short if on a 'non-entertainment' subject. If the audience in the cinemas is predominantly urban, it has to speak to them in the first instance. If the producers are not only urban but middle-class-oriented, their depiction even of rural life will tend to be fleeting and somewhat romanticised, even if quite possibly infused with genuine and patriotic motives of sympathy for the rural poor.

Anyone who has the opportunity frequently to view films made in such conditions—in fact, to view the films that might not be considered those available nationally for 'development support' will be struck by these tendencies. Both visually and in narration the film 'goes out to' the rural areas from a city, of course. Yet again, the villages of developing countries are filled with born, natural actors for purposes of development support communications. It is, however, very common indeed to find a film producer transporting out to a village from the city an entire cast of actors and actresses to play not 'features' but documentary roles.

d. Development support communications, we have stated earlier as a categorical premise, must be carefully audience-attuned; it requires quite scrupulous, and optimally researched attention to the socio-economic and socio-psychological environment of the people to whom it must speak, and to their level of absorptive capacity for innovations. The 'Western' training, or Westernised social background and continuing technological orientation of information personnel is almost bound to militate against this perspective and this creative priority.

A journalist turned government information officer who has this kind of 'Western' background is trained to report 'facts': not to try to motivate readers, change their attitudes, encourage them to adopt new techniques—indeed any such practices are traditionally frowned upon, and said to be the thin edge of the wedge towards '1984'. Yet the skilled practice of Development Support Communications calls for unceasing attention to how to reach, interest, and very purposively motivate and inform people.

A documentary film producer with a 'Western' orientation sees his craft as at its best when he is 'expressing himself' on film and sound—his own response to a situation or subject, presented to the cinematic equivalent of Robert Frost's 'unknown everybody'. We would be the first to insist that artistry and imaginative use of the film medium remains vital in Development Support Communications. But we would also insist that the very last desideratum is the self-expression of the producer or director in the usual 'Western' sense. It is in no way encouraging—in terms of the massive needs we have been describing to ask film-makers in developing countries what they would most like to produce, and to receive quite invariably descriptions of film ideas suitable for the audience-equivalent in their countries of avant-garde enthusiasts in Paris, London, New York and Montreal.

e. Scrupulous authenticity of detail and carefully thought out choice of accurate technical information are further requirements of Development Support Communications. It needs little elaboration that the great majority of present information workers, in whatever medium, have not had any training enabling them to translate development technology effectively into their media. Nor are they given the time or the sheer morale to have the very considerable patience that such detailed communications work requires. The reader who has had practical experience in educational television or radio, including the production of scientific or technical programmes, will appreciate these problems most readily. A film is being made about farming and requires shots of a particular kind of seed and its cultivation. That is so written in the script, with a location prescribed thirty miles outside the city. But the film unit is tired; it is underpaid; it is thoroughly over-worked; and there is a college demonstration plot almost inside the city. The shot is taken there. The villagers to whom the film is screened can spot the fake at once. The utility of the film has been almost destroyed.

Among the countless examples of such problems known to us, we can discern a further cause which is the present very wide 'communications gap' between national information personnel and the functional development implementers. Just as inside the UN Family programme and technical personnel have not always taken Public Information Officers very seriously, so too there is this attitude within national ministries and related development agencies. The development technicians often take the view that information people are largely nuisances and inaccurate, 'never available when we do need them and bothering us when we don't', or 'preoccupied with taking pictures of politicians'. Again the causation in a vicious circle is apparent. To date, no one has asked, encouraged, and equipped such information workers to reach that level of professional expertise in development support that would make development technicians regard them as serious co-professionals with skills badly needed to help programmes.

f. If the above factors militate strongly against any great optimism about national capability for support communication in project-implementation, we believe we must recognize certain other very practical problems. A key one is quite simply the size of the technical resources available within a given country receiving UN development assistance. In our experience, the existing equipment and potentially usable talent is very heavily taxed in producing what we have called broad, national development support materials, most especially in the medium of the film. In countries where there are governmental film units (and there are not in many countries), they are hard pressed to complete their annual quota of films required by different ministries, plus the inevitable emergency demands (a head of State visiting; a disaster; a war). As we have described, most of these films are very broad in content and can contribute to project implementation only in general climate-of-opinion improvement.

A further common difficulty is that the equipment and personnel resources which we need for project-level support communications are very severely diffused and dissipated within government structures. In many countries, there has been a historical tendency for each functional ministry to create its own information or Public Relations Division but for it to be starved of just that extra input of funds that might make it really viable. In the usual way within human authority-structures, if a central information service is then created, it may never quite get the resources it needs because the functional ministries are reluctant to support it at the expense of their own Public Information. For UN Family project implementation, which so often proceeds through specific sectoral ministries, this is a further difficulty.

Conclusions from the Above Appraisal

In the foregoing survey of national capabilities for this kind of communication work, we have been as realistic as our practical experience, now over many years and encompassing all regions, compels us to be. But we must emphasize that a great many of the problems we have described within national levels could be overcome—some quite quickly, others over a forward period of planned assistance. Broadly, there are four categories of need in improving the national resources available for Development Support Communications as earlier defined:

1. *Expansion and improvement of communication infrastructures* is an obvious need in many countries and has, of course, been the subject of great attention by UNESCO and International Telecommunication Union (ITU) in particular.[2] While stressing the need for this kind of assistance to continue and increase, we would add that there will be many instances where proper advance appraisal of the support communications needs of a given UN Family project

would suggest a specific assistance input of equipment and possibly short-term on job training personnel. This has been done, generally and to date, only in terms of supplying such basic items as cine-projectors, slide-projectors, darkroom gear and tape recorders. In specific instances, for projects with a large and relatively long-term communications element, we can envisage far more comprehensive inputs (and, as explained earlier, far more cost effective since a cine-projector without anything to project on it is not very useful).

2. *Orientation of national authorities towards DSC* is a second surely vital need, even for the effective implementation simply of UN-assisted projects (and we are assuming throughout this paper that we are also collectively concerned with helping to make all development more effective). From our own concrete experience, we cannot over-emphasize the importance of outside, UN Family assistance in this respect. For the reasons outlined earlier, and for many others which space prevents us, including the voices of the relatively few national information professionals who do not understand this kind of development communications work will have to be supplemented from outside.

3. *Training or retraining of national information personnel* in all the media in Development Support Communications is desperately needed in almost every country. What is required is nothing less than the development of a whole new discipline and professional expertise in this kind of information work with status, standards, methodology, and rational use of resources.

4. *Application of system and resources by the UN Family* to this new instrument of Development Support Communications will be essential, in each region, if we are to begin to move towards better project implementation. Within the UN Family we must create a body of professional expertise in these particular communications techniques, a counterpart to the (obviously numerically much larger) national resources cited earlier. We must stress that nothing in our experience in this work gives any grounds for believing that the hundreds of specific, project-tailored support communication components at this moment missing from UN-assisted projects will be supplied by national resources alone. A major UN assistance effort is required.

In earlier pages we have pointed towards the new system, methods and deployed resources which this effort will require. Work on it has already begun, both at Headquarters level and through the Development Support Communications Service in Asia now being expanded. In section E we offer a very compressed outline of the total system and method that are needed.

Methods and Systems for UN Development Support Communications Aid

It may be best to outline our UN Family needs by describing what ought to happen over a sample UN-assisted development project. For breadth of illustration let us suppose the project in question to be one with a large and comprehensive communications component encompassing many of the categories described earlier in this paper. Obviously, for projects with less communications complexities, there may not be need for all of the elements cited in this example. But the need of the specific approach will be there regardless.

1. At the stage of appraisal of a project request, it will automatically be examined for its support communications requirement. At the relevant Headquarters, this standard practice will be instituted by Programme chiefs. They should be able to draw on the resident advice of one Information Officer who has begun to specialise in Development Support Communications. In the region in which the requesting country is situated, the project papers will be studied by a staff member of the Development Support Communications Service based in that region, and already familiar with support communications problems and available national resources in the country concerned.

It is quite essential to work from regional level in this field, and if we in the UN Family are serious about this enormous neglected gap in the development process, we will as rapidly as possible develop this kind of DSC Service for each major region.

2. Research in the 'project community' will be indicated and carried out, as necessary, before final project formulation. The first 'act' of communication in a development project is in fact such research in the community of human beings among whom the innovations are to be diffused. The socio-economic information a DSC specialist needs about the community (or cadres to be formed) is also, in our opinion, essential to the proper formulation of the entire project. We know of very many cases of poorly formulated projects where, simply by having conducted DSC community research in advance of formulation, the project would quite certainly have been better designed and in some cases saved from virtual fiasco.

Properly staffed regional DSC Services for the UN Family will include on their strengths one specialist in social science research as it relates to development and the diffusion of innovations to work with national social scientists.

Depending on the size, the overall complexity, and the communications complexity of the project, DSC Service staff would make a field appraisal from their regional base, in the country concerned, in order to tailor their recommendations for the DSC component as closely as possible. In many such cases, staff would probably make the field survey together with the overall project consultant mission or other appraiser for the agency involved. At the earliest practicable stage, DSC staff would work with counterparts in the country concerned so that the communications component was planned from the outset as closely with the country's information specialists as with its project-sector specialists.

3. From the above appraisal and survey, a complete and detailed communications component would be evolved and negotiated with the national authorities and included in the PlanOps. This component would fully specify and stipulate responsibilities within the Government's various information media for the production or co-production of a detailed schedule of support communications materials (publication, lecture audio-visual aids, slides, films,

radio and/or TV programmes, and so forth). The materials would be specified, and planned relative to project phases and to communications media within the project infrastructure as well as the mass media. Due care would be given to support communications aids for project cadre training and to the aids those cadres would in turn need for diffusion of the innovations involved.

Having negotiated the best possible use of available national resources for the DSC programme required, the component in the PlanOps would further specify what assistance the UN would provide—which would vary from ancillary funds and some basic equipment, possibly to the complete shooting of a given complex film or films, and it would include short-term or resident communications experts, with on-job training counterparts as necessary. 'Second-phase' inputs of foreign-made communications materials, for example, slides or films, or publications that would be useful at later stages would also be specified.

The DSC component in the PlanOps would be properly budgeted for, stipulating UN and counterpart contributions, project phase by phase.

We are merely outlining the actual, highly technical details that ought to go into such component preparation. In many cases already known to us, for example, they would include written agreement as to the actual information to be disseminated since one of the serious troubles is that unless this is foreseen what may be several ministries simply never do agree on what they want to tell the project community.

4. The regional UN Family DSC Service, working with the appropriate UN Resident Representative and Agency Chief of Mission, and the agreed national counterparts, would then follow through on implementation of the project's DSC component. Advisory and production resources, based in the regional DSC Service would be brought to bear as planned—one of the Service's film units, for example, might have to assist with preparation of the scheduled film for a given project phase. By proper advance planning of all such DSC components, production resources based outside the region would be used to help the Service and the project where national resources would not be adequate.

5. It may be of interest, here, to mention that we envisage that feedback on a project to Headquarters and for donor countries, should also be serviced through the same regional base. We are in fact engaged, in Asia, on what we call 'double yield' operations, in which, for example, the still photography, sound recordings, and film footage prepared for direct project-support use are also used for this reportage function.

6. In many instances, support communications materials prepared for implementations of one project in one country can be of great value in another similarly placed country. One of the further responsibilities of the regional DSC Services would be to watch for such opportunities of 'intra-project support communications'—and indeed to plan in advance for them against the known schedule of such types of projects.

The above thumbnail sketch of a new system and approach for this aspect of UN development assistance clearly presupposes UN Family collective effort. We are openly envisaging a Development Support Communications Service in Asia to begin with—to which specialised agencies will allocate resident communication specialists to appraise, plan, and follow up on DSC components in their projects in the region. By this approach, we would build up a highly professional group of communications experts, each doubly specialist in a given sector of development, and serving the various Agencies accordingly. [End of Childers and Vajrathan text.]

Many ideas in the papers of Childers and Vajrathan have relevance to us today, but two especially stand out. First, there was the emphasis on *planning*. The authors noted the need to give communication support to civil servants, change agents, and to rural communities and that these communication efforts needed to be orchestrated. They also stressed the importance of *research*, especially for matching communication materials to communities. 'This may require,' they said, 'organized socio-economic research harnessing (practical, development-oriented) social scientists to assemble data about attitudes, motivational factors, etc.' And further, Childers and Vajrathan emphasized the difference between publicity and development support communication. Worth noting is their emphatic plea for 'the mobilization of properly trained communication personnel.'

2. The Extension Thread

The extension approach to development was used before either the concepts 'development' or 'development communication' appeared in the language of many of us. Jones and Garforth (1997) point, for example, to the hieroglyphs on Egyptian columns giving advice on how to avoid crop damage and loss of life from the flooding of the Nile. And, along with the establishment of agricultural societies and agricultural schools in Europe in the early 1800s, 'itinerant agriculturalists' emerged to give farmers information, advice and encouragement. This was predominantly a private sector initiative. The potato blight in Europe in 1845 led to the first 'official' extension system. The British Viceroy to Ireland, the Earl of Clarendon, wrote a letter to the Royal Agricultural Improvement Society of Ireland urging it to appoint itinerant lecturers to travel around to the peasant population, which relied heavily on potatoes in their diet, to show them how to improve their cultivation and to grow other nutritious crops. 'Lord Clarendon's practical instructors' were funded partly by landowners and charitable donations, but half from government-controlled funds (Jones and Garforth, 1997:5–6).

In contemporary times, extension refers to the process of linking researchers (or other producers of innovations) with potential users of research results. The idea has appeared prominently (though not exclusively) in the United States Land-Grant University system where the Smith-Lever Act of 1914 combined national, state and local governments with agricultural colleges and universities for the establishment of the Cooperative Extension Service. It historically has placed great emphasis on extending research-based recommendations and skills to rural families, with the ultimate goal of their adopting the practices and the new technology. Thus extension has often been associated with the phrase 'transfer of technology'—from the experts to the users. For example, agricultural researchers breed a new high yielding variety seed and extension's role is to get farmers to adopt it and to train farmers in the appropriate agricultural techniques. Similarly, following researchers' discoveries in food technology, the extension staff persuades families to adopt a new way to preserve food. (We are using agriculture as an example; similar situations exist in health, nutrition and other fields associated with community development.)

Extension has long been a major strategy for information and technology transfer in development activities. It is estimated that the World Bank has provided more than US$ 3 billion in direct support for extension, more than all other international donors combined (Ameur, 1994). The US system was 'exported' to India in the second half of the twentieth century largely through a US Agency for International Development project that helped established agricultural universities in most of India's states. Likewise, the World Bank and national governments have put large amounts of money into establishing 'training and visit' (T and V) extension systems throughout the Third World. T and V has attempted to streamline the traditional extension system through three kinds of concentration: (1) concentrating on a few 'contact farmers' in a service area, (2) concentrating on agriculture matters exclusively; and (3) concentrating on a few practices during each regular visit village extension worker.

In the contemporary USA, the scope of extension has broadened substantially both the kinds of subjects covered and the clientele served: Cornell University's extension programme in New York City is not *rural* at all. Extension people associated with Cornell are involved in water quality, small business enterprise training, and environmental issues. However, the conventional idea of extension exists widely around the world. In India, for example, it is estimated that there are approximately 90,000 extension workers in the public sector, and officially their principal responsibility is agricultural development and technology transfer.

A dominant assumption in the extension approach has been that individuals will adopt new practices and technology 'if only they understand what is advocated and know how to carry it out' (Andreasen,1995:9). For the past 50 years, diffusion and adoption of innovations have been central concepts in the transfer of technology, thanks to the scholarship of the late Everett Rogers and those who followed his path (Singhal and Dearing, 2006). Evolving out of research related to the adoption of corn varieties in the 1940s, the concepts have been applied to a wide range of innovations, from family planning to farming methods. For example, writing in a 2006 book focussed on Rogers' many contributions to the communication discipline, Ronny Adhikarya, who worked at the World Bank and at FAO, for example, says: 'I personally witnessed the widespread applications of diffusion theory in family planning communication programmes in 26 countries of Asia, Near East and Eastern Africa' and he acknowledged the influence of diffusion research in his FAO work on strategic extension campaigns (Adhikarya, 2006). Rogers estimated in 2003 that more than 5,200 articles had been published on diffusion. According to Rogers, 'No other field of behaviour science research represents more effort by more scholars in more disciplines in more nations' (Rogers, 2003:xviii).

Recently some agencies, practitioners and scholars have moved away from the traditional extension approach to technology transfer by re-conceptualizing the relationship between change agents (such as extension workers and health educators) and their target populations. This re-examination of the 'top-down' flow of information and technology from researchers to farmers and families includes raising issues such as: (1) Do the farmers' perceptions of their needs match those presumed by the researcher? (2) Are the researcher's results appropriate for the farmers' needs? (3) Does the farmer have knowledge that would be useful to the researcher? (4) How should researchers' and farmers' agendas be set? And (5) 'whose reality counts?' (Chambers, 1997).

In some places re-evaluating extension is accelerating because in its conventional form, extension service has been a very labour-intensive and a very expensive system. It is labour-intensive because the dominant pattern of interaction is person-to-person. We recently compiled a list of various other concerns about extension, and although most came from analysis of India's experience, our discussions with persons from other countries suggest that they apply to extension in many places. These issues include:

1. Direction of Information Flow
Information is supplied from the 'top' (scientists and officials) to the 'bottom' (farmers); and from the centre to the field. There is little 'feed-forward' (a process in which information obtained from population targets shapes or influences the information that is subsequently directed to the population) or feedback.

2. Relevance of Information
Information often is not relevant because the scientists/researchers do not respond to farmers' needs. The extension system is driven by the assumption that relevant technical knowledge *is* available.

3. Character of Agricultural Information
The messages tend to be narrowly suited to production of a few particular commodities rather than to the issue of farmers' profitability which may come through mixed agricultural systems.

4. Overall Character of Extension Information
Extension packages concentrate on technical and production aspects of agriculture ignoring the 'whole' farmer who is likely to have other important concerns such as his and his family's health and education.

5. Clientele
Extension efforts ignore particular agricultural populations such as women, tribals, operators of very small holdings, and non-landed agricultural workers.

6. Control of the System

Managers and scientists control the agenda of the research and extension system to the exclusion of being farmer-centred.

7. Methods Used to Reach Farmers

Emphasis is often on face-to-face contact, with relatively little attempt to integrate communication media and distance learning into the process.

8. Cost of System

Especially where extension is dominated by the Training and Visit (T and V) approach that was strongly advocated by the World Bank, a labour-intensive face-to-face contact system is very costly to sustain.

9. Lack of Results

While there is evidence of better management in some extension operations as a result of T and V, evidence of consistent success of extension programmes in increasing agricultural productivity is elusive.

10. Inadequately Trained Extension Agents

Extension personnel tend to be trained in technical areas but have not been effectively trained in communication.

11. Incentives for Extension Personnel

Extension agents (Village Extension Workers—VEWs) are generally poorly paid and are given few incentives to perform at the level expected by the system. 'Professionalization' has sometimes removed the VEW from providing input supplies (an income-producing activity), and, consequently, from status and earning power.

12. Evaluation and Monitoring of Extension

Better training, planning and computerization are necessary to effect better monitoring.

13. Extension Funding

Extension is under-funded, and that results in unfilled extension lines which results in inadequate coverage of farm populations.

14. Linkage to Research

The link itself is weak, and, where it exists at all, the relationship tends to be dominated by scientists. Their higher status results in putting *their* priorities first which may not reflect the needs in the field.

Extension systems have been adjusting to some of these criticisms, including the privatization of some extension organizations and the use of new information and communication technologies to increase efficiency and impact. One attempt was the launching of the Training and Visit (T and V) Extension System in the 1970s which attempted to correct some of deficiencies of the conventional extension system. It focussed on (1) restricting the material that an extension worker covered to a few agricultural only; (2) concentrating on covering only a very few of the most important and timely pieces of information related to the topic during an extension visit; and (3) concentrating its farmer training on a few 'contact' farmers who were expected to share the information and training with other farmers (but without any incentive to do so). The principal advocate and funder was the World Bank, with secondary roles played by FAO and the International Fund for Agricultural Development. In 2006, a World Bank Policy Research Working Paper prepared by Bank employees reviewed the history of T and V and reported on its lack of sustainability and 'ultimate abandonment' after 25 years and application in about 50 countries in Asia and Africa. In the document titled 'The Rise and Fall of Training and Visit Extension: An Asian Mini-drama with an African Epilogue' (Anderson et al., 2006).[3] The major conclusion is that T and V was unsustainable because of the staff-intensive high recurrent cost structure. The basic Benor and Harrison model (Benor and Harrison, 1977) also failed to take advantage of media such as radio which was contributing significantly to other contemporary extension efforts such as those in Masagana 99 in the Philippines. Masagana 99 was instrumental in moving the Philippines from rice-importing towards adopting high yielding rice cultivation and self-sufficiency in rice. It included extensive use of radio broadcasts for 'spot announcements' and training, and a variety of printed materials including a document (referred to as 'the Bible') that showed the 16-step process of rice production.

The World Bank report on T and V indicates that donor advocates of the system expected nations that adopted T and V to build its costs into their mainstream budgeting. However, those nations 'lack of conviction over the success of the approach at the farm level and competition for government resources resulted in those governments' unwillingness to continue their investment in the system. Contributing to the end was a report by the World Bank's own Operations Evaluation Department that suggested that evaluation studies of T and V were flawed and that T and V was 'unlikely to be the most appropriate approach for improving extension in many African countries.'[4] It was time to look at other options.

Reduced government financial support for extension has created a vacuum into which the private sector has sometimes moved—as a means of selling inputs to farmers and/or contracting for the farmers' product. Radio and television broadcasting and the on-rush of digital technologies have influenced strategies for reaching rural communities for transferring technology. For a comprehensive review of the role that information and communication technologies and especially telecentres are playing worldwide in extension and in the lives of rural people see Chapters 2 and 6 of Colle, 2007.

3. The Community Participation Thread

The idea of participation as an important approach in development communication stretches back to the late 1940s (as we shall see later in this section). However, it has been FAO, at least among the Special Agencies of the UN, that has been among the most active in pushing the concept into field practice. Likewise, FAO has taken a very active leadership role in exploring and testing ways of systematically using communication in development programmes. In 1989, the organization developed some useful suggestions that helped define development communication. These include:

What is the Idea behind Development Communication and What is it?

Development communication rests on the premise that successful rural development calls for the conscious and active participation of the intended beneficiaries at every stage of the development process; for in the final analysis, rural development cannot take place without changes in attitudes and behaviour among the people concerned.

To this end, development communication is the planned and systematic use of communication through interpersonal channels, and audio-visual and mass media:

- to collect and exchange information among all those concerned in planning a development initiative, with the aim of reaching a consensus on the development problems being faced and the options for their solution.
- to mobilize people for development action, and to assist in solving problems and misunderstandings that may arise during project implementation.
- to enhance the pedagogical and communication skills of development agents (at all levels) so that they may dialogue more effectively with their audiences.
- and last but, by no means least, to apply communication technology to training and extension programmes, particularly at the grassroots level, in order to improve their quality and impact.

What are the Problems that Development Communication can Help to Overcome?

1. Problems of designing projects that take properly into account the perceptions and capacities of the intended beneficiaries. Development communication can help to ensure that the design and action plan of a development project take into account the attitudes, perceived needs and capacities of the people which the project is trying to help. Many projects have failed in the past because assumptions were made about the willingness and capacity of rural people to absorb new technology and development infrastructures into their way of living and working. Abandoned irrigation schemes and settlement programmes, broken down equipment, and the slow adoption of improved crop varieties are examples that bear witness to this failure to bring about attitudinal and behavioural change.

As an adjunct and complement to the usual situation analysis that is done for project formulation, development communication helps to identify attitudes, felt needs, capacities, and constraints to the adoption of change. And through the dialogue and consultation process it employs, it naturally elicits the participation of the intended beneficiaries of a development action.

2. Problems of mobilizing rural people for development action and ensuring an information flow among all concerned with a development initiative. If a rural development project has been planned with its beneficiaries, their participation and mobilization are almost certain to follow quite naturally.

However, in any event, communication support during project implementation keeps people informed, helps to mobilize them, and to stimulate the more conservative to action. This is especially so when communication (in the form of audio-visual presentations, for example) is used to spread knowledge of successful development action taken by some communities and individuals to other communities and individuals that have not yet mobilized.

Furthermore, even the best project—designed with its beneficiaries—cannot be rigid. As it progresses, there will be need to review and refine its activities and introduce changes of emphasis. A good communication system can keep a dialogue open among those involved in a development project, thereby addressing problems as they arise. Such an ongoing information flow can also help to ensure coordination and proper orchestration of inputs and services to a development initiative.

Development communication spreads information about successful development experience as a stimulus to others, keeps a dialogue open among all concerned in a development project, and helps to smooth project implementation.

3. Problems of improving the reach and impact of rural training programmes.   Training at the grassroots level has become a major priority in recent years. At the same time, communication technology has been improving and becoming ever cheaper and easier to use in rural areas. Audio-visual media make it possible to:

- help overcome the barriers of illiteracy and incomprehension (by conveying ideas and practices in an audio and visual form);
- illustrate new ideas and techniques more effectively than by word-of-mouth alone, and thus improve the impact of extension and training;
- compress time (a whole crop cycle can be shown in a short presentation);
- compress space (events and practices in distant locations can be transferred to other places where they can be useful testimonials);
- standardize technical information (by creating audio-visual materials that illustrate the best available advice to farmers and having these materials used throughout the extension and farmer training chain, thereby ensuring that the technical information will not become distorted during its passage from its source to the smallest and most remote farmer).

Development communication applied to training and extension in rural areas increases their effectiveness and reach, and ensures that the best available technical information is standardized....

What Types of Development Initiatives Require Communication Inputs?

Any development initiative that depends for its success on rural people modifying their attitudes and behaviour and working with new knowledge and skills will normally benefit from communication support. So also will projects that have a multi-disciplinary nature, that is to say those which involve a number of subject-matter ministries and authorities, and which are therefore inherently difficult to manage. Communication can provide the linkages that will ensure coordinated management.

Are Development Communication Activities Always Planned as Part of a Development Project?
Not necessarily. There are also development communication projects *per se*. This is the case when, for example, assistance is being provided for institution-building such as creating or strengthening an agricultural or rural development communication unit, or providing assistance to rural broadcasting. Such institutions can often provide communication support to a number of agricultural and rural development projects in a country.

What are the Overall Considerations when Planning Communication Inputs?
Successful development communication calls for a well-defined strategy, systematic planning, and rigorous management. Experience has shown all too clearly that ad hoc communication inputs such as the provision of some audio-visual equipment, or the stand-alone production of some audio-visual or printed material has seldom made any measurable impact. It has also become clear that communication activities require a certain critical mass—of resources, intensity, and duration—if they are to realize their full potential in mobilizing people for development action and become self-sustaining in this role. This explains the minimal results when symbolic attention has been paid to development communication by including of some token equipment and expertise in the project.

A communication plan should be tailored to the particular conditions being faced. There are so many variables of a human, cultural and physical nature that a communication plan that worked for irrigation development in an arid zone of one country cannot effectively be transferred *in toto* to another country. For even if the principles remain the same, the details will almost certainly call for differences.

Who should Plan Communication Inputs?
Communication planning is a specialized field and calls for people who know communication processes and technology, and understand development issues and conditions in developing countries.

Development communication planners can often be made available by international development agencies, either from among their own staffs or by calling in consultants.

Communication planners may also be found locally in developing countries. There are increasing numbers of universities and institutions that are becoming involved in development communication and can provide expertise. Many NGOs in developing countries also have communication expertise that can be called upon (FAO, 1989).

FAO's approach forcefully inserts the idea of community participation into the development communication field. In the PRODERITH project in Mexico, one of FAO's most successful projects, the FAO approach could be described as follows:

Any development programme should be a complete and integrated response to the peasants' situation.... An integrated development programme could not be put into practice without the participation of the peasants in the process of identifying and analysing their problems, planning and implementing actions to resolve them, and monitoring and evaluating the results. (Fraser and S. Restrepo-Estrada, 1998:101)

FAO, of course, was not the first or only organization to promote participation of local people in development communication activities. During more than three decades beginning in the late 1940s, Puerto Rico's Division of Community Education was a significant pioneer in applying the concept systematically to development programmes. The story has been largely overlooked in the literature on community participation and one episode, in the accompanying box, helps explain the Division's approach.

Others have also been active in suggesting new approaches to the style of development communication. The late Paulo Freire gained international prominence with his 1968 manuscript *Pedagogy of the Oppressed* (Freire, 1970) with its emphasis on community participation and a bottom-up scenario for development. In the mid-1990s the World Bank established a policy of building participation into programmes where it was appropriate (World Bank, 1994). Nevertheless, participation as an operational principle diffused slowly through ministries and major development initiatives. However, by the turn of the twenty-first century the Rockefeller Foundation was able to publish a report by Alfonso Gumucio-Dagron called *Making Waves, Stories of Participatory Communication for Social Change* (Gumucio-Dagron, 2001) which contained '50 experiments in empowering people—to seize control of their own life stories and begin to change their circumstances of poverty, discrimination and exclusion' (from the Foreword, p. 1.)

Box 6.2 Bottom-up Development in Puerto Rico

Building a Bridge or People?

In the late 1940s there was a river near the community of Barranquitas in Puerto Rico. Torrential rains and flash floods roaring down from the mountain threatened the lives of several persons attempting to cross through the river. A schoolboy had once been swept downstream and narrowly escaped drowning or being battered on the rocks. As a result, if it looked like rain, mothers would not let their children go to school because they would have to cross the treacherous stream. For the same reason, when weather threatened, men of some 60 families stayed at home and lost wages. For decades, the people affected had asked, unsuccessfully, for the government to do something.

The Division of Community Education, created by Luis Munoz Marin, Puerto Rico's first popularly elected governor, agreed to help but not in the conventional 'we'll do it for you' way. The Division selected a respected man in the district and trained him as a Group Organizer. He began to discuss community problems with the people and to share with them simply-written booklets on life in Puerto Rico, on health, on new ways of doing things—*but not specifically on building a bridge across an unpredictable stream.*

For months he visited homes, showed films, and distributed posters and booklets. In December 1950, a group of neighbours raised the question as to why a government would spend a lot of money on movies, but nothing on helping provide people safe passage across the river. Between January and July 1951, the Group Organizer discussed a staggering idea with the people: they might do it themselves. And they did. They collected a small amount of money, recruited volunteers, arranged for donations of materials, and *in 22 days* had a bridge. At the official opening, it wasn't a government official who made the principal speech; it was the boy who had been swept down the river.

There was another outcome. The Division made a short documentary film called *El Puente* (The Bridge) and it was shot on location using the community's people, not professional actors, as the cast (Hanson, 1960).

4. The Population IEC and Health Communication Threads

Along with agricultural development, population issues have had a large influence in the evolution of development communication. The acronym IEC—Information, Education and Communication—has achieved greatest prominence in programmes designed to influence knowledge, motivation and behaviour related to contraception and family planning. National governments, NGOs, multi-national agencies, and the private sector have conducted many studies and interventions in which communication and population issues have been central components. These programmes, through their successes and failures, have enriched development communication through their practically-oriented explorations in message design, media use, incentives and other aspects of communication whose implications extend beyond population issues.

For several decades IEC has been associated with population and family planning programmes around the world. United Nations Population Fund (UNFPA) was among the first to use the term IEC when in 1969 it used the label for its communication activities. Specifically, IEC has referred most frequently to the use of information, education and communication to promote adoption of contraceptives or other practices to limit births.

Many will remember that the terms 'birth control' and 'family planning' frequently were used in regard to concerns about rapidly increasing populations. The challenge for communicators in public and private sector organizations was quite unambiguous: how can we most effectively persuade people (particularly women) to adopt new birth control methods? The traditional approach to IEC campaigns and community mobilization used information to try to influence people's contraceptive behaviour according to policies generated by governments and population authorities.

Changes Affecting IEC

A variety of issues have influenced the IEC approach during the past two decades. Among them were concerns about gender equality and the conditions of women and children. These sometimes became linked with human rights issues. Population issues also were linked to the AIDS situation, to providing assistance to infertile couples, and to development in general. Along with these issues was the introduction of different approaches to reaching populations including social mobilization, social marketing, advocacy, and interventions emphasizing participation and empowerment. Woven into these approaches were the questions: whom should communication programmes reach and (as Robert Chambers rhetorically suggested) 'whose reality counts'? Within many agencies, the emphasis began shifting from agency-dictated goals to goals jointly determined by the agency (or government) and the broader health-related needs of the people.

Among the most dramatic social changes related to population are recent fertility data. In the developed nations, the fertility rate has fallen from 2.8 to 1.5 since the 1950s. In the less developed nations, the rate has fallen from about 6 to under 3. This has led to the prediction of a scenario in which the world population may stabilize in 40 years at 7.7 billion, and *decline* thereafter. In 1998, for the first time in history, the number of persons over 60 years of age in a country (Italy) exceeded the number of children under 20.

One of the most important chronological points in the changes taking place in IEC was 'Cairo'. In 1994, the International Conference on Population and Development (ICPD) which was held in Cairo helped broaden the scope of population programmes. At the core is the concept of 'reproductive health' (RH).

> The ICPD defined reproductive health as a state of physical, mental and social well-being and not merely the absence of disease or infirmity in all matters relating to the reproductive system. Reproductive health therefore implies that people are able to have a satisfying and safe sex life and that they have the capability to reproduce and the freedom to decide if, when and how often to do so. (World Health Organization, 1997:xi)

Thus, reproductive health is at least concerned with: family planning, prevention of maternal and newborn deaths and disabilities, prevention and management of sexually transmitted disease and AIDS, harmful traditional practices such as female genital mutilation (FGM), rape, domestic violence, forced prostitution and human trafficking, infertility, malnutrition and anaemia, osteoporosis, uterine prolapse, reproductive tract infections and cancers.

The new definition of 'population programmes' has a potentially profound influence on how one approaches IEC. The Programme of Action of ICPD reflects the convergence of many issues that have significance for a communication agenda. Obviously the task for communicators associated with reproductive health programmes is substantially broader than generally perceived in IEC, including, once again, the question as to who the stakeholders are. The issue of reaching men has also broadened. Earlier, men were targets largely in the context of condom use; now men are being targeted because of their 'often dominant roles in decisions crucial to women's reproductive health' (Drennan, 1998).

This brings us to the process called *advocacy* which has become a key concept in developing reproductive health communication strategies and in other development communication contexts. The primary aim of advocacy, says Jan Servaes, is fostering public policies that support the solution of an issue or problem (Servaes, 2000:104). The stakeholders for advocacy include political, religious and community leaders as well as a wide range of institutions. Advocacy has become a key part of the activities of the Johns Hopkins University's Center for Communication Programs. The Hopkins people have built an 'A-Frame' symbol representing a model of advocacy that includes a six-step process—Analysis, Strategy, Mobilization, Action, Evaluation, and Continuity. Phyllis Piotrow, long-time head of the Center, says that:

> For reproductive health advocacy a vital need is giving voice to the silent majority that supports these programs, even in the face of sometimes vocal minority opposition.... Policy-makers will

support reproductive health programs adequately only if they feel a groundswell of demand from the grassroots. And grassroots organizations can demand this effectively only by making advocacy a top priority. (Piotrow, 2005)

Piotrow and her colleagues at Johns Hopkins Center for Communication Programs suggest that the next decades will see continuing rapid demographic, political and technological change that will require family planning and reproductive health communication programmes to adapt to a variety of dynamic situations. These include:

- changing audiences
- changing channels of communication
- changing behavioural science theory and research
- changing values and mandates
- changing organizational structures
- changing political environments and resources (Piotrow, Kincaid, Rimon II and Rinehart, 1997:187–188).

It is clear that RH and the related social and cultural issues demand a substantially more sophisticated and comprehensive approach to communication than occurred in IEC.

Reproductive health and communication in Ethiopia: an example of planning.   These new approaches have begun to take root in countries that are building their capacity to deal with population matters. Ethiopia is a good example. Ethiopia is the third most populous country in Africa. Its fertility rate of 7.0 children per woman raises official concern about achieving a steady pace of economic development and social well-being for the population as a whole. In 1993 Ethiopia adopted a National Population Policy and in 1997 became the first country in Africa to draft a national IEC and Advocacy Strategy in support of a National Population Policy. A six-day workshop, supported by UNFPA, was held in 1996 to draft the strategy.[5]

The contents of the document illustrate vividly the scope of activities that confront communication people in the country's official National Office of Population.

First, two 'thematic areas' are identified: (1) reproductive health and (2) population and development. Each thematic area is sub-divided as follows:

Reproductive health

- Safe motherhood
- Family planning
- STIs including HIV/AIDS
- Access and quality of RH services and care
- Gender issues

Population and development

- Rapid population growth
- Implementation of the National Population Policy
- Gender and development
- Research/data collection and dissemination
- Youth and development
- Other Population Policy priorities (migration and urbanization, environment, and special population sub-groups)

For each of these items, there is a list of priority issues. And for each priority, there is a programme goal, and for each goal there are IEC objectives and advocacy objectives. Here is an example.

Thematic Area: Reproductive Health

Programme Component: Safe Motherhood: Issue #3: High prevalence of reproductive health-related harmful practices: Women and girls are subjected to several harmful practices which can affect their reproductive health in a negative way. Early marriage, female genital mutilation, and harmful practices done with an intention of assisting labour, birth and recovery during postnatal period are widely practiced in Ethiopia.

Programme Goal: To reduce maternal and neonatal morbidity and mortality associated with harmful practices.

IEC Objectives: To increase awareness and knowledge about the health hazards of early marriage, female genital mutilation, and other malpractices, and bring about change in attitudes and behaviours among relevant segments of the population.

Advocacy Objectives:

(i) To mobilize the participation and support of religious and community leaders for actions leading to the elimination of FGM, early marriage, and other reproductive health-related harmful practices.

(ii) To increase the understanding on the need for data collection and research on harmful practices, and mobilize support for undertaking relevant data collection and analysis.

(iii) To gain support for raising the age of marriage to at least 18 years through the revision of existing legislation and regulations, and to have declared supportive regulations to abolish reproductive health-related harmful practices.

(iv) To mobilize support to bring about changes in religious and customary laws, practices, and norms that foster early marriage, FGM, and other reproductive health-related harmful practices.

The document goes on with charts identifying who the IEC audiences are and who the advocacy targets are, what the messages are for each and what channels need to be used for each population group identified. The document then proposes indicators of progress and impact.

The Ethiopian IEC and Advocacy Strategy illustrates a very complex communication enterprise that focusses on producing *outcomes* rather than outputs, includes a research effort that provides data for situational analysis and measures outcomes, involves a substantial variety of stakeholders (from adolescents to policy-makers) and media (to 'reach the ultimate audiences directly'), and extends over a five-year period. The strategy is especially distinguished by its attention to policy, laws, norms, advocacy and other matters that surround decisions and practices of people in relation to their reproductive behaviour. The lesson is that RH behaviour change involves far more changes than those of potential contraceptive users.

Dimensions of Communication in Reproductive Health (RH)

To put the discussion of communication and health into organizational terms, a health ministry or a health research organization concerned with behaviour change in today's environment might consider a comprehensive communication programme with at least the following ingredients.

(1) Promote public understanding of the wide range of issues that make up RH.
(2) Foster good public relations for the organization, particularly to gain and keep visibility and support from policy-makers, funders and the community.
(3) Conduct advocacy programmes in support of social, political and cultural changes that will contribute to norms and policies favourable to RH.
(4) Promote and sustain behavioural change among appropriate stakeholders including contraceptive users and influentials such as RH service administrators and front-line health workers.
(5) Share technical knowledge with the RH and communication professions.
(6) Build intra-organizational professional communications.

5. The Social Marketing Thread

Social marketing is a process that assumes that what has made McDonald's and Coca-Cola world class successes can also have a dramatic impact on the problems of high blood pressure, AIDS, child mortality in developing nations, and other circumstances related to patterns of behaviour. Social marketing has greatly influenced the way communication and information are incorporated in development programmes. For example, it has increased our sensitivity to the needs for research prior to developing and sending messages and it has shifted emphasis from the needs of the social change agent to the needs and perspectives of the beneficiary groups. Unfortunately social marketing has many detractors who equate social marketing with commercial marketing and especially with its excesses. However, when one gets away from the 'marketing' label the value of the approach stands out.

The following, written by Alan Andreasen, gives a glimpse of the characteristics of social marketing that distinguish it from commercial marketing and from advertising with which it is sometimes confused.

Lessons for Development Communicators

The lessons gleaned from the oral rehydration projects in Honduras and the Gambia underscore the importance of comprehensive communications planning to the success of social marketing campaigns. The crucial importance of audience research and the integration of media, especially interpersonal interactions and community-oriented promotional activities, was borne out by the results of longitudinal studies in both countries. The knowledge gained from these two research sites concerning the complexity of behaviour change, the importance of sustained communication efforts in maintaining new behaviours, and the challenge of institutionalizing systematic health (or, any other) communication strategy, has guided the expansion of such approaches in other countries.

Building upon their experiences in Honduras and the Gambia, AED and USAID expanded their health communication programmes to different settings during the 1980s. The Communication for Child Survival Project, or HEALTHCOM, was designed to improve health practices (for example, diarrhoeal disease control, immunization, child nutrition, maternal health and birth spacing, and control of acute respiratory infections) in selected sites throughout the Third World, and to refine further the practice of social marketing, as well as other development communication strategies. A five-step planning model was articulated, emphasizing the need for communication planners to remain in close contact with potential audiences through a variety of feedback mechanisms. Numerous assessment, planning, pretesting delivery and monitoring strategies were developed for this purpose.

The results obtained from a wide variety of HEALTHCOM sites in the past decade, as well as from other communication programmes, have yielded many other useful lessons for development communicators. These lessons, synthesized from an analysis compiled by the Academy for Educational Development for USAID, are:

Sustained Behaviour Change

Communication programmes must identify and stress the favourable consequences of any new behaviour. Furthermore, such consequences or benefits must be communicated in ways that are sensitive to the audience's needs and expectations. When the goal is to stimulate consumer demands, programme planners must coordinate their efforts with the supply structure to ensure that such demands are not frustrated.

Improved Consumer Research

Research which provides an effective base for planning should focus on consumer attitudes towards *perceived* problems, as well as the explanation for current practices. While most governments have difficulty affording the in-depth market research conducted by donor-funded projects, communication planners may choose to employ user-friendly rapid assessment techniques and to locate appropriate local partners to conduct necessary consumer research.

Media Selection

The selection of communication channels should be determined according to the results of audience research, rather than perceived assumptions regarding their conventional usefulness. For effective design, communication planners must have knowledge of the channels available, their potential reach, and the intended result of the messages. As changes in communication technology become more prevalent, such as the use of videos and interactive audio-conferencing, the training of production staff and field workers should become more consistent and individualized.

Community Focus

For most people to adopt a new behaviour, it must become an accepted cultural norm. For this reason, communication planners must pay attention to the role that communities play in determining and shaping health behaviours. For sustained long-term behavioural change to take place, the involvement of local community groups is often essential. The well-documented influence of community leaders and family members should also be considered through targeted programme research and message design.

Narrowing Communication Gaps

Communication programmes often produce dramatic initial effects, with subsequent levels of adoption presenting more of a challenge. Potential barriers such as physical access, adequacy of information, exposure to media, conflicting cultural beliefs, or lack of social support systems often stand in the way of behaviour change. The success of qualitative research methods such as in-depth interviews and focus group discussions in identifying such barriers has been demonstrated throughout HEALTHCOM sites, with continual analysis of target audience information used to tailor messages and other programme elements to specific audience needs.

Structured Interventions

Large-scale, intensive communication campaigns which mobilize social and political support are often attractive to planners. However, such campaigns may have several disadvantages. They can often deplete the resources used to deliver important services on a regular basis. More successful are those communication efforts which are fully integrated with the existing structure and are sustainable.

Prevention Messages

As communication campaigns stressing health and safety achieve success, increasing emphasis is likely to be placed on preventive behaviours of all kinds. This presents a new set of challenges to communicators, as prevention behaviours are often more complicated and difficult to identify and teach. They often require a greater change in everyday routines, and have no direct, immediate payoff.

Institutional Capacity

The most basic, effective strategy for the institutionalization of development communicators involves training, especially in the areas of formative research, strategy development, message design, and project monitoring. To be successful, however, this training must reach beyond the project counterparts to include groups in national and regional development institutions.

Long-term Planning

Many successful development communication programmes have wasted away because of lack of government commitment once donor funding ends. The challenge of political and financial commitment must be met if the programmes are to continue. Specific commitments to establishing personnel positions, budgets, and career tracks which will support future communication initiatives are critical. In planning for the long-term, project managers from donor agencies must discuss such issues with senior government officials during the project negotiation stage. Decision-makers may be persuaded by programme results data which demonstrate the cost-effectiveness of communication interventions. This difficult yet essential part of the institutionalization process will allow decision-makers to view communication programmes as an investment with tangible payoffs, rather than a continuing drain on the country's strained resources (Andreasen, 1995).

6. The Institution-Building Thread

The first five threads of development communication have dealt largely with various approaches that organizations have used in applying communication to development problems. Woven in and out among these is a thread one vital to them all. This is the institution-building that has provided developing nations with organizations, skills and facilities to carry out development communication.

Institution-building for communication in developing nations has taken different forms. For example, in the late 1960s, the Ford Foundation was active in India supporting training and resource development for the nation's family planning campaigns. (The Foundation supported the employment of elephants on whose flanks were painted the family planning logo.) The Ford Foundation also funded the creation of a modern agricultural communication centre at what is now the G.B. Pant University of Agriculture and Technology in Uttaranchal state. Two decades later, FAO was to contribute additional funding to elevate the centre into a Centre for the Advanced Study of Agricultural Communication. The Ford and FAO institution-building consisted of both training abroad to upgrade the communication competence of the faculty and providing facilities for the university to produce radio programmes and other resources for reaching the farm and rural population.

In Guatemala in the 1970s, the US Agency for International Development provided assistance that enabled the government to build two radio stations that were dedicated to supporting agricultural, nutrition and health activities in rural communities. In Indonesia in the 1980s, the Canadian Government supported efforts to institutionalize special units in most major broadcast stations that were especially focussed on development issues.

Other governments and foundations contributed to largely uncoordinated efforts to build the physical and human resources infrastructure that would allow developing nations to accelerate and broaden the reach and impact of communication media. Entering the twenty-first century, much of that effort was focussed on the creation of multi-purpose community telecentres and broadband infrastructure.

The UNESCO Role

UNESCO has been one of the most consistent agencies supporting institution-building for development communication. UNESCO's Third Medium Term Plan, adopted in 1989, set as one of its objectives 'to strengthen communication capacities in the developing countries so that they may participate more actively in the communication process' (Hancock, 2000). Although it has worked through other UN organizations such as the Population Fund (UNFPA) to provide communication training and technology, UNESCO's major contribution to development communication has been in enhancing the professional infrastructures in developing nations. Long time UNESCO official Alan Hancock explains it this way:

> Some of the earliest UNESCO programmes emphasised professional training (initially in film, then in radio and television), following a model of basic training at local and national levels, intermediate skills training at regional levels, and advanced training through overseas attachments and study tours. The tradition is still very strong, although it has been modified over the years by a rising emphasis on community based media practice, and the use of adapted, or appropriate media technologies. (ibid.:62)

UNESCO's leadership in building and strengthening communication infrastructures got an initial thrust from a 1958 declaration of the UN General Assembly calling 'for a "program of concrete action" to build up press, radio broadcasting, film and television facilities in countries in process of economic and social development' (Schramm, 1964). In 1962, UNESCO authorized the publication of a study that was designed to help give 'practical effect' to the mass media development programme that had been urged on all governments. The study was conducted by Stanford University's Wilbur Schramm and the study was published by the Stanford University Press as *Mass Media and National Development*, copyrighted by UNESCO. Schramm built the rationale for using mass media in the development of nations and in development projects. He offered 15 recommendations 'to developing nations and their friends and aiders, concerning what they might do about the mass media' (ibid.:253). It is noteworthy that Schramm included a section in the book on the necessity of communication research in developing nations. A UNESCO statement describing the book calls it 'A useful guide to government and industrial planners, economists, educators, mass-media specialists and others concerned with the welfare of people in developing nations.'

Wilbur Schramm entered the UNESCO picture again when, in 1965, its International Institute for Educational Planning (IIEP) undertook a worldwide research project 'to extract useful lessons from the accumulated experience of numerous countries which have been pioneering in the use of new educational media' (Schramm, 1967:253). Schramm was drafted to be the project director, with financing to be provided by the USAID. The three volumes published by UNESCO included 16 case studies ranging from the use of airborne instructional television (foreshadowing satellite television) in the United States to radio clubs in Niger (Schramm et al., 1967). A fourth volume contained a summary and conclusions, and, as reflected in its title, the volume served as a Memo to Educational Planners (Schramm, 1967).

In 1980, after years of international haggling over its mandate, UNESCO created the International Programme for the Development of Communication (IPDC) as its 'main operational instrument' for upgrading the communications capacity of developing nations. According to Hancock, more than US$ 22 million have been committed to 375 projects in more than 80 developing countries. Initially, funding only passed through the governments of developing nations but more recently IPDC has extended support to non-governmental bodies and professional associations.

Examples of UNESCO's support for building infrastructure in developing nations include the creation of regional training institutes (such as the Asia Pacific Institute for Broadcasting Development in Malaysia and India's Film and Television Institute in Poona) and backing the creation of news agencies particularly in Africa and Asia. Hancock notes that UNESCO's past six-year medium-term plan includes 'some US$ 25 million worth of projects, focussing primarily on the development of news agencies and rural newspapers in Africa, and on radio and communication training in Asia and the Pacific' (Hancock, 2000:70).

UNESCO's interest in local institution-building is demonstrated by its contribution of US$ 50,000 in 1998 to help Sri Lanka's Kothmale community radio station add an Internet facility to its system, thereby combining a new information technology with traditional community radio. UNESCO provided computer equipment and training while the Sri Lankan Government provided the Internet connectivity. In one application of the system, listeners request information which station staff try to provide on the air using Internet searches.

This accounting of institution-building activities is only meant to illustrate some of the initiatives undertaken during the past half century. For example, at the turn of the century, the Canadian Government's International Development Research Centre and governments in Europe have contributed consistently to the training of media people from developing nations, and, of course, there are developing nations themselves that have been instrumental in building the resources for doing development communication.

Paralleling (or a sub-component of) this thread is a strand that might be labelled ICT. Because of its prominence in the twenty-first century, we treat it here in a separate section.

7. The ICT Thread

Rogers asserts that the Internet 'has spread more rapidly than any other technology innovation in the history of mankind' (Rogers, 2003:xix). Yet, ICT have played a role in development for at least half a century. Rural radio forums, a product of the 1950s, continue today in some countries. Audio and video cassette technology, along with broadcasting, satellites and various audio-visual technologies, became part of the development communication tool kit in the last half of the twentieth century.[6] Heavily influencing the communication technology initiatives was an interest in distance learning projects. An early example in this history was Radio Sutatenza which began educational and cultural programming in Colombia in 1947. One of the most dramatic events in the half century was the use of a communication satellite in India to provide television programmes to the six most underdeveloped areas of the country. Although radio and television continue to be important 'new technologies' for some parts of the world, computers and the Internet are attracting substantial interest in developing nations. For example, Don Richardson suggests that:

> The time to act to support Internet knowledge and communication systems in developing countries is now. Today we truly live in a global village, but it is a village with elite information 'haves' and many information 'have-nots.'... Adopting a proactive strategy and acting to bring the Internet to rural and agricultural communities in developing countries will help enable rural people to face the unprecedented challenges brought by the changing global economy, political changes, environmental degradation and demographic pressures. (Richardson, 1997:69–70)

The value of information can be seen in more personal terms at the community level with real people. There are many stories from around the world that illustrate how valuable information and the new information technologies can be for someone in the community. This anecdote comes from Latin America. The story starts:

> Until a brilliant sunny day when the Internet reached his Ashaninka Indian village in central Peru, tribal leader Oswaldo Rosas could think of few benefits modern life had brought to his people.

The story goes on to tell of how through grants from the Canadian government, the local telephone company and a non-profit organization, things were changed by the introduction of a computer, portable generator, a satellite dish and a big screen monitor. Rosas and five other tribal leaders received eight weeks of computer training which led to developing their own Ashaninka web site (www.rcp.net.pe/ashaninka). With it they sold their organically grown oranges in Lima, 250 miles away, and boosted tribal revenue 10 per cent. Now, Rosas' hut also doubles as a tribal cybercafé (Faiola and Buckley, 2000).

The central and vital role communication and information play in the lives of people was officially recognized by the UN General Assembly in December 1997 when it endorsed a statement on the Universal Access to Basic Communication and Information Services. The statement concluded that the 'introduction and use of information and communication technology must become a priority effort of the United Nations in order to secure sustainable human development.' The statement also embraced the objective of establishing 'universal access to basic communication and information services for all.' In mid-2000, the eight major industrial nations (the G-8) meeting in Okinawa acknowledged that ICT 'is one of the most potent forces in shaping the twenty-first century [and] its revolutionary impact affects the way people live, learn and work, and the way government interacts with civil society.'

Emerging from the discussion was the Okinawa Charter on the Global Information Society. Its framers announced that 'this Charter represents a call to all, in both the public and private sectors, to bridge the international information and knowledge divide.' The Charter also renewed a commitment of the G-8 nations 'to the principle of inclusion: everyone, everywhere should be enabled to participate in and no one should be excluded from the benefits of the global information society.' The G-8 launched a major effort to strengthen all nations' potential to be part of this Information Age starting with a Digital Opportunity Task Force which reported to the G-8 in mid-2001 (DOT Force, 2001). The DOT noted the relationship between high priority international development goals and communication such as the Millennium Development Goals and emphasized that harnessing the power of information and communication technologies can contribute substantially to realizing *every one* of these goals; either directly (for instance, through greater availability of health and reproductive information, training of medical personnel and teachers, giving opportunity and voice to women, expanding access to education and training) or indirectly (through creating new economic opportunities that lift individuals, communities and nations out of poverty). Creating digital opportunities was not something that happens *after* addressing the 'core' development challenges; it was considered a key component of addressing those challenges in the twenty-first century.

The DOT report detailed four major thrusts for concerted international action:

(1) Fostering Policy, Regulatory and Network Readiness—through establishing and supporting both developing country and emerging economy *National eStrategies* including *eGovernment*, and universal participation in new international policy and technical issues raised by ICT and the Internet.

(2) Improving Connectivity Increasing Access and Lowering Costs—through establishing and supporting a range of targeted interventions as well as dedicated initiatives for the ICT inclusion of the Least Developed Countries.

(3) Building Human Capacity—through a range of targeted training, education, knowledge creation and sharing initiatives, as well as promote ICT for healthcare and in support against HIV/AIDS and other infectious and communicable diseases.

(4) Encouraging Participation in Global e-Commerce and other e-Networks—through enterprise and entrepreneurship for sustainable economic development, including poverty alleviation, and promote national and international effort to support the creation of local content and applications (DOT Force, 2001).

A related effort prompted by the Okinawa meeting was a study and report by the Digital Opportunity Initiative (DOI) that lays out a framework for action that developing countries and their partners could follow to gain benefits from the new information technologies and the systems associated with them.

The report established a 'strategic framework' to help guide stakeholders in investing in and implementing strategies that take advantage of the potential of ICT to accelerate social and economic development. The report lists five interrelated areas for intervention (DOT Force, 2001). These include:

- Infrastructure—deploying a core ICT network infrastructure, achieving relative ubiquity of access, and investing in strategically-focussed capacity to support high development priorities.
- Human capacity—building a critical mass of knowledge workers, increasing technical skills among users and strengthening local entrepreneurial and managerial capabilities.
- Policy—supporting a transparent and inclusive policy process, promoting fair and open competition, and strengthening institutional capacity to implement and enforce policies.
- Enterprise—improving access to financial capital, facilitating access to global and local markets, enforcing appropriate tax and property rights regimes, enabling efficient business processes and stimulating domestic demand for ICT.
- Content and applications—provide demand-driven information that is relevant to the needs and conditions experienced by local people.

The DOI report proceeded to provide evidence of how ICTs could contribute to individual development goals, including those related to health, education, economic opportunity, empowerment, participation and protection of the environment.

At a 2002 Special Session of the UN General Assembly on information technology and development, Secretary General Kofi Annan succinctly placed ICTs among the important tools of development. Opening the session, he declared:

A wide consensus has emerged on the potential of information and communications technologies to promote economic growth, combat poverty, and facilitate the integration of developing countries into the global economy. Seizing the opportunities of the digital revolution is one of the most pressing challenges we face.

In 2001 Annan had already created the UNICT Task Force, consisting of an 'inspiring group of government officials, industry experts, non-governmental organization leaders and others from every part of the world.' The principal mission of this Task Force was 'to tell, realistically, what ICT can and cannot do, especially in terms of making its benefits accessible and meaningful for all humanity, in particular the poor' (UNICT Task Force, 2001).

In 2005, the Task Force matched the potential of ICTs with the challenges of the Millennium Development Project in producing a document that identified five critical areas that needed to be addressed for the 'mainstreaming' of ICTs in meeting the MDGs. These, with a short 'outlook' for each, included:

1. Evidence of Impact—The case for mainstreaming ICT to meet the MDGs [must be made with] rigorous analysis and empirical evidence of development impact. Emphasis must shift from simple ICT access to more sophisticated data sets on the improved efficiency of ICT-enabled delivery of public and private services particularly in Lesser Developed Countries (LDC).
2. Policy Development—National e-strategies need to be linked far more explicitly to national economic development plans and vice versa. The special case of LDCs demands immediate and full integration of national e-strategies within the poverty reduction strategy process, accompanied by enhanced cooperation and coordination among donors.
3. Resource Mobilization—There remains a serious deficit in the current approaches and financing mechanisms for bridging the global digital divide. Flows of adequate funds will fail to materialize until scepticism among donor countries is countered, developing country prioritization is enacted, and the private sector is persuaded of profitable business models for investment.
4. Global Alliance for ICT and Development—An open, multi-stakeholder and forward-looking framework for employing ICT and media in accelerating the achievement of the MDGs is urgently required. The MDGs provide a common denominator and common agenda for the creation of a Global Alliance for ICT and Development drawn from actors both within and outside the ICT sector.
5. Global Campaign and Initiatives—The sheer ambition of the MDG challenge demands an unprecedented response at the global as well as at the national level. Scaling and replication of ICT efforts will require aggregation of knowledge and resources across markets, and innovative breakthrough approaches to meet key price points and economics of scope and scale for MDG delivery (UNICT Task Force, 2005:viii–ix).

By the middle of the decade, there was clearly a widespread consensus in the international community of the need to bring together development issues and ICTs.

The Attraction of ICT for Development

We digress briefly from the international scene related to ICT and development to note what it is about ICTs that attracts development organizations to them. Here we briefly distill some of the features that cause excitement among many planners of initiatives. These include the following—many of which are associated with the older media:

- Reaching many people simultaneously,
- Overcoming geographic boundaries,
- Overcoming social and literacy barriers,
- Providing frequency and repetition of contact,
- Storage of information for on-demand access,
- Capturing the reality of events, by depicting them graphically and in real time, and
- Greater efficiency (lower costs) in sending and receiving information.

In the 1990s, computers and digital networks exploded into the communication environment and provided additional dimensions to the list of ICT benefits. The newer technologies provided at least six additional features, including opportunities for

- Relatively convenient individual information *searching* through a vast array of information sources, on-demand and often 24 hours a day;
- Timely interaction between and among computer users that allows convenient and 'contemplated' exchanges: exchanges that are quick but not necessarily instantaneous;
- 'Broadcasting' of information to many by ordinary *individuals,* including easier 'bottom-up' and collaborative message initiation;
- Global reach almost constantly and instantly, and at relatively low cost;
- Convenient storage facilities for text, graphics, audio, video and data; and
- Intermixing of media forms and content.

These features of ICTs potentially translate into benefits in education and health, reducing social distance, better connections between governments and individuals, marketing advantages, and, overall, improved opportunities for information sharing. But there is still a more profound implication regarding ICTs. According to some analysts, writing and reading have long been symbols of, and contributors to, social *inequality* because these skills provide their holders with information and knowledge that lead to power and privilege. Now, 'the rise of multimedia should provide an important opportunity to level the playing field of literacy by restoring the status of more natural forms of audiovisual communication that are in some ways more broadly accessible' (Warschauer, 2003:116).

Box 6.3 The Internet and Village Development

ICTs on the ground

The potential of ICTs is illustrated in a report from Cambodia published in the *International Herald Tribune.* It tells of the village chief who is quoted as saying: 'I don't really know what the Internet is or how it works, but it is changing our lives.' The story goes on to tell about women who revived the village's traditional silk-weaving industry.

They sold scarves through the village's web site to customers around the world, and the profits are being plowed into a pig farm. The farm has generated new employment, possible spin-off industries and hoped-for profits that will go into a fund to pay for the villagers' medical care (Colle and Roman, 2005).

The World Bank and ICT in the new century.   In the mid-1960s the World Bank began supporting conventional telecommunications infrastructure development in various countries. In the 1990s, the Bank moved more decisively into ICT matters, including, for example, projects fostering a larger ICT role in education and in increasing the efficiency of government services. In recent years, according to Bank documents, total annual funding for ICT projects and for ICT-related project components averaged more than US$ 1.5 billion with a heavy concentration in Africa and Latin America. The Bank's lead unit for this was *info*Dev, created in 1995 to promote 'innovative projects that use ICTs for economic and social development, with special emphasis on the needs of the poor in developing economies' (Primo Braga et al., 2000). Averaging approximately US$ 200,000 each, *info*Dev has selected more than 200 projects in more than a hundred countries for funding.

Two programmes of *info*Dev merit attention here because they are especially relevant to building a supportive environment for ICT development. These are 'e-Readiness' and 'Country Gateways.'

e-Readiness.   e-Readiness is an assessment of a country's status regarding several aspects ICT development: its ICT infrastructure, the accessibility of ICT to the population, the suitability of the policy environment for ICT effectiveness, and everyday use of ICT. The *info*Dev programme became a major funder of countries that want to do such assessments. By the end of 2001 more than 130 assessments had been undertaken (with various funding), with repetition as many as six times in some countries. The key actors in doing or supporting e-Readiness studies in addition to *info*Dev were the UNDP, the World Economic Forum (WEF), the International Telecommunications Union, USAID, and the UK Department for International Development. More than 15 e-Readiness assessment tools have been developed in recent years but, according to Teresa Peters, Chairman of Bridges.org, at the *info*Dev Symposium in Washington in 2001, virtually no action. Another challenge in the e-Readiness world is gathering reliable data at the local level and building appropriate programmes there. The Global Network Readiness Project, a joint project of Harvard's Center for International Studies, the Markle Foundation, the WEF, IBM, the UNDP and the United Nations Foundation, formed a network of experts to provide advice to nations interested in moving into concrete strategies.

Country Gateways.   In September 2001, *info*Dev announced a Country Gateways programme and allocated US$ 1.8 million for fiscal year 2001. It is a partner to the World Bank's Development Gateway initiative which is directed by the Development Gateway Foundation, a public-private partnership created in December 2001 and whose Board of Directors represents civil society and public and private donors. The Development Gateway is an Internet portal for information on sustainable development and poverty reduction and expects to help fill the knowledge and communication needs of government officials and promote government quality and efficiency by providing information on best practices, networks for sharing solutions and experiences, and tools for analysis and problem solving. Its 'search engine' is dedicated to helping public, civil society and private sector people navigate the Internet to find useful information and resources. For one example: officials in a community in a developing nation wants to attract investors to the community. They need to advertise the community's assets and provide legal information and data on infrastructure and the local labour market. The Gateway provides an international 'platform' for diffusing this information widely.

When it was first introduced, the Gateway stirred up substantial controversies because some perceived it as a 'super-site' and a *gatekeeper* on development information, and some thought its management and control might not be impartial and beneficial to all. 'A measure of success of the Development Gateway Foundation,' says a Bank official, 'will be how much it helps connect existing Internet portals and networks and brings together more resources for government, civil society, and donor agency ICT initiatives.'

The Country Gateways are independently owned and operated partners of the Development Gateway. Each gateway is designed to provide country-level information and resources, and promote local content development and knowledge sharing. In some cases, Country Gateways will provide their nation with e-government, e-business, and e-learning, and, overall, contribute to better connectivity and use of ICT. *info*Dev provides funding for planning of gateways (an average of US$ 50,000, but up to US$100,000) and may also provide funding for start-up activity. By 2004, more than 50 country gateways joined in a Country Gateway Network that facilitates sharing of resources among the members.

The telecentre movement.   Emerging alongside the development of ICTs has been the telecentre movement (Badshah, Khan and Garrido, 2004; Latchem and Walker, 2001). While computers and networks have reached global penetration, many individuals, communities and regions have not shared in the benefits of ICTs. But, in 2005, experts guessed that there were as many as 150,000 to 200,000 public access centres where people could exchange messages, access web sites, and use other ICT resources. The challenge now is to increase the relevance and sustainability of those existing facilities and to expand the movement to those persons still on the margins. Community-based telecentres are part of that movement.

International organizations have a keen interest in telecentres because of three related assumptions. These are:

(1) Appropriate information can contribute significantly to development.
(2) Information technologies provide an important and potentially economical way for people to access that information.
(3) Telecentres are a viable way to link communities with the information and communication technologies.

Various international organizations have invested in the telecentre movement. These include: the ITU, Canada's International Development Research Centre, USAID, the Food and Agriculture Organization, the World Health Organization, UNESCO and the World Bank. Some national governments are also making large investments in telecentres, including Australia, Canada, Egypt,

Hungary, India, South Africa, Taiwan, Tunisia and Vietnam. In late 2001, Mexico announced plans for a major ICT and telecentre project called Systema e-México.

The private sector has also seen promise in providing information technology services for the public. However those tend to be enterprises such as cybercafés or telephone access points whose principal goal is to make a profit. In the development field, we generally consider a telecentre to be a public place where the motive of the telecentre operator is largely to foster community development. Basically, telecentres are shared public facilities that provide telecommunication services to persons who, for various reasons, do not have them available individually. Because of the great diversity of initiatives, making sharp distinctions between cybercafés and telecentres is hazardous, and there maybe many exceptions when one tries to do it. But we will take this step because they are different movements, and each can learn from the other.

Commercially-oriented cybercafés tend to be in the private sector and focus primarily on providing customers with the use of computers and especially connections with the Internet and the World Wide Web. Their clients tend to be more urban, more educated, and more economically well off than the clients of telecentres. By their nature, at this period of the telecentre movement, telecentres tend to be in the public sector and focus on more isolated people (like villagers), and lower income and less educated people. Thus, for our characterization of telecentres, we adopt the multi-purpose community telecentre idea suggested by the ITU and others. Typically, telecentres offer a broad range of services related to the needs of the community, some of which are free or subsidized by external bodies (such as governments or NGOs). These might include: desktop publishing, community newspapers, sales or rental of audio and video cassettes and DVDs, book lending, photocopying, faxing, and telephone services. While both cybercafés and telecentres might offer training in computer use, the telecentre is more likely to offer other kinds of training, non-formal education, and distance learning in agriculture, health, basic education and other fields. Their reason-for-being is consistent with the idea expressed by the Dot Force report noted above: 'Creating digital opportunities is not something that happens *after* addressing the 'core' development challenges; it is a key component of addressing those challenges in the 21st century.'

With this we offer a brief historical note. The idea of a community sharing computer technology emerged in the 1980s with the introduction of the telecottage in Scandinavia. The initial purpose of those telecottages was to fight against marginalization of remote rural places in the information society. This was before the Internet. In the mid-1990s a new breed of telecottages appeared in Hungary. Supported initially by the USAID, these were built around social and economic development, computers and the Internet. Hungarian telecottages were part of a more robust movement that marked the close of the twentieth century, with a variety of international organizations supporting the diffusion and adoption of ICTs and telecentres.

Cybercafés, however, are potentially relevant to the development communication enterprise. Francisco Proenza reminds us that there is much to learn from cybercafés even though they are not development-oriented. The small business cybercafés, he reports, have been expanding very rapidly worldwide. When we disregard cybercafés in the discussion of telecentres, we are ignoring the 'most replicable and sustainable governance structure known—that is, the privately-owned business' (Proenza, 2001). From cybercafés, he asserts, telecentres could learn a business-like approach to telecentre management, a key issue in assessing their sustainability.

Furthermore, Proenza says, government and NGO-run telecentres that find it difficult to sustain themselves often have easy access to funds, and spend more than they can afford on staff and superfluous services. Their motivation to be economical or to run their centres to meet their customers' needs 'is feeble'. On the other hand, if the owner of a commercial cybercafé is not committed to sustainability through demand-driven entrepreneurship, he will surely fail while others take over his place. Thus a key lesson for the telecentre movement lies in careful assessment of the market.

Telecentres might also look at the culture of the cybercafé to see what features could be adopted by the telecentre. For example, in many places the ambiance of the cybercafé is social and enjoyment: the café aspect is an important attraction for the persons who frequent the places. Computer games are popular. Even in fulfilling their development communication objectives, telecentres will need to be demand-driven.

Despite its commercial and narrow interests, the cybercafés phenomenon is important in the context of telecentres because cybercafés may discover that some development-related services are, in fact, profitable, either directly or indirectly (for example, attracting more traffic). Elsewhere we have explored this idea by suggesting that telecentres be viewed as 'communication shops' (Colle, 1998; Colle and Roman, 2004). Ultimately, the sustainability of the telecentre system is likely to depend on this kind of entrepreneurship.

We need also to note that there are major public sector initiatives around the world that have the unidimensional look of the cybercafé but without the coffee. We call them Information Access Points (IAP). Canada's Community Access Programme (CAP) that launched 10,000 CAP sites in rural and urban Canada is an example. We spoke with the head of a CAP site that only provided use of computers and connectivity to the Internet in a sparse bare room. It was not until they changed the *name* of the site from CAP to include a name with 'cybercafé' in it that people started to use the place. These kinds government-sponsored information technology access points that have proliferated throughout Canada and are emerging in places as widespread as Mexico, Egypt and India are important for the telecentre movement because they already have the public service mandate, and potentially they can expand into the broader development areas and services characteristic of telecentres, similar to the adaptation that took place when Hungary reconstructed the telecottage concept.

Some Common Threads

As one examines the trends in such sectors as health, agriculture, nutrition and the environment as well as the approaches being used by major sponsors and stakeholders there appears to be some convergence of views as to how communication can be used most effectively to promote economic and social development and especially improve the well-being of people who live in various degrees of poverty. The threads we have followed covering the last five decades convey a sense of evolving into a development communication fabric. One can discern in this fabric characteristics than can be said to help define what development communication is in this early twenty-first century. Following is a list of those characteristics.

1. Focus on Beneficiaries

Instead of starting with an innovation or a behaviour or an organization's priorities, increasingly communication interventions are emphasizing the individual or family or community as the centre of the development process. Childers referred to this as 'people-centred' as compared to agency or ministry-centred approaches.

2. Consideration of Various Stakeholders

In addition to focussing on those who are expected to be the primary targets for change-inducing communication, others are considered as targets because of their influence and their control over essential resources. These range from political and opinion leaders to clinic staffs and those in outreach systems such as the mass media and extension. Even those initiating a programme/project may also be considered as stakeholders. Hence the concept of advocacy reflects the importance of looking beyond mass-oriented strategies.

3. Participation

The ideas of 'targeting' and 'receivers' are modified (but not eliminated) so that *interactivity and sharing of power* within and among stakeholders' groups is an operational model guiding communication planning.

4. Emphasis on Outcomes

What and how many messages are sent out is less important than what is *perceived* by stakeholders and what changes take place in stakeholders' behaviour relative to development objectives.

5. Data Gathering and Analysis

While intuition and creativity continue to be valued, these are driven and inspired by systematic data collection and analysis. For example, an early step in a communication plan is to do a situational analysis that includes research on a variety of subjects related to behavioural change and communication resources. In the incubation of telecentres, we have already found that doing research on a community's information needs is vital to a telecentre's sustainability. Evaluation is another process that permeates the communication programme, with information being collected for pre-testing materials, monitoring progress, and measuring impact.

6. Systematic Models

The communication process involves specific and explicit sequential steps including situational analysis (research), planning, pre-testing, implementation and evaluation. The sequence is iterative and dynamic: results of the evaluation are fed back into the situational analysis to register changes in conditions upon which the original planning was based so that adjustments can be made in the steps that follow.

7. Strategy

Most development programmes deal with *voluntary* behaviour of stakeholders: farmers *choose* to adopt different varieties of seeds; families *choose* to change diets or visit health clinics; couples *choose* to accept or reject family planning. These kinds of situations challenge communication people to design strategies for providing appropriate information, through appropriate channels, at appropriate times, for the appropriate people. Thus a quality professionally-driven development communication programme is characterized by having a rational means for selecting communication objectives, content, channels and target groups that fit the voluntary nature of the behaviour change being proposed.

8. Multi-Channel Versatility

As the examples in the opening section of this paper and the ICT thread at the end illustrate, development communication is equipped with a broad range of information and communication techniques and technologies with which to attack poverty and underdevelopment.

An Agenda for the Future

Absent from most of the major documents and international meetings concerning communication and development, and especially more recently concerning ICTs and development, is reference to higher education institutions as significant players. With the exception of technical connectivity issues and building simple computers (such as those addressed by the India's Institutes of Technology and the Massachusetts Institute of Technology), computer training, and distance learning courses for college-level students, the record of higher education in information and communication technologies for development is not very bright.[7] A two year study commissioned by the World Bank and UNESCO concluded that the contribution of higher education to social and economic development in developing countries has been 'disappointing to date' including a failure to advance the public interest. One of the major obstacles is that 'the social and economic importance of higher education systems is insufficiently appreciated' (Task Force, 2000:93). However, a 2006 Harvard University study commissioned by the Word Bank suggested a shift in perceptions concerning; it noted the international community was coming to recognize higher education's value for development. It urged donors to increase investments in Africa's capacity—beginning with higher education, particularly in the sciences and technology (Bloom, Canning and Chan, 2006).

The record of university involvement with ICTs and the Millennium Development Goals is virtually invisible. In regard to supporting and helping sustain community telecentres, universities are widely perceived as irrelevant—if they are considered at all.

We raised this relevance issue in India when the National Alliance for Information and Communication Technologies for Basic Human Needs came into being in 2004. The National Alliance set a goal of bringing all of India's 600,000 villages into the modern 'information society' by 2007, the 60th anniversary of the nation's Independence. The National Alliance hopes to achieve its 'Mission 2007' primarily through the creation of a network of Rural Knowledge Centres (telecentres) across the country. When we proposed to an Alliance leader that the agricultural universities in India be explicitly included in the planning as partners for the knowledge centres, we received this terse response: 'The universities have failed miserably in many respects. Most university faculty have no clue to life outside the campus nor have they any social concerns. Sorry for being very forthright or even blunt.'

Especially with the support of colleges and universities in the LDCs, telecentres could be local institutions that parallel the local school system—providing a learning resource for reaching people like Nigar, whose situation in a New Delhi slum is described in the accompanying box— and perhaps like 160 millions other young people, mostly in rural areas around the world, who have been overlooked or abandoned by the conventional education system.

Box 6.4 Telecentres and Poverty Reduction

There is a young woman named Nigar who lives in a mostly Muslim slum in New Delhi. Separated from an abusive husband, Nigar and her two children struggle against the poverty that engulfs her home. It is through a local telecentre that she and other women in the community are breaking the isolation of their ghetto lives and learning about health and gaining vocational training including the use of computers. The Nigar story speaks to the first Millennium Development Goal: To reduce extreme poverty and, more specifically, to *cut in half the proportion of people living on less than a dollar a day and those who suffer from hunger* (UNESCO, 2004).

Let us be specific about the connection between universities and telecentres. First, a very large percentage of telecentres struggle for survival. The reasons vary, but prominent among them is the failure for telecentres to be *demand-driven*. And this happens because telecentre people often lack an understanding of the communities' information, education, and training needs, and the telecentre people often lack the know-how and resources to build the content and services that could respond to those needs. We can identify four specific ways in which higher education can contribute to the sustainability of telecentres that—unlike cybercafés—have a community development mission.[8]

Research

Research helps telecentres become demand-driven. Research can identify communities' needs for information and related services. Research must be a long-term process, not a single start-up activity, because needs change over time especially if the community is developing. Telecentres generally have neither the skills, time, motivation, nor interest in systematic research about the communities around them. Telecentres also need research to evaluate continuously how well they are serving the needs of their communities. Many universities have research capabilities that could be applied to these telecentre needs. Students and university faculties in a range of disciplines (from computer science to rural sociology) can apply their knowledge and training to ICT-related research that will better link telecentres to their communities.

Local and Relevant Content

Too much content on the web is not relevant to farmers and other rural people. Nor to the young women in the New Delhi slum. It is a common problem around the world, where externally-generated information often dominates locally-tailored material. This is where credible, useful and user-friendly information needs to be crafted. The UNDP has suggested that the most important reason for the failure of telecentres is their lack of suitable content. Universities such as agricultural universities have access to science-based information that could be tailored to regional, provincial and local agronomic, social, linguistic, and cultural characteristics, and could be matched with many of the education and training requirements related to the Millennium Development Goals. Also universities are in a good position to design and administer distance learning and self-paced learning packages that people including the poor, can use to negotiate successfully in contemporary society. Its students could work with local people to develop community-oriented databases, such as where to find a veterinarian, or bus schedules. Returning once again to the Delhi slum, we find that Nigar studied embroidery in a six-week course at the telecentre, and ended up teaching embroidery in the community. In South India, the Tamil Nadu University of Veterinary and Animal Sciences has produced video CDs on subjects ranging from remedial measures for infertility in cattle to 'Cream, Butter and Cheese'—all designed for rural populations who can view them at the Village Information Centre or in homes.

Information Management

People in telecentres need to be trained in how information can contribute to development. We have found telecentre managers who know a lot about computers but don't know how to link telecentre potential to health clinics for community health education, or to schools, agricultural extension, or local government. Likewise, telecentres need to make their communities aware of the value of information, such as agricultural marketing, micro enterprise management, or the chances for more education through distance learning. Awareness of the value of information will help the communities realize the value of the telecentre. Logically, universities have the capacity to teach and train, and these skills could be applied to these telecentre-related needs.

Human Resources

Telecentres need volunteers who can help make telecentres good places to visit—volunteers who can help people search and understand the basic rewards of a digital experience and help those people navigate the various media in the telecentre. A major challenge for telecentres is to 'gain, train, and retain' volunteers. Those in touch with today's young people are aware that they—especially college students—generally have the media and digital skills to be good volunteers. Volunteers are important in welcoming persons in special groups such as women and the elderly who are frequently shut out of access to ICTs and telecentres by culture. Universities have human resources such as students who could serve as telecentre interns, and faculty members who could serve as content and development advisors.

Benefits to Universities

Universities and telecentres have a logical affinity. In addition to the benefits that they can bring to telecentres, the universities can benefit from an affiliation with telecentres. Here are three ways.

(1) Telecentres provide universities with a means for reaching beyond their 'ivory tower' to extend their knowledge and learning resources to the surrounding communities and to other populations in the region. This includes translating, adapting, localizing and re-packaging information from external sources to fit the agronomic and cultural characteristics of those local communities. This function is especially vital to the worldwide priorities identified in the Millennium Development Goals. Ultimately this makes universities more relevant and better candidates for support from the public and private sector.

(2) Telecentres provide a laboratory for faculty and researchers to carry out ICT and extension-related research and development (R&D) projects especially involving issues ranging from HIV/AIDS to small business enterprises and poverty alleviation, and to universities' involvement with these issues. Telecentres, as extensions of the classroom, can also strengthen student understanding of issues ranging from computer applications and community development to e-Government and e-Commerce.

(3) Telecentres provide a learning environment for students as telecentre volunteers to gain practical experience in helping people in the community. In some countries college graduates have a public service obligation for one or two years. While it is often associated with military service, attention can be drawn to adding community service in telecentres as a means for discharging this obligation.

It is important to note that an active, visible and successful university ICT4D programme can have three additional outcomes. One is the simultaneous building of the university's own internal ICT infrastructure—which will contribute to the quality and efficiency of its academic and administrative functions. Second is the reshaping of its relationship to the outside world as a more active agent of change. This addresses the observation of the Task Force on Higher and Society that 'Unlike primary and secondary education, there is little in the way of a shared vision about the nature and the magnitude of the potential of contribution of higher education to development.' And third is the university's significant role in producing a new generation of leaders for telecentres and for other applications of communication for development.

Universities, ICT and Relevance

In considering the judgement that universities, especially those in developing nations, are irrelevant to the reality of the world around them, it is important to document cases in which universities *are* relevant. Here are two from India.

The first is a 1969 initiative in which the Ford Foundation helped build the capacity of the G.B. Pant University of Agriculture and Technology (then in Uttar Pradesh) to produce radio programmes for Indian farm families. Radio was the major 'ICT' of that time. In producing complete radio programmes and delivering them on tape to an All India Radio station (in Rampur), the university became the first non-governmental body in India to supply programmes for public consumption. Was it sustainable? Now, 35 years later, the university is serving more than 20 radio stations in the region.

The second case comes from Tamil Nadu where support from Canada's International Development Research Centre (IDRC) increased the capacity of the TN University of Veterinary and Animal Sciences (TANUVAS) to incubate and support three Village Information Centres (VICs) and six additional information centres especially serving Self Help Women's Groups. All are community-driven and some are fully supported by their surrounding communities. The university continues to play a partnership role through some training and advisory initiatives and supply of content (Colle and Roman, 2004).

In the process of supporting multi-purpose telecentres, universities can educate students about the potential of ICT4D and train them to apply ICTs to development issues in their communities, and ultimately to support local and national policies that build ICT resources into health, education, government, and economic programmes.

In a very practical way, initiatives that build the ICTD and ICT4D capacities of universities will influence the future character of higher education and help them become, and *be perceived as*, more relevant to the people of their countries.

Notes

1. The italicized leads in these paragraphs have been added to the original text for formatting purposes.
2. Italics in this section have been added to the original text.
3. Although the authors were Bank staff members, the report carries the note that 'the findings, interpretations, and conclusions expressed in the paper are entirely those of the authors [and] do not necessarily represent the view of the World Bank, its Executive Directors, or the countries.

4. Quoted in Anderson, Feder, and Ganguly, 2006, p. 21.
5. The following discussion is based on an unpublished document: National Population Information, Education, and Communication and Advocacy Strategy of the Government of the Federal Democratic Republic of Ethiopia (Draft), National Office of Population and UNFPA, Addis Ababa, 1997.
6. There is a vast literature on media but a convenient and concise treatment can be found in a pair of monographs issued by the Centre for the Study of Education in Developing Countries (CESO) in the Hague. These are Boeren (1994) and Boeren and Epskamp (1992).
7. A substantial number of university students have studied in distance learning courses throughout the world. The five largest programmes are based in developing countries. See Task Force, 2000:31. This agenda for the future has been adapted from Colle, 2005.
8. The power of the university + telecentres could be substantially increased if they make alliances with conventional libraries, which are beginning to reach out into the development field. Acknowledging the onset of a new digital era and rapid developments in information technology and digital communications, the theme of the 72nd International Federation of Library Associations and Institutions (IFLA) Congress 2006 was 'Libraries: Dynamic Engines for the Knowledge and Information Society. ' IFLA noted that 'It is time for libraries to work together with library scholars and professionals in order to fulfil the role and functions of 21st century information centres to meet the challenges of this fast moving world.'Papers presented at the Congress in Seoul included such titles as 'Information provision to farmers in Africa: the library-extension service linkage' and 'Forging partnerships between libraries and extension services for improved access to agriculture information: a case study in Sri Lanka.'

References

Adhikarya, R. 2006. 'Implementing Strategic Extension Campaigns: Applying Best Practices and Lessons Learned from Ev Rogers', in A. Singhal and J.W. Dearing (eds), *Communication of Innovations, A Journey with Ev Rogers*. New Delhi: Sage Publications.

Ameur, C. 1994. *Agricultural Extension, A Step Beyond the Next Step*. Washington: The World Bank.

Anderson, J.R., G. Feder and S. Ganguly. 2006. 'The Rise and Fall of Training and Visit Extension: An Asia Mini-drama with an African Epilogue', *World Bank Policy Research Working Paper* 3928, May 2006. Available online at: http://ideas.repec.org/p/wbk/wbrwps/3928.html.

Andreasen, A. 1995. *The Marketing of Social Change*. San Francisco: Jossey Bass.

Badshah, A., S. Khan and M. Garrido (eds). 2004. 'Connected for Development: Information Kiosks and Sustainability', *UN ICT Task Force Series 4*. Available online at: http://www.unicttaskforce.org/perl/documents.pl?id=1361.

Benor, D. and J.Q. Harrison. 1997. *Agricultural Extension: The Training and Visit System*. Washington: The World Bank.

Bloom, D., D. Canning, and K. Chan. 2006. *Higher Education and Economic Development in Africa*. Washington: The World Bank. Available online at: http://www.worldbank.org/afr/teia/pdfsHigher_Education_Econ_ Dev.pdf#search=%22BLOOM% 2C%20D.%2C%20CANNING%2C%20D.%20%26%20%20CHAN%2C%20K.%20(2006).%20The%20Role%20of%20Higher%20Education%20in%20Development.%20%09Cambridge%3A%20Harvard%20University.%22.

Boeren, A. 1994. 'In Other Words ... The Cultural Dimension of Communication for Development', *CESO paperback*, No. 19, Den Haag: CESO.

Boeren, A. and K. Epskamp (eds). 1992. 'The Empowerment of Culture: Development Communication and Popular Media', *CESO paperback*, No. 17, Den Haag: CESO.

Casmir, F. (ed.). 1991. *Communication in Development*. Norwood: Ablex.

Chambers, R. 1997. *Whose Reality Counts?* London: Intermediate Technology.

Colle, R. 1998. 'The Communication Shop: A Model for Private and Public Sector Collaboration Sustainable Too!', paper prepared for the *Don Snowden Program Conference: Partnerships and Participation in Telecommunications for Rural Development: Exploring What Works and Why*, Guelph, Ontario, Canada.

———. 2005. 'Building Developing Nations' Universities into the ICT4D Strategy', *International Journal of Education and Development using ICT* (1:1). Available online at: http://ijedict.dec.uwi.edu/viewarticle.php?id=13.

———. 2007. *Advocacy and Interventions, Readings in Communication and Development*. Available at http://hdl.handle.net/1813/7749.

Colle, R. and R. Roman. 2004. 'University-Based Telecenters', in A. Badshah, S. Khan and M. Garrido (eds). *Connected for Development: Information Kiosks and Sustainability, UN ICT Task Force Series 4*. Available online at: http://www.unicttaskforce.org/perl/documents.pl?id=1361.

———. 2005. *A Handbook for Telecenter Staffs*. Available online at: http://ip.cals.cornell.edu/commdev/handbook.cfm

DOI. 2001. *Creating a Development Dynamic, Final Report of the Digital Opportunity Initiative*, July. The DOI was sponsored by Accenture, the Markle Foundation and the United Nations Development Program.

DOT Force. 2001. 'Digital Opportunities for All: Meeting the Challenge', *Report of the Digital Opportunity Taks Force*. Available online at http://www.markle.org/dotforce.html.

Drennan, M. 1998. 'Reproductive Health: New Perspectives on Men's Participation', *Population Reports*, XXVI(2).

Faiola, A. and S. Buckley. 2000. 'Poor in Latin America Embrace Net's Promise'. Available online at http://www.washingtonpost.com.

FAO. 1989. *Guidelines on Communication for Rural Development*. Rome: FAO.

Fraser, C. and S. Restrepo-Estrada. 1998. *Communicating for Development. Human Change for Survival*. London: Tauris.

Freire, P. 1970. *Pedagogy of the Oppressed* (M. Bergman Ramos, Trans.). New York: Herder and Herder.

Gumucio-Dagron, A. 2001. *Making Waves. Stories of Participatory Communication for Social Change*. New York: Rockefeller Foundation.

Gumucio-Dagron, A. and T. Tufte (eds). 2006. *Communication for Social Change*. S. Orange, NJ: Social Change Consortium.

Hancock, A. 2000. 'UNESCO's Contributions to Communication, Culture and Development', in J. Servaes (ed.). *Walking on the Other Side of the Information Highway. Communication, Culture and Development in the 21st Century*. Penang: Southbound.

Hanson, E.P. 1960. *Puerto Rico, Land of Wonders*. New York: Alfred Knopf.

Hornik, R. 1989. 'Channel Effectiveness in Development Communication Programs', in R.E. Rice And C.K. Atkin (eds). *Public Communication Campaigns, 2nd ed*. Newbury Park, CA: Sage Publications.

Jones, G.E. and C. Garforth. 1997. 'The History, Development and Future of Agricultural Extension', in B.E. Swanson, R.P. Bentz and A.J. Sofranco (eds). *Improving Agricultural Extension: A Reference Manual*. Rome: Food and Agriculture Organization. Available online at http://www.fao.org/docrep/W5830E/w5830e00.htm.

Korten, David C. and Norman Uphoff. 1981. Bureaucratic Reorientation for Participatory Rural Development, World Bank Paper No. 1, Washington, DC: National Association Schools of Public Affairs and Administration.

Latchem, C. and D. Walker (eds). 2001. *Telecentres: Case Studies and Key Issues*. Vancouver, BC: The Commonwealth of Learning. Available online at http://www.col.org/colweb/site/pid/3337.

McKee, N., J. Bertrand and A. Becker-Benton. 2004. *Strategic Communication in the HIV/AIDS Epidemic*. New Delhi: Sage Publications.

Mody, B. 2003. *International and Development Communication*. New Delhi: Sage Publications.

Piotrow, P. 2005. 'A is for Advocacy'. Available online at http://www.infoforhealth.org/pr/advocacy/article.

Piotrow, P., L. Kincaid, J. Rimon II and W. Rinehart. 1997. *Health Communication. Lessons from Family Planning and Reproductive Health*. Westport, CT: Praeger.

Primo Braga, C.A. Roger S. Barga, David B. Lomet, Thomas Baby and Sanjay Agrawal. 2000. 'The Network Revolution, Opportunities and Challenges for Developing Countries', infoDev Working Paper, Washington: The World Bank. Available online at http://www.schoolnetafrica.netfileadmin/resourcesThe_Networking_Revolution.pdf#search=%22The%20Network%20Revolution%2C%20Opportunities%20and%20Challenges%20%22.

Proenza, F. 2001. 'Telecenter Sustainability: Myths, Challenges and Opportunities', *The Journal of Development Communication*, 12(2):94–109.

Richardson, D. 1997. *The Internet and Rural Development: An Integrated Approach*. Rome: Food and Agriculture Organization.

Rogers, E.M. 2003. *Diffusion of Innovation, 5th edition*. New York: Free Press.

Schramm, W. 1964. *Mass Media and National Development*. Stanford: Stanford University Press.

———. 1967. *The New Media: Memo to Educational Planners*. Paris: UNESCO.

Schramm, W., P.H. Coombs, F. Kahnert and J. Lyle. 1967. *New Educational Media in Actions, Case Studies for Planners*. Paris: UNESCO.

Servaes, J. 2000. 'Advocacy Strategies for Development Communication', in J. Servaes (ed.). *Walking on the Other Side of the Information Highway. Communication, Culture and Development in the 21st Century*. Penang: Southbound.

Singhal, A. and J.W. Dearing. 2006. *Communication of Innovations, A Journey with Ev Rogers*. New Delhi: Sage Publications.

Task Force on Higher Education and Society. 2000. *Higher Education in Developing Countries, Peril and Promise*. Washington: The World Bank.

UNESCO. 2004. 'Women and ICTs–Mediating Social Change' (Video). Available online at http://portal.unesco.org /ci/en/ev.php-URL_ID=18443&URL_DO=DO_TOPIC&URL_SECTION=201.html.

UNICT Task Force. 2001. 'United Nations ICT Task Force, Welcome'. Available online at http://www.unicttaskforce.org/ welcome.

UNICT Task Force. 2005. 'Innovation and Investment: Information and Communication Technologies and the Millennium Development Goals', Report prepared for the United Nations ICT Task Force in Support of the Science & Innovation Task Force of the United Nations Millennium Project. New York.

Warschauer, M. 2003. *Technology and Social Inclusion*. Cambridge: MIT Press.

World Bank. 1994. *The World Bank and Participation*. Washington: The World Bank.

World Health Organization. 1997. *Communicating Family Planning in Reproductive Health*. Geneva: WHO.

Development Communication Approaches in an International Perspective

7

JAN SERVAES AND PATCHANEE MALIKHAO

In this chapter, we present the general concepts which are normally referred to in discussions on development communication. We will address the topic from a historical perspective.

First, in theory, one observes a shift from modernization and dependency theories to more normative and holistic approaches. We have attempted to group these new insights as 'One World, Multiple Cultures' or 'Multiplicity'.

Secondly, also at the policy and planning level one can distinguish between different approaches which could be identified as the 'diffusion model' versus the 'participatory model'.

Thirdly, we will assess the changes which took place throughout the years.

Changing Theories of Development

Modernization

Historical Context

After the Second World War, the founding of the United Nations stimulated relations among sovereign states, especially the North Atlantic Nations and the developing nations, including the new states emerging out of a colonial past. During the Cold War period the superpowers—the United States and the former Soviet Union—tried to expand their own interests to the developing countries. In fact, the USA was defining development as the replica of its own political-economic system and opening the way for the transnational corporations. At the same time, the developing countries saw the 'welfare state' of the North Atlantic Nations as the ultimate goal of development. These nations were attracted by the new technology transfer and the model of a centralized state with careful economic planning and centrally directed development bureaucracies for agriculture, education and health as the most effective strategies to catch up with those industrialized countries.

Modernization and Development

The modernization paradigm, dominant in academic circles from around 1945 to 1965, supported the transferring of technology and the socio-political culture of the developed societies to the 'traditional' societies. Development was defined as economic *growth*. The central idea in the modernization perspective is the idea of evolution, which implies that development is conceived as first, directional and cumulative, secondly, predetermined and irreversible, thirdly, progressive, and fourthly, immanent with reference to the nation-state. The developed Western societies or modern societies seem to be the ultimate goals which the less developed societies strive to reach.

All societies would, passing through similar *stages,* evolve to a common point: the modern society. In order to be a modern society, the attitudes of 'backward' people—their traditionalism, bad taste, superstition, fatalism, etc.—which are obstacles and barriers in the traditional societies have to be removed. The differences among nations are explained in terms of the degree of development rather than the fundamental nature of each. Hence, the central problem of development was thought to revolve around the question of 'bridging the gap' and 'catching up' by means of imitation processes between *traditional and modern sectors,* between retarded and advanced or between 'barbarian' and civilized sectors and groups to the advantage of the latter. These two sectors, the traditional and the modern, were conceived of as two stages of development, co-existing in time, and in due course the differences between them were to disappear because of a natural urge towards equilibrium. The problem was to remove the obstacles or barriers, which were only to be found in the traditional society. These 'barriers' can be 'removed' through at least five mechanisms: through 'demonstration', whereby the developing world tries to 'catch up' with the more developed by adopting more advanced methods and techniques; through 'fusion', which is the combination and integration of distinct modern methods; through 'compression', whereby the developing countries attempt to accomplish the task of development in less time than it took the developed world; through 'prevention', that is, by learning from the 'errors' made by the developed countries; and through the 'adaptation' of modern practices to the local environment and culture. Consequently, the *means of modernization* were the massive transfer of capital, ideology, technology, and know-how, a worldwide Marshall Plan, a green revolution. The measures of progress were Gross National Product (GNP), literacy, industrial base, urbanization, and the like, all *quantifiable criteria.* Everett Rogers (1976:124) writes that although:

India, China, Persia, and Egypt were old, old centres of civilization ... their rich cultures had in fact provided the basis for contemporary Western Cultures ... their family life displayed a warmer intimacy and their artistic triumphs were greater, that was not development. It could not be measured in dollars and cents.

Another characteristic of modernization thought is the emphasis on *mono-disciplinary explanatory factors.* The oldest is the *economic* variant, associated with Walt Rostow (1953). As each discipline within the social sciences approaches the modernization process from its own expert point of view, the scholarship on modernization has become increasingly specialized. Therefore, the orthodox modernization theories fall into one or a combination of the following four categories: *stage theories, index theories* (of mainly economic variables), *differentiation theories* (largely advanced by sociologists and political scientists), and *diffusion theories* (advanced primarily by social psychologists, suggesting that the development process starts with the diffusion of certain ideas, motivations, attitudes or behaviours). Nonetheless, the economic root has always remained the essence of the modernization theory.

In practice modernization accelerated the Westernized elite structure or urbanization. With the help of foreign aid the rural backward areas needed to be developed in the area of agriculture, basic education, health, rural transportation, community development, and so forth. Therefore, the government service bureaucracies have been extended to the major urban centres. The broadcasting system was used mainly for entertainment and news. Radio was a channel for national campaigns to persuade the people in very specific health and agricultural practices. According to Robert White (1988:9):

> The most significant communication dimension of the modernization design in the developing world has been the rapid improvement of the transportation, which linked rural communities into market towns and regional cities. With improved transportation and sources of electric power, the opening of commercial consumer supply networks stretched out into towns and villages carrying with it the Western consumer culture and pop culture of films, radio and pop music. Although rural people in Bolivia or Sri Lanka may not have attained the consumption styles of American middle-class populations, their life did change profoundly. This was the real face of modernization.

Critique

Under the influence of the actual development in most Third World countries, which did not turn out to be so justified as the modernization theory predicted, the first *criticisms* began to be heard in the 1960s, particularly in *Latin America.* In a famous essay, the Mexican sociologist, Rodolfo Stavenhagen (1966) argued that the division into a traditional, agrarian sector and a modern, urban sector was the result of the same development process. In other words, growth and modernization had brought with them greater inequality and underdevelopment. Stavenhagen tested his theses against the situation in Mexico, while others came to similar conclusions for Brazil, and Chile.

The best known critic of the modernization theory is Gunder Frank (1969). His criticism is fundamental and three-fold: the progress paradigm is *empirically untenable,* has an *inadequate theoretical* foundation, and is, in practice, *incapable of generating a development* process in the Third World. Moreover, critics of the modernization paradigm charge that the complexity of the processes of change is too often ignored, that little attention is paid to the consequences of economic, political, and cultural macro-processes on the local level, and that the resistance against change and modernization cannot be explained only on the basis of traditional value orientations and norms, as many seem to imply. The critique did not only concern modernization theory as such, but the whole (Western) tradition of evolutionism and functionalism of which it forms part.

Therefore, referring to the offered unilinear and evolutive perspectives, and the endogenous character of the suggested development solutions, these critics argue that the modernization concept is a veiled synonym for '*westernization*,' namely the copying or implantation of Western mechanisms and institutions in a Third World context. Nowhere is this as clear as in the field of political science. Many Western scholars start from the assumption that the US or West-European political systems are the touchstones for the rest of the world. The rationale for President J.F. Kennedy's Peace Corps Act, for instance, was totally ingrained in this belief.

Dependency

Historical Context
The dependency paradigm played an important role in the movement for a New World Information and Communication Order from the late 1960s to the early 1980s. At that time, the new states in Africa, Asia and the success of socialist and popular movements in Cuba, China, Chile and other countries provided the goals for political, economic and cultural self-determination within the international community of nations. These new nations shared the ideas of being independent from the superpowers and moved to form the Non-Aligned Nations. The Non-Aligned Movement defined development as *political struggle*.

Dependency and Development
At a theoretical level, the dependency approach emerged from the convergence of two intellectual traditions: one often called neo-Marxism or structuralism, and the other rooted in the extensive Latin American debate on development that ultimately formed the ECLA tradition (the United Nations' Economic Commission for Latin America). Therefore, in contrast to the modernization theory, the dependency perspective was given birth in Latin America. The so-called 'father' of the dependency theory, however, is considered to be the American, Paul Baran (1957), who is spokesperson for the North American Monthly Review group. He was one of the first to articulate the thesis that development and underdevelopment are *interrelated processes*, that is, they are two sides of the same coin. In Baran's view, continued imperialist dependence after the end of the colonial period is ensured first and foremost by the reproduction of socio-economic and political structures at the periphery in accordance with the interests of the Centre powers. This is the main cause of the chronic backwardness of the developing countries, since the main interest of Western monopoly capitalism was to prevent, or, if that was impossible, to slow down and to control the economic development of underdeveloped countries. As Baran uncompromisingly

puts it, the irrationality of the present system will not be overcome so long as its basis, the capitalist system, continues to exist.

Some dependistas worked exclusively with economic variables, while others also took social and political factors into consideration in their research. Typically the scientific divisions of economics, political science, sociology, history and the like, which were being used in the West, were less rigidly distinguished in the Latin American division of scientific labour. Some stressed the sectoral and regional oppositions within the dependency system (for example, Sunkel); others (for example, Cardoso) were more concerned with possible class oppositions. Opinions also differed about one of the central elements in dependency theory, that is, the specific relationship between development and underdevelopment. While Frank observes what he termed 'a development towards underdevelopment', Cardoso argued that a certain degree of (dependent) capitalist development is possible.

However, as varied their approaches may be, all dependistas will agree to the basic idea exemplified in the following definition by Dos Santos (1970:231):

Dependence is a conditioning situation in which the economies of one group of countries are conditioned by the development and expansion of others. A relationship of interdependence between two or more economies or between such economies and the world trading system becomes a dependent relationship when some countries can expand through self-impulsion while others, being in a dependent position, can only expand as a reflection of the expansion of the dominant countries, which may have positive or negative effects on their immediate development. In either case, the basic situation of dependence causes these countries to be both backward and exploited. Dominant countries are endowed with technological, commercial, capital and socio-political predominance over dependent countries—the form of this predominance varying according to the particular historical moment—and can therefore exploit them, and extract part of the locally produced surplus. Dependence, then, is based upon an international division of labour which allows industrial development to take place in some countries while restricting it in others, whose growth is conditioned by and subjected to the power centres of the world.

Critique

Hence, according to the dependency theory, the most important hindrances to development are not the shortage of capital or management, as the modernization theorists contend, but must be sought in the present international system. The obstacles are thus not internal but external. This also means that development in the Centre determines and maintains the underdevelopment in the Periphery. The two poles are structurally connected to each other. To remove these external obstacles, they argue, each peripheral country should dissociate itself from the world market and opt for a self-reliant development strategy. To make this happen, most scholars advocated that a more or less revolutionary political transformation will be necessary. Therefore, one may say that the dependency paradigm in general as well as in its sub-sector of communication is characterized by a global approach, an emphasis on external factors and regional contradictions, a polarization between development and underdevelopment, a subjectivist or voluntaristic interpretation of history, and a primarily economically-oriented analytical method.

As a result, the only alternative for non-aligned nations was to *disassociate* themselves from the world market and achieve self-reliance, both economically and culturally. The *New International Economic Order* is one example of attempts towards this end. However, many non-aligned countries were simply too weak economically, and too indebted, to operate autonomously. As a result, attempts to legislate integral, coherent national communication policies failed because of the resistance of national and transnational media interests. As Friberg and Hettne (1985:212) point out, 'Self-reliance is a difficult option in the context of the present world order.' Because of this, McAnany (1983:4) characterized dependency theory as '... good on diagnosis of the problem ... but poor on prescription of the cure.' Dependency addressed the causes of underdevelopment, but did not provide ways of addressing that underdevelopment.

Multiplicity/Another Development

Historical Context

Since the demarcation of the First, Second and Third Worlds is breaking down and the crossover centre-periphery can be found in every region, there is a need for a new concept of development which emphasizes cultural identity and multidimensionality. For example, some countries may be dependent economically but have greater cultural 'power' in the region. Therefore, the previously held dependency perspective has become more difficult to support because of the growing interdependency of nations. The concept of *'another development'* was first articulated in the industrialized nations of northern Europe, particularly by the Dag Hammarskjold Foundation in Sweden and the Green political movement in Germany. This does not mean, however, that the 'another development' concepts and perspective is Western. It can also be traced back in Third World environments.

Multiplicity and Another Development

The Dag Hammarskjold Foundation established three foundations for another development: (1) Another Development is geared to the satisfaction of needs, beginning with the eradication of poverty; (2) Another development is endogenous and self-reliant; and (3) Another development is in harmony with the environment. Another development applies to all levels of all societies, not just the poor of the non-aligned world. It grew from dissatisfaction in the 'consumer society,' with what is sometimes termed 'overdevelopment' or even 'mal-development', as well as the growing disillusionment with the modernization approach.

The central idea, which is pointed out by almost everybody who is searching for new approaches towards development, is that there is *no universal path to development*, that development must be conceived as an *integral, multidimensional, and dialectic process* which can differ from one society to another. This does not mean, however, that one cannot attempt to define the general principles and priorities on which such a strategy can be based. Indeed, several authors have been trying to gather the core components for another development. From the search of these authors, we would cite six criteria as essential for 'another' development.

Such development must be based on the following principles:

(a) *Basic needs*: being geared to meeting human, material and non-material, needs.

(b) *Endogenous*: stemming from the heart of each society, which defines in sovereignty its values and the vision of its future.

(c) *Self-reliance*: implying that each society relies primarily on its own strength and resources in terms of its members' energies and its natural and cultural environment.

(d) *Ecology*: utilizing rationally resources of the biosphere in full awareness of the potential of local ecosystems, as well as the global and outer limits imposed on present and future generations.

(e) *Participative democracy*: as the true form of democracy: not merely government of the people and for the people, but also, and more fundamentally, 'by the people' at all levels of society.

(f) *Structural changes*: to be required, more often than not, in social relations, in economic activities and in their spatial distribution, as well as in the power structure, so as to realize the conditions of self-managements and participation in decision-making by all those affected by it, from the rural or urban community to the world as a whole.

In practice, adopting some or all of the above principles, new forms of communication have been emerging. Decentralized media systems and democratic communication institutions, such as Mahaweli community radio in Sri Lanka and Radio Enriquillo in the Dominican Republic, emphasize self-management by local communities. New concepts of media professionalism bring a greater knowledge of—and respect for—forms of people's communication, emphasize the recognition of and experience with new formats of journalism and broadcasting which are more consonant with the cultural identity of the community, and create greater awareness of the ways democratization of communication is taking, and can take, place.

Mixed Approaches

This review of three perspectives on development reveals a number of *shifts in scientific thought*:

1. from a more positivistic, quantitative, and comparative approach to a normative, qualitative and structural approach;

2. from highly prescribed and predictable processes to less predictable and change-oriented processes;

3. from an ethnocentric view to an indigenous view and then to a contextual and polycentric view;

4. from endogenism ('blame the victim') to exogenism ('blame the outsider') and then to globalism and holism;

5. from an economic interest to more universal and interdisciplinary interests;

6. from a primarily national frame of reference to an international perspective and then to combined levels of analysis;

7. from segmentary to holistic approaches and then to more problem-oriented approaches;
8. from an integrative and reformist strategy to revolutionary options and then to an integral vision of revolutionary and evolutionary change;
9. from technocratic/administrative views on development to more problem-posing and participatory perspectives.

Theoretical Approaches to Development Communication (Devcom)

Communication theories such as the 'diffusion of innovations', the 'two-step-flow', or the 'extension' approaches are quite congruent with the above modernization theory. According to Everett Rogers, one of the leading proponents of the diffusion theory, this perspective implies

> that the role of communication was (1) to transfer technological innovations from development agencies to their clients, and (2) to create an appetite for change through raising a "climate for modernization" among the members of the public (Rogers, 1986:49).

The elitist, vertical or *top-down orientation of the diffusion model* is obvious. However, the reality often proves much more complex than the theory. Therefore, many authors and development workers point out that decision-making and planning cannot be done by bureaucrats and policy-makers for the people but only by these 'experts' together with all concerned institutions and together with the people. In other words, in accordance with discussions on international political and academic forums like UNESCO, FAO or IAMCR, these people refer to newer insights on the role and place of communication for development which favours *two-way and horizontal communication*: 'The systematic utilization of appropriate communication and techniques to increase peoples' participation in development and to inform, motivate, and train rural population, mainly at the grass-root level' (FAO, 1987:4). Though it can be argued that this approach still remains 'paternalistic' or a social marketing strategy, it at least distinguishes between policy and planning-making at micro and macro levels.

Before we elaborate on the related changes in strategies and techniques, we summarize the major theoretical characteristics of both theoretical approaches to Development Communication: the Diffusion/Mechanistic Model and the Participatory/Organic Model.

The Diffusion Model

General
The 1950s was the *decade of the communication model*. Interestingly, one of the earliest and most influential of these came not from the social sciences or humanities, but from information

engineering. Shannon and Weaver's linear 'source-transmitter-channel-receiver-destination' model eclipsed the earlier, more organic, psychological and sociological approaches. Lasswell, Hofland, Newcomb, Schramm, Westley and Mclean, Berlo, and others each devised a model of communication as they conceived it. This profusion of communication models may be attributed to three reasons.

First, because they identified communication basically as the *transfer* of information (the stimulus) they were amenable to empirical methodology, thus establishing the basis for communication as a distinct and legitimate science.

Secondly, theorists focussed on the efficiency, or *effects*, of communication, (the response), thereby holding vast promise for manipulation or control of message 'receivers' by vested interests, or the 'sources'.

Finally, the communication models fit neatly into the nature and mechanics of mass or *mediated communication*, an emergent and powerful force at that time.

Therefore, in these years the discipline of communication was largely, and most importantly, its effects. The 'bullet' or 'hypodermic needle' effects of media were to be a quick and efficient answer to a myriad of social ills. Robert White (1982:30) writes 'This narrow emphasis on media and media effects has also led to a premise ... that media information is an all-powerful panacea for problems of human and socioeconomic development,' not to mention dilemmas of marketing and propaganda. Falling short of exuberant claims, direct effects became limited effects, minimal effects, conditional effects, and the 'two-step flow'.

More Specific Communication Approaches

In these years, more sociological, psychological, political, and cultural factors were considered in the view of modernization. The place and role of the communication processes in the modernization perspective was also further examined, with the American presidential election campaigns functioning as the theoretical framework.

These models saw the communication process as a message going from a sender to a receiver. Out of a study in Erie County, Ohio, of the 1940 US presidential elections came the idea of the so-called '*two step flow of communication*' (Lazarsfeld et al., 1944). Although the researchers expected to find that the mass media (radio and press) had a great influence on the election, they concluded that voting decisions were chiefly influenced by personal contacts and face to face persuasion. The first formulation of the two-step-flow hypothesis was the following: 'Ideas often flow from radio and print to opinion leaders and from these to less active sections of the population' (ibid.:151). Thus, two elements are involved: (a) the notion of a population divided into 'active' and 'passive' participants, or 'opinion leaders' and 'followers'; and (b) the notion of a two-step-flow of influence rather than a direct contact between 'stimulus' and 'respondent', (or the so-called bullet or hypodermic needle theory). Since that time the concept and role of 'personal influence' has acquired a high status in research on campaigns and diffusions, especially in the US. The general conclusion of this line of thought is that mass communication is less likely than personal influence to have a direct effect on social behaviour. Mass communication is important in spreading awareness of new possibilities and practices, but at the stage where decisions are being made about whether to adopt or not to adopt, personal communication was far more likely to be influential.

Therefore, we could characterize this era as '*sender- and media-centric*'. The new models, in conjunction with the obsession with the mass media, led to a conceptualization of communication as something one does to another. White (1984:2) argues this pro-media, pro-effects, and anti-egalitarian bias of communication theory '... has developed largely as an explanation of the power and effects of mass communication and does not provide adequate explanation of the factors of social change leading toward democratization.'

Building primarily on sociological research in agrarian societies, Everett Rogers (1962, 1983) stressed the *adoption and diffusion processes of cultural innovation*. Modernization is here conceived as a process of diffusion whereby individuals move from a traditional way of life to a more complex, more technically developed and more rapidly changing way of life. This approach is therefore concerned with the process of diffusion and adoption of innovations in a more systematic and planned way. He distinguishes between five phases in the diffusion process: awareness, interest, evaluation, trial and adoption. The role of the mass media is concentrated on the first stage of the process, whereas 'personal sources are most important at the evaluation stage in the adoption process' (Rogers, 1962:99). In a second edition of his work (Rogers and Schoemaker, 1973), there are only four crucial steps left in the process of diffusion and adoption: (a) the knowledge of the innovation itself (information), (b) the communication of the innovation (persuasion), (c) the decision to adopt or reject the innovation (adoption or rejection), and (d) the confirmation of the innovation by the individual.

Three more approaches contributed to the success of this diffusion model: that is, a psycho-sociological, institutional and technological interpretation of communication for modernization.

The *psycho-sociological or behaviouristic perspective* on communication and modernization is particularly concerned with the individual value and attitude change. Rokeach (1966) defined '*attitude*' as 'a relatively enduring organization of beliefs about an object or situation predisposing one to respond in some preferential manner'. 'Attitude change' would then be 'a change in predisposition, the change being either a change in the organization or structure of beliefs, or a change in the content of one or more of the beliefs entering into the attitude organization' (ibid.:530). Central in the view of Daniel Lerner (1958), one of the main representatives of this communication for modernization paradigm, is the concept of '*empathy*', that is, 'the capacity to see oneself in the other fellow's situation, ... which is an indispensable skill for people moving out of traditional settings'. The major hypothesis of his study was that 'high empathic is the predominant personal style only in modern society, which is distinctively industrial, urban, literate and participant' (ibid.:50). Central in his research design was the individual-psychological capacity of people to adjust themselves to modern environments. Empathic persons had a higher degree of mobility, meaning a high capacity for change, being future-oriented and rational, more than so-called traditional people. Therefore, according to Lerner, mobility stimulates urbanization, which increases literacy and consequently also economic and political participation.

Also the role and function of the mass media is carefully examined in this context: 'He (that is, the modern man, JS) places his trust in the mass media rather than in personal media for world news, and prefers national and international news rather than sports, religious or hometown news' (Inkeles and Smith, 1972:112). In other words, the media stimulate, in direct and indirect ways, mobility and economic development; they are the 'motivators' and 'movers' for change and modernization.

Wilbur Schramm (1964), building on Lerner, took a closer look on this *connection between mass communication and modernizing practices and institutions*. The modern communication media supplement and complement as 'mobility multipliers' the oral channels of a traditional society. Their development runs parallel to the development of other institutions of modern society, such as schools and industry, and is closely related to some of the indices of general social and economic growth, such as literacy, per capita income, and urbanization. So he claimed that 'a developing country should give special attention to combining mass media with interpersonal communication' (ibid.:263). In Schramm's opinion, mass media perform at least three functions: they are the 'watchdogs', 'policymakers', and 'teachers' for change and modernization.

A third, *technologically deterministic approach*, sees technology to be a value-free and politically neutral asset that can be used in every social and historical context. Within this perspective at least four different points of view can be distinguished. A first rather optimistic view shares the conviction that the development and application of technology can resolve all the varied problems of mankind. The second view comes the previous one to the opposite extreme, namely the conception that technology is the source of all what goes wrong in societies. A third variant expresses the view of technology as the pre-potent factor in development, it sees technology as the driving force to development. The fourth variant has become popular by Marshall McLuhan (1964). It views technology as an inexorable force in development, an irresistible as well as an overwhelming force. As McLuhan (1964:VIII) puts it: 'Any technology gradually creates a totally new human environment,' or, in other words: the medium is the message.

The 'Framework of Reference' of Modernization and Dependency

While supporters of the communication for modernization theory take the *nation-state* as their main framework of reference, dependistas believe in a predominantly *international level of analysis*. They argue that the domination of the Periphery by the Centre occurs through a combination of power components, that is, military, economics, politics, culture, and so on. The specific components of the domination of any nation at a given point of time vary from those of another as a result of the variations in numerous factors, including the resources of the Centre powers, the nature or structure of the Periphery nation, and the degree of resistance to domination. Nowadays the cultural and communication components are of great importance in continuing the dependent relationships. Because, as many scholars argue, we stand within the rather paradoxical situation that, as the Third World begins to emancipate itself economically and politically, cultural dominance increases. While the former colonialist was largely out to plunder economically profitable areas and showed often only moderate interest in political administration, the technological evolution of the communication media have contributed to a cultural and ideological dependence.

In many ways dependency is the antithesis of modernization, but at the level of communication it is a continuation of it. Dependency theory argues that the prevailing conditions in the non-aligned world are not a stage in the evolution towards development, but rather the result of extant international structures. In other words, whereas the modernization perspective holds that the causes of underdevelopment lay mainly *within* the developing nation, dependency theory postulates the reasons for underdevelopment are primarily *external* to the dependent society.

The Participatory Model

General

The participatory model incorporates the concepts in the emerging framework of multiplicity/another development. It stresses the importance of *cultural identity* of local communities and of *democratization and participation* at all levels—international, national, local and individual. It points to a strategy, not merely inclusive of, but largely emanating from, the traditional 'receivers'. Paulo Freire (1983:76) refers to this as the right of all people to individually and collectively speak their word:

> This is not the privilege of some few men, but the right of every man. Consequently, no one can say a true word alone—nor can he say it for another, in a prescriptive act which robs others of their words.

In order to share information, knowledge, trust, commitment, and a right attitude in development projects participation is very important in any decision-making process for development. 'This calls for new attitude for overcoming stereotyped thinking and to promote more understanding of diversity and plurality, with full respect for the dignity and equality of peoples living in different conditions and acting in different ways' (International Commission for the Study of Communication Problems, 1980:254). This model stresses reciprocal collaboration throughout all levels of participation. Listening to what the others say, respecting the counterpart's attitude, and having mutual trust are needed. Participation supporters do not underestimate the ability of the masses to develop themselves and their environment.

> Development efforts should be anchored on faith in the people's capacity to discern what is best to be done as they seek their liberation, and how to participate actively in the task of transforming society. The people are intelligent and have centuries of experience. Draw out their strength. Listen to them. (Xavier Institute, 1980:11)

Cultural Identity, Empowerment, and Participatory Communication

According to many authors, authentic participation directly addresses *power* and its distribution in society. Participation 'may not sit well with those who favour the status quo and thus they may be expected to resist such efforts of reallocation more power to the people' (Lozare, 1989:2). Therefore, development and participation are inextricably linked.

Participation involves the more equitable sharing of both political and economic power, which often decreases the advantage of certain groups. *Structural change* involves the redistribution of power. In mass communication areas, many communication experts agree that structural change should occur first in order to establish participatory communication policies. Mowlana and Wilson (1987:143), for instance, state:

> Communications policies are basically derivatives of the political, cultural and economic conditions and institutions under which they operate. They tend to legitimize the existing power relations in society, and therefore, they cannot be substantially changed unless there are fundamental structural changes in society that can alter these power relationships themselves.

Since dialogue and face to face interaction is inherent in participation, the development communicator will find him/herself spending more time in the field. It will take some time to develop rapport and trust. Continued contact, meeting commitments, keeping promises, and follow-up between visits is important. Development of social trust precedes task trust. Both parties will need patience. It is important to note that when we treat people the way we ourselves would like to be treated, we learn to work as a team, and this brings about rural commitment and motivation too. Thus honesty, trust, and commitment from the higher-ups bring honesty, trust, and commitment for the grassroots as well. This brings about true participation. And true participation brings about appropriate policies and planning for developing a country or community within its cultural and envir-onmental framework.

Consequently also the perspective on communication has changed. It is more concerned with *process and context,* that is, on the exchange of 'meanings,' and on the importance of this process, namely, the social relational patterns and social institutions that are the result of and are determined by the process. 'Another' communication 'favours multiplicity, smallness of scale, locality, de-institutionalization, interchange of sender-receiver roles (and) horizontality of communication links at all levels of society' (McQuail, 1983:97). As a result, the focus moves *from a 'communicator' to a more 'receiver-centric' orientation, with the resultant emphasis on meaning sought and ascribed rather than information transmitted.*

With this shift in focus, one is no longer attempting to create a need for the information one is disseminating, but one is rather disseminating information for which there is a need. Experts and development workers respond rather than dictate, they choose what is relevant to the context in which they are working. The emphasis is on information exchange rather than on the persuasion in the diffusion model.

Two Major Approaches to Participatory Communication

There are two major approaches to participatory communication which everybody today accepts as common sense. The first is the dialogical pedagogy of Paulo Freire, and the second involves the ideas of access, participation and self-management articulated in the UNESCO debates of the 1970s. Every communication project which calls itself participatory accepts these principles of democratic communication. Nonetheless there exists today a wide variety of practical experiences and intentions. Before moving on to explore these differences it is useful to briefly review the common ground.

The Freirian argument works by a dual theoretical strategy. He insists that subjugated peoples must be treated as fully human subjects in any political process. This implies dialogical communication. Although inspired to some extent by Sartre's existentialism—a respect for the autonomous personhood of each human being—the more important source is a theology that demands respect for otherness—in this case that of another human being. The second strategy is a moment of utopian hope derived from the early Marx that the human species has a destiny which is more than life as a fulfilment of material needs. Also from Marx is an insistence on collective solutions. Individual opportunity, Freire stresses, is no solution to general situations of poverty and cultural subjugation.

These ideas are deeply unpopular with elites, including elites in the Third World, but there is nonetheless widespread acceptance of Freire's notion of dialogic communication as a normative theory of participatory communication. One problem with Freire is that his theory of dialogical communication is based on group dialogue rather than such amplifying media as radio, print and television. Freire also gives little attention to the language or form of communication, devoting most of his discussion to the intentions of communication actions.

The second discourse about participatory communication is the UNESCO language about self-management, access and participation from the 1977 meeting in Belgrade, the former Yugoslavia. The final report of that meeting defines the terms in the following way:

Access refers to the use of media for public service. It may be defined in terms of the opportunities available to the public to choose varied and relevant programs and to have a means of feedback to transmit its reactions and demands to production organisations.

Participation implies a higher level of public involvement in communication systems. It includes the involvement of the public in the production process, and also in the management and planning of communication systems.

Participation may be no more than representation and consultation of the public in decision-making. On the other hand, *self-management* is the most advanced form of participation. In this case, the public exercises the power of decision-making within communication enterprises and is also fully involved in the formulation of communication policies and plans.

These ideas are important and widely accepted as a normative theory of alternative communication: it must involve access and participation. However, one should note some differences from Freire. The UNESCO discourse includes the idea of a gradual progression. Some amount of access may be allowed, but self-management may be postponed until some time in the future. Freire's theory allows for no such compromise. One either respects the culture of the other or falls back into domination and the 'banking' mode of imposed education. The UNESCO discourse talks in neutral terms about 'the public'. Freire talked about the oppressed. Finally, the UNESCO discourse puts the main focus on the institution. Participatory radio means a radio station that is self-managed by those participating in it.

Assessing the Changes

In his summary of the Asian development communication policies and planning, Peter Habermann reaches the following conclusions:

> The difficulties for the adoption of a viable development communication policy are caused very much by the fact that the planning of such a policy has to take into account that there is a horizontal and a vertical level which requires simultaneous approaches. The horizontal and vertical level consists of diversified institutions such as governmental developments, semi-governmental agencies (Rural Extension Service etc.), independent development organizations, and private media, which are all active in communication in one way or the other. The coordination of these institutions, e.g. the problem of assigning them to communicative tasks they are able to perform best becomes thus a major item of a meaningful development communication policy. The vertical level is defined by the need for a mutual information flow between the population base and the decision-making bodies. On this level even more institutions are involved because of the local and supra-local administrations which of course are active in handing out directives and in feeding back reports to the government. Coordination of development communication becomes a more difficult task on this level because with the exception of the governmental extensions no institution is really prepared until now to pick up the information from the grass root levels and feeding them back meaningfully to the administration (Habermann and G. de Fontgalland, 1978:173).

Neville Jayaweera, in the introduction of the follow-up on Habermann and de Fontgalland's publication, specifies that

> (a) the pursuit of the modernization model, as recommended by the modernization and diffusion theorists and policy-makers, was neither practicable nor desirable; (b) Third World societies should aim instead to satisfy the 'basic needs' of their people; (c) fundamental reforms in the structures of international trade and monetary institutions were a necessary condition of development; (d) likewise, fundamental structural reforms within Third World societies themselves, such as land reform, opportunities for political participation, decentralization etc., were a prerequisite for development; (e) reliance on foreign aid and capital intensive technology must give way to self-reliance and appropriate technology, and that the bias for industry must give way to a greater commitment to agriculture; and (f) development is unthinkable except within a framework of culture. (Jayaweera and Amunaguma, 1987:xvii)

In accordance with the findings of these and other scholars we perceive a number of changes in the field of communication for development which may have considerable *consequences for communication policy and planning-making*:

1. The Growth of a Deeper Understanding of the Nature of Communication Itself

The perspective on communication has changed. As explained above, early models in the 1950s and 1960s saw the communication process simply as a message going from a sender to a receiver, (that is, Laswell's classic S-M-R model). The emphasis was mainly sender- and media-centric; the stress laid on the freedom of the press, the absence of censorship, and so on. Since the 1970s, however, communication has become more receiver- and message-centric.

The emphasis now is more on the process of communication (that is, the exchange of meaning), *and on the significance of this process* (that is, the social relationships created by communication and the social institutions and context which result from such relationships).

2. A New Understanding of Communication as a Two-Way Process

With this shift in focus, one is no longer attempting to create a need for the information one is disseminating, but one is rather *disseminating information for which there is a need*. The emphasis is on information exchange rather than on the persuasion in the diffusion model.

The 'oligarchic' view of communication implied that freedom of information was a one-way right from a higher to a lower level, from the Centre to the Periphery, from an institution to an individual, from a communication-rich nation to a communication-poor one, and so on. Today, the interactive nature of communication is increasingly recognized. It is seen as fundamentally two-way rather than one-way, interactive and participatory rather than linear.

3. A New Understanding of Culture

The cultural perspective has become central to the debate on communication for development. Culture is not only the visible, non-natural environment of a person, but primarily his/her normative context. Consequently, one has moved away from a more traditional mechanistic approach that emphasized economic and materialistic criteria to more *multiple appreciations of holistic and complex perspectives*.

4. The Trend towards Participatory Democracy

The end of the colonial era has seen the rise of many independent states and the spread of democratic principles, even if only at the level of lip service. Though often ignored in practice, democracy is honoured in theory. Governments and/or powerful private interests still largely control the world's communication media, but they are more attuned to and aware of the democratic ideals than previously. At the same time, literacy levels have increased, and there has been a remarkable improvement in people's ability to handle and use communication technology. As a consequence, *more and more people can use communication media and can no longer be denied access to and participation in communication processes for the lack of communication and technical skills.*

5. Recognition of the Imbalance in Communication Resources or the Digital Divide

The disparity in communication resources between different parts of the world is increasingly recognized as a cause of concern. As the Centre nations develop their resources, the gap between Centre and Periphery becomes greater. *The plea for a more balanced and equal distribution of communication resources can only be discussed in terms of power at local, national and international levels.* The attempt by local power-elites to totally control the modern communication channels—press, broadcasting, education, and bureaucracy—does no longer ensure control of all the communication networks in a given society. Nor does control of the mass media ensure support for the controlling forces, nor for any mobilization around their objectives, nor for the effective repression of opposition.

Some may argue that thanks to the new ICTs, especially the Internet and World Wide Web, one has to re-address the debate on the digital divide; however, others remain sceptical and less optimistic.

6. The Growing Sense of Globalization and Cultural Hybridity

Perhaps the greatest impetus towards a new formulation of communication freedoms and the need for realistic communication policies and planning have come from the realization that the international flow of communication has become the main carrier of cultural globalization. This cultural hybridity can take place without perceptible dependent relationships.

7. A New Understanding of What is Happening within the Boundaries of the Nation-State

One has to accept that 'internal' and 'external' factors inhibiting development do not exist independently of each other. Thus, in order to understand and develop a proper strategy one must have an understanding of the class relationships of any particular peripheral social formation and the ways in which these structures articulate with the Centre on the one hand, and the producing classes in the Third World on the other. To dismiss Third World ruling classes, for example, as mere puppets whose interests are always mechanically synonymous with those of the Centre is to ignore the realities of a much more complex relationship. The very unevenness and contradictory nature of the capitalist development process necessarily produces *a constantly changing relationship*.

8. Recognition of the 'Impact' of Communication Technology

Some communication systems, (for example, audio- and video-taping, copying, radio broadcasting, and especially the Internet), have become *cheap* and so simple that the rationale for regulating and controlling them centrally, as well as the ability to do so, is no longer relevant. However, other systems, (for instance, satellites, remote sensing, trans-border data flows), remain *very expensive*. They are beyond the means of smaller countries and may not be 'suitable' to local environments.

9. From an Information Society to Knowledge Societies

Information has been seen as the leading growth sector in society, especially in advanced industrial economies. Its three strands—computing, telecommunications and broadcasting—have evolved historically as three separate sectors, and by means of digitization these sectors are now converging.

Throughout the past decade a gradual shift can be observed away from a technological in favour of more socio-economic and cultural definitions of the Information Society. The term Knowledge Societies (in plural as there are many roads) better coins this shift in emphasis *from ICTs as 'drivers' of change to a perspective where these technologies are regarded as tools which may provide a new potential for combining the information embedded in ICT systems with the creative potential and knowledge embodied in people*: 'These technologies do not create the transformations in society by themselves; they are designed and implemented by people in their social, economic, and technological contexts' (Mansell and Wehn, 1998:12).

True knowledge is more than information. It includes the meaning or interpretation of the information, and a lot of intangibles such as the tacit knowledge of experienced people that is not well articulated but often determines collective organizational competence. Knowledge is the sense that people make of information. Knowledge in society is not objective or static, but is ever changing and infused with the values and realities faced by those who have it.

Meaning is not something that is delivered to people, people create/interpret it themselves. If knowledge is to be effectively employed to help people, it needs to be interpreted and evaluated by those it is designed to help. That requires people to have access to information on the issues that affect their lives, and the capacity to make their own contributions to policy-making processes. Understanding the context in which knowledge moves—factors of control, selection, purpose, power, and capacity—is essential for understanding how societies can become better able to learn, generate and act on knowledge (for more details, see Breit and Servaes, 2005).

10. A New Understanding towards Integration of Distinct Means of Communication

Modern mass media and alternate or parallel networks of folk media or interpersonal communication channels are not mutually exclusive by definition. Contrary to the beliefs of diffusion theorists, they are *more effective if appropriately used in an integrated fashion, according to the needs and constraints of the local context.* The modern mass media, having been mechanically transplanted from abroad into Third World societies, enjoy varying and limited rates of penetration. They are seldom truly integrated into institutional structures, as occurs in some Western societies. However, they can be effectively combined, provided a functional division of labour is established between them, and provided the limits of the communication media are recognized.

11. The Recognition of Dualistic or Parallel Communication Structures

No longer governments or rulers are able to operate effectively, to control, censor, or to play the role of gatekeeper with regard to all communications networks at all times in a given society. *Both alternate and parallel networks, which may not always be active, often function through political, socio-cultural, religious or class structures or can be based upon secular, cultural, artistic, or folkloric channels.* These networks feature a highly participatory character, high rates of credibility, and a strong organic integration with other institutions deeply rooted in a given society.

Conclusion

It should be obvious by now that no all-embracing view on development is on offer. No theory has achieved and maintained explanatory dominance. Each of the above three theoretical perspectives still does find support among academics, policy-makers, international organizations, and the general public. In general, adopted and updated versions of the ideas upon which the modernization theory is built—economic growth, centralized planning, and the belief that under-development is rooted in mainly internal causes which can be solved by external (technological) 'aid'—are still shared by many development agencies and governments. A *revitalised modernization perspective* in which some of the errors of the past are acknowledged and efforts are made to deal in new ways, as outlined in the multiplicity view, *remains the dominant perspective in practice but becomes increasingly more difficult to defend in theory.* On the other side, while the multiplicity theory is gaining ground in academic spheres, in practice it is still looked upon as a sympathetic though idealistic side show.

References

Albrow, M. and E. King (eds). 1990. *Globalization, Knowledge and Society*. London: Sage Publications.

Axinn, G. 1988. *Guide on Alternative Extension Approaches*. Rome: FAO.

Balit, S. 1988. 'Rethinking Development Support Communication', *Development Communication Report*, 3:62.

Baran, P. 1957. *The Political Economy of Growth*. New York: Monthly Review Press.

Beltran, L.R. 1993. 'Communication for Development in Latin America: A Forty Years Appraisal.' Keynote speech at the Opening of the IV Roundtable on Development Communication, Instituto para America Latina (IPAL), February 23–26, Lima.

Berrigan, F. 1979. *Community Communications. The Role of Community Media in Development*. Paris: UNESCO.

Blomstrom, M. and B. Hettne. 1984. *Development Theory in Transition. The Dependency Debate and Beyond*. London: Zed.

Boafo, K. 1989. *Communication and Culture: African Perspectives*. Nairobi: ACCE.

Boyd-Barrett, O. 1982. 'Cultural Dependency and the Mass Media', in M. Gurevitch, T. Bennett, J. Curran and J. Woollacott (eds). *Culture, Society and the Media*. London: Methuen.

Breit, R. and J. Servaes (eds). 2005. *Information Society or Knowledge Societies? UNESCO in the Smart State*. Penang: Southbound.

Casmir, F. (ed.). 1991. *Communication in Development*. Norwood: Ablex.

Chilcote, R. and D. Johnson (eds). 1983. *Theories of Development. Mode of Production or Dependency?*. Beverly Hills: Sage Publications.

CINCO. 1987. *Comunicacion Dominante y Comunicacion Alternativa en Bolivia*. La Paz: CINCO/IDRC.

Clegg, S. 1989. *Frameworks of Power*. London: Sage Publications.

De Schutter, A. 1983. *Investigacion Participativa: una Opcion Metodologica para la Educacion de Adultos*. Mexico: Crefal.

Decker, P. 1989. *Que siga adelante ... The role of Grassroots Communications in Community Development: Experiences from Tijuana, Mexico*. Stanford: Center for Latin American Studies, Stanford University.

Dos Santos, T. 1970. 'The Structure of Dependency', *American Economic Review*, 60(21), May.

Escobar, A. and S. Alvarez (eds). 1992. *The Making of Social Movements in Latin America: Identity, Strategy and Democracy*. San Francisco: Westview.

Fals Borda, O. (ed.). 1985 . *The Challenge of Social Change*. London: Sage Publications.

Food and Agriculture Organization (FAO). 1987. *Perspectives on Communication for Rural Development*. Rome: FAO.

Fox, E. 1988. *Media and Politics in Latin America. The Struggle for Democracy*. London: Sage Publications.

Frank, A.G. 1969. *Latin America: Underdevelopment or Revolution*. New York: Monthly Review Press.

Freire, P. 1970. 'Cultural Action and Conscientization', *Harvard Educational Review*, 40(3).

———. 1983. *Pedagogy of the Oppressed*. New York: Seaburg Press.

Friberg, M. and B. Hettne. 1985. *The Greening of the World Development as Social Transformation*. Boulder: Westview.

Galtung, J. 1980. *The True Worlds. A Transnational Perspective*. New York: Free Press.

Graff, R.D. (ed.). 1983. *Communication for National Development. Lessons from Experience*. Cambridge: Oelgeschlager, Gunn & Hain.

Gunder, F. and M. Fuentes. 1988. 'Nine Theses on Social Movements', *IFDA Dossier*, 63:27–44.

Habermann, P. and G. de Fontgalland (eds). 1978. *Development Communication—Rhetoric and Reality*. Singapore: AMIC.

Hamelink, C. 1983. *Cultural Autonomy in Global Communications. Planning National Information Policy*. New York: Longman.

Hancock, A. 1992. *Communication Planning Revisited*. Paris: UNESCO.

Harrison, D. 1988. *The Sociology of Modernization and Development*. London: Unwin Hyman.

Hedebro, G. 1982. *Communication and Social Change in Developing Countries. A Critical View*. Ames: Iowa State University Press.

Hettne, B. 1982. *Development Theory and the Third World*. Stockholm: SAREC.

Hofmann, R. 1981. *Kommunikation und Entwicklung. Applikation eines Lateinamerikanischen Modells (Paulo Freire-Mario Kaplun) in Indonesien*. Frankfurt am Main: Peter Lang.

Hulme, D. and M. Turner. 1990. *Sociology and Development*. New York: Harvester Wheatsheaf.

Inkeles, A. and D. Smith. 1974. *Becoming Modern. Individual Change in Six Developing Countries*. Cambridge: Harvard University Press.

Jamias, J. (ed.). 1975. *Readings in Development Communication*. Laguna: UP at Los Banos.

Jayaweera, N. and S. Amunaguma (eds). 1987. *Rethinking Development Communication*. Singapore: AMIC.

Korten, D. (ed.). 1986. *Community Management: Asian Experience and Perspectives.* West Hartford: Kumarian Press.

Kumar, K. (ed.). 1988. 'Communication and Development', special issue of *Communication Research Trends*, 9(3).

Kunczik, M. 1985. *Massenmedien und Entwicklungsländer.* Köln: Böhlau.

Lazarsfeld, P., B. Berelson and H. Gaudet. 1944. *The People's Choice.* New York: Duell, Sloan and Pearce.

Lerner, D. 1958. *The Passing of Traditional Society. Modernizing the Middle East.* New York: Free Press.

Lerner, D. and W. Schramm (eds). 1967. *Communication and Change in the Developing Countries.* Honolulu: University Press of Hawaii.

Long, N. and A. Long (eds). 1992. *Battlefields of Knowledge. The Interlocking of Theory and Practice in Social Research and Development.* London: Routledge.

Louw, E. 1993. 'Participative Media: Whose Agendas? Some Thoughts on the Practices of Funding Agencies and the Consequent Empowering of Factions', *PCR-Newsletter*, 1(2):1–3.

Lozare, B. 1989. 'Power and Conflict: Hidden Dimensions of Communication, Participative Planning and Action.' Paper presented at 'Participation: A Key Concept in Communication for Change and Development, University of Poona, February, Pune.

MacBride, S. (ed.). 1980. *Many Voices, One World. Communication and Society. Today and Tomorrow.* Paris: UNESCO.

Mansell, R. and U. Wehn. 1998. *Knowledge Societies: Information Technology for Sustainable Development.* Oxford: Oxford University Press.

Martin-Barbero, J. 1993. *Communication, Culture and Hegemony. From the Media to Mediations.* London: Sage Publications.

Mattelart, A. 1983. *Transnationals and the Third World. The Struggle for Culture.* Massachusetts: Bergin and Garvey.

McAnany, E. 1983. 'From Modernization and Diffusion to Dependency and Beyond: Theory and Practice in Communication for Social Change in the 1980s.' Development Communications in the Third World, Proceedings of a Midwest Symposium, April, University of Illinois.

McAnany, E. (ed.). 1980. *Communications in the Rural Third World: The Role of Information in Development.* New York: Praeger.

McKee, N. 1983. *Social Mobilization and Social Marketing in Developing Communities. Lessons for Communicators.* Penang: Southbound.

McLaren, P. and P. Leonard. 1983. *Paulo Freire. A Critical Encounter.* London: Routledge.

McLuhan, M. 1964. *Understanding Media*, New York: Signet Books.

McQuail, D. 1983. *Mass Communication Theory.* London: Sage Publications.

Midgley, J. (ed.). 1986. *Community Participation, Social Development, and the State.* London: Methuen.

Moore, S. 1986. 'Participatory Communication in the Development Process', *The Third Channel*, 2.

Mowlana, H. and L. Wilson. 1987. *Communication and Development: A Global Assessment.* Paris: UNESCO.

O'Conner, A. 1990. 'Radio is Fundamental to Democracy', *Media Development*, 37(4).

O'Sullivan-Ryan, J. and M. Kaplun. 1979. *Communication Methods to Promote Grassroots Participation.* Paris: Unesco.

Perroux, F. 1983. *A New Concept of Development.* Paris: UNESCO.

Phildhrra. 1986. Participatory Research Guidebook, Philippine Partnership for the Development of Human Resources in Rural Areas. Laguna.

Pool, I.D.S. 1983. *Technologies of Freedom.* Cambridge: Belknap Press.

Robertson, R. 1992. *Globalization. Social Theory and Global Culture.* London: Sage Publications.

Rogers, E.M. 1962. *Diffusion of Innovations.* New York: Free Press.

———. 1976. *Communication and Development.* Beverly Hills: Sage Publications.

———. 1983. *The Diffusion of Innovations* (third ed.). New York: Free Press.

———. 1986. *Communication Technology: The New Media in Society.* New York: Free Press.

Rogers, E.M. and F. Schoemaker. 1973. *Communication of Innovations.* New York: Free Press.

Rokeach, M. 1966. 'Attitude Change and Behavioural Change', *Public Opinion Quarterly*, 30(4).

Rondinelli, D. 1993. *Development Projects as Policy Experiments. An Adaptive Approach to Development Administration.* London: Routledge.

Rostow, W.W. 1953. *The Process of Economic Growth.* Oxford: Clarendon Press.

Said, E. 1993. *Culture and Imperialism.* New York: Alfred Knopf.

Savio, R. (ed.). 1990. 'Communication, Participation and Democracy' (special issue), *Journal of the Society for International Development*, 2.

Schiller, H.I. 1976. *Communication and Cultural Domination.* New York: International Arts and Sciences Press.

Schramm, W. 1964. *Mass Media and National Development. The Role of Information in the Developing Countries.* Stanford: Stanford University Press.

Schramm, W. and D. Lerner (eds). 1976. *Communication and Change. The Last Ten Years—and the Next.* Honolulu: University Press of Hawaii.

Servaes, J. 1983. *Communication and Development. Some Theoretical Remarks.* Leuven: Acco.

——. 1987. *Media Aid. Naar een 'Ander' Communicatie- en Ontwikkelingsbeleid.* Leuven: Acco.

——. 1989. *One World, Multiple Cultures. A New Paradigm on Communication for Development.* Leuven: Acco.

——. 1999. *Communication for Development. One World, Multiple Cultures.* Cresskill: Hampton Press.

Sklair, L. 1991. *Sociology of the Global System.* New York: Harvester Wheatsheaf.

Somavia, J. 1981. 'The Democratization of Communication: From Minority Social Monopoly to Majority Social Representation', *Development Dialogue,* 2.

Spybey, T. 1992. *Social Change, Development and Dependency. Modernity, Colonialism and the Development of the West.* Cambridge: Polity Press.

Stavenhagen, R. 1966. Siete Tesis Equivocados Sobre América Latina, Desarrollo Indoamericano, 4.

Sunkel, O. (ed.). 1993. *Development from Within. Toward a Neostructuralist Approach for Latin America.* Boulder: Lynne Rienner.

Sunkel, O. and E. Fuenzalida. 1980. 'La Transnacionalizacion del Capitalismo y el Desarrollo Nacional', in O. Sunkel, E. Fuenzalida, F.H. Cardoso, et al., *Transnacionalizacion y Dependencia.* Madrid: Ed. Cultura Hispania.

Taylor, J. 1979. *From Modernization to Modes of Production.* London: Macmillan.

Tehranian, M. 1979. 'Development Theory and Communication Policy. The Changing Paradigm', in M. Voigt and G. Hanneman (eds). *Progress in Communication Sciences.* Vol. 1. Norwood: Ablex.

Thomas, P. 1993. 'Communication and Development: Freirean Cultural Politics in a Post-Modern Era', *PCR-Newsletter,* 1(1):2–3.

Thompson, J. 1990. *Ideology and Modern Culture. Critical Social Theory in the Era of Mass Communication.* Cambridge: Polity Press.

Ugboajah, F.O. (ed.). 1985. *Mass Communication, Culture and Society in West Africa.* München: Saur.

Van Nieuwenhuijze, C.A.O. 1982. *Development Begins at Home. Problems and Projects of the Sociology of Development.* Oxford: Pergamon Press.

Vogler, C. 1985. *The Nation State: The Neglected Dimension of Class.* Hants: Gower.

Wallerstein, I. 1979. *The Capitalist World Economy.* Cambridge: Cambridge University Press.

Wang, G. and W. Dissanayake (eds). 1984. *Continuity and Change in Communication Systems. An Asian Perspective.* Norwood: Ablex.

White, R. 1982. Contradictions in Contemporary Policies for Democratic Communication, Paper IAMCR Conference, September, Paris.

——. 1984. The Need for New Strategies of Research on the Democratization of Communication, Paper ICA Conference, May, San Francisco.

——. 1988. Media, Politics and Democracy in the Developing World, draft Centre for the Study of Communication and Culture, April, London.

Xavier Institute. 1980. *Development from Below.* Ranchi: Xavier Institute for Social Service.

The dominant paradigm of development underwent far-reaching interrogation and criticism in the 1970s by scholars and practitioners across disciplines and from around the globe. Perhaps the most significant challenge to the dominant paradigm of development communication came from Latin American scholars who deconstructed and rejected the premises, objectives, and methods of modernization and its attendant communication approaches. This early criticism stimulated a range of research projects that has resulted in a robust literature exploring participatory communication approaches to development. Participatory approaches gained momentum in the 1980s and 1990s and have evolved into a rich field standing in stark contrast to models and theories of the first development decades. In fact, scholars have noted that few contemporary development projects—regardless of theoretical orientation—are conducted without some sort of participatory component, even if this notion is honoured more on paper than in practice (Ascroft and Masilela 1994; Fraser and Restrepo-Estrada, 1998; Mato, 1999; White, 1994). Despite its widespread use, however, the concept of participatory communication is subject to loose interpretation that appears at best to be variable and contested and at worst misused and distorted (Arnst, 1996; Jacobson and Servaes, 1999).

Indeed, the Latin American challenge for scholars to embrace more appropriate, ethical, and responsive theories of development communication remains unrealized to some extent, creating a sense of conceptual and practical stagnation. One way of reinvigorating this field of study is to review the key elements of the challenge from Latin America and of the subsequent research that has refined our sense of participatory approaches of development communication. Such a review is intended to illuminate the conceptual directions that have been emphasized, elaborated, neglected, and ignored over time. By reviewing the variety of directions that have been explored over time, future paths of research and practice will be suggested for the continued theoretical advance of this field.

This chapter will begin with an abbreviated history of the challenge to the dominant paradigm of development communication that emerged from Latin America in the 1970s.[1] It will then provide a thematic review of the participatory communication research that has emerged since then, identifying the various directions taken by scholars in this field. Placing this thematic review into relief with the Latin American critique will provide a historical map of ideas and interests that will point to future directions. The final section of the chapter will conclude by recovering specific themes that hold the promise of advancing participatory development communication.

Challenging the Dominant Paradigm

In the 1970s, scholars from Latin America began deconstructing the dominant paradigm of communication for development and pointing to new directions for research. This section briefly summarizes this deconstruction and reconstruction, beginning with an examination of the assertions that development efforts were ideologically and materially related to neo-colonialism and the extension of capitalist relations. It continues by introducing key, alternative directions for development efforts, including notions of praxis, dialogue, and communication process.

Communication Domination

Prior to the 1970s, almost all of Latin American communication development theory and practice was based on concepts and models imported from the United States and Europe and used in ways that were both incommensurable with and detrimental to the region's social context (Beltrán, 1975). These concepts and models were guided philosophically by a combination of behaviourism and functionalism prevalent in the social sciences and by persuasion definitions of communication dating back to Aristotle in the humanities (Beltrán, 1980). The development programmes and research projects falling out of this philosophical frame tended to focus on individual attitudes and effects, while ignoring social, political, and economic structures that frequently stood in contradiction to development goals. Development was often defined in terms of the adoption of new behaviours or technologies, which were rarely, if ever, examined in terms of their social, political, and economic dimensions. Beltrán (1975) concluded, 'the classic diffusion model was based on an ideological framework that contradicts the reality of this region' (p. 190). This persuasion, attitude focus of research not only reflected the culture and philosophy of the Western tradition, it resulted in theories that blamed individuals, not systems, for continued underdevelopment.

But more than merely reflecting the intellectual and cultural history of Western research, early development projects were criticized as a form of domination and manipulation. Freire (1973b) analysed the term, 'extension', used in agricultural projects, in terms of its 'associative fields' and concluded that they invited 'mechanistic', 'transmission', and 'invasion' models of communication development. The vertical structure of many extension projects paralleled the hierarchical organization of landlord-peasant relations preceding it in Latin American *latifundios*, resulting in an unintended continuity of in-egalitarian relations. The sense that development projects frequently perpetuated the interests of dominant elites was echoed by numerous scholars at the 'First Latin American Seminar on Participatory Communication' sponsored in 1978 by CIESPAL (Center for Advanced Studies and Research for Latin America). Influenced by dependency theory that was prevalent at the time, scholars there concluded that uses of mass media in development imposed the interests of dominant classes on the majority of marginalized people, resulting in the reinforcement, reproduction, and legitimation of social and material relations of production (O'Sullivan-Ryan and Kaplún, 1978).[2]

The Latin American critique of the dominant paradigm, then, moved from the level of specific and misguided models of communication to the level of historical and global theories of domination and inequity. Early on, Latin American scholars suggested that development communication be interpreted from within a global framework guided by dependency theory (ibid.). That is, development projects should be analyzed as integral elements in a global system that actually act to maintain asymmetrical relations. Freire (1973a) went as far as to label the various top-down, modernization projects as 'assistentialism', or social and financial activities that attack symptoms, not causes, of social ills that function as disguised forms of colonial domination. These early suspicions have been confirmed by a more recent analysis of health and nutrition programmes in Latin America, which concluded that development projects functioned as an extension of the geopolitical struggle between the capitalist West and the communist East (Escobar, 1995). Moreover, the categories of assistance constructed by donor nations allowed 'institutions to distribute socially individuals and populations in ways consistent with the creation and reproduction of modern capitalist relations' (ibid.:107). The deconstruction of the dominant paradigm of development, then, was a protest against the perpetuation of historical inequities and a call for the invention of humane, egalitarian, and responsive communication theories and practices.

Toward Dialogic Praxis

Embracing the notion of praxis—self-reflexive, theoretically guided practice—was an immediate and obvious outcome of the Latin American critique of the dominant paradigm. The modernization project and its concomitant theories of development themselves had been shown to illustrate the inextricable connection between theory and practice (Beltrán, 1975, 1980; Escobar, 1995). Through its assumptions regarding the locus of social problems, models of communication as information transfer, methods that placed human objects under the antiseptic gaze of scientists, and findings that confirmed micro explanations of persistent underdevelopment, the modernization approach unconsciously demonstrated the reciprocal and self-confirming relationship between theory and practice. One of the earliest recommendations of the Latin

American critics was to acknowledge consciously this relationship, to turn away from scientific positions of objectivity and to embrace an orientation toward research as praxis.

Much of the inspiration for this shift came from the work of Freire (1970), whose experience in traditional pedagogy was seen as analogous to modernization approaches to development. In traditional pedagogy, teachers typically viewed students as objects characterized by some sort of deficiency and in need of knowledge that could be transferred to them in a linear fashion. Freire denounced this objectivist orientation as sadistic and oppressive, and claimed that humane practitioners could not view themselves as proprietors of knowledge and wisdom. In contrast to this oppressive pedagogy, Freire proposed a liberating approach that centred on praxis. Under this orientation, practitioners attempt to close the distance between teacher and student, development agent and client, researcher and researched in order to enter into a co-learning relationship guided by action and reflection. In a praxis approach to teaching, development, or research, people serve as their own examples in the struggle for and conquest of improved life chances.

The turn toward research praxis was a radical epistemological move that has been adopted and refined by scholars since then (for example, Fals Borda, 1988; Rahman, 1993). It posits that the combination of critical theory, situation analysis, and action create a fruitful dialectic for the construction of knowledge, which is systematically examined, altered, and expanded in practice. The elimination of the dichotomy between subject and object, combined with an action-reflection orientation toward inquiry resulted in a heightened moral awareness or *conscientização*. This liberating praxis generated 'thinking which perceives reality as process, as transformation, rather than as a static entity—thinking which does not separate itself from action, but constantly immerses itself in temporality without fear of the risks involved' (Freire, 1970:81). The turn toward praxis not only rejected dominant approaches to development as oppressive, it argued for integrating scholarship more directly with development practice.

While this turn provided both a philosophical and epistemological framework for scholarship, it also provided a practical, commensurate method in the form of dialogue. Dialogic communication was held in stark contrast to information transmission models emerging from Lasswell's (1964) 5-point question of who says what in what channel to whom with what effect. This required development researchers and practitioners to seek out the experiences, understandings, and aspirations of others to jointly construct reality and formulate actions (Beltran, 1980). Freire (1970, 1973a) provided concrete exercises for initiating critical dialogues to, in effect, deconstruct social contexts, separate out their constituent parts, and reconstruct a thematic universe for pursuing social transformation. Such a process resulted in a 'cultural synthesis' between development collaborators to arrive at mutually identified problems, needs, and guidelines for action.

Aside from its practical contribution, dialogue was promoted as an ethical communication choice within the development context. Freire (1970) argued that true humanization emerged from one's ability 'to name the world' in dialogic encounters. This humanization was not only denied to marginalized or oppressed peoples, but something that leaders and elites were prevented from attaining, as well, in prevailing communication environments. Grounded in

Buber's notion of 'I-Thou' communication, Freire argued that subject-object distinctions were impossible to maintain in true dialogue because one's sense of self and the world is elicited in interaction with others. The resulting fusion of identities and communal naming of the world did not emerge merely from an exchange of information, however, it required a moral commitment among dialogue partners. 'Being dialogic is not invading, not manipulating, not imposing orders. Being dialogic is pledging oneself to the constant transformation of reality' (Freire, 1973b:46). This highly developed sense of dialogue—simultaneously practical and rarefied—pushed scholars to conceptualize the phenomena of their study away from states—attitudes, and entities—media, toward process.

Communication as Process

More than any other aspect of the Latin American critique, the observation that communication was frequently conceptualized in static, rather than process, terms constituted the greatest challenge for development practitioners. Scholars from the north had been struggling with process models of communication since Berlo's (1960) work so convincingly argued in their favour. Yet Berlo's construction of the Sender-Message-Channel-Receiver model of communication demonstrated the tenacity of static, linear models that identified components amenable to survey research and development programme design. It also demonstrated the elusiveness of the dynamic, process nature of communication.

Latin American scholars introduced a phenomenological orientation, which radically altered the conceptualization, study, and practice of development communication.[3] Rather than focussing on the constituent parts of communication, Latin American scholars introduced more fluid and elastic concepts that centred on how-meaning-comes-to-be in its definition. These more fluid and meaning-centred conceptualizations of communication emphasized co-presence, intersubjectivity, phenomenological 'being in the world', and openness of interlocutors (Pasquali, 1963). This view introduced a sophisticated epistemology arguing that the understanding of social reality is produced between people, in material contexts, and in communication. Freire (1973b) captured the sense of the phenomenological orientation toward communication writing:

> One's consciousness, 'intentionality' toward the world, is always consciousness of, and in permanent movement toward reality.... This relationship constitutes, with this, a dialectical unity in which knowing-in-solidarity is generated in being and vice versa. For this reason, both objectivist and subjectivist explanations that break this dialectic, dichotomizing that which is not dichotomizable (subject-object), are not capable of understanding reality. (Freire, 1973b:85)

In other words, traditional development approaches of 'understanding reality' through the unilateral definition of problems, objectives, and solutions were criticized as violating the very essence of communication.

Pasquali (1963) went as far as stating that the notion of 'mass communication' was an oxymoron and that Latin American media constituted an 'information oligarchy' that cultivated a social context characterized by 'communicational atrophy'. Though his analysis was aimed at issues of media and culture broadly, the kinds of development communication projects typical of the period were consistent with his analysis. This fundamental criticism of static models of communication led to calls in development to abandon the 'vertical' approaches of information transmission and to adopt 'horizontal' projects emphasizing access, dialogue and participation (Beltrán, 1980). The Latin American critique of the dominant paradigm as an extension of domination and the call for more egalitarian and responsive approaches to development were followed by a robust body of research into participatory development communication, which is thematically summarized in the next section.

The Rise of Participatory Communication

In the decades following the Latin American call for participatory approaches to development communication, a wide range of theoretical responses emerged. At one end of the participatory spectrum, scholars coming out of the tradition of behaviourist, mass media effects tradition acknowledged the critique and have incorporated participatory dimensions—albeit to a limited extent—into their research. On the other end of the spectrum, scholars critical of traditional development communication research embraced participation virtually as utopian panacea for development. These distinct theoretical positions essentially mark ends on a continuum, where participation is conceptualized as either a means to an end, or as an end in and of itself. In this section I will present these two positions more fully before moving on to review a variety of other themes that reside somewhere between these two extremes.

Participation: Technical Means or Utopian End?

Almost as quickly as Latin American scholars articulated their objections to mainstream approaches to development communication, some of the leading figures of the dominant paradigm acknowledged the criticisms and reformed their projects (Lerner, 1976; Rogers, 1976; Schramm, 1976). They acknowledged that their conceptualization of development had been oversimplified by focussing narrowly on individuals as the locus for change, theorizing in a universal, evolutionary manner, ignoring cultural specificity, and emphasizing mass media. But this recognition did not lead to the wholesale rejection of their empiricist approach. In fact, Lerner (1976) defended social science's inviolable methodological assumptions of ontological continuity and social regularity, which were threatened by the Latin American rejection of objectivism and promotion of communication-as-process. Rather, dominant paradigm scholars acknowledged the general value of popular participation in development, recognized new uses of media to 'unlock local energies' (Lerner and Schramm, 1976:343), and expanded research to include interpersonal networks in addition to opinion leaders. To an extent, the concept of participation served to reform the dominant paradigm, making it—in the words of its proponents—more expansive, flexible, and humane (Rogers, 1993).

Such reformist approaches to participation are used by major institutions such as the World Bank and Mexico's dominant Institutional Revolutionary Party (PRI) (White, 1999; Mato, 1999). Their top-down efforts are supported by theoretical arguments that participation be conceptualized in ways that disassociate it from any particular ideology (Chu, 1987; 1994). By ideologically neutralizing it, participation is seen as compatible with social marketing, capitalist expansion, and global trade (Moemeka, 1994). In fact, King and Cushman (1994) have argued that participation be conceptualized on highly abstract level where a 'nation's people and its government' fashion themselves as global competitors participating in the arena of world trade. They discard the value of grass-roots participation, local knowledge, and cultural beliefs as 'old myths' that are incompatible with the contemporary reality of globalization.

Less dismissive of grass-roots participation but still consistent with empiricist, top-down approaches to development is recent research in entertainment-education (Singhal and Rogers, 1988; Storey, 1999). Rather than neutralizing the ideological element of participation, entertainment-education draws on findings emerging from cultural studies to advance predetermined objectives in areas such as 'reproductive health'. A sophisticated theoretical framework drawing from studies in reception and popular culture has been constructed to conceptualize texts as open systems activated by audience participants that render media products incapable of manipulation (Storey, 1999, 2000). Rather than using this assertion as the basis for promoting grass-roots communication broadly, the notion of 'open texts' has functioned primarily as a justification for expert-produced, entertainment-education products. Coupled with the theoretical contributions of Mikhail Bakhtin, this approach uses the concept of participation both to guide the development of 'pro-social content' through audience surveys and focus groups and more importantly to impute wide-ranging and long-term consequences via the 'social dialogue' of individuals, institutions, and culture. More than any other research genre, entertainment-education has used the concept of participation to bolster the administrative position of the dominant paradigm.

The apparent contradictions of using participatory elements to enhance the status of traditional development practices has received intense attention by communication scholars. A recent, historical analysis focussing on the discourse of development suggests that the Latin American call for participation constituted a counter discourse to the dominant paradigm that was 'easily co-opted by the established system and rendered ineffective or counter productive' (Escobar, 1999:326). Indeed, the most pernicious instances of instrumental uses of participation appear to be attached to large agencies connected to the state or to trans-national regimes such as the USAID or the World Bank (Mato, 1999; White, 1999). The role of scholars who have integrated participation into essentially top-down development theories has been interpreted as akin to engaging in a 'conspiracy theory' to redeem the dominant paradigm from the interrogation it experienced in the 1970s (Ascroft and Masilela, 1994; Lent, 1987). When put into practice, such uses of participatory communication exemplify, at best, passive collaboration, at worst, manipulative consultation done only to help advance a predetermined objective (Díaz Bordenave, 1994; Dudley, 1993). In fact, one development practitioner argues that any uses of participation will evolve into an 'insidious domination tactic' if incorporated into the development discourse due to its historical association with Western political hegemony (White, 1999).

Few scholars would agree with this extreme position, especially those reviewed above who advocate administrative uses of participation. Moreover, a group of scholars conceptualizing participation as an end in and of itself has articulated utopian visions of the role of people in their own development. These visions are premised on a somewhat romantic belief that peasants, Indians, and other marginalized persons possess local wisdom and a virtuous cultural ethos, and that participatory processes are inherently humanizing, liberating, and catalyzing (Dissanayake, 1985; Vargas, 1995; White, 1994). Beginning from such premises, scholars have prescribed totalizing processes of participatory communication where all interlocutors experience freedom and equal access to express feelings and experiences and to arrive at collective agendas for action (Díaz Bordenave, 1994; Kaplún, 1985; Nair and White, 1994a). Under these circumstances, all people are said to take ownership of communication and to experience empowering outcomes. These utopian visions of development communication have been called 'genuine' and 'authentic' participation, as opposed to the manipulative, pseudo-participation reviewed above.

The generalized premises and prescriptions of utopian scholars have been accompanied by equally optimistic renditions of participation by researchers who offer more concrete directions for development practice. For example, various phases in development—identifying problems, setting goals and objectives, planning procedures, assessing actions—have been identified, each one necessitating the full participation of intended beneficiaries (Kennedy, 1984; Midgley, 1986; Nair and White, 1994b). This has been accompanied by policy recommendations for the reorganization of major social institutions, such as the media system, in order to bring communication structures in line with participatory communication development approaches (Servaes, 1985). Placed on a continuum, these utopian, normative theories stand as polar opposites to the functional, administrative notions of participation advanced by scholars approaching development from a more conventional perspective.

The evolution of polarized conceptualizations of participatory development communication has been noted in a number of scholarly reviews that have distinguished the two poles in slightly different ways. In fact, early research in this area suggested that participatory communication function as both a means and an end in development, thus foreshadowing the distinct conceptual paths that would be followed in the decades to come (O'Sullivan-Ryan and Kaplún, 1978). A number of scholars have interpreted this means-end division as a convenient and fruitful way of guiding communication decisions in development projects (Chu, 1994; Decker, 1988; Kaplún, 1989; Rodriguez, 1994). That is, a limited role for communication—*participation-as-means*—may be appropriate in projects focussed on teaching skills, carrying out prescribed objectives, or producing highly polished media products. Under such circumstances, social impacts are viewed as ephemeral, goals are immediate, and interaction is formal. In contrast, an expansive role for communication—*participation-as-end*—is appropriate in projects aimed at organizing movements, transforming social relations, and empowering individuals. Under such circumstances, social impacts are perpetual, goals are long-range, and interaction is fluid. Other scholars noting the means-end continuum in the research have been more critical of the distinction, arguing that participation-as-means is nothing more than a thinly veiled reincarnation of the dominant paradigm (Melkote, 1991; Vargas, 1995; White, 1994). They argue that this approach invokes participatory communication in an instrumental, manipulative, dominating manner that undercuts its theoretical legitimacy. While they recognize the existence of the gradations in the evolution of the concept of participation, they reject the means-to-an-end perspective as an illegitimate appropriation. Regardless of the subtle distinctions characterizing the ends of this continuum, these scholars have noted that most theory development of participation has not been predominately means or end, teaching or organizing, pseudo or genuine, but some version that resides between the poles. The remainder of this section reviews major concepts and issues that have emerged over the years but that defy convenient location at either end of the conceptual continuum.

From General Theories to Concrete Practices

The bulk of theoretical research into participatory communication does not claim an exclusive means or ends focus, but does vary in terms of level of abstraction, issue of attention, or topic of interest. This section of the chapter briefly summarizes these various theoretical contributions moving from general and abstract scholarship to more applied and concrete research. This review will touch on the general notions of multiplicity, power, and popular mobilization, as well as specific attention to levels of participation, media applications, and concrete methods of inquiry. The purpose of doing this is to display the various degrees of participation that have emerged over the years and to stake out some of the dominant patterns of interest that this field has generated. Holding these general patterns in relief to the origins of interest in participatory communication will form the basis for making recommendations for future research.

One of the more general and fully articulated concepts to emerge from the participatory communication tradition is the notion of multiplicity in one world (Servaes, 1985, 1986, 1989). This approach recommends strong, grass-roots participation in development efforts, but explicitly rejects universal approaches to its application (Servaes, 1986, 1996a). Instead, it emphasizes the terms 'diversity' and 'pluralism', suggesting that nations and regions cultivate their own, responsive approaches to self-determined development goals that emerge out of participatory processes. The reluctance to advocate universal theorizing stems from the observation that even within fairly homogeneous cultures, competing political, social, and cultural interests and groups will be found (Servaes, 1985). The conflicts inherent in all social systems suggest that 'rigid and general strategies for participation are neither possible nor desirable. It is a process that unfolds in each unique situation' (Servaes, 1996a:23). Eschewing even 'general strategies for participation' constitutes a naive faith in the power of communication to negotiate stark political differences and casts multiplicity into a relativistic arena that has difficulty sustaining coherence within the larger discourse of development.

The strain on theoretical coherence is evident in the introduction of universal principles and totalizing concepts that accompany this relativized communication approach. The early multiplicity research, for example, claimed that a universal 'right to communicate' formed the basis for all multiplicity approaches to development communication (Servaes, 1986). Later scholars adopting the multiplicity framework reiterated this position and added that 'cultural processes' should be granted primacy in both the study and practice of development communication (White, 1994; Wildemeersch, 1999). Most recently, Servaes (1998) has suggested that a 'global ethics' grounded in principles of democracy and respect for human rights be adopted unilaterally by development agencies. This tension between a rejection of universal approaches and the advocacy of global principles is a contradiction that permeates the development communication field generally in its attempts to reconcile subjectivity/agency and structure/political economy (Dervin and Huesca, 1997, 1999). Moreover it is emblematic of a widespread reluctance among scholars to establish normative standards of participatory communication on philosophical grounds (Deetz, 1992). While this contradiction does represent theoretical incoherence, it more significantly demonstrates the desire to honour differential forms of human agency that generate diverse cultural practices, while reckoning with the material constraints of an undemocratic, profit-driven communication environment.

Another area of general, theoretical attention in participatory communication has centred more closely on those material constraints by focussing on the role of power in development. Early advocates of participatory approaches either ignored the issue of power or naively called for its general redistribution within and between nations. More recent research has focussed explicitly on power and conceptualized it in a nuanced and problematic way. For the most part, power has been theorized as both multi-centred—not one-dimensional—and asymmetrical (Servaes, 1996c; Tehranian, 1999). This role acknowledges the force of institutions and structures, but emphasizes the role of human agency in reproducing and transforming them (Tehranian, 1999). Within this generalized framework of power, participatory communication is seen by some as being a potential source of social transformation (Nair and White, 1994a; Riaño, 1994). By virtue of the differences—ethnic, gender, sexual, and the like—that multiple social actors bring development projects, participatory communication reveals how power functions to subordinate certain groups of people (Riaño, 1994). Furthermore, participation functions to cultivate 'generative power' where individuals and groups develop the capacity for action, which can be harnessed to reshape and transform conditions of subordination (Nair and White, 1994a). While mindful of the asymmetrical characteristics of power in society, these positions are generally optimistic regarding the prospects of transformation via participatory communication.

Less optimistic are scholars who see participation as either insufficient or problematic in and of itself, in terms of altering power relationships in society. For these scholars, participatory communication may be helpful in attaining structural transformations in the land tenure, political, or economic arrangements of society, which are viewed as the root sources of subordination (Hedebro, 1982; Lozare, 1994; Nerfin, 1977). As such, participatory communication is necessary but not sufficient for engaging and altering power relationships. In fact, participatory communication that is not guided toward an apriori structural goal, such as building progressive institutions or deconstructing dominating discourses, runs the risk of dissolving into a self-indulgent exercise or being co-opted by an established and elitist organization (Escobar, 1999; O'Connor, 1990). Worse yet, participatory communication by itself is capable of reproducing in-egalitarian power structures, especially in regard to gender relations (Wilkins, 1999, 2000). For these authors, the relationship between participatory communication and dominant power structures is neither transparent nor unproblematic.

An approach to the issue of participatory communication and power that most explicitly bridges the agency-structure divide is the scholarship that focusses on the role of participation in relation to popular movements. One position in this research argues that popular movements are inherently linked to participatory communication projects because 'liberation' is an axiomatic quality of participation (Riaño, 1994). That is, the openness required of participatory communication leads to awareness of differences that reveal inequalities and result in movements to address and transform them. A distinct but related perspective notes that participation emerges from popular movements that engage in structural reforms but rely on continual regeneration through broad social participation (Servaes, 1996b; White, 1994). Large-scale popular movements, therefore, serve as valuable laboratories for breaking through artificial boundaries that obscure the role of participatory communication in the transformation and reproduction of dominant relations. Some scholars have gone further and suggested that development research actively align itself with popular movements in order to yield insights that contribute directly to participatory, social change projects (Rahman, 1993; Servaes and Arnst, 1999). This nexus between participation and popular liberation movements constitutes an entry point for negotiating problematic issues of power.

Concrete Applications and Operationalizations

Research attending to abstract theoretical concerns of multiplicity, power, and mobilization demonstrates the negotiation of the means/end polarity in the participatory communication literature. But a range of scholarship focussed on more specific issues and concerns defies simple means/end classification, as well. This section of the chapter briefly reviews scholarship focussing on more concrete issues such as levels of participation, media applications, and research methods.

A number of researchers have worked to identify differential levels and intensities of participation in development projects. These scholars have identified stages of participation, ranging from initial access to communication resources to active identification of development issues and goals to full authority in project governance (Fraser and Restrepo-Estrada, 1998; Krohling-Peruzzo, 1996;

Servaes, 1996a). These stages are usually conceptualized as being guided either by contextual qualities of the participants themselves or by organizational constraints of the supporting development institutions. For example, Thapalia (1996) suggested that development practitioners cultivate a stronger, more directive role for themselves—something she labelled 'transformational leadership'—aimed at constructing a shared vision and commitment to action in a community. She argues for resurrecting the discredited notion of 'leadership' because egalitarian participation is frequently incommensurable with the desires and interests of local people. Like the constraints created by local cultural contexts, organizational characteristics impose limitations on participation, as well. Large development agencies most frequently implement participation on limited level, such as using focus groups in the initial phase of an information campaign, because of organizational goals and limitations on time and resources (McKee, 1994; Wilkins, 1999). The various levels identified by these researchers are conceptualized in a complex interaction with contextual and structural constraints that move beyond the binary means/end continuum suggested by other scholars. Furthermore, they are acutely concerned with concrete applications of participatory communication in development.

Another area of scholarship that has focussed on communication applications concerns participatory uses of media in development. Soon after the Latin American challenge to the dominant paradigm of development, scholars began focussing on participatory applications in media. Fuelled by a series of UNESCO meetings that led to the declaration for a New World Information and Communication Order, these scholars identified the concepts of access— to communication resources, participation—in planning, decision-making, and production, and self-management—collective ownership and policy-making—in media development (Berrigan, 1981; O'Sullivan-Ryan and Kaplún, 1978). Since then, systematic attention has been given to various aspects of participatory media, including audience involvement in message creation (Mody, 1991; Nair and White, 1993a, 1993b, 1994b; Thomas, 1994), identity construction (Rodriguez, 1994), and institution-building (Díaz Bordenave, 1985; Fadul, Lins da Silva and Santoro, 1982). In fact, an entire communication *subfield of 'alternative media' has spun off of the initial criticisms of the dominant paradigm and the subsequent calls for participatory approaches* to social change (see Atwood and McAnany, 1986; Huesca and Dervin, 1994; Reyes Matta, 1983; Simpson Grinberg, 1986).

While scholarly attention has been given to many abstract and concrete issues relevant to participatory communication, the area of research methods has been neglected to some extent (Ascroft and Masilela, 1994; Melkote, 1991). Recently this situation has begun to change, however, with scholars emphasizing the importance of advancing research methods that are commensurate with the philosophy and theory that underpins participatory communication for development (Dervin and Huesca, 1997, 1999; Jacobson, 1996; Servaes and Arnst, 1999; White, 1999). At the level of methodology, this requires thinking through the ontological and epistemological assumptions that mandate the dissolution of subject-object relations and lay the groundwork for participatory communication for development (Dervin and Huesca, 1999; Jacobson, 1993, 1996). It also requires the establishment of criteria of validity in order to fulfil the self-reflexive, evaluative dimension of research, as well as to advance comparative studies in the field. Such criteria might be imported from parallel communication theories, such as Habermas' ideal speech situation (Jacobson and Kolluri, 1999), or they might emerge from the practical outcomes of the research process itself (Escobar, 1999; Servaes and Arnst, 1999). At the level of method, an orientation towards participatory action research has been suggested as perhaps the most compatible approach to the study of participatory communication (Einsiedel, 1999; Escobar, 1999; Jacobson, 1993; White, 1999). Such methods are explicitly political, calling on researchers to align themselves with specific social actors and to embrace their goals and purposes. The recent attention to methodology and method may foreshadow renewed interest in conducting empirical research into participatory communication for development.

This brief sketch of the multiple issues receiving scholarly attention was intended to identify the major patterns shaping our understanding of participatory communication for development. By examining these patterns against the issues raised in the Latin American challenge to the dominant paradigm, I intend to identify some fruitful directions for future research in the concluding section of this chapter.

Revisiting Key Concepts

The future of participatory communication for development is uncertain because of serious practical and conceptual impediments facing it. Practical impediments include a lack of institutional support as the approach's long-range, time-consuming, and symbolic *conscientização*—empowerment—dimensions do not conform to the evaluative criteria of many development bureaucracies (Arnst, 1996; Fraser and Restrepo-Estrada, 1998; Servaes, 1998; Servaes and Arnst, 1999; Wilkins, 1999). These same scholars note that strong participatory projects transfer control from officials to beneficiaries and are often met with resistance from experts whose power is jeopardized. Conceptual impediments include definitional fuzziness, exemplified by the wide-ranging scholarship outlined above (Ascroft and Masilela, 1994; Jacobson, 1994; Vargas, 1995; White, 1994). Several scholars have noted that because of this definitional fuzziness, dominant communication patterns and oppressive social relationships can be and are reproduced under the guise of participation (Kaplún, 1985, 1989; Wilkins, 1999).

While the challenges to participatory communication for development appear formidable, reasons for optimism are provided by scholars who have documented renewed interest in this approach (Ascroft and Masilela, 1994; Fraser and Restrepo-Estrada, 1998; Melkote, 1993; Nair and White, 1993c; Vargas, 1995). Attention to participation as a component in development is being embraced by both small, non-governmental organizations as well as large institutions, albeit in problematic forms as documented above. The challenge before contemporary scholars is to continue advancing this area of theory and practice in light of the practical and conceptual impediments currently facing it. Such advancement can occur by revisiting key notions that have been pursued and neglected in the 30-year-old call to participatory communication.

On the conceptual level, scholars should redouble their efforts to base development practices and analysis on definitions of communication that emphasize its dynamic process nature. Much of the conceptual fuzziness in this field is due to instrumental adoptions and adaptations of participation in projects that are essentially attempts to improve information transfers and cloak them as communication. Furthermore, this fuzziness is compounded when participation is incorporated into applications clearly based on linear models of communication, such as 'message development'. Freezing communication action into static components effectively ignores the dynamic process roots of the Latin American challenge and slides back into the linear models that guided modernization and its top-down projects. Concerns about moving from state-entity concepts to process-dynamic models are evident not only in communication, but in other social science disciplines, as well (Bruner, 1986; Dervin, 1993; Fals Borda, 1991). Adopting process models as the foundation of theory and practice will provide conceptual guidance for negotiating the means-end polarity and for distinguishing participatory communication from information transfer.

Other conceptual components worthy of recovering and reinforcing are the ethical and political mandates that underpinned the Latin American call for participatory communication. These mandates have become obscured, if not lost altogether, as scholars have emphasized multiplicity, the primacy of culture, and other notions that have effectively relativized the meaning of participation. Although the early denunciations of the dominant paradigm called for dialogue, democracy, and participation, they did so with a clear sense of moral commitment to strive for social justice. The claim to moral authority was grounded in the liberation theology movement popular at the time but never claiming a prominent place in the theoretical challenges to the dominant paradigm. Consequently, the liberation theology connection to the call for participatory communication has been lost in all but a few research projects conducted in subsequent years (Díaz Bordenave, 1994; Fals Borda, 1988; Tehranian, 1999; Vargas, 1995). Nevertheless, the work of Freire—whose adult education project in Recife was modelled on Catholic base community meetings—has been infused consistently with references to theologians and declarations of faith and commitment to oppressed groups in society (Freire 1970, 1973b, 1997; Horton and Freire, 1990). The intensity of these dimensions were maintained in his most recent analyses of neo-liberal Brazil in the 1990s, when he suggested, 'It is urgent that the disowned unite and that we all fight in favour of liberation, transforming this offensive world into a more people-oriented one, from both a political and an ethical standpoint' (Freire, 1997:46). Strengthening the ethical and political grounds of participatory communication for development will function to enhance conceptual clarity and to reduce the likelihood that participatory projects will reproduce in-egalitarian relationships.

One practical step that researchers can take to advance the agenda of participatory communication for development is to begin aligning themselves with new social movements that have emerged recently worldwide. New social movements constitute a nexus where concerns for communication process, social justice, and broad participation converge as natural laboratories for exploring participatory communication for development. A number of researchers noted above have already identified popular movements as an arena worthy of scholarly attention. Their suggestion is further strengthened by the recent attention given to method and methodology, particularly those that advocate an action orientation to scholarship of and for social change. The intensive study of new social movements will not only give scholars direction in their research, it might address some of the issues of efficacy raised by development bureaucracies that demand demonstrable evidence of broad, material consequences of specific projects.

The concept of participatory communication for development is the most resilient and useful notion that has emerged from the challenges to the dominant paradigm of modernization. It has generated a diverse body of scholarship that has issued new challenges, identified problems, documented achievements, and advanced theoretical understanding. The past 30 years of research demonstrates substantial progress, but more than that, it contains important traces for the continued advancement of scholarship in this area.

Notes

1. Although this history draws primarily from Latin American authors, readers should note that the dominant paradigm of development received criticisms from across geographic boundaries. Flaws in the conceptualization and administration of diffusion of innovations projects, for example, were identified in both Africa and Asia (Röling, Ascroft and Chege, 1976; Shingi and Mody, 1976).
2. Dependency was a school of thought emerging in Latin America in the 1960s that explained underdevelopment as the result or byproduct of capitalist expansion. Furthermore, the development of underdevelopment was interpreted as part of a process of continuous political economic relations occurring globally between the developed north and the impoverished south, or what has been termed 'core-periphery' relations. Key authors include Cardoso and Faletto (1979) and Frank (1967).
3. Antonio Pasquali was fundamental in introducing Continental proponents of phenomenology to Latin American critics of the dominant paradigm of development communication. Relying most heavily on the work of Heidegger and Merleau-Ponty, Pasquali argued that knowledge of development needed to be generated phenomenologically, that is, through presuppositionless, intentional action in the world. This position undermined—on the most fundamental level—modernization approaches that assumed a separation between subject and object, researcher and development recipient.

References

Arnst, R. 1996. 'Participation Approaches to the Research Process', in J. Servaes, T.L. Jacobson and S.A. White (eds). *Participatory Communication for Social Change*, pp. 109–126. New Delhi: Sage Publications.

Ascroft, J. and S. Masilela. 1994. 'Participatory Decision Making in Third World Development', in S.A. White, K.S. Nair and J. Ascroft (eds). *Participatory Communication: Working for Change and Development*, pp. 259–294. New Delhi: Sage Publications.

Atwood, R. and E.G. McAnany (eds). 1986. *Communication and Latin American Society*. Madison: University of Wisconsin.

Beltrán, L.R. 1975. 'Research Ideologies in Conflict', *Journal of Communication*, 25:187–193.

———. 1980. 'A farewell to Aristotle: "Horizontal" Communication', *Communication*, 5:5–41.

Berlo, D. 1960. *The Process of Communication: An Introduction to Theory and Practice*. San Francisco: Holt, Rinehart and Winston.

Berrigan, F.J. 1981. *Community Communications: The Role of Community Media in Development.* Paris: UNESCO.

Bruner, E.M. 1986. 'Experience and Its Expressions', in V.W. Turner, and E.M. Bruner (eds). *The Anthropology of Experience,* pp. 3–30. Urbana: University of Illinois.

Cardoso, F.H. and E. Faletto. 1979. *Dependency and Development in Latin America* (M. Mattingly Urquidi, Trans.). Berkeley: University of California.

Chu, G.C. 1987. 'Development Communication in the Year 2000: Future Trends and Directions', in N. Jayaweera and S. Amunugama (eds). *Rethinking Development Communication,* pp. 95–107. Singapore: Asian Mass Communication Research and Information Centre.

———. 1994. 'Communication and Development: Some Emerging Theoretical Perspectives', in A. Moemeka (ed.), *Communicating for Development: A New Pan-disciplinary Perspective,* pp. 3–30. Albany: SUNY Press.

Decker, P. 1988. *Portable Video in Grass-roots Development.* Paper from the Institute for Communication Research. Stanford University.

Deetz, S.A. 1992. *Democracy in an Age of Corporate Colonization: Developments in Communication and the Politics of Everyday Life.* Albany: State University of New York.

Dervin, B. 1993. 'Verbing Communication: A Mandate for Disciplinary Invention', *Journal of Communication,* 43:45–54.

Dervin, B. and R. Huesca. 1997. 'Reaching for the Communicating in Participatory Communication', *The Journal of International Communication,* 4(2):46–74.

———. 1999. 'The Participatory Communication for Development Narrative: An Examination of Meta-theoretic Assumptions and Their Impacts', in T.L. Jacobson and J. Servaes (eds). *Theoretical Approaches to Participatory Communication,* pp. 169–210. Cresskill, NJ: Hampton Press.

Díaz Bordenave, J.E. 1985. *Comunicación y Sociedad [Communication and Society].* La Paz, Bolivia: CIMCA.

———. 1994. 'Participative Communication as a Part of Building the Participative Society', in S.A. White, K.S. Nair and J. Ascroft (eds). *Participatory Communication: Working for Change and Development,* pp. 35–48. New Delhi: Sage Publications.

Dissanayake, W. 1985. 'From a Piecemeal Approach to an Integrated Strategy for Development', *Media Development,* 4:20–22.

Dudley, E. 1993. *The Critical Villager: Beyond Community Participation.* London: Routledge.

Einsiedel, E.F. 1999. 'Action Research: Theoretical and Methodological Considerations for Development', in T.L. Jacobson and J. Servaes (eds). *Theoretical Approaches to Participatory Communication,* pp. 359–379. Cresskill, NJ: Hampton Press.

Escobar, A. 1995. *Encountering Development: The Making and Unmaking of the Third World.* Princeton: Princeton University Press.

———. 1999. 'Discourse and Power in Development: Michel Foucault and the Relevance of His Work to the Third World', in T.L. Jacobson and J. Servaes (eds). *Theoretical Approaches to Participatory Communication,* pp. 309–335. Cresskill, NJ: Hampton Press.

Fadul, A., C.E. Lins da Silva and L.F. Santoro. 1982. 'Documento Básico do IV Ciclo de Estudos Interdisiplinares da Comunicação' [Basic Document of the IV Cycle of Interdisciplinary Studies of Communication], in C.E. Lins da Silva (ed.). *Comunicação, Hegemonia, e Contra-Informação* [Communication, Hegemony, and Counter-Information], pp. 9–16. Sao Paulo: Cortel Editora/Intercom.

Fals Borda, O. 1988. *Knowledge and People's Power: Lessons with Peasants in Nicaragua, Mexico and Colombia.* New Delhi: Indian Social Institute.

———. 1991. *Knowledge and Social Movements.* Santa Cruz, CA: Merrill Publications.

Frank, A.G. 1967. *Capitalism and Underdevelopment in Latin America.* New York: Monthly Review Press.

Fraser, C. and S. Restrepo-Estrada. 1998. *Communicating for Development: Human Change for Survival.* London: I. B. Tauris Publishers.

Freire, P. 1970. *Pedagogy of the Oppressed* (M. Bergman Ramos, Trans.). New York: Herder and Herder.

———.1973a. *Education for Critical Consciousness.* New York: Seabury Press.

———. 1973b. *Extensión o Comunicación?* (L. Ronzoni, Trans.). Buenos Aires: Siglo XXI.

———. 1997. *Pedagogy of the Heart* (D. Macedo and A. Oliveira, Trans.). New York: Continuum.

Hedebro, G. 1982. *Communication and Social Change in Developing Nations.* Ames, IA: Iowa State University Press.

Horton, M. and P. Freire. 1990. *We Make the Road by Walking: Conversations on Education and Social Change.* Philadelphia: Temple University Press.

Huesca, R. and B. Dervin. 1994. 'Theory and Practice in Latin American Alternative Communication Research', *Journal of Communication*, 44(4):53–73.

Jacobson, T.L. 1993. 'A Pragmatist Account of Participatory Communication Research for National Development', *Communication Theory*, 3(3):214–230.

———. 1994. 'Modernization and Post-Modernization Approaches to Participatory Communication for Development', in S.A. White, K.S. Nair and J. Ascroft (eds). *Participatory Communication: Working for Change and Development*, pp. 60–75. New Delhi: Sage Publications.

———. 1996. 'Conclusion: Prospects for Theoretical Development', in J. Servaes, T.L. Jacobson and S.A. White (eds). *Participatory Communication for Social Change*, pp. 266–277. New Delhi: Sage Publications.

Jacobson, T.L. and S. Kolluri. 1999. 'Participatory Communication as Communicative Action', in T.L. Jacobson and J. Servaes (eds). *Theoretical Approaches to Participatory Communication*, pp. 265–280. Cresskill, NJ: Hampton Press.

Jacobson, T.L. and J. Servaes. 1999. 'Introduction', in T.L Jacobson, and J. Servaes (eds). *Theoretical Approaches to Participatory Communication*, pp. 1–13. Cresskill, NJ: Hampton Press.

Kaplún, M. 1985. *El Comunicador Popular* [The Popular Communicator]. Quito: Ciespal.

———. 1989. 'Video, Comunicación y Educación Popular: Derroteros Para una Búsqueda' [Video, Communication, and Popular Education: Action Plan for a Quest], in P. Valdeavellano (ed.). *El Video en la Educación Popular* [Video in Popular Education], pp. 37–58. Lima: Instituto Para América Latina.

Kennedy, T.W. 1984. 'Beyond Advocacy: An Animative Approach to Public Participation' (Doctoral dissertation, Cornell University, 0058), *Dissertation Abstracts International*, 45, 09A.

King, S.S. and D. Cushman. 1994. 'Communication in Development and Social Change: Old Myths and New Realities', in A. Moemeka (ed.). *Communicating for Development: A New Pan-disciplinary Perspective*, pp. 23–33. Albany: SUNY Press.

Krohling-Peruzzo, C.M. 1996. 'Participation in Community Communication', in J. Servaes, T.L. Jacobson and S.A. White (eds). *Participatory Communication for Social Change*, pp. 162–179. New Delhi: Sage Publications.

Lasswell, H.D. 1964 c,1948. 'The Structure and Function of Communication in Society', in L. Bryson (ed.). *The Communication of Ideas*, pp. 37–51. New York: Cooper Square Publishers.

Lent, J. 1987. 'Devcom: A View from the United States', in N. Jayaweera and S. Amunugama (eds). *Rethinking Development Communication*, pp. 20–41. Singapore: Asian Mass Communication Research and Information Centre.

Lerner, D. 1976. 'Toward a New Paradigm', in W. Schramm and D. Lerner (eds). *Communication and Change: The Last Ten Years—and the Next*, pp. 60–63. Honolulu: East-West Centre.

Lerner, D. and W. Schramm. 1976. 'Looking Forward', in W. Schramm, and D. Lerner (eds). *Communication and Change: The Last Ten Years—and the Next*, pp. 340–344. Honolulu: East-West Center.

Lozare, B.V. 1994. 'Power and Conflict: Hidden Dimensions of Communication, Participative Planning, and Action', in S.A. White, K.S. Nair and J. Ascroft (eds). *Participatory Communication: Working for Change and Development*, pp. 229–244. New Delhi: Sage Publications.

Mato, D. 1999. 'Problems of Social Participation in "Latin" America in the Age of Globalization: Theoretical and Case-Based Considerations for Practitioners and Researchers', in T.L. Jacobson and J. Servaes (eds). *Theoretical Approaches to Participatory Communication*, pp. 51–75. Cresskill, NJ: Hampton Press.

McKee, N. 1994. 'A Community-Based Learning Approach: Beyond Social Marketing', in S.A. White, K.S. Nair and J. Ascroft (eds). *Participatory Communication: Working for Change and Development*, pp. 194–228. New Delhi: Sage Publications.

Melkote, S.R. 1991. *Communication for Development in the Third World*. New Delhi: Sage Publications.

———. 1993. 'From Third World to First World: New Roles and Challenges for Development Communication', *Gazette*, 52:145–158.

Midgley, J. 1986. 'Community Participation: History, Concepts and Controversies', in J. Midgley (ed.). *Community Participation, Social Development and the State*, pp. 13–44. London: Methuen.

Mody, B. 1991. *Designing Messages for Development Communication: An Audience Participation-Based Approach*. New Delhi: Sage Publications.

Moemeka, A. A. 1994. 'Development Communication: A Historical and Conceptual Overview', in A. Moemeka (ed.). *Communicating for Development: A New Pan-disciplinary Perspective*, pp. 3–22. Albany: SUNY Press.

Nair, K.S. and S.A. White. 1993a. 'The Development Communication Process', in K.S. Nair and S.A. White (eds). *Perspectives on Development Communication*, pp. 47–70. New Delhi: Sage Publications.

Nair, K.S. and S.A. White. 1993b. 'Introduction', in K.S. Nair and S.A. White (eds). *Perspectives on Development Communication*, pp. 12–31. New Delhi: Sage Publications.
———. 1993c. 'Preface', in K.S. Nair and S.A. White (eds). *Perspectives on Development Communication*, pp. 9–11. New Delhi: Sage Publications.
———. 1994a. 'Participatory Development Communication as Cultural Renewal', in S.A. White, K.S. Nair and J. Ascroft (eds). *Participatory Communication: Working for Change and Development*, pp. 138–193. New Delhi: Sage Publications.
———. 1994b. 'Participatory Message Development: A Conceptual Framework', in S.A. White, K.S. Nair and J. Ascroft (eds). *Participatory Communication: Working for Change and Development*, pp. 345–358. New Delhi: Sage Publications.
Nerfin, M. 1977. 'Introduction', in M. Nerfin (ed.). *Another Development: Approaches and Strategies*, pp. 9–18. Uppsala: Dag Hammarskjöld Foundation.
O'connor, A. 1990. 'Radio is Fundamental to Democracy', *Media Development*, 4:3–4.
O'Sullivan-Ryan, J. and M. Kaplún. 1978. *Communication Methods to Promote Grass-Roots Participation: A Summary of Research Findings from Latin America, and an Annotated Bibliography*. Paris: UNESCO.
Pasquali, A. 1963. *Comunicación y Cultura de Masas*. Caracas: Universidad Central de Venezuela.
Rahman, M.A. 1993. People's *Self Development: Perspectives on Participatory Action Research*. London: Zed Books.
Reyes Matta, F. (ed.). 1983. *Comunicación Alternativa y Búsquedas Democráticas* [Alternative Communication and Democratic Quests]. Mexico City: Instituto Latinoamericano de Estudios Transnacionales y Fundación Friedrich Ebert.
Riaño, P. 1994. 'Women's Participation in Communication: Elements of a Framework', in P. Riaño (ed.). *Women in Grassroots Communication*, pp. 3–29. Thousand Oaks, CA: Sage Publications.
Rodriguez, C. 1994. 'A Process of Identity Deconstruction: Latin American Women Producing Video Stories', in P. Riaño (ed.). *Women in Grassroots Communication*, pp. 149–160. Thousand Oaks, CA: Sage Publications.
Rogers, E.M. 1976. 'Communication and Development: The Passing of the Dominant Paradigm', *Communication Research*, 3(2):213 240.
———. 1993. 'Perspectives on Development Communication', in K.S. Nair and S.A. White (eds). *Perspectives on Development Communication*, pp. 35–46 New Delhi: Sage Publications.
Röling, N.G., J. Ascroft and F.W. Chege. 1976. 'The Diffusion of Innovations and the Issue of Equity in Rural Development', in E.M. Rogers (ed.). *Communication and Development: Critical Perspectives*, pp. 63–79. Beverly Hills: Sage Publications.
Schramm, W. 1976. 'End of an Old Paradigm?', in W. Schramm and D. Lerner (eds). *Communication and Change: The Last Ten Years—and the Next*, pp. 45–48. Honolulu: East–West Center.
Servaes, J. 1985. 'Towards an Alternative Concept of Communication and Development', *Media Development*, 4:2–5.
———. 1986. 'Development Theory and Communication Policy: Power to the People!', *European Journal of Communication*, 1:203–229.
———. 1989. *One World, Multiple Cultures: A New Paradigm on Communication for Development*. Leuven: Acco.
———. 1996a. 'Introduction: Participatory Communication and Research in Development Settings', in J. Servaes, T.L. Jacobson and S.A. White (eds). *Participatory Communication for Social Change*, pp. 13–25. New Delhi: Sage Publications.
———. 1996b. 'Linking Theoretical Perspectives to Policy', in J. Servaes, T.L. Jacobson, and S.A. White (eds). *Participatory Communication for Social Change*, pp. 29–43. New Delhi: Sage Publications.
———. 1996c. 'Participatory Communication Research with New Social Movements: A Realistic Utopia', in J. Servaes, T.L. Jacobson and S.A. White (eds). *Participatory Communication for Social Change*, pp. 82–108. New Delhi: Sage Publications.
———. 1998. 'Human Rights, Participatory Communication and Cultural Freedom in a Global Perspective', *The Journal of International Communication*, 5(1 and 2):122–133.
Servaes, J. and R. Arnst. 1999. 'Principles of Participatory Communication Research: Its Strengths (!) and Weaknesses (?)', in T.L. Jacobson and J. Servaes (eds). *Theoretical Approaches to Participatory Communication*, pp. 107–130. Cresskill, NJ: Hampton Press.
Shingi, P.M. and B. Mody. 1976. 'The Communication Effects Gap: A Field Experiment on Television and Agricultural Ignorance in India', in E.M. Rogers (ed.). *Communication and Development: Critical Perspectives*, pp. 79–98. Beverly Hills: Sage Publications.
Simpson Grinberg, M. (ed.). 1986. *Comunicación Alternativa y Cambio Social* [Alternative Communication and Social Change]. Tlahuapan, Puebla, Mexico: Premiá Editora de Libros.
Singhal, A. and E.M. Rogers. 1988. 'Television Soap Operas for Development in India', *Gazette*, 41(2):109–126.

Storey, D. 1999. 'Popular Culture, Discourse, and Development', in T.L. Jacobson and J. Servaes (eds). *Theoretical Approaches to Participatory Communication*, pp. 337–358. Cresskill, NJ: Hampton Press.

———. 2000. 'A Discursive Perspective on Development Theory and Practice: Reconceptualizing the Role of Donor Agencies', in K.G. Wilkins (ed.). *Redeveloping Communication for Social Change: Theory, Practice, and Power*, pp. 103–117. Lanham, MD: Rowman and Littlefield Publishers.

Tehranian, M. 1999. *Global Communication and World Politics: Domination, Development and Discourse*. Boulder, CO: Lynne Rienner.

Thapalia, C.F. 1996. 'Animation and Leadership', in J. Servaes, T.L. Jacobson and S.A. White (eds). *Participatory Communication for Social Change*, pp. 150–161. New Delhi: Sage Publications.

Thomas, P. 1994. 'Participatory Message Development Communication: Philosophical Premises', in S.A. White, K.S. Nair and J. Ascroft (eds). *Participatory Communication: Working for Change and Development*, pp. 49–59. New Delhi: Sage Publications.

Vargas, L. 1995. *Social Uses and Radio Practices: The Use of Participatory Radio by Ethnic Minorities in Mexico*. Boulder, CO: Westview.

White, K. 1999. 'The Importance of Sensitivity to Culture in Development Work', in T.L. Jacobson and J. Servaes (eds). *Theoretical Approaches to Participatory Communication*, pp. 17–49. Cresskill, NJ: Hampton Press.

White, R. 1994. 'Participatory Development Communication as a Social-Cultural Process', in S.A. White, K.S. Nair and J. Ascroft (eds). *Participatory Communication: Working for Change and Development*, pp. 95–116. New Delhi: Sage Publications.

———. 1999. 'The Need for New Strategies of Research on the Democratization of Communication', in T.L. Jacobson and J. Servaes (eds). *Theoretical Approaches to Participatory Communication*, pp. 229–262 Cresskill, NJ: Hampton Press.

White, S.A. 1994. 'The Concept of Participation: Transforming Rhetoric to Reality', in S.A. White, K.S. Nair and J. Ascroft (eds). *Participatory Communication: Working for Change and Development*, pp. 15–32. New Delhi: Sage Publications.

Wildemeersch, D. 1999. 'Transcending the Limits of Traditional Research: Toward an Interpretive Approach to Development Communication and Education', in T.L. Jacobson and J. Servaes (eds). *Theoretical Approaches to Participatory Communication*, pp. 211–227. Cresskill, NJ: Hampton Press.

Wilkins, K.G. 1999. 'Development Discourse on Gender and Communication in Strategies for Social Change', *Journal of Communication*, 49:46–68.

———. 2000. 'Accounting for Power in Development Communication', in K.G. Wilkins (ed.). *Redeveloping Communication for Social Change: Theory, Practice, and Power*, pp. 197–210. Lanham, MD: Rowman and Littlefield Publishers.

Part III

Communication Policies, Strategies and Exemplars

Communication for Development Approaches of Some Governmental and Non-Governmental Agencies

9

JAN SERVAES

In this chapter, we first briefly present two communication models: the 'diffusion/mechanistic' versus the 'participatory/organic' communication model. These models should be seen as extremes on a continuum.

Secondly, also at the policy and planning level one can distinguish between different approaches, which build on the 'diffusion model' versus the 'participatory model'.

Thirdly, we will identify the communication strategies and policies of a number of national and international governmental and non-governmental agencies on the basis of the above made distinction.

Diffusion versus Participatory Model

The Main Characteristics of *the Diffusion Model* are:

1. Derived from a worldview of dominance over one's environment, the Western conception of communication is overwhelmingly oriented towards persuasion. Akin to the modernization paradigm in both theory and ideology, the communication approach is uni-directional, from the informed 'source' to the uninformed 'receiver'.

2. Congruent with the modernization philosophy, the diffusion and development support communication approaches tend to assign responsibility for the problem of under-development to peoples residing in those societies.

3. Development as modernization and communication as one-way persuasion reached their zenith through the diffusion of innovations, the two-step-flow, and other 'social marketing' strategies of attitude and behaviour change directed at 'underdeveloped' peoples.

4. Mass media play the pre-eminent role in the campaign of development through communication, and early predictions were of great effects. Bi-directional models and strategies such as feedback were added to render the initial message more effective.

5. Mass audiences were 'influenced' with predispositions towards development and social institutions. Such media technology has been taken either as the sole solution, the driving force, or simply a value-free tool in the process of development.

6. Research of the diffusion approach, like the modernization theory, suffers from an overemphasis on quantitative criteria to the exclusion of social and cultural factors. As a result, the manner in which foreign media hardware and software interact within a cultural context is largely unexplored.

The Main Characteristics of *the Participatory Model* are:

1. The participatory model sees people as the controlling actors or participants for development. People will have self-appreciation instead of self-depreciation. Development is meant to liberate and emancipate people. Local culture is respected.

2. The participatory model sees people as the nucleus of development. Development means lifting up the spirits of a local community to take pride in its own culture, intellect and environment. Development aims to educate and stimulate people to be active in self and communal improvements while maintaining a balanced ecology. Authentic participation, though widely espoused in the literature, is not in everyone's interest. Such programmes are not easily implemented, highly predictable, or readily controlled.

3. The participatory model emphasizes on the local community rather than the nation-state, on monistic universalism rather than nationalism, on spiritualism rather than secular humanism, on dialogue rather than monologue, and on emancipation rather than alienation.

4. Participation involves the redistribution of power. Participation aims at redistributing the elites' power so that a community can become a full-fledged democratic one. As such, it directly threatens those whose position and/or very existence depends upon power and its exercise over others. Reactions to such threats are sometimes overt, but most often are manifested as less visible, yet steady and continuous resistance.

DevCom Approaches in Intergovernmental and Non-Governmental Agencies

The theoretical changes in the perspective on development communication have also reached the level of policy-makers. As a result, different methodologies and terminologies have evolved, which often make it difficult for agencies, even though they share a common commitment to the overall goals of development communication, to identify common ground, arrive at a full understanding of each other's objectives, or to co-operate effectively in operational projects.

Communication theories such as the 'diffusion of innovations', the 'two-step-flow', or the 'extension' approaches are quite congruent with the elitist, vertical or top-down orientation of the diffusion model. However, the reality often proves much more complex than the theory.

During discussions on international political and academic forums new insights on the role and place of communication for development emerged which favour two-way and horizontal communication.

Therefore, in 1989, the UNESCO started a UNFPA-financed project on *Integrated Approaches to Development Communication*. Its objectives were to review the various approaches and methodologies, to identify their differences and common features, and to create a framework for integrated and co-operative action.

The project analyzed the following agencies and projects (for more details, see Mayo and Servaes, 1994):

Seven United Nations Agencies: The Food and Agriculture Organization (FAO) of the United Nations, International Labour Organization (ILO), United Nations Development Programme (UNDP), United Nations Educational, Scientific and Cultural Organization (UNESCO), United Nations Population Fund (UNFPA), United Nations Children Fund (UNICEF), World Health Organization (WHO);

Three Governmental Agencies: Agence de Coopération Culturelle et Technique/Agency for Cultural and Technical Co-operation (ACCT), Canadian International Development Agency (CIDA), United States Agency for International Development (USAID);

Nine Non-governmental Organizations: African Council for Communication Education/Conseil Africain d'Enseignement de Communication (ACCE), Asian Mass Communication and Information Centre (AMIC), Association Mondiale des Radiodiffuseurs Communautaires/World Association of Community Radio Broadcasters (AMARC), Friedrich Ebert Stiftung (FES), Instituto para America Latina (IPAL), Radio Nederland Training Centre (RNTC), Women's Feature Service (WFS), World Association for Christian Communication (WACC), Worldview International Foundation (WIF); and

Nine Case Studies: of development communication in action, presenting a range of strategies in different world regions: Brazilian Telenovelas, Expanded Programme on Immunisation (EPI) (Bangladesh), Inter Press Service (IPS), Kheda Communications Project (India), Mahaweli Community Radio (Sri Lanka), Radio Enriquillo (Dominican Republic), Rural Communication System for Development in Mexico's Tropical Wetlands (PRODERITH), Social Marketing Campaigns, West and Central Africa News Agencies Development/Developpement des Agences de Presse en Afrique de l'Ouest et Centrale (WANAD).

Table 9.1 identifies the major DevCom approaches for the above agencies and projects:

Table 9.1
Distinct DevCom Approaches and Media Strategies within the Diffusion Model and Participatory Model

	Diffusion of Innovations	Network Dev. Documentat	Social Marketing	Social Mobilization	DSC/Institut Development	Community Media
UN AGENCIES						
FAO	xxxxxxxx				xxxxxxxx	xxxxxxxx
ILO					xxxxxxxx	
UNDP					xxxxxxxx	
UNESCO		xxxxxxxx			xxxxxxxx	xxxxxxxx
UNFPA	xxxxxxxx	xxxxxxxx	xxxxxxxx			
UNICEF	xxxxxxxx	xxxxxxxx		xxxxxxxx	xxxxxxxx	xxxxxxxx
WHO	xxxxxxxx		xxxxxxxx			
GOVERNMENTAL AGENCIES						
ACCT		xxxxxxxx			xxxxxxxx	
AID	xxxxxxxx	xxxxxxxx	xxxxxxxx		xxxxxxxx	
CIDA		xxxxxxxx			xxxxxxxx	xxxxxxxx
DANIDA					xxxxxxxx	xxxxxxxx
NON-GOVERNMENTAL AGENCIES						
ACCE		xxxxxxxx				
AMARC		xxxxxxxx				xxxxxxxx
AMIC	xxxxxxxx	xxxxxxxx			xxxxxxxx	
FES		xxxxxxxx			xxxxxxxx	xxxxxxxx
IPAL		xxxxxxxx				xxxxxxxx
RNTC					xxxxxxxx	xxxxxxxx
WACC		xxxxxxxx			xxxxxxxx	xxxxxxxx
WFS		xxxxxxxx				
WIF				xxxxxxxx		xxxxxxxx
Case Studies						
AID Health Africa	xxxxxxxx		xxxxxxxx		xxxxxxxx	
Brazil Telenovela	xxxxxxxx		xxxxxxxx			
EPI Bangladesh	xxxxxxxx				xxxxxxxx	xxxxxxxx
IPS		xxxxxxxx			xxxxxxxx	
Kheda India	xxxxxxxx			xxxxxxxx		xxxxxxxx
Mahaweli Sri Lanka				xxxxxxxx	xxxxxxxx	xxxxxxxx
PRODERITH Mexico				xxxxxxxx	xxxxxxxx	xxxxxxxx
REnriquillo Dominican Rep.				xxxxxxxx	xxxxxxxx	xxxxxxxx
WANAD West-Africa		xxxxxxxx				

As noted already, a variety of theoretical models can be used to devise communication strategies for development. In contrast with the more economical- and politically-oriented approach in traditional perspectives on modernization and development, the central idea in alternative, more culturally-oriented versions of multiplicity and sustainable development is that there is no universal development model which leads to sustainability at all levels of society and the world, that development is an integral, multidimensional, and dialectic process that can differ from society to society, community to community, context to context. As each case and context is different, none has proven to be completely satisfactory. In other words, each society and community must attempt to delineate its own strategy to sustainable development. This implies that the development problem is a relative problem and that no one society can contend that it is 'developed' in every respect. Therefore, we believe that the scope and degree of interdependency must be addressed in relationship with the content of the concept of development.

Distinct development communication approaches and communication means used can be identified within organizations working at distinct societal and geographic levels. Some of these approaches can be grouped together under the heading of the above diffusion model, others under the participatory model. The major ones could be identified as the following (for more details, see Servaes and Malikhao, 2004):

Extension/Diffusion of Innovations as a Development Communications Approach: The Extension/ Diffusion of Innovation Approach is based on the modernization paradigm and Ev Rogers' diffusion theory. Extension is concerned with the staged process of technology transfer in a top-down fashion from researchers/experts (or other producers of innovations) to potential users of these research results. The conventional scope of extension remains in the agricultural field but the contemporary one has broadened to a wide range of subjects such as environmental issues, small business enterprise trainings, and technology transfer. Therefore, the clientele served can be urban people as well. *This approach is to inform the audience or to persuade a behavioral change in a predetermined way.*

Contemporary variations re-examine the messages, the needs of the audience, the initial knowledge of the audience and the agenda setting between the researchers and the farmers/ clientele.

Network Development and Documentation: The dominant approach requires networking through computerized satellite telecommunication links or the Internet as a basic infrastructure. The provision of analytical and contextualized flows of information regarding development events and issues through telecommunication services or the Internet are designed, implemented and researched to support the process of development.

In news reporting this kind of networking allows journalists from the global South to voice their views and exchange news events from their perspectives to counterbalance the mainstream traffic of data and information flows from the North. Not only this approach allows the peripheral-to-centre flow in the world system context, it also supports those in the peripheral-to-centre flow within the peripheral arenas itself. New actors are thus identified, such as women, rural people and children in the developing world. This approach could contribute to interesting spin-offs, such as online training programmes, distance education, information exchange and the establishment of alternative networks.

ICTs for Development: Information and Communication Technologies (ICTs), such as computer and telecommunication technology, especially the Internet, are used to bridge the information and knowledge divide between the haves and the have-nots. Having access to the digital highways helps improve access to education opportunities, increase transparency and efficiency in government services, enhance direct participation from the 'used-to-be-silent public' in the democratic process, increase trade and marketing opportunities, enhance community empowerment by giving a voice to voiceless groups (e.g. women) and vulnerable groups, such as those who live with HIV/AIDS, create networking and income opportunities for women, access to medical information for isolated communities and increase new employment opportunities.

In developing countries, the local appropriation of ICTs is a *telecentre or multi-media community centre* consisting of desktop publishing, community newspaper, sales or rentals of audio and video cassettes and DVDs, book lending, photocopying, faxing, and telephone services. Access to the Internet and World Wide Web can be optional. The use of the mobile and satellite telephony can help small entrepreneurs and rural farmers getting access to information needed to improve their livelihood.

ICTs can be powerful tools for sharing information, but they often cannot solve the development problems caused by the underlying social, economic and political issues, nor can they change the existing power structures as the information available is not necessarily knowledge. In order to become knowledge, the information has to make sense to the people who receive this information.

Training/Education and Capacity-Building/Strengthening: In co-operation with local training and development centres and universities vocational and follow-up training systems are developed, implemented and evaluated. This could be training for agency personnel and technicians, as well as the training of professional groups of journalists or development communicators. To improve the quality of output and bilateral communication flows, exchange programmes and networking are being developed. Communication manuals written by experts from First and Third World countries serve as a guideline for scriptwriters, journalists and educational radio workers. These handbooks and multi-media kits (both in hardcopy or digital) are often the outcome of workshops and conferences held with local experts and practitioners.

Social Marketing: Social marketing is the application of commercial marketing techniques to solve social problems. It is also a multi-disciplinary approach because it concerns education, community development, psychology and communication. Roy Colle states that it is 'a process that assumes that what made McDonald's and Coca-Cola a world class success can also have a dramatic impact on the problems of high blood pressure, AIDS, child mortality in developing nations, and other circumstances related to patterns of behavior' (see Colle's chapter).

The process involves the planning, implementation and monitoring of programmes to persuade the acceptance of social ideas. The basic elements of the process lie on *product, price, place, and promotion.* The 'product' concept may be an object, idea or behavioural change in a favourable way. The 'price' concept is comparable to that of the commercial sector but it is conceived in social cost terms, such as missed opportunities, deviation from the established cultural norm, and so forth. 'Place' refers to the channels through which the ideas or the product will be transmitted. 'Promotion' refers to the use of mediated or interpersonal communication to make the product known among the audience or target groups.

Social marketers commit themselves to people's health and well-being; are not profit-oriented and are seeking a larger market share than the commercial marketers.

Edutainment (EE):   Entertainment Education (EE) or the edutainment approach is a *hybrid* of participatory communication strategies and the diffusion model of communication. It combines the attraction of entertainment with educational messages to help educate, inform and encourage behaviour change to achieve development and social progress. This approach can employ traditional or indigenous media such as puppet shows, music and dance to promote issues in health care, literacy programmes, environmental protection and introducing agricultural practices.

These forms of communication can be integrated with electronic media such as radio, television, video and audio cassettes. The important point is that the programmes are produced locally to appeal to the local audience.

Another offshoot of this approach is applying the social marketing strategies to help embed the development issues in melodramatic soap operas for radio and television, which use real or fictional 'social models' to promote changes in lifestyles. These programmes are adapted to local cultural contexts and integrate entertainment with awareness-raising and education. It is often used in the raising of awareness in complex issues such as HIV/AIDS. It brings particular health issues such as sexual practices in a private manner to the people's home via the TV screen.

Health Communication: The best representative of the Health Communication approach is the World Health Organization (WHO). In the past WHO tended to employ development communication strategies based on the *social marketing approach and diffusion theory.* Current projects are more centred on bottom-up, grass-roots, and *participatory models of communication in a mixed media approach.*

Three main strategies are being employed in this new approach:

(*a*) *Advocacy*: Advocacy aims to foster public policies that are supportive of health such as the provision of biomedical care for treating illness, and prevention such as immunization, safe water and sanitation, maternal and child health and promoting of healthy lifestyles. Mass media and traditional media can play a strong advocacy role in creating public awareness and in bringing about action for health, and often target decision-makers as well as interest groups who in turn press for suitable policies. The effectiveness of their advocacy role, however, depends on the freedom the media enjoy and the influence they carry with the national political system and the public.

(*b*) *Empowerment*: This strategy emphasizes the role of the community members in planning and managing their own health care. Furthermore, there has been increasing realization that knowledge alone is not enough for behavioural change; empowering people aims not only at fostering healthy lifestyles but also at enabling them to mobilize social forces and to create conditions including health supportive public policies and responsive systems, that are conducive to healthy living.

(*c*) *Social support*: Since acceptance of new practices and favourable behavioural change need social approval, there is a need for building alliances between and networking with the many groups and agencies that work for and influence health and welfare. WHO organizes activities to train media professionals in health and in health education by running health promotion campaigns in all regions, and workshops at all levels and intensive courses to improve the planning and production of mass media programmes on priority health development subjects. WHO, furthermore, collaborates with UNESCO, UNICEF and other organizations on information exchange.

In other words, this new paradigm for health is *people-oriented*. A bottom-up process that pays due attention to the individual, the family and the community, but especially to the underprivileged and those who are at risk, such as women and children and the elderly.

Social mobilization: Social mobilization, an approach associated with UNICEF, is a process of bringing together all feasible and practical *inter-sectoral* social partners and allies to determine felt-needs and to raise awareness of, and demand for, a particular development objective. It involves enlisting the participation of all actors, including institutions, groups, networks and communities, in identifying, raising, and managing human and material resources, thereby increasing and strengthening *self-reliance* and sustainability of achievements. It is a planned process that relies heavily on communication.

At the policy level, advocacy is used to assure the high level of public commitment necessary to undertake action by fostering a knowledgeable and supportive environment for decision-making, as well as the allocation of adequate resources to attain the campaign's goals and objectives.

At the grass-roots level, the primary aim is to inform and motivate community members through multiple channels, and to sustain the latter's active participation.

Information, Education and Communication (IEC): For several decades IEC has been associated with *population and family planning* programmes around the world. UNFPA was among the first to use the term IEC in 1969 in labelling its communication activities. Specifically, IEC has referred most frequently to the use of information, education and communication to promote adoption of contraceptives or other practices to limit births.

The information component brings facts and issues to the attention of an audience in order to stimulate discussion. It also concerns the technical and statistical aspects of development. Population information programme strategies in the future gear towards improving databases and research, linking population to environmental and other development issues, identifying the role of women in population and development, reiterating the case for family planning, maintaining media attention and political commitment and applying new technology to population information programmes.

The education component fosters knowledge and thorough understanding of problems and possible solutions. The formal and non-formal education subcomponents are to strengthen human resources by curriculum design and training to sensitize awareness and foster critical thinking of development issues and facilitate life-long educational goals.

The communication component is to influence attitudes, disseminate knowledge and to bring about a desired and voluntary change in behaviour.

In 1994, the IEC approach was linked with the concept of *reproductive health*. The focus on the use of condoms in males shifted to a focus on gender inequality, as males often decide on behalf of women. IEC has become a close tie with advocacy in developing reproductive health communication strategies and in other development communication contexts.

Institution-building: The Institution-building approach provides developing nations with organizations, skills and facilities to carry out development communication. There are many national and international institutions that use this approach, for instance the Ford Foundation, FAO, USAID, and the Canadian Government. However, UNESCO is the UN-agency closely associated with this approach.

For the Ford Foundation and FAO institution-building took place at the G.B. Pant University of Agriculture and Technology in Uttar Pradesh State in India in the late 1960s and 1980s respectively. The work consisted of both training the staff abroad to upgrade the communication competence, and providing facilities for the university to produce radio programmes and other resources for reaching the farm and rural population. In 1970s, the USAID assisted the Guatemalan Government in building two radio stations that were dedicated to supporting agricultural, nutrition, and health activities in rural communities. In the 1980s, the Canadian Government supported Indonesia to institutionalize special units in most major broadcast stations that were especially focussed on development issues.

Knowledge, Attitudes and Practices (KAP): Development communicators work to bring about change in the behaviour of people reached in the projects they undertake. Knowledge and attitude are internal factors that affect how human beings act. There are also other internal factors such as perceived social pressure/norms, gender, and so forth. An *enabling environment* such as the education system, policy and legislation, cultural factors, service provision, religion, socio-political factors, physical environment and organizational environment can also influence the knowledge and attitudes of the target groups.

Knowledge is internalized learning based on scientific facts, experiences and/or traditional beliefs. Experience shows that knowledge is necessary but not sufficient to produce behaviour change, which only occurs when perceptions, motivation, skills and the social environment also interact.

Attitudes in this perspective are feelings, opinions or values that an individual holds about a particular issue, problem or concern.

Development Support Communication (DSC):   The Development Support Communication (DSC) approach is the systematic utilization of appropriate communication channels and techniques to increase people's participation in development and to inform, motivate, and train rural populations, mainly at the grassroots level.

This concept is one of the central ones in FAO's approach to Communication for Development. The DSC Branch was one of a sub-programme within FAO's Rural Development Programme. It emphasizes a multi-media approach, especially the integration of traditional and popular media, and campaign strategies.

There are two major lines of actions. A majority of DSC field interventions still deal with communication components that support a variety of rural development, but increasingly DSC operations became stand-alone projects. A new line is the support to national institutions in an effort to build in-country capacity to deal with all aspects of Communication for Development: from policy advice to appropriate communication research, from the definition of national communication policies and strategies, to the development of multi-media approaches and the choice of culture-specific media mixes.

HIV/AIDS Community Approach: The HIV/AIDS pandemic is cause and consequence of underdevelopment. For the past three decades of its existence, there appears to be growing consensus that focussing on the risky behaviours of individuals is insufficient when not taking into account the social determinants and deep-seated inequalities driving the epidemic. The UNAIDS framework was published in December 1999 following an intensive consultation process in Asia, Africa, Latin America and the Caribbean. Its conclusions were that:

- The simple, linear relationship between individual knowledge and action, which underpinned many earlier interventions, does not take into account the variation among the political, socio-economic and cultural contexts that prevail in the regions.
- External decision-making processes that cater to rigid, narrowly focussed and short-term interests tend to overlook the benefits of long-term, internally derived, broad-based solutions.

- There is an assumption that decisions about HIV/AIDS prevention are based on rational, volitional thinking with no regard for more true-to-life emotional responses to engaging in sexual behaviour.
- There is an assumption that creating awareness through media campaigns will necessarily lead to behaviour change.
- There is an assumption that a simple strategy designed to trigger an once-in-a-lifetime behaviour, such as immunization, would be adequate for changing and maintaining complex, life-long behaviours, such as consistent condom use.
- There is a nearly exclusive focus on condom promotion to the exclusion of the need to address the importance and centrality of social contexts, including government policy, socio-economic status, culture, gender relations and spirituality.
- Approaches based on traditional family planning and population programme strategies tend to target HIV/AIDS prevention to women, so that women, rather than men, are encouraged to initiate the use of condoms.

UNAIDS identified five interrelated factors in communications for HIV/AIDS preventative health behaviour: government policy, socio-economic status, culture, gender relations, and spirituality. These domains formed the basis of *a new framework* that could be used as a flexible guide in the development of HIV/AIDS communications interventions. Individual health behaviour is recognized as a component of this set of domains, rather than primary focus of health behaviour change. UNAIDS emphasizes that community consultation occurs in all phases of HIV/AIDS policy design, programme implementation and evaluation as well as protection for civic society and community groups. The importance of HIV information is recognized, with adequate HIV prevention and care information presented as a human rights issue.

Community Participation: C4D rests on the premise that successful sustainable development calls for the conscious and active participation of the intended beneficiaries at every stage of the development process; for in the final analysis, development cannot take place without changes in attitudes and behaviour among all the people concerned. Participation involves the more equitable sharing of both political and economic power, which often decreases the advantage of certain groups. Structural change involves the redistribution of power.

Media used in participatory communication are among other things: interactive film and video, community radio and newspapers. The main theme is empowering people to make their own decisions. The *conscientization approach* of Freire (1983) showed how people will galvanize themselves into action to address their priority problems.

The distinct DevCom approaches and media used have been summarized in the enclosed matrices (in Table 9.1). Some of these approaches can be grouped together under the heading of the diffusion model, others under the participatory model.

The Diffusion Model

The Diffusion Model mainly builds on approaches such as Development Support Communication (DSC), multimedia and campaign strategies, training and research.

Organizations adopting this model stress the need for careful planning of communication and implementation, but also emphasize the importance of creativity and flexibility in the planning process.

1. The DSC Process Model

Broken down to its essential elements, the systematic approach, which is thought to be particularly appropriate for multimedia campaigns, comprises the following four stages:

(a) *Needs Assessment/Information Gathering:* Determine key development priorities through field surveys, community consensus, interviews with field specialists and subject matter specialists; assess media channels available to potential target groups; ascertain whether technology transfer inputs are readily available.

(b) *Decision Making/Strategy Development:* Prioritize needs, select the most important and establish development or project objectives to be addressed; identify target groups, carry out baseline knowledge, attitudes, practices (KAP) survey, conduct focus group sessions, determine multimedia mix and message design strategies.

(c) *Implementation:* Draw up an action plan, produce and field test samples of media materials, revise and finalize material, train field staff in content and use of material, distribute material, and monitor campaign as it unfolds.

(d) *Evaluation:* Carry out small-scale field evaluations at strategic points during campaign to suggest where 'in course' changes may be warranted; conduct full scale ex-post or post-campaign impact evaluation survey and use as preparation or feed-forward for future campaigns.

2. Multimedia Approaches

No single media is better than any other. Therefore, multimedia approaches are considered the most effective, and that behavioural change is seldom the result of exposure to media alone. Therefore, audience research, which, among other things, establishes a knowledge base regarding the type of media rural people have access to, those they like and those they would love to own, determines to a large extent the proposed choice of media.

At the regional level, already existing telecommunication systems can be modified, adapted and expanded to serve the needs of local and national groups. By using existing infrastructure, no new expensive technology is needed. Setting up regional television news exchange networks implies reaching consensus between authorities and TV corporations to make use of already existing satellite services and ground stations wherever possible. If additional infrastructure is necessary, it is important to implement the economically, socially and culturally most preferable hardware.

(a) *Rural radio*: Radio is generally agreed to be the most useful mass medium in rural development projects. Although television is more prestigious, powerful and persuasive, radio is more widely available in rural areas, cheaper and easier in production and reception, quicker, simpler, less monopolized and can more easily facilitate localized information.

(b) *Group media*: Among the group media, video is increasing its popularity. Though video is highly effective, it also calls for a careful strategy and skilled producers.

Audio-visual media in general make it possible to:

- help overcome barriers of illiteracy and incomprehension, by conveying ideas and practices in audio and visual formats;
- illustrate new ideas and techniques more effectively than by word-of-mouth alone, and thus improve the impact of extension and training;
- compress time, as for instance a whole crop cycle can be shown in a short presentation;
- compress space, as events and practices in distant locations can be transferred to other places where they can be useful testimonials;
- standardize technical information, by creating audio-visual material that illustrate the best available advice to farmers and by having this material used throughout the extension and farmer training chain, thereby ensuring that the technical information will not become distorted during its passage from its source to the smallest and most remote farmer.

(c) *Interpersonal communication*: Interpersonal communication skills do also play a major role in rural communication programmes. Interpersonal communication moves beyond a good understanding of the technical subject matter. It also calls for knowledge and skills concerned with empathy, group and individual psychology, and group dynamics. It requires sensitivity to the needs and views of others, listening skills, and attitudes favourable to working with people as a trusted helper, rather than an agent of authority telling people what to do. Proper training of development staff in this area is therefore also stressed.

(d) *Traditional and popular media*: Village and street theatre, puppets, songs, dances and storytelling have become familiar media used either in mass or group settings.

3. The Campaign Strategy

The multi-channel communication campaigns are seen as an effective strategy in the arsenal of DSC mechanisms, as they spur action in areas of high development priority. These campaigns usually involve broadcasting, village-based group media, and intensive use of interpersonal communication techniques through institutional channels such as extension workers, community workers, and so forth. The campaigns are usually carried out at a national or regional level over a short period of time, focus on a specific topic of high development priority and have a limited set of objectives, for instance, expanding rice production through increased cultivation of swamp farms in Sierra Leone, a two-month campaign.

Furthermore, one has to recognize, first the importance of good project management, because studies indicated that many projects failed due to poor management, and, secondly, the training of trainers. Two additional components or sub-systems of the campaign approach are therefore: (1) the 'Management Plan' aimed at coordinating people and events, and (2) the 'Staff Training Plan' which is adapted from the UNDP model.

4. Training

In co-operation with local training and development centres, initial and follow-up training systems are developed, implemented and evaluated. This concerns training for broadcasting personnel and agency technicians, as well as the training of journalists. Within the central objective to improve the quality of output and bilateral communication flows, exchange programmes are set up. Communication manuals written by experts from First and Third World countries serve as a guideline for scriptwriters, journalists and educational radio workers. These handbooks often are the result of workshops and conferences held between local experts from different regions.

5. Research

In close co-operation with regional centres, and the more practically-oriented broadcasting unions, communication systems are developed. This decentralized approach is regarded as essential for the development of socio-cultural autonomous and situation-specific methods and strategies. Apart from conveying modern methods of training in programme production and engineering, efforts are made to design blueprints for media laws and regulations.

Conferences held between different experts aim at projecting and forecasting consequences of local and international communication developments from an interdisciplinary point of view. The outcome of these meetings serve as a starting point for further research.

The Participatory Model

The *participatory model* calls for upward, transactive, open and radical forms of planning that encompass both grassroots collective actions (that is, small-scale planning and large-scale planning in the small), and large-scale processes (i.e., planning in the large). This kind of planning and research is centrally conceived with human growth, learning processes through mobilization, and the basic aim is to involve the people under study to co-operate with one another in the planning and research process, with the planner or researcher as a facilitator and participant.

Participatory communication methods employed, include:

1. A Participatory Approach to Evaluation

Participatory communication projects always emphasize democratic participation in its operations. Therefore, the project staff is inclined towards a participatory approach to evaluation. The assumption is that if staff is directly involved in the determination of evaluation results, they will also be more committed to carrying out the recommendations. Thus the staff is involved at various stages of the evaluation process—selection of objectives, development of the methodology, data collection and analysis. However, the process attempts to balance the in-depth knowledge of the project's operations with the research experience and independent perspective of 'outside' facilitators of the evaluation.

2. A Participatory Approach to Research

Data collection is carried out with the involvement of project staff and local people. Six methods are normally used to collect data: (a) surveys, (b) community meetings, (c) focus groups, (d) analysis of programming, (e) document analysis and (f) participatory observation.

3. Quantitative and Qualitative Research Methods

Research methods employed focus on a combination and interpretation of quantitative and qualitative data. For quantitative data, clear-cut conventions exist as to what can be done with data and how data should be collected. Sometimes some of these conventions, like inter-coder reliability, cannot be met, due to the specific situations in which the research is executed, for instance, the 'inexperience' of the interviewers with the above conventions. However, most of these methodological problems in the quantitative part of the research can be corrected through the qualitative research findings. The collection of qualitative data assists in formulating the specific content of the questionnaires by identifying the most important key variables or sensitizing concepts under which more specific data can be explored. It also aids in controlling the quantitative data. And, even more significantly, qualitative data enlivens and makes more concrete the statistical pictures which come out of survey information.

Some standards of data collection, such as a high degree of statistical reliability, can sometimes not be met. First, because most data are gathered by associates of the project, rather than by independent observers and, secondly, because many of them are inexperienced in the protocols of data collection, though there may be a provision of training. It is agreeable that problems with quantitative measurements can be corrected through more in-depth qualitative research, and careful data analysis and interpretation. Participatory researchers also believe that qualitative data broaden the findings suggested by the statistical data.

4. A Community-Based Approach

Why does the community have such trust and support for participatory projects? 'Because the people that work with it are valuable resources.' 'Because they have the support and acceptance of the people.' 'Because they make continual efforts toward improvement, as in this evaluation.' These are the three answers most frequently cited by respondents during a participatory evaluation. They are the three basic elements by which a democratic organization can transcend its limitations, redefine vision: a team that values people, works to revise its practice, and ensures that the people recognize this project as their own.

5. Community Participation

The audience needs to express their needs and wishes. The organization of the project is democratic. This means that the population can co-operate in the development of programmes. Access for anyone to the microphones or other resources is all important. People express their feedback and their own ideas. Access for farmers in remote villages is made easier through the 'unidad movil'—a mobile recording unit. Most important is to gain the trust of the people.

Therefore, one could call the conventional strategies 'diffusion/mechanistic' models, as the human being is considered as just a 'thing', while participatory strategies are more 'organic', spiritually-oriented and 'human', they believe in the humanness, the importance of people (see Table 9.2: Mechanistic versus Organic Model). Both models should be regarded as opposite positions on a continuum.

Table 9.2
Mechanistic versus Organic Model

	Mechanistic Model	Organic Model
OVERALL OBJECTIVES		
Motive for Co-operation	People need to be helped. Charity.	People are able to help themselves. Empowerment.
Assumption about target group	People lack abilities and resources to develop themselves. They are helpless.	People do have abilities to develop themselves. These can be mobilized.
Attitudes towards problems	Problem solving.	Problem posing.
Attitude towards participation	Means to achieve ends.	A never-ending process.
Objective of policy-makers or researchers	Implementation of project objectives.	Striving towards a common vision and understanding of self-development.
Learning relationship	Teacher-student; know–all versus know-nothing. Paternalistic.	Everybody is a teacher and student at the same time; everybody has something of interest to share.
Valuation of knowledge	Western knowledge is superior.	Traditional knowledge is equally relevant.

(*Table 9.2 continued*)

(*Table 9.2 continued*)

	Mechanistic Model	Organic Model
Agent of change	Policy-maker or researcher.	People themselves.
People seen as	Targets, objects.	Subjects, actors.
'Leadership position'	Project leader.	Coordinator, animator, facilitator.
Selection of 'leaders'	Appointed by higher authority.	Preferably selected by people themselves.
'Leadership' qualifications	Decision-making, management, authoritative.	Co-operation, delegation, receptive, adaptability to new circumstances.
Relation with people and colleagues:	Expert-counterpart; authority-centred.	Shared Leadership; shared responsibility.
POLICY AND PLANNING		
Design criteria	Productivity and economic growth.	Needs and criteria for well-being formulated by people themselves.
Organizational structure:	Hierarchical, vertical.	Horizontal, two-way.
Type of work	Technical-economic.	Educational-organizational.
Approach to work	Executing tasks.	Listening to people. Facilitating.
Organization of work	Formal, static.	Informal, dynamic.
Mode of communication	Monologue; consultation.	Dialogue
COMMUNICATION PROJECTS		
Type of media used	Mainly mass media.	Mixed and integrated media use; also interpersonal communication.
Direction of ideas and information	Top-down; one-way.	Bottom-up; two-way.
IMPLEMENTATION AND EVALUATION		
Planning format	Blueprint. Project approach.	Open-ended. Process approach.
Change seen as	Improvement.	Transformation.
Time perspective	Short term.	Long term.
Effect of absence of leader	Project activities slow down.	Development process continues.
Initiative for Evaluation	By funding agency or higher authority.	Usually initiated by people themselves.
Type of solutions	Symptom curing; evolutionary change.	Aimed at elimination of root causes; structural change.

Conclusion

It should be obvious by now that *no all-embracing view on development* is on offer. No theory has achieved and maintained explanatory dominance. Each of the above three theoretical perspectives still does find support among academics, policy-makers, international organizations, and the general public.

In general, adopted and updated versions of the ideas upon which the modernization theory is built—economic growth, centralized planning, and the belief that underdevelopment is rooted in mainly internal causes which can be solved by external, technological 'aid'—are still shared by many development agencies and governments. A *revitalized modernization perspective* in which some of the errors of the past are acknowledged and efforts are made to deal in new ways—as outlined in the multiplicity view—remains the dominant perspective in practice but becomes increasingly more difficult to defend in theory. On the other side, while the multiplicity theory is gaining ground in academic spheres, in practice it is still looked upon as a sympathetic though idealistic side-show.

At a more applied level, several perspectives on communication for development could be adopted and pursued.

A first perspective could be of *communication as a process*, often seen in metaphor as the fabric of society. It is not confined to the media or to messages, but to their interaction in a network of social relationships. By extension, the reception, evaluation and use of media messages, from whatever source, are as important as their means of production and transmission.

A second perspective is of *communications media as a mixed system of mass communication and interpersonal channels*, with mutual impact and reinforcement. In other words, the mass media should not be seen in isolation from other conduits.

Another perspective of communications in the development process is from an *intersectoral and interagency* concern. This view is not confined to information or broadcasting organizations and ministries, but extends to all sectors, and its success in influencing and sustaining development depends to a large extent on the adequacy of mechanisms for integration and co-ordination.

References

Freire, P. 1983. *Pedagogy of the Opressed.* New York: Seabury Press.

Mayo, J. and J. Servaes (eds). 1994. *Approaches to Development Communication. A Training and Orientation Kit.* Volumes 1 + 2. New York/Paris: UNFPA/UNESCO (@ 800pp. + video + diskette).

Servaes, J. and P. Malikhao. 2004. *Communication and Sustainable Development.* Rome: FAO.

UNESCO's Contributions to Cultural Diversity and Communication for Development

10

UNESCO

The United Nations Educational, Scientific and Cultural Organization (UNESCO) has been concerned with communication since its inception in 1946, as reflected in Article 1.2 of the Constitution, which invites the Organization to 'collaborate in the work of advancing the mutual knowledge and understanding of peoples, through all means of mass communication, and to that end recommend such international agreements as may be necessary to promote the free flow of ideas by word and image'. UNESCO is also recognized by the United Nations General Assembly as possessing the lead mandate in the field of social communication (in parallel to the technical mandate of the International Telecommunication Union [ITU]). Unlike many other organizations, therefore, UNESCO sees communication as a major programme in its own right, not only as a support to, or as a vector of, the development process.

The main orientations of UNESCO's Sector for Communication and Information have, in recent years, been in line with the main policy development of other leading United Nations agencies dedicated to Human Development. In order to meet the major challenges posed by the development of the new Information and Communication Technologies (ICTs) in the years to come, UNESCO provided a platform for international policy discussion and guidelines for action on the preservation of information and universal access to it, on the ethical, legal and societal consequences of ICT developments (especially with the Information For All Programme), and also providing training, networking and supporting indigenous knowledge.

Policy Changes after 1989

The Third Medium Term Plan, adopted by UNESCO's General Conference in 1989, after the end of the Cold War, set the objective 'to render more operational the concern of the Organisation to ensure a free flow of information at international as well as national levels, and its wider and better balanced dissemination, without any obstacle to the freedom of expression, and to strengthen communication capacities in the developing countries, so that they may participate more actively in the communication process'. Within the framework Communication in the Service of Humanity UNESCO committed itself to programmes that promote and monitor the exercise of free expression, support media pluralism and diversity, and emphasize professional and material exchange. In an effort to strengthen the South-North dialogue, the strategy called for a better dialogue and equilibrium between and among regions, and a more regular flow of programmes and materials across economic and cultural frontiers.

The second area of commitment reinforced UNESCO's long-standing work in support of the developing countries, primarily through infrastructure building and training, concentrated on the activities of the International Programme for the Development of Communication (IPDC).

The third focus of attention centred on the new communication technologies, their socio-cultural impact, development potential and relevance to UNESCO's spheres of competence, as well as on the need for users and audiences to become media-literate.

The Fourth Medium Term Plan for 1996–2001 reinforced these objectives and added An Agenda for Peace: conflict prevention, emergency assistance and post-conflict peace-building. Freedom of expression is an overarching theme.

These are new fields of action for UNESCO. With regard to conflict prevention, UNESCO strengthened its clearing-house function for the exchange of information on current research and experience concerning the means of ensuring the early detection and peaceful settlement of conflicts.

With regard to emergency assistance, UNESCO has become a strong advocate in the international community of the idea that humanitarian assistance cannot be reduced merely to the supply of food, medicine and blankets; that there must be a close link between the concepts of 'relief', 'rehabilitation' and 'long term development'; and that emergency operations must include from the beginning, a local training component. This idea has gained ground: there is growing recognition of the principle that the victims of conflicts have an equally inalienable right to education as all other human beings. UNESCO's strategy therefore consists in endeavouring to set up temporary educational structures in emergency situations, particularly for displaced persons and refugees. The Organization's role can only be as a catalyst: it is not so much to build schools or print school textbooks as to assess priority education needs, formulate strategies to meet them in conjunction with the Office of the United Nations High Commissioner for Refugees (UNHCR), UNICEF and FAO and contribute to the formulation of consolidated appeals for international humanitarian assistance coordinated by the United Nations Office for the Coordination of Humanitarian Affairs (UNOCHA).

While education is one of the high priorities in emergency situations, assistance to the independent media can prove to be fundamental to the reconciliation process. To counter warmongering propaganda and incitement to hatred in triggering and aggravating conflict,

UNESCO continues, as it has done in the Balkans and elsewhere, to support, together with the United Nations and professional organizations, local media whose independence of the parties to the conflict is internationally acknowledged, which provide non-partisan information and which defend the values of peaceful co-existence and mutual understanding.

It is most of all during the reconstruction period following the conclusion of peace agreements, however, that vast fields of action open up to UNESCO: peace-building, especially the building of civil peace, can rest only on genuine national consensus, that is on the widespread desire to plan and construct peace together. That implies a considerable effort to sensitize and educate the main actors in civil society, and here education, science, culture and communication all have their part to play. It does not just mean rebuilding the institutions destroyed during a conflict— even if that is a priority objective; it means doing so in such a way that the foundations of a democratic, pluralist and participatory society are laid at the same time.

Here again, education—in its broadest sense—has a key role to play, not only in building the bases of democratic citizenship; not only in alleviating the psychological after-effects of conflict for young people; but also in ensuring that all sections of the population who have been excluded because of their age or sex, their ethnic origin or religious beliefs, their political or economic situation or their geographical position are given a real opportunity to be brought back into social and working life.

Communication is therefore an essential tool for reconstructing civil societies torn apart by conflict: freedom of the press, pluralism and independence of the media, development of community newspapers and radio stations are crucial to the re-establishment of social bonds and to the reconciliation process.

UNESCO's 31st General Conference (Paris, October–November 2001), held only a few weeks after September 11, broke new ground with the adoption of a Universal Declaration on Cultural Diversity. Adopted by acclamation, it is the first major international standard-setting instrument conceived to promote cultural diversity. Its adoption confirms the view that 'intercultural dialogue is the best guarantee for peace, rejecting the ideas that conflicts between cultures and civilizations are inevitable', said UNESCO Director-General Koïchiro Matsuura at the closing session of the General Conference. 'Our behaviour has shown how much dialogue between cultures and civilizations is not only possible but fertile and can lead to consensus on questions of the highest importance'. Creation draws on the roots of cultural tradition, but flourishes in contact with other cultures. For this reason, heritage in all its forms must be preserved, enhanced and handed on to future generations as a record of human experience and aspirations, so as to foster creativity in all its diversity to inspire genuine dialogue among cultures,' the Declaration states in its 7th Article (Universal Declaration on Cultural Diversity, 2001).

For the first time the international community has endowed itself with a comprehensive standard-setting instrument, which 'elevates cultural diversity to the rank of common heritage of humanity, as necessary for the human race as is biodiversity in the natural world. This makes the protection of cultural diversity an ethical imperative inseparable from human dignity,' Mr Matsuura said.

ICTs were also at the heart of the General Conference debates and are expected to play a key role in all of UNESCO's fields of competence. The General Conference stressed that equitable access to cyberspace should enable better expression of cultural diversity in all its forms, including multilingualism, and called on UNESCO to continue its work on a standard-setting instrument on cyberspace.

UNESCO aims at increasing the contribution of media and information to the process of social integration and development, in general, with particular emphasis on poverty and illiteracy eradication, good governance, gender issues, empowering women and young people, research and media education through forms of advisory service to member states, conferences, meetings, seminars, publications/documentation and training.

At the request of the 1998 United Nations Round Table, several new publications and documents compiled 15 years of UNESCO experience in supporting grassroots community media. This collection of information allows improving the internal governance of community radio settings, facilitating preparations for establishing new associative broadcasting projects and establishing adequate relations with national regulatory authorities. In particular, UNESCO was requested to update the current publication *Approaches to Development.*

Several publications, including *A Comprehensive Legal Survey on Public Service Broadcasting in Leading Public Service Broadcasting, Public Broadcasting, Why, How?, The Community Radio Handbook* or the innovative worldwide survey on the economics of national cinemato-graphies represent important references to the professionals concerned.

Looking Back and Forward: The Evolution of Development Communication

UNESCO has gradually moved from a technical assistance agency to a leading agency in the field of development communication. It has integrated and combined different traditions and approaches.

The Professional Tradition

The first study on the professional training of communicators (journalists) was undertaken in 1949. In the same year, UNESCO commissioned a film-maker to train Chinese village educators in animation techniques for the preparation of cartoon films. Thus, the oldest tradition of UNESCO's communication involvement is the professional: focussed on the development of communication infrastructures, especially in developing countries, and including not only press, broadcasting or film institutions, but also a range of training or research centres and networks.

Some of the earliest UNESCO programmes emphasized professional training (initially in film, then in radio and television), following a model of basic training at local and national levels, intermediate skills training at regional levels, and advanced training through overseas attachments and study tours. The tradition is still very strong, although it has been modified over the years by a rising emphasis on community-based media practices, and the use of adapted, or appropriate media technologies.

Professional Networks

UNESCO's action is based on partnerships and alliances within and outside the United Nations system. For example, the organization of the United Nations Round Table on Communication for Development, which is held every two years since 1988, sees a gathering of about 50 experts and colleagues for a unique occasion to exchange experiences and information. UNESCO has also co-operated with the Global Knowledge Network (GKN) for the United Nations Task Force on Information and Communication Technology as well as with the International Telecommunications Union (ITU) in the organization of the World Summit on the Information Society (WSIS) in both Geneva (2003) and Tunis (2005).

Another strong feature of the UNESCO programme is its emphasis on varied professional networks, organized both at regional levels and by media. It is through such networks that it vocalizes its concerns, and identifies human resources for project development; it is also from such networks that its ideas are drawn in the first place. Even when international political divisions have been at their most acute, professional and academic contacts have generally been maintained.

It is also mostly through these networks that links with different theoretical and normative traditions have been maintained. For example, communication research in UNESCO has long been identified with the International Association for Media and Communication Research (IAMCR), a body originally created under UNESCO auspices. Similar associations exist, and enjoy a comparable relationship, in the various world regions (for example *Asia Media Information Centre (AMIC)* in Asia, *African Council for Communication Education (ACCE)* in Africa, Asociación Latinoamericana de Investigadores de la Comunicación (*ALAIC*) in Latin America, *ECREA* in Europe); in the majority of cases these links have been acknowledged by the granting of a formal status of association. It is through this academic network that many conceptual dimensions of dependency theory, participatory theory, or of critical research, have been exercised and reinforced: the same network has also been largely responsible for carrying out global research projects on information flow, or for providing contributions to such compendia as the World Communication Report (a reference guide for the first time produced in 1989).

Comparable relationships reinforce other traditions in the professional community (for example links with the IIC—International Institute of Communication, with CILECT—a nongovernmental organization grouping film and television training schools, or JOURNET, a global network for professional education in journalism and media). There are similar networks for journalists (whose consultative regional meetings were assisted for many years by UNESCO), for press freedom and monitoring groups, or for documentalists (through the COMNET international communication documentation network). In this way, a variety of traditions can co-exist.

Mass Media Tradition

Another tradition, which concerns the role of mass media in development, is historically based upon modernization (and later upon diffusion of innovation) theories. Wilbur Schramm originally wrote his study 'Mass Media and National Development' for UNESCO's International Institute for Educational Planning, and it is as much concerned with the use of media within formal instructional processes as it is with informal mass media programmes: this pedagogical approach evolved into a further communication channel for UNESCO over the years, moving from televised instruction to patterns of distance education and educational technology.

Each of these strands is still retained in UNESCO's programme, whether of mediated instruction (at both formal and informal educational levels), or of applied communication in an orthodox development communication tradition (for health education, preventive education, functional literacy programmes, and above all, population communication under *UNFPA* auspices). There have, however, been shifts of emphasis over the years.

The Division of the Development of Communication participated in a large number of seminars and workshops in close co-operation with other United Nations agencies offering its communication expertise for preventive health information in Africa and Asia. In 2000, and in close co-operation with UNAIDS, an innovative health care information methodology was developed through investigative journalism in East Africa.

Instructional Media-Theoretical Tradition

UNESCO's work in instructional media followed US and European trends in instructional design as a whole; in its early days, it was based on the assumption that mass media might be used as fundamental educational tools, at times replacing the classroom or group teacher. This led to a debate on the relative merits of direct teaching by television, as compared with the use of media as enrichment (reflecting an ongoing pedagogical debate, in which the US and Europe were largely polarized). At a later stage, the accent was placed upon evolving patterns of distance learning, using a multimedia approach within a carefully structured package of teaching and learning aids, including correspondence, residential tuition, and self-instructional materials. This debate was, however, mostly outside the development communication context, apart from its tendency (when coming down to the specifics of media production) to follow a production formula based upon stepped message design strategies, similar to advertising or development campaigns.

The applied developmental programme has been reinforced by the conclusions of the Jomtien meeting on 'Education for All', and by the UNICEF-supported initiative on a Third Channel for education. Currently, there is a great deal of emphasis on models of distance learning, initially at the higher education level, but translated increasingly into other levels, especially technical and vocational.

The exponential growth of the Internet has evoked a renewed interest on the part of national authorities and the public in general, in the concept of Distance Learning and Youth Media Education for their integration in formal and informal school curricula. UNESCO has therefore started a series of research programmes on Media Literacy aiming to promote critical approaches of youngsters towards the media. After lengthy consultations and the realization of a worldwide survey to identify the regional needs in a diversity of approaches to this issue, three main sets of actions were defined, aiming to: 1) ensure better co-operation between researchers and practitioners—teachers and radio/TV producers particularly in Asia and Africa; 2) develop regional educational methods, curriculum and learning tools; and 3) provide normative advice for new and updated national laws and regulations.

With a policy of continued development and a strong will to be more and more participative, UNESCO is inviting researchers and practitioners, journalists, civil servants or teachers to contribute actively to UNESCO orientations and programmes.

Population Communication

The majority of UNESCO-supported population communication projects fell into two distinct categories: (a) programmes developed for national or regional communication training institutions; and (b) the provision of communication technology and skills to national population programmes.

Programmes instituted in journalism schools may illustrate the first category. These set out to create an awareness of population issues among students of journalism in the hope that they would be able, at a later date, to make a meaningful contribution to national programme awareness creation efforts. The second category of projects envisages audio-visual equipment procurement in the first instance, followed by local staff training. Such training, however, is not necessarily limited to the use of equipment, but can be extended to cover all aspects of communication skills, including those involved in inter-personal communication. Looked at from another dimension, training also encompasses the creation of awareness of relevant population subject matter content.

Clearly, UNESCO's technical competence for executing projects, which provide communication technology and skills to national population programmes, is specific. However, in some instances, UNESCO accepts responsibility for project management as well as for the development of technological skills. Hence liability extends to awareness creation and the enlistment of political support at the highest levels, as well as actual activity implementation at community level. Consequently, while the objectives would appear to be concentrated on technical skills training, actual programme inputs also encompass grassroot activities.

While this is probably the closest parallel to the applied development communication approach dominant in other agencies, the impact of the wider UNESCO communication debate (and of the events behind it) upon development strategies cannot be ignored.

Communication Research

From the 1960s, there has been a substantial communication research tradition in UNESCO with topics ranging from rural radio and farm forums to satellites and Internet, and their application for educational media. In November 2001, this was articulated with greater clarity and some changes of direction at an expert meeting at Leicester University. Members of the expert panel had in common their belief in a critical and qualitative research tradition, an interest in new development paradigms, and above all, a compelling interest in UNESCO's policy research.

Research has always fulfilled an important role in UNESCO's communication work, particularly now with the convergence and multiplicity of communication channels. But UNESCO is also interested in researching communication as a social process, not merely as a technical imposition on society, an entertainment industry, means of advertising campaigns nor as a mass media extension of the human voice or pen.

UNESCO therefore works closely with its partners, the International Association of Mass Communication Research, the European Consortium for Communications Research, the International Clearinghouse on Children and Violence on the Screen, and various university scholars and research institutes.

UNESCO's ongoing research activities in the field of communication will focus on the following areas: (a) infoethics and universal access to information and knowledge; (b) linguistic and cultural diversity in media and information networks; (c) ICTs and peoples with disabilities; (d) gender and ICTs; (e) press freedom and freedom of expression in the information society; and (f) education, particularly media literacy and training in and for the information society.

Community Media

The experience gained from many projects and studies has demonstrated the fact that community radio is one of the most effective (and not very costly) means of communication for development, especially in rural communities, as well as of social participation, of information and advice on literacy, health, child care, improved agricultural methods, vocational training and protection of the environment.

Since 1996 UNESCO has worked with the Global Knowledge Partnership to promote Community Multimedia Centres (CMCs) that aim to integrate Community Radio and Telecentres in multipurpose communities.

The CMC addresses the digital divide in Least Developed Countries (LDCs) seeking to ensure that information, communication and knowledge become the basic tools of the poor in improving their own lives through an approach that is cost-effective, country differentiated and empowerment-oriented.

The pilot CMC project, implemented in 2001 with notable success, at Kothmale Community Radio in Sri Lanka, has served as a model for further pilot projects now being launched in Latin America, Caribbean, Africa and Asia. The CMC programme was debated and endorsed at an international seminar in Sri Lanka.

Decentralization

An accelerated process of decentralization also stressed the practical needs of communication for development, with Regional Advisers for Communication posted to 10 field offices to help contextualize the new communication strategy. These advisers work directly with regional organizations and the professional and non-governmental community.

Much of the work of UNESCO also focusses on regional strategies—through co-ordinating mechanisms like the Information Society Programme in Latin America and the Caribbean (INFOLAC), the Regional Network for the Exchange of Information and Experience in Science and Technology (CARSTIN) in the Caribbean or the Regional Network for the Exchange of Information and Experiences in Science and Technology in Asia and the Pacific (ASTINFO). In the Intergovernmental Informatics Programme (IIP), informatics networks are pursued in the Arab States (Regional Informatics Network for the Arab States—RINAS), Africa (Regional Informatics Network for Africa—RINAF), South and Central Asia (Regional Informatics Network for South and Central Asia—RINSCA), South-East Asia and the Pacific (Regional Informatics Network for South-East Asia and the Pacific—RINSEAP). In the IIP, a new developmental programme for Africa has been established to expand the use of informatics (especially in education) under the title INFORMAFRICA. Regional advisory services have also been provided in the area of population communication under a programme funded by UNFPA since the early 1970s. While this programme has made some advances towards systematizing communication planning and strategy formulation, its main impact has probably been made at the level of training.

In the future, it is expected that a more varied approach will develop, following the establishment of inter-agency teams for population programmes, and the extension of upstream planning activities.

The International Programme for the Development of Communication (IPDC)

UNESCO's main operational instrument for upgrading the communication capacity of developing countries is the International Programme for the Development of Communication (IPDC). Originally proposed by the United States as a mechanism for channelling both multilateral and bilateral aid, it was evaluated alongside a second, radically different proposal, for a communication research, training and operational institute. What finally emerged was an Intergovernmental Council, having some autonomy from UNESCO, but ultimately dependent upon it for its staff, management resources and programme execution. Its main feature was a Special Account facility, which could receive voluntary contributions, thus providing an alternative funding source for communication projects in the Third World. Even though IPDC's resources remained limited, they were relatively secure. In the early 1990s, for example, as other funding sources were drying up in the face of international recession, the Special Account remained constant, even if static. In the late 1980s, the IPDC began a two-edged administrative reform process: on the one hand, seeking to expand its financial base through extra-budgetary arrangements, and on the other to streamline its working methods, leading to more effective selection and decision-making mechanisms.

Most recently the IPDC has devoted considerable attention to widening its membership base and increasing access by the non-governmental and professional communities (who can now apply more directly for project support, without a governmental filter), thus emphasizing pluralism in project generation, management and financing. This new focus links the programme more directly with the emphasis of UNESCO as a whole on media pluralism and independence, and on the development of the private media sector in the developing world, especially Africa. Following the Windhoek seminar on media independence and pluralism in Africa, a number of projects featuring private and non-governmental initiatives were developed for external financing, and a similar effort occurred following the 1992 Kazakhstan seminar, involving the Central Asian Republics, as well as a wider Asian community.

Over the last 20 years, following the decisions and guidelines of the IPDC Intergovernmental Council and its Bureau, the Programme has made considerable efforts to improve its working methods and to refocus its 900 projects on the most urgent priorities in communication development in more than 130 developing countries. These efforts of the IPDC have had a remarkable impact on a broad range of fields covering, among others, the promotion of press freedom, media independence and pluralism; community media, development of human resources for the media, modernization of national and regional news agencies, radio as well as television organizations; and new information and communication technologies (ICTs). About 50 countries have contributed US$ 85 million to the IPDC activities through IPDC Special Account and under funds-in-trust arrangements. Denmark, Germany, Finland, France, India, Italy, Japan, Republic of Korea, Russia, Luxembourg, the Netherlands, Norway, Sweden and Switzerland have made the biggest voluntary contributions.

Projects and Activities

News Exchanges, Agencies and Sources

The principal sources of diversified news are the news agencies themselves, but the main obstacle to a balanced dissemination has been the dominating role played by a few international news agencies, compounded by the lack of national news agencies and operations in most developing countries. In addition to the regional news agency development projects set up in three sub-regions of Africa (WANAD, SEANAD, and CANAD), UNESCO has assisted in the planning and development of a number of national news agencies, notably in Bangladesh, China, Mongolia, Morocco, Nepal, Pakistan, Philippines, Tanzania, Tunisia and Zimbabwe.

Reacting to the fact that several African national news agencies had shut down by the turn of the century and that others were nearing closure, urgent studies were undertaken to analyse the situation and identify possible solutions. The classical model of newsgathering and dissemination had been undermined by the Internet and by other factors. A workshop in Amman in January 2000, brought together 13 news agencies from Asia, the Caribbean, Eastern and Central Europe and the Middle East.

Community Media and Internet

UNESCO has assisted over 40 rural newspapers in Africa, some of which are printed on offset with a circulation from 10,000 to 40,000 per week, others employing desktop publishing techniques.

Community radio has taken on increased importance in the last two decades, partly as a reaction to mainstream media and the need to reach dispersed regions, and partly because of new, low-cost technology now available, such as the UNESCO designed low-power FM transmitter. These transmitters are now serving community radio stations in Cape Verde, Ghana, Kenya, St Lucia, Jamaica, Bhutan, Philippines, Sri Lanka, Tonga and Niue.

The Mahaweli Community Radio project in Sri Lanka has been particularly productive, not only in terms of setting up a permanent community radio unit, but also in institutionalizing this under a new ministerial organ, the Rural Communication Centre, responsible for the development and expansion of community radio stations, including broadcasting licences, training, research and experimentation with new technology. The project, which is further described as a case study, has served as inspiration for similar developments in other countries. Thus, in the Philippines, the Tambuli project was designed for implementation by the Foundation of Rural Broadcasters. Twelve FM Community stations were targeted over a four-year period. Although these will be linked to major city stations for news dissemination, they operate mainly at the community level under the management of community associations. Another project, for the development of Bhutan Broadcasting Services, has included FM transmission as a service for the capital and its outlying regions, for outside broadcasting, and for experimentation prior to the installation of a microwave network to be coupled with an FM network in the major regions.

UNESCO's international initiative for Community Multimedia Centres (CMCs) aims to promote community empowerment and to address the digital divide by combining community broadcasting with the Internet and related technologies.

A CMC combines community radio by local people in local languages with community telecentre facilities such as computers with Internet and e-mail, phone, fax and photocopying services. The radio, low-cost and easy to operate, not only informs, educates and entertains, but also empowers the community by giving a strong public voice to the voiceless and so encourages greater accountability in civil affairs. The walk-in community telecentre offering Internet access allows even the most remote village to communicate and exchange information with the rest of the world. With training, communities can locally access, manage, produce and communicate information for development.

The Internet and associated technologies are pivotal to full and effective membership of the knowledge society. However, disparities of access, language barriers, the cost of the technologies and of connectivity, lack of awareness and motivation are creating a growing digital divide which, for many, hampers vital access to these important new resources.

Development of Communication Technology

Over the past 10 years, a UNESCO sub-programme has been devoted to the design of low-cost, easy-to-assemble technical facilities that can be set up and maintained in developing countries without constant resources to foreign aid and expensive spare-parts and replacement. The most prominent development has been the design (with Mallard Concepts) of a 10 to 100 watt FM transmitter that can be powered by a car battery or solar panel. The transmitter, which costs about US$ 2,000, has been installed in a number of projects in Africa and Asia.

A major problem in many developing countries is the shortage of publications in local languages—and this is also an underlying difficulty of literacy and post-literacy programmes. UNESCO has consequently collaborated in the development of a software called AFRALPHA, designed to enable all African languages to be transcribed for printing in various forms and it is now being applied in a number of countries, including Mali, Burkina Faso and Congo.

Similar initiatives are being undertaken in Asia, where UNESCO, in co-operation with the Asian Institute of Technology, organized a workshop in Bangkok for over 100 informatics and language specialists to discuss the computerization of Asian non-Latin alphabets and scripts. The difficulties posed in computerizing these scripts are considerable, and the workshop focussed on the possibilities of a universal font maker, the electronic transmission of digitized alphabets and the problems of adapting these techniques to professional photocomposition and printing processes.

Conclusion

UNESCO's interest in communication is holistic, encompassing all aspects of the discipline—technological, social, political, and cultural. Clearly, the majority of UN agencies have some interest in communication—whether in its technical aspects (like ITU), its industrial (like United Nations Industrial Development Organization [UNIDO]), or in its potential contribution to specific fields—of agriculture, health, population, the workplace (FAO, WHO, UNFPA, ILO). But in the case of UNESCO, the interest is more in seeing how those individual dimensions come together, in communities and social systems, both local and international. That is UNESCO's strength—most probably also one reason for the controversies into which the Organization has on occasions been drawn.

UNESCO's brief is to monitor the information society as a whole, not a single perspective. For this reason UNESCO has a special obligation to collaborate with all the other organizations—multilateral and bilateral, international and regional, intergovernmental and non-governmental—which have a specific mandate to pursue. At times, UNESCO's contribution is no more than as a source of information, or of informants. On other occasions it plays a more prominent role: in promoting South-North dialogue, in reinforcing communication capacity in the developing countries, or in monitoring a free flow of information.

But to make the free flow of information more than a catchphrase involves movement, information flow and networking in all directions and among many partners, traditional and modern. It also requires inter-sectorality and inter-disciplinarity. UNESCO's traditional fields—education, science and culture—are much stronger when they are underpinned by a thorough competence in information skills, and one of UNESCO's recent priorities has been to combat the inertia and resistance of a vertically organized system, in favour of a transversal approach. New technologies, like the satellite, can only realize their social applications through this kind of inter-disciplinarity, and it should be no surprise that UNESCO now has projects in preparation in Africa, India and Latin America that depend upon satellite technologies to educate at a distance.

The links between the programmes of the Communication Sector, juxtaposing communication, information and informatics, need to be further consolidated, moving from a structural to a conceptual level that would mirror the emergence of a global information society.

Reference

Universal Declaration on Cultural Diversity. Adopted by the General Conference of the United Nations Educational, Scientific and Cultural Organization at its thirty-first session on 2 November 2001. Available online at http://www.ohchr.org/english/law/diversity.htm.

Making a Difference through Development Communication: Some Evidence-based Results from FAO Field Projects

11

GARY COLDEVIN*

Background

FAO's mandate as a specialized UN Agency has been largely to raise levels of nutrition, improve agricultural productivity, better the lives of rural populations and contribute to the growth of the world economy (FAO, 2006). At the heart of its efforts in the developing world has been the promotion of sustained food security throughout the year. Set against a current background of an estimated 1.2 billion people living on less than $1 a day, with about 75 per cent of these 'absolute poor' living in rural areas where they mostly depend on agriculture for their food, income, and employment (CIDA, 2003), the key preoccupations of FAO have assumed mounting importance. Indeed, reducing both poverty and hunger in rural areas will depend heavily on the sustainable development of agriculture. The challenge for the Agency is thus to lead international efforts to defeat under-nourishment and play a dominant role in the 2001 Millennium Development Goal (MDG) Target concerned with significantly lessening the proportion of those who suffer from hunger.

The 1996 World Food Summit, out of which the MDG hunger reduction target was derived, set a goal of reducing by half the number of hungry people in the developing world—about 400 million people—by the year 2015. The progress achieved during much of the 1990s has made this goal appear to be a daunting task. In the 1990/92 period for example, the number of

*In collaboration with the Communication for Development Group of the Food and Agriculture Organization (FAO) of the United Nations.

undernourished in developing countries was estimated at 817 million people; by 1999–2001 the number had dropped to 798 million or a decrease of only 19 million overall. At the regional level the number of under-nourished mostly declined in Asia, the Pacific and Latin America, but largely increased in Africa (FAO, 2004). The total net reduction of slightly over 2 million per year for the nine year period is thus disappointingly slow when the achievement of the 2015 MDG target will require, on average, an annual reduction of 26 million. These results dramatically suggest that unless more effective solutions are found for increasing food production among the hungry and most vulnerable, and better distribution of it, the goal of the 1996 World Food Summit may never be realized. As Sen (1998:204) wryly notes, 'The contemporary age is not short of terrible and nasty happenings, but the persistence of extensive hunger in a world of unprecedented prosperity is surely the worst'. And even more sobering, looking further down the road, from a base of slightly over six billion people as the twentieth century ended, the world's population may exceed eight billion by 2025 and food needs in developing countries—which will account for 98 per cent of the population increase—will more than double (Crowder, 2000).

A growing number of development specialists and agencies argue that appropriate use of ICTs for accelerating the dissemination of research-based recommendations, blending them with indigenous practices, and rendering them locally useable though small media adaptation, and especially radio, may well provide part of the solution towards reducing the chronic food deficits and reducing poverty (Balit, 2004; Girard, 2003; Ilboudo and Castello, 2003; IDRC, 1999; Richardson, 1997; van der Stichele and Bie, 1997; Woods, 1996). Put more succinctly by FAO, the challenge in assisting farmers to sustainably produce more food implies the need for new technologies, new skills, changed attitudes and practices, and new ways to collaborate. All of this requires that farmers have access to relevant information and knowledge (Crowder, 2000).

The purpose of this chapter is to provide an overview of the FAO Communication for Development Group's work, arguably the foremost practitioner of applied communication for agricultural and other areas of rural development, like forestry, environment, nutrition, over the past 35 years. In particular, the focus will be on projects that have included quantitative evaluation studies and which have produced concrete results. During this period the role of communication has undergone a 180 degree shift from a one-way, top-down transfer of messages by extension agents to farmers, to a social process which starts with farmers and brings together both groups in a two-way sharing of information among communication equals—in short, participatory communication. Along with communication, it is also now widely accepted that a parallel investment in 'human capital' through education and training of adults is essential for project success (Fraser and Villet, 1994). Awareness raising, knowledge acquisition, attitude change, confidence-building, participation in decision-making, and action, all require processes of education and communication. In this spirit, the chapter includes an overview of parallel movements in participatory adult learning, notably Farmer Field Schools developed by FAO, and the opportunities for combining participatory methods to refine both communication and learning as partners in supporting project implementation.[1]

Development Support Communication at FAO—The 1970s and 1980s

In carrying out its fieldwork, much of FAO's early communication activities were subsumed within two main areas: (1) information dissemination and motivation, and (2) training for field workers and rural producers (Coldevin, 1987; Fraser, 1983). The gathering movement towards participatory audience involvement inherent to communication for development was assumed to be a subset of each.

Information dissemination and motivation, as the most basic areas of communication for development, are concerned with simply informing rural people of new ideas, services and technologies for improving their quality of life.[2] Given that about one-third of adults in the developing world are illiterate (PRB, 1999), with the regional disparities being most acute in Africa—34 per cent male and 54 per cent female—the broadcast media, principally radio, have performed a major service in this role.[3] Not surprisingly, with the advent of the transistor receiver, and lowering of prices, radio—either battery operated or wound-up by hand—became the ubiquitous medium for rural communication, a status that it is likely to retain well into the twenty-first century. But while much of the emphasis in the 1970s was on supporting open broadcast with a national or regional reach, a number of disadvantages were noted. Typically, it was conducted without involving farmers or extension in its programming, and was literally 'open' in the sense that broadcasts were directed at unorganized audiences.

In the face of the criticism that by 'attempting to reach everyone, it reaches no one', open broadcasts for educational purposes, including agricultural programming, was given low priority, averaging less than 5 per cent of total broadcasting hours (FAO, 1981). As a stand-alone medium, however, radio's main value was in reaching a lot of people quickly with fairly simple messages. With the current surge of community radio stations that invite audience participation, a rejuvenation appears to be under way. Particularly in Africa, 'Radio remains the most popular, accessible, and cost-effective means of communication for rural people. Radio can overcome the barriers of distance, illiteracy and language diversity better than any other medium' (FAO, 1996:9). And when linked with the Internet and relevant websites, the new media mix will go a long way towards bridging the digital divide (Girard, 2003; Ilboudo and Castello, 2003).

Radio, whether national, regional or local in reach, has also formed the main-stay for many multimedia campaigns, the most powerful of communication strategies for disseminating information and building motivation. Communication theory has tended to support the case for multimedia use based on the premise that having access to at least two channels allows a production team to present and reinforce the same points in different ways and with varied emphasis. Individuals also differ in their processing of information from different media; some learn better from, and prefer, visual media than audio and vice versa. In general, evidence from controlled classroom studies suggests that providing a variety of reinforcing channels caters to both learning styles and learning preferences (World Bank, 1983). Practical evidence from the field to reinforce the experimental classroom findings, however, especially in rural development, is rare (see Case 1 for one such example).

Campaigns have been used in virtually every facet of rural development, and examples abound in agriculture. One of the better known case studies, 'Masagana 99', was undertaken in the Philippines during 1974 (Sison, 1985). 'Masagana' translates as 'bountiful harvest' with the project objective to increase rice production up to 99 sacks (50 kg) of un-milled rice per hectare. The channel mix included radio broadcasting, a variety of print materials (bulletins, posters), and intensively trained farm technologists. Radio was used in three ways: (a) jingles and spot messages for motivation, (b) information through a daily 30-minute farm programme and (c) instructional courses through the existing Farmers' University of the Air. Prior to the campaign the Philippines had to import a substantial part of its rice to meet national requirements. Following the campaign, 1974 rice yields had increased by 28 per cent over the previous year and by 1976 a 40 per cent rise was registered over 1973 pre-campaign levels. During 1977, national requirements were more than met and the country began exporting its excess harvest.

Case 1

Multimedia Advantage in Communication Campaigns

During 1988 FAO was asked to assist the mountain Kingdom of Lesotho in southern Africa toward increasing sorghum production, a drought resistant crop grown by farmers in a dry region of the country. An assessment of their information and skills upgrading needs was undertaken by extension officers and subject matter specialists through group discussions. Priorities which emerged were to increase farmers' knowledge of recommended seeds, better methods of sorghum production, and reduction of post-harvest losses. A baseline KAP and media use survey was then taken with a stratified sampling of 161 farmers who were later classified as belonging to one of a) the full campaign communities, b) radio only communities, and c) a 'control' community where the campaign was not held. The full campaign which ran for nearly 4 months was kicked-off by a nutritionist who gave cooking demonstrations and explained the nutritional value of sorghum. This was followed by radio programs aired once per week, distribution of illustrated leaflets, and communication teams using slide-tape programs

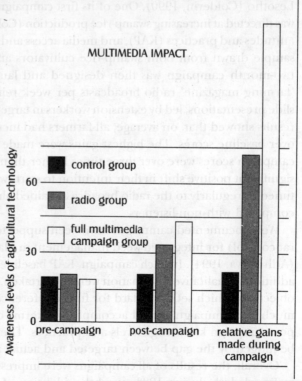

MULTIMEDIA IMPACT

control group
radio group
full multimedia campaign group

Awareness levels of agricultural technology

60

30

0

pre-campaign   post-campaign   relative gains made during campaign

(*Case 1 continued*)

(*Case 1 continued*)

> as a basis for follow-up discussion with small groups of farmers. Posters and handouts were also given during these sessions and practical demonstrations were held when possible. An impact survey was taken immediately following the campaign. When compared with baseline levels, farmers who participated in the 'full campaign' achieved a relative gain of 130 per cent in their knowledge of recommended sorghum seeds, production methods, and post-harvest loss reduction. The 'radio only' group achieved a solid knowledge gain of 70 per cent, while the 'control group', which did not experience the campaign directly, had a relative increase of about 20 per cent, ostensibly through spin-off or secondary word-of-mouth effects with neighbours and friends who were part of the radio only group. The almost doubling of the impact of the multimedia approach in relation to the single medium effects of radio brings into sharp relief the power—and wisdom—of using a mutually reinforcing multimedia mix backed up with interpersonal support at the village level.
>
> *Source:* Coldevin, G. (1990). *Communication Strategies for Rural Development: A Case Study of the Use Campaigns in Lesotho.* Rome: FAO.

FAO has also accumulated a strong legacy in implementing and validating this powerful delivery strategy in a variety of topics ranging from stamping out rinderpest viruses in 34 countries across West, Central and East Africa (Villet, 1988), to increasing maize and sorghum production in Lesotho (Coldevin, 1990). One of its first campaigns, carried out during 1984 in Sierra Leone, was directed at increasing swamp-rice production (Coldevin, 1986). A baseline survey of knowledge, attitudes and practices (KAP), and media access and preferences was undertaken with a stratified sample drawn from both swamp-rice cultivators and uniquely upland farmers. A nation-wide two-month campaign was then designed and launched involving a mix of four 15-minute 'farming magazine' radio broadcasts per week reinforced by posters, pamphlets, and sound-slide presentations, led by extension workers in targeted villages near swamp areas. Post-campaign results showed that, on average, all farmers had increased their knowledge levels by 60 per cent over baseline scores. The highest gains were made by upland or non-rice farmers whose after-campaign scores were over three times higher than baseline levels. This group also indicated a significant positive shift in their intention to start swamp-rice farming. And overall, farmers who tuned in regularly to the radio broadcasts gained almost twice the amount of information when compared with non-listeners.

Well documented campaigns have been supported by FAO in Bangladesh and Malaysia (for rat control) for integrated weed management in Malaysia, and for pest surveillance in Thailand (Adhikarya, 1994). In each campaign, KAP baseline surveys as well as focus group interviews for additional qualitative information were undertaken. An interesting variation in setting campaign objectives, which set a standard for future reference, was the use of a targeted estimate of how much the campaign should accomplish in terms of shifts in each indicator included, like in post-campaign knowledge levels and practices. The rate of success of the campaign could then be judged by the gap between targeted and actual achievements.

Overall, the results of all campaigns were impressive. For example, the rat control campaign in Bangladesh during 1983 raised the adoption of rat control practices among wheat farmers from 10 to 32 per cent, resulting in an average harvest gain of 54 kg per hectare in treated fields.

A follow-up campaign in 1984 with all types of farmers showed 47 per cent practicing rat control before and 67 per cent after the exercise with average overall harvest gains of 44 kg per hectare.

Training for Field Workers and Rural Producers

Communication for Development interventions for training extension workers have been mainly directed towards perfecting their interpersonal communications skills, and, more recently, in facilitating participatory involvement of farmers in defining their own problems, reaching consensus on actions to be taken, information and skills development required to carry out the actions, and mechanisms for seeking research assistance on technical problems for which there is no ready solution available locally. In this cycle, extension workers have the prime responsibility for selecting and interpreting farmers' requests to research agencies and for disseminating the results back to farmers.

Training for rural producers, typical involving extension or subject matter specialists as the vital interpersonal link, has tended to rely on group media such as slides, film-strips, audio-cassettes, flip-charts, village theatre and video. In the hands of a trained facilitator these media add punch and authority to a presentation. Perhaps the most advantageous aspect of group media is the possibility for immediate feedback from the audience and establishment of a two-way flow of information. Participants' level of understanding can be tested, central points can be repeated where necessary, and discussions can be started with a view towards initiating action on agreed upon development problems.

Cases abound where FAO has used film-strips and slides with sound commentaries in virtually all areas of its mandate (FAO, 1981). Normally the presentations are reinforced by booklets, which depict the visuals used in the script with accompanying dialogue. Routinely, the booklets become manuals in their own right. The pre-recorded audio-cassette is another low-cost medium, which FAO has promoted extensively. The cassette's chief advantage over radio is the control that a group facilitator has over the information flow and the ability to start and stop at will, and repeat messages. Cassette recording is also an easy way to bring farmers' questions and information needs to the attention of extension and research. Folk media in the form of popular singers and musicians have also proven highly effective for focussing community attention on population issues (FAO, 1994).

Of all the group media, however, video has emerged as the medium of choice for supporting participatory farmer training in a variety of FAO rural development projects (Coldevin, 1988). Its many advantages are unequalled by any other medium, namely, its production 'immediacy' with instant replay in the field to check on shooting details, its ability to add on commentary in local languages, its ease of editing, and its 'show anywhere, anytime' flexibility using battery or generator operated playback equipment where electricity is lacking. During extensive long-term projects in Peru, Mexico and Mali, FAO has perfected a complete learning package that combines video with discussion, simple printed materials, and practical fieldwork. Often referred to as a model for international reference, the efficiency of the methodology has been evaluated by the World Bank in terms of both training costs (ranging from 1/3 to 1/5 the costs of traditional training; Balit, Rios and Masias, 1996) and high internal rate of return (Fraser and Restrepo-Estrada, 1997). More recent examples include training for women farmers in Jamaica where video was combined with drama performances, oral testimonies and printed material (Protz, 1998).

Communication for Development in the 1990s: Evolution of a Participatory Model

The importance of popular participation in planning and executing projects was largely postulated during the 1970s (see for example, Freire, 1972). In a ground-breaking article on development communication, Rogers (1976) suggested that the passing of the 'dominant paradigm' of top-down planning would signal a shift towards self-development wherein villagers and urban poor would be the priority audiences, and self-reliance and building on local resources would be emphasized. The role of communication in this process would be '(1) providing technical information about development problems and possibilities, and about appropriate innovations in answer to local requests, and (2) circulating information about the self-development accomplishments of local groups so that other such groups might profit from others' experience' (ibid.:141). Despite these early predictions, rural communication systems continued to service the transfer of technology or 'TOT' model in which information passed from researchers to farmers through the extension system (Ramirez, 1995). At least a decade would pass before participatory methodologies began to gain acceptance. And where they were tentatively introduced, most projects up to end of the 1980s were mainly concerned with having beneficiaries discuss how to implement projects. The later adoption of full 'interactive participation' (Pretty, 1995:61), involved beneficiaries deciding which development initiatives should be pursued, whether the initiatives were feasible—and prioritizing those that were—and only then deciding how to carry them out, all the while keeping in mind the requirements for sustainability and ultimately 'self-mobilization' upon project completion (see typology Table 11.1).

Table 11.1
A Typology of Participation

Type	Characteristics of Each Type
Passive participation	People participate by being told by an administration or project management what is going to happen or has already happened.
Participation in information giving	People participate by answering questions posed by researchers using questionnaire surveys or similar approaches, but do not have the opportunity to influence proceedings. The findings of the research are not shared with the participants or checked for accuracy by them.

(*Table 11.1 continued*)

(*Table 11.1 continued*)

Type	Characteristics of Each Type
Participation by consultation	People participate by being consulted on their views. External professionals define both problems and solutions, and may (but are not obliged to) modify these in the light of people's responses. However, local people do not share in decision-making.
Participation for material incentives	People participate by providing resources—for example labour, or land—in return for food, cash or other material incentives. Much on-farm research falls in this category, as farmers provide the location but are not involved in the experimentation or the process of learning. It is very common to see this called participation, yet people have no stake in prolonging activities when the incentives end.
Functional participation	People participate by forming groups to meet predetermined objectives related to the project, which can involve the development or promotion of externally initiated social organization. Such involvement tends to come after major decisions have been made, rather than during the planning stage.
Interactive participation	People participate in joint analysis, which leads to action plans and the formation of new local institutions or the strengthening of existing ones. It tends to involve interdisciplinary methodologies that seek multiple perspectives and make use of systematic and structured learning processes. These groups have control over local decisions, and so people have a stake in maintaining structures or practices.
Self-mobilization	People participate by taking initiatives independent of external institutions to change systems. They develop contacts with external institutions for resources and technical advice they need, but retain control over how resources are used.

Source: Pretty, 1995.

From the Drawing Board to Implementation

Forerunner Trials in the Philippines

One of FAO's early exercises in 'interactive' participatory communication for development was carried out over a three-year period in the Philippines from 1991–1994 (Coldevin, 1995).[4] The UNDP funded project was implemented by the Applied Communication Division (ACD) of the Philippine Council for Agriculture, Forestry and Natural Resources Research and Development (PCARRD), and five of its 15 Regional Applied Communication Offices (RACOs).[5] Building on the mounting literature in participatory rural appraisal (PRA), and refinement of its methodology (for example, Chambers, 1992), the over-riding goal of the project was to take the ACD and each of the five RACOs through prototype exercises in setting priorities for technology transfer in carefully selected, isolated and economically depressed pilot-communities, called barangays, one per region. This involved bottom-up needs assessment through a number of PRA tools, social and livelihood mapping, seasonal calendar, problem trees, key informant panels, media access and preferences, and quantitative baseline KAP surveys, which served as diagnostic profiles for the framing of communication support objectives. A variety of multi-channel communication approaches were then implemented, spearheaded by a new lead-medium in the form of community audio-tower systems or CATS[6], in each participating barangay. 'Broadcasting associations' were subsequently formed to manage, produce and broadcast programmes created by thematic sub-committees, like agriculture, health, cooperatives and youth, on a weekly schedule (Ramirez and Stuart, 1994). Case 2 highlights one example from the project wherein a multimedia campaign was launched to promote increased rice production.

Case 2
Multimedia Campaign Propels Record Rice Harvests in the Philippines

The 'barangay' or community of Tulungatung near Zamboanga City, on the island of Mindanao, is an agriculturally depressed area. Prior to a multimedia campaign launched in 1993, average annual rice yields were only about 60 per cent of that produced in the larger Ayala District in which it was located. In preparation for the campaign, farming families were involved in participatory rural appraisals about their farming systems and determining which agricultural technologies were most urgently needed. They also determined which media they wanted to use and the times and places when they could get together to learn. As the focal point for systematically getting out relevant messages in line with the agricultural calendar, a community audio-tower system (CATS) was set up and operated by local farmers and extension agents.

The campaign covered an area with 93 hectares of rice. During the campaign to promote increased rice production, a 4-month School of the Air (SoA) was run with three CATS broadcasts per week, along with print support and field demonstrations by specialists covering all facets of rice farming, including integrated pest management. Knowledge level scores among the rice farmers rose from a baseline average of 55 per cent prior to the campaign to 92 per cent following it. And adoption of key technologies rose from a baseline level of 46 per cent to a post-campaign high of 68 per cent, mainly because of the simple, low-cost nature of the practices being promoted. For example, one of the first challenges was to control a severe infestation of 'black bug' which had been a major rice pest in the area during the previous six years. A cheap but effective repellent in the form of neem-leaf abstract was recommended and a vigorous effort was made to increase the local supply of neem plants. By the end of the campaign the outbreak of the pest was brought well under control, largely through the information and motivation provided by the CATS.

As for bottom-line results, the rice yield during the 1992 wet season immediately prior to the campaign was 43 cavans/ha (see Table below). Following the campaign, by 1994 the wet season yields had more than doubled to 90 cavans/ha, nearly equal to that produced in the relatively well-off Ayala district at large. Translated into monetary terms, at the going 1994 selling rate of 3.5 pesos per kilo, the wet season harvest increase per hectare in 1994 over 1992 levels amounted to Ps7,238, or about US$ 290.

(*Case 2 continued*)

(*Case 2 continued*)

WET SEASON RICE PRODUCTION LEVELS
(average cavans/hectare)

Year	Non-Campaign Area	Full Campaign Area
1992	76	43
1993	82	58
1994	96	90

Source: Coldevin, G. (1995). *Farmer-First Approaches to Communication: A Case Study from the Philippines.* Rome: FAO.

The SADC (South African Development Community) Regional Centre of Communication for Development

The SADC Centre of Communication for Development based in Harare officially began operations during mid-1996, assisted by a 4-year FAO project. Its opening marked the first regional multi-purpose communication facility for rural development in Southern Africa, serving all 14 countries under the SADC mantle. The Centre's mandate is broad and encompasses providing communication advice, setting up linkages, a clearinghouse for documentation, production of information and discussion materials, and training for all development sectors with an emphasis thus far on agriculture, health, sanitation, and environment.

The Centre has carved out its principal aim as 'facilitating people's participation at all levels of the development effort to identify and implement appropriate policies, programs and technologies to prevent and reduce poverty in order to improve people's livelihood in a sustainable way' (Anyaegbunam et al., 1998:10). A revitalized methodology, Participatory Rural Communication Appraisal or PRCA, has been developed as the basis for dialoguing with people using a mix of qualitative and quantitative research. Qualitative aspects of PRCA refer to developing a profile of a given community's needs, opportunities, problems and solutions, its key interaction groups, traditional and modern communication networks, and influential sources of information. This front-end portion of PRCA also provides basic indicators and sharpens the focus for framing quantitative baseline surveys of awareness, knowledge, attitudes and practices or AKAP of the development problem(s) to be addressed. Results of the full PRCA in turn make it possible to formulate specific AKAP objectives, segment key interaction groups, plan problem-solving communication strategies and approaches, design messages, select appropriate media and interpersonal channels, and develop and pre-test materials. PRCA also sets the basis for monitoring and adjusting a communication programme or campaign as it unfolds, and for measuring its immediate AKAP outcomes and longer term impact after completion.

The Centre's main draw thus far has been a series of 'Action Programme' or AP workshops, initially lasting 10 weeks, but now reduced to seven following a market research survey. Each workshop presently comprises an initial two-week introductory session in Harare—theory of communication for development, preparation for field PRCA, and baseline AKAP surveys—two weeks of field research at project sites in participating countries, and back to Harare for a final three weeks of analysis of field research, communication strategy design, setting objectives, message content, media-mix, preparation of a sample of media material, and budget and work plan to carry out an actual communication programme or campaign for a given project. Eight such AP workshops have been given thus far—for the most part focussing on multimedia communication campaigns—each with an average of about 25 middle-level communication and extension personnel drawn from about four to five organizations, like UN Agencies, Government Ministries, NGOs. Following each AP workshop, the Centre provided backstopping as the various field projects are undertaken.[7]

Only one evaluation study has been documented on the success of the applied field projects. In this case, a pilot communication action plan was developed around introducing a new variety of millet into the northern region of Namibia during 1996 (SADC, 1999). A pre-implementation survey of technology awareness and practices was conducted, followed by an On Farm Trial and Demonstration Programme (OFTDP). Two sets of coloured flip-charts were produced for use by extension technicians on key-OFTDP topics. At the end of pilot programme in 1998 an outcomes survey revealed that, in comparison with non-participating farmers, the OFTDP farmers were much more aware of the recommended technologies for millet production, for instance, 74 per cent of the OFTDP group knew about the benefits of fertilizers versus only seven per cent of those who had not participated. And almost half of the OFTDP trained farmers found that the use of flip-charts helped them to better understand the farming concepts, thereby demonstrating that even simple visual media can provide significant pay-offs in terms of learning gains.

Networking through Village Telecentres

While the call for 'networking' became the 1990s' mantra, sub-Saharan Africa in particular has faced deepening marginalization. According to data provided by IDRC in 1999, excluding South Africa, only one African in 9,000 had access to the Internet, while around the world the average was one person in 40 (IDRC, 1999). By 2002 the situation had not improved much, if at all. About 10 per cent of the world was online at the time or about 606 million people. Of these, 62 per cent were North American or European, 31 per cent were from Asia/Pacific and five per cent were Latin American, leaving about one per cent in Africa with over half of this taken up by South Africa and virtually none in the rural areas (Girard, 2003). IDRC responded with project 'Acacia', designed to encourage access to ICTs by low-income groups in cities and the countryside, to provide tools and techniques that make it easier for low-income groups to use ICTs, and to adapt applications and services to meet community needs. The vehicle for doing this was through the establishment of multimedia community centres or 'telecentres' accessible within an hour of home by foot.[8] Most of its emphasis thus far has been on urban telecentres—which have been mushrooming—with typical services offered consisting of telephone, fax, photocopying, e-mail, Internet, and small group training in ICT proficiencies, like in information data navigation, networking, Website design. Pilot telecentres were also being tried out in a limited number of rural settings, for instance in two communities in Mozambique; one each in Mali and Uganda.

FAO has been actively supporting the use of ICTs for agricultural development (Richardson, 1997; Richardson and Paisley, 1998) through rural telecentres, and other means (such as co-operatives and farmer associations), although the pace has been much slower than the explosion in urban settings. Rural Multipurpose Community Telecentres (RMCTs) provide much or all of the capability of their urban counterparts as well as access to more traditional media such as audio and video playback equipment. Typically, they can also serve as venues for formal and non-formal distance education training for extension and subject matter specialists. As information 'depots' or 'hubs' they can place regional, national and international information at the fingertips of agricultural development workers—information on markets, weather, crops, livestock production and natural resource protection (Crowder et al., 1998). Undoubtedly, as they become more developed and wide-spread, PRA/PRCA principles will be applied to bring crystallized farmer group's technology information needs to telecentres, tapping the relevant data bases available through the Internet that provide usable recommendations, and then packaging the results to respond to local demands and disseminating it through a variety of conventional media, and especially radio for maximum reach. Special efforts have been made to increase the access of rural women to the Net, and using it as a powerful vehicle in their agenda of advancement (FAO, 2002).

Much of the debate revolving around RMCTs has been in establishing the link from the global networks to national, town, and finally to village levels, the latter referred to by some as 'the last mile' of connectivity (van der Stichele and Bie, 1997) and others, 'the first mile' (Moetsabi in Richardson and Paisley, 1998). Costs appear to be the main constraint. IDRC estimates that if a wired land-based network is to be put into place, the expense for connecting rural subscribers in Africa will be five to 10 times higher than that of city-dwellers. The cost of equipment, and training of those to operate it, must also be factored in. But the issues of connectivity, start-up costs and sustainability can be solved, according to Woods (1996) through establishing rural telecentres as a 'Community Utility', accessible on a pay-to-use basis. Based on IDRC's experience, however, the report card on making RMCTs financially viable is still in the making. Others more optimistically suggest that trend is clearly wireless, mobile, multimedia and broadband ICTs, with costs dropping appreciable (Crowder, 2000).[9]

FAO's initial experience with Internet-based ICTs started in Latin America in the early 1990s when farmer-operated information networks were established in Chile and Mexico. Linkages were established with agricultural producers, farmer associations, extension services and NGOs. The networks provided data on seeds, inputs, markets, weather forecasts, and credit facilities, among other essential topics. All told, the networks have proven an effective way for farmers to access local, regional, national and even global sources. By knowing market price information in larger centres, they have also increased profitability in setting local crop selling rates, and a base for better planning of quantities to plant in the future (ibid.). Building on the experiences in Latin America, FAO recently carried out a study to design a farmer-operated network, or FarmNet, with the Uganda National Farmers' Association (UNFA). The study found that the best approach would be to enhance existing communication efforts through face to face meetings, audio listening groups, local radio, publications and other media with the use of a simple e-mail-based communication system. UNFA members overwhelmingly indicated the need for information on markets, improved agricultural technologies, and weather conditions.

A more recent FAO development has been the Virtual Extension, Research and Communication Network or VERCON, designed as an open network to improve communication between research and extension, and, for those with Internet access, farmers themselves. Prototype software was developed which can be readily adapted locally to improve the flow of information between extension and research departments. A VERCON project was tested in Egypt during 2001–2002 and officially launched in 2003 (FAO, 2003). Another FAO project is under development in Mali to link four rural radio stations to the Internet. The overall focus of the latter initiative is to train radio producers to collect and package scientific and technical information available on the Internet for broadcasting to rural audiences in formats and languages they easily comprehend. At the same time, locally relevant agricultural information that is collected through radio reports and field interviews is formatted and disseminated through the Internet.

Finally, a pilot VERCON project was initiated in Bhutan during 2005 to test gathering farmers' information needs through participatory methods out of three regional extension centres, moving the information requests via Internet to the Central Ministry of Agriculture for recommendations and solutions which would be posted on a specially designed Website and accessed by extension officers and farmers around the regional centres. Other menu items would feature seasonal technology recommendations, marketing information, and weather reports. A variety of local media such as radio, posters and pamphlets will be used for dissemination of the information to the wider farming community.

Parallel Evolution of a Participatory Adult Learning Model

Hand in hand with the development of participatory theory and practice in communication has been a recognition of the importance of indigenous knowledge bases accumulated by farmers, and an examination of how new research recommendations might best fit into them. This reversal of the uni-directional passing on of research findings through extension to farmers, long advocated under the training and visit system (Benor and Cleaver, 1989), now implies that 'farmers are the ones who must control the learning and be able to access information according to specific needs, times and means' (Ramirez and Stuart, 1994:4). Previously technologies were typically finalized in research institutions before farmers got to see them, essentially leaving them three choices: adoption, adaptation or rejection. When farmers make choices about what technologies are needed, and the knowledge and skills required to use them through what Rogers (1992; 1996) terms 'a critical reflection on experience', the roles of research and extension are dramatically changed. Under the new paradigm, the 'assertion of a knowledge gap, or a disparity between "experts" and local people is wrong—unless the "experts", through cooperation and learning from local people, can apply their knowledge in the context and to the benefit of local "expertise"'(Servaes and Arnst, 1992:18).

Along with the levelling of extension services to match farmer demands, the shift from teaching to learning with them through practical applications has assumed vital importance. Roling and Pretty (1997:183) put the case succinctly. 'It is important to recognize that local people are always involved in active learning, in (re)inventing technologies, in adapting their farming systems and livelihood strategies. Understanding and supporting these processes of agricultural innovation and experimentation have become an important focus in facilitating more sustainable agriculture with its strong locality-specific nature'. One of the more successful of these methodologies has been the Farmer Field School or FFS pioneered by FAO (FAO, 2000; Gallagher, 2000).

FFSs were first established in Indonesia in 1989 as part of an FAO Integrated Pest Management (IPM) project. Courses take place in the field, field conditions define the curriculum, and real field problems are observed from planting of a crop to harvesting. An FFS is usually initiated by someone who has had experience at growing the crop concerned. For this reason, most IPM programmes have begun with training extension field staff in basic technical skills for managing an IPM crop. Each school lasts for one cropping season, with a group of about 25 people meeting on a weekly basis to study and make decisions based on the cropping calendar, like on seeding, fertilizing, weeding, curbing pest encroachment. Instead of listening to lectures or watching demonstrations, farmers observe, record and discuss what is happening in the field. This discover-learning approach generates a deep understanding of ecological concepts and their practical application.

An FFS is always held in the community where the farmers live, with the extension officer travelling to the site on the day when the school meets. The field used for study is usually small, and either provided by the community or some other arrangement so that farmers can carry out risk-free management decisions that they might not otherwise attempt on their own farms. All field schools include field-based pre-and post-tests for the participants. Those with high attendance rates and who master the tests are awarded a certificate. Graduates routinely take over the job of extension facilitator by doing farmer-to-farmer training or most of the functions of a follow-up season's training. The effects of IPM methods taught in FFSs are also compared with conventional practices. Case 3 describes one notable example drawn from Indonesia in 1993.

Case 3

Comparison of Inputs and Outputs of Farmer Field School versus Non-Field School Trained Rice Farmers in Indonesia

A controlled FAO study was conducted in West Sumatra, Indonesia, during the wet season of 1992–1993 (December to May). The study compared costs of rice farming inputs and outputs among ten farmers who had participated in integrated pest management (IPM) farmer field schools during the previous wet season with

(*Case 3 continued*)

(Case 3 continued)

practices and outputs of ten farmers who had never participated in FFSs. The two groups of farmers were matched by location, farm size and land tenure. The only treatment variable was the IPM–FFS training.

Observations and discussions with both sets of farmers were held on a weekly basis. IPM training had stressed 'Growing a Healthy Crop' (improved seed varieties, balanced fertilization, proper plant spacing in straight rows), 'Conservation of Beneficial Insects' (low pesticide use), and Weekly Field Observations to Determine Management Actions. The foregoing training focal points were determined to be the major differences between IPM and non-IPM farmers.

The comparative results on a number of key variables based on actual harvests are tabulated below.

Variable	Average Budget for 10 Non-IPM Farmers (in Rupiahs)	Average Budget for 10 IPM Trained Farmers (in Rupiahs)
Pre-Harvest Labour/Ha	414,660	384,656
Harvest Labour/Ha	657,730	659,851
Total Inputs/Ha	163,268	139,819
Total Production Costs/Ha	820,998	799,670
Total Output in Kg/Ha	5,741	6,953

Overall, the IPM farmers achieved 21 per cent more rice harvest yield on a per hectare basis (6.9 tons versus 5.7 tons), for 97 per cent of production costs, when compared to their non-IPM farmer counterparts. The significantly lower 'input' costs for IPM farmers were largely attributed to minimal usage of commercial pesticides. Labour costs were also slightly lower for IPM farmers, possibly because of better land management practices.

Source: FAO (1993). *IPM Farmer Training: The Indonesian Case,* Jogyakarta: FAO—IPM Secretariat.

Hard Lessons Learned for the Road Ahead

1. Participatory Communication using Best Practices in Adult Learning should be Built-in from the Start of a Project.[10]

The literature is rife with confirmative statements to this effect. Two examples will suffice:

If the goal of the development effort is to assist the poor, the endeavour should begin in their context, not in the planning office, not in the research station, and not from theories and constructs of far-removed institutions.... The claim is not that rural farmers are the foremost experts in macro-level planning but they are often the most qualified to decide how, or if, a given project's planning and objectives applies at the local level.... Participation is not a supplementary mechanism 'diffused' to expedite external agendas, or a means to an end. It is a legitimate goal in itself. (Servaes and Arnst, 1992:18)

Access to and control of information sources are essential for poor people to participate fully in decisions affecting their lives and communities. Sustained social change is impossible without their full participation (Rockefeller Foundation, 2000:2).

Unfortunately, all too often when communication is included, it is treated as an 'add-on' type of materials production component to assist project objectives that may be well off the mark. Simply stated, communication with target groups in the planning stage gives a better project design and better chances of making it successful.

2. Indigenous Knowledge and Practice should be Incorporated Early on

The adage of 'start with what people already know and build on what they have' subsumes the notion that 'indigenous knowledge can provide a different understanding and analysis of a situation which was formulated in response to the environment and relevant cultural issues' (Servaes and Anrst, 1992:18). Further, 'the location-specific nature of sustainable agriculture implies that extension must make use of farmers' knowledge and work together with farmers' (Roling and Pretty, 1997:186). And finally, 'experiences from around the world have shown that new "scientific technologies" are not always the best strategy to adopt. Farmers' indigenous agricultural practices offer many answers and the best of both knowledge areas needs to be considered to meet local needs' (Protz, 1998:2).

3. Multi-Channel Approaches are Much more Effective than any Single Medium Application and should be Part of any Communication Strategy

Communication theory has tended to support the case for multimedia use based on the premise that having access to at least two channels allows a production team to present and reinforce the same points in different ways and with varied emphasis. Individuals also differ in their processing of information from different media; some learn better from and prefer visual media than audio, and vice versa. In general, evidence from controlled classroom studies suggests that providing a variety of reinforcing channels caters to both learning styles and learning preferences (World Bank, 1983). Practical evidence from the field to reinforce the experimental classroom findings, however, especially in rural development, is rare (See Coldevin, 1986 and Coldevin, 1990 for two FAO field-based examples).

4. Provide Adequate Funding from the Start for Communication and Learning Components

A rule of thumb estimate is to budget 10 per cent (Fraser and Villet, 1994) but large projects may require proportionately less and smaller ones more. But based on the limited evidence thus far, training and technical support for ICT-related projects will need substantially more funding than previously allotted for conventional media. Norrish (in Richardson and Paisley, 1998) for example, points out that an average of 24 per cent of the funding for a World Bank information technology component was spent on training and technical support.

5. Set Longer Project Running Times for Communication and Learning Focussed Efforts

Although not a new theme, building human capacity takes time, usually much more than provided for in a typical five year project. Balit (1988) notes that the most successful of FAO's projects with a communication for development component have had a running time of seven to 10 years. Benor and Cleaver (1989) go even further when suggesting that support to extension systems should be designed with a long term perspective (15 years at least). As they sceptically conclude, 'The continent of Africa is littered with five-year projects, abandoned on "completion" by farmers' (ibid.:2).

6. Given the Location-Specific Nature of the Participatory Communication Process, a 'Small is Beautiful' Approach should have Projects Focussing at the Community Level

While a number of communities may be included in a given project, individual attention should be stressed such that each would build on its own strengths and unique opportunities. As Roling and Pretty (1997) conclude from their review of extension's role in sustainable agricultural development, 'Most successes are still localized. They are simply islands of success' (Roling and Pretty, 1997:181). And undoubtedly, it is much easier to encourage and facilitate what we might call the four pillars of collaborative development at the individual village level, namely, multi-stakeholder involvement or pluralism, transparent negotiations, representational participation, and accountability (Anderson et al., 1998; Ramirez, 1998).[11]

7. Plan for Gender Sensitivity in Communication Strategies and Media Content, Particularly with Regard to Rural Women's Concerns

As Balit (1999) points out, women farmers are responsible for half of the world's food production and in most developing countries produce from 60 per cent to 80 per cent of food destined for household food consumption. The 'feminization of agriculture' means that rural women are key actors on the development agenda. PRCA applications should address social, economic, cultural, and time constraints faced by women in producing and preparing food and factor these into the design of communication messages, the choice of appropriate channels to use, and best timing and locations for delivery.

8. Build in Both Qualitative and Quantitative Baseline Measures as the Comparative Benchmark for Evaluating Project Impact Later On

The issue of the lack of evaluation continues to undermine the perception of the value of participatory communication and learning project components. Assessing and taking credit for outcomes and longer term impact which rightly accrue from communication and learning activities, such as changes in awareness, knowledge, attitudes, skills and behaviour, should be applied more frequently. Time and time again, one reads that a true assessment of the value of communication and training was not possible due to the lack of a baseline or a benchmark survey. And even in the background research for this paper, only a small percentage of FAO field projects had built in baseline and outcomes surveys; even fewer had included a control group for comparing the results of the communication interventions.

Incorporating both qualitative and quantitative baseline measures such as those advocated in PRCA ensures that shifts in indicators can be measured during project implementation upon its completion, and well after to probe longer term impact. Inferences as to the effects of media and learning strategies on agricultural production levels—as a result of practice changes—can also be made, like the results of IPM–FFS on increases in rice production in Indonesia. In short, we need to consolidate a portfolio of validated best practices to better enable project decision-makers to harness the power of communication interventions. Put succinctly by Balit (2004: 19), '… the only way to convince decision-makers to devote additional resources to communication is by providing them with concrete examples of the impact and cost-benefits of communication. And, we must speak their language. Is this not what we do when we work with rural people?'

One way to encourage more evaluation, and to curb the contention that it is such a time consuming process, is to choose and apply only those PRA tools that will yield useful information; and the turn-around time for baseline quantitative surveys can be reduced by choosing smaller, but representative, samples and asking only what needs to be asked for formulating a communication strategy and media-mix.

The issue of evaluation is taking on mounting importance since the day has arrived when donors want hard evidence of the results of their project investments. Anecdotal, narrative descriptions of outcomes and impacts will no longer do. Results-Based Management or RBM has been around at least since 1999 (CIDA, 1999). This methodology which sets specific inputs, activities, outputs, outcomes and impact performance indicators is being applied by CIDA, SIDA, USAID and some UN Agencies, like UNFPA. Assuredly most development agencies will follow. Mainstreaming gender into RBM and factoring it into the evaluation grid of project indicators is another very positive step in this movement.

9. How to Best Achieve Sustainability should be Discussed and Planned before Implementation Begins

The question of how to best achieve sustainability following project completion remains a constant challenge but some answers are starting to emerge. Among those that we consider key triggers for successful development are:

- a community focus with beneficiary participation for setting achievable project objectives and creating local buy-in from the start;
- extension communication and learning approaches that build on indigenous know-how and mainly consult research on technical problems for which there are no effective local solutions available;
- sufficient time is allotted to allow project objectives to become routine; follow-on activities use local resources—staff, media equipment and facilities, and fall within the means of extension, and the community, to afford them.

Three decades of research and practice building mostly on traditional media are now being rapidly morphed into the drive to network the rural areas of the developing world. Whether this popular surge succeeds is far from certain and will be largely determined around issues of band-width and Wi-Fi connectivity. In the interim, conventional wisdom would dictate that the information power of ubiquitous radio supported by the Internet and reinforced with simple, well-illustrated print and localized extension services—which have served so well in the past—will continue to get the job done.

Notes

1. Education and training are no longer seen simply as processes of transferring knowledge or information, but rather as means to empower people to become critical thinkers and problem solvers who are better able to help themselves, and engage with others in order to learn, share information and address problems and priorities. This is very important for farmers whose ability to cope with the unpredictable is often the key to survival (FAO/World Bank, 2000).
2. More recently, Ramirez and Quarry (2003) refer to this function as 'communication for sharing knowledge'.
3. Although there are some examples of open television broadcasting in rural development, like in India, generally its use has been limited because of high production costs and low access among rural populations (FAO, 1989). Video, on the other hand, has rapidly emerged as perhaps the most effective medium for a variety of information and training purposes.
4. Another advance made by FAO in the Philippines during this period was the undertaking of a modified version of RAAKS (rapid appraisal of agricultural knowledge systems) for visualizing farmers' communication networks in two barangays up to municipal level (Ramirez, 1995).
5. Assistance to the project was also provided by the College of Development Communication (CDC), University of the Philippines, Los Baños (UPLB). Development Communication as an academic discipline was first introduced and has continued to flourish at UPLB since 1954.

6. Each CATS consisted of a karaoke system, two microphones, and a 500-watt amplifier housed in a studio and connected to four 100-watt loudspeakers attached to a metal tower. Total cost: US$ 2,000. Construction of studio housing and towers was provided by the communities. 'Broadcasts' can reach up to a two kilometre radius.

7. Other popular one to two week workshops include Gender and Communication, Participatory Research Techniques, Quantitative Baseline Surveys, Village Theatre in Development, and Participatory Rural Radio.

8. While a 'telecentre' may be the common descriptor for such a facility, a variety of other terms is used such as Multi-Purpose Telecentre (MPTC), Multi-Purpose Community Telecentre (MPCT), and Multi-Purpose Communication Centre (MPCC). IDRC has reduced it to Multipurpose Community Telecentre or MCT. UNESCO calls them Community Multimedia Centres (CMCs).

9. Certainly mobile phones have made tremendous inroads during the first five years of the twenty-first century. The UN had set a goal of 50 per cent access by 2015 but the World Bank reports that 77 per cent of the World's population already lives within range of a mobile network (*The Economist*, 12 March 2005). Cell phones are increasingly considered as the major low-tech vehicle for bridging the digital divide gap. Mobile phones are widely shared by villagers and are especially useful for farmers who can call several markets, cut out the middleman, and work out where to get the best prices on their own.

10. Common adult learning principles applied to rural producers can be summarized as follows:
    - Farmers are relevancy oriented. They want to work on projects that reflect their immediate needs and interests.
    - Farmers bring a foundation of experience and knowledge to any training situation. They want to connect this background to new learning.
    - Farmers are goal-oriented; they want to see the reason for learning—or adopting new technologies—and how this relates to the agricultural production and/or improved livelihoods.
    - Farmers are practical and prefer 'learning by doing'.
    - Farmers are pressed for time. They want to be able to immediately apply the skills learned to their immediate situation or else they forget them. The 'use it or loose it' phenomenon is especially critical when complex skills capacity-building is involved.

11. Pretty's (1995) top levels in his typology of participation, namely, interactive participation and self-mobilization are also best initiated at the individual community level.

References

Adhikarya, R. 1994. *Strategic Extension Campaign: A Participatory-Oriented Method of Agricultural Extension*. Rome: FAO.

Anderson, J., J. Clement and L.V. Crowder. 1998. 'Accommodating Conflicting Interests in Forestry Concepts Emerging from Pluralism', *Unasylva*, 49.

Anyaegbunam, C., P. Mefalopulos and T. Moetsabi. 1998. *Participatory Rural Appraisal: Starting with the People*. Harare: SADC Centre of Communication for Development.

Balit, S. 1988. 'Rethinking Development Support Communication', *Development Communication Report*, 62.

———.1999. *Voices for Change: Rural Women and Communication*. Rome: FAO.

———. 2004. *Communication for Isolated and Marginalized Groups*. Rome: FAO.

Balit, S., C. Rios and L. Masias. 1996. *Communication for Development in Latin America: A Regional Experience*. Rome: FAO.

Benor, D. and K. Cleaver. 1989. 'Training and Visit System of Agricultural Extension', *Interpaks Exchange*, 6(2):1–3.

Chambers, R. 1992. *Rural Appraisal: Rapid, Relaxed and Participatory*. Sussex University, Brighton: Institute of Development Studies.

———. *Promoting Sustainable Rural Development Through Agriculture*. Hull, Canada: CIDA.

Coldevin, G. 1986. 'Evaluation in Rural Development Communication—A Case Study from West Africa', *Media in Education and Development*, 19:112–118.

———. 1987. *Perspectives on Communication for Rural Development*. Rome: FAO.

———. 1988. 'Video Applications in Rural Development', *Educational Media International*, 25(4):225–229.

———. 1990. *Communication Strategies for Rural Development: A Case Study of the Use of Campaigns in Lesotho*. Rome: FAO.

Coldevin, G. 1995. *Farmer-first Approaches to Communication: A Case Study from the Philippines.* Rome: FAO.

CIDA. 1999. *Results-Based Management in CIDA: An Introductory Guide to the Concepts and Principle.* Hull. Canada: CIDA.

Crowder, Loy Van and the Communication for Development Group Extension, Education and Communication Service (SDRE) FAO Research, Extension and Training Division. 1998. *Knowledge and Information for Food Security in Africa: From Traditional Media to the Internet.* Rome, FAO.

———. 2000. *Farmer Information Networks (FARMNets)—A Tool for Sustainable Agricultural Production and Improved Food Security in Developing Countries.* Rome: FAO.

FAO. 1981. *Communication for Rural Development.* Rome: FAO.

———. 1989. *Guidelines on Communication for Rural Development.* Rome: FAO.

———. 1993. *IPM Farmer Training: The Indonesia Case.* Jogyakarta: FAO–IPM Secretariat.

———. 1994. *Applying DSC Methodologies to Population Issues: A Case Study in Malawi.* Rome: FAO.

———. 1996. *Development of Rural Radio in Africa.* Rome: FAO.

———. 2000. *Community Integrated Pest Management.* Rome: FAO.

———. 2001. 'Participatory Communication', paper presented at the UNFPA Roundtable on Development Communication. November. Managua.

———. 2002. *Harnessing ICTs for Advancement of Rural Women: FAO Perspectives and Strategic Actions.* Rome: FAO.

———. 2003. *Virtual Extension, Research and Communication Network (VERCON).* Rome: FAO.

———. 2004. *Follow-up to the World Food Summit: Report on the Progress in the Implementation of the Plan of Action.* Rome: FAO.

———. 2006. *FAO's Mandate.* Available online at http://www.fao.org. (Downloaded on 15 August 2006).

FAO/World Bank. 2000. *Agricultural Knowledge and Information Systems for Rural Development (AKIS/RD), Strategic Vision and Guiding Principles.* Rome: FAO.

Fraser, C. 1983. 'Adopting Communication Technologies for Rural Development', *CERES*, 95.

Fraser, C. and Restrepo-Estrada. 1997. *Communication for Rural Development in Mexico: In Good Times and Bad.* Rome: FAO.

Fraser, C. and J. Villet. 1994. *Communication: A Key to Human Development.* Rome: FAO.

Freire, P. 1972. *Pedagogy of the Oppressed.* London: Penguin.

Gallagher, K. 2000. *Farmers' Field Schools (FFS): A Group Extension Process Based on Adult Non-Formal Education Methods.* Rome: FAO Global IPM Facility.

Girard, B. 2003. 'Radio and the Internet: Mixing media to bridge the divide', in B. Girard (ed.). *The one to watch: Radio, new ICTs and interactivity,* Chapter 1. Rome: FAO.

Ilboudo, J.P. and R. Del Castello. 2003. 'Linking Rural Radio to New ICTs in Africa: Bridging the Rural Digital Divide', in B. Girard (ed.). *The one to watch: Radio, new ICTs and interactivity,* Chapter 1. Rome: FAO.

IDRC. 1999. *Internet for All: The Promise of Telecentres in Africa.* Ottawa: IDRC.

Population Reference Bureau (PRB). 1999. Country Profiles for Population and Reproductive Health, Population Reference Bureau at www.prb.org

Pretty, J. 1995. *Regenerating Agriculture: Policies and Practice for Sustainability and Self-Reliance.* London: Earthscan Publications. p. 61.

Protz, M. 1998. 'Developing Sustainable Agricultural Technologies with Rural Women in Jamaica: A Participatory Media Approach'. Available online at http://www.fao.org/sd/CDdirect/CDan0020.htm

Ramirez, R. 1995. *Understanding Farmers' Communication Networks: An Experience in the Philippines.* Rome: FAO.

———. 1998. 'Participatory Learning and Approaches for Managing Pluralism', *Unasylva,* 49.

Ramirez, R. and T. Stuart. 1994. 'Farmers Control Communication Campaigns', *ILEIA Newsletter,* March.

Ramirez, R. and W. Quarry. 2003. *Communication for Development: A Medium for Innovation in Natural Resource Management.* Ottawa: IDRC.

Richardson, D. 1997. *The Internet and Rural and Agricultural Development: An Integrated Approach.* Rome: FAO.

Richardson, D. and L. Paisley (eds). 1998. *The First Mile of Connectivity: Advancing Telecommunication for Rural Development through a Participatory Communication Approach.* Rome: FAO.

Rockefeller Foundation. 2000. *Special Programs: Communication for Social Change.* New York: Rockefeller Foundation.

Rogers, A. 1992. *Adult Learning for Development.* London: Cassell.

———. 1996. 'Participatory Training Using Critical Reflection on Experience in Agricultural Extension Training', in L. van Crowder (ed.). *Training for Agriculture and Rural Development 1995–96,* pp. 86–103. Rome: FAO.

Rogers, E. 1976. 'Communication and Development: The Passing of the Dominant Paradigm', in E. Rogers (ed.). *Communication and Development—Critical Perspectives,* pp. 121–148. Beverly Hills, CA: Sage Publications.

Roling, N. and J. Pretty. 1997. 'Extension's Role in Sustainable Development', *Improving Agricultural Extension: A Reference Manual*, pp. 181–191. Rome: FAO.

SADC. 1999. *A Case Study on the Use of Participatory Communication in Support of the On-Farm Trial and Demonstration Program in the Kavango Region of Namibia*. Harare: SADC.

Sen, A. 1998. *Development as Freedom*. New York: Alfred A. Knopf.

Servaes, J. and R. Arnst. 1992. 'Participatory Communication for Social Change: Reasons for Optimism in the Year 2000', *Development Communication Report*, 79:18–20.

Sison, O. 1985. *Factors Associated with the Successful Transfer of Rice Technology in the Philippines Masagana 99 Program*. Rome: FAO.

The Economist: 12 March 2005. The Real Digital Divide, p. 11.

Van der Stichele, P. and S. Bie. 1997. *The Last Mile: How Can Farmers Take Advantage of New Media?* Rome: FAO.

Villet, J. 1988. *African Rinderpest Campaign Guide*. Rome: FAO.

Woods, B. 1996. 'A Public Good, A Private Responsibility', *CERES*, 28(2):23–27.

World Bank. 1983. Basic Education and Agricultural Extension, World Bank Staff Working Paper 564. World Bank, Washington.

Involving People, Evolving Behaviour: The UNICEF Experience[1]

12

NEILL McKEE, ERMA MANONCOURT,
CHIN SAIK YOON AND RACHEL CARNEGIE

Practitioners of development communication often set out to change the behaviour of people reached in the projects they undertake. The behaviour may range from getting farmers to adopt a new cropping technique, to persuading mothers to feed their babies boiled water. Their approach may be top-down or participatory, as the occasion requires. It is unlikely that farmers will respond to non-participative interventions in altering their cropping practices, just as it is unlikely that mothers with critically ill babies will respond to lengthy participatory processes when seeking treatment.

Communicators working to change or develop people's behaviour have found it a highly complex activity to engage in. Goals often remain elusive in spite of their best efforts. Many development communication campaigns succeed admirably in raising awareness about a particular issue while failing abysmally, at the same time, to bring about the sustained behaviour change such awareness is suppose to trigger. For example in anti-tobacco campaigns, smokers may quickly learn about the dangers of smoking, but continue to consume the same number of cigarettes that they did prior to their exposure to the messages of the campaign.

Why are people's behaviours so difficult to change? Why do development communication interventions often fail short of their behaviour altering goals?

While some of the answers and solutions may be found within the discipline of development communication, many others seem to lie well beyond its confines. It seems interventions in development communication must be integrated with a number of other efforts so as to nurture new behaviour in people. Once motivated with information and awareness about a new practice, people need to learn and master new skills to enable them to apply it. At the same time, their environment needs to evolve in such a way that they are encouraged to practise their new skills and knowledge. In other words, interventions in development communication must be integrated and coordinated with other interventions in education and policy advocacy and implementation aimed at nurturing the new behaviour.

It seems, on another front, that individuals in developing communities enjoy less freedom to make strictly personal decisions when considering whether to adopt a new behaviour, than their counterparts in developed countries. In making such decisions, the individuals in developing countries will consider more deeply the interests and views of their family, peers and community alongside their own preferences. As such, campaigns must aim to reach beyond the individuals, whose behaviour we are interested in, to include the people who influence the individuals and their behaviour.

Underpinning these personal and communal decisions are the values that lie at the core of the community. Shared values define so much of daily life in developing societies that development practitioners must take time to identify and appreciate them. These values are the cardinal reference points of people as they filter new information, learn new skills, discard old practices and beliefs, evolve their environment, and decide upon action.

This integrated approach towards involving people in evolving behaviour is summarized in the model in Figure 12.1.

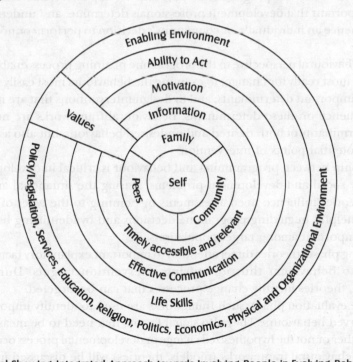

Figure 12.1 A Model Showing Integrated Approach towards Involving People in Evolving Behaviour

This contribution will focus on the two outer rings of the diagram: 'Enabling environment' and 'Ability to act'.

The inner two rings of 'Information' and 'Motivation' are the forte of development communicators and have been covered in depth in the preceding sections of this publication.

However, before we turn to these two topics, let us first review briefly the main theories for behaviour change from the interrelated perspectives offered by sociology, psychology and anthropology.

Theories and Frameworks for Behavioural Change

Understanding people and their behaviour is one of the keys to successful development programmes. The actions and practices of an intended beneficiary or a stakeholder can directly affect the evolution of many social and health-related problems. The political and social sciences, especially the disciplines of sociology, psychology and anthropology, have contributed much to our understanding of why people behave the way they do and the respective roles of their motivations, fears, social pressure, environmental factors, and others, on individual and collective behaviour. In order to increase programme impact, and develop interventions that are strategically applied, it is important that development professionals determine, and understand, the various factors that influence an individual's, or community's decision to perform or not perform specific behaviours.

Applying a behavioural perspective to the programme planning process enables one to identify the populations most ready for change; to examine the behaviours most easily influenced, along with their most important determinants; and to design interventions that are most likely to have the desired influence on these determinants. Behavioural frameworks are not only useful for identifying determinants of both desired and undesired behaviour, but also assist programmers in identifying potential points of intervention.

The relationship between programming and behaviour is critical in developing programmes that address key social and development problems. During the situational analysis phase of a programme, theories influence need assessments by pointing to the types of information that would be most helpful in guiding programme decisions and by identifying behavioural factors that are more important among target populations.

In the planning phase, theories direct attention to important explanatory factors (how different factors relate to behaviour) thus identifying intervention targets. During programme implementation, theories identify change processes that can be targeted.

As part of the evaluation phase, such frameworks are used to identify important explanatory factors for observed behaviours. They also signal factors that need to be measured, in order to understand whether or not the hypothesized change or developmental process occurred as planned.

A variety of behavioural frameworks (models, theories) will be discussed in this chapter but for illustration purposes, emphasis will be placed on health programmes and consequently the use of health behaviour examples. Nonetheless, the reader is reminded that the discussion that follows has a wider application to other social and development programmes.

Although one often hears the term 'health behaviour', it has different meanings depending on one's professional training. For programming purposes, distinguishing between health-directed and health-related behaviour is useful. The former refers to observable acts that are undertaken with a specific health outcome in mind. In direct contrast, health-related behaviours are those actions that a person does that may have health implications, but are not undertaken with a specific health objective in mind.

Box 12.1 Key Definitions

Behaviour is defined as: 'an observable act, such as stepping on a weighing scale'. Technically speaking, a behaviour category is used to refer to a composite of discrete actions. For example: 'weighing a baby' is composed of several actions: 'putting the child in a harness,' 'calibrating the scale measurement,' 'calculating the kilograms on a scale', etc.

Behavioural determinants are factors that either influence or cause an action to occur, or not occur. Also referred to as mediating factors, they may be internal (anxieties, beliefs, etc.) or external (peer pressure, supportive setting, etc.). In the example of 'losing weight', the determinants could be internal (like an individual's personal attitude towards being overweight) and/or external (like having close friends who are on diets). Research has shown that these factors will vary in importance for different behaviours and across different settings; therefore a clear understanding of when, where and under what conditions the desired behaviour should occur (or undesired practices should cease) needs to be determined.

A discussion of behavioural terminology is incomplete without mention of two key internal behavioural determinants, knowledge and attitudes, that affect how human beings act.

Attitudes are feelings, opinions or values that an individual holds about a particular issue, problem or concern.

Knowledge is internalized learning based on scientific fact, experience and/or traditional beliefs. Experience shows that knowledge is necessary but not sufficient to produce behaviour change, which occurs when perceptions, motivation, skills and the social environment also interact.

When formulating interventions, it is important to clarify who is the subject of the action—by age or cultural group, gender, religion, ethnicity or some other characteristic. Decisions about which groups to target help us make choices from amongst the variety of theoretical models and conceptual frameworks that are based on empirical programme experience. Realizing that change in society occurs at many societal levels, programme staff are often faced with choices as to whom they should direct their efforts—individuals, families or households, communities or the wider society as a whole. In practice, these choices are influenced by time and resource considerations and should be informed by an understanding of behaviour as a developmental and change process. Knowledge of the available theories or models can also guide programme planning and clarify the relationships between different factors that influence individual, interpersonal and group behaviour.

Box 12.2 Key Definitions: Female Genital Mutilation (FGM)

UNICEF's Sara Communication Initiative for the adolescent girl in Eastern and Southern Africa has researched attitudes and produced materials on FGM. Through focus group discussions, communities aired their views on the issue and identified any positive elements related to the practice. Many believed that, as a rite of passage, the ceremonies as a whole gave a sense of cultural identity to young people and provided a form of family life education to young girls. People were aware of the negative impact on the girls' and women's health, yet girls highlighted the anxiety caused by resisting the practice individually, since an uncircumcised girl may be mocked and considered potentially unmarriageable within her community.

The debate in the focus groups centred on whether it was possible to reject the negative while retaining the positive elements of this rite of passage. People also considered who would be the most likely and effective initiators of change within the community as a whole. The Sara film and books reflect these research findings, and seek to stimulate debate on FGM at community level and also advocate for greater support at policy level.

Some Theoretical Frameworks that Explain Individual Behaviour

Health Belief Model (HBM)

The Health Belief Model is the most common and well-known theory in the field of public health and has been used more widely than any other to guide behaviour interventions in development programmes. Developed in the early 1950s by Godfrey Hochbaum and other social psychologists at the US Public Health Service, it was used to explain patients' responses to tuberculosis preventive actions. The HBM model is based on the premise that one's personal thoughts and feelings control one's actions. It proposes that health behaviour is therefore determined by internal cues (perceptions or beliefs), or external cues (for example, reactions of friends, mass media campaigns, and so forth), that trigger the need to act. It specifically hypothesizes that individual behaviour is determined by several internal factors:

- Belief about one's chances or risk of getting an illness or being directly affected by a particular problem or illness (perceived susceptibility);
- Belief or one's opinions about the seriousness of a given problem or illness (perceived severity);
- Belief about the efficacy of an action to reduce risk or severity (perceived benefits) compared to one's opinion about the tangible or psychological risks or costs for proposed action (perceived barriers).

According to the HBM, the first two beliefs jointly form one's conviction and influence the degree to which an individual may be motivated to act on a given problem. The theory also suggests that the above reflections and thoughts are triggered by both internal influences (like sweating, nervousness, and so forth) and external influences (like reactions by other people and/or opinions of significant others, media, and so forth). These are labelled as 'cues to action'.

Once an individual is motivated to act, the actual behaviour undertaken will be determined by a third factor—a personal perception of 'cost-benefit'. This framework further explains that before deciding to act, individuals consider whether or not the benefits (positive aspects) outweigh the barriers (negative aspects) of a particular behaviour.

In a more recent formulation of this theory, the concept of self-efficacy has been added. This addition takes into account individual beliefs or personal perceptions of one's own ability to undertake a particular action.

Theory of Reasoned Action (TRA) and Personal Behaviour (TPB)

Similar to the HBM model, the Theory of Reasoned Personal Behaviour also supports the notion that one's thoughts and perceptions are important determinants of behaviour. Developed by Fishbein and Ajzen (1980), this theory added a new dimension to our understanding of behaviour by introducing the concept of behavioural intent. According to their behaviour research, the most critical factor in determining whether individuals will actually perform a desired behaviour is their behavioural intent. Behavioural intent reflects the level of commitment that an individual has to undertake a desired behaviour and likelihood that an individual will perform the desired behaviour: It is influenced by personal attitudes and perceived social pressure/norms.

In later formulations of TRA, the concept of perceived behavioural control was added to the framework. This concept identifies beliefs that individuals have about available resources and obstacles to performing a desired behaviour and their impact (or power) in either facilitating or inhibiting the behaviour. This was an attempt to reflect that factors outside an individual's control could also affect actual performances of a particular behaviour.

Clearly, this theory acknowledges the joint influence of attitudes, norms and perceived control in affecting behavioural intention as a motivating force in the behaviour process. It also clarifies that perceptions of control, similar to behavioural intention, have a direct influence on one's taking action. However, the relevant importance of each of these dimensions is dependent on the behaviour goal, itself. TPB posits that individuals who have positive attitudes towards performing a particular behaviour, and who believe that 'significant others' are in favour of or support the desired action, will more likely attempt a particular behaviour. For some people, their own personal attitudes will have a greater influence on their behaviour than perceived social pressure, and vice versa for others.

Stages of Change Theory

The Stages of Change Theory is based on the premise that behaviour change is a process and explains the psychological processes that people undergo are iterative in nature. Assuming that individuals experience different levels of motivation to change, Prochaska et al. (1992) suggest that interventions should be matched to individuals at their respective stages in the change process. It also suggests that behaviour change can be characterized by five stages: pre-contemplation (no thoughts about change), contemplation, decision/determination, action and maintenance.

The theory, conceived as a circular model, allows for individuals to enter at any stage and takes into account that the stages, themselves, may appear different, given different situations. While these stages can be used to explain why people behave as they do, they can also inform intervention design and communication messages that can be tailored accordingly.

Some Theoretical Frameworks which Explain Interpersonal Behaviour

Social Cognitive Theory (SCT)

Originally developed as Social Learning Theory in 1986, Albert Bandura later expanded his work to evolve the Social Cognitive Theory (SCT) (1995). As such, the SCT assumes that individuals interact constantly with their social environment and that they influence, and are influenced by their social milieu—friends, family, co-workers, and so forth. Central to this theory is the premise that behaviour is a result of a three-way, reciprocal interaction between personal factors (that is, one's own feelings and reactions) and environmental influences (like thoughts, advice and feelings of 'significant others'). In contrast to the previously discussed conceptual models, this theory emphasizes the role of one's own experiences and observations of others and the results of their actions on personal behaviour. SCT explains human behaviour as a multi-dimensional and reciprocal process. It uses four concepts that can be used to guide programme development and behavioural interventions at an interpersonal level: reciprocal determinism, behavioural capability, outcome expectations and self-efficacy.

SCT is centred on the premise that people learn their behaviours from their own experiences (trial and error) and the results of their actions, and by observing, others.

Observations, and consequently effective role models, are important in learning new behaviours. Empirical study shows that the more similar a role model is to a particular target group, the more the group will identify with the model and try to emulate his or her behaviour.

Practice, trial and error, is the most powerful source of learning. It takes into account that the individual's mastery of tasks is important and that the more they practice and are able to accomplish a particular task, the more motivated they will be to attempt a desired action.

According to Bandura, one's sense of self-efficacy is also learnt through emotional reactions or feelings about a situation or from persuasive arguments and encouragement by credible people within an appropriate social context.

Social Experience Model

Using a human development perspective, Bloomberg et al. (1994:455) developed a framework for understanding the critical interaction between elements of the social environment and health. They concentrated on the concept of social experience, and the ways in which the immediate and wider environment of an individual can affect his/her behaviour. This theoretical model emphasizes that human behaviour is the result of interactions with 'significant others' and the ways that one is treated due to his/her status or membership in a particular group. It also explains that social context and relationships in which one is involved influences his/her self-perceptions of personal competencies and expectations and can ultimately affect various social or health outcomes.

According to Bloomberg and his colleagues, an individual's socio-demographic background plus his/her own personal traits determine the social context of interactions with others. They noted that factors such as environment resources, parental education, family income, and occupational status are key socio-demographic characteristics that play a role. More importantly, this theory suggests that the opinions and behaviours of one's friends, family, or social network influence one's own personal perceptions and actions. This social experience has a direct impact on one's actions and ultimately, social, health and other development outcomes.

Social Network and Social Support Theory

The theory explains the mechanisms by which social interactions can promote or inhibit individual and collective behaviour. As defined by Israel (1985) and Israel and Schurman (1990) and other researchers, a social network is person-centred and refers to the set of linkages and social relationships between people. An understanding of network theory enables programmers to better analyse how friends, families and other significant people might impact on the same individuals and groups that they are trying to influence. In developing appropriate interventions, the following network characteristics should be considered: size and number of members, frequency of contact and strength of the bond between members; extent to which everyone knows each other and extent to which resources and support are exchanged between members.

Social support, on the other hand, refers to the content of these relationships, that is, what is actually being shared or transmitted during different interactions. As such, assistance provided or exchanged through interpersonal and other social relationships can be characterized into four types of supportive action: emotional support, instrumental support such as tangible aid or services, appraisal support such as feedback and constructive criticism, and informational support in the form of advice or suggestions, so on and so forth.

Some Theoretical Frameworks which Explain Community or Societal Behaviour

Diffusion of Innovations (DOI)

Based on his study of collective human behaviour and responsiveness to novelty and the introduction of change, Everett Rogers (1986, 1995) developed a theoretical model entitled the Diffusion of Innovations Theory. Based on agricultural extension work in USA and East Africa, this theory explains the progression over time by which members of a community or society adopt new, or different, ideas and practices. It is based on the premise that social change or changes in human behaviour can be understood by the way that individuals and groups respond to new or different ideas and behaviours that are introduced. The theory also provides insight into the impact of social influence on individual and household behaviour.

Commonly referred to as 'innovations', these new ideas can in fact be technologies, attitudes, behaviours, policies, practices or even programmes. Experience has taught us that these innovations are not always recognized initially as being necessary, useful, or important, by the target population. Their acceptance, and adoption, on a wide-scale basis begins slowly, as a few people or groups try the idea out first before it gradually spreads to others, as a social momentum may be created or the social climate becomes more accommodating. The theory also posits that the adoption is a process. All eventual adopters pass through five stages: (a) awareness of the innovation; (b) interest in it; (c) trying it out; (d) making a decision to accept or reject, and (e) adopting or adapting the innovation into one's daily life.

Conceptual Model of Community Empowerment

Many theorists are not satisfied with individual behaviour change alone. They maintain that we should be more concerned with empowerment of people for long-term change (Freire, 1970; Wallerstein, 1992; Steckler et al., 1993). A review of literature (mainly health education articles) reveals that there are a variety of definitions for the concept of 'empowerment'. For some it is:

- Largely a personal process in which individuals develop and employ necessary knowledge, competence and confidence for making their own decisions/voices heard, or,
- Participatory competence: the ability to be heard by those in power, or,
- A social process of recognizing, promoting and enhancing people's abilities to meet their own needs, solve their own problems and mobilize the necessary resources in order to feel in control.

Central to an understanding of the community empowerment process is the recognition that communities are composed of individuals and organizations that interact in a variety of social networks. This interdependence supports the notion that changes in one part of the social system has rippling effects in other parts. As a result, development programmes that aim to facilitate community ownership, competence and commitment to change must explore the concept of empowerment at three levels of practice: individual, organizational and community. They are distinguished as follows:

- Individual empowerment has a focus on personal efficacy and competence. It also takes into account one's sense of mastery and/or control over a situation.
- Organizational empowerment emphasizes processes that enable individuals to increase control within a formalized structure, and the organization itself to influence policies and decisions in the larger community. In practice, it also provides opportunities for individual growth and access to decision-making processes.
- Community empowerment centres on collective action and control that is based on participation of both individuals and organizations within a specific social context. Some of its benefits, on a group level, are greater economic independence and social recognition.

In summary, there are a variety of theoretical models from which development workers can choose. None of these have proven completely satisfactory in the field of international development. Many practitioners find that they can achieve the greatest understanding by combining more than one theory or developing their own conceptual framework. What follows in this book is such an attempt. It is not a theory, but it does offer insight in the form of a model which can be easily understood by professionals in many fields and it does answer some of the criticism sometimes made, that theories of behaviour are too Western and geared to the individual.

Strengthening People's Life Skills

The term 'life skills' is applied in a variety of ways in the context of different programmes. In some cases it is taken to refer to practical, technical skills, such as mixing oral re-hydration solution or putting on a condom. In other cases, it refers to entrepreneurial or livelihood skills, necessary for economic survival. In the school context, it is sometimes taken to mean the essential skills of basic education, including literacy, numeracy, and technical skills in health education. In this section, however, the discussion of life skills focusses on what are often termed psychosocial competencies. These are the skills which enable individuals to think and behave in a pro-active and constructive way in dealing with themselves, relating to others and succeeding in the wider society. Life skills are required both in everyday circumstances and, particularly, in specific risk situations.

The most accessible way to explain life skills is perhaps to provide a list of life skills which have been identified by different programmes around the world. The Mental Health Promotion Unit of the World Health Organization in Geneva has analysed the content of numerous life skills programmes in schools around the globe, and has found that there are five basic life skills areas which frequently appear (WHO/MNH, 1994). These life skills areas provide a starting point. Later in this chapter we will examine whether life skills have a cross-cultural relevance and the ways in which they can be adapted.

Each basic life skill area leads to a multitude of other skills to be developed and practised. For example, developing critical thinking skills can strengthen people's ability to clarify their values and assess risks more effectively. After developing basic communication skills, young people can go on to learn about negotiation skills, assertiveness and resisting peer pressure. Learning decision-making skills can be further refined with additional activities to practise setting realistic goals for the future.

Clearly, different dimensions of life skills are appropriate for different age groups. For example, in the case of communication skills, while young children might aim for clear expression and the ability to speak and listen in turn, older children need more advanced skills in negotiation. Adolescents, and indeed adults, could refine this still further and should be able to combine communication skills and problem-solving skills for conflict resolution.

Life skills are required by people for their healthy development by enabling them to:

- Acquire a sense of self-worth and self-efficacy;
- Build supportive relationships with family and friends;
- Promote healthy living;
- Cope with the stresses and pressures of daily life;
- Deal with conflicting values and norms for behaviour.

The acquisition of life skills is clearly linked to the development of values. Of most significance are the attitudes relating to the individual's perception of self and others. The enhancement of life skills goes hand-in-hand with the promotion of self-esteem, self-control and personal responsibility. It also involves, crucially, both a respect for others, regardless of race, sex, religion or life style, and a sense of the individual's responsibility for the group, be it family, friends or community.

These general attitudes need to be combined with efforts to clarify one's own set of values. In many regions, vast population growth, urban migration and exposure to alternative values through new information channels, have challenged traditional family and community structures which formerly raised young people within their own particular cultural system. In many cases, the social and sexual mores of the modern world are in direct conflict with traditional values. Within societies there is often moral ambivalence, when what is practised contradicts what is preached. All these factors lead to feelings of confusion and alienation for young people attempting to make sense of their world, feelings which may manifest themselves in risky behaviours.

Life Skills Learning Process

What most clearly defines a 'life skills approach' from other health promotion initiatives is the teaching and learning approach. In life skills programmes the emphasis is more on process rather than on content; on how something is learned, rather than what is learned; on how to think, not what to think. Life skills are not a set of technical skills that can be taught on the basis of information transferred from the teacher to the pupil. Nor should life skills be taught in isolation. They need to be dealt with holistically, taking into account the social, cultural and economic context of the learners' lives, with application to real life concerns.

Considering the health and social issues addressed within life skills programmes, the information content is, of course, significant. However, effective learning is likely to depend more on the methods employed than on the information component of the programme. 'The methods used are what most clearly distinguishes life skills programmes from information dissemination initiatives, such as teaching "facts for life"' (WHO/MNH, 1994:3). This educational approach involves participatory and active learning methods. The objective is to create an environment conducive to experiential learning of life skills.

Defining knowledge as a 'process of inquiry' (Freire, 1973:46), in which the learner is the active agent in creating knowledge, is the key issue which demarcates active learning in life skills education from conventional, didactic approaches. 'The central, and indispensable, component of active learning is the "inner" activity in which the learner constructs and reconstructs his system of knowledge, skills and values. It is this structure which enables him to order new experiences, and thus to attach meaning both to the outside world and to his role in it' (Somerset, 1988:151).

It must be acknowledged that, for learners of all ages, their experiences will not always be easy or positive. Applying life skills to their real life involves taking risks. If young people refuse to smoke, take drugs or alcohol, they might risk ostracism from their social group. If a person, concerned about his or her partner's sexual history, insists on condom use, he or she might risk rejection. This is why life skills education should always include time to practise skills in a safe learning environment. This is an opportunity to test out other people's reactions to new behaviours.

Obviously all efforts should be made to create as supportive an environment as possible, through parallel work with parents and the community. However, it must be acknowledged that use of life skills is, in itself, a risk-taking venture, since it potentially alters the individual's relationship with others, challenging their values, roles and power relations. This underlines the importance of life skills education as a long-term, sequential and developmentally appropriate intervention. To support the learning and practice of life skills, they should always be taught first in the context of low risk, non-threatening situations, to provide opportunities for positive feedback from the application of life skills. The skills should then be explored and practised in progressively more challenging or threatening situations over time. It is the confidence gained in the practise of skills in low risk situations which helps people to persevere with their intended action when people do not respond favourably to their behaviour.

Box 12.3 Zimbabwe School AIDS Action Programme

The School AIDS Action Programme in Zimbabwe provides an interesting example of an attempt to take a life skills approach from small-scale intervention into a national programme, introduced through the formal education system. With HIV/AIDS prevention as its primary objective, the programme has a broad foundation in the development of life skills.

The Curriculum Development Unit of the Ministry of Education developed the programme in partnership with UNICEF. Its main impetus has been on the research, development and dissemination of student textbooks, teachers' manuals and supplementary materials, combined with teacher training.

The programme targets all students from primary Grade 4 to the highest secondary class. It is compulsory in the school curriculum and has one weekly period timetabled. The textbooks are graded and incremental. As the students mature, so the topics move from 'bad touches' to actual rape, from making friends to physical relationships.

The textbooks used are issue-oriented and pose a series of scenarios requiring students to explore feelings, examine alternatives, think through situations, take decisions and make judgements. The books

(*Box 12.3 continued*)

(Box 12.3 continued)

avoid talking down to students and do not prescribe answers to problems. The material provides situations that help students confront issues that enable them to make decisions about their own sexual values and interpersonal relationships. (UNICEF Harare, 1994)

This approach demonstrates how HIV/AIDS education can be planned around life-skills development, rather than pure information transfer.

The greatest challenge lies in teacher education, in being able to transform didactic teachers into facilitators. In-service teacher training is provided through a 'cascade' model, each level training a lower level, from national down to school level, although this inevitably tends to get weaker as it moves downwards. To provide further stimulus and support to teachers and to promote school interaction, 'demonstration' schools receive targeted training and serve a local cluster of schools. However, established teachers have found it difficult to transform their conventional approaches, fearing that greater student participation could lead to a loss of control.

Pre-service training is conducted in all teachers' colleges. This incorporates factual information on HIV/AIDS as well as training in the participatory, life-skills approach used by this programme. It also targets the college students themselves as a group at risk.

In a preliminary evaluation study on the text books and implementation in Grade 7, students 'were unanimous in viewing the book as useful, enjoyable, appropriate and, in the main, relevant to their experience,' although many expressed embarrassment at having to discuss these issues with adult teachers, who were themselves also uneasy with the material (Chisuo, 1995:30–31). However, the study highlights the difficulties which participatory methods present to teachers. Rather than introducing the books as a separate lesson, many teachers have tended to integrate the lessons into other core subjects, returning to their conventional, didactic approaches. This necessarily inhibits the development of life skills. Future development of the programme will focus on teacher training and monitoring mechanisms.

Source: UNICEF Harare, 1994:1–19.

Summary of Lessons Learned

Experience of life skills programmes around the world has provided a number of key lessons learned which are summarized here:

- Life skills need to be learnt in an integrated, holistic manner, since real-life problems require a range of psychosocial skills. Life skills programmes should be developed to address the 'whole person' within his or her environment.
- Life skills education is a long-term process and requires follow-up activities to ensure that learners continue, over time, to apply their life skills in different contexts and have a chance to reflect on their experiences.
- Learners, their families and communities, need to be involved in identifying risky behaviours and the related life skills which are significant to them, to ensure the relevance of the programme and its cultural appropriateness.
- In programme planning, implementation, monitoring and managing, all efforts should be made to promote community ownership of the programme for long-term sustainability.

- Learners require opportunities for practice of skills and positive reinforcement. Consultation and parallel life skills training with other family members, parents, peers and the community can aim to make the environment more supportive.
- Early interventions with children of primary school age enable them to acquire life skills before they may become involved in risk-taking behaviours.
- Both qualitative and quantitative research are an essential part of the whole process of life skills programme development, implementation and maintenance.
- The participatory, active learning approach required for life skills education makes new demands on the abilities of educators. Teacher/facilitator training and follow-up support need to be given priority.
- When designing risk-reduction programmes, on AIDS, substance abuse, and so forth, the life skills required to address the issue should form the central focus. These life skills will then define the learning objectives, the content, materials and educational methods, as well as the behavioural outcomes to be evaluated.
- Work with the media, to promote positive life skills modelling, helps to provide other sources of motivation and examples for the acquisition and practice of life skills, especially for young people.
- Life skills programmes should be underpinned by a human rights stance, giving special consideration to the promotion of the Rights of the Child, and the prevention of gender, racial and other forms of discrimination.
- While strengthening the capabilities of individuals, life skills programme developers should also recognize the importance of wider environmental factors which can constrain people's behaviour and limit their choices. Agencies need to collaborate, working simultaneously at a structural level to promote a more positive environment.

Creating an Enabling Environment

All too often, people wanting to make changes in their lives face the resistance of their family, peers and community. Health services are often inadequate for their needs or insensitive to their situation. The education system often fails them. They may also face religious, cultural, economic, or social pressures—or a lack of structural and legislative support—that constrain their freedom to choose healthy and safe options.

All too often, programmes designed to improve people's lives have focussed on the 'vulnerable individual', exhorting them to change their lifestyles. Such programmes not infrequently ignore the wider environment and the forces which push people into doing things that undermine their health, such as having unwanted or unsafe sex, using drugs, being subjected to female genital mutilation (FGM) or using breast-milk substitutes.

At the same time, health promotion programmes can gain far greater impact by building on existing cultural, social and other factors which support safe and healthy choices, for example, in discouraging the use of tobacco or alcohol.

When programming for behaviour development and change we therefore need to think in much broader terms, beyond the individual whose behaviour we are concerned about. Programmes that aim to decrease the number of people who smoke, the number of people injured in car accidents, the number of children who remain without immunization, the number of teenage girls becoming pregnant, have to do much more than develop individuals' knowledge, motivation and skills to be effective. They have to focus on creating a supportive and enabling environment for these individuals. Such programmes need to build on those aspects of the environment which are supportive to positive behaviours and minimize or change those which are negative or resistant.

Analysing the Environment

There are two major dimensions of the environment to consider, that overlap and are interrelated. The first refers to the 'immediate environment' of parents and family, friends and community members, where interpersonal communication is the major influence on behaviour. Then there are those factors in the 'wider environment', such as culture and religion, health and education systems, news and entertainment media, which both influence and are influenced by pervading social values.

The first part of the chapter gives an overview of the need for an enabling environment. The second part examines how different factors in the environment affect or determine people's behaviour and reviews various interventions which have sought to make the environment more supportive. These environmental factors include:

- Policy and legislation,
- Service provision,
- Education system,
- Cultural factors,
- Socio-political factors,
- Socio-economic factors, and
- Physical environment.

While each factor is discussed separately, in programming terms they need to be addressed in an integrated way, reflecting the manner in which they relate to a specific issue.

In many countries the plethora of parallel projects by governments, NGOs and other agencies may fail to achieve their potential impact at the macro level if they are not delivered within a consistent policy environment, which achieves synergy through coordinated action. The efforts of individual programmes can ultimately only be sustained and expanded when underpinned by supportive policy and legislation. Such legislation must also be held by the political will to enforce its provisions. Development organizations have a crucial role to play through advocacy in strengthening this political commitment.

There are many examples of effective development of policy and legislation in the creation of an enabling environment for change. In fact, in many instances, getting new policies passed has been relatively easy. More difficult has been effectively implementing their provisions. As such, policy and the development of national laws can usually only provide a framework for change, except in relatively clear examples, easily enforced by the authorities, such as the enactment and enforcement of car seat belt legislation.

Box 12.4 Using VIPP: The Case of Zambia

Since its introduction through UNICEF in early 1994, Visualisation in Participatory Programmes (VIPP) has made great strides in Zambia, building upon the foundations of participatory training that already existed in the country. VIPP methodologies have been used for strengthening teams, project planning, strategy development, managing meetings, generating information, and training trainers. Over 300 facilitators at various levels in government, NGOs, and international development agencies have been trained in the use of VIPP, and several partner organisations have espoused the methods for their own programmes.

VIPP has been used with numerous different types of groups and organisations to develop strategies on a range of issues, including: promoting girls' retention in school, improving youth access to media about HIV/AIDS, problem-solving with street children in urban areas, community-based planning, and capacity building for health reforms in Zambia. VIPP has also been used within UNICEF's Zambia country office to strengthen its own internal management and planning, and for staff team building.

VIPP methods are particularly appropriate to raise difficult issues. For example, an adolescent involved with HIV/AIDS education for youth in Zambia uses a VIPP card to anonymously ask: 'How can I be sure that my partner is wearing a condom?' Police officers and Lusaka street children have frankly exchanged their perceptions of each other, and at the same time defined common ground. Youths have collaborated with senior health providers to better define their needs in reproductive health service provision. Staff members have been able to raise their fear about speaking up in front of their manager in a manner that allows for constructive exploration of this issue in the workplace.

A preliminary evaluation of VIPP's application in Zambia conducted in 1996 indicated that VIPP is most effective for mid-level decision-makers who are often better at talking about the need for participation than at practising it in their own working environments.

Source: Whitney and Wyss, 1998.

Service Provision

No matter what we do to give people clear and accurate information, to motivate them to change existing practices or to adopt an innovation, and to assist them in developing the skills needed for positive change, our efforts will be largely in vain unless there is a commensurate improvement in the quality of services made available to support such behaviours. Such services include health and education provision, safe water supply, sanitation facilities and waste disposal, and agricultural extension services. These services need to be affordable and accessible, and of a standard to meet the needs of the client community. As the illustration of the 'Education for All' policy showed, service delivery factors must be tackled in conjunction with policy and legislative change.

Box 12.5 Interpersonal Communication and Service Delivery

In Bangladesh, the Expanded Programme on Immunisation (EPI) had achieved 62 per cent coverage by 1991. However, statistics indicated that dropout levels were still very high. A large-scale, qualitative study revealed that much of this was due to the poor quality of communication between service-providers and clientele. Vaccinators allowed relatives and people with higher status to jump places in lines. They seldom counselled on possible side effects and treated poorer people rudely. It was found that, on average, they spent 21 seconds with each child and caretaker. Very little use was made of the thousands of flip charts and flash cards produced to support interpersonal communication. A more in-depth analysis of the same data indicated that there was little difference in performance between those field workers who had undergone training programmes and those who had learned on the job. This led to the formulation of an interpersonal communication (IPC) training strategy for field workers and their supervisors.

Sources: EPI (1991); Griffey-Brechin (1993); MOHFW (May 1994).

Education Systems

Although education is part of service provision, it merits a separate discussion, given its formative role in determining people's behavioural patterns. For those who have been to school, their educational experience is probably the most significant determinant of the way in which they receive, process and use information. Many examples exist of educational initiatives which promote the development of life skills, including the capacity for critical thinking, decision-making and problem-solving. In this light, such education systems can be seen to develop the capacity of people to work proactively within and upon their environment for constructive change. The key to this transformation lies in the quality of the educational process. The way in which the learner experiences the learning process can either encourage or inhibit positive behavioural development and change. However, while globally many education systems are working actively to improve the quality of teaching, it remains a fact that the majority of educational environments serve only to promote passivity in learners.

A bleak but influential view of this educational approach was taken by Paulo Freire who characterized it as a 'pedagogy of oppression' (Freire, 1973). He sensed that such forms of education can keep people locked in a closed world in a 'culture of silence'. In this context, education becomes a series of facts passed on from the 'knowledgeable' teacher to the 'ignorant' student through rote learning. This follows what Freire called the 'banking concept' of education, whereby teachers believe their role is to 'fill' their students with knowledge. Education suffers from 'narration sickness'. 'Narration leads the students to memorize mechanically the narrated content. Worse still, it turns them into containers, into receptacles to be filled by the teacher' (ibid.:45).

Where the education system itself is rigid and autocratic, from the style of management at the top, down to delivery in the classroom, it may appear resistant to change. The way society is organized can be reflected and reinforced by the way people are educated: either enforcing acquiescence within a hierarchy or, conversely, encouraging a democratic openness and questioning. However, education systems can be mobilized to challenge social norms and become a catalyst in changing the way people think and behave. For instance, educational initiatives in the North promoting citizenship education aim to help young people gain a sense of community responsibility, challenging pervasive individualism. Educational reform is possible, albeit slow and incremental.

Many sectoral programmes, particularly in health, water and sanitation, and agriculture, seek to use school systems as a key channel for disseminating their messages. However, such information will likely remain unused unless the learning process encourages enquiry and innovation. Outreach will also be limited unless more students are retained in the school system. Two key issues therefore govern the potential of the education system to contribute to creating an enabling environment. The first relates to the continuing quest for improving quality in teaching; the second to increasing access to and retention in schools.

The education system provides the most crucial point of interface between individuals and their environment. A positive educational experience can prepare people to participate in creating a more supportive environment, in redefining the terms on which they live. For example, disadvantaged groups, who have learnt about the rights to equality before the law, can work individually or collectively to challenge social practice and to lobby for changes in policy and legislation. In terms of programming for an 'enabling environment', investment in education becomes the central priority, for education opens the way for people themselves to influence their environment and widen their options for action.

Box 12.6 Mobilizing for Education for All in Bangladesh

A year after the World Conference on 'Education for All', held in Jomtien, Thailand in 1990, not a great deal had been achieved in Bangladesh. There was a great deal of rhetoric and disagreement over the strategies required to bring education to a population of 110 million which was less than 25 per cent literate. UNICEF was still giving emphasis to the provision of educational materials, curriculum development and teacher training. There had been much energy and concentration on mass education in the past, with little progress. The government, academics and NGOs were at odds as to the reasons for the lack of progress, each tending to blame the other. Compulsory primary education was declared by the President at Jomtien, but no one believed that it was enforceable or achievable. The call for 'Education for All' remained a hollow cry.

Participatory Planning

A breakthrough came in April 1991. UNICEF organised a participatory planning workshop using a method called Visualisation in Participatory Programmes (VIPP). High-level government, NGO staff and academics attended, along with participants from UNICEF and UNESCO. In three days, participants worked through the essential steps to be taken in mobilizing for Basic Education in Bangladesh and developed a multimedia and multi-partnership plan of action for advocacy, social mobilization and programme communication.

(*Box 12.6 continued*)

(*Box 12.6 continued*)

This initial planning workshop was followed by training in VIPP facilitation for key government, NGO and UNICEF staff involved in education. This training initiated a whole sequence of participatory planning processes, right down to the lowest administrative level. For the first time, people in lower level posts had a say in what was needed to mobilize the educational bureaucracy, social partners, parents and children.

Determining the Value of Education

A qualitative research study was carried out on the perception and value of education. After a great deal of discussion, it was decided that before launching a major communication initiative for accelerating the provision of educational services and quality of services, more should be known about what parents and children think and believe about schools and school personnel, revealing deep-seated perceptions, beliefs and values. The information from this research was used in the formulation of mass media, traditional media and interpersonal communication messages aimed at various stakeholders in the educational process.

Launching a Movement

In 1992, the Prime Minister launched the 'Education for All' movement in a major national conference attended by people from all relevant sectors and all parts of the country. The conference was a lively affair, with a great deal of debate, which sparked new initiatives. At the above event, a communication symbol for 'Education for All' was unveiled. The final symbol, with the girl slightly ahead of the boy because of her historic disadvantage, was adopted as the best concept to promote basic education for all in Bangladesh. Today, it is used by all major partners in the movement and can be seen throughout the country. It is easily recognisable and communicates a message, even to illiterates.

Cultural Factors

In development programmes the role of culture is often ignored, for example, in analyses of social change which take a purely economic and political perspective. In other instances, where the influence of culture is acknowledged, it is still considered to be either sacrosanct (in representing a 'unique' traditional culture) or immutable, and certainly not within the domain of the development programmer. However, cultural values form the overriding determinant of behaviour, which cuts across all other factors. People's behaviour is guided by their personal values, governed by the pervading cultural values of their social group.

A holistic approach to creating a supportive environment recognizes the complexity and interrelationship of the various factors determining behaviour, of which culture plays a very significant and influential part. As for our discussion, we can adopt a working definition of 'culture' as a set of values and practices shared by a group. The domain of such a culture is therefore determined by the number of people of communities who identify with and subscribe to its shared set of values and practices. This results in layers of cultures and subcultures within a single society.

As with the other factors in this section, the discussion of culture and behavioural change merits a whole book in itself. However, the review of gender programmes offers some general lessons which can be applied more broadly to other aspects of culture. It emphasizes the value of a programmer's role as a listener, learning about people's culture through formative research. This insight allows initiatives to tap into the evolutionary process of culture, building on the value and behavioural shifts that communities believe are desirable and possible. Such work can be reinforced by establishing alliances with other agents in society, particularly harnessing the power of the mass media.

However, as culture exists as a set of values and practices shared by a group, change cannot be imposed from without, but will evolve within communities through a participatory process, in which people are enabled to become more objectively conscious and to consider possible transformations.

This finally brings us to the ethical issues which a programmer needs to consider when dealing with cultural issues. Community participants need to be fully conscious that efforts to reform their culture may lead to social disruption. It is they, not the programmer, who carry the risk in challenging their cultural norms. As with the example of FGM, interventions concerned with culture are more appropriate in addressing the community as a whole, on all its levels, rather than isolated, and possibly vulnerable, groups within the community.

Finally it is worth remembering that programmers too, from whatever society, may subscribe to an 'international development' culture, their own shared set of values, which could also benefit from a regular, critical scrutiny. In its worst manifestation, this could be portrayed as a sense of cultural superiority, implicit in same policy statements, 'particularly when programmes involve "educating" a "target population"' (Allen and Thomas, 1992:338). Our guard against this is to adopt a listening stance and approach our work with communities as a process of mutual learning.

Conclusion: Integrating for Change

This brief review of the many processes and factors that must converge in order to facilitate behaviour change, strongly suggests the importance of adopting integrated approaches in designing development communication programmes. It calls into question the current trend of using the words 'information' and 'knowledge' to mean the same thing. It also questions the marketing hype which suggests that knowledge can be downloaded from appliances plugged into the Internet. And that there are technological shortcuts to change and development.

This review also emphasizes to policy-makers and programme directors the importance of building effective and responsive communication elements into development programmes right from the start of all projects. While communication on its own will not bring about change and development, neither will change happen without development communication. We need to integrate all our efforts.

Note

1. This contribution is synthesized from the book: *Involving People, Evolving Behaviour* edited by Neill McKee, Erma Manoncourt, Chin Saik Yoon, Rachel Carnegie and co-published by Southbound, Penang and UNICEF, New York in 2000 (ISBN 983-9054-22-8, 14.5 × 22 cm, 272 pages). E-mail book enquiries to chin@south.pc.my.

References

Allen, T. and A. Thomas (eds). 1992. *Poverty and Development in the 1990s*. Oxford: Oxford University Press.

Bandura, A. 1995. *Social Foundations of Thought and Action: A Social Cognitive Theory*. New Jersey: Prentice-Hall, Englewood Cliffs.

Bloomberg, L., J. Meyers and M. Braverman. 1994. 'The Importance of Social Interaction: A New Perspective on Some Epidemiology, Social Risk Factors and Health', *Health Education Quarterly*, 21(4):447–63.

Chisuo, L. 1995. *Report on an Evaluation of the Implementation of Grade 7 AIDS Action Programme Book 'Let's Talk' in Schools in Zimbabwe*. Harare: UNICEF.

EPI. 1991. 'Needs assessment study of field workers involved in the Expanded Programme on Immunisation', Directorate General of Health Services, Ministry of Health and Family Welfare, Government of Bangladesh.

Fishbein, M. and I. Ajzen. 1980. *Understanding Attitudes and Predicting Social Behaviour*. New Jersey: Prentice-Hall.

Freire, P. 1970. *Pedagogy of the Oppressed*. Baltimore: Penguin.

———. 1973. *Pedagogy of the Oppressed*. Hagerstown, MN: Harper and Row.

Griffey-Brechin, S.J. 1993. 'Evaluating health-worker performance: The relationship between knowledge and practice of counselling related activities of field workers in the National Expanded Programme on Immunisation in Bangladesh'. New Orleans: Ph.D. dissertation, School of Public Health and Tropical Medicine, Department of International health and Development, Tulane University.

Israel, B.A. 1985. 'Social Networks and Social Support: Implications for Natural Helper and Community Level Intervention', *Health Education Quarterly*, 12:65–80.

Israel, B.A. and S.J. Schurman. 1990. 'Social Support, Control and the Stress Process', in K. Glantz, F.M. Lewis and B. Rimer (eds). *Health Behaviour and Health Education: Theory, Research and Practice*. San Francisco: Jossey-Bass.

MOHFW (Ministry of Health and Family Welfare). 1994. 'Generic curriculum: Interpersonal communication and counselling training'. Interpersonal Communication and Counselling Training Forum, Generic Curriculum Task Force, MOHFW, Government of Bangladesh.

Prochaska, J.O., C.C. Diclemente and J.C. Norcross. 1992. 'In Search of How People Change: Applications to Addictive Behaviours', *American Psychologist*, 47:1102–14.

Rogers, E.M. 1986. *Communication of Innovations*. New York: The Free Press.

———. 1995. *Diffusion of Innovations* (fourth edition). New York: The Free Press.

Somerset, A. 1988. *Child-to-Child: A Survey*. London: Child-to-Child Trust.

Steckler, A.B., B.A. Israel, L. Dawson and E. Eng. 1993. 'Community Health Development: An Anthology of the Works of Guy W. Steuart', *Health Education Quarterly*, Suppl. 1.

UNICEF Harare. 1994. *Report of Study Tour of School AIDS Education Programme in Zimbabwe.* Harare: UNICEF.

Wallerstein, N. 1992. 'Powerlessness, Empowerment, and Health Implications for Health Promotion Programs', *American Journal of Health Promotion,* 6.

Whitney, B. and E. Wyss. 1998. *A Process Evaluation of VIPP in Zambia.* Nairobi: UNICEF East and Southern Africa Regional Office.

WHO/MNH. 1994. 'Life Skills Education in Schools, Parts 1 & 2'. *Introduction and Guidelines to Facilitate the Development and Implementation of Life Skills Programmes,* WHO/MNH/PSF/93.7A. Eve. 1. Geneva: Division of Mental Health, World Health Organization.

Part IV

Special Case: HIV/AIDS Campaigns

Part IV

Special Case: HIV/AIDS Campaigns

Rural HIV/AIDS Communication/ Intervention: From Using Models to Using Frameworks and Common Principles

13

RICO LIE

Introduction

Rural livelihoods change rapidly because of the HIV/AIDS epidemic. The consequences for people living with HIV/AIDS are devastating. Many people pass away in early phases of their lives. The pandemic touches communities, and rural societies at large, at the heart of their functioning. Among the consequences are, for instance, an increasing amount of orphans, a lack of knowledge sharing from generation to generation, inability to work the land and generate enough income, children being withdrawn from schools to help generate income, out-migration to urban areas, and so forth. Communities need to learn to live with these consequences.

HIV/AIDS is a socially complex problem covering many different sectors of rural life. It is complex in at least six different ways. First, HIV/AIDS is more than a health issue and affects all sectors of life. Many countries acknowledge this—at least in principles—through their multi-sectoral approaches, for instance, Tanzania: Tanzania Commission for HIV/AIDS, 2003; Uganda: Uganda AIDS Commission, 1993. Second, it is complex in the sense that it involves a multi-stakeholder process. Stakeholders include governments, non-governmental organizations and civil society at large, media, media organizations and journalists, medical technicians, doctors and health workers, commercial and non-commercial medicine companies and, of course, people living with HIV/AIDS and their close ones. As such and third, it is also a trans-disciplinary problem. Dealing with different stakeholders from different sectors calls for a trans-disciplinary approach; bringing together perspectives and knowledges of all actors involved. Such an integrated perspective on change also calls for participatory action research or participatory communication research; enabling all actors to be heard and to co-own a change process.

Fourth, the pandemic has to deal with the delicate topic of sex. Sex is in many countries and cultures a taboo issue and difficult to discuss. Addressing HIV/AIDS means talking about sexuality, personal relationships, gender relations, emotions and feelings. Fifth, the issue of HIV/AIDS deals with social stigmatization and discrimination. These are deeply rooted social mechanisms and difficult to change. Stigma and discrimination often result in people being hesitant to disclose their status and not seeking testing and care services. Sixth, and consequently, the problem is not always surfaced, figures are unknown or unreliable. Moreover, these figures might be distracting in the sense that they draw attention to highly infected areas that are known. By overestimating the figures in these areas, it draws attention away from other areas in the world where the problem is not on the public agenda yet, where its severity is not recognized yet, but where the near future might be even more devastating than in the known highly infected areas.

The HIV/AIDS epidemic, as a complex problem, calls for as complex communicative development approach. Such a trans-disciplinary approach should thus first of all accommodate a multi-stakeholder and a multi-sectoral approach. Second, the approach must be sensitive to issues such as stigmatization, discrimination, norms and values.

Shifts in HIV/AIDS Communication

Seen from a bird view perspective, HIV/AIDS communication interventions have not been very successful. The epidemic continues to spread, despite the many efforts to change the situation. In the global fight against HIV/AIDS, relevant elements or aspects have too often been isolated. Examples of such isolated or reductionist approaches are for instance: (a) the focus and emphasis on particular high-risk groups, which often resulted in blaming the group's (sub)culture, (b) considering HIV/AIDS primarily as a health problem, (c) selecting the mass media as the most important communication prevention tool, for instance, in campaign programmes and (d) not including the commitment of all stakeholders involved. These kind of isolated and non-integrative approaches might have contributed to raising levels of awareness, but overall they have not been very successful in changing the spread of the epidemic. Moreover, isolated approaches and especially isolated mass media approaches that aim at certain groups like homosexuals or AIDS-orphans contribute to an increased stigmatization and discrimination.

This chapter addresses responses to the ineffectiveness of past approaches through identifying three shifts in thinking about appropriate HIV/AIDS communication: (1) a shift away from mainstream HIV/AIDS mass media campaigning towards culturally appropriate responses to HIV/AIDS and the use of local community media; (2) a shift away from seeing HIV/AIDS primarily as a health problem towards seeing it as a development problem and (3) a shift from a primary focus on behavioural change to a primary focus on social change. These shifts overlap and are connected. As a consequence of these shifts in the underlying philosophical principles and paradigmatic thinking about communication, a shift in research and intervention strategies is also suggested. This shift concerns an evolutionary moving on from the use of dominant or theoretical models to loose conceptual frameworks and common principles.

From National to Local Media Forms

After unsuccessful attempts to use the national mass media in the early post-World War II period to bring about development—through aiming at individual changes in attitudes and behaviour or modernization approach—there was a shift towards using local media and local dialogue for local change. Participatory approaches and interactive 'solutions' based on interpersonal communication became the mainstream approach to local development and change. Next to the trend of hyper interests in ICTs, Internet and e-health, e-government and e-democracy there seems to be a parallel renewed interest in alternative, small-scale and community media. In the 1970s the idea to use community media for social development was new. A landmark publication in this regard is the UNESCO Berrigan report from 1979 (Berrigan, 1979). This report was of course published in the days when issues concerning access to and participation in the media were relatively new. The use of video was highlighted as a small-scale participatory medium to voice local concerns and initiate dialogue. A much used example here is the Fogo Island-project. Building on Freire's ideas, video was used on Fogo Island in the New Foundlands in Canada to show the views of the people on the island to the Canadian people and the Canadian government and stimulate dialogue. The project showed through film how the inhabitants of the island opposed a resettlement to the mainland of Canada.

The Berrigan report on the Fogo Island project marked the beginning of an alternative media methodology, which became more structured during the 1970s. This alternative audio-visual media methodology not only found its way into a social learning approach, but also found grounding in an institutional way through the acknowledgement and establishment of local community media. A good example of how audio-visual media can be used in a social learning approach is through Visual Problem Appraisal (VPA). This method is developed by Loes Witteveen (Witteveen et al., 2003) to address complex and delicate multi-stakeholder problems. Through a set of documentaries and filmed interviews VPA allows trainees to learn in semi-interaction with the real stakeholders. At the institutional level the emphasis on local community media has been ongoing since the 1970s, and became more structured during the following decades. Local community media empower in the sense that they work with low access thresholds for the receivers to become senders and that they respect local cultures. Besides serving a community and providing an alternative for mainstream media, they can also be seen as an integral part of civil society. As such they can become important institutional actors in HIV/AIDS communication interventions. In the last 10 years, our understanding of the role and functioning of this kind of media has deepened (see for instance Carpentier, Lie and Servaes, 2003; Jankowski and Prehn, 2002; Kwame Boafo, 2000).

From Deliberate to Undeliberate Use of Mass Media

Deliberate HIV/AIDS mass media strategies, as far as they aim at change, are mainly effective in the field of *awareness raising*. They can set aspects of the public agenda and create attention or interest. National HIV/AIDS campaigns often use the mass media in various ways to get the message known to the public. These kinds of large-scale communication campaigns often have very weak effects on actual behavioural change.

On the other hand, it is not so much the deliberate use of mass media for achieving individual behavioural change, as well the *undeliberate use* for achieving social change that could be of interest. 'Most viewers watch by the clock and not by the program' (Gerbner, 1979:216) is a well-known statement by George Gerbner. His cultivation theory addresses that mass media, especially television is non-selective media. As such it has no direct effect on attitudes and behaviour, but they do function as instruments of 'enculturation'. Media content is diverse and diffuse, and media is consulted in similar diversified and diffuse ways. These mass media messages form a continuous blanket surrounding us. Effects are not about isolated messages, but about the whole blanket. Effects are to be found in a shared audio-visual culture. This culture is only at a very basic level controllable by the individual. He or she can turn the media off or on, but the flow of messages continues, even if the individual media is turned off. This continuous reference to culture, is one of the reasons why edutainment has become a popular HIV/AIDS communication strategy. The strategy uses for instance popular television and radio programmes like soap operas, to incorporate information about HIV/AIDS (see for instance Singhal and Rogers, 1999, 2003; Tufte, 2003a; Vaughan et al., 2000).

From a Health Problem to a Cultural Embedded Development Problem

In line with the above, the mainstream view on HIV/AIDS communication in so far as it has been using the mass media, has been campaigning, but we now know that campaigning alone does not bring about any real change. We now also know that we need to move beyond awareness. So what comes after awareness? What if everybody knows that the HIV-virus leads to AIDS and that AIDS will kill? What if everybody knows how the virus is transmitted? What if everybody knows how to prevent oneself from getting infected, but HIV/AIDS continues to spread anyway? How can we use communication and audio-visual media in a more appropriate and effective way? Can local community media in an undeliberate way be of help in bringing about social change?

There are different routes to take here. On the one hand we should continue raising levels of awareness. Awareness might in some cases lead to direct behaviour change. Moreover, in some rural areas people might still be unaware of the issues. Learning basic facts about HIV/AIDS and how you can prevent yourself from getting it remains important. But knowing in many cases is not enough reason to change behaviour. We need to move beyond that. If it is the social/cultural that is the focus of change, then change intervention programmes must also focus on what is circulating within the social domain; what is shared within the community. An edutainment programme—even if it uses folk media such as story-telling, theatre or puppetry—that incorporates HIV/AIDS themes, will not change any individual behaviour directly, but it will address the climate; set a frame for discussion. It is here that social change takes place, not at the individual level, but in circulated culture; in shared beliefs.

Moreover, and maybe even more important is that HIV/AIDS is now among us, and a daily fact of living in many rural areas. Prevention, awareness raising and attitude change towards issues such as promiscuity, unprotected sex and other gender-related issues remain important, but care and support, hope and providing a future are key words for those living with HIV/AIDS. 'Improving the quality of life' not only relates to People Living with HIV/AIDS (PLWHA), but also to their close ones and the people they leave behind when they pass away, often in a too early stage of their life. Social learning here refers to learning about a new way of life; about adaptations and learning to deal with new situations. HIV/AIDS causes very unstable rural economies. It affects production and income-generation and can lead to food insecurity. It is in this area that we have now come to recognize that HIV/AIDS is far more than a health issue. It changes society in all sectors and all aspects of individual and collective life (see for instance Qamar, 2003).

Relatively little is known about HIV/AIDS and its impact in remote, rural areas. Not only are situations often unknown, but sometimes deliberately ignored and not acknowledged. It is difficult to generalize about the rural unknown, but it is clear that the rural unknown is always culture-specific. Not only in the sense that ways of life, worldviews and religions differ, but also in the sense that rural cultures differ from urban cultures. The UK-based organization *Creative Exchange* has addressed this. The organization recognizes that culture operates at three levels in development:

- as a context in which development takes place;
- as a rich source of locally appropriate content for communication programmes; and
- as a method of building dialogue, enabling expression and promoting participation by beneficiaries (Creative Exchange, 2004).

UNESCO also calls for a culturally appropriate response to HIV/AIDS prevention and care.

> On the basis of the Mexico Declaration of 1982, culture is broadly understood within UNESCO to include: ways of life, traditions and beliefs, representations of health and disease, perceptions of life and death, sexual norms and practices, power and gender relations, family structures, languages and means of communication; as well as arts and creativity. (UNESCO, 2004)

Mass media theory has also moved into this direction of cultural embedded communication (see, for instance, Baran and Davis, 2003 for an overview of more culture-oriented theories of communication; see also Lie, 2003). Some even speak of a cultural turn and the development of cultural—media—studies as a new discipline is in itself an indicator for the cultural paradigm shift.

To work in these culture-specific rural areas means that prevention, care and support need to be appropriate. This again calls for involvement, commitment, knowledge and action sharing, building dialogue, engagement and empowerment. Such a call can be translated into approaches such as peer groups approaches and locally-owned and culturally embedded media forms—community media—and ways of communicating. HIV/AIDS is a highly cultural-sensitive issue. Sexual relations, life and death, emotions and actions are perceived differently in different parts of the world.

Towards Appropriate and Effective HIV/AIDS Communication and Change Strategies

The Communication for Development Roundtable that was co-organized by the UNFPA, the Rockefeller Foundation, UNESCO and Panos in 2001 in Nicaragua had a special focus on HIV/AIDS communication and evaluation. The subsequent report makes a distinction between three paradigms in HIV/AIDS communication:

(a) *Behaviour Change Communication*: drawing on socio-psychological approaches and persuasive communication theory and aiming at individual behaviour change; originally starting from diffusion theory (Rogers, 1962), mass media campaigning and social marketing; also focussing on social learning theory, play theory, negotiation theory;

(b) *Communication for Social Change*: drawing on socio-anthropological and development theory; originally starting from conscientization, dialogical communication and liberating pedagogy (Freire, 1970), empowerment; focusses on communication rights and grassroot social movements and NGOs; institutional, social, community and cultural-oriented; also focussing on globalization theory, political-economy theory and cultural studies and;

(c) *Advocacy Communication*: 'involves organized attempts to influence the political climate, policy and programme decisions, public perceptions of social norms, funding decisions and community support and empowerment towards specific issues' (UNFPA, 2002:52; see also Servaes and Malikhao, 2004; Tufte, 2003b; McKee, Bertrand and Becker-Benton, 2004).

The general opinion is that the three paradigms in HIV/AIDS communication should work together. It is important to realize that you cannot achieve behavioural change without the other two paradigms. First of all you need to have the support of stakeholders, especially policy-makers and other decision-makers. Without core actor support and commitment it will be difficult to achieve change. Change here relates to a change in climate, a change in culture and atmosphere. Governments, governmental organizations, as well as NGOs working in a variety of human sectors need to work together and adopt and embrace the issues as their field of action.

The above-mentioned report, and especially the Rockefeller Foundation calls for a shift away from behaviour change to social change. McKee, Bertrand and Becker-Benton (2004:41 a.f.)

even talk about a paradigm shift from behaviour change to social change. The statement is that behaviour change depends in most cases on social change. Social issues such as norms and values, stigmatization and discrimination, prejudices and stereotypes, hegemonies and ideologies, gender roles and sexual relations, power relations and domination, form, within a specific cultural, political and economic context the magnetic fields that pull people into certain behavioural directions.

Box 13.1 From Behavioural Change to Social Change

This approach attempts to rebalance strategic approaches to communication and change by taking the overriding emphasis:

- Away from people as the objects for change ... and on to people and communities as the agents of their own change;
- Away from designing, testing and delivering messages ... and on to supporting dialogue and debate on the key issues of concern;
- Away from the conveying of information from technical experts ... and on to sensitively placing that information into the dialogue and debate;
- Away from a focus on individual behaviours ... and on to social norms, policies, culture and a supportive environment;
- Away from persuading people to do something ... and on to negotiating the best way forward in a partnership process;

Away from technical experts in 'outside' agencies dominating and guiding the process ... and on to the people most affected by the issues of concern playing a central role.

Source: The Rockefeller Foundation, 1999.

Although Panos criticizes the above stating that little of the above is new, that participatory, people-centred communication is now the mainstream, that the arguments create artificial boundaries, and that good approaches focus on appropriate mixes of the different paradigms (Panos, 2001:7–8), the listing does provide a checklist for appropriate interventions. It might be true that some of the issues are old news, but that is not the case for calling for a shift from individual to social behaviour. The HIV/AIDS problematic has shown that a direct behaviour change approach is not very effective and the above looks for alternatives by emphasizing the importance of a social focus, next to an individual, psychological and advocacy focus.

Airhihenbuwa and Obregon (2000) reinforce this point by concluding their article in which they critically assess theories and models that are used in health communication for HIV/AIDS as follows:

This examination of theories and models commonly used in health communication and promotion clearly shows that HIV/AIDS communication often is based on the behaviour and decision-making process of so-called rational individuals who follow an established linear path from awareness to attitude to action. However, decisions about preventing HIV/AIDS are based on cultural norms that often mediate individual decisions in ways that individuals may not always realize. Moreover, decisions about HIV/AIDS often are based on emotion and thus may not follow any pre-established pattern of decision making advanced in most of the theories and models. (Airhihenbuwa and Obregon 2000:12)

In addition to seeing culture as being important, it also needs to be said that culture is not something that can simply be added to the situation. Culture is text, not context. A situation cannot exist without culture. Culture is rooted in situations. It is the underlying base of action, not a coat around it (see for instance Lie, 2003). It is therefore important to move from culturally-sensitive to culturally-embedded communication.

From a Culturally-Embedded Communication Analysis to Action

Culturally-embedded communication research is important to analyse the specific situations of the rural unknown. This research is trans-disciplinary to incorporate different perspectives from different involved actors (see Lie, 2004). Research empowers a multi-stakeholder process by making change processes rooted in knowledge. It is also in this respect that research and intervention need to merge.

Many reports plead for a shift away form the behavioural-oriented communication models (for example, Panos, 2003; UNAIDS and Penn State, 1999; UNFPA, 2002) to what UNAIDS calls a framework. The UNAIDS report makes a plea for a new context-based direction for a communications framework and formulates it as follows:

The major finding was that five domains of context are virtually universal factors in communications for HIV/AIDS preventive health behaviour: *government policy*, *socioeconomic status*, *culture*, *gender relations*, and *spirituality*. These interrelated domains formed the basis of a new framework that could be used as a flexible guide in the development of HIV/AIDS communications interventions. Individual health behaviour is recognized as a component of this set of domains, rather than the primary focus of health behaviour change. (UNAIDS and Penn State, 1999:12)

The much-discussed Panos report concludes as follows:

To move this thinking forward we outline three areas which urgently require more emphasis, thought and attention. Within each of these areas we highlight the challenges in fostering the debate and social mobilisation that have characterised past successful responses. At *policy level*, particularly amongst donors, these include longer-term engagement, greater inclusiveness in consultation, more participatory decision-making and greater transparency. Within *the media*, these include the beginnings of a critical reappraisal of media training, and also the importance of working on media structure, legislation and regulation. And within *civil society*, there is a need to increase emphasis on advocacy, and on more sophisticated relations with the media. (Panos, 2003:1)

It is this evolution from a dominant use of theoretical models to the use of a loose conceptual framework in HIV/AIDS communication research/interventions that is addressed in the remaining parts of this paper.

From Models to Frameworks and Common Principles

Theoretical models that are used to guide a research or intervention perspective provide a prefabricated and bounded way of thinking. Theoretical models are either linear, circular or spiral in construction. They are circular to indicate that communication can never be a linear process; they are spiral to indicate that we are moving forward. But, they all set out the lines of thought for us. In many cases this might be very helpful, but they often block creativity when it comes to research/intervention. They are not situation-sensitive enough and lack cultural grounding. They also simplify complex situations and do, as such, no justice to that complexity. For instance there is no strategic health communication model that frames the HIV/AIDS problematic as a complex development problem. On the other hand, we do need handles and entries to deal with the complexity. One way of trying to grasp it and keep respecting the existing complexity is working with *frameworks* and *common principles*, instead of a dominant use of theoretical models.

The Role of a Conceptual Framework and Theory

Frameworks, and I specifically mean conceptual frameworks here, provide central concepts that guide the researcher's, the facilitator's, or the media producer's way of looking and dealing with the problematic. A conceptual framework is a framework, not a model. Its purpose is to frame situations through the use of carefully selected concepts. For instance, the original SMR (Sender→Message→Reciever) communication model includes direction and it implicitly includes assumptions about effects in a linear way. An SMR framework on the other hand only frames a situation with the use of the three concepts: sender, message, receiver. In this case we can talk for instance about participation and access by referring to the extent to which it is possible for receivers to become senders and produce messages. In the SMR framework, there is no linear direction, whereas in the case of the SMR model there is.

Actually starting from the original SMR-model I developed in Lie (2003) such a conceptual framework for the study of localizing/globalizing cultural identities. Based on literature study, the framework incorporates the concepts of *production, regulation, representation, consumption* and (*counter*)*action*. These concepts are related to each other in many different ways, and one could adopt theories based on, or linking these concepts prior to a situational analysis. For instance cultural imperialism theory, the Frankfurter Schule and political economy theory would all emphasize the power aspects in the concepts of *production* and *regulation*. Neo-Marxist theory (for instance Gramsci, 1971) also emphasizes the existence of dominant structures and cultures and that one culture could be superior to another in a hegemonic way. *Representation* in these theories would be an instrument for ideological control and *consumption* is thus never free. It seems impossible to escape mass cultural consumption. *Counteraction* is marginalized in this theoretical thinking. These concepts are thus theoretically framed from a political-economy perspective.

Theory on cultural hybridity, multi-culturalism or creolization would emphasize different relationships between the concepts in the framework or would look at the concepts using other definitions. Looking at the interplay of the concepts, multi-cultural theory would emphasize the mixing of cultures through processes of *consumption* and in processes of *representation*. It could also lead to the study of the relationship between *production* and *representation*, for example, through a content analysis of cultural media products. Cross-cultural psychology would look at the conceptual model through the individual; looking at, for instance, how the individual can communicate or behave in cultures that are unknown to him or her. Actor-oriented, critical and interpretative theory like symbolic inter-actionalism, phenomenology and ethnographic cultural studies focussing on processes of social construction, would probably centre the concepts of *action* and *consumption*, trying to make sense of people making sense of the surrounding world, for instance, through studying daily-life consumption patterns.

The point here to make is that we need all this linking of concepts through different theories to make sense of, and understand processes of globalizing/localizing cultural identities. In one case, one particular theory might be more applicable than in another case. It might also be that in one particular era, or in one particular department or sector, one particular theory is dominant as a paradigm. Concepts can be linked through different theories and the difficulty is that through adopting a theory prior to the research situation, one looks at reality through a biased glass. In the case of HIV/AIDS, looking at the problem through awareness raising theories and behavioural change theories and models, have not led to stopping the epidemic from spreading. So instead of starting from a dominant theoretical model, the idea is to start with a loose conceptual framework and having a broad knowledge of different theories related to the relationships between the concepts. To a certain extent, these theories can be made explicit, because it is always important to realize one's theoretical bias. Adopting one, as a main theoretical perspective is an option and is always a worthwhile academic endeavour. However, I am arguing for another possible way to approach research-related interventions.

The argument is that a dominant use of mono-theoretical models sets boundaries for creativity, narrows possibilities of 'finding new ways of seeing things', limits the developments towards fundamental cultural appropriateness and thus creates the risk of developing inappropriate interventions. This is especially important for HIV/AIDS interventions where the use of dominant models have failed to change behaviour and where it is now high time to look for alternative approaches.

The role of a conceptual framework is thus to organize our observations and reasoning. A conceptual framework tells us where to look in reality. A theory tells us how to look in reality. Theory guides the reasoning. Reasoning means connecting concepts through theory. For instance: If a conceptual framework includes, among others, the concepts of 'technological innovations' and 'development', there are different theories that can connect these concepts. One way of connecting the concepts is through theories on divides, for instance, through a digital/social divide theory such as the knowledge gap theory. Another way of connecting the concepts is through theories of social learning; learning about technological innovations in a participatory way can lead to sustainable development. A modernization theory would argue that technological innovation is development as it pushes the economy in the right direction. The concepts can thus be linked through different theoretical perspectives.

The idea is further to let the research/intervention field decide which theoretical connections are of relevance—within a biased context. It is for instance, possible that a government emphasizes the modernization theory, an NGO emphasizes the divide theory and an academic researcher emphasizes the social learning theory. All theoretical perspectives can thus be found in the field with the different stakeholders. The theory is thus to be found within the conceptual framework. This of course implies that the researcher should have a broad knowledge of social science theories and recognize them in the field.

How to Develop a Conceptual Framework?

Concepts that could be of interest to develop a rural HIV/AIDS communication framework are for instance: religion, power, stigma, risk, gender, sexuality, parenthood, livelihood. Many more can be added here. In developing such a framework there seem to be two possibilities. Either you develop such a conceptual framework from behind the desk, based on literature study and with limit knowledge of the specific situations. This might be the case if donors give specific conceptual directions or if it is not possible to visit the field beforehand.

Another way of developing such a conceptual framework is in interaction with the local situation. In this case such a conceptual framework can be an outcome of a first rapid field appraisal. Ideas about central concepts are collected through informal exploratory interviewing, basic observations, in stakeholder meetings and community forums. This phase sets the stage for the focus of analysis and intervention.

An additional important function of such a conceptual framework is that it offers the tools for the relational questions that you want to see answered, for instance, how is stigma related to gender and what is the role of religion here. Short-term research is a first step to learn about context-specific issues as they are related to HIV/AIDS in a specific rural area. This kind of research cannot be standardized and can in itself become an action tool for change; like become participatory action research or action ethnographic research that emphasizes the cultural embedding in a more central way (see, for instance, Beebe, 2001; Handwerker, 2001; Tacchi et al., 2003).

Common Principles

Working with guiding or common principles is an additional way of dealing with the complexity. Where conceptual frameworks are mainly meant to be guiding and analytical tools—they help to guide and analyse—the use of checklists are also aiming at change through interventions. They are of relevance in an action approach; an approach where research and action are combined. Common principles summarize the rationale and the philosophy behind the research/intervention. They are basic generalizations about appropriate research/intervention and are used as guides for reasoning and a basis for conduct. Common means in this case shared by the different stakeholders.

The following list, developed by Ricardo Gómez and Benjamín Casadiego in 2002, is an example of such a checklist that can be used for developing appropriate communication strategies:

1. Offer concrete solutions.
2. Move forward at the pace of the community.
3. Learn from mistakes.
4. Localize globalized communication.
5. Work with a gender perspective.
6. Let people speak with their own voice.
7. Generate new knowledge.

According to Ricardo Ramirez, 'most practitioners in Communication for Development have moved beyond the need for unifying theories and models, and onto sets of *guiding principles* that are adjusted to local contexts' (FAOcomm discussion forum, 11/09/2003). He shared with the above list the following extension to the list (additions in italics):

1. Offer concrete solutions *and use realistic technologies.*
2. Move forward at the pace of the community.
3. Learn from mistakes.
4. Localize globalized communication.
5. Work with a gender perspective.
6. Let people speak with their own voice.
7. Generate new knowledge *and promote local content.*
8. *Address info costs: who pays?*
9. *Ensure equitable access.*
10. *Strengthen existing policies and systems.*
11. *Build capacity.*
12. *Build knowledge partnerships.*

Alfonso Gumucio also brought forward some of these principles on the same list discussion (FAOcomm discussion forum, 19/09/2003):

(a) Language and cultural pertinence, respect for diversity.
(b) Community ownership.
(c) Local content, rather than imposed agendas.
(d) Appropriate technology, better to 'appropriate' by communities (socially, technically, economically).
(e) Convergence and networking.
(f) Processes, rather than products.
(g) Strategic thinking, not patches.
(h) Being accountable to the community, not to donors.
(i) Dialogue and debate, rather than 'dissemination'.
(j) Communication is not equal to media.
(k) Communication is not the same thing as 'communications', ... among other.

Don Richardson contributed with the following principles (Richardson, 10/09/03):

1. Start communicating, early in the life of a project or programme, with all the parties involved.
2. All the activities under the consultation and communication process should:

    (a) contribute to the social, environmental, and financial sustainability of the initiative,
    (b) be flexible and adapt to local needs and conditions,
    (c) promote the participation of the stakeholders throughout the life of the initiative, and
    (d) be conducted in a transparent and open manner.

3. Provide full information promptly to encourage fair and informed decision.
4. Support consultation to the maximum by responding to information requests fully and quickly.
5. Provide opportunities for people to inform each other within the context of the initiative, and to offer advice and guidance to the initiative.
6. Help in identifying and understanding the diversity of perspectives, values, and interest.
7. Strive to work with stakeholders to identify how best the consultation and communication process can help to guide the flow of discussion.
8. Develop areas of common ground, understand where differences exist, and the underlying reasons for them.
9. Establish clear and realistic timetables for facilitating discussion, and arriving at decisions.
10. Be sensitive to the limited resources available to people and groups, and provide tools and resources for building stakeholder capacity to participate where feasible.

11. Provide information in plain language.
12. Give practical help to people and groups to take part with particular attention to equal opportunity.
13. Provide frequent feedback.
14. Stimulate constructive exchange of views.
15. Frequently monitor and evaluate the process.
16. Share with stakeholders the responsibility for effective consultation and communication.

UNESCO (2004) also recognized the difference between using dominant theoretical models and using checklists and came up with the following five criteria that should always be fulfilled for HIV/AIDS projects, programmes and strategies to be effective:

- Cultural-appropriateness;
- Fully respect of universally-agreed human rights;
- Gender-responsiveness;
- Age-responsiveness, and;
- Involvement of people living with HIV/AIDS at every stage.

How to Develop a List of Common Principles?

Lists of common principles are developed in an early stage of a project. They can be based on studies done in other areas or in related sectors, and build on the lessons learned from those research/intervention projects.

Working on common principles in a multi-stakeholder process also has a motivating and stimulating effect. It can promote the co-ownership of projects. Developing a list of common principles could be a social learning process in itself and could therefore take years to accomplish. However, the idea here is not only to build on dialogue, but also, and maybe even more so, on studies done in related areas. In-depth social learning about the issues at stake takes place in the research/intervention phase of the project. Here the aim is to build the philosophical grounding for the project and make an inventory of concrete problems.

As a start and based on lessons learned from the literature study done for this chapter, common principles that are specifically relevant for rural HIV/AIDS communication research/interventions could include the following:

- *Approach HIV/AIDS as a multi-sectoral development problem, not as a health problem:* This is one of the most important lessons learned from previous HIV/AIDS communication/interventions. This also implies to be active beyond awareness issues.
- *Use a trans-disciplinary approach:* Ensure that perspectives from scientists (social and technical), community members, governments, NGOs and other relevant stakeholders are represented,

addressed and respected. A *multi-stakeholder process* explicitly includes political commit-ment and strong leadership, but also involvement and dedication of local organizations, such as local farmer groups/organizations.

- *Don't use theoretical models of change in a dominant way; use a conceptual framework instead:* The conceptual framework works as a guide for focus and emphasis in change processes. Establish in this regard also an *appropriate mix* of focussing on advocacy communication, behavioural change communication and communication for social change.
- *Use a list of common principles:* A list of common principles grounds the philosophy of the project in an explicit way. All stakeholders should share the list of principles.
- *Work in a culturally-embedded way:* Culture is text, not context. Culture cannot be added to an analytic situation. Culture is the basis of a situation.

Concluding Remarks

We need to move beyond awareness issues. Awareness does not automatically lead to change. Knowing about HIV/AIDS, how the virus is transmitted, and how one can prevent oneself will not be enough. HIV/AIDS is in many areas a fact of life with far-reaching socio-economic consequences.

This chapter argued that HIV/AIDS is now to be seen as a culturally-embedded development problem and called for appropriate communications/interventions and learning processes. It offered a concrete proposal for an alternative approach focussing on social change instead of behavioural change. A plea was made for using a conceptual framework parallel to a list of common principles. This alternative approach intrinsically accommodates a multi-sectoral, multi-stakeholder and trans-disciplinary approach.

Note

1. This continuous and all surrounding flow of mass media messages might be different in remote rural areas where mass media is scarce. Alternative and community media might have a less surrounding character in some areas. However, in other areas, especially television might be viewed in a collective way (for example, out-door television viewing and watching or listening to community media) and in these cases a flow of audio-visual culture does exist.

References

Airhihenbuwa, C.O. and R. Obregon. 2000. 'A Critical Assessment of Theories/Models Used in Health Communication for HIV/AIDS', *Journal of Health Communication*, 5(supplement): 5–15.

Baran, S.J. and D.K. Davis. 2003. *Mass Communication Theory: Foundations, Ferment, and Future*. Belmont, CA, USA: Thomson/Wadsworth.

Beebe, J. 2001. *Rapid Assessment Process. An Introduction.* Lauham: Rowman and Littlefield Publishers.

Berrigan, F.J. 1979. 'Community Communications: The Role of Community Media in Development', *Reports and Papers on Mass Communication.* No. 90. Paris, France: UNESCO.

Carpentier, N., R. Lie and J. Servaes. 2003. 'Community Media: Muting the Democratic Media Discourse?', *Continuum: Journal of Media and Cultural Studies,* 17(1):51–68.

Creative Exchange. 2004. Available at http://www.creativexchange.org.

FAOcomm discussion forum. September 2003. Available online at http://www.comminit.com/majordomo/faocomm/maillist.html.

Freire, P. 1970. *Pedagogy of the Oppressed* (M. Bergman Ramos, Trans.). New York: Herder and Herder.

Gerbner, G. 1979. 'Television's Influence on Values and Behaviour', *Massacommunicatie,* 7(6): 215–222.

Gómez, R. and B. Casadiego. 2002. 'Letter to Aunt Ofelia. Seven Proposals for Human Development Using New Information and Communication Technologies'. Available online at http://www.idrc.ca/pan/ricardo/publications/ofelia_eng.htm.

Gramsci, Antonio. 1971. *Selections from the Prison Notebooks of Antonio Gramsci.* London : Lawrence and Wishart.

Handwerker, W.P. 2001. *Quick Ethnography. A Guide to Rapid Multi-Method Research.* Walnut Creek: AltaMira Press.

Jankowski, N. and O. Prehn (eds). 2002. *Community Media in the Information Age: Perspectives and Prospects.* Cresskill, New Jersey: Hampton Press.

Kwame Boafo, S.T. 2000. *Promoting Community Media in Africa.* Paris: UNESCO.

Lie, R. 2003. *Spaces of Intercultural Communication. An Interdisciplinary Introduction to Communication, Culture, and Globalizing/Localizing Identities.* Cresskill, New Jersey: Hampton Press.

———. 2004. 'ICTs for Agricultural Development. An Exercise in Interdisciplinarity'. Paper presented at the International Conference Communication and Democracy: Perspectives for a New World, IAMCR (International Association for Media and Communication Research), 25–30 July 2004, Porto Alegre, Brazil.

McKee, N., J.T. Bertrand and A. Becker-Benton. 2004. *Strategic Communication in the HIV/AIDS Epidemic.* London: Sage Publications.

Panos. 2001. Background Paper for Communication for Development Roundtable. November, Nicaragua. Available online at http://comminit.com/roundtable2/cdr_nov22.pdf.

———. 2003. *Missing the Message. Twenty Years of Learning from HIV/AIDS.* London: The Panos Institute. Available online at http://www.afroaidsinfo.org/public/Home/missingmessage.pdf.

Qamar, M.K. 2003. *Facing the Challenge of an HIV/AIDS Epidemic: Agricultural Extension Services in Sub-Saharan Africa.* Rome: FAO, Extension, Education and Communication Service, Research, Extension and Training Division, Sustainable Development Department .

Richardson. 2003. FAO comm discussion forum, 10/09/2003.

Rockfeller Foundation. 1999. 'Communication for Social Change: A Position Paper and Conference Report'. New York: Rockfeller Foundation.

Rogers, E.M. 1962. *Diffusion of Innovations.* New York: Free Press.

Servaes, J. and P. Malikhao. 2004. 'Communication and Sustainable Development'. Background Paper, 9th United Nations Roundtable on Communication for Development, FAO, Rome.

Singhal, A. and E.M. Rogers. 1999. *Entertainment-Education: A Communication Strategy for Social Change.* Mahwah, N.J.: Erlbaum.

———. 2003. *Combating AIDS. Communication Strategies in Action.* London: Sage Publications.

Tacchi, J., D. Slater and G. Hearn. 2003. *Ethnographic Action Research Handbook.* New Delhi: UNESCO. Available online at http://unescodelhi.nic.in/publications/ear.pdf.

Tufte, T. 2003a. 'Edutainment in HIV/AIDS Prevention. Building on the Soul City Experience in South Africa', in J. Servaes (ed.). *Approaches to Development. Studies on Communication for Development.* Paris: UNESCO.

———. 2003b. 'HIV/AIDS, Globalisation and Ontological Security. Key Communication Challenges in HIV/AIDS Prevention'. Paper presented at the 11th FELAFACS Conference, 4–8 October 2003, Puerto Rico.

Uganda AIDS Commission. 1993. *The Multi-Sectoral Approach to Aids Control in Uganda.* Available online at http://www.aidsuganda.org/pdf/maca_executive_summary.pdf.

UNAIDS. 2003. Janzania Commission for HIV/AIDS, 2003. Available online at http://www.unaids.org/en/regions/countries/countries/tanzania.asp.

UNAIDS and Penn State. 1999. *Communications Framework for HIV/AIDS. A New Direction*. Available online at http://www.unaids.org/html/pub/Publications/IRC-pub01/JC335-CommFramew_en_pdf.pdf.

UNESCO. 2004. AIDS and Culture. Available online at http://portal.unesco.org/en/ev.php URL_ID=2932&URL_DO=DO_TOPIC&URL_SECTION=201.html.

UNFPA. 2002. 'Communication for Development'. Roundtable Report. Focus on HIV/AIDS Communication and Evaluation, UNFPA, New York. Available online at http://www.comminit.com/pdf/C4DRoundtableReport.pdf.

Vaughan, P.W., E.M. Rogers, A. Singhal and R.M. Swalehe. 2000. 'Entertainment-Education and HIV/AIDS Prevention: A Field Experiment in Tanzania', *Journal of Health Communication*, 5(suppl.):81–100.

Witteveen, L.M., B. Enserink and A. Ramachandran. 2003. 'People on Stage, A Visual Problem Appraisal of Kerala's Coast'. Conference proceedings, People and the Sea II—Conflicts, Threats and Opportunities, MARE September 2003, Amsterdam, The Netherlands.

Religion and HIV/AIDS Prevention in Thailand

14

PATCHANEE MALIKHAO

Introduction

The AIDS pandemic came to the Thai public's attention in 1984. It has since spread from men who had sex with men, to injecting drug users, to sex workers, to the male population at large, and finally to the partners of the males and their children. A survey conducted in 2002 by UNAIDS, UNICEF and WHO found that, at the end of 2001, there were 650,000 infected adults (that is 15–49 years of age), 220,000 of these were females. In addition, there were 21,000 children (0–15 years) who got infected and the ratio of male:female who live with HIV/AIDS has shifted from 4:1 to 2:1 during the last decade.

During the eighth National AIDS Conference in 2002, Mr Thaksin Shinawatra, the former Prime Minister of Thailand admitted that there were about 700,000 people living with HIV and AIDS. However, he hoped that the numbers would decrease in 2002–2006. He argued that, compared to 1991, when there had been 140,000 new cases, Thailand had been able to reduce the newly infected rate to 29,000 cases in 2000. The premier hoped to further reduce the rate down to 17,000 people in 2006. An update, presented on 12 July 2004 during the 15th International AIDS Conference in Bangkok, indicated that one estimated 19,000 new infections in 2003, reflecting a remarkable decline over a 12-year period (*The Correspondent*, 2004a:3).

However, the Prime Minister indirectly admitted in his speech in 2001 that the prevention of HIV/AIDS has been successful among certain groups only. There were indications that the epidemic was spreading among young adults. Prevention campaigns among drug users had not been successful either. He then called for a holistic approach aimed at preventing the risk behaviour in each group. During the 2004 15th International AIDS Conference, the Premier reiterated that, though one had tried to reduce the epidemic during the past two decades, new infections had been reported on an ongoing basis. He estimated that Thailand would need at least US$ 1 million for 5 years to combat the disease (*The Correspondent*, 2004b:4).

The above statements indicate that the AIDS epidemic continues to be a major problem in Thailand. Though the official AIDS policies have changed from an individualistic approach (increasing information/awareness) during 1992–1996 to a collective social approach during 1997–2001, no substantial changes have been noticed.

Put in a development perspective, HIV/AIDS prevention could be seen as a stream of globalization which affects each local environment differently, because it implies cultural and political changes in addition to the obvious health issues (Barnett and Whiteside, 2002:353). In each developing nation-state, poverty, gender, power, budgets, culture and political administration contribute to the alarming spread of HIV/AIDS. The Western or so-called developed world calls for either the ABC (*Abstinence or delay sexual debut, Be faithful or reduction in number of partners and Condom use* where one is unwilling or unable to practice A or B) strategy or the CNN (use Condoms, use sterile Needles and Negotiate for a safer sex) strategy to solve the problem. The first strategy has a tight relationship with religious institutions which emphasize abstinence and monogamous behaviour, the latter on safer sex and dialogues (*The Correspondent*, 2004c:5). The developing world has responded by adapting these prevention strategies recommended by major United Nations agencies such as WHO, UNICEF and UNAIDS into their own cultural settings. This process is called localization.

This chapter starts from the Localization as Development Paradigm which studies how the locals respond to global concepts and strategies of HIV/AIDS prevention. The *global-local* can be looked at from four different perspectives:

1. the transfer of HIV/AIDS prevention concepts from the UN agencies and global religious institutions such as the Vatican and the Christian Connections for International health or the CCH (global/centre) to Thailand as a national recipient (local/periphery);
2. the transfer of HIV/AIDS prevention as development messages from the Thai government, the local UN agencies and the global religious institutions (global/centre) to the Thai religious institutions such as the Ecumenical Churches and the *Sangha* (Thai Buddhist body) (local/periphery);
3. the transfer of the HIV/AIDS prevention as development messages in a religious context from the Thai religious institutions (global/centre) to the Thai communities under study (local/periphery);
4. the transfer of the HIV/AIDS prevention messages and related religious morality from the Thai religious leaders (global/centre) to the Thai individuals in the communities under study.

Thailand is an interesting case because of its socially accepted practices of commercial sex; its hierarchical and patriarchal culture and its attempt to devise a community-based approach to tackle this so-called 'societal immune deficiency syndrome' (Wasi, n.d.:12) on the assumption that a strong or cohesive community will help eradicate poverty, ignorance, unemployment and other socio-cultural factors that help spread HIV/AIDS.

Two Thai communities with HIV/AIDS prevention messages in their rituals, rites and sermons in two religious contexts—Buddhism and Christianity—have been studied. Both communities not only adopt the Western concepts of HIV/AIDS prevention, such as persuading people to use condoms, spreading knowledge about HIV/AIDS, preaching faithfulness to people, and so forth, but they also adapt national strategies to involve the people in their holistic campaigns/activities against HIV/AIDS as part of a community development project. How these Western development messages of HIV/AIDS prevention get localized in a culture like Thailand has been studied. How the Western morality (which has a strong hold on Christian moral ethics) on HIV/AIDS prevention has been adapted in a Thai Buddhist-dominated moral ethics to prevent them from engaging in risk-taking sexual behaviours has also been studied. In other words, this research aimed to explore how the ABC or the CNN concept is adapted to fit a Thai Buddhist cultural context. The study of a Thai Christian community is meant as a triangulation to compare the differences or sameness in the localization process.

Background

Thai Culture, the Key Concept

Culture can be described as a framework with four distinguishable but interrelated analytical components: a worldview (*Weltanschauung*), a value system, a system of symbolic representations, and a social organizational system (Servaes, 1999:12). Servaes studied Thai culture along these lines and described it as a village culture with mutual trust and informal social relationships among the inner groups, but with distrust and formality or business-like positions towards the outer groups. Thais believe that supernatural power (other than their religion) will protect them in their dealings with the outer groups. Power is thus the core of the Thai worldview. Power exists in the hierarchical structure of the language use according to age, gender and social status. In this way, Thais do not approach prostitution from a moral criterion but from a power perspective (Mulder, 1990:44).

Komin studied the differences in values of a group of religious (Buddhist) Thais and non-religious (Buddhist) Thais. The two groups were identified on the basis of their visits to temples and listening to Buddhist sermons. She found that urban Thais are less religious than rural Thais. Rural Thais are more socially-oriented and the urban Thais are more self-oriented. This explains peer group influence in drinking and unsafe sex behaviours of the rurals.

HIV/AIDS Prevention in a Global and a Thai Cultural Context

Much AIDS research during the 1980s and early 1990s focussed on collecting numbers of sexual partners, the frequency of sexual practices, and so forth. Previous experience with sexually transmitted diseases showed that the relationship between preferable attitude and preferable behaviours is neither simple, nor linear or causal (see Maticka-Tyndale et al., 1997; Sandfort, 1998; Sukda, 2000; Timmins et al., 1998). It was assumed that decisions about HIV/AIDS prevention were based on rational, volitional thinking with no regard for more true to life emotional responses to engaging in sexual practices (Servaes and Malikhao, 2004).

Since the 1990s, the research trend has shifted, as was observed by the Panos Institute, UNFPA, UNESCO and the Rockefeller Foundation at the conclusion of their Communication for Development Roundtable in HIV/AIDS communication in Nicaragua in 2001. Their overall conclusion was that people should be seen as 'the agents of their own change; address social norms, policies, culture and supportive environments; cautiously transfer accurate information through dialogue and debate; and negotiating the best way forward in a partnership process' (Panos, 2003:10).

Several researchers in Africa and South-East Asia proved that altering people's attitudes towards safe sex and condom use in order to change their risky behaviours cannot be applied without considering the cultural settings in which the interventions take place (Jemmott and Jemmott 1994:169; Lyttleton, 2000; Ntseane, 2004). In Thailand, the Thai unofficial sexual norm is known to help spread the HIV virus since the pre- and extramarital sexual relations are accepted for Thai men; for most women they are not, and in many cases, extramarital sexual relations are tolerated by the females (Boonmongkol et al., 1998:47, 52; Saengtienchai et al., 1999:80–81). Moreover, socio-economic factors such as poverty help spread the disease in two ways: firstly, the locals are forced to seek cheap advice from self-proclaimed doctors who use tainted needles, and secondly, poverty in combination with the moral gratitude towards parents forces females in the North-eastern and Northern part of the country (which are the two poorest parts of Thailand), into prostitution. When poverty is combined with the patriarchy of the Thai culture, female prostitutes are assumed to accept unsafe sex practices (Lyttleton, 2000:173–188). Sexual inequality also drives wives and casual girlfriends into non-negotiable positions for condom use (Boonmongkol et al., 1998:52).

The Persistence of the HIV/AIDS Issue in Thailand

As mentioned, the AIDS pandemic has spread from men who have sex with men, to injecting drug users, to sex workers, to the male population at large and finally to the partners of the males and their children.

In other words, the AIDS epidemic continues to be a major problem in Thailand; despite the various efforts of a number of political administrations to combat the epidemic. In 1998 Pimpawan Boonmongkol, Penchan Pradapmuk, and Sansanee Raungsaun, in their State-of-the-Art Review of Socio-economic and Behavioural Research on AIDS, identified the following groups/factors that encourage risk behaviour:

Men who have sex with men group:

They did not have adequate knowledge of HIV transmissions. Only 20 per cent of homosexuals used condoms with strangers. Male sex workers lack negotiating power to use condoms with customers.

Drug injectors:

They exchanged syringes among small groups. They did not know the correct way of sterilizing the syringes. They have more than one sexual partner, and 70 per cent of them did not use condoms on a regular basis.

Sex workers:

They lack bargaining power for safe sex with customers. Some customers physically abused them when they wanted to use condoms. The entrepreneur did not allow virgin sex workers to use condoms for their first sexual intercourse with customers. Most sex workers do not understand how HIV is transmitted. Latent prostitution is on the rise due to tighter control by local authorities. Restaurants, bars, houses, truck parking, and so forth, have become places of commercial sex. Customers had to commit fast intercourse for fear that they would get caught; they tended not to use condoms. Bad quality condoms also contribute to non-safe sex behaviour. Authorities, enforcing the use of condoms in brothels, also contribute to an increase in risk behaviour.

Adult males:

Some were treated by local traditional doctors and were subjected to shared syringes. Most of them had sexual relations with prostitutes before and after marriage. Some refused to use condoms with their wives and regular sexual partners, but used them with sex workers. Some did not use condoms with latent sex workers. They do not discuss sex issues with their wives. Peer groups support one another to get drunk and later visit sex workers in group. Migration also causes males to visit sex workers. Furthermore, a lack of knowledge about HIV transmissions and the proper use of condoms are contributing to risk behaviour.

Adult females:

Some were treated by local traditional doctors in similar ways as the male group (see above). Some had more than one sexual partner and did not use condoms (2.7 per cent of samples). Many were ignorant about their own husband's risk behaviour. Especially single women lacked knowledge on safe sex, birth control and the bargaining power for safe sex. Women were victims of the double cultural standard: the accepted men's premarital sex behaviour versus the insistence on the female's premarital virginity. Virgin females did not have adequate knowledge about sex because they assumed it to be a matter for married women.

Adolescents:

They tend to have their first sexual intercourse more with girlfriends than with sex workers. They tend not to use condoms, either with sex workers or with sexual partners. They lack knowledge about HIV transmission from sexual partners. Female adolescents had difficulty negotiating the use of condoms because they were 'culturally' expected to know nothing about sexuality. (Boonmongkol et al., 1998:32–55)

Previous Social Science Research on HIV/AIDS Prevention in Thailand

Previous social science research on HIV/AIDS prevention undertaken in Thailand has tended to focus on the following:

The Effect of Mediated Campaigns on HIV/AIDS Prevention

Research done during 1990–1999 adopted various media theories to conduct descriptive research without reflecting on the existing values of the Thai sexuality, worldview and beliefs. Examples of these kinds of research are Foo-Inlong (1991) 'Media Exposure of Labours in the Industrial Estate in Prathumthani Province on AIDS Prevention and Control' and Thongthai (1994) on 'Knowledge, Media exposure and AIDS-related Risky Behaviours' (Sthapitanonda et al., 2003:41–53).

Sexuality and Behavioural Research for HIV/AIDS Prevention

A number of quantitative research projects have been undertaken by the Ministry of Public Health and UNAIDS to show relationships of non-condom use and sexually transmitted disease and HIV contraction or evaluation of counselling techniques, health care, and so forth (UNAIDS, 1998, 1999a, 2000). What one gains is that there has been a shift from paid sex towards, mostly, unsafe casual sex among adolescents in the 2000s. Thai youngsters, under peer group influence, consume methamphetamines and alcohol and may lose their volition control on safer sex practices (Boonyabuddhi, 2001:14–19). Field work revealed that preferable attitudes towards monogamy of Thai men do not correspond to their constant patronage of commercial sex under the peer group pressure; the knowledge of HIV/AIDS transmission and prevention does not correspond to the perception of being at risk for HIV infection; and the misperception that HIV/AIDS is contagious from sex workers only (Maticka-Tyndale et al., 1997).

Aheto and Gbesemete reported their focus group discussion finding that married men disapproved condom use with their wives (Aheto and Gbesemete, 2004). This supported Boonmongkol et al.'s work that non-condom sex is associated with intimacy and trust; not with ignorance on HIV/AIDS (Boonmongkol et al., 1998:32–55).

Studies on the Effect of Religion on Sexual Behaviours, and HIV/AIDS Prevention

(a) Religiosity.   Reynolds and Tanner (1995:45–47) stated:

Religious rules provide ways of do's and don'ts in human's life cycle such as age of marriage and conception for Christians, obligation to have marital intercourse for Jews and remarriage of widows for Hindus. Religious practices enhance as well as reduce the risk of diseases, for instance, more alcoholics have been cured by being converted to Catholicism (to practice abstinence) than by medical programmes. In contrary, HIV/AIDS prevention is difficult to implement among Muslim homosexuals because the religious teaching disapproves anal intercourse.

McGuire points out many symbolic representations of religion in terms of discourses that we can observe and analyse such as rituals, symbols, religious experiences, and so forth (McGuire, 2002:124–125). The concept of religiosity encompasses many facets of symbolic representations. Religiosity can be measured as discussed by Glock and Stark (1968) in five different dimensions: belief, practice, experience, knowledge and consequence. The belief dimension is belief in the essence of a religion. The practice dimension is expressed through participation in rituals; the experience through subjective feelings and perceptions; the knowledge dimension through understanding of the basic philosophy of the religion; and the consequence through the commitment manifested in everyday life (Glock and Stark quoted in Marsh 1996:482).

(b) Sexual Morality. Morality is encoded in both Christian and Buddhist traditions (Weeks, 1995: 47; Payutto, 1998:104). Morality and sexual behaviour have a close relationship. Weeks pointed out that immorality in the English language has a connotation of sexual misbehaviour (Weeks, 1995:47). Rawls (1980:515–572) stated that one should select fundamental ethical principles that maximize the long-term interest of most members in the community, from the utilitarianism point of view. In the case of HIV/AIDS prevention, it is morally wrong to spread viruses to someone else by not practicing safe sex practice—not allowing body fluid of the two partners to contact while having intercourse; using condoms as safe sex practice is thus morally right because one can prevent the virus from spreading further to other people in the community, and it is also wrong for a person who is at risk of being HIV infected not to provide information that may prevent the spouse or partner from suffering or death (Jonson, 1988:30–43). People who have moral ethics do not have to be religious (ibid.:18).

Also quantitative research on the relationship between religiousness or religiosity and sexual behaviours is important for the HIV/AIDS prevention. Chantavanich et al. (2000:12), for instance, found a significant difference between the Buddhist and the Christian respondents with regards to safe sex practice and casual sex.

One can conclude that gender, poverty and age are factors in risk-taking behaviours. One can see that traditional values towards sex together with the lack of awareness of HIV/AIDS transmission do put Thais at risk in their sex practices. This leads again to the importance of the Thai culture studies.

Religious Institutions and HIV/AIDS Prevention

Global Perspectives

There are a number of different religions attempting to deal with HIV/AIDS, such as Buddhism, Christianity and Islam. They all employ humanitarian strategies within their particular rites and rituals. Not only the preventive messages, the religious leaders have also worked on the moral responsibility or sexual morality of the people who attend the services, as stated in the do's and don'ts of the religion's fundamental morality. The Christians' ABC is controversial in a global context. The A (abstinence from sexual intercourse before marriage) and the B (be faithful to your partner) have been promoted but the C (condom use) has not been widely supported by all Christian denominations. Churches by and large are traditionally promoters of abstinence before marriage and monogamy after it (Paterson, n.d.:4) but conservative/fundamentalist Christians such as some Evangelical churches are against condom promotion because they think condoms promote immoral behaviours (Mosley, 2003:3). In other words, condoms are associated with promiscuity and infidelity (Long and Plater, 2004:1). The Roman Catholic Churches are not promoters of condom use because it is a method of contraception that goes against the Catholic teachings; the Vatican promotes chastity as the best method of fighting HIV (Quintero, 2004:4; Logie, 1994). The Ecumenical churches and non-Roman Catholic bodies are more supportive of the condom use as they stated that they do not 'contradict the public health messages' (Paterson, n.d.:4). They also promote the idea that HIV/AIDS is not a sin; encourage dialogues with PLWHA; and reflect Christian moral ethics in the HIV/AIDS issue; and create community which includes the PLWHA (Paterson, n.d.:6). The other approach is the C (condom use) N (sterile needles) N (safer sex negotiation) which is less religious and focuses more on the safer sex and condom use. It is promoted by UNESCO (see Viddhanaphuti, 1999). The CNN strategy is discussed in detail in the HIV/AIDS Prevention Programme Archive which is advised by US-based scientists from the US Centers for Disease Control and Prevention, Beth Israel Medical Centre, Emory University, Medical College of Wisconsin and California State University at Long Beach (see Card et al., 2001). The World Health Organization (WHO) supports the ABC approach and part of the CNN approach (the access of sterile injecting equipments) (WHO, 2003:16). The United Nations Children's Fund (UNICEF) and the Joint United Nations Programme on HIV/AIDS (UNAIDS) supports the religious leaders all over the world to use the ABC approach in their prevention programmes (UNICEF, World Conference of Religions for Peace and UNAIDS, 2004: 9). The United Nations Population Fund (UNFPA) is supportive of part of the CNN approach such as the communication for safer sex, reduction of gender inequality, condom use; it does not discuss the access of sterile needles in its approach (UNFPA, n.d.). In sum, the United Nations as a global body promotes both ABC and CNN approaches. At the same time, the United Nations has been calling for compassion, leadership and moral responsibility in dealing with HIV/AIDS. Since HIV/AIDS is a threat to the growth of a community and is seen as a morality problem, UNICEF and UNAIDS have called for the shaping of social values and public opinion by using trusted and respected members of the society: religious leaders (UNICEF, World Conference of Religions for Peace, and UNAID, 2004:60).

Local Perspectives

In local settings there were critiques on the ABC approach. The locals believe that even excluding the issue of condom use, practice of being abstinent or being faithful is not simple because this approach is, among other issues, silent on gender inequality. Long and Plater reported that 61 per cent of women living with HIV and AIDS in Africa had never had sex with more than one man; they got infected even though they were faithful (Long and Plater, 2004:1). The success in Uganda and Senegal was due to open dialogues and a societal change at the community level, together with applying the ABC approach, not the injection of the ABC in a social marketing fashion (Panos, 2003:12–13). Therefore, a community-based approach is the right answer to tackle the HIV/AIDS problem. Religious leaders are expected to support fidelity and abstinence among people who attend temples and churches, and those who participate in religious activities/ ceremonies and reach out to the people who have not accessed them (Brewster-Lee, 2003: 11–13; Stecker, 2003:15–16).

Religious leaders are respected in a community and have potential to serve as effective resource persons because of their credibility and trustworthiness:

UNICEF and UNAIDS (2003:9) state the role of religious leaders:

Religious leaders are in the unique position of being able to alter the course of the epidemic Why? Because religious leaders can:

- Shape social value;
- Promote responsible behaviour that respects the dignity of all persons and defends the sanctity of life;
- Increase public knowledge and influence opinion;
- Support enlightened attitudes, opinions, policies and laws;
- Redirect charitable resources for spiritual and social care and raise new funds for prevention and for care and support;
- Promote action from the grass roots up to the national level.

A Response from Thai Religious Institutions

The opening speech of the Thai Minister of Public Health, Ms Sudarat Kaeyuraphan, during the 'Para-liturgical Celebration on Inter-faith Cooperation Activities' session of the 15th International AIDS Conference (on 13 July 2004) was illuminating the engagement of religion in HIV/AIDS prevention. She stated that in combating AIDS:

> Religion is comparable to the spiritual and mental pillar of humankind as reflected in our culture and way of lives, largely at the community level. With its significant role, the religious institution has a great opportunity to invest in human life by allocating its resources early enough to conduct effective large scale strategic intervention. (Inter-Faith Networking on AIDS, 2004:2)

She also emphasized the importance of religion for loving, caring and sharing to assure that people living with HIV/AIDS (PLWHA) were cared and loved for and did not suffer from stigma and discrimination. According to her, all sectors of society were working closely with religious organizations to prioritize HIV/AIDS interventions. She guaranteed the commitment from the highest levels of government and all sectors of society, including religious institutions, to necessary resources, people and funding (ibid.:2–3).

Apart from caring and providing counselling for PLWHA, the religious leaders in Thailand encourage people in their community to have compassion towards PLWHA, training and giving information to the public on the disease, its transmission and prevention by organizing seminars for males, females and adolescents. They show Western slides, films and video tapes to help the locals understand the HIV virus and AIDS. They also organize mobile exhibitions on HIV/AIDS and mobilize PLWHA to present their life stories of how they contracted HIV. They involve local health officials and teachers in teaching people how to use condoms. They raise funds for the PLWHA. They also involve the participant in self-reliant activities in the form of community development projects to help relief them from poverty. Each religious approach calls for morality as stated in the Holy Bible or the Holy Qur'an in the case of Islam (The Balm in Gilead, 2004:2–5), or in the moral precepts of Buddha in the case of Buddhism (UNICEF, 2003a:10–24).

Since there is no known Muslim HIV/AIDS project in Thailand, the focus of this study has been on the Christian and Buddhist approaches that have been in existence for many years.

The Christian Approach in Thailand.   Christianity was introduced to Thailand in 1582 when three Franciscan Discalced missionaries sailed from Macau to Thailand. Their aim was to learn the local language and prepare themselves for evangelization (Bressan, 2000:158–159). According to historical accounts, in 1682 several French missionaries were visiting sick locals on a daily basis (ibid.:166). That was when Ayutthya was the capital of Thailand.

The Catholic Church, through the Catholic Commission for Health and Pastoral Care, has set up the 'Catholic Committee on HIV/AIDS' in 1990. There have been about 28 Catholic organizations working voluntarily on AIDS since 1989. Their strategies mainly focus on hospices for AIDS patients and orphans; they are not prominent with regards to holistic HIV/AIDS preventive projects (Catholic Committee on HIV/AIDS, 2004).

According to an account of the Church of Christ in Thailand (2004:14, 23–26) in this so-called Ratanakosin period (when Krungthep or Bangkok is the capital of Thailand), there were three groups of Protestant missionaries coming from the US. The American Board of Commissioner for Foreign Mission (ABCFM) sent its first missionary to Bangkok in 1831 to investigate the possibility of propagating Christianity in Thailand. Later it sent a group of missionaries to work in 1834. The American Presbyterians came in 1837 and The American Baptists came in 1851. After the Second World War, only the Siamese Presbyterians based in Bangkok remained flourishing and could merge with the so-called Loatian Presbyterians in Chiang Mai to become the Church of Christ in Thailand in 1921 (The Church of Christ in Thailand, 2004:30). It has provided, among other services, Christian education and Christian public health services.

The Christian institution built a stronghold in the North. They have Christian hospitals, the Pa-yup University, private Christian schools and churches. There are more than 60 churches in Chiang Rai alone (Christian Mission Region 2 Chiang Rai n.d.). The headquarters of the AIDS Ministry, which branch out the HIV/AIDS prevention and care network to other parts of the North, is situated in Chiang Mai, the capital city of the North. The prevalence of high death tolls resulted in the establishment of the AIDS Ministry in Chiang Mai in 1991 by the Church of Christ in Thailand (Sae Tang and Nantachaipan, 2001: 3). Later the Lamtharn Church (a fictitious name) in Chiang Rai started its own HIV/AIDS prevention and care project in 1995 (Lamtharn, 2006:50). Lamtharn church is praised by its headquarters as an example of a strong community with a successful HIV/AIDS prevention and is a place to visit (Wutthi, 2005).

Christian organizations in Thailand started to work on HIV/AIDS before the establishment of an AIDS policy; their activities have included AIDS education activities, prevention services, home-based care, counselling, testing and anonymous clinics (Porapakkham et al., 1995:35).

The Church of Christ in Thailand established its AIDS Ministry, also known as Christian AIDS Ministry or CAM, in 1991. The CAM staff is mainly theologically-trained and has pastoral experience (Sae Tang and Nantachaipan, 2001:3). In 1993 CAM was the pioneer in home care projects for people living with HIV/AIDS. Their strategic plan has shifted over the past decade from home care to a more community or holistic approach to facilitate the integration of people living with HIV/AIDS in the community and to encourage community organizations to support them and their families, and in preventing the spread of HIV infections in their communities (ibid.). The approach of CAM is in line with the Ecumenical churches regarding the promotion of the ABC concepts (Wutthi, 2005).

The Buddhist Approaches in Thailand. Since Buddhism is a non-God religion, the rituals and rites which express the symbolic representations of the people's worldview are different from those of Christianity. These challenge this author to research the effectiveness of each approach to HIV/AIDS prevention.

Buddhism is the mainstream religion in Thailand, as 97 per cent of the population claims to be Buddhists. There are more than 30,000 temples situated all over the country. These temples house more than 200,000 monks and novices altogether (Visalo, 2003:6). Traditionally monks are supposed to study *Pali* (the ancient language in which Buddha taught in India) text, the dharma (doctrines/ultimate reality), *Vinaya* (disciplines), and practice mediation to uplift their spiritual well-being (Klausner, 1993:160). In the contemporary concept, monks cannot detach themselves from being the populace's leader of spirituality. While the urban monks' roles are often limited to the study of *Pali*, meditation, teaching dharma, performing rites and ceremonies, village monks have been organizing various projects. Village monks who practice selflessness are also expected to devote themselves to social work. These monks are called '*pra nakpattana*' or monk-developers (Jackson, 2003:206–215).

Buddhist monks started to engage in rural development in 1957 (Nozaki, 2003:105). HIV/AIDS care and prevention projects are one of the projects run by about 50 monks and nuns across the country. The monks got involved in HIV/AIDS issues due to their role as spiritual refuge in the time of AIDS crisis (Norwegian Church AID and UNICEF, 2004:1). There are two Buddhist approaches to HIV/AIDS prevention and care. One is the *hospice care* founded by the *Phra Bat Nampu* Temple in 1988 (UPI, 1998:8). The other approach formed in the same year is a community approach known as the *Sangha Metta* (the Compassionate Buddhist Monks) Project which got later funded by UNICEF, Thailand. This group emphasizes a *community-based prevention and care* (Punyakammo, 2004).

In 1992, The Monks against AIDS network formed in Mae Jan district, Chiang Rai, started working on HIV/AIDS in line with the Sangha Metta Project. Its preventive approach mixes the ABC approach with the Buddhist morality precepts. They try to convey to Thai people through their preaching in the HIV/AIDS crisis adherence to the Five Precepts: (1) abstain from taking life, (2) abstain from stealing, (3) abstain from sexual misconduct, (4) abstain from false speech, and (5) abstain from intoxicants that cloud the mind.

Communication Strategies on HIV/AIDS Prevention

From a Media Advocacy and Social Marketing Approach

The initial official 'answer' of Thailand to the emergence of the first AIDS case in 1984 was *silence*. The government was afraid that it would affect tourism and cause a public panic (Baltimore Sun, 2002:2). This policy changed gradually from avoidance to acceptance in the late 1980s. The Thai government, then, assigned the Ministry of Public Health to play an official role in the national AIDS campaigns. Between 1989 and 1992 the '100 per cent condom use in brothels' campaign was launched. The campaign was to prevent sex clients from purchasing sexual services unless they use a condom. The former Prime Minister Thaksin Shinawatra stated at the 2001 seventh meeting of the Association of Southeast Asian Nations (ASEAN) in Brunei that this was the most significant strategy change. The 100 per cent condom strategy was officially adopted in 1991 when the Prime Minister took the chair of the National AIDS committee. It took the government six more years to set up the National AIDS Foundation in 1997.

A summary of 26 research projects on mass media and HIV/AIDS in Thailand, executed during 1990–1996, concluded that negative messages to frighten the public were the most prominent communication strategy applied in this period, mainly transmitted through governmental ads on television. *The messages brand the people who contracted HIV negatively.* The public's reaction was to negate or ignore news about HIV/AIDS, and to discriminate against the infected people. This created misunderstanding among the public and caused anxiety and hopelessness among the infected people (Sthapitanonda et al., 2003:37–53).

Ms Prudence Borthwick, the UNICEF coordinator for the AIDS in Thailand project, commented that:

> It soon became apparent in Thailand, as elsewhere, that lurid photographic enlargements of herpes zoster blisters or other opportunistic infections displayed as clinical models of disease prevention were not the best way for the public to be informed about HIV/AIDS.(Borthwick, 1999:209–210)

The social marketing approach has gradually shifted to the use of positive campaign strategies. Top-down approaches, such as those giving moral support, avoiding branding names or creating emotional appeal, are widely used now by the Ministry of Public Health and other governmental organizations (Sthapitanonda et al., 2003:178–179).

However, from 1997 onwards another shift became visible, which got referred to as the bottom-up approach.… towards a Community-based Approach. 1997 was a bad year for the Thai economy. Thailand had to devalue its currency and sign a contract to get loans from the IMF. These events raised the public awareness on the failure of imposing Western concepts of democracy, industrialization, and modernization and so forth without reflecting on the set of values and the worldview of the Thais. Thailand, then, turned to aim for a more sustainable or 'sufficient' economy and civic society, as stated for the first time in 1998 in the National Agenda proposed by Praves Wasi, one of the leading scholars and Buddhist activists in Thailand (Wasi, 2003:1).

> Sufficient economy' is a concept of King Bhumibol, the King of Thailand. It advocates an endogenous approach based on the Buddhist philosophy to become self-reliant on the basis of integrating strong communities, the environment, culture, quality of life, generosity, compassion and local intellect. (ibid.:4–5)

Praves Wasi defined a strong community as a community where the people:

... get organized and share the same objectives; they provide mutual assistance; together they go through different learning experiences and develop good management systems. Strong communities are capable of resolving poverty issues, conserving natural resources and prevention and solving social ills such as violence, substance abuse, and prostitute recruitment. (Wasi, n.d:10)

The community-based development approach is thus seen as a solution to the cause of the HIV/AIDS epidemic. Therefore, a UNAIDS report on funding priorities for the HIV/AIDS crisis in Thailand stated that:

In the national AIDS control and prevention plan (1997–2001), the AIDS programme budget is not solely a financing source for HIV/AIDS control. Rather, it is a catalyst for mobilizing and reorienting the use of resources from public and private sectors, families and the community at large.(UNAIDS, n.d:14)

One can see that *the national AIDS policy has changed over a decade from an individualistic approach (increasing info/awareness) to a collective social approach* as one can see the paradigm shift from the National AIDS Plan during 1992–1996 to the strategic plan during 1997–2001. (Poolcharoen, 1998:39)

The Thai government has been funding a number of NGO agencies, such as the Population and Community Development Association, to promote self-reliant projects. Apart from the governmental funding agencies, there are also foreign-funded NGOs and self-organized groups or grassroots groups emerging in order to help alleviate the problem.

Self-help groups which represent people living with HIV/AIDS (PLWHA) in the Northern region can be classified into *five categories*:

(1) Self-organizing groups, such as the New Life Friends (formed by the widows of AIDS patients);
(2) Groups initiated and supported by NGOs such as the Wednesday Friends Group, that is coordinated by the Thai Red Cross Society since 1991 and supported by the Thai-Australian Northern AIDS Prevention and Care Program (NAPAC) since 1993;
(3) Groups initiated and supported by community hospitals;
(4) Groups initiated and supported by religious institutions such as Buddhist temples and the Christian Churches in Thailand; and
(5) Groups formed by local institutions such as the Rajaphat educational institutes and Chiang Mai University (compiled from Borthwick, 1999:220–221; Poolcharoen, 1998:42–43).

Some groups are networking with one another and with governmental organizations. This author studied the Sankampang Ruam Jai Group (see Malikhao, 2004), which is an example of networking between the Sankampang hospital, the Sankangpla temple, the Public Health Bureau and the Labour Department, and which gets support from the Sanga Metta Project funded by UNICEF. The group also gets advice from the Christian Churches of Thailand in terms of home visit and counselling techniques.

The 'AIDS Colony' versus the 'Community' Approach

The most famous abbot who devoted his life to HIV/AIDS is Ven. *Athorn Prachanart* (a.k.a. *Chao Khun Alongkot Tikapanyo* or *Phra Udom Prachathorn*), the abbot of *Wat Phra Bhat Nam Phu* in Lopburi Province. He advocated *the hospice approach*, which emphasizes on the admission of the symptomatic or terminal-stage AIDS patients into his hospice. This hospice, also called AIDS city, operates since 1992 with the support of the International Network of Engaged Buddhists and AusAID (UNICEF, 2003b:1–4). He received monthly donations from the public for a total of about 1,200,000 *Baht* and a monthly budget of 100,000 *Baht* from the government (*Wat Pra Bath Namphu*, 2004). In 1998, he caught the media's attention when he, together with the Thai Agricultural and Cooperatives Ministry, aimed to construct the world's first 'AIDS colony', in a centre about 100 kilometres North of Bangkok. This centre would shelter approximately 10,000 AIDS patients. HIV activists denounced his plan because they thought this would ostracize the AIDS patients and it would project the image that AIDS patients were difficult to care for (UPI, 1998:8).

In about the same year, another group of laymen and monks formed the Sangha Metta (the Compassionate Buddhist Monks) Project chaired by Mr M, an Australian who spent 30 years of his life as a Buddhist monk. This group insists on having *HIV/AIDS patients living in the same community as others* while trying to increase awareness, knowledge and cooperation of the villagers to distinguish fears, stigma and discrimination. M explained his alternative approach as follows:

While Wat Phra Baht Nam Phu was initially intended to provide a place where people with HIV/AIDS who are unable to care for themselves, or who don't have families to care for them, can go for shelter and treatment. It has become known nationally as a place where people with HIV/AIDS can go. Consequently, people from all over Thailand are drawn there once they find they are HIV positive, rather than caring for themselves or investigating family support. In some cases, this precludes development of self-care and home-based care. As the work of the hospice is highly publicized, the problem has arisen where the public associates HIV and AIDS with 'worse case scenarios' of sick and dying people with severe symptoms. Because of the large number of patients, quality all round treatment and care is also a challenge. Another problem the hospice faces is a high monthly operating cost, approximately Baht 3 million per month, which necessitates constant and time-consuming fund-raising. (UNICEF, 2003b:4–5)

HIV/AIDS Prevention in Two Thai Villages

Two separate villages in the northern part of Thailand (Chiang Rai province), where the numbers of people who died of AIDS are the highest in the country (Ministry of Public Health 2004), were selected for the study (for more details, see Malikhao, 2006a).[2]

The Christian community of Lamtharn Christ Church (a fictitious name), led by Rev. Wichit (a fictitious name) is living in Lamtharn village. About one-third of the 1,297 villagers are Christians. They are a Thai ethnic minority whose ancestors had migrated from China. They had been converted into Christianity in 1921.Though separated by about 40 kilometres from the Sangha Metta project, they sometimes work with it and the Monk against AIDS network in Mae Jan, Chiang Rai on HIV/AIDS prevention and care.

The Buddhist community around the Tonnam temple (a fictitious name) is lead by Phra Akom (a fictitious name), the abbot who is also the president of the national Sangha Metta Project and member of the Monks against AIDS network in Chiang Rai. In 2002 this village of 1,228 inhabitants received an award from the Thai government for setting an example for others in development projects (Tonnam, 2004).

In both villages, both males and females were interviewed separately from their partners. Also semi-structured in-depth interviews of key informants, such as religious leaders, village headmen, local health officers and staff of the AIDS Preventive programmes were conducted to gain a more detailed understanding of their motives towards the HIV/AIDS preventive campaigns, sexual morality, interpretation and adaptation of the ABC and CNN concepts, and the identity of each community. Thirdly, participatory observation of official and unofficial religious practices was conducted to help analyse different discourses on the ABC and CNN concepts at different local levels. In addition, most religious activities were photographed.

Research Results

Lamtharn Christian Village.   Lamtharn village was named by the Christian villagers who moved to this area in 1941 (Lamtharn Christ Church, 2006:17). It is an area that covers half the area of *moo* 1 (meaning a village), and half of *moo* 5. *Moo* 1 has 631 inhabitants and *moo* 5 has 648 inhabitants (Treeaekanukul, 2004). Inhabitants of both *moos* are Buddhists and Christians. There are 78 households that make 343 Christians in the household registration. There are quite a few Buddhists living in Lamtharn village. The community was built around the Lamtharn church. The denomination of this church is Presbyterian. The people migrated from Mosha city in Yunnan province, the South of China 65 years ago (Lamtharn, 2006:14). They call themselves *Dai Ya* and still maintain their identity by wearing costumes on special occasions and most of them can speak *Dai Ya*. An American Presbyterian missionary named Rev. William Clifton Dodd came to Yunnan to convert them from animistic beliefs into Christianity (The Church of Christ in Thailand, 2004:44). Later the people migrated down to Myanmar and Chiang Rai.

There were 43 males and 60 females being interviewed. That means the entire population in the village was interviewed. The middle-aged adults were the highest (45.63 per cent). The second ranked were the adolescents who accounted for 28.16 per cent of the sample. The young adults ranked third (16.50 per cent) and the senior adults ranked last (9.71 per cent) (see Table 14. A1 in appendix).

People who had only primary education were the largest (42.72 per cent) group, and the people with junior high school qualification ranked second (20.39 per cent). In this village those who had a tertiary education were higher than those in the Buddhist village (which is 12.62 per cent[see Table 14. A3 in appendix]).

Most people earned their living by being labourers (26.21 per cent). Students ranked second— 22.33 per cent. The third were the self-employed people (13.59 per cent). The unemployed accounted for 17.48 per cent of the population (see Table 14.A5 in appendix).

The people who lived below the poverty line were 30.39 per cent of the population, whose income is 1,230 Baht per head per month according to the World Bank Thailand Office (The World Bank Thailand Office, 2005:4). People with a low income were the highest (52.94 per cent). People who earn more than 15,000 Baht a month accounted for only 2.94 per cent of the population (38.47 Baht = 1 US$) (see Table 14.A7 in appendix).

Tonnam Buddhist Village. The people under study migrated in 1858 from Lampoon during a drought to settle near a big lake. There are 397 households that make a total population of 1,274 people. The people speak a Northern dialect but understand standard Thai. Most of the studied but one claimed to be Buddhist. The person who claimed to be a non-believer, whose house is about 300 metres from the temple, stated that she had seen many adultery cases among devout Buddhists in the village. Therefore, she lost her faith. Those who claimed to be Buddhist practice 'popular Buddhism' which is a mixture of Animism, Brahmanism and Buddhism. People revered the abbot of the Tonnam temple highly. He presided over most religious ceremonies and local meetings.

Ninety-three males and 78 females were interviewed. Middle-aged adults (41–56 years old) were the largest group (39.13 per cent). Second largest was that of young adults, between 27–40 years of age, who account for 26.09 per cent. The third and fourth largest groups were those of the adolescents (21.12 per cent) and the senior adults, between 57 to 65 years of age (13.66 per cent). This age range represents the population age range quite well (see Table 14.A2 in appendix). Like the Christians, the respondents did not have high education. People with primary education were the largest group (57.14 per cent). People who finished junior high school ranked second (18.63 per cent). People with no schooling accounted for 8.07 per cent. People who got a diploma or a bachelors degree were a small minority. They formed 0.62 per cent and 4.97 per cent of the population (see Table 14.A4 in appendix).

The education level corresponds well with the occupation of the population. Agriculturists and labourers were the highest and second highest numbers. They were 25.63 per cent and 18.13 per cent of the sample size respectively. The unemployed accounted for 8.13 per cent of the population (see Table 14. A6 in appendix).

As was more or less the same for the Christian village, about one-third (31.01 per cent) of the population were living below the poverty line. The low income group that earned between 3,000 and 5,000 Baht a month was the largest group. They accounted for 46.84 per cent of the population. The highest income group, earning more than 15,000 Baht a month, accounted only for 1.27 per cent of the population (see Table 14.A8 in appendix).

A Comparison of Results from the Two Villages

Religiosity Level.   The Christians were more religious than the Buddhists. No one in the Christian group had a low religiosity score, while 21.74 per cent of the Buddhists had. The number of Christians with high religiosity scores was almost four times more than the Buddhists with high religiosity scores (80.38 per cent to 16.15 per cent). From participatory observation and in-depth interviews I learned that the Christians believe in God and rely on the power of God to guide them in anything they do (see also Wichit, 2005). Though some Buddhists believe in spirits and ghosts for their protection and good luck, most of them do not think that they need power outside of themselves to lead their life (Akom, 2005). The Buddhists tended to adhere to rites and rituals but did not understand the philosophical part of their own religion. The community leaders in the Buddhist village did not understand the core of their religion. Only two Buddhist monks understood it. In contrary, all Christian community leaders who were interviewed understood the essence of their own religion.

Knowledge about HIV/AIDS Transmission and Risky Practices.   In both villages people who have a low level of knowledge about HIV/AIDS transmission and risky practices were in the minority. This can be a good indication of the effectiveness of the campaigns run by the religious leaders together with the public health office and local hospitals. 46.60 per cent of Christian respondents and 23.60 per cent of the Buddhist respondents had a high level of knowledge. 52.43 per cent of the Christians and 69.57 per cent of the Buddhists had a medium knowledge level. This proves that religious difference does not influence knowledge difference.

Sexual Morality.   Respondents responded to two different scenarios narrated by this author/researcher, the summaries of which are as follows:

a) If you were a married person who once had an extramarital sex without using a condom, you realized you had a chance of contracting HIV virus, which of the following would you have done (a) inform your partner about it, (b) use condoms, or (c) abstain from sex?

21.09 per cent of the Buddhist respondents and 11.35 per cent of the Christians would not tell their spouse. According to the reasons given by the respondents, most of them did not want to have a quarrel and had to divorce. While 81.40 per cent of the Christians stated that they would use condoms, 78.99 per cent of the Buddhists stated they would. Only 4.08 per cent of the

Christian respondents and 6.9 per cent of the Buddhist respondents said that they would abstain from sex. One can conclude that religious difference did not make a significant difference on HIV prevention among married couples.

b) If you just lived together with a friend who did not know that you were a drug addict, you had used a needle injection once, you realised you had a chance of passing HIV virus to your partner, you would: (a) inform your partner about it, (b) use condoms based on what happened, or (c) use condoms based on false excuses.

In this case the Buddhist respondents would inform their partners and use condoms more than the Christians. It was noticed that 11.58 per cent of the Christian respondents ask their partners to use condoms on false excuses such as irregular menstruation, and so forth, while only 4.14 per cent of the Buddhist respondents did that. From this one cannot conclude that religions alone have an affect on sexual morality. The main factor is the pattern of relationship. Those who did not want to inform their spouses and pretended as if nothing happened tended to inform the informal partners. They gave an explanation that when married it was difficult to split because of the children. They would not upset the spouses and risk breaking up. The same person would inform a casual partner because the commitment was not that strong. They could break up and therefore dared to tell the partners and took the risk of breaking up.

Knowledge of Safer Sex Practices.   The Buddhists on average had a better understanding of safer sex practices than the Christians. Safer sex practices are a newer concept than safe sex. That's why most of them don't know about it. This author/researcher did also ask the respondents what they know about safe sex. The top four lists are 'condom use', 'monogamy', 'having a blood check before having sex', and 'no sex at all'. One teenager from the Christian village gave another definition of safer sex. According to him, safer sex is having sex in a massage parlour because they always provide condoms. So, having sex there is safe (smile).

The Localization of the ABC Concept.   More than 90 per cent of respondents agreed with the concept of abstinence and be faithful in both religion categories. When asked about agreement to use condoms in case one cannot keep the first two concepts, 88.75 per cent of the Buddhists and only 75 per cent of the Christians were positive about condom use. The answers of people who said no to condom use can be grouped under three categories: condoms may leak; people who are monogamous do not need condoms; condoms help married people to cheat on their partners and support pre-marital sex.

Condom Use of Respondents.   What people say is not always what they do. Buddhists who used condoms at least once were only 35.71 per cent compared to 39.44 per cent of the Christians. The percentages are quite low compared to their positive attitude towards condom use. It cannot yet be concluded that the reasons the respondents did not use condoms up to even 50 per cent means that they all are monogamous because from literature one knows that some married men and single men do practice polygamy. From what happened in real life, women are more in line with a monogamous relationship in this patriarchal culture; they have been infected by their partner. Indeed, there is a significant difference between males and females in both religious groups. Only 27.5 per cent of the Christian females who answered this question used condoms while 54.84 per cent of the males used them. This result is suggesting that the Christian males are about two times more active than the females. In the Buddhist group, the males used three times more condoms than the females as one can see that 56.67 per cent of Buddhist males used condoms while 16.67 per cent of females used them. This lead to a further question on gender inequality.

Attitude towards Gender.   Three questions were compiled to help understand whether the attitude towards gender in the current Thai culture has changed due to globalization.

'It is all right for married men to have sex with somebody else other than their wives'.

The Christians and the Buddhists both disagreed (79.61 per cent and 63.39 per cent respectively), but 30.43 per cent of the Buddhists strongly disagreed with extramarital affairs of married men while only 11.65 per cent of the Christian disagreed strongly.

'It is all right for single men to buy sex from sex workers'.

Respondents tended to agree that single men might buy sex. There is no significant difference between Christians and Buddhists (48.54 per cent and 46.54 per cent respectively).

'A woman who keeps her virginity before marriage is a good person'.

Both Christians and Buddhists agreed that good is equal to virginity for females (73.33 per cent of the Christian respondents and 68.32 per cent of the Buddhist respondents agreed).

Preliminary Conclusions

In the two villages under study, AIDS cases were high in the past. The mode of HIV transmission has been heterosexual intercourse. Some interviewees in the Buddhist village stated that about 10 years ago people died of AIDS like falling leaves. In the Christian village, every household had at least one member who died of AIDS complications. Most women in both villages contracted HIV from their husbands. Some men contracted HIV from their wives. Yupin, one of the members of the Buddhist women's club committee, recounted about her brothers-in-law who died of AIDS:

> He was a good-looking man. Of course, he was a philanderer. After he had died, there were a number of women in both our village and in the neighbouring village, who died of AIDS. (Yupin, 2005)

Nuansri from the Christian village talked about her brother and his wife who also died of AIDS:

My brother visited sex workers and his wife contracted HIV from him. After he died, she moved southwards and re-married a military man. She did not tell her new husband how her late husband died. When he knew, he committed suicide. Later she died and left a son. I am the carer.

There are no cases of drug injectors found among the samples in the Buddhist village. According to the head of the anti-drug committee of the Buddhist village, volunteer neighbourhood watchers help spy on those who use drugs and report them to the police. Those who were drug addicts were arrested and sent to a rehabilitation camp where monks and other speakers came to boost their morality (Somchai, 2005).

This doesn't mean that everybody is against drugs in this region. One telling story is the killing of a former headman who got shot dead by maffiosi because he was believed to be in favour of eradicating the drug problem (Nakhorn, 2005). One man in the Christian village admitted to have injected drugs for more then 20 years.

Impact of Religion

Religion does shape the worldview of the people. The Christian interviewees do believe in God and look at Buddhism as satanic because Buddhists 'worship statues'. The Christians believed that the only way to reach God is to become a Christian. This creates a strong sense of being chosen and that makes the community stronger. But at the same time this also initiates discrimination towards people from other religions. The saying that 'we Christians are more faithful than the Buddhists because we believe in God' and 'monogamy is the best policy because God taught us so' proved to be a cliché when the findings are presented. There is no difference between the two religious groups regarding sexual morality and condom use. From observations and interviews, Christian married males are more polygamous than the Buddhists. Only three men in the Buddhist sample had extramarital affairs while eight men in the Christian sample/ population had extramarital affairs. One of the church elders admitted to visiting sex workers whenever he had a chance and his spouse still does not know anything about it. One Christian man announced proudly during an interview that he was the Casanova of the Lamtharn village because he has had a wife and seven regular mistresses and a few casual girlfriends and nine children from all the women! He did not support those children.

Though the number of people who passed the prevention programmes in the Buddhist village was lower than that of the Christian one (12 people out of 161 Buddhists attended while 66 out of 103 Christians attended), the Buddhists had better knowledge of risky practices and safer sex. Phra Akom stated that he used the strategy of creating seeds to educate further. He hand-picked the youth groups to be a spearhead in educating others. He also organizes a network with the people living with HIV/AIDS and has a meeting every month to let them speak to the villagers about their experiences. The Christians had more knowledge on HIV transmission maybe because they used movies and audio-visual media to inform the participants on HIV/AIDS. No one in the Buddhist village ever mentioned having watched audio-visual aids from the monks; while the monks claimed to use a multimedia approach.

Strong Communities?

The Christian community had their own credit union. They refused the 'one million baht a tambon' loan from the Thaksin government. They could save up to 3 million baht in total. The pastor initiated several projects to support the income of the housewives such as repacking iodine coated salt for retail, raising biopigs, making mats, and so forth. He also received funds from the government each year to run HIV/AIDS prevention campaigns. The pastor earns his salary from donations of 10 per cent from the church members' income. He is in the high income group. He cannot work on a computer. He needs someone to be his secretary. He is a low-tech man. The relationship among the villagers is strong. Any problem could be solved through the Chair of the church committee. The villagers will take turn hosting the church members to come and worship in their houses on Sunday afternoons. They will cook and eat together after the worship. Most of the women attend. They stick together and help each other. The pastor once preached them to be kind to people from other religions.

The Buddhist community follows the Thaksin policy. They have their own community radio where 4–5 volunteers work. Phra Akom also has his programme in the morning to teach the people about old traditional Lanna (Northern Thai) culture. They have their own community bank and they have a committee to distribute loans to the villagers. According to Wilai, the volunteer worker and Chair of the women's group, 80 per cent of the loan was used in a positive way. The other 20 per cent was a loan to buy luxurious goods. The villagers also have their own self-sustainable projects, such as making pork sausages and handicraft such as embroidery or ratten basket weaving.

Phra Akom stated that this community was strong before he came. He started to campaign for hygienic practices, in line with the Public Health Promotion project, stop drinking habits, and awarded certificates to 'AIDS free families'. He provides a dharma room in a local hospital to give mental counselling to PLWHA. The monk gets only 500 Baht a month from the government for being an abbot. He also gets financial support from the government to support HIV/AIDS prevention and care projects.

He is a high tech monk who uses PowerPoint presentations, has a laptop and a desktop, an MP3 player, a video and a digital camera.

The ABC Approach

Even though people were quite positive about the ABC concepts, the actual condom use is low. It shows that there is no causality between what one knows and what one practices. The people who were against the condom use in the ABC concept actually responded positively when asked their opinion about condom use. Some stated 'it is safe, it protects you from HIV/AIDS'. Some senior adults in both villages do not know condoms at all. Some stated that they did not even know on which part of the body you use a condom.

People believed that their partners were faithful and that makes people not at risk of getting HIV/AIDS. Most of the people being interviewed stated that women were more faithful than men. Women whose husbands visit sex workers or have mistresses can do nothing about it. In the Christian village, there were a few men who left their wives to live with a mistress. This author interviewed Pan who left his wife for a year and came back. He stated the following reason for coming back home:

'I am old now and she (the mistress) is also old. I am also afraid of AIDS' (Pan, 2005).

Saroj, who admitted to have had mistresses, stated:

'Yeh, I had mistresses but I stopped now. I am old. Many friends of mine died of AIDS so I was scared' (Saroj, 2005).

The pastor of the Lamtharn Church gave an interview stating that condoms should be used to prevent the already infected spouse to transfer the HIV virus to his/her partner. In his view 'Abstinence' and 'Be faithful' is the best policy (Wichit, 2005). The pastor and the AIDS prevention staff emphasized on delaying pre-marital sex in training sessions. From in-depth interviews we learned that even some adolescent males who were active in the HIV/AIDS campaign and who agreed that abstinence is best, admitted that they already had sex. One of the Christian male youth members stated that he had sex with his girlfriend and he ejaculated outside to prevent pregnancy. A few more Christian male youths admitted to have had pre-marital sex but all the female youths reported to practice abstinence.

Contrary to the local church's condom policy under study, the director of CAM in Chiang Mai emphasized condom use on the basis that Thai men are not faithful. He does not think that promoting condoms will help the youth violating pre-marital sex because the youth already know about sex. He then turned to teach life skills. He said he did not mean to teach people to practice pre-marital sex but the staff should have given them proper knowledge. The staff must give the youth choices. Of course they do talk about 'Abstinence' and 'Be faithful' as moral practice but if the teenagers cannot practice then they must know how to prevent HIV/AIDS properly (Wutthi, 2005). He stated that 50 per cent of the Christian churches in Thailand are still conservative. Some church elders who preach about abstinence and faithfulness were caught in a buy-sex from female students in one of the Northern provinces. He himself finds these people hypocrites (ibid.). The headmen and public health volunteers in the Christian village did a good job in promoting the condom use. One of the headmen knows of the ABC concept.

One of the Buddhist youth members admitted to have had pre-marital sex and had to let his girlfriend abort their baby. Later he became an advocate of abstinence. He stated in an interview that about 30 per cent of the youth already practiced pre-marital sex. On the other hand, the head of the female youth strongly advocates abstinence and is against masturbation. She was one of the speakers in the youth camp. Phra Akom supports this group to practice traditional Northern style dance. The monk said he could not speak openly about condom use because monks have to adhere to celibacy. He let the public health office teach the people. He supports people to adhere to the third and fifth precepts of Buddhism. That's why some of the respondents added another concept to the ABC, that it should be ABCN—*Abstinence, Be faithful, use Condoms and use Non-intoxicants*. The people in the Christian village also consider the influence of alcohol more important than sexual morality or good knowledge. Respondents who often drink reported not to use condoms when they get drunk and engage in sex.

Other Factors

According to the Christians, drinking in moderation is allowed but what this author observed was that the Thai Christian males often drink together after work. They drink liquor distilled from rice which is very strong. From the Buddhist side, even though consuming alcohol is not allowed at all, most males drink after work.

To be able to interview them this author had to make an appointment on their sober day.

One of the reasons people in both villages think that abstinence is not doable is that teenagers have a looser bond from their parents than before. They go to big cities to study and live in dormitories. Chandra from the Buddhist village stated:

'They moved from a rural area to an urban place. They feel lonely. They fall in love easily. And they watch TV or porno films via pirated CDs or DVDs' (Chandra, 2005).

Blame the Media?

Most of the people blame the media for portraying the Western culture which promotes consumerism. Respondents also mention new communication technologies, such as Internet and mobile phones, make people contact one another easier than 10 years ago. Supote, one of the senior schoolteachers, said that the Buddhist village was on the verge of no return. People do not want to bike or walk. Everyone rides on a motorcycle. He used the example that the Rotary Club in Bankok provided 35 bicycles for students but asked for a 200 Baht transport fee. Only 13 bicycles got borrowed. Students prefer to buy a modern motorcycle, a second-hand one costs more than 20,000 Baht. Supote and the headman of the Buddhist village blame the Chartichai government in the 1990s to spoil the villagers with the 'changing the war zones into the market place policy'. This created a big real estate boom. Poor people in Chiang Rai sold their land and lived like kings for a while then became destitute because they didn't know how to handle money. This helped spread AIDS. Supote recounted about one head of *tambon* who died of AIDS:

He was very rich. He owned lots of land. He was the one who welcome those ministers who visited Chiang Rai. He lived in luxury. He could not eat rice soup in Chiang Rai because there was no singer. He had to go to Chiangmai (about 200 km away) to have a supper with live music there. Later he contracted HIV. Those people who wanted to gun him down did not need to waste the bullets. Later the creditors seized all the assets. (Supote, 2005)

Gender Inequality and Sexual Behaviour

People still prefer abstinence in single females but single males can exercise their sex drive with sex workers. During the time of my fieldwork, there were no brothels. They had disappeared and commercial sex had moved in 'grey zones' like karaoke bars, restaurants, and even department stores where salespersons sell casual sex (Wutthi, 2005). According to the Thai tradition, violating a single female by touching her is called *Phid Phee*—offending the ancestor ghosts—and the males need to pay a fine. During the time that this author was doing her field work, one Buddhist married man was caught drunk and dangling from a window of a single female neighbour and he had to pay a fine of 5,000 Baht for committing a *Phid Phee*.

For some Buddhists being interviewed, visiting sex workers is not violating the 'no commit adultery' precept nor the *Phid Phee* tradition because the sex workers give consent. Some Christians shared this view. But some Christians said it was wrong according to the Bible. Phra Akom stated it was normal for single men to visit sex workers (Akom, 2005).

Even though one-third of the people under study live below the poverty line, there is no evidence of reusing condoms. In the Buddhist village there has been a constant supply of condoms but only 40 per cent of them got taken away from the public health office (Chandra, 2005).

Looking at the attitude towards gender inequality, this author found that it has not changed much though. The findings are in line with the work of Vanlandingham et al. in 1998. They summarize their report as follows:

In the Thai context, these specific cultural features include a conception of male gender that places much emphasis on sexual drive and impulsiveness, a lack of emphasis on companionship within marriage, a view of commercial sex activity as a normal form of male entertainment, little stigma for regular commercial sex visitation by unmarried men, widespread acceptance by men and tolerance by some women of occasional commercial sex visitation by married men, a high value on harmonic social relations within a peer group context. All of these features serve to support the practice of extramarital sexual relations with commercial sex workers'. (p. 17)

Appendix

Table 14.A1
Age Group of the Christians

Age Group	Freq.	Per cent	Cum.
adolescents	29	28.16	28.16
early-aged adults	17	16.50	44.66
middle-aged adults	47	45.63	90.29
senior adults	10	9.71	100.00
Total	103	100.00	

Table 14.A2
Age Group of the Buddhists

Age Group	Freq.	Per cent	Cum.
adolescents	34	21.12	21.12
early-aged adults	42	26.09	47.20
middle-aged adults	63	39.13	86.34
senior adults	22	13.66	100.00
Total	161	100.00	

Table 14.A3
Level of Education of the Christians

Level of Education	Freq.	Per cent	Cum.
no schooling	15	14.56	14.56
primary	44	42.72	57.28
junior high	21	20.39	77.67
senior high	9	8.74	86.41
diploma	1	0.97	87.38
bachelor	13	12.62	100.00
Total	103	100.00	

Table 14.A4
Level of Education of the Buddhists

Level of Education	Freq.	Per cent	Cum.
no schooling	13	8.07	8.07
primary	92	57.14	65.22
junior high	30	18.63	83.85
senior high	17	10.56	94.41
diploma	1	0.62	95.03
bachelor	8	4.97	100.00
Total	161	100.00	

Table 14.A5
Occupation of the Christians

Occupation	Freq.	Per cent	Cum.
agriculturist	4	3.88	3.88
labourer	27	26.21	30.10
low-ranked gov officials	4	3.88	33.98
high-ranked gov officials	1	0.97	34.95
employee	12	11.65	46.60

(*Table 14.A5 continued*)

(*Table 14.A5 continued*)

self-employed	14	13.59	60.19
student	23	22.33	82.52
unemployed	18	17.48	100.00
Total	103	100.00	

Table 14.A6
Occupation of the Buddhists

Occupation	Freq.	Per cent	Cum.
religious practitioner	1	0.63	0.63
agriculturist	41	25.63	26.25
labourer	29	18.13	44.38
low-ranked gov off	4	2.50	46.88
high-ranked gov off		0.63	47.50
employee	16	10.00	57.50
self-employed	25	15.63	73.13
student	27	16.88	90.00
unemployed	13	8.13	98.13
retired with pension	3	1.88	100.00
Total	160	100.00	

Table 14.A7
Level of Income per Head per Year of the Christians

Level of Income per Head per Month	Freq.	Per cent	Cum.
below poverty line	31	30.39	30.39
low income	54	52.94	83.33
fairly low income	8	7.84	91.18
average income	6	5.88	97.06
high income	3	2.94	100.00
Total	102	100.00	

Table 14.A8
Level of Income per Head per Year of the Buddhists

Level of Income per Head per Month	Freq.	Per cent	Cum.
below poverty line	49	31.01	31.01
low income	74	46.84	77.85
fairly low income	22	13.92	91.77
average income	10	6.33	98.10
fairly high income	1	0.63	98.73
high income	2	1.27	100.00
Total	158	100.00	

Notes

1. To protect the confidentiality of the respondents, names of key informants and villages are fictitious.
2. This author/research is still working on more variables and inferential statistics as part of her Ph.D. thesis. At this stage only descriptive statistics have been included.

References

Aheto, D. and K. Gbesemete. 2004. 'Rural Perspectives on HIV/AIDS Prevention: A Comparative Study of Thailand and Ghana'. Available online at http://www.sciencedirect.com/science?_ob=ArticleURL&_aset (Downloaded in November 2004).

Akom, P. 2005. Interview. Chiang Rai: Tonnam Temple. 10 September.

Baltimore Sun. 2002. 'Fighting AIDS in Asia—In Thailand, the Armed Forces Help Beat Back an Epidemic'. Available online at www.utopia-asia.com/aidsth.htm (Downloaded on 15 October 2003).

Barnett, T. and A. Whiteside. 2002. AIDS in the Twenty-first Century: Disease and Globlaization. New York: Palgrave Macmillan.

Boonmongkol, P., P. Pradupmuk and S. Raungsaun. 1998. State of the Art Review in Socio-economic and Behaviour Research on AIDS. Mahidol University. Bangkok: Roongsaeng Press.

Boonyabuddhi, N. 2001. 'Sex, AIDS and STDs among Youth in the Year 2001', AIDSNet Newsletter, 3(1): 14–19.

Borthwick, P. 1999. 'Developing Culturally Appropriate HIV/AIDS Education Programs in Northern Thailand', in P. Jackson and N. Cook (eds). Genders and Sexualities in Modern Thailand, pp. 206–225. Chiang Mai: Silkworm Books.

Bressan, L. 2000. A Meeting of Worlds: The Interaction of Christian Missionaries and Thai Culture (first ed.). Bangkok: Assumption University Press.

Brewster-Lee, D. 2003. 'AIDS Prevention—A Faith-Based Perspective', The CCIH Forum (13): 28.

Card, J.J., T. Benner, J.P. Shields and N. Feinstein. 2001. 'The HIV/AIDS Prevention Program Archive (HAPPA): A Collection of Promising Prevention Programs in a Box', AIDS Education and Prevention, 13(1): 1–28.

Catholic Committe on HIV/AIDS Under Catholic Bishop's Conference of Thailand. 2004.

Chandra. 2005, September 9. Interview. Chiang Rai: Tonnam village.

Chantavanich, S., S. Paul, P. Wangsiripaisal, P. Suwannachot, A. Amaraphibal and A. Beesey. 2000. Cross-border Migration and HIV Vulnerability in the Thai–Myanmar Border Sangkhlaburi and Ranong. Bangkok: Asian Research Center for Migration, Institute of Asian Studies.

Christian Misssion Region 2. (n.d.). Christian Mission Region 2 from 2003–2007. Chiang Rai: The Church of Christ in Thailand.

Directory 2004. Catholic Services to People Living with HIV/AIDS. Bangkok: Suchart Press.

Glock, C.Y. and R. Stark. 1968. 'Dimensions of Religious Commitment', in R. Robertson (ed.). Sociology of Religion. Harmondsworth: Penguin.

Hill, P.C. and R.W. Hood, Jr. 1999. Measures of Religiosity (first ed.). Birmingham, Alabama: Religious Education Press.

Inter-Faith Networking on AIDS. 2004. Access for All: The Faith Community Responding. Bangkok: Inter-Faith Networking on AIDS.

Jackson, P. 2003. Buddhadasa, Theravada Buddhism and Modernist Reform in Thailand. Chiang Mai: Silkworm Books.

Jemmott III, J.B. and L.S. Jemmott. 1994. 'Interventions for Adolescents in Community Settings', in R.J. DiClemente and J.L. Peterson (eds). Preventing AIDS: Theories and Methods of Behavioural Interventions, pp. 141–174. New York: Plenum Press.

Jonson, E.P. 1988. AIDS: Myths, Facts & Ethics (first ed.). Sydney: Pergamon Press.

Klausner, W. 1993. 'Popular Buddhism in North East Thailand', in W. Klausner (ed.). Reflections on Thai Culture, pp. 159–176. Bangkok: The Siam Society under Royal Patronage.

Lamtharn Christ Church. 2006. 65 years of Lamtharn. Chiang Rai, Thailand: Lamtharn Christ Church.

Logie, D. 1994. 'Does God Want Orphans?' Available online at http://bmj.bmjjournals.com/cgi/content/full/309/6954/614 (Downloaded on 24 February 2005).

Long, C. and K. Plater. 2004, July 14. *ABC not as easy as 1-2-3. Access For All: The Faith Community Responds*, p. 4. Bangkok: Ecumenical Advocacy Alliance.

Lyttleton, C. 2000. *Endangered Relations: Negotiating Sex and AIDS in Thailand* (first ed.). Amsterdam: The Harwood Academic Publishers.

Malikhao. P. 2004. 'An HIV/AIDS Prevention Programme from a Thai Buddhist Perspective: A Case Study of the Sankampang Ruam Jai Group, Chiangmai, Thailand', presented in Postgraduate Research Conference 2004: School of Social Science, University of Queensland.

———. 2006a. Field Work Report. Australia: School of Social Science, University of Queensland.

———. 2006b. 'A Comparative Study of Two Thai Communities with Differing Buddhist versus Christian Participatory Approaches to HIV/AIDS Prevention'. Paper presented at World Congress on Communication for Development, 25–27 October 2006, Rome.

Marsh, I. 1996. *Making Sense of Society: An Introduction to Sociology* (first ed.). London: Longman.

Maticka-Tyndale, E., D. Elkins, M. Haswell-Elkins, D. Rujkarakorn, T. Kuyyakanond and K. Stam. 1997. 'Contexts and Patterns of Men's Commercial Sexual Partnerships in Northeastern Thailand: Implications for AIDS Prevention', *Social Science and Medicine*, 44(2): 199–213.

McGuire, M. 2002. *Religion: The Social Context*. Belmont, CA: Wadsworth Thomson Learning.

Ministry of Public Health. 2004. *AIDS Patients According to District and Province*, Bangkok: Ministry of Public Health.

Mosley, W.H. 2003. 'The ABCs of HIV/AIDS Prevention—Seeking the Evidence and Telling the Truth', The CCIH Forum (13).

Mulder, N. 1990. 'Inside Thai Society: An interpretation of everyday life'. Bangkok: DK Books.

Nakhorn. 2005, September. Interview. Chiang Rai: Tonnam village.

Norwegian Church AID and UNICEF. 2004. *Buddhism and AIDS Prevention, Invitation to Buddhist Pre Conference Integrating Interfaith Statements into the XV International AIDS Conference*. Bangkok.

Nozaki, A. 2003. 'Buddhist Way of Rural Development in Thailand', in A. Nozaki and C. Baker (eds). *Village Communities, States, and Traders: Essays in Honour of Chatthip Nartsupha* (first ed.), pp. 93–110. Bangkok: Sangsan Publishing House.

Ntseane, P.G. 2004. 'Cultural Dimensions of Sexuality: Empowerment Challenge for HIV/AIDS Prevention in Botswana', Chiang Mai, Thailand.

Nuansri. 2005, November. Interview. Chiang Rai: Lamtharn village.

Pan. 2005. November. Interview. Chiang Rai: Lamtharn village.

Panos. 2003. *Missing the Message?: 20 Years of Learning from HIV/AIDS*. London: The Panos Institute.

Paterson, G. (n.d.). *Church Leadership & HIV/AIDS: The New Commitment*. Geneva, Switzerland: Ecumenical Advocacy Alliance.

Payutto, P. 1998. *Sustainable Development*. Bangkok: Buddhadham Foundation.

Poolcharoen, W. 1998. 'Experience from Thailand', in Partners in Prevention: International Case Studies of Effective Health Promotion Practice in HIV/AIDS. Available online at http://www.unaids.org.

Porapakkham, Y., S. Pramarnpol, S. Athibhoddhi and R. Bernhard. 1995. *The Evolution of HIV/AIDS Policy in Thailand: 1984–1994*. ASEAN Institute for Health Development, Mahidol University Kenan Institute.

Punyakammo, S. 2004. *The Cause of AIDS and Buddhism in the Time of AIDS*. Chiang Mai: the Sangha Metta Project.

Quintero, M. 2004, July 13. 'Does the Condom Fit?: Use of Condoms Debated in Faith-Based Communities', *Access For All: The Faith Community Responds*, p. 4.

Rawls, J. 1980. 'Kantian Constructivism in Moral Theory', *The Journal of Philosophy*, 77(9): 515–572.

Reynolds, V. and R. Tanner. 1995. *The Social Ecology of Religion*. New York and Oxford: Oxford University Press.

Sae Tang, P. and P. Nantachaipan. 2001. *A Synthesis of Knowledge from Direct Experience: Home Care for HIV Infected Persons, AIDS Patients and Their Families, The Church of Christ in Thailand AIDS Ministry (1991–2000)*. Chiang Mai: the Church of Christ in Thailand, AIDS Ministry.

Saengtienchai, C., J. Knodel, M. Vanlandingham and A. Pramualtratana. 1999. 'Prostitutes are Better than Lovers: Wives' Views on the Extramarital Behavior of Thai Men', in P. Jackson and N. Cook (eds). *Genders & Sexualities in Modern Thailand*, pp. 78–92. Chiang Mai: Silkworm Books.

Sandfort, T. 1998. 'Homosexual and Bisexual Behaviours in European Countries', in M. Hubert, N. Bajos and T. Sandfort (eds). *Sexual Behaviour and HIV/AIDS in Europe* (first ed.), pp. 68–105. London: UCL Press.

Saroj. 2005 September. Interview. Chiang Rai: Lamtharn village.

Servaes, J. 1999. *Communication for Development: One World, Multiple Cultures* (first ed.). Cresskill, New Jersey: Hampton Press, Inc.

Servaes, J. and P. Malikhao. 2004. *Communication and Sustainable Development.* Rome: FAO.

Somchai. 2005. October 1. Interview. Chiangrai: Tonnam village.

Stecker, C.C. 2003. 'Doing A & B Well: Behavioural Change with Youth in an Era of HIV/AIDS', The CCIH Forum13: 28.

Sthapitanonda, P., K. Kunphai, P. Jatiket and P. Jatiket. 2003. *Health Communication: The Potential of Mass Media for Health Promotion* (Thai language). Bangkok: Chulalongkorn University Book Centre.

Sukda, S. 2000. *Sexual Values and Risk Behaviour of Students in State University.* Bangkok: Chulalongkorn University, Bangkok.

Supote. 2005. October 10. Interview. Chiang Rai: Tonnam village.

The Balm in Gilead. 2004. *A Theological Call to Action.* New York: The Balm in Gilead Inc.

The Church of Christ in Thailand. 2004. *Seventy Years of Blessings: The Church of Christ in Thailand 1934–2004.* Bangkok: The Church of Christ in Thailand.

The Correspondent. 2004a. July 12. 'Access for All in AIDS Prevention at the 15th International AIDS Conference', *The Correspondent:*1–3.

———. 2004b. July 12. 'HIV/AIDS in Thailand', *The Correspondent:*3

———. 2004c. July 15. 'CNN vs ABC: the Life You Can Choose', *The Correspondent:* 12.

Timmins, P., C. Gallois, M. McCamish and D.J. Terry. 1998. 'Sources of Information about HIV/AIDS and Perceived Risk of Infection among Heterosexual Young Adults: 1989 and 1994', *Australian Journal of Social Issue,* 33(2): 179–198.

Tonnam village. 2004. *Village Funds and National Urban Community 'Tonnam'.* Unpublished manuscript. Chiang Rai, Thailand.

Treeaekanukul, L. 2004. Lamtharn Christ Church (fictitious name) and the Christian Community, Chiang Rai.

UNAIDS. (n.d.). *Funding Priorities for the HIV/AIDS Crisis in Thailand.* UNAIDS.

———. 1998. 'Connecting Lower HIV Infection Rates with Changes in Sexual Behaviour in Thailand: Data Collection and Comparison'. Geneva: UNAIDS.

———. 1999a. 'Reducing Girls' Vulnerability to HIV/AIDS: The Thai Approach (case study)'. Geneva: UNAIDS.

———. 1999b. 'UNAIDS and Nongovernmental Organizations'. Geneva: Joint United Nations Programme on HIV/AIDS.

———. 2000a. 'HIV and Health-Care Reform in Phayao'. Geneva: UNAIDS.

———. 2000b. 'HIV and Health-care reform in Phayao: from crisis to opportunity'. Geneva: UNAIDS.

———. 2000c. 'Evaluation of the 100% Condom Programme in Thailand'. Geneva: UNAIDS and AIDS Division, Ministry of Public Health, Thailand.

———. 2004. 'World AIDS Campaign 2004'. Available online at http://wac@unaids.org (Accessed on 12 November 2004).

UNAIDS, UNICEF and WHO. 2002. 'Epidemiological Fact Sheets on HIV/AIDS and Sexually Transmitted Infections in Thailand'. Available online at www.unaids.org (Downloaded in November 2003).

UNFPA. (n.d.). *Preventing HIV/AIDS among Adolescents through Integrated Communication Programming.* New York: United Nations Population Fund.

UNICEF. 2003a. 'Strategy Monitoring & Evaluation Framework Buddhist Leadership Initiative.'Available online at www.unicef.org.

———. 2003b, August 25–29. 'Buddhist Participation in Community and National Responses to HIV/AIDS Report of Proceedings of Regional Seminar'. Paper presented at the Buddhist Participation in Community and National Responses to HIV/AIDS, Bangkok.

UNICEF and UNAIDS. 2003. 'How to Prevent HIV Infection.' Available online at www.unicef.org/aids.

UNICEF, World Conference of Religions for Peace, and UNAIDS. 2004. *What Religious Leaders Can Do about HIV/AIDS: Action for Children and Young People.* New York: UNICEF, World Conference of Religions for Peace and UNAIDS.

UPI. 1998. 'Thai "AIDS Colony" Scheme Draws Fire', in *Utopia Asia 2003.* Available online at http://www.utopia.asia.com/aidsth.htm (Accessed on 15 December 2003).

Vanlandingham, M., J. Knodel, C. Saengtienchai and A. Pramualtratana. 1998. 'In the company of friends: Peer influence on Thai male extramarital sex'. *Social Science and Medicine,* 47(12): 1993–2011.

Viddhanaphuti, C. 1999. *A Cultural Approach to HIV/AIDS Prevention and Care*. Chiang Mai, Thailand: UNESCO.

Visalo, P. 2003. *Thai Buddhism in the Future: Trend and Ways Out of Crisis* (in Thai language). Bangkok: Sodsri-Saritwong Foundation.

Wasi, P. (n.d.). *AIDS and the Revolution in Humanity. In Buddhism in the Time of AIDS*. Chiang Mai: The Sangha Metta Project.

Wasi, P. 2003. *Sufficient Economy and Civic Society* (in Thai language). Bangkok: Mau Chao Ban.

Wat Phra Bapu Namphu. 2004. AIDS, the Danger that we have to realise for today prevention of the youngsters [brochure].

Weeks, J. 1995. *Invented Moralities: Sexual Values in an Age of Uncertainty* (first ed.). Oxford: Polity Press.

WHO. 2003. *Global Health-Sector Strategy for HIV/AIDS 2003–2007*. Geneva, Switzerland: World Health Organization.

Wichit.2005. In-depth interview 15th September 2005.

Wilai. 2005, September. Interview. Chiang Rai: Tonnam village.

Wutthi. S. 2005, December 20. Interview. Chaing Mai: CAM office.

Yupin. 2005. September. Interview. Chiang Rai: Tonnam village.

Fighting AIDS with Edutainment: Building on the Soul City Experience in South Africa

15

THOMAS TUFTE

Introduction

How do you communicate about HIV/AIDS on a large scale? How do you make people not just knowledgeable about HIV/AIDS but really make them change behaviour and especially take preventive measures to avoid the spread of the disease? How do you communication-wise address the underlying development problems which call for a communication strategy for social change? These are key questions that many governments, NGOs/Community-Based Organizations (CBOs) and multilateral and bilateral development agencies—despite more than 25 years of experience—still are debating. There is no consensus on how to go about the fight against HIV/AIDS, but in the midst of these struggles to curb the pandemic, edutainment, also known as entertainment-education, has gained growing prominence as a communication strategy which can respond to both the more behavioural challenges as well as the challenges of articulating social change via communication. The issue in this chapter is thus to explore what roles edutainment can play in developing successful strategies in the fight against HIV/AIDS.

First, a general introduction to edutainment will uncover how edutainment is defined and how it can be distinguished into three distinct 'generations' which all draw on the same communication tools. Secondly, the theory will be countered by the experience of using edutainment in the South African NGO 'Soul City Institute of Health and Development Communication'. As the longest running South African multimedia experience in the fight against HIV/AIDS, Soul City is seen as a successful example of edutainment in the fight against HIV/AIDS. However, what exactly does their success consist in? Soul City is a multimedia communication vehicle which combines the production of TV-fiction with radio drama and with a massive production and subsequent distribution of print materials through newspapers and through educational systems as well as through civil society. All the media products circle around the same fictional universe, a fictional township called Soul City. The same characters have thus been appearing and reappearing on TV, in radio and in print through the past almost 15 years. Since 1999 there has also been a strong advocacy component in Soul City's communication vehicle. Since Soul City began broadcasting on TV in 1994, HIV/AIDS has been a recurrent issue amongst their thematic foci, present in all campaigns so far. Thirdly, the chapter will conclude by highlighting a number of critical issues to address in the further development of edutainment as a strategy to fight HIV/AIDS.

The hypothesis of this chapter is that—based on the Soul City experience, and with a further elaboration and adaptation of the edutainment strategy to the complex issue of HIV/AIDS— edutainment can become an even more powerful instrument in combating HIV/AIDS then it already is. This is based on two assumptions: 1. Conceptual clarity is lacking and could be improved in a lot of the work with edutainment. Both researchers and practitioners need to further develop an understanding of the implications the different edutainment approaches entail; 2. In order to increase more sustained social change with edutainment strategies in the fight against HIV/AIDS, increased activities and work is required within what I call the 'third generation' of edutainment approaches—that is where edutainment strategies comply mostly with the principles of communication for social change.

Prior to entering further into the case of Soul City, let me briefly introduce the field of edutainment.

Edutainment

As the field of communication for development evolved in the post-war era and onwards, edutainment evolved as a communication tool used particularly in health communication, but also in other fields as agricultural development and more recently even in conflict resolution and peace-building. The actual use of mass media and particularly television series and radio drama for educational purposes and to spread messages has thus been around for a long time.

At the core of edutainment lies the use of drama and entertainment for educational purposes. Most often it is done by integrating instructive or best practices into a fictional narrative, often a radio drama or a television series, and thereby communicating to the audiences how they can tackle specific issues, often health issues, in their everyday life. A large part of the entertainment value of the drama lies in the moral dilemmas and drama that are spun around the problems that are articulated by the health problem the characters may have. In many countries, these radio drama and television series have obtained very high ratings, thus securing high reach and exposure of the problems and messages that are to be communicated. For example in 1999, with their fourth television series, Soul City managed to reach 16.2 million South Africans. 79 per cent of the 16–24-year-olds watched Soul City, 71 per cent of the 25–35-year-olds and the percentage gradually decreased to 49 per cent of the 46-year-olds and over (Soul City 4—Impact Evaluation, 2000).

At a strategic level, the aim with edutainment varies; from promoting individual behaviour change to supporting social change; from enhancing social mobilization to articulating peoples participation and empowering minority or marginalized groups to collective action. The main point to emphasize here is that edutainment can and is being used as a strategic tool with a varying diversity of agendas. There is thus abundance and diversity in current communication practice which can sustain the argument that edutainment is not just one uniform communication strategy, that of social marketing conceived as far back as in the 1930s (see Tufte, 2005). It is much more. Considering the characteristic integration of entertainment with education and also recognizing the multiple epistemological, theoretical and methodological foundations informing the field, my proposed definition of edutainment (elaborated upon in Tufte, 2005) is:

> Edutainment is the use of entertainment as a communicative practice crafted to strategically communicate about development issues in a manner and with a purpose that can range from the more narrowly defined social marketing of individual behaviours to the liberating and citizen-driven articulation of social change agendas.

The edutainment practices we observe today reflect many epistemologies, methodologies and overall objectives within strategic communication. Epistemologically, the foundations are from scholars and strategists rooted in different schools of thought. As a means of storytelling, the edutainment practices reflect varying cultural traditions, and strategically, edutainment reflect a breadth of organizational traditions, trajectories, priorities and constraints. Furthermore, varying political agendas influence edutainment objectives. Finally, varying media infrastructures and a breadth in the choice of communication tools use result if very different implementation strategies (See for example: Bouman, 1999; Fuenzalida, 1994; Gao, 2005; La Pastina, 1999; McKee et al., 2004; Parker, 2005; Skeie, 2005; Singhal et al., 2004). In an attempt to organize the differing practices of edutainment, I have previously argued to break the field of entertainment-education, or edutainment, down into three generations (Tufte, 2005). As assembled in Box 15.1, the distinctions refer to different conceptualizations of problem definition, notion of change, culture, education and of the audience, the levels of society where interventions are sought, and so forth. First generation edutainment refers not least to the strong tradition of social marketing used in health communication since the 1970s and still very prevalent. Here the focus is on individual behaviour change. The second generation edutainment refers to those strategies—as Soul City—that have a broader scope than the first generation. Acknowledging the complexity of social, health and other developmental problems, second generation edutainment connects the focus on individual behaviour change with the participatory paradigm, although still in a restricted manner compared to the ideals of participation, as for example, Paulo Freire formulated them (Freire, 1968). However, second generation edutainment is the paradigmatic bridge-builder between two previously very separate schools of thought; the more marketing- and diffusion-oriented school and the participatory school of thought. Thus, the third generation edutainment define the problems dealt as more fundamental social critique of a specific development problem, leading to aim of challenging power relations, advocating social change and placing empowerment and citizen participation at the core of the strategy. It is the form of edutainment which is reflected in the 'forum theatre' of Augusto Boal and his followers (Boal, 1979; Singhal, 2004) or in the work of the Nicaraguan NGO '*Puntos de Encuentro*' (see Rodriguez, 2005). The key distinctions between the three generations of edutainment (or entertainment-education) are reflected in Box 15.1.

Box 15.1 (De–)Constructing the Field of Entertainment-Education

Entertainment-Education	1st Generation	2nd Generation	3rd Generation
Definition of Problem	Lack of Information	Lack of Information and Skills Inappropriate Contexts Structural Inequalities	Structural Inequalities Power Relations Social Conflict
Notion of Entertainment	Instrument: Tool for Message Conveying	Dynamic Genre: Tool for Change	Process: Popular Culture Genre as Form of Expression
Notion of Culture	Culture as Barrier	Culture as Ally	Culture as 'Way of Life'
Notion of Catalyst	External Change Agent Targeting X	External Catalyst in Partnership with Community	Internal Community Member
Notion of Education	Banking Pedagogy Persuasion	Life Skills, Didactics	Liberating Pedagogy
Notion of Audience	Segments Target Groups Passive	Participants Target Groups Active	Citizens Active
What is Communicated?	Messages	Messages and Situations	Social Issues and Problems
Notion of Change	Individual Behaviour Social Norms	Individual Behaviour Social Norms Structural Conditions	Individual Behaviour Social Norms Power Relations Structural Conditions
Expected Outcome	Change in Norms and Individual Behaviour Numerical Result	Change in Norms and Individual Behaviour Public and Private Debate	Articulation of Social and Political Process Structural Change Collective Action
Duration of Intervention	Short Term	Short and Long Term	Short and Long Term

In the case of HIV/AIDS, the issue is complex and must be presented as such. A lot of HIV/AIDS communication can be identified as having the characteristics of first generation edutainment, with a focus on individual behaviour change—which often has been about the promotion of condoms. However, considering the complexity of the issue, which will be elaborated upon below, part of the problem in the fight against HIV/AIDS has been the narrow definition of the problem and the subsequent narrow edutainment response. HIV/AIDS is obviously a significantly different and more difficult communicative challenge than for example communicating about tobacco and arguing for the audiences to stop smoking.

The point of highlighting Soul City's edutainment model in this chapter is due to the fact that Soul City has responded—in terms of communication—to some of the complexity that HIV/AIDS poses, behaviourally, socially, politically. In practice this is seen in their bridging between traditionally very separate paradigms encountered within theories and methods of communication for development. Soul City's edutainment vehicle is developed and used within the social reality of South Africa, elaborating excellent social marketing strategies and combining them with participatory components that promote dialogue, challenge power structures and promote community-based action. The advocacy part of Soul City's communication strategy—an element which was formally institutionalized into their work in 1999—coincides with a growing international trend towards social change agendas, within the field of communication for development (Gumucio-Dagron and Tufte, 2006; Papa, Singhal and Papa, 2006). Unlike many communication interventions, the point with Soul City is that it operates strategically within three interlinked units of change: the individual, the community and the broader society. As such, it reflects a holistic, multilevel and culture-sensitive communication strategy which lies in line with the principles argued, by UNAIDS in their communication framework (UNAIDS/Penn State, 1999; Airhihenbuwa and Obregon, 2000), by Panos in for example their summary report of 20 years of HIV/AIDS communication (Panos, 2003) and increasingly also by others in the development community. However, before exploring Soul City's communication practice more in detail, let me first present some of the communication challenges that HIV/AIDS poses today.

HIV/AIDS

The Present Situation

The impact of the HIV/AIDS pandemic is well known. Some 40 million people are living with HIV/AIDS, over 25 million of them in sub-Saharan Africa. Over 20 million people are dead of AIDS since the beginning of the epidemic (Panos, 2005). While in Southern Africa HIV/AIDS is a devastating epidemic striking and affecting all sectors of society, it is in Asia a 'ticking bomb', with scary statistics and perspectives, considering not least the epidemiological developments in India and China. The impact of HIV/AIDS so far has been tremendous in Africa. Estimates in 1991 predicted that in sub-Saharan Africa, by the end of the decade, nine million people would be infected and five million would die (Piot in UNAIDS, 2000:7).The figures in 2000 were more than three times that size indicating that the impact of HIV/AIDS in the 1990 had been almost *threefold underestimated*. As Kofi Annan said at the UN Security Council meeting in January of 2000: 'The impact of AIDS is no less destructive than war itself, and by some measures, far worse'.

The underestimation of HIV/AIDS in the 1990s has had catastrophic consequences, resulting in a situation now where the pandemic not only requires urgent but also substantial and long-term responses to be efficiently combated. This is happening, with the establishment of the Global Fund and with growing budgets amongst both the bilateral and multilateral agencies, in addition to also a growing international civil society involved in the fight against HIV/AIDS. Also, at country level, national action plans have been developed most places, as have poverty reduction strategy papers. Part of the recent impetus in the fight against HIV/AIDS has been the WHO-driven '3 by 5' campaign, which aimed at getting three million AIDS-struck people into a treatment programme by the end of 2005. This came to dominate the HIV/AIDS agenda in a very powerful manner in these years, where funding for prevention activities came to suffer and loose substantial international attention. The 'trench war' of 'either prevention or treatment' was revived during the '3 by 5' campaign. Treatment focus was in focus to a degree that the Working Group under the UN Millennium Project in 2005 stated:

> As the United Nations General Assembly Special Session (UNGASS) Declaration of Commitment stated, prevention must be the mainstay of the response to the epidemic, as only by preventing new infection can the epidemic eventually be brought under control. The long-over-due-drive to expand treatment—energized by the WHO/UNAIDS initiative to provide antiretroviral therapy to 3 million people by 2005 and large influxes of funds—has mobilized activists, national governments, and the United Nations system, and now dominates the AIDS agenda at all levels. Every effort must now be made to bring the same sense of urgency and excitement to meeting ambitious prevention goals. Unless prevention remains a fundamental priority of leaders, donors and those who battle the epidemic on the ground, tens of millions more will become infected and the need for treatment will grow inexorably. As is now widely recognized, treatment can assist prevention in important ways, but treatment alone will not bring the epidemic under control. (UN Millenium Project, 2005:4)

We can observe that HIV/AIDS has achieved growing political attention but at the same time, a strong disagreement exists on what to prioritize—prevention or treatment. The ideal scenario is to have room for both.

Communication-wise, the growing political attention to HIV/AIDS could and should consequently result in ambitious, long-term responses bringing the mainstream practice of communication strategies beyond the traditional concept of short-term campaigning. Long-term responses, I would argue, would entail a process-oriented ongoing perspective with no fixed time-frame. Soul City is an example of this sort of ongoing perspective, as is for example the Nicaragua NGO 'Puntos de Encuentro' or the Tanzanian 'FEMINA Health Information Project'. However, the funding mechanisms, both to these examples and to the field in general, follow short-term cycles of one to three years, most commonly.

The Complexity of HIV/AIDS

A core challenge, when wanting to design, implement and evaluate HIV/AIDS communication programmes, is to recognize the complexity of HIV/AIDS and strategize and plan accordingly. Panos, one of the oldest and most important international NGOs in the field of HIV/AIDS communication and prevention, has since 1986 been arguing for a number of key aspects to be considered when addressing the issue of HIV/AIDS prevention. These issues, highlighted below, reflect the Panos analysis, and have been reconfirmed in their most recent AIDS Programme 2001–2005 (Panos, 2001). The issues are:

- HIV/AIDS is both a cause and consequence of poverty and underdevelopment;
- Discrimination and stigma;
- Sexual equality;
- Openness and deep-rooted change;
- Political leadership;
- A chronic crisis, not an emergency;
- Money is only part of the answer, and can be an obstacle to HIV prevention
- Informed public debate.

While Panos focuses on articulating public debate, there are many other methodological approaches whereby to respond to this analysis of the causes—one is the use of edutainment. Fundamentally, the crucial issue is to understand the theoretical underpinnings of the method chosen, understand how communication works but equally—as the above eight points suggest— understand the nature of the pandemic and the social, cultural, political and economic contexts within which it has be able to spread so dramatically. Recognizing—and profoundly understanding—these contexts is the first step in designing any communication strategy.

HIV/AIDS Communication and Programming

The new priority the international community currently is giving to HIV/AIDS is being accompanied by an ongoing critical re-examination of the effectiveness of existing HIV/AIDS prevention programmes. One of the early but influential processes of re-examination of HIV/AIDS communication was the theoretically innovative communication framework which UNAIDS has developed. The process was conducted by UNAIDS between 1998 and 2000. In 1998–1999 UNAIDS conducted a major analysis of communications programming which involved consultations in all major regions of the world and which culminated in the publication of *A Communications Framework for HIV/AIDS: A New Direction* in late 1999.

Based on a review of the literature and of experiences in the field, participants in the global consultations noted that most current theories and models of HIV communication programming did not provide an adequate foundation on which to develop communications interventions for HIV/AIDS in the regions. They further noted the inadequacy and limitations of current theories and the models derived from them (UNAIDS, 1999). As such, they resonate with what Soul City, in practice, experienced. Chief among the weaknesses they identified were:

- The simple, linear relationship between individual knowledge and action, which underpinned many earlier interventions, does not take into account the variation among the political, socio-economic and cultural contexts that prevail in the regions;
- External decision-making processes that cater to rigid, narrowly focussed and short-term interests tend to overlook the benefits of long term, internally derived, broad-based solutions;
- There is an assumption that decisions about HIV/AIDS prevention are based on rational, volitional thinking with no regard for more true-to-life emotional responses to engaging in sexual behaviour;
- There is an assumption that creating awareness through media campaigns will necessarily lead to behaviour change;
- There is an assumption that a simple strategy designed to trigger a once in a lifetime behaviour, such as immunization, would be adequate for changing and maintaining complex, lifelong behaviours, such as consistent condom use;
- There is a nearly exclusive focus on condom promotion to the exclusion of the need to address the importance and centrality of social contexts, including government policy, socio-economic status, culture, gender relations and spirituality; and
- Approaches based on traditional family planning and population programme strategies tend to target HIV/AIDS prevention to women, so that women, rather than men, are encouraged to initiate the use of condoms.

The findings, despite being from the turn of the millennium, remain very relevant and still strike the core challenges in HIV/AIDS communication. Many of the points highlighted were reaffirmed in the final declaration of the UN-Roundtable on Communication for Development held in Nicaragua in November 2001 (www.comminit.com/roundtable2/index.html) and again in the report Panos wrote in 2003 retrieving key lessons learnt from 20 years of HIV/AIDS communication. This document title 'Missing the Message' hints at the core challenge (Panos, 2003). The findings of the UNAIDS report are also seen in the ongoing analysis and debates articulated in and by a network facilitated by the Rockefeller Foundation (RF) from 1996–2003 and since by the Communication for Social Change Consortium, headed by Denise Gray-Felder, who also led the debate while working in RF. This network has—in a series of Bellagio-meetings— brought together communication experts, researchers and practitioners, including grassroots and community-based NGOs through to international NGOs and major multilateral and bilateral organizations(Rockefeller Foundation, 1997, 1999). The network, dealing more broadly with communication for social change, has in its debates about communication for social change emphasized that while mass education campaigns aimed at changing individual behaviour play an essential role in AIDS prevention, they are highly unlikely to be successful or sustainable unless they are accompanied by deep-rooted social changes which will only result from internally-driven change processes, including informed and inclusive public debate (all relevant documentation assembled on the CFSC Consortium website: www.communicationforsocialchange.org).

Many millions of dollars have been spent on individually targeted education campaigns, and many of these campaigns have had important impacts. Increasingly, as these different networks and debates show, concern is mounting that these campaigns are at best insufficient, in achieving the kind of long-term, sustainable and rooted changes in society that are required for HIV/AIDS to be confronted. While the critical analysis has developed over the past years the growing focus now is on how to transform the critique and recommendations into practice: country-level implementation of strategies that reflect the lessons learnt is the core challenge now. This is reflected in the thematic focus for the 10th UN-Roundtable held by UNESCO in Ethiopia in February 2007 but also in the whole set-up of the first World Congress on Communication for Development which brings together researchers, policy-makers and programme implementers. In emphasizing the need for better implementation, a growing tendency seen is to relate HIV/AIDS challenges with those of *good governance* and *accountability*. This is seen in DFID's recent policy paper on governance which is being followed up by other bilateral donors that also are developing policy papers on governance issues. Focussing on governance and connecting HIV/AIDS to governance issues is not least a way to try to hold governments accountable to implement, what often on paper, are fine words.

What the above overview of current policy debates and actual development trends within HIV/AIDS communication and programming illustrates is that the HIV/AIDS communication debate has advanced far beyond a discussion only about individual behaviour change—at least at the level of policy and advocacy. However, the fact is that this more overall discursive level is not always translated into practice. This is where one big challenge lies.

Soul City's Edutainment Model

It is in the context of the above theoretical and methodological preoccupations and discussions that Soul City proves a useful case to analyse. The results of Soul City are visible and substantial: massive awareness raising and change in behaviour, social mobilization, public debate in the media and influence on legislation are some of the visible results (Goldstein et al., 2005). Soul City has developed into an innovative and important agent in the poverty-oriented work around health, HIV/AIDS, women's and children's rights in South Africa. In recent years Soul City has furthermore set up a regional programme, so their experience with edutainment can be shared with NGOs in neighbouring countries in order to further advance the Soul City approach to edutainment. As to the HIV/AIDS-related content, a development can also be detected, not least in an integrated approach which increasingly connects prevention, treatment, care and support into the overall prevention strategy.

The Edutainment Vehicle

Contrary to rational communication of information through, for example, news genres, the point about using the narrative and melodramatic is to articulate emotional engagement. By using melodrama to draw attention, recognition and identification the aim is to promote insight and change of attitude and behaviour.

The guiding communicative principle for Soul City is edutainment, their denomination of entertainment-education. Garth Japhet has developed a model that explains the main principles of the 'Edutainment Vehicle' (Japhet, 1999—the revised and updated version is presented in Figure 15.1). The Edutainment Model proposed by Japhet argues for a cyclical communication strategy, where a number of inputs are fed into the media vehicle which then results in a number of outputs. The overall process and the outputs in particular are then evaluated which then serves as a key input into the next phase of the ongoing vehicle.

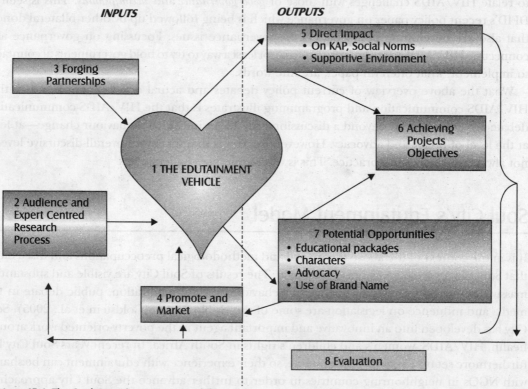

Figure 15.1 The Soul City Edutainment Model

As for inputs, there are two key *inputs: the audience and expert centred research process*, the formative research, and *the partnerships* established with civil society, government, private sector, international partners and others. In a very participatory process, messages are developed and worked into the creative products, the media narratives, being both TV, radio and print. Long and in-depth formative research, taking up to 18 months prior to the design and production of media products, has been a way for Soul City to engage all relevant segments of society, including lay audience as well as experts, in the research process, developing messages that are consistent with the audience knowledge, opinion and needs.

Soul City emphasizes that the edutainment model is generic, and that any narrative form can be applied in the media vehicle. It could also be popular theatre, music or any other form of popular cultural narrative. Soul City has had the opportunity to work in prime time and with the mass media and believe firmly in the efficiency of this. However, the medium may well be another if this opportunity is not possible.

The media vehicle results in two key types of *output: the direct output,* being the changes in knowledge, attitude, social norms and intermediate and direct practices—the traditional KAP-distinction can be nuanced substantially, which Soul City also emphasizes—as well as the development of a supportive environment favouring these mentioned changes.

The *development of potential opportunities.* These potential opportunities, made possible due to the media intervention, contain a number of interesting opportunities, of some of which Soul City have come far in making use of, while others still are being developed further. These include educational packages, advocacy at both community and national level, and the development and use of their brand name.

When operationalized, the edutainment model is put into practice in the course of five phases as shown in Box 15.2.

Box 15.2 Steps to Develop an Edutainment Project

Phase 1	Research and Planning. This is topic research involving target audience and other stakeholders.
Phase 2	Development of the narrative. This involved message design, integration of message into chosen form of entertainment, pre-testing with target audience and other role-players. Finally it involve modification as a result of pre-testing.
Phase 3	Production.
Phase 4	Implementation and Promotion. This includes promoting, popularizing and getting the most out of the edutainment during implementation. Thus, large parts of advocacy takes place at this stage.
Phase 5	Evaluation. The communication initiative is evaluated on an ongoing basis, and each final evaluation serves as input into the next campaign.

Source: Japhet, 1999:233.

In the training manual, Japhet also sets up a rough estimate of how much time to use on each phase 25 per cent on phase 1, 50 per cent on the development of the whole project and the narrative, mere 15 per cent on the production and 10 per cent on the implementation and promotion. The evaluation is considered ongoing, despite the fact that in Soul City 4 anenormous evaluation was carried out, consuming large amounts of time and money (Goldstein et al., 2005).

So far Soul City campaigns have been launched seven times between 1994 and 2005. The issues treated so far have, among others, been women's and children's rights, HIV/AIDS, TB, land rights, housing, energy, alcohol, tobacco, personal finance, depression and traffic. It is thus quite apparent that Soul City is operating with a broad definition of public health which brings them around a variety of subjects.

With regard to HIV/AIDS, it has been a recurrent theme throughout the campaigns, and it has been dealt with in a multitude of ways within the broad spectrum of prevention, care, support and treatment—working around issues of stigma and taboo, silence, discrimination, pain, fear, doubt, and so forth.

The many Soul City campaigns have not been alike. They have grown in size, but first and foremost, in complexity and impact, with Soul City 4 as the most influential campaign and most thoroughly evaluated campaign to date. Communication-wise they have been very learning processes, for Soul City as well as for edutainment-practitioners and scholars around the world.

If we take a close look at the underlying discourse seen in Soul City documents—evaluations and articles—it remains closely linked to the discourse encountered in diffusion theory and in what is generally known as the transmission model of communication (Bouman, 1999:47). This would be equivalent to the first generation edutainment as outlined in Figure 15.1. Soul City's material speak of diffusion, persuasion, impact, messages, and so forth. It is a language which lies far from the discourse of participatory communication which speaks of people as key agents of change, emancipation, dialogue, balanced ecology and of communication processes where the output—the produced meaning—is not highly predictable nor readily controlled. This kind of rapid analysis of Soul City's material, including the edutainment manual, the evaluations and of a number of other documents by Soul City all points towards a paradigmatic belonging of Soul City to the transmission model.

However, despite these paradigmatic connotations, Soul City's practice *is* different. It deals with issues and concerns such as social mobilization, empowerment, advocacy and active and multiple audience reception, and this language is also present in Soul City discourse. This wording corresponds well to the reception model of communication and especially to participatory models of communication. In practice Soul City works both with the individual and with the broader communities and with society as units of change.

However, overall, there is a discrepancy between Soul City's written representation of their work on one side, and their practice on the other.

The fact is that Soul City has been developed as a health communication project, but mainly by health scholars and with no substantial participation of communication scholars. As such the scientific connotations in the communication discourse they apply seemingly plays less of a role in their practice. The point is that the nuanced understanding of audiences encountered in their practice resonates very much with the notion of audience found in what in media studies is known as reception theory. Here the audience is conceived of as actively using the media, again largely resonating with the notion of audience used in participatory communication strategies.

Seen in retrospective, Soul City has from the outset in 1992 had some basic principles guiding their work. Some of them refer to the inputs in the edutainment models, others are direct impacts and opportunities Soul City ambitiously and deliberately have pursued from the outset. These basic principles are:

- Soul City is conceived as an ongoing vehicle, recurrent and building up a quality brand around the name of Soul City.
- Soul City applies a multimedia strategy, combining TV-series with radio programmes in numerous languages, newspaper booklets, adult education material, and so forth.
- Soul City emphasizes substantial formative research as well as summative research.
- Soul City promotes community activism and enhancing strategic partnerships.
- Soul City develops materials and courses, training and education, in the issues of concern
- Soul City works with advocacy both on community level as at the national level.

If we refer Soul City's discourse and choice of wording, as well as their outlined principles, with the three generations of edutainment outlined in Figure 15.1, some of their statements point towards a first generation edutainment vehicle. This is particularly the case in their consistent focus on messages and messaging, as well as on individual behaviour and social norms (Goldstein et al., 2005). In their expected outcomes, Soul City somewhat covers the full panorama—first generation with change in norms and individual behaviour assessed in numerical results; second generation in also emphasizing 'talk' or rather public and private debate; and finally, third generation with articulations of social and political processes, structural change and collective action. However, a couple of concepts which to my best judgement places Soul City as a bridge-building second generation edutainment vehicle lies in their notions of entertainment, education and notion of catalyst. In entertainment, it comes clearly through in Soul City's material and general discourse that they consider their fictionalized entertaining narratives as examples of a dynamic genre which is an ideal too for change. It's not everything, but it is visually and conceptually placed in the heart of their edutainment vehicle. By conducting a rather participatory formative research process, they furthermore contextualize this dynamic genre—as a tool for change—within the lives and minds of the potential target audience. This moves beyond the first generation edutainment, which has a somewhat more instrumental approach, but does on the other hand not place them in the third generation where the narrative and genre chosen typically allows for popular participation throughout the process.

The same issues count regarding the notion of catalyst. Here Soul City works along the characteristics of the second generation: 'external catalyst in partnership with community'. They are more than the first generation external change agent targeting 'X' group of people, but not so much that they are to be considered an internal community member. The partnerships with the communities, reflected in the partnerships they establish with networks from civil society, and others, are crucial for their intervention. As for their notion of education, it moves beyond the persuasive strategies and the Freirean principles of 'banking pedagogy' but, on the other hand, does not practice a 'liberating pedagogy'. They work along the lines of life skills and didactics in their pedagogical approach.

In this way, a deeper analysis of Soul City's practice of edutainment could further unfold. In general terms, such analytical exercises can prove useful to deconstruct the epistemological, theoretical, methodological and technical underpinnings which always will guide and influence an edutainment intervention. It is this sort of further deconstruction of the field of edutainment practice which could contribute to a further conceptual clarity, or at least to a discussion about the concepts that guide the edutainment practice. The above rapid analysis has pointed to placing Soul City in the so-called second generation edutainment.

Evaluating the Impact

As mentioned above, the evaluation of Soul City's fourth intervention is the largest evaluation conducted of Soul City's work to date. It was based on the fact that Soul City obtained an European Union (EU) grant to conduct a comprehensive evaluation. The external evaluation reports lie on Soul City's webpage, but the Goldstein et al. article published in the *Journal of Health Communication* is a furthering and a summary of the evaluation, written by four core staff members of Soul City.

A number of results provide strong indications of how the Soul City 4 communication strategy impacted on the audiences. HIV/AIDS was one of the four major issues addressed in the media products. Forty-three per cent of the people who watched the Soul City television series spoke more openly about HIV and AIDS as compared to 25 per cent of people who did not watch Soul City. Thirty-eight per cent of people who have been exposed to three Soul City sources were found to use condoms more often as compared to 6 per cent who had not watch Soul City at all (Soul City 4—Impact Evaluation).

What most of the evaluations of Soul City's intervention have been able to document emphasize predominantly quantitative outcomes such as reach, ratings, quantifiable relations between exposure to Soul City media products and the degree of change in social norms, attitudes and to some degree also behaviour (Soul City 4—Impact Evaluation: AIDS, 2000). In two sentinel site studies, Soul City 4 studied more in-depth the impact of their media vehicle. In relation to HIV/AIDS four actions were measured, and radio proven particularly influential on influencing these actions: 'Soul City radio appeared to be a particularly effective vehicle for encouraging respondents to take measures to try to find out more about HIV/AIDS, assist someone who is HIV positive, using condoms or going for an HIV/AIDS test' (CASE, 2000).

One of the innovative elements in the Soul City 4 evaluation was that of assessing the outcome of the advocacy communication component, or 'local policy changes attributable to Soul City' (Goldstein et al., 2005:471). This showed that Soul City has been able to articulate social mobilization in support of transmitting, in their fictional TV-drama, references to a delayed

'Domestic Violence Act' which, thanks to the popular support and insistence of Soul City broadcasting reference to it, resulted in a speeding up of the final ratification of the Act in parliament. As such, Soul City's advocacy communication had proven successful, paving the way for a further elaboration of advocacy communication as a tool to articulate social change processes with edutainment strategies.

Some of the lessons that can be learnt from Soul City's edutainment strategy are:

- edutainment recognizes the strengths and relevance of basing communication strategies in the popular culture of the audiences
- fictional genres have shown particularly useful and efficient, contrary to what often is (not) obtained through the more traditional journalistic spread of information
- successful edutainment strategies require a strong advocacy component
- there is a need to further develop follow up activities to edutainment campaigns.

Conclusions and Recommendations

Soul City has managed to create a communication model that transcends the traditional focus on individual behaviour change, and has combined a focus on individual behaviour change with the need to address the larger social, political, economic and media environments the individual is situated within. However, another range of issues should be included, focussing on exploring and understanding the full process of the communication strategy, from the formative research, script development, pre-testing, production, broadcasting, reception and summative research.

On the basis of the large, EU-funded evaluation of Soul City 4, and following my own participation in the international advisory panel to the Soul City 4 evaluation, a number of issues have been identified as needing further research as well as operational testing. My overall argument is that both Soul City as the international health communication community can benefit from an in-depth qualitative analysis of the role of Soul City media product in the lives of the audience. By drawing on new media theory as reception analysis and audience ethnography, the hypothesis is that an increased understanding can be obtained as to the relation between communication interventions and both individual and social change. The impossible question to get a full answer to in health communication is 'what is the causal link between a communication intervention and individual and social change?' This question remains a key driver behind what donors, local governments and practitioners themselves need and wish to clarify.

In exploring a whole range of qualitative research methodologies, brought in especially from newer media and communication theory, there exists a still largely unexplored potential to further advance the field of health communication in general and HIV/AIDS communication in particular. A number of recommendations can be made as pertinent points for Soul City to pursue in order to develop their edutainment model even further. These are:

- Conduct audience ethnography. To further explore the media use in everyday life and how the media flow relates to the everyday life of the audience.
- Conduct qualitative reception analysis referent the produced television and radio programmes, and the print material, to better understand processes of identification, meaning-making and the establishment of para-social relationships between characters and audience.
- Carry out content analysis of Soul City programmes to supplement the reception analysis
- Develop qualitative indicators for impact and outcome evaluations. This will be related to the above mentioned fields of research, but must be treated as a separate issue.
- Analyse the impact of long-term communication strategies over time. In the case of Soul City a retrospective of their impact from 1994 and until today would be very useful.

Recommendations

Given the lessons learnt from Soul City on how to use edutainment for HIV/AIDS communication and programming, a number of more general recommendations can be made both to researchers and practitioners:

1. Further Development of Communication Strategies: Clarify Epistemology, Substantiate Theory and Improve Methodology

This recommendation is three-fold. A well-developed communication strategy is obviously the strategy that manages to be efficient, also cost-effective, and achieve the objectives, most often a change of behaviour. However, many of the mistakes and inefficient strategies in the past can—in addition to the given limitations of communicative action *per se*—be attributed to poorly designed strategies. Often, there is no clear epistemological stand, and equally no clear theory informing the chosen methodology. Finally, classical shortcomings lie in not prioritizing formative and summative research and giving no attention or very little attention to the use of qualitative methods. Developing qualitative indicators for impact assessments is thus an issue which only recently is being given attention amongst international organizations working in this field. Almost no NGOs/CBOs and governments have in practice incorporated such indicators in their HIV/AIDS communication programming.

2. Understanding HIV/AIDS

Given the socio-cultural and political-economic complexities of the rise and spread of HIV/AIDS, and given the diversity in perceptions and explanations surrounding the pandemic in different countries, it is crucial to obtain a clear, holistic and localized understanding of all crucial issues that must condition any HIV/AIDS communication and prevention in any country. In other words, although communication strategies at the overall level are generic, no strategy will work if it is not carefully developed in context of local conditions. These include:

- The meanings (stigma, fear and denial) attached to HIV/AIDS in the respective settings.
- The sexual practices and the inherent gender roles and relations of target audiences.
- The local institutional capacity to tackle the HIV/AIDS problematic (with particular focus on the health and educational systems).
- The national policies and communication practices informing and guiding HIV/AIDS prevention in the chosen countries.

The above is far from an exhaustive listing, but indicates some elements that recurrently emerge as fundamentals in striving for a deeper insight into the how's and why's of the continuously expanding pandemic.

3. Advocacy and Accountability

As the case of Soul City's fourth intervention in 1999–2000 showed, advocacy communication can be a powerful dimension of an edutainment strategy. Following the breakthrough experience in 1999 Soul City established an advocacy office, which develops the advocacy dimensions of the continuing efforts. The field of advocacy ties in with the growing mobilization and organization of civil societies in AIDS-affected countries and is thus closely associated with questions of citizenship, rights and voice and visibility in the public sphere. A growing dimension is seen in the trans-national advocacy networks and their ability to articulate social change. This moves beyond edutainment strategies, although it indeed connects herewith given that a growing number of organizations that use edutainment are engaging in trans-national networks. What advocacy ultimately is about is to influence governance and make governments accountable to their constituencies of voters/citizens/people.

Although dealing with a range of tools, methodologies, genres and formats that together compose the generic values of edutainment as a widely successful and used communication strategy, edutainment, as any communication intervention, is far from value-free. We, as communication scholars and researchers, must improve our ability to deconstruct and understand the stakeholder interests—be they ideological, political, humanistic or religious—that underpin chosen strategies. Although there is urgent need for increased coordination and moving forward together in the fight against HIV/AIDS this can only happen if we—in addition to the first recommendation about conceptual and epistemological clarity—each stakeholder speaks, acts and commits to the common cause.

References

Airhihenbuwa, C.O. and R. Obregon. 2000. 'A critical assessment of theories/models used in health communication for HIV/AIDS', *Journal of Health Communication*, 5:5–15.

Boal, Augusto. 1979. *The Theatre of the Oppressed*. New York: Urizen Books.

Bouman, Martine. 1999. *The Turtle and the Peacock. The Entertainment Education Strategy on Television*. Netherlands: Thesis Wageningen Agricultural University.

CASE, 2000. Evaluation of Soul City. Cape Town.

Cody, M., A. Singhal, E. Rogers and M. Sabido (eds). 2005. *Entertainment-Education and Social Change*. Mahwah, M: Lawrence Erlbaum Associates.

Freire, Paulo. 1968. *Pedagogy of the Oppressed*. New York: Seabury Press.

Fuenzalida, Valerio 1994. *La apropriación educative de la telenovela*. Santiago: CPU.

Gao, Melissa Yun. 2005. *Participatory Communication Research and HIV/AIDS Control: A Study among Gay Men and MSM in Chengdu, China*. Unpublished Ph.D. thesis. The University of Newcastle, Australia.

Goldstein, Susan, Shereen Usdin, Esca Scheepers, and Garth Japhet. 2005. 'Communicating HIV and AIDS, What Works? A Report on the Impact Evaluation of Soul City's Fourth Series'. *Journal of Health Communication-International Perspectives*.

Gumucio-Dagron, Alfonso and Thomas Tufte (eds). 2006. *The Communication for Social Change Anthology. Historical and Contemporary Readings*. New Jersey: The Communication for Social Change Consortium.

Japhet, Garth. 1999. *Edutainment. How to Make Edutainment Work for You: A Step by Step Guide to Designing and Managing an Edutainment Project for Social Development*. Johannesburg: Soul City. 230 p.

La Pastina, Antonio. 1999. *The telenovela way of knowledge: An ethnographic reception study among rural viewers in Brazil*. Unpublished Ph.D. dissertation. Austin, Texas: University of Texas at Austin, Dept. of Radio-TV-Film.

McKee, Neill, Jane T. Bertrand and Antje Becker-Benton. 2004. *Strategic Communication in the HIV/AIDS Epidemic*. New Delhi: Sage Publications.

Panos. February 2001. *HIV/AIDS: Social Change Through Public Debate—The Panos AIDS Programme: 2001-2005*. Working paper for partners. London.

———. 2003. *Missing the Message—20 years of HIV/AIDS Communication*. Panos, London. Available online at www.panos.org.

———. 2005. *Reporting Aids. An analysis of media environments in Southern Africa*. London.

Papa, M., A. Singhal and W.H. Papa. 2006. *Organizing for Social Change. A Dialectic Journey of Theory and Praxis*. New Delhi: Sage Publications.

Parker, Warren. 2005. *Ideology, Hegemony and HIV/AIDS: The Appropriation of Indigenous and Global Spheres*. Unpublished Ph.D. thesis. University of Kwazulu-Natal, South Africa.

Rockefeller Foundation. 1997. *Communications and Social Change: Forging Strategies for the 21st Century*. New York.

———. 1999. *Communication for Social Change: A Position Paper and Conference Report*. New York.

Rodriguez, Clemencia. 2005. 'From the Sandinista Revolution to Telenovelas: The case of Puntos de Encuentro', in Oscar Hemer and Thomas Tufte (eds). *Media and Glocal Change—Rethinking Communication for Development*. Buenos Aires and Gothenburg: CLACSO and NORDICOM.

Singhal, A. 2004. 'Entertainment-Education Through Participatory Theatre: Freirean Strategies for Empowering the Oppressed', in M. Cody, A. Singhal, E. Rogers and M. Sabido (eds). *Entertainment-Education and Social Change*. Mahwah, M: Lawrence Erlbaum Associates.

Singhal, Arvind, Michael J. Cody, Everett Rogers and Miguel Sabido (eds). 2004. *Entertainment-Education and Social Change*. New Jersey: Lawrence Erlbaum Associates.

Skeie, Silje Sjøvaag. 2005. 'Narratives for peace—using entertainment-education in the promotion of a culture of peace', *Transformator–tidsskrift for fredsforskning. 3. årgang. 2/2004*, page 63–81. Oslo: PROION.

Soul City 4—Impact Evaluation: AIDS. October 2000. Johannesburg.

———. 2005. 'Entertainment-Education in Development Communication. Between Marketing Behaviours and Empowering People', in Oscar Hemer and Thomas Tufte (eds). *Media and Glocal Change. Rethinking Communication for Development*. Buenos Aires and Gothenburg: CLACSO and NORDICOM.

Tufte, T. 2005. 'Entertainment-Education in Development Communication. Between Marketing Behaviour and Empowering People', in O. Hemer and T. Tufte (eds). *Media & Global Change. Rethinking Communication for Development*, pp. 159–174. Goteborg: Nordicon.

UN Millennium Project, Working Group on HIV/AIDS. 2005. New York.

UNAIDS/Penn State. 1999. C.O. Airhihenbuwa, B. Makinwa, M. Frith and R. Obregon (eds). *Communications Framework for HIV/AIDS: A New Direction*. Geneva: UNAIDS.

UNAIDS. 2000, June. *Report on the Global HIV/AIDS Epidemic*. Geneva: UNAIDS.

Part V

More Complexity Added:
Community Media
and Conflict Resolution

Making Community Media Work: Community Media Identities and Their Articulation in an Antwerp Neighbourhood Development Project

16

NICO CARPENTIER, RICO LIE AND JAN SERVAES

Defining Community Media

The concept of 'community media' (CM) has shown to be, in its long theoretical and empirical tradition,[1] highly elusive. The multiplicity of media organizations that carry this name has caused most mono-theoretical approaches to focus on certain characteristics, while ignoring other aspects of the identity of community media. This theoretical problem necessitates the use of different approaches towards the definition of community media, which will allow for a complementary emphasis on different aspects of the identity of 'community media'. This contribution has two aims: it firstly combines four theoretical approaches in order to capture both the diversity and specificity of these community media. Secondly it aims to show the applicability of these combined approaches by analysing and evaluating a mixed media project in a North Belgian town.

None of the four approaches discussed below can be considered as giving a sufficient overview when applied independently, as we postulate that the only way to capture the diversity that characterizes community media is the simultaneous application of these four approaches. This does not exclude the sometimes-strong interrelationship between the four approaches, especially when comparing the two media-centred approaches one and two, and the two more society-centred approaches three and four. Differences within the two media-centred approaches and the two society-centred approaches are based on the application of a more essentialist theoretical framework, as opposed to a more relationalist theoretical framework. In approaches one and three, the identity of community media is defined as autonomous, while in approaches two and four this identity is defined in relationship to other identities. These relationships can be summarized in Table 16.1.

Table 16.1
Positioning the Four Theoretical Approaches

	Media-centred	Society-centred
Autonomous Identity of CM (Essentialist)	Approach I: Serving the community	Approach III: Part of civil society
Identity of CM in relation to other identities (Relationalist)	Approach II: An alternative to mainstream	Approach IV: Rhizome

Implementing these four approaches also allows highlighting a series of arguments stressing the importance of community media in a wide range of areas; at the same time, they can, and will, be used to analyse the weaknesses of and threats to community media. After a brief description of each approach, they are then operationalized, directing the analysis of both the arguments emphasizing the importance of community media and the arguments uncovering any weaknesses and threats. This analysis will lead to a summarizing table containing both sets of arguments.

A promising starting point for the theoretical analysis is given by the 'working definition' of community radio adopted by AMARC-Europe, the European branch of the World Association of Community Radio Broadcasters;[2] an organization that encompasses a wide range of radio practices in the different continents. In Latin America, the AMARC constituents are termed popular radio, educational radio, miners' radio, or peasants' radio. In Africa, they refer to local rural radio, while in Europe it is often called associative radio, free radio, neighbourhood radio, or community radio. Asians speak of radio for development, and of community radio, in Oceania of aboriginal radio, public radio and of community radio (Servaes, 1999:259). Attempting to avoid a prescriptive definition, AMARC-Europe (1994:4) labels a community radio station as '*a "non-profit" station, currently broadcasting, which offers a service to the community in which it is located, or to which it broadcasts, while promoting the participation of this community in the radio*'.

Multi-Theoretical Approaches

1. Approach One: Serving a Community

In AMARC's working definition, it is nevertheless clear that there is a strong emphasis on the concept of 'community'. Moreover, the geographical aspect is explicitly highlighted ('*in which it is located*'), although other types of relationships between medium and community are often mentioned ('*to which it broadcasts*').

Within the disciplines of sociology and anthropology, the concept of 'community' has a long history. Already in the 19th century, Tönnies (1963) theorized a distinction between community and society: where 'community' is defined by the presence of close and concrete human ties and by a collective identity, the prevalent feature of 'society' is the absence of identifying group relations (Martin-Barbero, 1993:29). Morris and Morten (1998:12–13) exemplify Tönnies' distinction by using the concepts 'communion' and 'association'; community thus refers to the '*notion of a big family*', while society '*represents a colder, unattached and more fragmented way of living devoid of cooperation and social cohesion. Instead of a sense of neighbourliness, people are isolated.*'

As Leunissen (1986) argues, conceptualizations of community refer predominantly to geography and ethnicity as structuring notions of the collective identity or the group relations. These structural conceptualizations of community are put firstly into perspective by introducing the concept of the 'community of interest', which emphasizes the importance of other factors in structuring a community. Although one cannot explicitly assume that a group of people has common interests[3] (see Clark, 1973:411 a.f.), the communality of interest can form the conditions of possibility for the emergence or existence of a community. A similar argument can be made for Wenger's (1999) so-called 'communities of practices', which are composed out of the informal arenas of family, work and friendship networks and so forth (see also Hewson, 2005: 17). Especially the analysis of the impact of information and communication technologies (ICT) on everyday life has shown that communities are not only formed in geographically defined spaces, but also in cyberspace, such as so-called user groups. Jones (1995) has shown that such 'virtual' or 'on-line' communities have similar characteristics as the geography-based communities.[4] Verschueren (2006) therefore argues that the differences between offline and online behaviour appear to be of degree rather than of kind. The 'new' communities have further altered the rather fixed idea about space, clearly showing that geographical nearness is not in all cases a necessary condition for, or quality of, 'community.' As Lewis (1993a:13) remarks, a 'community of interest' can extend '*across conurbations, nations and continents*'. What is a defining feature for 'community' is the direct and frequent contact between the members and the feeling of 'belonging' and 'sharing'.

A second type of re-conceptualization is based upon the emphasis of the subjective construction of community, where Lindlof's (1988) concept of 'interpretative community' and Cohen's (1989) 'community of meaning' are relevant. Although Lindlof's re-conceptualization is specifically aimed at redefining the audience as a community, both re-conceptualizations approach the concept of 'community' from within. Cohen pleads for, in line with the above, '*a shift away from the structure of community towards a symbolic construction of community and in order to do so, takes culture, rather than structure as point of departure*' (ibid.:70). Community is not something that is imposed on people from the outside and that, like a machine, punches structure in big metal plates. A community is actively constructed by its members and those members derive an identity from this construction. People extract a 'community identity' from their own constructed social communication structure. These different conceptualizations are summarized in Table 16.2.

Table 16.2
Defining Community

Community as close and concrete human ties, as 'communion', as a collective identity, with identifying group relations		
Traditional	Re-conceptualization 1	Re-conceptualization 2
	Supplementing the geographical with the non-geographical	Supplementing the structural/material with the cultural
• Geography	• Community of interest	• Interpretative community
• Ethnicity	• Community of practice	• Community of meaning
	• Virtual or on-line community	

Community media are thus oriented towards a community (Fraser and Restrepo, 2000; Sjöberg, 1994; Sundaraj, 2000), regardless of the exact nature of this community—defined geographically/ spatially, ethnically (Husband, 1994) or otherwise—but the relationship between the community medium and the actual community transcends 'ordinary' one-way communication, where '*topics are chosen in the same way, by professional communicators, and targeted towards the apparent needs and interests of the audience*' (Berrigan, 1979:7). As is illustrated in AMARC's working definition, especially by the segment stating that community media should be '*promoting the participation of this community*', relationships between broadcaster and community are defined by the concept of two-way communication. Access by the community and participation of the community are to be considered key defining factors (Gumucio, 2001; O'Sullivan-Ryan and Kaplun, 1979; Savio, 1990), as Berrigan (1979:8) eloquently summarizes: '*[Community media] are media to which members of the community have access, for information, education, entertainment, when they want access. They are media in which the community participates, as planners, producers, performers. They are the means of expression of the community, rather than for the community.*' Referring to the 1977 meeting in Belgrade, Berrigan (1979:18) (partially) links access to the reception of information, education, and entertainment considered relevant by/for the community: '*[Access] may be defined in terms of the opportunities available to the public to choose varied and relevant programs, and to have a means of feedback to transmit its reactions and demands to production organizations.*' Others limit access to mass media and see it as '*the processes that permit users to provide relatively open and unedited input to the mass media*' (Lewis, 1993a:12) or as '*the relation to the public and the established broadcasting institutions*' (Prehn, 1992:259). Both the production- and reception-approaches of 'access' are considered relevant to the definition of 'community media' and are incorporated in Table 16.3.

Table 16.3
Access and Participation of the Community

Production Perspective	Reception Perspective
Access to the content producing organization	Access to the content considered relevant

(*Table 16.3 continued*)

(*Table 16.3 continued*)

Production Perspective	Reception Perspective
→ Ability to produce content and have it broadcast	→ Ability to receive and interpret content
Participation in the produced content	
→ Co-deciding on content	
Participation in the content producing organization	
→ Co-deciding on policy	→ Evaluating the content

Participation is seen here, following Pateman (1972:71), as a process where the individual members, of a community, have a certain degree of power to influence or determine the outcome of that process. Community media not only allow but also facilitate the participation of members of the community in both the produced content and the content producing organization. Prehn illustrates this as follows: '*participation implies a wider range of activities related to involving people directly in station programming, administration and policy activities*' (Prehn, 1992:259).

A. The Importance of Community Media in Approach One: Validating and Empowering the Community

In this first approach the relationship between the broadcaster and the community is placed in the foreground. By choosing a specific community as a target group, the concept of community itself is validated and strengthened. The audience is not defined as an aggregate of individuals who only share socio-demographic or economic characteristics, but instead as a collective of people holding a series of identifying group relations. In this fashion, the situation of the audience, as part of complex set of social structures, is emphasized, deepening and bridging the traditional state-citizen and medium-audience dichotomies that tend to articulate the public and the audience as an aggregate of individuals.

Moreover, the aim of community media in approach one to serve the community is often translated as enabling and facilitating access and participation by members of the community. 'Ordinary people'[5] are given the opportunity to have their voices heard. Topics that are considered relevant for the community can be discussed by members of that community, thus empowering those people by signifying that their statements are considered important enough to be broadcast. Especially societal groups that are misrepresented, disadvantaged, stigmatized, or even repressed can benefit from using the channels of communication opened by community media, strengthening their internal identity, manifesting this identity to the outside world, and thus enabling social change and/or development.

B. Threats to Community Media in Approach One: Which Community?

This orientation towards a community also creates a situation of dependency towards this community, as two-way communication demands two partners more or less equally interested in communicating. While the dominant discourse on media is based on one-way communication, raising the community's interest to go beyond this limited form of communication does not speak for itself, due to what can be called the lack of two-way communication skills and interest. This problem is strengthened even more by the diffusion of specific technologies oriented towards one-way communication and the lack of technologies facilitating two-way communication.

Moreover, the concept of 'community'—central to the identity of community media—has often been reduced to its geographical meaning. This reduction has trapped community media in the position of small-scale local media, gradually de-emphasizing their role towards serving the community and eventually copying commercial media formats in their efforts to survive.

2. Approach Two: Community Media as an Alternative to Mainstream Media

A second approach to defining community media is based on the concept of alternative media. This concept introduces a distinction between mainstream and alternative media, where alternative media are seen as a supplement to mainstream media (Atton, 2002; Atton and Couldry, 2003; Couldry and Curran 2003; O'Sullivan, 1994). As alternative media are sometimes defined in a negative relationship towards mainstream media, the contingency of this concept should be emphasized: what is considered 'alternative' at a certain point in time could be defined as mainstream at another point in time. The societal context in which alternative media function is inseparable from the concept of 'alternative media' and can serve as a starting point for the definition of alternative media. Present day mainstream media are usually considered to be:

- Large-scaled and geared towards large, homogeneous (segments of) audiences
- State-owned organizations or commercial companies.
- Vertically structured organizations staffed by professionals.
- Carriers of dominant discourses and representations.

Alternative media can take a (or several) opposite position(s) on these matters:

- Small-scaled and oriented towards specific communities, possibly disadvantaged groups, respecting their diversity.
- Independent from state and market.
- Horizontally structured, allowing for the facilitation of audience access and participation within the frame of democratization and multiplicity.
- Carriers of non-dominant, (possibly counter-hegemonic) discourses and representations, stressing the importance of self-representation.

A more elaborate description of these different domains is given by Lewis (1993a: 12), as seen in Table 16.4.

Table 16.4
Defining Alternative Media[6]

Domain	Examples of the Domain
Motive or purpose	• Rejection of commercial motives • Assertion of human, cultural, educational ends
Sources of funding	• Rejection of state or municipal grants • Rejection of advertising revenue
Regulatory dispensation	• Supervised by distinct institutions • Independent/'free'
Organizational structure	• Horizontal organization • Allowing 'full' participation • Democratization of communication
Criticizing professional practices	• Encouraging voluntary engagement • Access and participation for non-professionals • Different criteria for news selection
Message content	• Supplementing or contradicting dominant discourses or representations
Relationship with audience and/or consumers	• Degree of user/consumer control • Allowing the needs and goals to be articulated by the audience/ consumers themselves • Democratization of communication
Composition of the audience	• Young people, women, rural populations • Diversity and multiplicity
Range of diffusion	• Local rather than regional or national
Nature of research methodology	• Qualitative, ethnographical and long term research

Source: Lewis, 1993a:12.

A. The Importance of Community Media in Approach Two: Supplementing, Contesting and Resisting Mainstream Media Discourse

This second approach of community media defines these media as an alternative to mainstream media, supplementing mainstream media both on the organizational as on the content level. At the organizational level, the existence of community media shows that media can exist independently from state and market. As the pressure on large-scale mainstream media in order to become more market-oriented tends to be considerable, community media show that 'the third way' is still open for media organizations. The same argument can be applied for the (internal) structure of the media organization, as large scale mainstream media organizations have a tendency towards a more vertical structure. Again, the more horizontally structured community media show that alternative ways of organization, and more balanced and/or horizontal structures, remain actual possibilities.

On the content level, community media can offer representations and discourses that vary from those originating from the mainstream media. The main reason for this difference can be found at the higher level of participation of different societal groups and communities and the aim to provide '*air space to local cultural manifestations, to ethnic minority groups, to the hot political issues in the neighborhood or locality*' (Jankowski, 1994:3). Mainstream media tend to be oriented towards different types of elites, as is the case, for instance, in mainstream news broadcasts favouring government sources, often resulting in what is often called structural bias (see McNair, 1998:75 a.f.). The orientation of community media towards giving voice to various older and newer social movements, minorities, and sub/counter-cultures and the emphasis on self-representation, can result in a more diverse content, signifying the multiplicity of societal voices (Van de Donk et al., 2004).

At the same time, the critical stance towards the production values of the 'professional' working in mainstream media leads to a diversity of formats and genres and creates room for experimentation with content and form. In this fashion, community media can be rightfully seen as a breeding ground for innovation, later often recuperated by mainstream media.

B. Threats to Community Media in Approach Two: From Alternative to Marginal?

When community media are situated in an antagonistic relationship towards mainstream media, community media may find themselves in a less advantageous position. Being small scale, independent, and horizontally structured organizations that carry non-dominant discourses and representations hardly guarantees financial and organizational stability.

Especially when the antagonistic relationship between public and commercial media is placed in the context of competition and these media try to hegemonise their identities at the expense of community media, the latter usually pay the price. Community media are then articulated as unprofessional, inefficient, limited in their capacity to reach large audiences and as marginal as some of the societal groups to whom they try to give voice. In this fashion, the need for an alternative is denied, as mainstream media are deemed to cover all functions considered relevant to society. One of the main consequences of marginalizing the alternative (or connotating it negatively, for instance as naïve, irrelevant or superfluous) is the low political priority given to what is considered to be 'marginal', causing a downward spiral for community media.

3. Approach Three: Linking Community Media to the Civil Society

The explicit positioning of community media as independent from state and market supports the articulation of community media as part of civil society. Civil society is deemed important for a variety of reasons, summarized here by Keane (1998:xviii):

- Civil society gives preferential treatment to individuals' daily freedom from violence;
- the importance of enabling groups and individuals freely within the law to define and express their various social identities;
- the impossibility, especially in the era of computerized networks of communication media, of nurturing 'freedom of communication' without a plurality of variously seized non-state communications media;

- the superiority of politically regulated and socially constrained markets as devices for eliminating all those factors of production that fail to perform according to current standards of efficiency.
- But of special interest [...] is the subject of democracy or, more precisely, the intellectual and political need to revive the democratic imagination.

By defining community media as part of civil society, these media can be considered the '*third voice*' (Servaes, 1999:260) between state media and private commercial media. One of the clearest examples of this articulation can be found in the introduction of Girard's (1992) 'a passion for radio', where he formulates the following answer to the question of '*a passion for [community] radio?*':

The answer to that question can be found in a third type of radio—an alternative to commercial and state radio. Often referred to as community radio, its most distinguishing characteristic is its commitment to community participation at all levels. While listeners of commercial radio are able to participate in the programming in limited ways—via open line telephone shows or by requesting a favourite song, for example—community radio listeners are the producers, managers, directors and even owners of the stations. (ibid.:2)

A starting point for defining community media as part of civil society can be found in Thompson's (1995) model describing the public and private domains in contemporary Western societies, where organizations related to the state are seen as constituting the public domain. Privately owned economic organizations geared towards profit, and personal and family relations are considered to be part of the private domain. Based on this distinction, civil society can be defined as a group of intermediate organizations, separate from the privately owned economic organizations operating in the market economy, personal and family relations[7] and from the state and quasi-state organizations. Table 16.5 shows the positioning of civil society in-between the private and public domain.

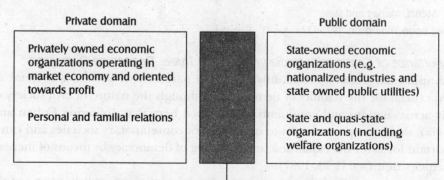

Private domain

> Privately owned economic organizations operating in market economy and oriented towards profit
>
> Personal and familial relations

Public domain

> State-owned economic organizations (e.g. nationalized industries and state owned public utilities)
>
> State and quasi-state organizations (including welfare organizations)

Intermediate organizations (e.g. charities, political parties and pressure groups, co-operatively owned enterprises, etc)

Figure 16.1 Private and Public Domains in Contemporary Western Societies
Source: Thompson, 1995: 122.

Although the nature and structure of civil society varies across regions and continents, this Western-inspired model tends to be applicable in most continents, as the neo-liberal market economy has become the predominant form of organizing society. Even in societies where the public domain is to be considered repressive towards civil society, different forms of what Lewis (1993b:127) named '*pockets of resistance*' emerge, as could well be illustrated by the existence of the Samizdat in the former U.S.S.R.

When reworking Thompson's model for the specificity of media organizations, a series of changes should be implemented to the model. Media deregulation, or more generally, the impact of the neo-liberal discourse on media policies, has prompted public broadcasting organizations, in some continents, to adopt more market- and efficiency-driven approaches. This includes an increased emphasis on audience maximization (see Ang, 1991), thus orienting these broadcasting companies' efforts (even) more towards the societal level, and less to the community level. The reworked model in Figure 16.2 also shows how this reorientation has allowed the market-driven approach to penetrate the public domain.

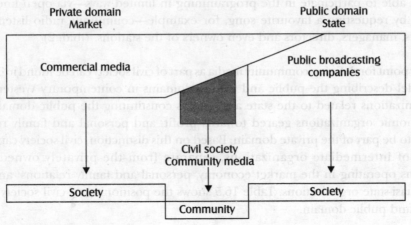

Figure 16.2 Media, Market and State
Source: Based upon Thompson, 1995:122.

A. The Importance of Community Media in Approach Three: Deepening Democracy

The third approach defines community media as part of civil society, a societal segment considered crucial for the viability of democracy. Although the nature of civil society can vary extensively across nations and continents, it is argued here that, following Cohen and Arato (1992:vii–viii), this concept is relevant to most types of contemporary societies and can be seen as an important locus for the expansion or deepening of democracy by means of increasing the level of participation (see Held, 1987).

Community media can firstly be seen as an 'ordinary' part of civil society, as one of the many types of organizations that is active in the field of civil society. The democratization *of* media, as Wasko and Mosco (1992:7) call this, allows citizens to be active in one of many (micro-)spheres relevant to daily life and to exert their rights to communicate. Secondly, as different political philosophers (from Rousseau, J.S. Mill and Wollstonecraft onwards) have pointed out, these forms of micro-participation are to be considered important, because they allow people to learn and adopt democratic and/or civic attitudes, thus strengthening, the possible forms, of macro-participation. Verba and Nie (1987:3) summarize this as follows: '*a participatory polity may rest on a participatory society*'. Held (1987:280) uses another catchy phrase to exemplify this: '*we learn to participate by participating.*'

When the specificity of broadcasters and their potential role as, one of the, major public sphere(s) is brought into focus and community media are not defined as just 'ordinary' parts of civil society, these media become important because they contribute to what Wasko and Mosco (1992:13) call the democratization *through* media. Community media offer different societal groups and communities the opportunity for extensive participation in public debate and for self-representation in the (or a) public sphere, thus entering the realm of enabling and facilitating macro-participation (Thomas, 2007).

B. Threats to Community Media in Approach Three: A Viable Civil Society?

This approach also allows a foregrounding of the struggle between community media, as part of civil society, the state and the market. Commercial, and public, media tend to see community media as '*contenders in a Darwinistic struggle among commercially oriented media*' (Prehn, 1992:266). The rejection of advertising as a prime source of income by community media places them in a financially hazardous situation, sometimes making them limp from one financial crisis to another.

The situation for community media becomes even worse when they, as part of civil society, are considered to be a threat to a repressive state. The objectives of community media can cause some state apparatus to interfere, placing staff in sometimes life-threatening situations. The example below contains a fragment of an email alert, among others mailed to the 'Development and Media'-mailing list, giving an accurate description of the dangers community media collaborators face in Haiti.

Box 16.1 Community Media in Haiti

According to information collected by RSF, on 23 December, Caraïbes FM, a Port-au-Prince radio station, suspended its news programs after having received telephone threats from mass organizations close to the Lavalas Family Party (currently in power). 'We are always targeted by these organizations ... when they invite us to their press conferences,' explained newsroom director Carlo Sainristil. The station also decided to suspend the program 'ranmase' (summary), a weekly political news program which has also been the target of threats. Sainristil also said that he and several journalists received disturbing telephone calls in recent months. A manager for Radio Kiskeya, another Port-au-Prince station, also claimed that his station received anonymous telephone threats in recent months.

Moreover, on 28 December, Amos Duboirant, the director of Rotation FM radio station, which broadcasts from the town of Lascahobas (in central Haiti), denounced the threats and intimidation against his station. Speaking on the air on another radio station, he reported that armed men connected to the municipality had surrounded Rotation FM's premises on 27 December, after the station denounced the unhealthiness in the city during the end of year holidays.

(*Box 16.1 continued*)

(*Box 16.1 continued*)

Dominique, director of the Radio Haïti Inter private station, was killed on 3 April as he was arriving at his station, located in the Delmas neighborhood (in Port-au-Prince's north-east). The station's guard was also killed in the attack (see IFEX alerts of 18, 7, 5 and 4 April 2000). A well-known political commentator in Haiti because of his constant commitment to democracy, Dominique had received death threats on several occasions. Radio Haïti Inter's director had disclosed several cases in which he implicated politicians and business people on his program 'Inter Actualités'. On 3 October, Radio Haïti Inter's personnel demonstrated against the slow progress of the investigation. At the time, the journalist's wife, Michelle Montas, said: 'I do not know the source of the barrier, but one clearly exists'.

Originator: Reporters sans frontières (RSF)
Date: 2001-01-03

When focussing on the internal functioning of community media, it should be emphasized that '*making democracy work*', to quote the title of one of Putnam's (1993) main publications, is a very difficult task that needs constant attention. The ongoing power struggle at the Pacifica network (USA) can be considered a textbook example. Organizations that are horizontally structured and oriented towards community participation have to deal with a certain degree of inefficiency, sometimes making their functioning and the realization of their objectives impossible or perverting these objectives. As Held (1987:281) puts it: 'it is at least questionable whether participation per se leads to consistent and desirable political outcomes'.

4. Approach Four: Community Media as Rhizome

Both the civil society and alternative media approaches have been fiercely criticized. When discussing the notion of alternative media Downing et al. (2001:ix) critiques its '*oxymoronic*' nature: '*everything, at some point, is alternative to something else*', thus legitimizing his decision to focus on 'radical alternative media'. Rodriguez (2001:20) develops a similar argument and even suggests abandoning the notion of alternative media altogether, in favour of 'citizen's media'. And although relationist approaches to civil society do exist, as can be found in for instance Walzer's (1998) work, this theoretical position has been criticized for its focus on the autonomous identity of the different actors and its ignoring of the contingency and interdependency of these identities.

For this reason the (relationist) civil society approach towards CM is radicalized building on Deleuze and Guattari's model of the rhizome (1987) and combined with the relationist approach of community media as alternative media. The theory of the rhizome is based on the juxtaposition of rhizomatic and arbolic thinking.[8] The arbolic is linear, hierarchic and sedentary, and could be represented as '*the tree-like structure of genealogy, branches that continue to subdivide into smaller and lesser categories*' (Wray, 1998:3). It is, according to Deleuze and Guattari, the philosophy of the state. On the other hand, the rhizomatic is non-linear, anarchic and nomadic. '*Unlike trees or their roots, the rhizome connects any point to any other point ...*' (Deleuze and Guattari, 1987: 19).

The image of the rhizome allows incorporating the high level of contingency that characterizes community media. Both their embeddedness in a fluid civil society, as part of a larger network, and their antagonistic relationship towards the state and the market, as 'alternative' to mainstream public and commercial media, make the identity of community media highly elusive. In this approach it is argued that this elusiveness and contingency, as is the case for a rhizome, forms its main defining element.

As rhizomes, community media tend to cut across borders and build linkages between pre-existing gaps: '*a rhizome ceaselessly establishes connections between semiotic chains, organizations of power and circumstances relative to the arts, sciences and social struggles*' (ibid.:7). In the case of community media, these connections apply not only to the pivotal role community media (can) play in civil society, but also to the linkages community media—and other civil organizations—can establish with, segments of, the state and the market, without losing their proper identity. In this sense, community media do not operate completely outside the market and/or the state, although the identity of community media is often defined in an antagonistic relationship, as being an alternative to the mainstream, towards the market and the state. Community media also establish different types of relationships with the market and/or the state, often for reasons of survival. At the same time they can be seen as potentially destabilizing—'de-territorialising' in Deleuze and Guattari's theory—the rigidities and certainties of public and commercial media organizations. The visualization of both the elusiveness of the rhizomatic network, and its de-territorializing potential towards the more rigid media organizations in the public and private domain can be found in Figure 16.3.

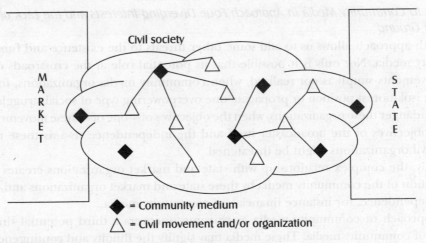

Figure 16.3 Civil Society and Community Media as Rhizome

A. The Importance of Community Media in Approach Four: Connecting Civil Society

This fourth approach builds further onto the importance that is attributed to civil society and—in relation to—democracy. In contrast to the third approach, the main emphasis for describing the importance of community media is not their role as part of the public sphere, but the catalyzing role they can play by functioning as the crossroads where people from different types of movements and struggles meet and collaborate, such as people from different women's, peasants', students', and/or anti-racist movements. In this fashion community media not only function as an instrument giving voice to a group of people related to a specific issue and/or, but also can function as a catalyst, grouping people active in different types of struggle for equality—or other issues.

Especially in the field of radical democratic theory, ample emphasis is attributed to the necessity for linking diverse democratic struggles in order to allow the '*common articulation of, for example, antiracism, antisexism and anticapitalism*', as one of the proponents puts it (Mouffe, 1997:18). She continues by stressing the need to establish an equivalence between these different struggles, as it is not considered sufficient to establish '*a mere alliance*' (ibid.:19) but deemed necessary to modify '*the very identity of these struggles ... in order that the defense of workers' interests is not pursued at the cost of the rights of women, immigrants or consumers*' (ibid.).

The approach of community media as rhizomatic also makes it possible to highlight the fluidity and contingency of (community) media organizations, in contrast to the rigid ways mainstream public and commercial media often—have to—function. Because of the elusive identity of community media, they can—by their mere existence and functioning—question and destabilize the rigidities and certainties of public and commercial media organizations. At the same time, this elusiveness makes community media, as a whole, hard to control and to encapsulate in legislation, thus guaranteeing their independence.

B. Threats to Community Media in Approach Four: Diverging Interests and the Lack of a Clear 'Common Ground'

This fourth approach allows us to add some other threats to the existence and functioning of community media. Not only is it possible that its potential role at the crossroads of different social movements simply is not realized, when community media organizations, for instance, choose an isolationist position or propagate one overpowering type of social struggle. This role can also endanger these organizations, when the objectives of—one of—these movements conflict with the objectives of the broadcaster itself and the independence vis-à-vis these movements and/or civil organizations might be threatened.

Secondly, the complex relationship with state and market organizations creates the risk of incorporation of the community media by these state and market organizations and/or the loss of the independence, for instance financial, of community media.

The approach of community media as rhizome uncovers a third potential threat to the existence of community media. These media may signify the fluidity and contingency of media organizations, in contrast to the rigidities and certainties of public and commercial media organizations. At the same time this elusiveness might prevent the existence of a 'common ground' on which policy may act. This lack of a clear 'common ground', unifying and structuring community media as such, also complicates the functioning of the organizations representing community media—such as, for instance, AMARC—and has prevented in the past the emergence of a well-defined community media movement.

The four approaches and the deduced arguments showing the importance and weaknesses of community media are summarized in Table 16.5. This overview articulates community media as an important but vulnerable type of media organization.

Table 16.5
Summarizing the Four Theoretical Approaches

Approaches to	1	2	3	4
Community media	Serving a community	Community media as an alternative to mainstream media	Linking community media to the civil society	Community media as rhizome
Importance of community media	• Validating and strengthening the community • Treating the audience as situated in a community • Enabling and facilitating access and participation by members of that community • Topics that are considered relevant for the community can be discussed by members of that community • Opening a channel of communication for misrepresented, stigmatized or repressed societal groups	• Community media show that 'the third way' is still open for media organizations • Alternative ways of organization, and more balanced and/or horizontal structures remain an actual possibility • Community media can offer representations and discourses that vary from those originating from mainstream media • Emphasis on self-representation, resulting in a multiplicity of societal voices • Diversity of formats and genres—room for experiments	• Importance of civil society (as such) for democracy, with community media as part of civil society • Democratization of media in relation to micro- & macro-participation· • Democratization extensive part-icipation in public debate and opportunities for self-representation in the (or a) public sphere	• Community media as the crossroads where people from different types of movements and struggles meet and collaborate • Deepening democracy by linking diverse democratic struggles • Highlighting the fluidity and contingency of media organizations • Questioning and destabilizing the rigidities and certainties

(*Table 16.5 continued*)

(*Table 16.5 continued*)

Approaches to	1	2	3	4
				of public and commercial media organizations, making at the same time room for collaboration and partnerships • Elusiveness makes community media (as a whole) hard to control and to encapsulate—guaranteeing their independence
Threats to Community media	• Dependency towards the community • Raising the community's interest for two-way communication when the dominant media discourse is based on one-way communication • Lack of two-way communication skills and interest • Lack of technology facilitating two-way communication • Reduction of	• Lack of financial and organizational stability, being small-scale, independent and horizontally structured organizations • Articulated as un-professional, inefficient, limited in their capacity to reach large audiences and as marginal as some of the societal groups they try to give voice to • Low political priority given to the 'marginal'	• Community media as contenders among commercially oriented media • Rejection of advertising as a prime source of income leads to financially hazardous situations • Dangers caused by a repressive state· • Dealing with a certain degree of inefficiency· • Making democracy work requires constant attention	• Not realizing its role as crossroads • Diverging or conflicting objectives with civic organizations, threatening the medium's independence towards these organizations • Incorporation by state and market organizations,

(*Table 16.5 continued*)

(*Table 16.5 continued*)

Approaches to	1	2	3	4
	community to its geographical meaning, trapping community media in the position of small-scale local media, gradually de-emphasizing their role towards serving the community			loss of independence towards these organizations • Lack of a clear 'common ground' leading to lack of policy efforts, complicating the functioning of representative organizations and preventing the emergence of a well-defined community media movement

A Belgian Case Study: Kijk de Wijk—Look My Neighbourhood

In this part the resulting multi-theoretical approach is put to work as a toolbox for the analysis of a mixed media neighbourhood development project, which is aimed at improving the social and economic texture in a North Belgian town.

1. Societal Context

The 'Kijk De Wijk'-project[9] is situated in an area of Antwerp called Seefhoek, which is part of the North Belgian city's 19th century industrial belt. Though Antwerp is considered to be one of the centres of gravity of the Belgian economy—because of its large harbour and key role in the trade of diamonds, to name but two—different areas of this town with 500,000 inhabitants are considered to be deprived. A complex set of societal problems, complemented with a very high number of votes for the extreme right-wing party '*Vlaams Blok*'[10] have prompted policy-makers at different levels to invest in these areas, in order to improve living conditions and the social and economic texture. These funding opportunities included the use of the European Regional Development Fund (ERDF) and the North Belgian Social Impulse Fund (SIF), with the Cultural Projects Fund (CPF) as one of its programmes.

2. A Brief Sketch of KdW

A group of social organizations[11]—with among them one of the few community radio stations left in North Belgium—Radio Centraal in Antwerp—applied for a CPF-funding for the KdW-project. The project has two main objectives: to give media training to people living in the Seefhoek-area, and to improve the image of that area. In order to achieve these objectives a series of activities is planned, including audio and video training workshops, radio broadcasts on Radio Centraal, photo exhibitions, making—and distribution—of a neighbourhood newspaper and the development of a web-site giving an overview of the produced content, and a virtual impression of a neighbourhood in the making.

At the time of writing 11 media training workshops have been organized:

- Three workshops for eight members of 'Brandpunt 23'—a local working group for 'social photography'—discussing technical and content-related aspects of social photography with two professional photographers.
- Three workshops for a group of 12 young asylum seekers, introducing them to the relevant techniques and allowing them to make a series of video and audio documentaries related to the topic of travel.
- One workshop for a group of six children, in collaboration with a Gynaika-project. Gynaika uses a bus to organize a series of multimedia and art workshops located at different squares in Antwerp. The collaboration enabled a small group of children to interview bystanders.
- One workshop—'How to be famous I'—for the, regular and occasional, visitors of the 'Oude Badhuis', allowing about 25 local youngsters to use a basement television studio, specifically constructed for the occasion, after a short training. Images were made at a neighbouring square the day before and used as a 'teaser' to attract the attention of potential participants. The day of the actual workshop, when the site, the 'Oude Badhuis', was an open house, the participants registered and interviewed the other visitors. They also edited the material themselves, which was broadcast using an internal television circuit.
- Three workshops—'How to be famous II'—for 10 regular visitors of the PCS, training them in the use of audio and video equipment, after which they were allowed to take the

equipment home. The collected material was then edited, resulting in a 30-minutes news broadcast about the neighbourhood.

These workshops were complemented with the exhibition 'Great people' and three neighbourhood newspapers. In the 'Great people' exhibition 12 'local heroes' were photographed and interviewed. These pictures were enlarged to a 5 × 3 metres format and put on display on different locations, where the interviews could be heard through speakers hidden in a cellar window, a tree, a letter box, or through an open window in a nearby house. During the opening of the exhibition artists who were born in the Seefhoek performed and several hundred inhabitants[12] paraded—accompanied by local brass bands—from picture to picture. In the three newspapers, printed on 15,000 copies and distributed in the neighbourhood,[13] residents told their life- and living-stories. These residents were also portrayed in the newspapers by one of the teachers of the 'social photography'-workshop.

Other activities, such as a new series of workshops, two 'ordinary' radio broadcasts, one live low-power radio broadcast in the neighbourhood itself,[14] a subproject with the collaboration of the residents of an estate in the Seefhoek, the virtual neighbourhood web-site, one new neighbourhood newspaper and the closing exhibition, still have to take place.

3. More on the Objectives of KdW

As mentioned before, the two main objectives of this project are giving media training to people who live in the Seefhoek-area, and improving the image of that area. Both objectives are interrelated, as the residents are trained in the use of media technology, in order to control themselves the image of their area being (re-)created. As is mentioned in the application text: '*the aim is to allow the participants to function in complete autonomy when registering and interpreting the events deemed important by him/herself in their immediate neighbourhood.*' In one of the letters to the residents, one of the trainers writes: '*We would like to record the changes, on photo, film, though radio and a newspaper. But we would like to be able to choose the changes. We would like to see the neighbourhood change the way the inhabitants think the neighbourhood should change.*' The combination of both objectives will result in a virtual image of a new Seefhoek, (partially) based on the content produced by the residents that will serve as a '*plan, project and program for the future*'.

At the same time the training workshops and the learning process that lies behind the creation of the different media products, serves a series of more independent objectives:

Helping the participants understand the functioning of the mass media, mainly through an analysis of media power, based on a combination of a political economy approach and a more culturally inspired critique on media representation. In the letter mentioned above, the trainer writes: '*We think it is important that people gain more power over the media. Television for instance is often made for financial reasons and not for the pleasure of the viewers. It is important that we really experience how media work. That way we can all become little journalists.*'

Changing the perceived participants' cultural and political passivity and disinterest. This objective is summarized in the application dossier as follows: '*The democratic level of our society will increase when citizens have a more nuanced view on different problems and when they function less as a individual and more as a community.*'

Improving the participants' opportunities on the labour market. As the Seefhoek is characterized by a level of unemployment that lies well above the town's average and the educational level lies well below average, it is claimed that this project will increase, to a certain extent, the educational level of the participants and hence their labour opportunities.

The so-called creation of a new image of the Seefhoek also serves a number of purposes that can be seen as independent from the media training of the residents. As mentioned above, the project is financed by the Social Impulse Fund, which aims at strengthening the social and economic texture of the city, at improving living conditions and indirectly at decreasing support for the extreme-right. The KdW-project ambitiously aims at creating a new plan for the Seefhoek and the realization of this ambition is the responsibility of the coordinating organizations—and not of the participants—as the concept of participation is strongly oriented to the creation of a series of mutually independent media products.

Both objectives are included in the Figure 16.4.

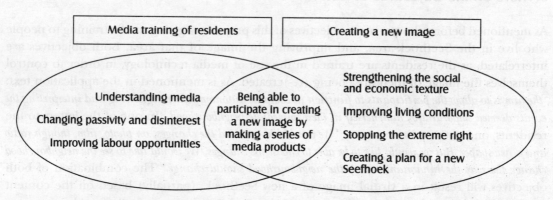

Figure 16.4   Objectives of the KdW-Project

Within the articulation of these objectives, main structuring components of the KdW-project are firstly 'participation and empowerment oriented towards social change', and secondly 'media synergy without media centrality'. The project explicitly aims to empower 'ordinary people' by teaching them the tools of the trade and offering them the opportunity to get acquainted with semi-professional audio and video equipment. This allows the participants to become '*little journalists*', or in other words, to break the barrier between the professional media elite and the 'ordinary people'. By taking hold of some of the basic communicative tools, they are placed in a position that they can tell and record their live- and living-stories, with the clear intention to promote social change. This intention is not only realized by denouncing local problems, but also by showing that 'ordinary people' are capable of using the technology and journalistic conventions for analyzing these local problems and for telling their own stories. In the case of the three PSC-workshops, the news broadcast contained items on refugees/asylum seekers and dilapidation on the one hand, but also featured a local writer and a local photographer talking about their work.

The second structuring component—media synergy without media centrality—refers to the use of mixed media as carriers of compatible meanings. The pictures and interviews used in the 'Great people' exhibition were for instance also used in one of the KdW-newspapers, and will feature on the project's website. The interviews will also be used for a radio broadcast. The emphasis on mixed media prevents that the media organizations involved become the starting point of the project. The community radio station 'Radio Centraal' is one of the partners of the project, but is not considered to be central to the project. Based on its expertise related to media technology and its knowledge of the functioning of alternative and mainstream media, it can adequately contribute to the project, without dominating and/or monopolizing it, and the participants.

4. Analysis and Synthesis

The KdW-project is to a very high degree oriented towards the *local community*. The project aims to give voice to the inhabitants of one of the most deprived areas of Antwerp in drafting a new, still virtual, neighbourhood, thus using a geographical approach to the concept of community. Access and participation of the members of the community in the use of different media are facilitated by training-workshops, where the participants are not only offered an opportunity to get acquainted with media technology, but also stimulated to discuss the problems they consider relevant to the community's well-being. At the same time the logic of project funding, combined with the lack of financial resources and time to invest in large training–workshops limits the degree of participation of the inhabitants. For reasons of efficiency and time–management the workshops are highly structured, though nevertheless improvised, and the involvement of the participants in certain domains, such as editing, is kept rather limited.

When confronted with this criticism, one of the project coordinators expressed the intention to increase the level of participation in the workshops to come, in the production of the fourth newspaper and in subproject in the estate. In the case of the newspaper it is being considered to ask the participants of the workshops to interview other residents and write articles on issues of their choice.

The discourses used during the workshops and in the media products are strongly related to the *alternative-mainstream* dichotomy. The analysis made of the North Belgian mainstream media can be considered critical, when it comes to their—commercial—intentions, their lack of interest for the 'real' problems of 'ordinary people' and their disinterest in a problem-solving role. For this reason(s) the KdW-project can be linked to the analysis made in the sphere of civic/public journalism, although it is more related to 'participatory journalism'.[15] At the same time KdW offers a set of 'alternative voices and images' that contrast with the representations used and created by mainstream media. The inhabitants are represented, and allowed to represent themselves, as critical and creative citizens, showing great interest in the evolution of their neighbourhood. Being outside mainstream media also creates problems of financial stability and continuity, which results in a relatively small number of workshops with a relatively small number of participants for a relatively limited amount of time. This problem is explicitly recognized by one of the KdW-coordinators:

As long as there is no alternative medium, through which we can give these realizations news value, by confronting them with an audience of listeners and viewers, we will stay in the margins of the world of communication. And the participants will remain—despite our efforts—ordinary people. He also expresses the need for the creating of a form of 'permanent follow-up' for the project: 'The young Deborah, the old Adriaan and the participants from the Open House belong to a target group (not the right phrase, but still …) that cannot act independently in reporting the issues and stories they find relevant. They do not have the means (yet), as the teachers and equipment are gone. Hence the idea of a cybercafé for the continuation and permanent *follow-up of the project. Up to now, we've only shown them the possibilities.…*

Thirdly KdW explicitly aims to improve the *democratic (local) culture*, by creating a more critical stance towards the functioning of the mass media and towards local problems as perceived by the inhabitants. Moreover, the project offers the participants a tool for social change, by teaching them a way to tell, structure and record their stories. Although participation at certain levels is rather limited and the teacher-participant relation sometimes echoes the 'professional elite'-'ordinary people' relation,[16] the residents of the Seefhoek are empowered to have their voices heard. Especially the mixed media approach and the use of a *network* of different organizations—ranging from a local working group for social photography to an Antwerp community radio station—should be considered a major strength. From this viewpoint, the project takes on the role of a crossroads, bringing together people from different organizations and from different backgrounds. Although this situation also sometimes creates differences of opinion and/or strategy, it also enables different social struggles to meet, thus further deepening (local) democracy. Furthermore, the strategic alliance with some of the Belgian and Antwerp government bodies—financing the project—has allowed these civil society organizations to cut across the traditional borders between state, market and civil society, without fundamentally weakening their identity construction as different or alternative from state and market organizations. By breaking with a more isolationist tradition the organizations, and especially the community radio station in question, are given the opportunity to expose the outside world to their combined democratic discourses, potentially destabilizing mainstream media discourses.

5. A Brief Note on Methodology

This evaluation of the KdW-project is based on the analysis of the available documents, provided by the two project coordinators, which were also interviewed. The text-analysis was supplemented by an analysis of the recordings of two of the PSC-workshops. One of the researchers was also present, as an observer, during the third PSC-workshop. The four theoretical approaches discussed above were used as sensitizing concepts, structuring the analysis and the brief report.

The results of the analysis were then mailed to the two coordinators for feedback, allowing them to give their view on the analysis. In the next phase this feedback was analysed, and relevant changes and additions were implemented. As the KdW-project is an ongoing project, the research should be, partially, defined as interventionist, as it is, also, aimed at identifying the factors that delimit the residents' participation, thus attempting to increase the level of participation of this project.

Strategies for Change

In the final part of this text, we focus on a series of possible strategies to improve the situation of community media. By using a combination of four theoretical approaches, we have not only shown the importance of community media, but also their vulnerability. For this reason, the conclusion of this chapter discusses a series of strategies oriented towards improving the situation of community media. These strategies are deduced from the theoretical framework, from the summarizing table that was used as a tool for the analysis of the Belgian case, and from the Belgian case itself. It is contended that these strategies should take into account both the diversity and the specificity of community media.

We suggest two types of strategies. The first strategy is aimed towards strengthening the niches community media often are located in, being caught in the uneasy position between market and state. The second strategy focuses more at the societal context in which community media function: by enlarging the network (or rhizome) community media are part of, their democratic function within civil society can be realized to a higher degree.

1. Strengthening the Niches

In order to improve the position of their community media, several countries have established media funds, specifically oriented towards direct project funding, and privileging community media. Examples are the French 'Fonds de soutien à l'expression radiophonique' and the South-Belgian 'Fonds d'aide à la création radiophonique'.[17] These, community, media funds could also function on a more transnational level, allowing community media from a specific continent, or different continents to apply for direct project subsidies.

A second point of attention is the quality of legislation and its enforcement in different countries and continents. This legislation might not be limited to the protection of human rights in their widest sense, but also to the recognition of the specificity and difference of community media on technical, organizational and content-related levels. As community media often find themselves in a more vulnerable position than market and state, or public, media, and their relation towards the state and market is also sometimes problematic, specific legislation is needed for their protection. This area includes access to good quality frequencies, the necessary technical equipment at a reasonable price, the presence of alternatives for, usually expensive, technical innovations, and the legal acceptance of organizational structures that are used by community media. All these would help facilitate the position of their volunteers, at the same time allowing for decent housing and protecting the independence and safety of the community media and their staff.

2. Enlarging the Network/Rhizome

At the same time, policies could be oriented towards the important role community media can play for reaching, maintaining, and deepening the level of democratization. This democratic function is especially related to their role as a nodal point in the network of civil society. The first step in improving the strength of the rhizome is improving the network between the different community media themselves, an aim that could be realized by the structural—financial—support for the representative organizations of community media, at the national and international level. This could allow these representative organizations, among others, to increase the number of 'regional offices'—covering a limited group of countries—to organize the exchange of programmes using different carriers, and the ability to exchange community media staff. In these ways, the contacts between community media collaborators from different countries and/ or continents might be established, thus stimulating organizational learning and networking.

Furthermore, the number of connections between community media and non-media civil organizations should be increased. Project funding specifically aimed at the collaboration of media and non-media organizations should be given priority. Contacts between the staff—working on compatible issues—of these different organizations should be stimulated. Exchange programmes for training community media staff by members of the non-media civil organizations in the areas of their expertise, and vice versa, should be organized. In this fashion, the opportunities for partnerships between media and non-media organizations are increased and the media-centrality that still, sometimes partially, characterizes most media organizations would be diminished.

Finally, the importance of the connections between public mainstream media and community media should be stressed. The rhizomatic approach allows breaking through the rigid separations that are created by the antagonistic position towards mainstream media—approach II—and towards the market and the state as such—approach III. The fourth approach creates more room for both the deterritorializing of mainstream media and at the same time enabling the collaboration with state and/or market organizations. Partnerships between, especially public, mainstream media could strengthen the rather problematic, vulnerable and isolated position of community media and allow mainstream media a unique form of organizational learning.

These different strategies, when implemented with the up-most respect for diversity and specificity, can allow community media to remain in a position where they can continue to serve their community, act as an alternative to mainstream media discourse, push for democratization in and through media, and function as a crossroads of civil society.

Notes

1. See for instance Janowitz (1967) early work on the community press.
2. The World Association of Community Radio Broadcasters is usually referred to by its French acronym AMARC, or the 'Association Mondiale des Radio diffuseurs Communautaires'. The AMARC website can be found at: http://www.amarc.org
3. In sociology, a group of people that is formed based on common interests is usually referred to as a 'collectivity' (Merton, 1968:353). A collectivity does not always have direct interaction, but is often only based on a common goal or interest. The people who belong to a collectivity do not need to know each other, and one cannot always identify direct interaction between them.
4. Hollander (2000:372) correctly argues that geographically based communities can also use digital technologies, which implies that a clear dichotomy between 'virtual' and 'real life' communities is not tenable.
5. In other words: people who are not part of a societal elite (including politicians, experts, and media professionals) and those not considered to be celebrities.
6. Table 16.4 is partially based on the list Lewis (1993a:12) mentions. Some of the examples were added by us.
7. When defining civil society, Cohen and Arato (1992:ix) explicitly include what they call the intimate sphere. The exact nature of civil society, and the question, which spheres to include is beyond the objectives of this text.
8. Deleuze and Guattari's thought is situated within the field of epistemology. Here we focus more on organizational structures that are seen as the sedimentation of the arbolic and/or rhizomatic ways of thinking.
9. 'Kijk de Wijk' can be translated as 'Look My Neighborhood' and will be abbreviated as KdW.
10. At the community council elections on 8 October 2000, 33 per cent of the Antwerp population (inhabitants that were entitled to vote) voted 'Vlaams Blok'. At the national parliamentary elections of 18 May 2003, 30.46 per cent of the Antwerp canton voted 'Vlaams Blok' (for the Chamber of Representatives), and at the Flemish parliamentary elections of 13 June 2004, 34.88 per cent voted 'Vlaams Blok.' On 14 November 2004, after having three of its linked organisations convicted on the grounds of inciting for racism, the 'Vlaams Blok' changed its name into 'Vlaams Belang'.
11. These organizations are: Het Oude Badhuis ('the Old Bathing House'–a social centre), Brandpunt 23 ('Focus 23'— a local working group for 'social photography'), Kzinix (an organization working on audio-visual projects), Het Noordelijk Halfrond ('The Northern Hemisphere'—an organization placing cultural activities in a social change framework), PSC ('Protestant Social Center'), AMAS ('Antwerp Minor Asylum Seekers'—an organization giving support to minor asylum seekers) and Grote Goesting ('Great Desire'—a theatre production in collaboration with local residents).
12. Other inhabitants showed their dissatisfaction with the presence of non-white 'local heroes'.
13. Especially the third newspaper met with resistance from one of the other local newspapers (the 'Wijkgazet'). The 'Wijkgazet' is also funded by the SIF and uses a more traditional approach, combining semi-political communication and the distribution of local information by a professional redaction. It was feared that the 'populist' approach of the KdW-newspaper would increase the support for the 'Vlaams Blok', instead of diminishing it.
14. This can consequently be considered as a form of neighbourhood radio.
15. Participatory journalism' is linked with what McQuail (1994:131–132) calls the democratic-participant media theory.

16. This for instance happens when a teacher uses technical jargon that is beyond the comprehension of the participants. The participants also define the teachers as professionals—because they are seen to possess 'professional knowledge'—despite the efforts of the teachers and their different—sometimes opposite—self-identification.

17. 'Fonds de soutien à l'expression radiophonique' and 'Fonds d'aide à la création radiophonique' can be translated as support funds for the radiophonic expression or creation.

References

AMARC-Europe. 1994. *One Europe—Many Voices. Democracy and Access to Communication, Conference report AMARC-Europe Pan-European conference of community radio broadcasters, Ljubljana, Slovenia, 15–18 September 1994*. Sheffield: AMARC.

Ang, I. 1991. *Desperately Seeking the Audience*. London/New York: Routledge.

Atton, C. 2002. *Alternative Media*. London: Sage Publications.

Atton, C. and N. Couldry (eds). 2003. 'Special Issue on Alternative Media', *Media Culture & Society*, 25(5):579–86.

Berrigan, F.J. 1979. *Community Communications. The Role of Community Media in Development*. Paris: UNESCO.

Clark, D.B. 1973. 'The Concept of Community: A Reexamination', *Sociological Review*, 21:397–417.

Cohen, A.P. 1989. *The Symbolic Construction of Community*. London: Routledge.

Cohen, J. and A. Arato. 1992. *Civil Society and Political Theory*. London: MIT Press.

Couldry, N. and J. Curran (eds). 2003. *Contesting media power: alternative media in a networked world*. Lanham, Md.: Rowman & Littlefield.

Deleuze, G. and F. Guattari. 1987. *A Thousand Plateaus. Capitalism and Schizophrenia*. Minneapolis: University of Minnesota Press.

Downing, J., with T.V. Ford, G. Gil and L. Stein. 2001. *Radical Media: Rebellious Communication and Social Movements*. Thousand Oaks, CA: Sage Publications.

Fraser, C. and E.S. Restrepo. 2000. *Community Radio Handbook*. Paris: UNESCO.

Girard, B. (ed.). 1992. *A Passion for Radio*. Montréal: Black Rose Books.

Gumucio, D.A. 2001. *Making Waves. Stories of participatory communication for social change*. New York: Rockefeller Foundation.

Held, D. 1987. *Models of Democracy*. Cambridge: Polity Press.

Hewson, C. 2005. *Local and Community Television in the United Kingdom: A New Beginning? A Policy Review*. Lincoln: University of Lincoln.

Hollander, E. 2000. 'Online Communities as Community Media. A Theoretical and Analytical Framework for the Study of Digital Community Networks', *Communications: The European Journal of Communication Research*, 25(4):371–386.

Husband, C. 1994. *A Richer Vision. The Development of Ethnic Minority Media in Western Democracies*. Paris: UNESCO.

Jankowski, N. 1994. 'International Perspectives on Community Radio', in AMARC-Europe (ed.). *One Europe—Many Voices. Democracy and Access to Communication. Conference report AMARC-Europe Pan-European conference of community radio broadcasters*. Ljubljana, Slovenia, 15–18 September 1994 (pp. 2–3). Sheffield: AMARC.

Janowitz, M. 1967. *The Community Press in an Urban Setting. The Social Elements of Urbanism*. Chicago and London: The University of Chicago Press.

Jones, S.G. 1995. 'Understanding Community in the Information Age', in S.G. Jones (ed.). *CyberSociety; Computer-mediated Communication and Community*, pp. 10–35. London: Sage Publications.

Keane, J. 1998. *Democracy and Civil Society*. London: University of Westminster Press.

Leunissen, J. 1986. '"Community" en "Community Development" bij de Australische Aborigines', in M. Van Bakel, A. Borsboom and H. Dagmar (eds). *Traditie in Verandering; Nederlandse Bijdragen aan Antropologisch onderzoek in Oceani*, pp. 57–82. Leiden: DSWO Press.

Lewis, P. 1993a. 'Approach to the Alternative Media Impact Study', in P. Lewis (ed.). *Alternative Media: Linking Global and Local*, pp. 11–14. Paris: UNESCO.

———. 1993b. 'Conclusion', in P. Lewis (ed.). *Alternative Media: Linking Global and Local*, pp. 127–128. Paris: UNESCO.

Lindlof, T.R. 1988. 'Media Audiences as Interpretative Communities', *Communication Yearbook*, 11:81–107.

Martin-Barbero, J. 1993. *Communication, Culture and Hegemony. From the Media to Mediations*. London, Newbury Park, New Delhi: Sage Publications.

McNair, B. 1998. *The Sociology of Journalism*. London, New York, Sydney, Auckland: Arnold.

McQuail, D. 1994. *Mass Communication Theory*. London, Thousand Oaks and New Delhi: Sage Publications.

Merton, R.K. 1968. *Social Theory and Social Structure*. New York: The Free Press.

Morris, A. and G. Morton. 1998. *Locality, Community and Nation*. London: Hodder and Stoughton.

Mouffe, C. 1997. *The Return of the Political*. London: Verso.

O'Sullivan, T. 1994. 'Alternative media', in T. O'Sullivan, J. Hartley, D. Saunders, M. Montgomery and M. Fiske (eds). *Key Concepts in Communication and Cultural Studies, 2nd Edition*. London: Routledge.

O'Sullivan-Ryan, J. and M. Kaplun. 1979. *Communication Methods to Promote Grass-Roots Participation*. Paris: UNESCO.

Pateman, C. 1972. *Participation and Democratic Theory*. Cambridge: Cambridge University Press.

Prehn, O. 1992. 'From Small Scale Utopism to Large Scale Pragmatism', in N. Jankowski, O. Prehn and J. Stappers (eds). *The People's Voice. Local Radio and Television in Europe*, pp. 247–268. London, Paris, Rome: John Libbey.

Putnam, R.D. 1993. *Making Democracy Work*. Princeton: Princeton University Press.

Rodriguez, C. 2001. *Fissures in the Mediascape: An International Study of Citizens' Media*. Cresskill, New Jersey: Hampton Press.

Savio, R. (ed.). 1990. 'Communication, Participation and Democracy', *Development, Journal of the Society for International Development*, 2:7–123.

Servaes, J. 1999. *Communication for Development. One World, Multiple Cultures*. Cresskill, New Jersey: Hampton Press.

Sjöberg, M. (ed.). 1994. *Community Radio in Western Europe*. Sheffield: AMARC-Europe.

Sundaraj, V. 2000. 'New Age, New Challenges. UNDA and Its Mission in Radio, Television and Audiovisuals', in J. Servaes (ed.). *Walking on the Other Side of the Information Highway. Communication, Culture and Development in the 21st Century*, pp. 86–100. Penang: Southbound.

Thomas, P. 2007. 'The Right to Information Movement and Community Radio in India: Observations on the Theory and Social Practice of Participatory Communication', *Communication for Development and Social Change*, 1(1): 33–48.

Thompson, J.B. 1995. *The Media and Modernity. A Social Theory of the Media*. Cambridge: Polity Press.

Tönnies, F. 1963. *Community and Society*. London: Harper and Row.

Van de Donk, B.D. Loader, P.G. Nixon and D. Rucht. 2004. *Cyber Protest: New Media, Citizens and Social Movements*. London, NY: Routledge.

Verba, S. and N. Nie. 1987. *Participation in America. Political Democracy & Social Equality*. Chicago: University of Chicago Press.

Verschueren, P. 2006. 'From Virtual to Everday Life', in J. Servaes and N. Carpentier (eds). *Towards a Sustainable Information Society: Deconstructing WSIS*, pp. 169–184. Bristol: Intellect.

Walzer, M. 1998. 'The Idea of Civil Society. A Path to Social Reconstruction', in E.J. Doinne Jr. (ed.). *Community Works: the Revival of Civil Society in America*, pp. 124–143. Washington, D.C.: Brookings Institution Press.

Wasko, J. and Mosco, V. (eds). 1992. *Democratic Communications in the Information Age*. Toronto and Norwood, NJ: Garamond Press and Ablex.

Wenger, Etienne. 1999. *Communities of Practice: Learning, Meaning and Identity*. Cambridge: Cambridge University Press.

Wray, S. 1998. *Rhizomes, Nomads and Resistant Internet Use*. Available online at http://sth.hgkz.ch/rhizom/texte/rhizomesnomadsrestantuse.html (Downloaded on 1 February 2001).

Working with Media in Areas Affected by Ethno-political Conflict

17

GEORGIOS TERZIS AND MYRIA VASSILIADOU

Introduction

The world has witnessed around 250 armed conflicts in the twentieth century, during which over 110 million people have been killed, and many times that number wounded, crippled and mutilated. By the end of the century, some figures suggested the existence of 233 groups in 93 countries, representing fully one-sixth of humanity, engaged in political or military struggles, from which more than 20 million refugees were in flight (Manoff, 1998). The first years into the new millennium have shown no indication as to a global shift towards the decrease of such phenomena.

The multi-layered and complex factors relating to the escalation and violent eruption of ethno-political conflicts are discussed widely in literature and are not our focus hereafter. Nevertheless, the following categories could provide one of many ways of categorizing such factors: structural including economic, social, and political issues relating to wealth distribution and inter-ethnic relations; facilitating including the degree of politicization and ethnic consciousness and, triggering including sharp economic shocks, inter-group tension and the collapse of central authority (Costy and Gilbert, 1998:12). It is precisely the instrumental role of the media in the public 'negotiation' of these factors that is of interest here. 'Hate' media for example—or media's attempts for sensationalist reporting with an emphasis on attacking the 'other', can be present and influential in the formation of all these factors. For Hamelink (1997:32), it is through the media that national or ethnic propagandists can 'suggest to their audiences that "the others" pose fundamental threats to security and well-being of the society and that the only effective means of escaping this threat, is the elimination of this great danger.' Interestingly, despite evidence supporting a more 'selective effects' approach, many organizations which include the UN, the EU, the Council of Europe, the World Bank, and the Danish, Dutch, Norwegian, Swiss, UK and US governments, among others, spend considerable amounts of political capital and money in support of their belief that specially 'designed' peace-building media interventions can have a positive impact for a non-violent outcome of conflicts.

This chapter builds on mainstream arguments of how the media have a potential role in conflict situations by contributing towards the creation of environments of hate and violence as well as by being involved in the promotion of positive conflict transformation ones. Although we do not enter here into a discussion of these arguments [for more details see Howard et al., 2003], we recognize that these two implicit media paths are not necessarily oppositional and mutually exclusive, but can rather coexist in most media landscapes. They are used here as basic tools for the further analysis of the ways in which the multiple and multilayered roles of the media can be contextualized. The focus of this chapter is based on case studies around the world investigated by the authors and includes practical approaches to be taken in relation to the creation of positive conflict transformation environments. The emphasis is therefore on descriptive 'guidelines' which can be further contextualized into theoretical frameworks surrounding these issues.

Media and Peace-building Interventions

This chapter is part of a larger project and is based on fieldwork and research undertaken as part of the Cyprus-Greece-Turkey Media Programme of the international NGO, *Search for Common Ground,* and the analysis of 13 cases where media peace-building projects have been carried out in conflict areas around the world (these being, Afghanistan, Benin, Cambodia, Central Asia, Colombia, DG Congo, Indonesia, Kenya, Macedonia, Rwanda, Senegal and Sierra Leone). In some instances we visited the field, and conducted both observations of the projects and in-depth interviews with the organizers and implementers, and in others we conducted extensive and repetitive telephone interviews as well as collected secondary material. (The complete outcomes of this research are published in *The Power of the Media, a Handbook for Peace-builders* by the European Centre for Conflict Prevention in co-operation with the European Centre for Common Ground and Institute for Media, Policy and Civil Society [EIMPACS].)

The idea behind media interventions and peace-building is clearly a problematic link to make. The mainstream line of thought behind 'media and peace-building' goes that journalists are not supposed to 'take sides' on the conflict in question, other than the side of 'peace' (Galtung, 1998; Lynch and McGoldrick, 2005). The questions we were repeatedly confronted with during this fieldwork and in the context of the particular case studies revolved around:

- Who defines peace?
- How is peace conceptualized?
- How many types of peace exist for the various stakeholders and how do these apply in particular conflict areas?

- On which criteria, premises and priorities are journalists' choices based over the target audience and/or the issues to be addressed?
- Which accountability systems are held in place in order to take into consideration for eventual fallbacks? Who decides if media interventions are indeed 'constructive'?
- Eventually, should media interventions take place at all?
- Which are the defining conditions for such interventions and what is the justification for the [often international] organization's presence in areas of conflict? To which extent are they imposing their own value-system while attempting to introduce a media culture of peace?
- To which extent are these media interventions funding driven and in which ways does it affect the process and the outcome?

The diversity of debates in relation to such questions abounds and there certainly cannot exist one approach alone for media interventions in areas of conflict, since no two ethno-political conflicts or media environments are the same. The guidelines provided below are built upon our constant reflections of such questions in an effort to give an overall picture of possibilities in relation to media intervention projects and at the same time attempt to promote more critical approaches towards practical conflict management and transformation.

In the following section, the various stages of media intervention projects are discussed. The 'Pre-Project Assessment' section, deals with the first stage of conducting media peace-building projects, that is, feasibility studies and pre-project assessment work. The 'Project Planning/ Design' section categorizes media projects into three broad categories, namely training, provision of hardware, and media content and provides a comprehensive outline of questions and themes that need to be addressed before a project takes place. Finally, 'Monitoring, Evaluating, and Leaving Projects' addresses three challenging and often controversial stages of any media [and other] peace-building project: that of implementation, evaluation, and sustainability. It points to important issues to consider throughout these three stages and provides guidelines on how these can be carried out most effectively.

1. Pre-Project Assessment and Planning

Feasibility Study

The mission of the multi-dimensional Pre-Project Assessment process proposed here is to find out more about (a) the conflict situation per se, (b) the media environment and whether that allows the space for media-based intervention for peaceful conflict transformation, (c) if so, to identify the type of this intervention based on the overall results of the previous two. The answers to the following sets of questions are crucial in providing guidance for finding the necessary tools for shaping the appropriate communication strategy:

'Assessing' the Conflict.   A set of questions needs to be answered at this level:

1. What is the conflict about? What is the history of the conflict and as told by whom? What is the *current* level of ethnic, political and economic tensions? Instead of simply assuming that the conflict is ethnic, and focussing only on that, one needs to look at important variables in the case such as land disputes, poverty, religious fundamentalism, mine risks, power struggles [class, and 'race' would be the most obvious examples], gender relations [rape, wife battering], child abuse, amongst others; thus look at other forms of identity beyond ethnicity (which tends to be defined as fixed) and account for mutations. The identification of power structures in terms of ethnicity, class, age, and gender amongst others, as well as the most dominant values and accepted social norms are vital data on which to base any potential project.

2. What is the time-line of the conflict: Pre-Conflict (Latent), Open Conflict, and (or) Post-Conflict? Although quite simplistic, such time-lines can provide an indication on how to proceed. One way this could be approached is in terms of what the official line is, what the international community says, how the people experience it and so on.

3. Who are the parties involved [directly and indirectly] and what are their goals? These parties need not necessarily be only two, bipolar and opposing—the dangers of assuming so are outlined elsewhere (Howard et al., 2003). There are local, regional, national, and international, official and unofficial, public and private, players often involved, some of whom may or may not have contrasting aims.

4. What is the current state of the military, political and religious authorities and economies of the opposing sides? What are their positions? To which extent do they communicate these positions? To which extent are some more affiliated and connected than others? How are their power structures shaped?

5. Are there any political negotiations 'Track One' going on at the moment? If so, are they secret, known but closed-door, or open?

6. What are the views of the peoples on the various sides of the conflict? What do they perceive to be the reasons for the conflict, as necessary factors for its resolution and as a desirable solution? What are their needs for security, identity and development?

7. Who is working towards peace-building and the prevention of violence? How do they work? What are the options they are discussing? Who are they supported by financially? Why? Upon the embarkation on a new project, it is often the case that peace-builders and peace activities are ignored or underestimated. In order to have a sustainable project, an understanding of their objectives as well as a functioning working relationship with them is desirable.

8. In particular, is there a grassroot peace movement 'Track Two'? If so, what is the relationship between the official level/political elites 'Track One' and civil society 'Track Two'? Is there sufficient communication between them? Would the political bodies and other local elites and civil society encourage the entry of a Peace Media Project into the media environment(s)?

9. How can the peace-media project avoid acting and being perceived as a top-down, 'foreign'-imposed solution process? What are the possibilities for grassroots community involvement in such project and how can this intervention best serve the people involved?

'Assessing' the Media Landscape.   A second set of questions needs to be answered at this level:

1. Which communication avenues are available? Who owns/controls them? The diversity of the media needs to be explored and assessed and the support of the commercial sector for a variety of independent media, which are widely available to the public needs to be explored.
2. What are the audience ratings for different media and what is level of access—media penetration of different media? How do variables such as age, gender and social class affect access to the media?
3. How does the *inter-media agenda setting* work in the countries involved? In other words, which media are considered prestigious enough and set the news agenda for the other media outlets? *Which sources are trusted by the local people?* To which extent are state media the major source of information for the public? To which extent are public service media regarded by the minority groups especially as non-credible and as supporting the dominant ethnic group's cultural and political agendas.
4. What is the legal framework in which the media in the country operate [media law, freedom of speech, and so on]?
5. What is the journalists' 'professional culture' like? What is the strength of the professional unions of journalists?
6. What is the economic framework that the local media work in? What are [if any] the economic barriers to the development of an independent media? In case where there is an independent media culture established at a preliminary level, have there been any economic setbacks suffered in the process?
7. What is the approach of the different media outlets to the conflict? What is the degree of media ethnic segregation and partisanship?
8. What is the level of public, media and media-broker diplomacy? {Public Diplomacy is defined as the use of media and other mass communication from official sources from both sides for confrontational propaganda; Media Diplomacy is defined as the use of the media from officials from both sides for purposes of conflict resolution, Media-broker Diplomacy is defined as the use of media from journalists as a tool of the negotiations (Gilboa, 2000: 275–309).

'Assessing' the Needs for the Prospective Project.   Answers to the questions of the two previous sections provide guidance on how to proceed with the following:

1. What is the logistical/time-frame, material/technical, and human resource requirements in the country(ies) in conflict for establishing a Peace Media initiative?

2. Is training necessary for the implementation of the project? What type of training? By whom? For whom?

3. Is the establishment of new media necessary or can the project work with existing ones?

4. Are partnerships between local and international media important to be established?

5. Is the distribution of media hardware to the local media and the population important, and if so what kind?

6. Which one [or combination] of different media and media genres formats will be appropriate?

7. Is the creation of new media productions important for this project? What will the specific content of these productions be? What will the outlet be?

8. What will the method of production be and who will produce it?

9. How can a balance between the opposing parties be best maintained?

10. How can the sustainability (commercial or voluntary) of the project be assured?

11. What is the 'opportunity cost'? In other words, what other projects [media or other] for the positive transformation of the conflict could be achieved with the same effort and money?

12. What will the appropriate time for implementing media projects be?

Also important to this multi-dimensional assessment is *designing the questions* according to the local variables. Such a case-specific approach would allow the implemented strategies to vary widely according to the nature of the conflict, the cultural geography of the field and the local media landscape. Finally, it is not only the questions which are important to the assessment, but the selection of the people asking those questions and who they choose to ask. The bottom line is to identify the local and international power structures at various levels and thus first be aware of 'who says what to whom and why' and the researcher's own positionality in the process.

2. Project Planning–Design

In order to design and carry out the project, it is important to recognize that various inter-players need to collaborate, some more than others. The political, economic, cultural, religious, and educational variables of the area of concern need to be taken into consideration upon embarking on the implementation of the project. Training journalists can be ineffective in a totalitarian environment; using the print media for a population with high illiteracy rates will not have the desired affects; neither will use of television as a medium for the project in areas where most people have no access to television sets, or even electricity. Upon designing the project, consideration needs to be paid to the whole political and socio-economic landscape of the area. Cultures of democracy and tolerance, financial media independence, and applied, fair legislation are all indicators that the project is more likely to have a long-lasting effect. This, clearly, creates a paradox and a dilemma since it is in those particular environments that these types of media projects are mostly needed.

Prior to embarking on a project, it is advisable for a pilot programme to be used as a pre-testing method. Thus, a session for training, an episode for a potential soap opera, or a documentary can all be prepared for targeted focus groups and their reactions, comments and thoughts must be recorded and analysed. This will ensure that the media intervention/project planned and the most suitable format of programming is selected. Further, this will enable the organizers and implementers of the project to clearly specify their objectives:

'So-called "catch-all"' projects in which one attempts to address all possible objectives or demands are most likely the result of a lack of focus. Projects should therefore have one main objective [fit one category]. However, and as for other project activities, one must be aware of possible effects along other axes. An institution-building project may, for example, have both positive and adverse effects on an imminent or ongoing conflict. This must be considered in advance, monitored throughout the implementation period, and systematically evaluated in retrospect. (Eknes and Endresen, 1999)

The types of media projects can fall into three broad categories: Training, Projects Targeting Media Content and Provision of Media Hardware.

Training

Given the generally low level of formal qualifications in the media, training and seminars are becoming very important for journalists and other media personnel. There are indeed three main categories of people that could benefit from training.

First, media technical staff can be trained in printing, recording, editing, sound maintenance, and so on. Second, judges, lawyers, and civil servants can be trained in press law issues, freedom of speech, censorship, diversity, international conventions protecting journalists, assisting in changing restrictive media laws, mainstreaming human rights and gender. Third and finally, journalists and journalism students can be trained on safety instructions, standard journalism skills, media management, community media, human rights and ethnic minorities reporting, gender issues reporting, health-emergency or humanitarian reporting, web-based and non-mainstream source reporting, conflict resolution theories, conflict analysis reporting, media and media-broker diplomacy.

All the above training topics can be adopted for international journalists covering conflicts as well as local journalists in a conflict area. Furthermore, they can be adjusted to the needs of aid workers and grassroots peace movements interested in working with media for peace-oriented programming in workshops, community radio, television or the press.

Projects Targeting Media Content

It has already been suggested at the beginning of this chapter that there is a diversity of media and genres formats available to carry out the intended media content. The conflict situation and the state of the local media landscape will determine which one (or combination) of those media and genres is more appropriate.

In fact, a discussion of the ways in which media can contribute towards peace-building cannot stop at journalism but needs to incorporate all mass media forms and genres distributed to mass audiences by any given technological means. These can include hard-news journalism, the Internet and Internet dialogues, advertising and public service announcements, public relations, television and radio programmes, including inter-ethnic peace reporting soap operas, comedies, drama series, documentaries, movies, roundtable talk-shows, peace songs, call-in shows on the radio, wall posters and matchbooks, cartoons on television and in magazines, video dialogue, street theatre, popular music, editorial exchange, and social marketing.

Provision of Media Hardware

Because of the partial or complete destruction of the media infrastructure in areas of conflict the provision of media hardware is increasingly been recognized as an important area of humanitarian assistance. Provisions could include financial and technical support to local print and broadcast media to re-establish themselves. It is usually preferable to support and strengthen existing local media, but this assumes their editorial independence and ability to reach the affected population. The most common strategy, in case the former conditions do not exist, is to set up a new media facility which usually presupposes the co-operation of the local authorities.

Furthermore, donating newspaper paper and printing machines, distributing radios and batteries or solar radios to the local population, donating computers and free access to Internet, setting up Internet portals for exchange of information and chat rooms for exchanges of opinion, donating mobile phones when absolutely necessary for the communication of the journalists, subsidizing newspaper supplements, subsidizing the printing of training materials, providing office equipment and creating Virtual Warehouses for the support of local media in importing the most suitable and cheapest equipment are some of the strategies.

These provisions are accompanied with the appropriate training in order for the local media industry to function during the conflict while paying attention not to create long-term dependencies. [Adapted and expanded from DFID, 2000:18–28.]

3. Choosing Partners and Staff

No single organization can achieve any of the above alone. In order to realize the feasibility studies, the trainings, creation of media content and provision of hardware, questions such as the following regarding the choice of partners and staff need to be addressed:

1. What is the perspective of the individual/organization they represent in relation to the conflict?
2. What is their background in terms of the conflict? How professionally [un]involved are they in the situation?
3. How respected is the individual/organization in the wider society? How much are they recognized by the society for their integrity and impartiality?
4. To which extent might the employment of these individuals and organizations run the risk of undermining other local media?

5. How well do they understand the local media environment?

6. What types of contacts do they have with editors and media broadcasting corporations?

7. What types of contacts/relationship with the information or other ministries of the host government do they have?

8. How much do they charge for their services and is that 'reasonable'? It is important to note here that foreign organizations working in conflict areas need to take the local salaries into consideration. Often, the salaries of journalists are lower whereas that of locals working for international non-governmental organizations are higher than average. Although some changes in the local salary market are unavoidable, creating hostilities, competition, and jealousies amongst the locals must be kept to a minimum. Consideration ought to be given to the extent to which these salaries are sustainable on a longer term basis and not only for the duration of the direct emergency situation.

9. How can expert translators be approached and act as interpreters between locals and expatriates, and as monitors of the broadcasts or newspaper coverage?

4. Monitoring and Evaluating

It has this far been established and elaborated that pre-project assessment, evaluation and feasibility studies are vital to the development, implementation, and sustainability of any media project for peace-building purposes. Once the project starts, monitoring and evaluation are vital for ensuring that both quality and strength of the objectives and goals set out at the initial stage are maintained, and to ensure that key information is not being understood or interpreted by the audience/participants in ways not intended. Ongoing monitoring and project evaluation, as well as post-project assessment are important aspects of the project process itself. It is important that monitoring and evaluation are conducted in a systematic and regular basis and that the results are used to provide feedback on how to sustain the project's impact and develop further projects in a manner that addresses the needs of local people and project participants.

The information generated by ongoing and post-project assessment serves a number of important purposes. In the short run, objectives of the assessment provide both feedback on progress towards programme and activity objectives, and give information for future programme planning. In the longer term, such assessment efforts ensure the sustainability and continuity of programmes and the fulfilment of the organization's broader objectives. They also contribute towards verifying whether or not conflict resolution strategies are guiding programming.

It is often the case that evaluation and assessment are time consuming, expensive, and difficult because 'measuring' and evaluating media impact is such a complex process. A primary consideration at this point ought to be that 'evaluations have to be put into perspective in relation to other political, economical and social trends in a region. In other words, they must be based in a regional context, not only in the context of the particular conflict setting where the project is carried out' (Galama and van Tongeren, 2002:22). One cannot thus assume that the resulting effects of any project are isolated from events within the conflict and the region in general.

Evaluation through the production of reliable information, tools and methods that will facilitate action is necessary as is a more effective response on the part of policy-makers, operational actors and donors. Also several institutions [international, regional, and local] across disciplines and geographical boundaries need to be brought together in order to narrow the knowledge gap and facilitate dialogue. Local capacity for research, information gathering and analysis in conflict areas needs to be developed and encouraged through the transferring of skills to local researchers. The local constituencies and capacities for media peace-building need to be identified, reinforced and respected.

Evaluating conflict resolution programmes is far from easy. Most conflict resolution training and practice involves multiple goals, diverse participants, shifting time frames, and seeks to change behaviours, perceptions, and/or institutional practices. In addition, there is often uncertainty about the relationship between the direct effects a project may have on those who participate in its activities and its more indirect impact on the wider conflict in which the projects are embedded—the problem of transfer of any impact from the participants to the wider population (Kelman, 1995).

When carrying out any form of assessment during (to make sure that the intervention is carried out effectively and to make adjustments based on changes in the situation that may develop) or after a project has been completed (to revisit the whole process in a reflective manner and be able to build on the outcomes), the following questions can serve as guidelines that evaluators need to answer:

- What are the objectives of the project?
- To which extent has the project in question fulfilled its objectives?
- What precise activities corresponded to the project objectives?
- How will success be measured given the difficulty in setting measurable indicators? How can we broaden the set of criteria by which the project is evaluated, to include poverty, social injustice, and participation?
- What have the challenges and barriers been in the whole process of carrying out the project? In which ways could they have been avoided?
- Which results of the projects have not been anticipated? To which extent do these contribute or work against the primary aims of the project?
- Which part of the project has worked best and why?
- What is the ('tangible') social and political impact of the project?
- Is continued media support advisable?
- Has the number of people involved in it been increased? Has the number of people involved in peace processes increased?

- Has it contributed towards engaging people in activities which influence peace agreements?
- Has it contributed towards the more positive dialogue and communication of the authorities and civil society in ways that promote peace, reconciliation, or settlement? What about dialogue and communication amongst formal political structures? To which extent did it influence policies?
- Has it been a process which is likely to be sustainable? How can this be best tested?
- Has the project introduced constructive peacemaking methods and disseminated them in an effective manner?
- What changes has the project led to? How do these relate to the conflict? Would these changes have taken place without this project? To which extent do these changes contribute towards peace-building or conflict?
- How does the project affect the community and/or various individuals within it? How does it foster relationships?

A successful and reflective project evaluation rests on a self-conscious effort to articulate the most significant goals of different groups of participants and to track goal evolution in the course of a project. Further, an evaluation points to operational criteria of success linked to specific project activities and seeks solid evidence to determine the degree to which they have been met. It addresses the question of transfer, the ways in which direct work with only a small number of project participants is expected to have more extensive, indirect effects on the course of the wider conflict in which a project is embedded. It further leads to the development of multiple criteria of success and failure and it helps practitioners define future, stage-appropriate activities, which variously build on what has been successful and/or modifies activities in light of what has not. Finally, a successful evaluation helps disputants, interveners and funders to imagine good enough conflict management not by asking whether they have fully resolved a complicated conflict but whether they have improved conditions sufficiently that the parties in the conflict are more likely to develop the capacity to manage a conflict constructively in the future (for an extensive discussion, see Ross, 2001).

Evaluation methods for ongoing monitoring and post-project assessment need not be restricted to short written reports, although these are very important part of the process as well. Rather, innovative and creative methodologies and methods could be less 'traditional' and 'user-friendly' in order for practitioners and policy-makers to find it accessible. Given the implementers' often immense overload, such methods can be more reliable at times and less restraining. It is important thus to be flexible and acknowledge that the type of evaluation to be conducted needs to be adjusted to the needs and types of programme as well as media formats. The following are just some of the examples of diverse methodologies one can consider:

1. Pre- and post-tests to assess efficacy of training seminars.
2. Exposure scale to assess exposure to violence.
3. Impact scale to assess psychological difficulties.

4. Direct observation.
5. Focus group discussions with various groups of interest. This can become part of the project itself.
6. Narrative descriptions of traditional beliefs and healing methods.
7. Process descriptions of community entry and relationship building.
8. Pictorial and narrative description of community projects.
9. Records of sensitization meetings and media interviews.
10. Promotion of ways and methods of collaboration between academics and practitioners.

It has thus far been established that evaluation is both necessary and difficult to carry out. The following discussion concentrates around issues which frequently occur during the implementation, monitoring, and evaluation of media projects and it is based on data collected through interviews with people involved in the media projects presented in this volume as well as on existing literature on the topic.

First, it cannot be stressed enough that when international organizations turn up in a country to help, they need to identify the local, regional and international power structures. Many examples of attempts to create media programming as well as other forms of peace-building efforts demonstrate that these programmes run the risk of the existing power structures taking control of the programme/project. In fact, these power structures can be accentuated through emphasizing 'Otherhood' within communities and thus creating conflict within an ethnic group. Evaluation in itself is an activity which is part of these power structures and cannot be regarded as a neutral activity. Some parties will regard it with scepticism and some others will not and this is something to be remembered at all stages and process of the project.

Second, the question of who should carry out the evaluation often creates heated debates amongst peace workers [activists, practitioners, donors, academics and so on]. The criteria and indicators guiding the appraisal of the outcomes, as well as the party establishing them are issues with conflicting answers. The very idea of attributing progress to intervention is a very problematic theme which results in rigorous dialogue amongst social scientists developing evaluation systems. In addition, the needs of the donors, the government [authorities], the local community and the implementers of these projects for evaluations are different. The party regarded as the beneficiary of the information gleaned during the evaluation will also affect the methodologies used for it. Thus, donors often require that traditional quantitative measurements be used for the evaluation of peace-building projects. This can be a highly problematic approach as different evaluation methodologies suit different projects: 'for example, a local radio station may be evaluated by quantitative indications such as the number of hours of programming or listener numbers. Although not without relevance, such indicators do not say much about qualitative indicators such as substance, programme profile and impact. Indicators may therefore be relevant, or irrelevant, depending on what one wants to evaluate. The key to relevant and useful evaluation is to have a clear understanding of the initial objective of the project' (Eknes and Endresen, 1999:44). It is thus highly recommended that operators, donors, organizers, implementers, and evaluators work together and co-operate in order for the best possible outcome to emerge and they need to be able to distinguish between quantifiable and qualitative results.

Third, one way of dealing with concerns such as editorial standards is to have them monitored by expatriates without a stake in the local political situation. Thus, a degree of expatriate 'protection' available to local journalists who would otherwise be liable to pressure from local vested interests is ensured. These are the people who are likely to face less restraints and difficulties in terms of communication means, visas, accessibility to information and so on. During times of conflict, and especially in emergency situations, many international non-governmental organizations tend to employ expatriates to fulfil the needs for the evaluation and implementation programmes [often due to apparent lack of other options]. The problem here is that a main part of programme development is supposed to involve building local capacity and that must not be easily compromised. In addition, people who no longer live in the community can often lose touch rapidly and are often unfamiliar with current uses of phrases and words.

Fourth, the establishment of editorial checking systems in *local languages*, especially when the editorial standards are not very high, is again a complicated process. The station or other medium, can become involved in local prejudices and biases, which will leave it susceptible to pressure from the authorities. Further issues to consider include: what can be done when words/concepts are not directly translatable and an international/foreign correspondent or evaluator needs to use them? Even when the words/concepts are indeed translatable and/or used, persons from different sites, classes, and/or or levels of education have different use for them; and how does one make sure they are used in a manner which is accessible and understood by most? These are issues to constantly reflect upon.

Finally, the question arising from attempting to carry out well-designed evaluation is how can we answer questions that we don't know we should be asking and how can we be confident that respondents are not saying what they think we want to hear in such politically and socially sensitive circumstances with such extreme power dynamics? The answer lies again in cultural understanding, analysis and sensitivity. 'In certain cultures, it may be considered impolite to answer in the negative, so "yes/no" questions should be avoided. Open-ended questionnaires, however, may prove too time-consuming to process in a rapid manner' (Hieber, 2001:16).

5. Leaving the Project: Sustainability and 'Handover' Strategy

In order to ensure that a media intervention project is not driven primarily by funding, and that its implementers do not impose their own value-system while attempting to introduce a media 'culture of peace', but rather that they are interested predominantly in the project's sustainability of the project, a 'handover strategy' must be an integral part of the project design and objectives. Handing over the project to local community groups or professional organizations and the implementation of this strategy will enable the organization to incorporate local capacity-building as an integral part of the project strategy. It appears that the media projects which incorporate such strategies are rare.

Indeed, all media projects are interventions. As interventions, they make a difference (to the better or worse); by leaving the conflict area abruptly, there are unavoidable consequences and changes in the region. Care must be taken with expectations often rising with particular types of programmes. Local people might rely on these activities in various practical and psychological ways which must be considered and the ethics of project sustainability need to be taken very seriously indeed.

Instead of an epilogue: An Ecological Approach

This chapter has argued that efforts conceptualized media interventions for the positive transformation of conflicts ought to be parts of a concerted action to shift the governance culture in which the media operate because the environment in which the media content is received is extremely important for its 'interpretation'. Experience in the field of media and conflict transformation proves that efforts limited only to the media often fail to address some of the 'structural' factors that gave rise to the conflict in the first place, and because of that these factors most of the times 'neutralise' even the best efforts of media peace-building interventions. The design and implementation of these interventions should be extended to include governmental and non-governmental organizations, political leaders, businesses (including media owners), public opinion leaders, teachers and academics, and marginalized sections of the society. It is through this ecological holistic approach that media cultures can eventually be transformed and become a transforming force themselves.

References

Costy, A. and S. Gilbert. 1998. *Conflict Prevention and the European Union: Mapping the Actors, Instruments, and Institutions.* London: International Alert.

DFID. 2000. *Working with the Media in Conflicts and Other Disasters.* London: Department for International Development.

Eknes, A. and Lena C. Endresen. 1999. *Local Media Support.* Oslo, Norway: Fafo.

Galama, A. and Paul van Tongeren. 2002. *Towards Better Peace-building; On Lessons Learned, Evaluation Practices and Aid and Conflict.* Utrecht: European Centre for Conflict Prevention.

Galtung, J. 1998. 'High Road, Low Road—Charting the Course for Peace Journalism', *Track Two*, 7(4):7–10.

Gilboa, E. 2000. 'Mass Communication and Diplomacy: A Theoretical Framework', *Communication Theory*, 10(3): 275–309.

Hamelink, C. 1997. 'Media, Ethnic Conflict and Culpability', in J. Servaes and R. Lie (eds). *Media in Transition.* Leuven/Amersfoort: ACCO.

Hieber, L. 2001. *Lifeline Media: Reaching Populations in Crisis; A Guide to Developing Media Projects in Conflict Situations.* Versoix, Switzerland: Media Action International.

Howard, R., F. Rolt, H. Van de Veen and J. Verhoeven (eds). 2003. *The Power of the Media, A Handbook for Peacebuilders.* Utrecht: ECCP.

Kelman, Herbert. 1995. 'Contributions of an Unofficial Conflict Resolution Effort to the Israeli-Palestinian Breakthrough', *Negotiation Journal*, 11(1):19–27.

Lynch, J. and A. McGoldrick. 2005. *Peace Journalism*, Gloucestershire: Hawthorn Press.

Manoff, R. 1998. 'Role Plays' *Track Two*, 7(4):11–15.
Ross, M.H. 2001. 'Conceptualising Success in Conflict Resolution Intervention: Evaluation Guidelines'. Presentation to the Annual Meeting of the International Society for Political Psychology, July 2001, Cuernavaca, Mexico.

Conclusion

JAN SERVAES

All those involved in the analysis and application of communication for development and social change would probably agree that in essence, development communication is the nurturing of knowledge aimed at creating a consensus for action that takes into account the interests, needs and capacities of all concerned. It is thus a social process. Communication media and ICTs are important tools in achieving this process but their use is not an end in itself—interpersonal communication must also play a fundamental role.

This basic consensus on communication for development and social change has been interpreted and applied in different ways throughout the past century. Both at theory and research levels, as well as at the levels of policy and planning-making and implementation, divergent perspectives are on offer.

The relationship between the practical application of communication processes and technologies in achieving positive and measurable development outcomes is an emerging subject of research, discussion and conjecture. While media professionals, opinion-shapers and development assistance policy-makers have often sought to utilize communication systems for social mobilization and change, a lack of understanding of the complexity of behavioural, societal and cultural factors on end-user consumption patterns has more often led to ineffective, or even counterproductive, outcomes.

Experienced practitioners and scholars point to the need for a close study of society and culture in formulating communication and outreach strategies, thus ensuring that target audiences are reached in an appropriate manner to effect knowledge transfer. This is particularly urgent among developing countries, where access to information supporting health, agriculture, HIV/AIDS, literacy and other initiatives, can be vital, and where a lack of resources has rendered the sharing of information and knowledge difficult, and the reaching of consensus, problematic.

In establishing communication for development programmes, professionals have, in the past, often laboured under a misunderstanding commonly held by policy-makers relating to the nature of the discipline. Lay persons, understandably, confuse the subject with public relations, public information, corporate communications and other media-related activities. However, while communication for development and social change may incorporate skill-sets from those areas of information dissemination, the subject reaches far deeper and broader into the entire communication process.

Communication for Development and Social Change is a multi-faceted, multi-dimensional and participatory process through which people are empowered to control their own destinies. Culture is central to development and deserves greater emphasis in communication for development and social change.

Policy-makers, academics and practitioners alike should recognize that communication is a process, not a product or a set of technologies. It includes formal (for example, campaigns) and informal (for example, community participation), direct (for example, media exposure) and indirect (for example, communication in social networks) forms of communication.

In other words, communication must be seen as an essential element of every development and social change project. Communication needs to be applied in different ways and at distinct levels according to the needs and characteristics of the context or community.

Hopefully, this book has offered perceptive insights and vivid examples to prove that the field of communication for development and social change is indeed vibrant.

Bibliography and Select Readings*

Aabenhus, O. and J. Wijayananda. 1985. *Community Radio and Rural Development. Four Essays.* Colombo: Mahaweli Community Radio.

Adhikarya, R. 1994. *Strategic Extension Campaign: A Participatory-Oriented Method of Agricultural Extension.* Rome: FAO.

Agrawal, B.C. (ed.). 1985. *Anthropological Methods for Communication Research: Experiences and Encounters During SITE.* New Delhi: Concept Publishing Company.

Agunga, R., S.B. Aiyeru and F. Annor-Frempong. 2005. 'Communication for Local Participation in Project Planning: A Study of Rural Development Workers in Ghana and Nigeria', *The Journal of Development Communication*, 16(2): 1–14.

Ajzen, I. and M. Fishbein. 1997. *Understanding Attitudes and Predicting Social Behavior.* New York: Prentice-Hall.

Albrow, M. and E. King (eds). 1990. *Globalization, Knowledge and Society.* London: Sage Publications.

Alfaro Moreno, R.M. 1993. *Una Comunicacion para otro Desarrollo.* Lima: Calandria.

Allen T. and A. Thomas (eds). 1992. *Poverty and Development in the 1990s.* Oxford: Oxford University Press.

Alleyne, M.D. 1995. *International Power and International Communication.* London: Macmillan.

Alonso Mielgo, A. and E.Y Sevilla Guzmán. 1995. 'El Discurso Ecotecnocrático de la Sustentabilidad', in A. Cadenas Marín (ed.). *Agricultura y Desarrollo Sostenible*, pp. 91–120. Madrid: Ministerio de Agricultura, Pesca y Alimentación.

Amin, S. 1997. *Capitalism in the Age of Globalization: The Management of Contemporary Society.* Delhi: Madhyam Books.

Anderson, B. 1983. *Imagined Communities: Reflections on the Origin and Spread of Nationalism.* London: Verso.

Andreasen, A. 1995. *The Marketing of Social Change.* San Francisco: Jossey Bass Publishers.

Anyaeghunam, C., P. Mefalopulos and T. Moetsabi. 1998. *Participatory Rural Appraisal: Starting with the People.* Harare: SADC Centre of Communication for Development.

————. 2004. *Participatory Rural Communication Appraisal: Starting with the People.* Rome: SADC Centre of Communication for Development and FAO.

Appadurai, A. 1993. 'Disjuncture and Difference in the Global Cultural Economy', *Public Culture*, 2(2):1–24.

————. 1996. *Modernity at Large. Cultural Dimensions of Globalization.* Minneapolis: University of Minnesota Press.

Arnst, R. 1996. 'Participation Approaches to the Research Process', in J. Servaes, T.L. Jacobson and S.A.White (eds). *Participatory Communication for Social Change*, pp. 109–126. New Delhi: Sage Publications.

Ascroft, J. and S. Masilela. 1994. 'Participatory Decision Making in Third World Development', in S.A. White, K.S. Nair and J. Ascroft (eds). *Participatory Communication: Working for Change and Development*, pp. 259–294. New Delhi: Sage Publications.

Ashcroft, B., G. Griffiths and H. Tiffin. 1998. *Key Concepts in Post-Colonial Studies.* London: Routledge.

Atwood, R. and E.G. McAnany (eds). 1986. *Communication and Latin American Society.* Madison: University of Wisconsin.

Aubel, J. and D. Sihalathavong. 2001. 'Participatory Communication to Strengthen the Role of Grandmothers in Child Health', *Journal of International Communication*, 7(2):76–97.

Axford, B. 1995. *The Global System. Economics, Politics and Culture.* Cambridge: Polity Press.

Balit, S. 1988. 'Rethinking Development Support Communication', *Development Communication Report*, 3:62.

————. 1998. 'Listening to Farmers: Communication for Participation and Change in Latin America', FAO. Available online at http://www.fao.org/sd/CDdirect/CDan0018.htm (Downloaded on 14.04.2006).

————. 1999. *Voices for Change: Rural Women and Communication.* Rome: FAO.

————. 2004. 'Communication for Isolated and Marginalized Groups Blending the Old and the New', Communication for Development Roundtable Report. Rome: FAO.

Balit, S., C. Rios and L. Masias. 1996. *Communication for Development in Latin America: A Regional Experience.* Rome: FAO.

*Contributors: Rico Lie, Jan Servaes and Adinda Van Hemelrijck in collaboration with Nico Carpentier, Gustavo Cimadevilla and Sara Wendy Ferreira for non-English entries.

Balit, S. and L. Grenna. 2006. 'Listening and Learning: Measuring the Impact of Communication for Development', *An Online Forum*. London: Department for International Development (DFID).

Ballantyne, P. 1988. 'Collecting and Propagating Local Development Content', Report of a project carried out by IICD in association with the Tanzania Commission for Science and Technology and funded by the UK Department for International Development (DFID), Synthesis and Conclusions, 2000. The Hague: International Institute for Communication and Development.

Banuri, T. 1990. 'Modernization and its Discontents: A Cultural Perspective on Theories of Development', in F. Marglin and S. Marglin (eds). *Dominating Knowledge: Development, Culture, and Resistance*, pp. 73–101. Oxford: Clarendon Press.

Barbero, J.M. 1993. *Communication, Culture and Hegemony. From the Media to Mediations*. London: Sage Publications.

Bauman, Zygmunt. 1998. *Globalization. The Human Consequences*. New York: Columbia University Press.

Bayardo, Rubens and Monica Lacarrieu (eds). 1999. *La dinamica global/local. Cultura y comun icacion: nuevos desafios*. Buenos Aires: Ediciones Ciccus La Crujia.

Becker, J., G. Hedebro and L. Paldan (eds). 1986. *Communication and Domination*. Norwood: Ablex.

Behrstock, J. 1986. *The Eighth Case. Troubled Times at the United Nations*. New York: University Press of America.

Bell, C. and H. Newby. 1971. *Community Studies. An Introduction to the Sociology of the Local Community*. London: Allen and Unwin.

Bell, D.A. 1996. 'The East Asian Challenge to Human Rights: Reflections on an East West Dialogue', *Human Rights Quarterly*, 18(3):641–667.

Beltran, S.L.R. 1974. 'Rural Development and Social Communication: Relationships and Strategies', proceedings at the Corner-CIAT International Symposium on Communication Strategies on Rural Development, Cali, Colombia, 17–22 March. Ithaca, pp. 11–27. NY: Cornell University.

———. 1993a. 'Communication for Development in Latin America: A Forty Years Appraisal', Keynote speech at the Opening of the IV Roundtable on Development Communication, Instituto para America Latina (IPAL), Lima, 23–26 February.

———. 1993b. 'Communication for Development In Latin America: A Forty Years Appraisal', in D. Nostbakken and C. Morrow (eds). *Cultural Expression in the Global Village*, pp. 9–31. Penang: Southbound.

Benhabib, S. 1995. 'Cultural Complexity, Moral Interdependence, and the Global Dialogical Community', in M. Nussbaum and J. Glover (eds). *Women, Culture and Development. A Study of Human Capabilities*, pp. 235–255. Oxford: Clarendon Press.

Benor, D. and K. Cleaver. 1989. 'Training and Visit System of Agricultural Extension', *Interpaks Exchange*, 6(2):1–3.

Berger, M.T. 2004. *The Battle for Asia*. London: Routledge-Curzon.

Berger, P. and T. Luckmann. 1967. *The Social Construction of Reality*. New York: Doubleday.

Berque, P., E. Foy and B. Girard. 1993. *La Passion Radio. 23 Expériences de Radio Participative et Communautaire á Travers le Monde*. Paris: Syros.

Berrigan, F.J. 1977. *Access: Some Western Models of Community Media*. Paris: UNESCO.

———. 1979. *Community Communications. The Role of Community Media in Development*. Paris: UNESCO.

Bery, R. 2003. 'Participatory Video that Empowers', in S.A. White (ed.). *Participatory Video*. London: Sage Publications.

Berting, J., Peter R. Bachr, Herman Burgers, Cees Flinterman, Barbara De Klerk, Rob Kroes, Cornelis A. Van Minnen and Koo Vanderwal. 1990. *Human Rights in a Pluralist World*. Westport: Meckler.

Besette, G. 2004. *Involving the Community: A Guide to Participatory Development Communication*. Penang: Southbound/IDRC.

Besette, G. and C.V. Rajasunderam (eds). 1996. *Participatory Development Communication: A West-African Agenda*. Penang: Southbound.

Bhabha, H.K. 1994. *The Location of Culture*. London: Routledge.

Blanchard, M. 1986. *Exporting the First Amendment*. White Plains: Longman.

Blomstrom, M. and B. Hettne. 1984. *Development Theory in Transition. The Dependency Debate and Beyond*. London: Zed Books.

Boafo, K. 1989. *Communication and Culture: African Perspectives*. Nairobi: ACCE.

——— (ed.). 2000a. *Media & HIV/AIDS in East and Southern Africa: A Resource Book*. Paris: UNESCO.

——— (ed.). 2000b. *Promoting Community Media in Africa*. Paris: UNESCO.

Boeren, A. 1994. *In Other Words ... The Cultural Dimension of Communication for Development* (CESO paperback no. 19). Den Haag: CESO.

Boeren, A. and K. Epskamp (eds). 1992. *The Empowerment of Culture: Development Communication and Popular Media* (CESO paperback no. 17). Den Haag: CESO.

Booker, D. 2003. 'Facilitating Participatory Video: India's NGOs', in S.A. White (ed.). *Participatory Video*, pp. 322–334. London: Sage Publications.

Bordenave, J.D. 1992. 'La Campaña como Intervención Social', *Revista Chasqui*, Quito, 41.

Botes, L. and D. Van Rensburg. 2000. 'Community Participation in Development: Nine Plagues and Twelve Commandments', *Community Development Journal*, 35(1):41–58.

Bouman, M. 1998. 'The Turtle and the Peacock. The Entertainment Education Strategy on Television', Ph.D. Thesis. Netherlands: Wageningen Agricultural University.

Box, L., A. Mossanne, E. Sizoo and N. Vink. 1993. *Culture and Communication: The Forgotten Dimension in Development Cooperation* (Bulletin 329). Amsterdam: KIT.

Boyd-Barrett, O. 1977. 'Media Imperialism: Towards an International Framework for the Analysis of Media Systems', in J. Curran, M. Gurevitch and J. Woollacott (eds). *Mass Communication and Society*. London: Arnold.

———. 1980. *The International News Agencies*. London: Constable.

———. 1982. 'Cultural Dependency and the Mass Media', in M. Gurevitch, T. Bennett, J. Curran and J. Woollacott (eds). *Culture, Society and the Media*. London: Methuen.

———. 1998. 'Media Imperialism Reformulated', in D.K. Thussu (ed.). *Electronic Empires. Global Media and Local Resistance*, pp. 157–176. London: Arnold.

——— (ed.). 2001. *Final report of the Workshop on News Agencies in the Era of the Internet*. Paris: UNESCO.

Braman, S. and A. Sreberny-Mohammadi (eds). 1996. *Globalization, Communication and Transnational Civil Society*. Cresskill: Hampton Press.

Brandner, R. 1999. *Interculturality: A Philosophical Approach, Colloquium, Towards a Constructive Pluralism*. Paris: UNESCO.

Bras Fernandez Callou, A. 2001. 'Comunicação rural e educação na era das tecnologias do virtual: proposição para um debate', in G. Cimadevilla (Coor.), *Comunicación, Tecnología y Desarrollo. Discusiones y Perspectivas desde el sur*, pp. 283–93. Río Cuarto: UNRC-ALAIC-RED MERCOMSUR.

Brislin, R. and T. Yoshida. 1994. *Intercultural Communication Training: An Introduction*. London: Sage Publications.

Buell, F. 1994. *National Culture and the New Global System*. Baltimore: The Johns Hopkins University Press.

Busso, M., M. Cicowiez and L. Gasparini. 2005. 'Ethnicity and the Millennium Development Goals', Report for CEDLAS, Universidad Nacional de La Plata, Colombia: Formato Communicación/Diseño Ltda.

Cabañero-Verzosa, C. 2005a. 'Counting on Communication: The Uganda Nutrition and Early Childhood Development Project', World Bank Working Paper No. 59. Washington D.C.: The World Bank.

———. 2005b. *Strategic Communication for Development Projects*. Washington D.C.: The World Bank.

Cabello, R. 1982. 'La Perspectiva del Desarrollo Humano en Comunicación', in G. Cabezas, A. Rosario, P.G. Llorente, E. Contreras and J. Ros (eds). *La Emisora Popular*. Quito: Editora Andina.

Cadiz, M.C. 1994. *Communication and Participatory Development: A Review of Concepts, Approaches and Lessons*. Laguna: University of the Philippines.

Camilo, M., M.C. Mata and J. Servaes. 1990. *Autoevaluacion de Radio Enriquillo*. Oegstgeest: Cebemo.

Canclini, N.G. 1982. *Las Culturas Populares en el Capitalismo*. Mexico: Nueva Imagen.

———. 1989. *Culturas Hibridas*. Mexico DF: Grijalbo.

Cantor, M. and J. Cantor. 1986. 'The Internationalization of TV Entertainment', in S. Thomas (ed.). *Studies in Communication*. Norwood, NJ.: Ablex Publications.

Cantu, A. 1997. 'Los Referentes. Una Versión de los 90 Obre los Líderes de Opinión', in G. Cimadevilla (Coor.), *La Bocina que Parla. Antecedentes y Perspectivas de los Estudios de Comunicación Rural*. Río Cuarto: INTA-UNRC.

———. 1998. 'El Papel de los Medios de Comunicación en la Difusión de Tecnología', *Temas y Problemas de Comunicación*, 7:98–107. Río Cuarto: UNRC.

———. 2001. 'De Noticias y Audiencias: Algunas Hipótesis para Avanzar en su Comprensión', in G. Cimadevilla (Coor.), *Comunicación, Tecnología y Desarrollo. Discusiones y Perspectivas desde el sur*, pp. 135–145. Río Cuarto: UNRC-ALAIC-RED MERCOMSUR.

Cantu, A. and G. Cimadevilla. 1997. 'Campos, Medios y Escritorios. Del Trabajo Interpersonal a la Terciarización Extensionista en el INTA', Revista *Cronía*, 1(2):9–15, UNRC.

Capila, A. 2002. 'Images of Women in the Folk Songs of Garhwal Himalayas: A Participatory Research', *Concept's Discovering Himalayas Series No. 6*. New Delhi: Concept Publishing Company.

Cardoso, F.H. and E. Faletto. 1969. *Dependencia y Desarrollo en América Latina*. Mexico: Siglo XXI.

———. 1979. *Dependency and Development in Latin America* (M. Mattingly Urquidi, Trans.). Berkeley: University of California.

Carey, J.W. 1989. *Communication as Culture; Essays on Media and Society*. Boston: Unwin Hyman.

Carniglia, E. 1997. 'Las Radios Regionales. Estructuras, Disponibilidades y Perspectivas para la Difusión del Desarrollo Rural Sustentable', in G. Cimadevilla (Coor.), *La Bocina que Parla. Antecedentes y Perspectivas de los Estudios de Comunicación Rural*. Río Cuarto: INTA-UNRC.

———. 2001. 'Hermes y Ceres, en un mismo surco. Sobre la comunicación en un esquema analítico del desarrollo', in G. Cimadevilla (Coor.), *Comunicación, Tecnología y Desarrollo. Discusiones y Perspectivas desde el sur*, pp. 31–56. Río Cuarto: UNRC-ALAIC-RED MERCOMSUR.

Carpentier, N., R. Lie and J. Servaes. 2001. *Making Community Media Work*. Paris: UNESCO.

Casmir, F. (ed.). 1991. *Communication in Development*. Norwood: Ablex.

Castaneda, M. and R.M. Alfaro (eds). 2003. *Relaciones entre Estado y Sociedad Civil. Concertación o vigilancia?*, Lima: Calandria.

Castles, S. 2000. *Ethnicity and Globalization: From Migrant Worker to Transnational Citizen*. London: Sage Publications.

Chambers, R. 1992. *Rural Appraisal: Rapid, Relaxed and Participatory*. Sussex University, Brighton: Institute of Development Studies.

Chan, J.M. 1994. 'National Responses and Accessibility to Star TV in Asia', *Journal of Communication*, 44(3):70–88.

Chenchabi, R. 1981. *L'Influence des Politiques Culturelles et de la Communication sur les Styles du Développement*. Paris: UNESCO.

Chew, S.C. and R.A. Denemark (eds). 1996. *The Underdevelopment of Development: Essays in Honor of Andre Gunder Frank*. Newbury Park: Sage Publications.

Chilcote, R. and D. Johnson (eds). 1983. *Theories of Development. Mode of Production or Dependency?*, Beverly Hills: Sage Publications.

Chisuo, L. 1995. *Report on an Evaluation of the Implementation of Grade 7 AIDS Action Programme Book "Let's Talk" in Schools in Zimbabwe*. Harare: UNICEF.

Chitty, N. (ed.). 1994. 'Local Visions of the Global', *Journal of International Communication*, 1(2) (special issue).

Chu, G.C. 1987. 'Development Communication in the Year 2000: Future Trends and Directions', in N. Jayaweera and S. Amunugama (eds). *Rethinking Development Communication*, pp. 95–107. Singapore: Asian Mass Communication Research and Information Centre.

———. 1994. 'Communication and Development: Some Emerging Theoretical Perspectives', in A. Moemeka (ed.). *Communicating for Development: A New Pan-disciplinary Perspective*, pp. 34–53. Albany: SUNY Press.

CIDA. 1999. *Results-Based Management in CIDA: An Introductory Guide to the Concepts and Principles*. Hull: CIDA.

CIESPAL. 1983. *Comunicacion Popular Educativa*. Quito: CIESPAL.

Cimadevilla, G. 1997a. 'El Viejo Sueño de lo Colectivo. Ante la Escasez de Interacción e Información entre los Actores Técnicos del Agro', *Revista Cronía*, 1(2), Facultad de Ciencias Humanas. Río Cuarto: UNRC.

——— (ed.). 1997b. *La Bocina que Parla. Antecedentes y Perspectivas de los Estudios de Comunicación Rural*. Río Cuarto: INTA-UNRC.

———. 1999a. 'Nuevas Preguntas y Reformulación del Modelo para una Teoría de la Difusión de Innovaciones', in A. Bras Fernandes Callou, *Comunicação Rural e o Novo Espaço Agrário*. Recife: UFRPE-INTERCOM.

———. 1999b. 'Para Poner en Agenda la Problemática Ambiental', *Revista Fractais*, 3: 119–134.

——— (Coor.). 2001. *Comunicación, Tecnología y Desarrollo. Discusiones y Perspectivas desde el sur*. Río Cuarto: UNRC-ALAIC-RED MERCOMSUR.

Cimadevilla, G. (ed.). 2001. *Comunicación, Tecnología y Desarrollo. Discusiones y Perspectivas desde el sur*. Río Cuarto: UNRC-ALAIC–RED MERCOMSUR.

——— (ed.). 2004. *Dominios. Crítica a la razón intervencionista, la comunicación y el desarrollo sustentable*. Buenos Aires: Prometeo Libros.

Cimadevilla, G. and E. Carniglia. 1992. 'La Escenografía del Desarrollo Sustentable', *Revista Medio Ambiente y Modernización*, 40. Buenos Aires: IIED-AL.

Cimadevilla, G. 1995a. 'Cambio Tecnológico y Perdurabilidad Hipodérmica', *Temas y Problemas de Comunicación*, 5. Río Cuarto: Depto. Cs. de la Comunicación.

———. 1995b. 'El Efecto Paradoja en la Comunicación Rural', *Revista de la Universidad Nacional de Río Cuarto*, 15(1). Río Cuarto: UNRC.

———. 2004. *Comunicación, Ruralidad u Desarrollo. Mitos, paradigmas y dispositivos del cambio*. Río Cuarto: INTA-UNRC.

Cimadevilla, G., E. Carniglia and A. Cantu. 1997. *La Bocina que Parla. Antecedentes y Perspectivas de los Estudios de Comunicación Rural*. Río Cuarto: UNRC-INTA.

Cimadevilla, G. and E. Severina. 1993. 'Privatización o Estatismo: Coyuntura Actual y Crisis en la Extensión Rural', in G. Magela Braga and M.M. Krohling Kunsch (eds). *Comunicação Rural. Discurso e Prática*, pp. 141–155. Viçosa: UFV-INTERCOM.

Cinco. 1987. *Comunicacion Dominante y Comunicacion Alternativa en Bolivia*. La Paz: Cinco/IDRC.

Cioffi-Revilla, C., R. Merritt and D. Zinnes. 1985. *Communication and Interaction in Global Politics*. Beverly Hills: Sage Publications.

Clark, D.B. 1973. 'The Concept of Community: A Reexamination', *Sociological Review*, 21:397–417.

Cleaver, H. 1998. *The Zapatistas and the Electronic Fabric of Struggle*. http://www.eco.utexas.edu/faculty/Cleaver/zaps.html

Clegg, S. 1989. *Frameworks of Power*. London: Sage Publications.

Cochrane, A. and K. Pain. 2000. 'A Globalizing Society?' in D. Held (ed.). *A Globalizing World? Culture, Economic, Politics*, pp. 5–45. London: Routledge in association with The Open University.

Codesria. 2005. Special Issue, 11th Cosesria General Assembly, 'Rethinking African Development: Beyond Impasse, Towards Alternatives', Codesria Bulletin (3 & 4). Dakar: Codesria.

Cohen, A.P. *The Symbolic Construction of Community*. London: Routledge.

Cohen, J. and A. Arato. 1992. *Civil Society and Political Theory*. London: MIT Press.

Cohen, S., A. Hoekman and W. Gikonyo. 1999. International Seminar on ICPD Advocacy in the Global Information and Knowledge Management Age. New York: UNFPA.

Coldevin, G. 1986. 'Evaluation in Rural Development Communications—A Case Study from West Africa', *Media in Education and Development*, 19:112–118.

———. 1987. *Perspectives on Communication for Rural Development*. Rome: FAO.

———. 1988. 'Video Applications in Rural Development', *Educational Media International*, 25(4):225–229.

———. 1990. *Communication Strategies for Rural Development: A Case Study of the Use of Campaigns in Lesotho*. Rome: FAO.

———. 1995. *Farmer-first Approaches to Communication: A Case Study from the Philippines*. Rome: FAO.

Coldevin, G. and FAO. 2001. 'Participatory Communication and Adult Learning for Rural Development', *Journal of International Communication*, 7(2):51–69.

Colin, R. 1981. *La Communication Sociale et la Participation Populaire au Dévelopement entre Tradition et Modernité*. Paris: UNESCO, Division de l'étude du développement.

Contreras, E. 1993. Evaluación de Proyectos de Comunicación. Quito: CIESPAL.

Coquery-Vidrovitch, C. and S. Nedelec (eds). *Tiers Monde: l'Informel en Question*. Paris: Ed. l'Harmattan.

Costa–Lascoux, J., M-A. Hily and G. Vermes (eds). 2000. *Pluralité des Cultures et Dynamiques Identitaires*. Paris : L'Harmattan.

Cris. 2005. *Assessing Communication Rights: A Handbook*. London, WACC.

Crocker, S. 2003. 'The Fogo Process: Participatory Communication in a Globalizing World', in S.A. White (ed.). *Participatory Video*, pp. 122–141. London: Sage Publications.

Crowder, L. van. 1998. *Knowledge and Information for Food Security in Africa: From Traditional Media to the Internet*. Rome, FAO.

———. 2000. *Farmer Information Networks (FARMNets)—A Tool for Sustainable Agricultural Production and Improved Food Security in Developing Countries*. Rome: FAO.

Davenport, T.H. 1998. *Ecologia da Informação: Por que só a Tecnologia Não Basta para o Sucesso na Era da Informação*. São Paulo: Futura.

de, D., B. Jirli and K. Ghadei (eds). 2004. *National Workshop on Communication Support for Sustaining Extension Services*. Varanasi: Ganga Kaveri.

de Cuellar, J.P. 1995. 'Our Creative Diversity'. Report of the World Commission on Culture and Development. Paris: UNESCO.

de Keizer, B. and J.A. Haro (eds). 1995. *Participación Comunitaria en Salud: Evaluación de Experiencias y Tareas para el Futuro*. Hermosillo, Mexico: El Colegio de Sonora-Organización Panamericana de la Salud.

de Melo, J.M. and M.C. Gobbi (eds). 2004. *Pensamento Comunicacional Latino-Americano. De Pesquisa-Denúncia ao Pragmatismo Utópico.* São Paulo: UMESP.

de Schutter, A. 1983. *Investigacion Participativa: una Opcion Metodologica para la Educacion de Adultos.* Mexico: Crefal.

de Villers, G. (ed.). 1992. 'Le Pauvre, le Hors la Loi, le Métis: la Question de l'Économie Informelle en Afrique', *Les Cahiers du CEDAF*–ASDOC Studies, 6.

Decker, P. 1988. 'Portable Video in Grass-roots Development', Paper from the Institute for Communication Research, Stanford University.

———. 1989. *Que siga adelante ... The Role of Grassroots Communications in Community Development: Experiences from Tijuana, Mexico.* Stanford: Center for Latin American Studies, Stanford University.

Deetz, S.A. 1992. *Democracy in an Age of Corporate Colonization: Developments in Communication and the Politics of Everyday Life.* Albany: State University of New York.

Dervin, B. and R. Huesca. 1997. 'Reaching for the Communicating in Participatory Communication', *The Journal of International Communication,* 4(2):46–74.

———. 1999. 'The Participatory Communication for Development Narrative: An Examination of Meta–theoretic Assumptions and Their Impacts', in T.L. Jacobson and J. Servaes (eds). *Theoretical Approaches to Participatory Communication,* pp. 169–210. Cresskill, NJ: Hampton Press.

Díaz Bordenave, J.E. 1985. *Comunicación y Sociedad* [Communication and Society], La Paz. Bolivia: Cimca.

———. 1994. 'Participative Communication as a Part of Building the Participative Society', in S.A. White, K.S. Nair and J. Ascroft (eds). *Participatory Communication: Working for Change and Development,* pp. 35–48. New Delhi: Sage Publications.

Dimitriu, A. 2001. 'Magallanes en Bermudas: Turismo, Organización Espacial y Crisis', in G. Cimadevilla (Coor.), *Comunicación, Tecnología y Desarrollo. Discusiones y Perspectivas desde el sur.* Río Cuarto: UNRC-ALAIC-RED MERCOMSUR.

Diouf, M. 1988. 'La Culture, la Communication, l'Education et la Science et la Technique dans les Stratégies de Développement en Afrique au Sud du Sahara'. Grand programme I *Réflexion sur les problèmes mondiaux et études prospectives,* 17, Paris: UNESCO.

Dissanayake, W. (ed.). 1994. *Colonialism and Nationalism in Asian Cinema.* Bloomington: Indiana University Press.

DOI. 2001. 'Creating a Development Dynamic'. Final Report of the Digital Opportunity Initiative, July. The DOI was sponsored by Accenture, the Markle Foundation and the United Nations Development Program.

Donders, Y. 1999. 'Human Rights, Culture and Development'. Report of the conference organised by Women for Women's Human Rights and Novib, Istanbul, 25–27 November 1998. The Hague: Novib.

Donnelly, J. 1989. *Universal Human Rights. In: Theory & Practice.* Ithaca: Cornell University Press.

———. 1993. *International Human Rights.* Boulder: Westview Press.

Dorfman, A. and A. Mattelart. 1975. *How to Read Donald Duck: Imperialist Ideology in the Disney Comic.* New York: International General Editions.

DOT Force. Digital Opportunities for All: Meeting the Challenge. Report of the Digital Opportunity Tasks Force. 2001. http://www.markle.org/dotforce.html.

Doty, R.L. 1996. *Imperial Encounters: The Politics of Representation in North-South Relations.* Minneapolis: University of Minnesota Press.

Downing, J. 2001. *Radical Media: Rebellious Communication and Social Movements.* Thousand Oaks, California: Sage Publications.

Du Gay, P. (ed.). 1997. *Production of Cultures/Cultures of Production.* London: Sage Publications (book 4 in the series Culture, Media and Identities).

Dudley, E. 1993. *The Critical Villager: Beyond Community Participation.* London: Routledge.

Dudley, M.J. 2003a. 'Voice, Visibility and Transparency', in S.A. White (ed.). *Participatory Video,* pp. 145–156. London: Sage Publications.

———. 2003b. 'The Transformative Power of Video: Ideas, Images, Process and Outcomes', in S.A. White (ed.). *Participatory Video.* London: Sage Publications.

Durer, H. 2006. *Ways of Perception: On Visual and Intercultural Communication.* Bangkok: White Lotus Press.

During, S. (ed.). 1993. *The Cultural Studies Reader.* London: Routledge.

Eade, D. (ed.). 2003. *Development Methods and Approaches: Critical Reflections.* Oxford: Oxfam UK.

Einsiedel, E.F. 1999. 'Action Research: Theoretical and Methodological Considerations for Development', in T.L. Jacobson and J. Servaes (eds). *Theoretical Approaches to Participatory Communication*, pp. 359–379. Cresskill, NJ: Hampton Press.

Elliott, J.A. 1994. *An Introduction to Sustainable Development*. London: Routledge.

Epskamp, K., H. Gould and D.A. Jelincic (eds). 2000. *Culture and Development vs. Cultural Development* (Special issue of Culturelink). Zagreb: Institute for International Relations.

Eriksen, Thomas Hylland. 1993. *Ethnicity and Nationalism. Anthropological Perspectives*. London: Pluto Press.

Escobar, A. 1987. 'Power and Visibility: The Invention and Management of Development in the Third World'. Doctoral Dissertation. Berkeley: University of California.

———. 1995. *Encountering Development: The Making and Unmaking of the Third World*. Princeton. NJ: Princeton University Press.

———. 1999. 'Discourse and Power in Development: Michel Foucault and the Relevance of His Work to the Third World', in T.L. Jacobson and J. Servaes (eds). *Theoretical Approaches to Participatory Communication*, pp. 309–335. Cresskill, NJ: Hampton Press.

Escobar, A. and S. Alvarez (eds). 1992. *The Making of Social Movements in Latin America: Identity, Strategy and Democracy*. San Francisco: Westview.

Eurich, C. 1980. *Kommunikative Partizipation und Partizipativekomunikationsforschung*. Frankfurt: Rita G. Fischer Verlag.

Fair, J.E. 1989. '29 Years of Theory and Research on Media and Development: The Dominant Paradigm Impact', *Gazette*, 44:129–150.

Fair, J.E. and H. Shah. 1997. 'Continuities and Discontinuities in Communication and Development Research since 1958', *Journal of International Communication*, 4(2):3–23.

Fals Borda, O. (ed.). 1985. *The Challenge of Social Change*. London: Sage Publications.

———. 1988. *Knowledge and People's Power: Lessons with Peasants in Nicaragua, Mexico and Colombia*. New Delhi: Indian Social Institute.

———. 1991. *Knowledge and Social Movements*. Santa Cruz, CA: Merrill Publications.

FAO. 1981. *Communication for Rural Development*. Rome: FAO.

———. 1984. *Expert Consultation on Communication for Development*. Rome: FAO.

———. 1989. *Guidelines on Communication for Rural Development*. Rome: FAO.

———. 1994. *Applying DSC Methodologies to Population Issues: A Case Study in Malawi*. Rome: FAO.

———. 1996. *Development of Rural Radio in Africa*. Rome: FAO.

———. 1999. *Le Centre de Services de Production Audiovisuelle (CESPA) au Mali*. Rome: FAO.

———. 2000. *Virtual Extension, Research and Communication Network* (VERCON). Rome: FAO.

FAO World Bank. 2000. *Agricultural Knowledge and Information Systems for Rural Development (AKIS/RD), Strategic Vision and Guiding Principles*. Rome: FAO.

———. 2003. *Revisiting the 'Magic Box': Case Studies in Local Appropriation of Information and Communication Technologies (ICTs)*. Rome: FAO.

———. 2005. 'Communication for Development Roundtable Report', Focus on Sustainable Development. 9th United Nations Communication for Development Roundtable, 6–9 September 2004, Rome.

Featherstone, M. (ed.). 1990. *Global Culture; Nationalism, Globalization and Modernity*. London: Sage Publications.

Fett, J.H. 1993. 'Pesquisa em Comunicação para o Desenvolvimento Rural', in G.M. Braga and K.M. Kunsch (eds). *Comunicação Rural: Discurso e Prática*, pp. 43–53. Viçosa: UFV.

Figuera, M.E., D.L. Kincaid, M. Rani and G. Lewis. 2002. 'Communication for Social Change: An Integrated Model for Measuring the Process and its Outcomes'. Communication for Social Change Working Papers Series (1). New York: Rockefeller Foundation and Johns Hopkins University Center for Communication Programs.

Fitzgerald, T.K. 1993. *Metaphors of Identity: A Culture-Communication Dialogue*. Albany: State University of New York Press.

Flores, T. 2001. 'Comunicación Ambiental para el Desarrollo Sostenible en Latinoamérica', in G. Cimadevilla (Coor.), *Comunicación, Tecnología y Desarrollo. Discusiones y Perspectivas desde el sur*. Río Cuarto: UNRC-ALAIC-RED MERCOMSUR.

Fourie, P. J. and L. Van Audenhove (eds). 2003. 'Globalisation, Regionalisation and the Information Society', special issue of *Communicatio*, (29/1 & 2) Unisa: University of South Africa. *Communicatio*

Fox, E. 1988. *Media and Politics in Latin America. The Struggle for Democracy*. London: Sage Publications.

Frank, A.G. 1967. *Capitalism and Underdevelopment in Latin America*. New York: Monthly Review Press.

———. 1969. *Latin America: Underdevelopment or Revolution*. New York: Monthly Review Press.

Fraser, C. 1993. *Adopting Communication Technologies for Rural Development*, CERES, 95.

Fraser, C. and S. Restrepo-Estrada. 1996. *Communication for Rural Development in Mexico. In Good Times and in Bad.* Rome: Food and Agriculture Organization of the United Nations.

———. 1998. *Communicating for Development. Human Change for Survival.* London: Tauris.

———. 2001. *Community Radio Handbook.* Paris: UNESCO.

Fraser, C. and J. Villet. 1994. *Communication: A Key to Human Development.* Rome: FAO.

Freire, P. 1970. 'Cultural Action and Conscientization', *Harvard Educational Review*, 40(3).

———. 1970a. *Pedagogy of the Oppressed* (M. Bergman Ramos, Trans.). New York: Herder and Herder.

———. 1973b. *Extension o Comunicacion? La Concientizacion en el Medio Rural.* Mexico: Siglo XXI.

———. 1997. *Pedagogy of the Heart* (D. Macedo and A. Oliveira, Trans.). New York: Continuum.

Freitas Maneti Dencker, A. and K.M. Krohling, 1994. *Comunicação e Meio Ambiente*. São Paulo: INTERCOM-IMS.

Friedman, J. 1994. *Cultural Identity and Global Process*. London: Sage Publications.

Friedman, S. and S. Ammassari. 1999. *Community Participation and Empowerment: The Millennium Challenge for UNICEF and Its Partners*. New York: UNICEF.

Fukuda-Parr, S. (ed.). 2004. *Cultural Liberty in Today's Diverse World. Human Development Report 2004*. New York: UNDP.

Gadihoke, S. 2003. 'The Struggle to "Empower": A Woman Behind the Camera', in S.A. White (ed.). *Participatory Video.* London: Sage Publications.

Gallagher, K. 2000. *Farmers' Field Schools (FFS): A Group Extension Process Based on Adult Non-Formal Education Methods.* Rome: FAO Global IPM Facility.

Galtung, J. 1980. *The True Worlds. A Transnational Perspective*. New York: Free Press.

———. 1994. *Human Rights in Another Key*. Cambridge: Polity Press.

Garbo, G. 1986. *A World of Difference. The International Distribution of Information*. Paris: UNESCO.

García Canclini, N. 1990. *Hybrid Cultures*. Minneapolis: University of Minnesota Press.

———. 1999. *La globalización imaginada*. México: Editorial Paidós.

Gardels, N. (ed.). 1977. *The Changing Global Order*. Oxford: Blackwell.

Garreton, Manuel (ed.). 1999. *América Latina: un espacio cultural en un mundo globalizado*, Bogotá: Convenio Andrés Bello.

Geertz, C. 1973. *The Interpretation of Cultures*. New York: Basic Books.

Gellner, E. 1983. *Nations and Nationalism*. Oxford: Blackwell.

Gendelsones, C. 2002. *Communicating for Development: Experience in the Urban Environment*. London: ITDG Publishing.

Gerbner, G. and M. Siefert (eds). 1983. *World Communications. A Handbook*. New York: Longman.

Gerbner, G., H. Mowlana and K. Nordenstreng (eds). 1993. *The Global Media Debate. Its Rise, Fall, and Renewal*. Norwood: Ablex.

Giddens, A. 1990. *The Consequences of Modernity*. Cambridge: Polity Press.

Ginsburg, F. 1991. 'Indigenous Media: Faustian Contract Or Global Village?, *Cultural Anthropology*, 6(1):92–112.

———. 1992. 'Indigenous Media: Faustian Contract Or Global Village?', in G. Marcus (ed.). *Rereading Cultural Anthropology*, pp. 356–376. Durham.

Girard, B. (ed.). 1992a. *A Passion for Radio*. Montréal: Black Rose Books.

——— (ed.). 1992b. *Radio Apasionados. 21 Experiencias de Radio Comunitaria en el Mundo*. Quito: CIESPAL (Montreal: AMARC).

———. 2001. 'Next-Generation Radio: Communication Technologies for Democracy and Development', *Journal of International Communication*, 7(2):70–75.

Golding, P. and P. Harris (eds). 1997. *Beyond Cultural Imperialism. Globalization, Communication and the New International Order*. London: Sage Publications.

Gomez, R. 2001. 'Latino América en el Salón de los Espejos de Internet', in G. Cimadevilla (Coor.), *Comunicación, Tecnología y Desarrollo. Discusiones y Perspectivas desde el sur*, Río Cuarto: UNRC-ALAIC-RED MERCOMSUR.

———. 2003. 'Magic Roots: Children Explore Participatory Video', in S.A. White (ed.). *Participatory Video*, pp. 171–184. London: Sage Publications.

González vela, H. 1999. 'A Extensão Rural e o Pensamento Internacional', in H. González vela (ed.). *A Extensão Rural no Mercosul*. Cruz Alta: UNICRUZ.

Goonasekera, A. and L. Chun Wah (eds). 2001. *Asian Communication Handbook 2001*. Singapore: Asian Media Information and Communication Centre (AMIC).

Graff, R.D. (ed.). 1983. *Communication for National Development. Lessons from Experience*. Cambridge: Oelgeschlager, Gunn and Hain.

Graham, G. 2004. *Eight Theories of Ethics*. London: Routledge.

Granzberg, G. 1982. 'Television as Storyteller: The Algonkian Indians of Central Canada', *Journal of Communication*, 32(1):43–52.

Grillo, Mabel, Silvina Berti and Adriana Rizzo. 1998. *Discursos locales*. Rio Cuarto: Universidad Nacional de Rio Cuarto.

Guidi, P. 2003. 'Guatemalan Mayan Women and Participatory Visual Media', in S.A.White (ed.). *Participatory Video*, pp. 252–270. London: Sage Publications.

Gumucio Dagron, A. 2001. *Making Waves. Stories of Participatory Communication for Social Change*. New York: Rockefeller Foundation.

Gumucio, A. and T. Tufte (eds). 2006. *Communication for Social Change Anthology: Historical and Contemporary Readings*. New Jersey: Communication for Social Change Consortium.

Gunaratne, S. A. 2005. *The Dao of the Press: A Humanocentric Theory*. Cresskill: Hampton Press.

Gunder, F. and M. Fuentes. 1988. 'Nine Theses on Social Movements', *IFDA Dossier*, 63:27–44.

Habermann, P. and G. De Fontgalland (eds). 1978. *Development Communication—Rhetoric and Reality*. Singapore: AMIC.

Hachten, W. 1981. *World News Prism. Changing Media, Clashing Ideologies*. Ames: Iowa State University Press.

Hachten, W.A. and J.F. Scotton. 2007. *The World News Prism: Global Information in a Satellite Age*. Malden: Blackwell Publishing.

Hall, S. 1992. 'The Question of Cultural Identity', in S. Hall, D. Held and T. McGrew (eds). *Modernity and its Future*, pp. 274–316. Cambridge: Polity Press.

———— (series ed.). 1997. *Culture, Media and Identities*. London: Sage Publications (series of 6 books).

Halleck, D.D. 2002. *Handheld Visions: The Impossible Possibility of Community Media*. NY: Fordham University Press.

Hamelink, C. 1983. *Cultural Autonomy in Global Communications. Planning National Information Policy*. New York: Longman.

Hamelink, C.J. 1994a. *The Politics of World Communication; A Human Rights Perspective*. London: Sage Publications.

————. 1994b. *Trends in World Communication: On Disempowerment and Self-empowerment*. Penang: Southbound.

————. 1997. 'MacBride with Hindsight', in P. Golding and P. Harris (eds). *Beyond Cultural Imperialism. Globalization, Communication and the New International Order*, pp. 69–93. London: Sage Publications.

————. 2004. *Human Rights for Communicators*. Cresskill: Hampton Press.

Hancock, A. 1982. 'La Planification de la Communication au Service du Développement: Recherche d'un Cadre Opérationel', *Monographies sur la Planification de la Communication*, 2.

————. 1992. *Communication Planning Revisited*. Paris: UNESCO.

————. 2000. 'UNESCO's Contributions to Communication, Culture and Development', in J. Servaes (ed.). *Walking on the Other Side of the Information Highway. Communication, Culture and Development in the 21st Century*, pp. 61–73. Penang: Southbound.

Hannerz, U. 1987. 'The World in Creolization', *Africa; Journal of the International African Institute*, 57(4):546–559.

————. 1992. *Cultural Complexity; Studies in the Social Organization of Meaning*. New York: Columbia University Press.

————. 1996. *Transnational Connections*. London: Routledge.

Harindranath, R. 2006. *Perspectives on Global Cultures*. Berkshire: Open University Press.

Harris, M. 1999. *Theories of Culture in Postmodern Times*. London: Altamira Press.

Harrison, D. 1988. *The Sociology of Modernization and Development*. London: Unwin Hyman.

Harrison, L.E. and S.P. Huntington (eds). 2000. *Culture Matters: How Values Shape Human Progress*. New York: Basic Books.

Hedebro, G. 1982. *Communication and Social Change in Developing Countries. A Critical View*. Ames: Iowa State University Press.

Held, D. 1987. *Models of Democracy*. Cambridge: Polity Press.

———— (ed.). 2000. *A Globalizing World? Culture, Economics, Politics*. London: Routledge in association with The Open University.

Held, D., A. McGrew, D. Goldblatt and J. Perraton. 1999. *Global Transformations. Politics, Economics and Culture.* Cambridge: Polity Press.

Held, D. and P. Hirst. 2001. Globalization after 11 September. The argument of our time. Open Democracy dialogues. Available online at http://www.opendemocracy.net/articles/View.jsp?id=637.

Hemer, O. and T. Tufte (eds). 2006. *Media and Glocal Change. Rethinking Communication for Development.* Gotebeorg: NORDICOM, Clacso Books.

Herman, Edward and Robert McChesney. 1997. *The Global Media. The new missionaries of corporate capitalism.* London: Cassell.

Hettne, B. 1982. *Development Theory and the Third World.* Stockholm: SAREC.

Hirst, P. and G. Thompson. 1996. *Globalization in Question: The International Economy and the Possibilities of Governance.* London: Polity Press.

Hofmann, R. 1981. *Kommunikation und Entwicklung. Applikation eines Lateinamerikanischen Modells (Paulo Freire–Mario Kaplun) in Indonesien.* Frankfurt am Main: Peter Lang.

Hofstede, G. and G.-J. Hofstede. 2005. *Cultures and Organizations. Software of the Mind.* New York: McGraw-Hill.

Hollander, E. 2000. 'Online Communities as Community Media. A Theoretical and Analytical Framework for the Study of Digital Community Networks', *Communications: the European Journal of Communication Research*, 25(4):371–386.

Holton, R.J. 1998. *Globalization and the Nation-State.* London: Macmillan.

Hornik, R. 1988. *Development Communication: Information, Agriculture, and Nutrition in the Third World.* New York: Longman.

———. 1989. 'Channel Effectiveness in Development Communication Programs', in R.E. Rice and C.K. Atkin (eds). *Public Communication Campaigns*, 2nd ed. Newbury Park, CA: Sage Publications.

Horton, M. and P. Freire. 1990. *We Make the Road by Walking: Conversations on Education and Social Change.* Philadelphia: Temple University Press.

Howard, P.L. 2003. 'Beyond the "grim resisters": Towards more effective Gender Mainstreaming through Stakeholder Participation', in D. Eade (ed.). *Development Methods and Approaches: Critical Reflections.* Oxford: Oxfam UK.

Howard, R., F. Rolt, H. an de Veen and J. Verhoeven. 2003. *The Power of the Media: A Handbook for Peacebuilders.* Amsterdam: ECCP, ECCG & IMPACS.

Howell, W.J. 1986. *World Broadcasting in the Age of the Satellite.* Norwood: Ablex.

Howes, D. (ed.). 1996. *Cross-Cultural Consumption. Global Markets, Local Realities.* London: Routledge.

Hudson, H.E. 2006. *From Rural Village to Global Village: Telecommunications for Development in the Information Age.* Mahwah, NJ: Lawrence Erlbaum Associates.

Huesca, R. 1995. 'A Procedural View of Participatory Communication: Lessons from Bolivian Tin Miners' Radio', *Media, Culture & Society*, 17:101–119.

———. 2001. 'Conceptual Contributions of New Social Movements to Development Communication Research', *Communication Theory*, 11(4):415–433.

———. 2002. 'Participatory Approaches to Communication and Development', in W.B. Gudykunst and B. Mody (eds). *Handbook of International and Intercultural Communication.* London: Sage Publications.

———. 2003. 'Participatory Approaches to Communication for Development', in B. Mody (ed.). *International and Development Communication: A 21st Century Perspective*, pp. 209–226. Thousand Oaks, CA: Sage Publications.

Huesca, R. and B. Dervin. 1994. 'Theory and Practice in Latin American Alternative Communication Research', *Journal of Communication*, 44(4):53–73.

Hulme, D. and M. Turner. 1990. *Sociology and Development.* New York: Harvester Wheatsheaf.

Husband, C. 1994. *A Richer Vision. The Development of Ethnic Minority Media in Western Democracies.* Paris: UNESCO.

Hussein, S.M. 1980. *Main Forms of Traditional Communication: Egypt, International Commission for the Study of Communication Problems*, 93. Paris: UNESCO.

Inter-American Development Bank. 2006. 'The Politics of Policies: Economic and Social Progress in Latin America', 2006 Report. Washington D.C.: IDB and David Rockefeller Center for Latin American Studies.

Jacobson, T.L. 1993. 'A Pragmatist Account of Participatory Communication Research for National Development', *Communication Theory*, 3(3):214–230.

———. 1994. 'Modernization and Post-Modernization Approaches to Participatory Communication for Development', in S.A. White, K.S. Nair and J. Ascroft (eds). *Participatory Communication: Working for Change and Development*, pp. 60–75. New Delhi: Sage Publications.

Jacobson, T.L. and S. Kolluri. 1999. 'Participatory Communication as Communicative Action', in T.L. Jacobson, J. Servaes (eds). *Theoretical Approaches to Participatory Communication*, pp. 265–280. Cresskill, NJ: Hampton Press.

Jacobson, T.L. and J. Servaes (eds). 1999. *Theoretical Approaches to Participatory Communication*. Cresskill: Hampton Press.

Jallov, B. 2004. 'Community Radio for Empowerment and Impact', *The Journal of Development Communication*, 15(2). Kuala Lumpur: Asian Institute for Development Communication (Aidcom).

Jameson, K.P. and C.K. Wilber (eds). 1996. *The Political Economy of Development and Underdevelopment*. NY: McGraw-Hill.

Jamias, J. (ed.). 1975. *Readings in Development Communication*. Laguna: UP at Los Banos.

Jandt, F.E. 1995. *Intercultural Communication. An Introduction*. London: Sage Publications.

Jankowski, N. 1994. 'International Perspectives on Community Radio', in AMARC-EUROPE, One Europe-Many Voices. Democracy and Access to Communication. Conference Report, AMARC-Europe Pan-European conference of community radio broadcasters, Ljubljana, Slovenia, 15–18 September 1994, pp. 2–3. Sheffield: AMARC.

Janowitz, M. 1967. *The Community Press in an Urban Setting. The Social Elements of Urbanism, Chicago and London*: The University of Chicago Press.

Japhet, G. 1999. *Edutainment. How to Make Edutainment Work for You: a Step by Step Guide to Designing and Managing an Edutainment Project for Social Development*. Johannesburg: Soul City.

Jayaweera, N. and S. Amunugama (eds). 1987. *Rethinking Development Communication*. Singapore: AMIC.

Johnston, H. and B. Klandermans (eds). 1995. *Social Movements and Culture*. London: University College Press.

Jones, G.E. and C. Garforth. 1997. 'The History, Development and Future of Agricultural Extension', in B.E. Swanson, R.P. Bentz and A.J. Sofranco (eds). *Improving Agricultural Extension: A Reference Manual*, pp. 2–12. Rome: Food and Agriculture Organization.

Jones, S.G. 1995. 'Understanding Community in the Information Age', in S.G. Jones (ed.). *CyberSociety; Computer-mediated Communication and Community*, pp. 10–35. London: Sage Publications.

Jussawalla, M. and D.M. Lamberton. 1982. *Communication Economics and Development*. New York: Pergamon Press, with The East-West Center, Hawaii.

Kamlongera, C. and P. Mefalopulos. 2002. *Participatory Communication Strategy Design*. SADC (Centre of Communication for Development) and FAO Harare.

Kaplun, M. 1992. *A la Educacion por la Comunicacion: La Practica de la Comunicacion Educativa*, Santiago: UNESCO/Orealc.

Keane, J. 1998. *Democracy and Civil Society*. London: University of Westminster Press.

Khadka, N.B. 2000. 'The Participatory Development Communication Paradigm: Communication Challenges and Change', *Australian Journal of Communication*, 27(3):105–122.

Kidd, W. 2002. *Culture and Identity*. New York: Palgrave.

Kiiti, N. 2003. 'Guiding Hands and the Power of the Video Camera', in S.A. White (ed.). *Participatory Video*. London: Sage Publications.

Kincaid, D.L. and M.E. Figueroa. 2004. 'Communication for Development and Social Change', in C. Beck (ed.). *Communication Yearbook*. Newbury Park, CA: Sage Publications.

King, A.D. (ed.). 1991. *Culture, Globalization and the World-System*. London: Macmillan.

Knapp, M. and J. Daly (eds). 2002. *Handbook of Interpersonal Communication*. Thousand Oaks: Sage Publications.

Korten, D. (ed.). 1986. *Community Management: Asian Experience and Perspectives*. West Hartford: Kumarian Press.

Kottak, C.P. 1990. *Prime Time Society; An Anthropological Analysis of Television and Culture*. Belmont: Wadsworth.

Kotze, D.A. (ed.). 1997. *Development Administration and Management: A Holistic Approach*. Pretoria: J.L. van Schaik.

Kraidg, Marwan. 2003. 'Glocalisation as an International Communication Framework', *Journal of International Communication*, 9(2):29–49.

Krohling-Peruzzo, C.M. 1996. 'Participation in Community Communication', in J. Servaes, T.L. Jacobson and S.A. White (eds). *Participatory Communication for Social Change*, pp. 162–179. New Delhi: Sage Publications.

Kumar, K. (ed.). 1988. 'Communication and Development', special issue of *Communication Research Trends*, 9(3).

Kunczik, M. 1985. *Massenmedien und Entwicklungsländer*. Köln: Böhlau.

Ladmiral, J.R. and E. Lipiansky. 1989. *La communication interculturelle*. Paris: Armand Colin.

Larsen, P. (ed.). 1990. *Import/Export: International Flow of Television Fiction, Reports and Papers on Mass Communication, no. 104*, Paris: UNESCO.

Latchem, C. and D., Walker. (eds). 2001. *Telecentres: Case Studies and Key Issues*. Vancouver, BC: The Commonwealth of Learning Publication.

Lazarsfeld, P., B. Berelson and H. Gaudet. 1944. *The People's Choice*. New York: Duell, Sloan and Pearce.

Lee, C.C. 1980. *Media Imperialism Reconsidered: The Homogenizing of Television Culture*. London: Sage Publications.

Lee, P. (ed.). 1986. *Communication for All. The Church and the New World Information and Communication*. New York: Orbis.

———. 2004. *Many Voices, One Vision: The Right to Communicate in Practice*. Penang, Malaysia: Southbound, London: WACC.

Leeson, K. 1984. *International Communications. Blueprint for Policy*. Amsterdam: North Holland Publishing Company.

Leeuwis, C. 2000. 'Reconceptualising Participation for Sustainable Rural Development. Towards a Negotiation approach', *Development and Change*, 31(5).

Leeuwis, C. with contributions from A. Van Den Ban. 2004. *Communication for Rural Innovation. Rethinking Agricultural Extension*. Oxford: Blackwell Publishing.

Leeuwis, C. and R. Pyburn (eds). 2002. *Wheelbarrows Full of Frogs. Social Learning in Rural Resource Management*. Assen: Koninklijke Van Gorcum.

Lefebre, E. 2004. 'The Impact of their adoption on small- and medium-sized enterprises', *Information and Communication Technologies for Development in Africa* (Vol IV).

Lerner, D. 1958. *The Passing of Traditional Society: Modernizing the Middle East*. New York: Free Press.

———. 1976. 'Toward a New Paradigm', in W. Schramm and D. Lerner (eds). *Communication and Change: The Last Ten Years—and the Next*, pp. 60–63. Honolulu: East-West Center.

Lerner, D. and W. Schramm (eds). 1967. *Communication and Change in the Developing Countries*, Honolulu: University Press of Hawaii.

———. 1976. 'Looking Forward', in W. Schramm and D. Lerner (eds). *Communication and Change: The Last Ten Years—and the Next*, pp. 340–344. Honolulu: East-West Center.

Lewis, P. (ed.). 1993. Alternative Media: Linking Global and Local, Reports and Papers on Mass Communication, no. 107. Paris: UNESCO.

Lewis, G. 2001. 'Development Communication Debates in Thailand Since the 1997 Crisis', *Journal of International Communication*, 7(2):115–130.

Lie, R. 2001. 'Globalisation, Development and "Communication for Localisation"', *Journal of International Communication* 7(2):14–24.

———. 2003. *Spaces of Intercultural Communication. An Interdisciplinary Introduction to Communication, Culture, and Globalising/Localising Identities*.

Liebes, T. and E. Katz. 1990. *The Export of Meaning: Cross-Cultural Readings of 'Dallas'*. New York: Oxford University Press.

Lindlof, T.R. 1988. 'Media Audiences as Interpretative Communities', *Communication Yearbook*, 11:81–107.

Logan, R. 1995. 'En Busca de una Teoría: Público, Medio Ambiente y Medios de Comunicación', *Comunicación y Sociedad*, VIII(2).

Long, N. and A. Long (eds). 1992. *Battlefields of Knowledge. The Interlocking of Theory and Practice in Social Research and Development*. London: Routledge.

Long, N. and M. Villarreal. 1993. 'Exploring Development Interfaces: From the Transfer of Knowledge to the Transformation of Meaning', in F. Schuurman (ed.). *Beyond the Impasse: New Directions in Development Theory*, pp. 162–178. London: Zed Books.

Louw, Eric. 2005. *The Media and Political Process*. London: Sage Publications.

Lozare, B.V. 1994. 'Power and Conflict: Hidden Dimensions of Communication, Participative Planning and Action', in S.A. White, K.S. Nair and J. Ascroft (eds). *Participatory Communication: Working for Change and Development*. pp. 229–244. New Delhi: Sage Publications.

Lull, J. 1995. *Media, Communication, Culture. A Global Approach*. Cambridge: Polity Press.

Macbride, S. 1980. *Many Voices, One World*. Kogan Page: London/UNESCO.

Magela Braga, G. and M. Krohling Kunsch. 1980. *Comunicação Rural. Discurso e Prática*. Viçosa: UFV-INTERCOM.

Malik, M. 1983. 'Traditional Forms of Communication and the Mass Media in India', *Communication and Society*, 13.

Malikhao, Patchanee. 2005. 'HIV/AIDS prevention campaigns from a Thai Buddhist perspective', *Media Development*, 52(2): 57–62.

Mansell, R. and U. When. 1998. *Knowledge Societies: Information Technology for Sustainable Development*. Oxford: Oxford University Press.

Manyozo, Linje Patrick. 2006. Doing Radio with Local People: A Development Broadcasting Approach (unpublished).

Manyozo, L. 2006. 'Manifesto for Development Communication: Nora Quebral and the Los Banos School of Development Communication', *Asian Journal of Communication*, 16(1): 79–99. Singapore: Routledge.

Martín Barbero, J. 1987. *De los Medios a las Mediaciones*. Mexico: Gustavo Gili.

———. 1993. *Communication, Culture and Hegemony; From the Media to Mediations*. London: Sage Publications.

Martin, W.J. 1995. *The Global Information Society*. Hampshire: Aslib Gower.

Masini, E. and J. Galtung (eds). 1979. *Visiones de Sociedades Deseables*. Mexico: CEESTEM.

Massey, D. and P. Jess (eds). 1995. *A Place in the World? Places, Cultures and Globalization*. Oxford: Oxford University Press.

Massoni, S.H. and M. Mascotti. 2001. 'Apuntes para la Comunicación en un Mundo Fluido: Mediación es no Mediar', in G. Cimadevilla (Coor.). *Comunicación, Tecnología y Desarrollo. Discusiones y Perspectivas desde el sur*. Río Cuarto: UNRC-ALAIC-RED MERCOMSUR.

Massoni, S.H. (s.d.). 2002. *La Comunicacion como Herramienta Estrategica em los Planes de Desarrollo Rural*. Buenos Aires INTA.

Mata, M.C. 1985. *Radio Enriquillo en Dialogo con el Pueblo*. QUITO: ALER.

———. 1990a. *Cómo Evaluar Nuestras Prácticas*. QUITO: ALER.

———. 1990b. *Nociones para Pensar la Comunicación y la Cultura Masiva*. Buenos Aires: La Crujia.

——— (ed.). 1995. *Mujer y Radio Popular*. QUITO: ALER.

Mathie, A. and G. Cunningham. 2003. 'From Clients to Citizens: Asset-Based Community Development as a Strategy for Community-Driven Development', *Development in Practice*, 13(5):474–486.

Mato, D. (ed.). 1994. *Diversidad Cultural y Construcción de Identidades*. Caracas: Tropikos.

———. 2001. *Globalización, cultura y transformaciones sociales*. Buenos Aires: Consejo Latinoamericano de Ciencias Sociales.

———. 2003. *Políticas sy Identidades y Diferencias Sociales*. Caracas: FACES-UVC.

Matta, F.R. 1979. *La Comunicacion Transnacional y la Respuesta Alternativa*. Mexico: ILET.

Mattelart, A. 1976. *Multinationales et Systèmes de Communication*. Paris: Anthropos.

———. 1983. *Transnationals and the Third World. The Struggle for Culture*. Massachusetts: Bergin and Garvey Publishers.

———. 1992. *La Communication–Monde*. Paris: Editions La Découverte.

Mattelart, A., X. D Elcourt and M. Mattelart. 1984. *International Image Markets. In Search of an Alternative Perspective*. London: Comedia.

Mayo, J. and J. Servaes (eds). 1994. *Approaches to Development Communication. A Training and Orientation Kit*. Volumes 1 + 2, UNFPA/UNESCO, New York/Paris (@ 800pp. + video + diskette).

Mazzei, L. and G. Scuppa. 2006. 'The Role of Communication in Large Infrastructure: The Bumbuna Hydroelectric Project in Post-Conflict Sierra Leone', World Bank Working Paper No. 84, Washington D.C.: The World Bank.

———. 1983. 'From Modernization and Diffusion to Dependency and Beyond: Theory and Practice in Communication for Social Change in the 1980s, Development Communications in the Third World', Proceedings of a Midwest Symposium, University of Illinois, April.

McAnany, E. (ed.). 1980. *Communications in the Rural Third World: The Role of Information in Development*. New York: Praeger.

McCarthy, J. 2004. *Enacting Participatory Development*. London: Earthscan Publications.

McKee, N. 1992. *Social Mobilization and Social Marketing in Developing Communities. Lessons for Communicators*. Penang: Southbound.

———. 1994. 'A Community-Based Learning Approach: Beyond Social Marketing', in S.A. White, K.S. Nair and J. Ascroft (eds). *Participatory Communication: Working for Change and Development*, pp. 194–228. New Delhi: Sage Publications.

McKee, N., E. Manoncourt, S.Y. Chin and R. Carnegie. (eds). 2000. *Involving People Evolving Behavior*. Penang: Southbound Publishers.

McLaren, P. and P. Leonard (eds). 1993. *Paulo Freire. A Critical Encounter*. London: Routledge.

McLuhan, M. and B.R. Power. 1989. *The Global Village: Transformation in World Life and Media in the 21th Century*. New York: Oxford University Press.

McPhail, T. 1987. *Electronic Colonialism: The Future of International Broadcasting and Communication*. Beverly Hills: Sage Publications.

McPhail, T. L. 2006. *Global Communication: Theories, Stakeholders, and Trends*. Malden: Blackwell.

McQuail, D. 1994. *Mass Communication Theory*. London, Thousand Oaks and New Delhi: Sage Publications.

———. 2005. *McQuail's Mass Communication Theory*. London, Thousand Oaks and New Delhi: Sage Publications.

Mefalopulos, P. and C. Kamlongera. 2004. *Participatory Communication Strategy Design: A Handbook*. Rome: FAO.

Meikle, J. 2002. *Future Active: Activism and the Interne*. Annandale: N.S.W. Pluto Press.

Melkote, S.R. 1991. *Communication for Development in the Third World: Theory and Practice.* London: Sage Publications.

———. 1993. *From Third World to First World: New Roles and Challenges for Development Communication, Gazette,* 52:145–158.

Melkote, S.R. 2002. 'Theories of Development Communication', in W.B. Gudykunst and B. Mody (eds). *Handbook of International and Intercultural Communication.* London: Sage Publications.

Melkote, S.R. and S. Rao (eds). 2001. *Critical Issues in Communication. Looking Inward for Answers.* New Delhi: Sage Publications.

Melkote, S.R. and H.L. Steeves. 2001. *Communication for Development in the Third World: Theory and Practice for Empowerment.* London: Sage Publications.

Melo, J.M. de (org.). 1996. *Identidades Culturais Latinoamericanas em Tempo de Comunicação Global,* Série UNESCO/UMESP.

———. 2001. *Mídia e Folclore—O Estudo da Folkcomunicação Segundo Luiz Beltrão,* Série UNESCO/UMESP.

Melo, J.M. de, I. Epstein, C. Sanches and S. Barbosa (orgs.). 2001. Mídia e Saúde, Série UNESCO/UMESP.

Melo, J.M. de and J. Brittes (orgs.). 1998. *A Trajetória Comunicacional de Luis Ramiro Beltrán,* Série Anais da Escola Latino-Americana de Comunicação.

Melo, J.M. de and M.C. Gobbi (orgs.). 1999. *Gênese do Pensamento Comunicacional Latino-Americano: Ciespal, Icinform, Ininco (O Protagonismo Das Instituições Pioneiras)*, Série Anais da Escola Latino-Americana de Comunicação.

———. 2000. Contribuições Brasileiras ao Pensamento Comunicacional Latino-Americano: Décio Pignatari, Muniz Sodré E Sérgio Caparelli, Série Anais da Escola Latino-Americana de Comunicação.

Melo, J.M. de, M.C. Gobbi and M. dos Santos. (orgs.). 2001. Contribuições Brasileiras ao Pensamento Comunicacional Latino-Americano—Décio Pignatari, Muniz Sodré e Sérgio Capparelli, Série UNESCO/UMESP.

Melo, J.M. de and W. Kunsch. (orgs.). 1998. De Belém a Bagé: Imagens Midiáticas do Natal Brasileiro, Série UNESCO/UMESP.

Melo, J.M. de and P da Rocha Dias. (orgs.). 1999. Comunicação, Cultura, Mediações-O Percurso Intelectual de Jesús Martín-Barbero, Série Anais da Escola Latino-Americana de Comunicação.

Melo, J.M. de and A. Queiroz. (orgs.). 1998. Identidade da Imprensa Brasileira no Final do Século: Das Estratégias Comunicacionais dos Enraizamentos Culturais, Série UNESCO/UMESP.

Melucci, A. 1992. 'Liberation or Meaning? Social Movements, Culture and Democracy', in J.N. Pieterse (ed.). *Emancipations Modern and Postmodern,* pp. 43–77. London: Newbury Park, New Delhi: Sage Publications.

Merrill. J. 1983. *Global Journalism.* New York: Longman.

Meyrowitz, Joshua. 1985. *No sense of place.* Oxford: Oxford University Press.

Midgley, J. (ed.). 1986. *Community Participation, Social Development, and the State.* London: Methuen.

Miege, B. 1995. *La Pensée Communicationnelle.* Grenoble: Presses Universitaires de Grenoble.

Mignot-Lefebvre, Y. (ed.). 1994. 'Technologies de Communication et d'Information au Sud: la Mondialisation Forcée' (special issue), *Revue Tiers-Monde,* 35(138) April–June: 6–76.

Miller, Daniel (ed.). 1995. *Worlds apart. Modernity through the prism of the local.* London: Routledge.

Minkler, M. (ed.). 1999. *Community Organizing and Community Building for Health,* New Brunswick: Rutgers University Press.

Mittelman, James H. (ed.). 1996. *Globalization: Critical reflections.* London: Routledge.

Mody, B. 1991. *Designing Messages for Development Communication: An Audience Participation-Based Approach.* New Delhi: Sage Publications.

——— (ed.). 1997. 'Communication and Development: Beyond Panaceas', *The Journal of International Communication,* 4(2):138.

——— (ed.). 2003. *International and Development Communication: A 21st Century Perspective.* Thousand Oaks, CA: Sage Publications.

Moemeka, A.A. 1994. 'Development Communication: A Historical and Conceptual Overview', in A.A. Moemeka, (ed.). *Communicating for Development: A New Pan–disciplinary Perspective,* pp. 3–22. Albany: SUNY Press.

——— (ed.). 1994. *Communicating for Development. A New Pan–Disciplinary Perspective.* Albany: State University of New York Press.

Mohanty, C.T. 1992 'Under Western Eyes. Feminist Scholarship and Colonial Discourses', in C.T. Mohanty, A. Russo and L. Torres (eds). *Third World Women and the Politics of Feminism,* pp. 51–80. Bloomington and Indianapolis: Indiana University Press.

Monga, C. 1994. *Anthropologie de la Colère. Société Civile et Démocratie en Afrique Noire.* Paris: Ed. l'Harmattan.

Moore, S. 1986. 'Participatory Communication in the Development Process', *The Third Channel,* 2.

Morris, A., G. Morton. 1998. *Locality, Community and Nation.* London: Hodder and Stoughton.

Mowlana, H. 1996. *Global Communication in Transition; The End of Diversity?* London: Sage Publications.

———. 1997. *Global Information and World Communication. New Frontiers in International Relations,* Second Edition. London: Sage Publications.

Mowlana, H. and L.J. Wilson. 1987. *Communication and Development: A Global Assessment.* Paris: UNESCO.

———. 1990. 'Communication, Technologie et Développement', *Etudes et documents d'information,* 101, Paris: UNESCO.

Mozammel, M. and G. Schechter. 2005. *Strategic Communication for Community-Driven Development: A Practical Guide for Project Managers and Communication Practitioners.* Washington, D.C.: World Bank.

Nair, K.S. and S.A. White. 1993. 'The Development Communication Process', in K.S. Nair and S.A. White (eds). *Perspectives on Development Communication,* pp. 47–70. New Delhi: Sage Publications.

———. 1994a. 'Participatory Development Communication as Cultural Renewal', in S.A.White, K.S. Nair and J. Ascroft (eds). *Participatory Communication: Working for Change and Development,* pp. 138–193. New Delhi: Sage Publications.

———. 1994b. 'Participatory Message Development: A Conceptual Framework', in S.A. White, K.S. Nair and J. Ascroft (eds). *Participatory Communication: Working for Change and Development,* pp. 345–358. New Delhi: Sage Publications.

Narayan, D., R. Patel, K. Schafft, A. Rademacher and S. Koch-Scholte. 1999. *Can Anyone Hear Us? Voices from 47 Countries.* Washington, DC: World Bank.

Narayan, U. 1997. *Dislocating Cultures. Identities, Traditions and Third World Feminism.* New York: Routledge.

Nederveen Pieterse, J. 1994. *Globalisation as Hybridisation, International Sociology,* 9(2):161–184.

———. 1995. 'The Cultural Turn in Development: Questions of Power', *The European Journal of Development Research,* 7(1):176–192.

Neveu, E. 1994. *Une Société de Communication?.* Paris: Montchrestien.

Nordenstreng, K. 1984. *The Mass Media Declaration of UNESCO.* Norwood: Ablex.

Nordenstreng, K. and H. Schiller (eds). 1979. *National Sovereignty and International Communication.* Norwood: Ablex.

Nostbakken, D. and C. Morrow (eds). 1993. *Cultural Expression in the Global Village.* Penang: Southbound.

Obregon, R. and J. Rivera. 2001. 'Participatory Communication in a High School Setting: Lessons Learned and Development Alternatives from a Development Communication Project in Colombia', *Journal of International Communication,* 7(2):98–114.

O'Connor, A. 1990a. 'Radio is Fundamental to Democracy', *Media Development,* 37(4): 8–160.

——— (ed.). 1990b. *Community Radio in Bolivia: The Miners' Radio Stations.* New York: The Edwin Mellen Press.

Omoto, A. (ed.). 2005. *Processes of Community Change and Social Action.* Mahwah: Lea.

Osaghae, E. 2004. *Special Issue on Globalisation, Diversity and Citizenship, Identity, Culture and Politics: An Afro-Asian Dialogue* 5(1 and 2): Colombo: ICES & CODESRIA.

O'Sullivan-Ryan, J. and M. Kaplún. 1978. *Communication Methods to Promote Grass-Roots Participation: A Summary of Research Findings from Latin America, and an Annotated Bibliography.* Paris: UNESCO.

Padovani, C. (ed.). 2001. *Comunicazione Globale. Democrazia, sovranitá, culture.* Torino: UTET Libreria.

Pang, L. 2005. *Cultural Control and Globalization in Asia.* London: Routledge.

Panos. 2000. *Setting Agendas: The Changing Roles of Development Communication in the Knowledge Age.* London: Panos Institute.

———. 2003. *Missing the Message? 20 Years of Learnning from HIV/AIDS.* London: Panos Institute.

———. 2005. *Reporting AIDS: An Analysis of Media Environments in Southern Africa.* Panos Case Studies, London: Panos.

Papa, M.J., A. Singhal, S. Law, S. Pant, S. Sood, E.M. Rogers and C.L. Shefner-Rogers. 2001. 'Entertainment-education and Social Change: An Analysis of Parasocial Interaction, Social Learning, Collective Efficacy, and Paradoxical Communication', *Journal of Communication,* 50(4):31–55.

Papa, M.J., A. Singhal and W. Papa. 2006. *Organizing for Social Change. A Dialectic Journey of Theory and Praxis.* New Delhi: Sage Publications.

Parks, W. 2005. *Who Measures Change? An Introduction to Participatory Monitoring and Evaluation of Communication for Social Change.* South Orange NJ: Communication For Social Change Consortium.

Pasquali, A. 1970. *Communicacion y Cultura de Masas.* Caracas: Avila.

———. 1980. *Comprender la Comunicacion.* Caracas: Avila.

Pateman, C. 1972. *Participation and Democratic Theory.* Cambridge: Cambridge University Press.

Perez de Cuellar, J. (ed.). 1995. *Our Creative Diversity. Report of the World Commission on Culture and Development.* Paris: UNESCO.

Petracci, M. and H. Muraro. 2001. 'Circuitos Comunicacionales de Información Sobre los Modos de Contagio y Prevención del VIH/SIDA', in G. Cimadevilla (Coor.), *Comunicación, Tecnología y Desarrollo. Discusiones y Perspectivas desde el sur*, pp. 267–281. Río Cuarto: UNRC-ALAIC-RED MERCOMSUR.

Pfiester, A., P. Roman and R.D. Colle. 2000. 'The Role Participation in Telecentre Initiatives: Building the Digital Bridge', *The Journal of Development Communication*, 11(2):62–75.

Phildhrra. Participatory Research Guidebook, 1986. Philippine Partnership for the Development of Human Resources in Rural A·cas, Laguna.

Phonekeo, K. 1990. *L'Education, la Culture, la Communication, la Science et la Technologie dans la Stratégie du Développement de la République Démocratique Populaire Lao, Grand programme I Réflexion sur les problèmes mondiaux et études prospectives*, 62. Paris: UNESCO.

Piotrow, P.T., D.L. Kincaid, J. Rimon II and W. Rinehart. 1997. *Health Communication: Lessons from Family Planning and Reproductive Health*. Westport, CT: Praeger.

Plummer, J. and J.G. Taylor. 2004. *Community Participation in China*. Earthscan Publications.

Prehn, O. 1991. 'From Small Scale Utopism to Large Scale Pragmatism', in N. Jankowski, O. Prehn, J. Stappers (eds). *The People's Voice. Local Radio and Television in Europe*, pp. 247–268. London, Paris, Rome: John Libbey.

Preiswerk, R. 1980. 'Identité Culturelle, Self-reliance et Besoins Fondamentaux', in P. Spitz, J. Galtung, R. Preiswerk, G. Berthourd, M. Guillaume, G. Rist, A. Allain, J.-P. Bärfuss, G. Eienne and L. Kanemann (eds). *Il Faut Manger pour Vivre ...'*. Paris: Presses Universitaires de France.

Primo Barga, C.A., S. Roger Barga, David B. Lomet, Thomas Baby and Sanjay Agarwal. 2000. The Network Revolution, Opportunities and Challenges for Developing Countries, *info*Dev Working Paper. Washington: The World Bank.

Protz, M. 1998. 'Developing Sustainable Agricultural Technologies with Rural Women in Jamaica: A Participatory Media Approach', in L. van Crowder (ed.). *Training for Agriculture and Rural Development 1997–98*, pp. 35–47. Rome: FAO.

Putnam, R.D. 1993. *Making Democracy Work*. Princeton: Princeton University Press.

Rahman, M.A. 1993. *People's Self Development: Perspectives on Participatory Action Research*. London: Zed Books.

Ramirez, R. 1995. *Understanding Farmers' Communication Networks: An Experience in the Philippines*. Rome: FAO.

———. 1998. 'Participatory Learning and Approaches for Managing Pluralism', Unasylva, 49.

Ramirez, R. and T. Stuart. 1994. 'Farmers Control Communication Campaigns', *ILEIA Newsletter*, March.

Ramirez, R. and W. Quarry. 2004. *Communication for Development: A Medium for Innovation in Natural Resource Management*. Ottawa: International Development Research Centre.

Ratzan, S. (ed.). 1993. *Effective Health Communication for the 90s*. Washington: Taylor and Francis.

Ravindran, D.J. 1998. *Human Rights Praxis: A Resource Book for Study, Action and Reflection*. Bangkok: The Asian Forum for Human Rights and Development.

Reeves, G. 1993. *Communications and the 'Third World'*. London: Routledge.

Regan, C. (ed.). 2002. *Development in an Unequal World*. Birmingham: Tide, 80:20.

Reimão, S. (org.) 2000. *Televisão na América Latina—7 Estudos*, Série UNESCO/UMESP.

Reyes Matta, F. 1986. 'Alternative Communication: Solidarity and Development in the Face of Transnational Expansion', in R. Atwood and E. McAnany (eds). *Communication and Latin American Society. Trends in Critical Research 1960–1985*, pp. 190–214. Madisn: University of Wisconson Press.

Riaño, P. 1994. 'Women's Participation in Communication: Elements of a Framework', in P. Riaño (ed.). *Women in Grassroots Communication*, pp. 3–29. Thousand Oaks, CA: Sage Publications.

Ribeiro, A.R. 1998. *Meio Ambiente e Dinâmica de Inovações na Agricultura*. São Paulo: Anna Blume/Fapes.

Rice, R. and C. Atkin. 1996. 'Principios de las Campañas de Comunicación Pública de Éxito', in J. Bryant and D. Zillmann (eds). *Los Efectos de los Medios de Comunicación. Investigaciones y Teorías*. Barcelona: Paidós.

Richardson, D. 1997. *The Internet and Rural and Agricultural Development: An Integrated Approach*. Rome: FAO.

Richstad, J. and M. Anderson (eds). 1981. *Crisis in International News*. New York: Columbia University Press.

Roach, C. 1996. 'The MacBride Round Table on Communication', in P. Thomas and P. Lee (eds). *Media Development*, special issue on Alternative Communication Networks, XLIII(3): 19–20.

Robertson, R. 1992. *Globalization. Social Theory and Global Culture*. London: Sage Publications.

Rochefort, M. 1998. *Redes e Sistemas: Ensinando Sobre o Urbano e a Região*. São Paulo: Hucitec.

Rockefeller Foundation. 1997. *Communications and Social Change: Forging Strategies for the 21st Century*. New York.

Rockefeller Foundation. 1999. *Communication for Social Change: A Position Paper and Conference Report.* New York.

————. 2000. *Special Programs: Communication for Social Change.* New York: Rockefeller Foundation.

Rodríguez, C. 2001. *Fissures in the Mediascape: An International Study of Citizen's Media.* Cresskill NJ: Hampton Press.

Rogers, A. 1992. *Adults Learning for Development.* London: Cassell.

————. 1996. 'Participatory Training Using Critical Reflection on Experience in Agricultural Extension Training', in L. van Crowder (ed.). *Training for Agriculture and Rural Development 1995–96,* pp. 86–103. Rome: FAO.

Rogers, E.M. 1962. *Diffusion of Innovations.* New York: Free Press.

————. 1976a. 'Communication and Development: The Passing of the Dominant Paradigm'. *Communication Research,* 3(2):213–240.

————. 1976b. 'Communication and Development: The Passing of the Dominant Paradigm', in E. Rogers (ed.). *Communication and Development—Critical Perspectives,* pp. 121–148. Beverly Hills, CA: Sage Publications.

————. 1986a. *Communication of Innovations.* New York: The Free Press.

————. 1986b. *Communication Technology: The New Media in Society.* New York: The Free Press.

————. 1993. 'Perspectives on Development Communication', in K.S. Nair and S.A. White (eds). *Perspectives on Development Communication,* pp. 35–46. New Delhi: Sage Publications.

Rogers, E.M. and F. Schoemaker. 1973. *Communication of Innovations.* New York: The Free Press.

Rogers, E.M. (ed.). 1976. *Communication and Development.* Beverly Hills: Sage Publications.

Rogers, E.M. and F. Balle (eds). 1985. *The Media Revolution in America and Western Europe.* Norwood. Ablex.

Röling, N.G. and J. Pretty. 1997. 'Extension's Role in Sustainable Development', in *Improving Agricultural Extension: A Reference Manual,* pp. 181–191. Rome: FAO.

Rondinelli, D. 1993. *Development Projects as Policy Experiments. An Adaptive Approach to Development Administration.* London: Routledge.

Rosenau, J. 1980. *The Study of Global Interdependence.* London: Francis Pinter.

————. 1987. *Along the Domestic–Foreign Frontier.* Cambridge: Cambridge University Press.

Rowlands, J. 2003. 'Beyond the Comfort Zone: Some issues, Questions and Challenges in Thinking about Development Approaches and Methods', in D. Eade (ed.). *Development Methods and Approaches: Critical Reflections,* pp. 165–186. Oxford: Oxfam UK.

Said, E. 1985. *Orientalism.* Harmondsworth: Penguin Books.

————. 1993. *Culture and Imperialism.* New York: Alfred Knopf.

Sainath, P. 1996. *Everybody Loves a Good Drought: Stories from India's Poorest Districts.* New Delhi: Penguin Books.

————. 2001. 'None So Blind as Those Who Will Not See', *The UNESCO Courier,* June:44–46.

Salomón, J. 1996. *Una Búsqueda Incierta. Ciencia, Tecnología y Desarrollo,* México: Fondo de Cultura Económica-CIDE-ONU.

Salzman, P.C. 1996. 'The Electronic Trojan Horse: Television in the Globalization of Paramodern Cultures', in L. Arizpe (ed.). *The Cultural Dimensions of Global Change: An Anthropological Approach,* pp. 197–216. Paris: UNESCO.

Samarajiva, R. 1987. 'The Murky Beginnings of the Communication and Development Field: Voice of America and the Passing of Traditional Society', in N. Jayaweera and S. Amunaguma (eds). *Rethinking Development Communication.* Singapore: AMIC.

Samovar, L.A. and R.E. Porter. 1995. *Communication between Cultures.* Belmont: Wadsworth.

Savio, R. (ed.). 1990. 'Communication, Participation and Democracy', *Development, Journal of the Society for International Development,* 2:7–10.

Schech, S. and J. Haggis. 2000. *Culture and Development.* Oxford: Blackwell.

Schiller, H.I. 1969. *Mass Communications and American Empire.* Boston: Beacon Press.

————. 1976. *Communication and Cultural Domination.* New York: International Arts and Sciences Press.

Schramm, W. 1964. *Mass Media and National Development.* Stanford: Stanford University Press.

————. 1976. 'End of an Old Paradigm?', in W. Schramm and D. Lerner (eds). *Communication and Change: The Last Ten Years—and the Next,* pp. 45–48. Honolulu: East-West Center.

Schramm, W., Nelson and M.T. Betham. 1981. *Bold Experiment: The Story of Educational Television in American Samoa,* Stanford, California: Stanford University Press.

Schramm, W. and D. Lerner (eds). 1976. *Communication and Change. The Last Ten Years—and the Next.* Honolulu: University Press of Hawaii.

Segall, M.H., P. Dasen, J. Berry and Y. Poortinga. 1990. *Human Behavior in Global Perspective.* Oxford: Pergamon.

Sen, A. 1999. *Development as Freedom*. New York: Random House.

Servaes, J. 1983. *Communication and Development. Some Theoretical Remarks*. Leuven: Acco.

———. 1989. 'Cultural Identity and Modes of Communication', in J. Anderson (ed.). *Communication Yearbook*, 12, pp. 383–416. Beverly Hills: Sage Publications.

———. 1989. *One World, Multiple Cultures. A New Paradigm on Communication for Development*. Leuven: Acco.

———. 1996a. 'Linking Theoretical Perspectives to Policy', in J. Servaes, T.L. Jacobson and S.A. White (eds). *Participatory Communication for Social Change*, pp. 29–43. New Delhi: Sage Publications.

———. 1996b. 'Participatory Communication Research with New Social Movements: A Realistic Utopia', in J. Servaes, T.L. Jacobson and S.A. White (eds). *Participatory Communication for Social Change*, pp. 82–108. New Delhi: Sage Publications.

———. 1997. 'Mass Media and Fragmented Identities', in J. Servaes and R. Lie (eds). *Media and Politics in Transition. Cultural Identity in the Age of Globalization*, pp. 77–88. Leuven: ACCO.

———. 1998. 'Human Rights, Participatory Communication and Cultural Freedom in a Global Perspective', *Journal of International Communication*, 5(1 and 2):122–133.

———. 1999. *Communication for Development. One World, Multiple Cultures*. Cresskill: Hampton Press.

———. 2000. 'Comunicación para el Desarrollo. Tres Paradigmas, Dos Modelos', *Temas y Problemas de Comunicación*, 8(10):5–28.

——— (ed.). 2000. *Walking on the Other Side of the Information Highway. Communication, Culture and Development in the 21st Century*. Penang: Southbound.

———. 2001a. 'El Mundo, Nuestro Pueblo ... Una Perspectiva Culturalista Hacia la Comunicación para el Cambio Social', in G. Cimadevilla (Coor.), *Comunicación, Tecnología y Desarrollo. Discusiones y Perspectivas desde el sur*. pp. 3–12. Río Cuarto: UNRC-ALAIC-RED MERCOMSUR.

———. 2001b. 'Participatory Communication (Research) for Social Change: Old and New Challenges', *Journal of International Communication*, 7(2):5–13.

———. 2005. Ideas and Ideologies in Development Communication: Mapping the Paradigm Shift, Paper presented at the Department of Community Resource Management Extension, Delhi.

Servaes, J. and R. Arnst. 1999. 'Principles of Participatory Communication Research: Its Strengths (!) and Weaknesses (?)', in T.L. Jacobson and J. Servaes (eds). *Theoretical Approaches to Participatory Communication*, pp. 107–130. Cresskill, NJ: Hampton Press.

Servaes, J. and P. Malikhao. 1998. 'A Critical Examination of a UNESCO Study on Television Flows in Europe and Asia', in S. Melkote, P. Shields and B. Agrawal (eds). *International Satellite Broadcasting in South Asia. Political, Economic and Cultural Implications*, pp. 273–294. Lanham: University Press of America.

Servaes, J., T.L. Jacobson and S.A. White (eds). 1996. *Participatory Communication for Social Change*. London: Sage Publications.

Servaes, J. and R. Lie (eds). 1997. *Media and Politics in Transition. Cultural Identity in the Age of Globalization*. Leuven: Acco.

Servaes, J. and N. Carpentier (eds). 2006. *Deconstructing WSIS: Towards a Sustainable Agenda for the Future Information Society*, ECCR Book Series. Bristol: Intellect.

Sherry, J.L. 1997. 'Pro-Social Soap Operas for Development: A Review of Research and Theory, Communication and Development: Beyond Panacea', *Journal of International Communication*. Special Issue, 4(2):75–102.

Silva, Da. G. 2001. 'Globo Rural: Entre a Globalização e a Segmentação', in G. Cimadevilla (Coor.), *Comunicación, Tecnología y Desarrollo. Discusiones y Perspectivas desde el sur*. Río Cuarto: UNRC-ALAIC-RED MERCOMSUR.

Simpson-Grinberg, M. (ed.). 1986. *Comunicación Alternativa y Cambio Social* [Alternative Communication and Social Change. Tlahuapan, Puebla, Mexico: Premiá Editora de Libros.

Sinclair, J. 1999. *Latin American Television. A Global View*. Oxford: Oxford University Press.

Sinclair, J., E. Jacka and S. Cunningham (eds). 1996. *New Patterns in Global Television. Peripheral Vision*. Oxford: Oxford University Press.

Singh, J.P. 2003. 'Communication Technology and Development: Instrumental, Institutional, Participatory and Strategic Approaches', in B. Mody (ed.). *International and Development Communication: A 21st Century Perspective*. Thousand Oaks. CA: Sage Publications.

Singhal, Arvind. 2000. HIV/AIDS and Communication for Behaviour and Social Change: Programme Experiences, Examples and Ways Forward. International Workshop, UNAIDS, Department of Policy and Strategy, July.

Singhal, A. and E.M. Rogers. 1988. 'Television Soap Operas for Development in India', *Gazette*, 41(2):109–126.

———. 1999. *Entertainment-Education: A Communication Strategy for Social Change*. Mahwah, NJ: Lawrence Earlbaum Associates.

———. 2001. 'The Entertainment-Education Strategy in Communication Campaigns', in R.E. Rice and C. Atkin (eds). *Public Communication Campaigns*, Third Edition, pp. 343–356. Thousand Oaks, CA: Sage Publications.

Singhal, A., S. Usdin, E. Scheepers, S. Goldstein and G. Japhet. 2005. 'Harnessing the Entertainment-Education Strategy in Development Communication by Integrating Program Design, Social Mobilization and Advocacy', in Okigbo Charles and Eribo Festus (eds). *Development and Communication in Africa*, pp. 141–153. Boulder: Rowman and Littlefield.

Singhal, A. and E.M. Rogers. 2002. *Combating AIDS, Communication Strategies in Action*. New Delhi: Sage Publications.

Singhal, A., M.J. Cody, E.M. Rogers and M. Sabido (eds). 2004. *Entertainment-Education and Social Change: History, Research, and Practice*. Mahwah NJ: Lawrence Erlbaum Associates.

Sison, O. 1985. *Factors Associated with the Successful Transfer of Rice Technology in the Philippines Masagana 99 Programme*. Rome: FAO.

Sjöberg, M. (ed.). 1994. *Community Radio in Western Europe*. Sheffield: AMARC-Europe.

Smith, A. 1980. *The Geopolitics of Information. How Western Culture Dominates the World*. London: Faber and Faber.

Snyder, L.B. 2003. 'Development Communication Campaigns', in B. Mody (ed.). *International and Development Communication: A 21st Century Perspective*. Thousand Oaks, CA: Sage Publications.

Somavia, J. 1980. 'Perspectivas del Informe MacBride', *Media Development*, 27(4).

Sosale, S. 2002. 'Communication and Development in the International and Global "Eras": Understanding Continuities and Changes', *Journal of International Communication*, 8(2).

Splichal, S. and J. Wasko (eds). 1993. *Communication and Democracy*. Norwood: Ablex.

Sposato, S. and W.A. Smith. 2005. *Radio: A Post Nine Eleven Strategy for Reaching the World's Poor*. Lanham M.D.: University Press of America.

Spybey, T. 1992. *Social Change, Development and Dependency. Modernity, Colonialism and the Development of the West*. Cambridge: Polity Press.

———. 1995. *Globalization and World Society*. Cambridge: Polity Press.

Srampickal, S.J. 2006. 'Development and Participatory Communication', *Communication Research Trends*, 25(2):3–32, Santa Clara CA: Centre for the Study of Communication and Culture (CSCC).

Sreberny-Mohammadi A., D. Winseck and J. McKenna. 1997. *Media in Global Context. A Reader*. London: Arnold.

Stavenhagen, R. 1966. 'Siete Tesis Equivocados Sobre América Latina', *Desarrollo Indoamericano*, 4:144–166.

Steckler, A.B., B.A. Israel, L. Dawson and E. Eng. 1993. 'Community Health Development: An Anthology of the Works of Guy W. Steuart', *Health Education Quarterly*, Suppl. 1.

Steeves, L. 2002. 'Participatory Approaches to Communication for Development', in W.B. Gudykunst and B. Mody (eds). *Handbook of International and Intercultural Communication*. London: Sage Publications.

Steeves, H.L. 2003. 'Development Communication as Marketing, Collective Resistance and Spiritual Awakening: A Feminist Critique', in B. Mody (ed.). *International and Development Communication: A 21st Century Perspective*. Thousand Oaks, CA: Sage Publications.

Sterling, C. 1984. *International Telecommunications and Information Policy*. Washington: Communications Press.

Stevenson, R. 1988. *Communication, Development, and the Third World*. New York: Longman.

Storey, D. 1999. 'Popular Culture, Discourse and Development', in T.L. Jacobson and J. Servaes (eds). *Theoretical Approaches to Participatory Communication*, pp. 337–358. Cresskill, NJ: Hampton Press.

———. 2000. 'A Discursive Perspective on Development Theory and Practice: Reconceptualizing the Role of Donor Agencies', in K.G. Wilkins (ed.). *Redeveloping Communication for Social Change: Theory, Practice, and Power*. pp. 103–111. Lanham, MD: Rowman and Littlefield Publishers.

Stover, W. 1984. *Information Technology in the Third World. Can it Lead to Human National Development?* Boulder: Westview.

Strathern, Marlyn (ed.). 1995. *Shifting Contexts. Transformations in Anthropological Knowledge*. London: Routledge.

Sunkel, O. and E. Fuenzalida. 1980. 'La Transnacionalizacion del Capitalismo y el Desarrollo Nacional', in O. Sunkel, E. Fuenzalida, F.H. Cardoso et al. (eds). *Transnacionalizacion y Dependencia*. Madrid: Ed. Cultura Hispania.

Sunkel, O. and P. Paz. 1970. *El Subdesarrollo Latinoamericano y la Teoria del Desarrollo*. Mexico: Siglo XXI.

Sunkel, O. (ed.). 1993. *Development from Within. Toward a Neostructuralist Approach for Latin America*. Boulder: Lynne Rienner.

Sustainable Development Department. 2006. *Sustaining Development for All: Expanding Access to Economic Activity and Social Services*. Washington D.C.: Inter-American Development Bank.

Tauk Santos, M.S. 2001. 'Internet: Uma Nova Cultura que Emerge do Campo Interdisciplinar das Ciencias da Informação e da Comunicação', in G. Cimadevilla (Coor.), *Comunicación, Tecnología y Desarrollo. Discusiones y Perspectivas desde el sur*, pp. 163–170. Río Cuarto: UNRC-ALAIC-RED MERCOMSUR.

Taylor P. 1997. *Investigating Culture and Identity*. London: Collins Educational.

Tehranian, M. 1979. 'Development Theory and Communication Policy. The Changing Paradigm', in M. Voigt and G. Hanneman (eds). *Progress in Communication Sciences*, Vol. 1. Norwood: Ablex.

———. 1999. *Global Communication and World Politics: Domination, Development and Discourse*. Boulder, CO: Lynne Rienner.

Therborn, Göran. 1999. *Globalizations and Modernities: Experiences and Perspectives of Europe and Latin America*. Stockholm: FRN, Swedish Council for Planning and Coordination of Research.

Thioune, R.M. 2003. 'Opportunities and Challenges for Community Development', *Information and Communication Technologies for Development in Africa* (Vol I).

Thomas, P. 1994. 'Participatory Message Development Communication: Philosophical Premises', in S.A. White, K.S. Nair and J. Ascroft (eds). *Participatory Communication: Working for Change and Development*, pp. 49–59. New Delhi: Sage Publications.

Thomas, P. and P. Lee (eds). 1996. 'Media Development', special issue on *Alternative Communication Networks*, XLIII(3).

Thomas-Slayter, B. and G. Sodikoff. 2003. 'Sustainable Investments: Women's Contributions to Natural Resource Management Projects in Africa', in D. Eade (ed.). *Development Methods and Approaches: Critical Reflections*, pp. 143–166. Oxford: Oxfam UK.

Thompson, J.B. 1995. *The Media and Modernity: A Social Theory of the Media*. Cambridge: Polity Press.

Thornton, R. 2001. 'La Vigencia de la Radio. Cuando la Educación y el Desarrollo Importan', in G. Cimadevilla (Coor.), *Comunicación, Tecnología y Desarrollo. Discusiones y Perspectivas desde el sur*. Río Cuarto: UNRC-Alaic-RED Mercomsur.

Tirvassen, R. 1994. 'Communication et Développement', *Langues et développement*, 3.

Tomasevski, K. 1993. *Development Aid and Human Rights Revisited*. London: Pinter.

Tomlinson, J. 1991. *Cultural Imperialism*. London: Pinter Publishers.

———. 1993. *Cultural Imperialism: An Introduction*. Baltimore: The Johns Hopkins University Press.

———. 1997a. 'Cultural Globalization and Cultural Imperialism', in A. Mohammadi (ed.). *International Communication and Globalization. A Critical Introduction*, pp. 170–190. London: Sage Publications.

———. 1997b. *Internationalisation, Globalisation and Cultural Imperialism*. London: Pinter Publishers.

———. 1999. *Globalization and Culture*. Cambridge: Polity Press.

Tönnies, F. 1963. *Community and Society*. London: Harper and Row.

Torero, M. and J. von Braun (eds). 2006. *Information and Communication Technologies for Development and Poverty Reduction*. Baltimore: The John Hopkins University Press.

Torres, R.M. 1989. *Educacion Popular y Comunicacion Popular*. Quito: Centro de Investigaciones.

Traber, M. (ed.). 1986. *The Myth of the Information Revolution*. London: Sage Publications.

Trespidi, M.A. 2001. 'Divergencias Comunicacionales que Inhiben Convergencias Esenciales para Lograr el Desarrollo', in G. Cimadevilla (Coor.), *Comunicación, Tecnología y Desarrollo. Discusiones y Perspectivas desde el sur*. Río Cuarto: UNRC-Alaic-Red Mercomsur.

Tufte, T. 2000. *Living with the Rubbish Queen—Telenovelas, Culture and Modernity in Brazil*. Luton: University of Luton Press.

———. 2001. 'Entertainment-Education and Participation', *Journal of International Communication*, 7(2).

Tunstall, J. 1977. *The Media are American; Anglo-American, Media in the World*. USA: Colombia University Press.

Turner, B. 1994. *Orientalism, Postmodernism and Globalism*. London: Routledge.

Turner, C. (ed.). 1993. *Tradition and Change. Contemporary Art of Asia and the Pacific*. Brisbane: University of Queensland Press.

Ugboajah, F.O. (ed.). 1985. *Mass Communication, Culture and Society in West Africa*. München: Saur.

Underwood, C. and B. Jabre. 2003. 'Arab Women Speak Out: Self-Empowerment Via Video', in S.A. White (ed.). *Participatory Video*, pp. 235–251. London: Sage Publications.

UNESCO. 1989. *World Communication Report*. Paris: UNESCO.

———. 1994a. *TV Transnationalization: Europe and Asia*. Paris: UNESCO.

———. 1994b. *The futures of Cultures*. Paris: UNESCO.

———. 1995. *Public Service Broadcasting: Cultural and Educational Dimensions*. Paris: UNESCO.

———. 1997a. 'Towards a World Report on Culture and Development: Constructing Cultural Statistics and Indicators'. Report of the Workshop on Cultural Indicators of Development, Paris: UNRISD & UNESCO.

———. 1997b. *World Communication Report: The Media and the Challenges of the New Technologies*. Paris: UNESCO.

———. 1999. *World Communication and Information Report 1999–2000*. Paris: UNESCO.

——— (s.d.). *Historical Background of The Mass Media Declaration*. Paris: UNESCO.

UNFPA. 2002. 'Communication for Development'. Round Table Report: Focus on HIV/AIDS Communication and Evaluation, November 26–28, 2001, Managua, Nicaragua. Organized by UNFPA with The Rockefeller Foundation, UNESCO and The Panos Institute, New York: UNFPA.

Ungpakorn, Ji Giles (ed.). 2003. *Radicalising Thailand. New Political Perspectives*. Bangkok: Institute of Asian Studies. Chulalongkorn University.

United Nations Development Programme. 2006. Communication for Empowerment: Developing Media Strategies in Support of Vulnerable Groups, Oslo, Norway, www.worldbank.org/wbi/news/docs/Severinoonfreepress.htm

Valle, C. (ed.). 2000. *Communication and the Globalisation of Poverty*. London: World Association for Christian Communication.

van der Stichele, P. and S. Bie. 1997. *The Last Mile: How Can Farmers Take Advantage of New Media?*, Rome: FAO.

van Dinh, T. 1987. *Independence. Liberation. Revolution. An Approach to the Understanding of the Third World*. Norwood: Ablex.

van Nieuwenhuijze, C.A.O. 1982. *Development Begins at Home. Problems and Projects of the Sociology of Development*. Oxford: Pergamon Press.

Vargas, L. 1995. *Social Uses and Radio Practices: The Use of Participatory Radio by Ethnic Minorities in Mexico*. Boulder, CO: Westview.

Varghese, K. 2003. 'Beyond Community Video', in S.A. White (ed.). *Participatory Video*. London: Sage Publications.

Varis, T. 1973. *International Inventory of Television Programme Structure and the Flow of TV Programmes between Nations*. University of Tampere: Institute of Journalism and Mass Communication.

———. 1984. 'The International Flow of Television Programs', *Journal of Communication*, 34:143–152.

——— (ed.). 1986. *International Flow of Television Programmes*. Paris: UNESCO.

Varis, T. and K. Nordenstreng. 1974. *Television Traffic—A One-Way Street?* Paris: UNESCO.

Verba, S. and N. Nie. 1987. *Participation in America. Political Democracy and Social Equality*. Chicago: University of Chicago Press.

Vincent, R.C., K. Nordenstreng and M. Iraber (eds). 1998. *Towards Equity in Global Communication*, MacBride Update. Cresskill: Hampton Press.

Vincent, R. and A. Byrne. 2006. 'Enhancing Learning in Development Partnerships', *Development in Practice*, 16(5): 385–399.

WACC. 2001. *Media Ownership and Citizen Access. A Global Overview*. London: World Association for Christian Communication.

———. 2006. 'Communication for Development and Social Justice', *Journal of the World Association for Christian Communication*, Media Development, 53(3):4–48.

Waisbord, S. 2000. *Family Trees of Theories, Methodologies and Strategies in Development Communication: Convergences and Differences*. New York: Rockefeller Foundation.

Wang, G. 1998. 'Protecting the Local Cultural Industry: A Regulatory Myth in the Global Age', in A. Goonasekera and P.S.N. Lee (eds). *TV Without Borders: Asia Speaks Out*, pp. 259–273. Singapore: AMIC.

Wang, G. and W. Dissanayake (eds). 1984. *Continuity and Change in Communication Systems. An Asian Perspective*. Norwood: Ablex.

Wang, G., J. Servaes and A. Goonasekera (eds). 2000. *The New Communications Landscape. Demystifying Media Globalization*. London: Routledge.

Wangvivatana, S. (ed.). 2005. *Media Reform Going Backwards?* Bangkok: Thai Broadcast Journalist's Association and Friedrich-Ebert-Stiftung.

Warnock, K. and R. Wickremesinghe (eds). 2005. *Information and Communication Technologies and Large-Scale Poverty Reduction: Lessons Learned from Asia, Africa, Latin America and the Caribbean*. London: Panos.

Wasko, J. and V. Mosco (eds). 1992. *Democratic Communications in the Information Age*. Toronto and Norwood, NJ: Garamond Press and Ablex.

Waters, M. 1995. *Globalization*. London: Routledge.

Wells, A.F. 1972. *Picture Tube Imperialism? The Impact of US Television on Latin America*. New York: Orbis.

Werbner, P. and T. Modood (eds). 1997. *Debating Cultural Hybridity: Multi-Cultural Identities and the Politics of Anti-Racism*. London: Zed Books.

White, K. 1999. 'The Importance of Sensitivity to Culture in Development Work', in T.L. Jacobson and J. Servaes (eds). *Theoretical Approaches to Participatory Communication*, pp. 17–49. Cresskill, NJ: Hampton Press.

White, R. 1994. 'Participatory Development Communication as a Social–Cultural Process', in S.A. White, K.S. Nair and J. Ascroft (eds). *Participatory Communication: Working for Change and Development*, pp. 95–116. New Delhi: Sage Publications.

———. 1999. 'The Need for New Strategies of Research on the Democratization of Communication', in T.L. Jacobson and J. Servaes (eds). *Theoretical Approaches to Participatory Communication*, pp. 229–262. Cresskill, NJ: Hampton Press.

White, R.A. 2004. 'Is Empowerment the Answer? Current Theory and Research on Development Communication', *Gazette: The International Journal for Communication Studies*, 66(1):7–24.

White, S.A. 1994. 'The Concept of Participation: Transforming Rhetoric to Reality', in S.A. White, K.S. Nair and J. Ascroft (eds). *Participatory Communication: Working for Change and Development*, pp. 15–32. New Delhi: Sage Publications.

———. (ed.). 2000. *The Art of Facilitating Participation*. London: Sage Publications.

———. 2003a. 'Involving People in a Participatory Process', in S.A. White (ed.). *Participatory Video*, pp. 63–101. London: Sage Publications.

———. 2003b. 'Participatory Video: A Process that Transforms the Self and the Other', in S.A. White (ed.). *Participatory Video*. London: Sage Publications.

———. 2003c. 'Video Kaleidoscope: A World's Eye View of Video Power', in S.A. White (ed.). *Participatory Video*. London: Sage Publications.

White, S.A., K.S. Nair and J. Ascroft (eds). 1994. *Participatory Communication. Working for Change and Development*. London: Sage Publications.

Whyte, W.F. 1984. *Learning from the Field. A Guide from Experience*. London: Sage Publications.

Wieczorek-Zeul, H. 2006. *Recht—Demokratie—Frieden. Politik fur Entwicklung*. Bonn: Bundesministerium fur wirtschaftliche Zusammenarbeit und Entwicklung.

Wilkins, K.G. 1999. 'Development Discourse on Gender and Communication in Strategies for Social Change', *Journal of Communication*, 49:46–68.

———. 2000a. 'Accounting for Power in Development Communication', in K.G. Wilkins (ed.). *Redeveloping Communication for Social Change: Theory, Practice, and Power*, pp. 197–210. Lanham, MD: Rowman and Littlefield Publishers.

———. 2000b. *Redeveloping Communication for Social Change: Theory, Practice, and Power*. Lanham MD: Rowman and Littlefield Publishers.

Wilson, Rob and Wimal Dissanayake. 1996. *Global/Local. Cultural Production and the Transnational Imaginary*. London: Duke University Press.

World Bank. 1994. *The World Bank and Participation*. Washington: World Bank.

World Health Organization. 1997. *Communicating Family Planning in Reproductive Health*. Geneva: WHO.

WSIS. 2005. Discussion papers. 'Information and Communication Technologies and Large-scale Poverty Reduction: Lessons from Asia, Africa, Latin America and the Caribbean'. London: Panos.

Xavier Institute. 1980. *Development from Below*. Ranchi: Xavier Institute for Social Service.

Xinn, G. 1988. *Guide on Alternative Extension Approaches*. Rome: FAO.

Yahaya, M.K. and B.R. Olajide. 2003. 'Challenges of Entertainment-Education: Format Utilisation for Agricultural Information Dissemination in Nigeria', *Journal of International Communication*, 9(1):127–142.

Zoller, H.M. 2005. 'Health Activism: Communication Theory and Action for Social Change', *Communication Theory*, 15(4):341–364.

About the Editor and Contributors

Editor

Jan Servaes (Ph.D., 1987, Catholic University of Louvain, Belgium) is Professor and Chair of the Department of Communication at the University of Massachusetts at Amherst (USA), Editor-in-Chief of *Communication for Development and Social Change: A Global Journal* (Hampton Press), Associate Editor of *Telematics and Informatics: An International Journal on Telecommunications and Internet Technology* (Elsevier), Editor of the Southbound Book Series *Communication for Development and Social Change*, and Editor of the Hampton Book Series *Communication, Globalization and Cultural Identity*. He chaired the Scientific Committee for the World Congress on Communication for Development (Rome, 25–27 October 2006), organized by the World Bank, FAO and the Communication Initiative.

Servaes has taught International Communication and Development Communication in Australia (Brisbane), Belgium (Brussels and Antwerp), the USA (Cornell), the Netherlands (Nijmegen) and Thailand (Thammasat, Bangkok).

He has been President of the European Consortium for Communications Research (ECCR, www.eccr.info) and Vice-President of the International Association for Media and Communication Research (IAMCR, www.iamcr.net), in charge of Academic Publications and Research, from 2000 to 2004.

Servaes has undertaken research, development, and advisory work around the world and is known as the author of journal articles and books on such topics as international and development communication; ICT and media policies; intercultural communication and language; participation and social change; and human rights and conflict management. Some of his most recent book titles include:

- Servaes, J. 2002. *Communication for Development. One World, Multiple Cultures*, Cresskill: Hampton Press.
- ———. (ed.). 2003. *Approaches to Development. Studies on Communication for Development*, Paris: UNESCO Publishing House.
- ———. (ed.). 2003. *The European Information Society: A Reality Check*, Intellect, Bristol: ECCR Book Series.

- Servaes, J. and N. Carpentier (eds). 2006. *Towards a Sustainable European Information Society*, Intellect, Bristol: ECCR Book Series.
- Shi-Xu, M. Kienpointner and J. Servaes (eds). 2005. *Read the Cultural Other. Forms of Otherness in the Discourses of Hong Kong's Decolonisation*, Berlin: Mouton de Gruyter.
- Thomas P. and J. Servaes (eds). 2006. *Intellectual Property Rights and Communications in Asia*, New Delhi: Sage Publications.
- Servaes, J. and S. Liu (eds). 2007. *Moving Targets. Mapping the Paths between Communication, Technology and Social Change in Communities*, Penang: Southbound.

E-mail: freenet002@gmail.com

Contributors

Rachel Carnegie has worked in the field of communication and health promotion for 21 years. She lived and worked in South Asia for eight years, and, from a UK base, she has worked as an independent adviser, undertaking extended assignments in East and Southern Africa and in South and South East Asia. The main focus of her work is on HIV and AIDS programmes for children and youth.

Carnegie has worked with a range of multilateral organizations and NGOs. For UNICEF, she was responsible for developing the *Meena Communication Initiative* for the South Asian girl child, as writer and creative director from 1991–1994 and remaining as a consultant to the initiative until 2005. She has supported the development of UNICEF's life skills-based education programmes in a number of countries, including Building Resources Across Communities (BRAC) in Bangladesh, formerly known as the Bangladesh Rural Advancement Committee. Carnegie has evaluated and edited training materials for UNICEF's faith-based initiatives with the Buddhist and Muslim leadership in Asia.

Carnegie's most recent work has involved an evaluation of UNICEF's humanitarian programme in Northern Uganda, an evaluation of a school-based HIV and AIDS programme in Zambia with the International HIV/AIDS Alliance, and a mentoring role with NGOs promoting child-centred approaches to HIV and AIDS in Uganda and Kenya.

In addition to being an editor and co-author of *Involving People, Evolving Behaviour* (2000), Carnegie is author of a number of resource books and training manuals on health promotion and Child-to-Child approaches, including *The River of Hope: Helping children to cope with the impact of HIV and AIDS, Healthlink Worldwide* (2006) and *Things Change: A Resource Book for Working with Youth and Communities on Female Genital Cutting* (Maskew Millar Longman, 2003).

E-mail: rcarnegie@rcmg.freeserve.co.uk

Nico Carpentier (Ph.D., University of Antwerp, Belgium) is a media sociologist working at the Free (VUB) and Catholic (KUB) Universities of Brussels, Belgium. He is Co-Director of the VUB research centre CEMESO and an Executive Board member of the European Communication Research and Education Association (ECREA). His theoretical focus is on discourse theory. His research interests are situated in the relationship between media and journalism, and especially towards social domains as war and conflict, ideology, participation and democracy.

His publications include the following books and articles: *Médias et citoyens sur la même longueur d'onde. Initatives journalistiques favorisantant la participation citoyenne* (2002, in Dutch and French, with B. Grévisse and M. Harzimont); *BBC's Video Nation as a Participatory Media Practice* (2003); *Media in movement, 22 Journalistic Experiments to Enhance Citizen Participation* (2004, in Dutch and French, with B. Grévisse); *The Ungraspable Audience* (ed.) (2004, combined Dutch and English, with C. Pauwels and O. Van Oost); *Identity, Contingency and Rigidity* (2005); *Towards a Sustainable Information Society. Deconstructing WSIS* (ed.) (2006, with J. Servaes); *Reclaiming the Media: Communication Rights and Democratic Media Roles* (ed., 2007 with B. Cammaerts) and *Discourse Theory and Cultural Analysis. Media, Arts and Literature* (ed., 2007 with E. Spinoy).

E-mail: Nico.Carpentier@kubrussel.ac.be

Gary Coldevin (Ph.D., University of Washington, Seattle, USA) is a full-time international consultant specializing in ICTs for development and distance education. Previously, he was a Professor for 25 years in the Graduate Programme in Educational Technology, Concordia University, Montreal. He has collaborated with FAO over a 20-year period, principally as an information campaign specialist, on several assignments in Africa and Asia. Currently based in the Philippines, his research interests are focussed on the design, delivery, and quantitative evaluation of a mix of low- to high-end technologies for development, and emerging best practices.

E-mail: gcoldevin@hotmail.com

For more information on the FAO Communication for Development Group contact: Senior Officer, Communication for Development (SDWDD), Food and Agriculture Organization of the United Nations, Viale delle Terme di Caracalla, 00100 Rome, Italy.

E-mail: ComDev@fao.org

Royal D. Colle (Ph.D., Cornell University, Ithaca, USA) is a Professor Emeritus at Cornell University where he has been on the faculty for more than 40 years. He has lived and worked abroad in countries ranging from India and Indonesia to Western Samoa and Guatemala. Colle has served as a consultant for a variety of international organizations including the World Bank, WHO, FAO, the UN, UNFPA, UNESCO, USAID, and the Ford Foundation. His work has focused on institution-building related to communication; the design of communication strategies for development programmes; and innovative uses of information technology for development. His most recent projects have been in Asia and Africa working on university-supported telecentre systems. He is co-author of *A Handbook for Telecenter Staffs* and author of an online book *Advocacy and Interventions, Readings in Development Communication*, 2007.

E-mail: rdc4@cornell.edu

Alfonso Gumucio-Dagron (Bolivia, 1950) is a communication specialist, photographer, filmmaker and writer with years of experience working in development programmes in Africa, Asia,

South Pacific, Latin America and The Caribbean with UN organizations (UNICEF, UNDP, FAO, UNESCO), foundations (Rockefeller Foundation), bi-laterals (AusAid) and NGOs (Conservation International). He is currently the Managing Director for Programmes at the Communication for Social Change Consortium and the author of various studies on communication such as *Communication for Social Change Anthology* (2006) (co-edited with Thomas Tufte), *Making Waves, Participatory Development for Social Change* (2001), and 20 other books of poetry, narrative and essays on communication, cinema and literature. He directed a dozen of documentary films on cultural and social issues in various countries.

E-mail: Gumucio@CFSC.org

Robert Huesca (Ph.D., Ohio State University, Columbus, USA) is Professor in the Department of Communication at Trinity University in San Antonio, Texas. His research interests include alternative media and participatory communication for social change. His research on international and development communication issues has been published in a number of books and journals, including Communication Studies, Gazette, Journal of Communication, Media, Culture and Society, and the Handbook of International and Intercultural Communication.

E-mail: rhuesca@trinity.edu

Rico Lie (Ph.D. 2000, Catholic University of Brussels, Belgium) is a social anthropologist working at the Department of Communication Science, which is based at the Wageningen University in The Netherlands. He previously worked at the University of Brussels in Belgium and the Universities of Nijmegen and Leiden in The Netherlands. In Wageningen he is an assistant professor in international communication and interested in the areas of development communication and intercultural communication. He is author of the book *Spaces of Intercultural Communication. An Interdisciplinary Introduction to Communication, Culture and Globalizing/Localizing Identities* (2003, Hampton Press, USA).

E-mail: Rico.Lie@wur.nl

Patchanee Malikhao is a senior consultant and researcher in mass communication and printing technology. She has been involved in projects for both public and private, national and international organizations, such as Agfa Gevaert, AMIC, the Europe-Asia Foundation, UNESCO, Chulalongkorn University, Bangkok, and the Rochester Institute of Technology. She is currently enrolled as a Ph.D. student at the University of Queensland and finishing a research project on HIV/AIDS prevention campaigns in two villages in Thailand.

E-mail: pmalikhao@gmail.com

Erma Manoncourt (Ph.D. in Public Health, University of North Carolina, Chapel Hill, USA) is the Country Representative for the UNICEF in the Arab Republic of Egypt, since January 2005. UNICEF-Egypt's present programme of cooperation focuses on girls' education, early child development and quality education, including school sanitation. Another major area of focus is child protection with initiatives on children at risk, combating child labour, street children, female genital cutting, and violence against children. Prior to her current assignment, she served in the India Country Office where she spent five years overseeing and coordinating technical programming for the largest UNICEF country programme in the world. In her previous positions, Dr. Manoncourt has also served as an assistant professor at the Tulane University School of Public Health and Tropical Medicine in New Orleans, Louisiana and Director of a Regional Support Center for the Caribbean and Southern United States before joining the United Nations in 1995.

As a public health specialist, she has worked more than 10 years in sub-Saharan Africa and the Caribbean in the areas of community-based development, nutrition and health programming. A key focus of her work has been on promoting behaviour and social change through participatory methodologies and approaches.

E-mail: emanoncourt@unicef.org

Neill McKee is an international development Programme Manager from Canada with 38 years of experience, 17 of those years based in developing countries/emerging economies. He is presently based in Moscow, Russia, as head of Healthy Russia 2020, a USAID-funded project of the Center for Communication Programs (CCP), Johns Hopkins University's Bloomberg School of Public Health. He manages a team in the design and development of country-specific initiatives and tools in health system improvement, cost analysis and advocacy, social mobilization and behaviour change communication in the fields of HIV/AIDS, reproductive health and family planning, and youth health lifestyles. McKee also served as Senior Advisor for HIV/AIDS and adolescent health communication at CCP, Baltimore, from 2001 to early 2004.

McKee worked for UNICEF from 1990 to 2000, serving as Regional Communication Advisor and HIV/AIDS Network Coordinator in Eastern and Southern Africa (1994–1999) based in Nairobi, and as Chief of Basic Education and Adolescent Development, Uganda (1999–2000). Besides being editor and co-author of *Involving People, Evolving Behaviour* (2000) McKee is author of *Social Mobilization and Social Marketing in Developing Communities*, Southbound (1993) and *Strategic Communication in the HIV/AIDS Epidemic* (Sage, 2004), he is also co-creator of VIPP (Visualisation in Participatory Programmes), a participatory planning and training methodology which has become popular through many parts of the world.

E-mail: nmckee@jhuccp.org

Sujatha Sosale (Ph.D., University of Minnesota, Minneapolis, USA) serves on the faculty of the School of Journalism and Mass Communication, The University of Iowa, USA. She teaches courses in the areas of international communication, and globalization and journalism. Her latest works include the book *Communication, Development, and Democracy: Mapping a Discourse* (in press).

E-mail: sujatha-sosale@uiowa.edu

Georgios Terzis (Ph.D., Catholic University Brussels, Belgium) is an associate professor at Vesalius College, Vrije Universiteit Brussel in Belgium (*www.vesalius.edu*) and the chair of the journalism

studies section of the European Communication Research and Education Association (*www.journalismstudies.edu*). He studied Journalism and Mass Communication in Belgium, Greece, UK, USA and The Netherlands. He worked as a foreign correspondent for Greek Media and as a course leader for the European Journalism Centre (*www.ejc.nl*), training journalists from all over the world on EU affairs. He also worked for Search for Common Ground (*www.sfcg.org*) and organized Media and Conflict Resolution programmes and trainings for journalists and journalism students from Angola, Cyprus, Greece, the Middle East, Sri Lanka and Turkey.

E-mail: Georgios.Terzis@vub.ac.be

Pradip Thomas Thomas (Ph.D. University of Leicester, UK) is Associate Professor at the School of Journalism and Communication, University of Queensland, Australia. Before he was Director, Studies and Publications at the World Association for Christian Communication in London, England. His research interests include Intellectual Property Rights and the Media and the Political Economy of Communications. His 2006 publications include two co-edited volumes, (with Jan Servaes), *Intellectual Property Rights and Communication in Asia: Conflicting Traditions,* Sage and (with Issac Mazondei), *Indigenous Knowledge Systems and Intellectual Property Rights in the 21st Century: Perspectives from Southern Africa,* CODESRIA.

E-mail: pradip.thomas@uq.edu.au

Thomas Tufte (Ph.D.,) is Professor in Communcation at Roskilde University, Denmark. Since the inception in 1999 he was a frequent lecturer at the masters in communication for development at Malmoe University, Sweden. UNESCO Chair in Communication at Universidad de Barcelona, 2003.

Recent publications include: *The Communication for Social Change Anthology—Historical and Contemporary Readings* (2006, co-ed.); *Media and Glocal Change—Rethinking Communication for Development* (2005, co-ed.); *The Media, The Minorities and the Multicultural Society—Scandinavian Perspectives* (2003, ed.) and *Living with the Rubbish Queen—Telenovelas, Culture and Modernity in Brazil* (2000).

E-mail: tufte@hum.ku.dk

Adinda Van Hemelrijck is an applied researcher and process advisor in organizational and social change processes at OXFAM in Boston, USA. She is an anthropologist with a research interest and experience in participatory communication, monitoring and evaluation, and the gender and development approach. She has worked for a Belgian NGO in Indonesia, the Belgian Special Evaluator for Development Cooperation, at the research centre Communication for Social Change at the Catholic University of Brussels, as well as for organizations from the social profit sector in Belgium, and most recently at the department of communication and innovation studies at the Wageningen University in the Netherlands. She also studied international relations and European decision-making, with a focus on international cooperation.

E-mail: adindavanh@yahoo.com

Myria Vassiliadou (Ph.D., University of Kent at Canterbury, UK) worked as an Assistant Professor of Sociology and Gender Studies at Intercollege, Cyprus for over a decade (*http://www.intercollege.ac.cy*). She is a founding member and the Director of the Board of the Mediterranean Institute of Gender Studies (*http://www.medinstgenderstudies.org*) and is also a Summer Fellow at the Solomon Asch Centre for Study of Ethnopolitical Conflict, University of Pennsylvania, USA. For the last two years, she has been attached to the European Commission as a National Expert at the Directorate of Social Sciences and Humanities of DG Research (*http://ec.europa.eu/research/social-sciences/index_en.htm*). She has worked extensively in the area of gender, conflict and the media. She has been involved in various non-governmental organizations and has published in books and journals.

E-mail: fa895638@SKYNET.be

Chris Verschooten (Ph.D., Catholic University of Brussels, Belgium) is Assistant Professor at the Department of Communication at the KU Brussels. She teaches Communication and International Relations, Intercultural Communication and International Communication. Her main focus is on South Asia. Her research interests include Dalits and Indian politics, Indo-Pakistan relations, foreign policy, women issues and communication.

E-mail: Chris.Verschooten@kubrussel.ac.be

Chin Saik Yoon has been a practitioner of participatory communication for development over the past 30 years. His fieldwork has been undertaken mainly in the Asian and Arab regions. He is the publisher of Southbound, a scholarly press that specializes in titles that concern development information and communication issues. Chin is the editor-in-chief of the first two editions of the *Digital Review of Asia Pacific* that analysed the ways in which information and communication technologies have been deployed across 29 economies in the region to support social and economic activities. His recent work has been in the building of incident command systems in Southeast Asia to prepare for outbreaks of infectious diseases, particularly avian influenza.

E-mail: chin@south.pc.my

Index